Liferay Portal Enterprise Intranets

A practical guide to building a complete corporate intranet with Liferay

Jonas X. Yuan

BIRMINGHAM - MUMBAI

Liferay Portal Enterprise Intranets

First published: April 2008

Production Reference: 1220408

Published by Packt Publishing Ltd.
32 Lincoln Road
Olton
Birmingham, B27 6PA, UK.

ISBN 978-1-847192-72-1

www.packtpub.com

Cover Image by Vinayak Chittar (vinayak.chittar@gmail.com)

Credits

Author Jonas Yuan	**Project Manager** Abhijeet Deobhakta
Reviewer C.J.S Hayward	**Project Coordinator** Abhijeet Deobhakta
Senior Acquisition Editor David Barnes	**Indexer** Hemangini Bari
Development Editor Ved Jha	**Proofreader** Nina Hasso
Technical Editor Usha Iyer	**Production Coordinator** Shantanu Zagade
Copy Editor Sumathi Sridhar	**Cover Work** Shantanu Zagade
Editorial Team Leader Mithil Kulkarni	

About the Author

Jonas X. Yuan is a senior technical analyst at CIGNEX. Jonas holds a Ph. D in Computer Science from the University of Zurich, where he focused on Integrity Control in Federated Database Systems. He earned his M.S and B.S. degrees from China, where he conducted research on expert systems for predicting landslides. Jonas is experienced in Systems Development Lifecycle (SDLC). Previously, he has worked as a Project Manager and a Technical Architect in Web GIS (Geographic Information System). He has extensive, hands on skills in J2EE technologies. Specifically, he had developed a BPEL (Business Process Execution Language) Engine called BPELPower from scratch at NASA data center. He also has experiences on content management related to the medical-legal area. Furthermore, he is an expert in Content Management Systems (CMS) such as Alfresco, Portals such as Liferay and full integration of Liferay, Alfresco, LDAP and SSO.

I would like to thank team members at Liferay, especially thank Bryan Cheung, Jorge Ferrer, Michael Young, Raymond Auge, Brian Chan, Jerry Niu, Ed Shin, Craig Kaneko and Brian Kim of Liferay for providing me with valuable information and all the support.

My special thanks to all my team members at CIGNEX for making this book a reality. I would like to thank Navin Nagiah, CEO of CIGNEX for his encouragement and great support; without him, this book would not have been written. Furthermore thanks to Munwar Shariff and Mike W. Walker for introducing me to the publishers. Amit Babaria, Harish Ramachandran, Jarred Parris, and our sales and presales team at CIGNEX helped me understand what the customers' demands are. Our consulting team at CIGNEX, Srini Sridhar, Zakir Laliwala, Harshad Bakshi and Zankar Shah presented me with the various flavors of Liferay implementations with real-life examples. I am thankful to them.

I sincerely thank and appreciate David Barnes and Ved Prakash Jha, Senior Acquisition Editor and Development Editor respectively at Packt Publishing for criticizing and fixing my writing style. Thanks to Abhijeet Deobhakta, and Usha Iyer and entire team at Packt Publishing and it was really joyful working with them.

Last but not least, I would like to thank my parents and my wife, Linda, for their love, understanding and encouragement. A special thanks to my wonderful and understanding kid Josua.

About the Reviewer

C.J.S. Hayward is an author and IT professional who loves to create. He holds a master's degrees in math (UIUC) and theology (Cambridge). His main site, JonathansCorner.com, showcases different creations: short stories and Socratic dialogue, science fiction and fantasy, CGI and OSS, musing and mystic spark, a role playing world and a four dimensional maze, novellas, artwork, poetry, philosophy and theology, dreamlike vision and energetic endeavors, plus a game review for meatspace. (His works are available in print from CJSHayward.com.) He has lived in the U.S., Malaysia, England, and France and is a parishioner of St. Innocent of Moscow Russian Orthodox Church.

Table of Contents

Chapter 2: Set-up The Home PageAnd Navigation Structure for The Intranet — 21

Preface

When you plan to build an amazing website based on a portal, you may commonly consider a lot of questions. Some of them would look like the following:

- Are you planning to build a website with an open source enterprise portal solution using SOA framework, ESB and Web 2.0 technologies?

- Do you want to add collaborative tools, such as Wikis, Blogs, Discussion Forums, Shared Calendar, RSS, mail, Tagging, and instant messaging in the same website?

- Do you want to manage, publish and maintain web contents and documents in the same website?

- Are you eager to integrate with LDAP, SSO and third-party systems like JBoss jBPM, Alfresco, Orbeon Forms, and Pentaho BI/Reporting in the same website?

Obviously Liferay would be the best choice in terms of answering the above questions. Liferay Portal is one of the most mature portal frameworks in the market and offers the above basic benefits. Liferay is backed by a comprehensive professional services network and it offers custom development, training, and support across the world.

As the world's leading open source portal platform, Liferay provides a unified web interface to data and tools scattered across many sources. Within Liferay portal, a portal interface is composed of a number of portlets — self contained interactive elements that are written to a particular standard. Since portlets are developed independently of the portal itself, and loosely coupled with the portal, they are apparently SOA (Service-Oriented Architecture).

Liferay has a wide range of portlets freely available for things like: Blogs, Calendar, Document Library, Image Gallery, Mail, Message Boards, Polls, RSS feeds, Wiki, and many others. Liferay Portal also ships with Liferay Journal CMS (Content Management Systems), which provides basic ECMS (Enterprise Content Management Systems) features. If you need robust enterprise content management system then you can integrate it with Alfresco. Liferay is good portal on top for small team collaboration. The data for events can be specific to a small group within a company. In any organization, some data will be relevant at a team level—and other data, across the whole business. Liferay has very good support for such things.

As the world's leading open source enterprise portal solution, Liferay portal uses the latest in Java, J2EE, and Web 2.0 technologies in order to deliver solutions to enterprises across both public and private sectors. Meanwhile, Journal CMS publishes, manages, and maintains web content and document libraries. In addition, Collaboration Suite takes advantage of the benefits of virtualized work environment for collaboration.

This book is your complete guide to build an intranet with Liferay —assess your needs, install the software, start using it, deploy portlets, customize as per your requirements and train users. The book focuses on leveraging the Liferay framework by configuring the XML files without changing the underlying java code.

What This Book Covers

Chapter 1 introduces Liferay.

Chapter 2 discusses how to set up the home page and navigate the structure of the intranet.

Chapter 3 investigates security and access model. It describes how to bring to users in the portal: application of full access control security model; administration of users, user groups, organizations and locations; authentication of Liferay portals, and moreover, usage of security permissions and roles.

Chapter 4 describes discussion Forums. Message Board (discussion Forum) provides support for sticky posts, statistics, recent posts, RSS, email-based subscriptions, avatars, threads management, and full fine-grained permissions. Tagging system provides support to tag web content, documents, Message Board threads and more, and dynamically publish content by tags.

Chapter 5 describes Wikis. Liferay Wiki is a straightforward Wiki solution with categories; classic Wiki, HTML, or plain text modes; WYSIWYG editing; page history and versioning; and permissions. Moreover, the Web Form portlet allows a web administrator to define a form to be published in the website; the Polls portlet allows users or administrators to create multiple choice polls that keep track of votes and display results on the page.

Chapter 6 describes Internal Bloggings. Blogs provide features including RSS support, user and guest comments, brows-able categories, tags and labels, and an entry rating system; RSS portlet has subscription ability to frequently read RSS feeds from within the portal framework. Furthermore, WYSIWGs (What You See Is What You Get editors) edit web content, including Blogs' content.

Chapter 7 introduces Shared Calendars. A calendar portlet provides the ability to display calendar information and to allow users to create, manage, and search for events. Workflow portlet provides the ability to manage instances and tasks, and furthermore, integrate with users, groups and roles. In addition, WSRP proxy portlet, IFrame portlet and Flash portlet are also included as well.

Chapter 8 investigates documents repositories. It does not only introduce document library, images gallery and content management including articles, templates and structure, but it also discusses content publication.

Chapter 9 presents chat and instant messaging. It first introduces chat portlet and its related features, such as AJAX and XMPP servers. Then it introduces mail portlet and its related features, such as IMAP. Finally, it briefly introduces SMS and the usage of SMS text messenger — sending SMS text messages.

Chapter 10 discusses others tools which would be useful to build a personalized web site.

Chapter 11 presents how to roll out to other teams. It principally introduces community administration, community virtual hosting, portal publishing and staging and a set of community tools.

Chapter 12 introduces search functionalities: OpenSearch, Journal content search, sitemaps protocol, Google search and Google maps.

Chapter 13 concludes the book. It mainly describes ongoing admin tasks, including admin portlet, enterprise admin portlet, managing password policies, updating the system–level settings, and monitoring users' activities,, and full integration approach to Liferay, Alfresco, LDAP and SSO.

What You Need for This Book

This book uses Liferay portal version 4.4 and 5.0. with the following settings:

- MySQL database 5.0
- Java SE 6.0
- Liferay portal bundled with Tomcat 6.0

Optionally, you can also work in both Windows and Linux with the following settings:

- Java SE 5.0
- Liferay portal bundled with Tomcat 5.5
- MySQL database 5.0

You can use one of the following options for Servlet containers and full Java EE application servers to install Liferay Portal:

- Geronimo + Tomcat
- Glassfish for AIX
- Glassfish for Linux
- Glassfish for OSX
- Glassfish for Solaris
- Glassfish for Solaris (x86)
- Glassfish for Windows
- JBoss + Jetty 4.0
- JBoss + Tomcat 4.0
- JBoss + Tomcat 4.2
- Jetty
- JOnAS + Jetty
- JOnAS + Tomcat
- Pramati
- Resin
- Tomcat 5.5 for JDK 1.4
- Tomcat 5.5 for JDK 5.0
- Tomcat 6.0

The applications servers (or Servlet containers) that Liferay Portal can run on include:

- Borland ES 6.5
- Apache Geronimo 2.x
- Sun GlassFish 2 UR1
- JBoss 4.0.x, 4.2.x
- JOnAS 4.8.x
- JRun 4 Updater 3
- OracleAS 10.1.3.x
- Orion 2.0.7
- Pramati 5.0
- RexIP 2.5
- SUN JSAS 9.1
- WebLogic 8.1 SP4, 9.2, 10
- WebSphere 5.1, 6.0.x, 6.1.x
- Jetty 5.1.10
- Resin 3.0.19
- Tomcat 5.0.x/5.5.x/6.0.x

Databases that Liferay portal can run on include:

- Apache Derby
- IBM DB2
- Firebird
- Hypersonic
- Informix
- InterBase
- JDataStore
- MySQL
- Oracle
- PostgresSQL
- SAP
- SQL Server
- Sybase

Operating systems that Liferay portal can run on include:

- LINUX (Debian, RedHat, SUSE, Ubuntu, and so on)
- UNIX (AIX, FreeBSD, HP-UX, OS X, Solaris, and so)
- WINDOWS
- MAC OS X

Who is This Book for

This book is for beginners to Liferay and "Do-It-Yourselfers" who want to develop a simple but powerful corporate Intranet. The book assumes technical confidence but does not require specialist administrator or developer skills.

Conventions

In this book, you will find a number of styles of text that distinguish between different kinds of information. Here are some examples of these styles, and an explanation of their meaning.

Code words in text are shown as follows: "We can include other contexts through the use of the `include` directive."

A block of code will be set as follows:

```
<swimlane name="user_admin">
    <assignment class="com.liferay.jbpm.handler.
IdentityAssignmentHandler"
                                config-type="field">
        <type>role</type>
        <companyId>liferay.com</companyId>
        <id>1001</id>
```

New terms and **important words** are introduced in a bold-type font. Words that you see on the screen, in menus or dialog boxes for example, appear in our text like this: "clicking the **Next** button moves you to the next screen".

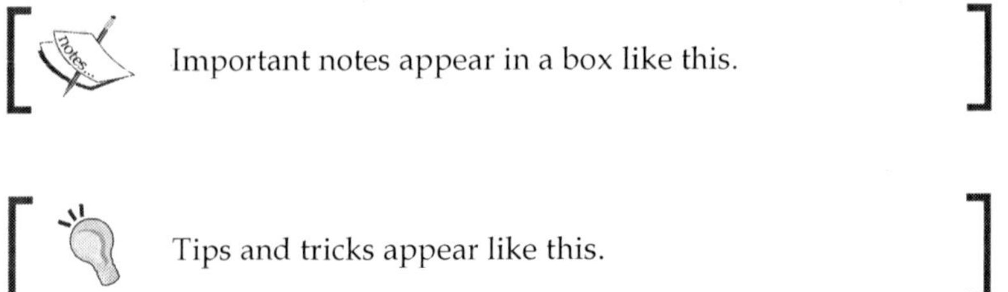

[Important notes appear in a box like this.]

[Tips and tricks appear like this.]

Reader Feedback

Feedback from our readers is always welcome. Let us know what you think about this book, what you liked or may have disliked. Reader feedback is important for us to develop titles that you really get the most out of.

To send us general feedback, simply drop an email to feedback@packtpub.com, making sure to mention the book title in the subject of your message.

If there is a book that you need and would like to see us publish, please send us a note in the **SUGGEST A TITLE** form on www.packtpub.com or email suggest@packtpub.com.

If there is a topic that you have expertise in and you are interested in either writing or contributing to a book, see our author guide on www.packtpub.com/authors.

Customer Support

Now that you are the proud owner of a PACKT book, we have a number of things to help you to get the most from your purchase.

Downloading the Example Code for the Book

Visit http://www.packtpub.com/files/code/2721_Code.zip to directly download the example code.

The downloadable files contain instructions on how to use them.

Errata

Although we have taken every care to ensure the accuracy of our contents, mistakes do happen. If you find a mistake in one of our books—maybe a mistake in text or code—we would be grateful if you would report this to us. By doing this you can save other readers from frustration, and help to improve subsequent versions of this book. If you find any errata, report them by visiting http://www.packtpub.com/support, selecting your book, clicking on the **Submit Errata** link, and entering the details of your errata. Once your errata are verified, your submission will be accepted and the errata are added to the list of existing errata. The existing errata can be viewed by selecting your title from http://www.packtpub.com/support.

Questions

You can contact us at `questions@packtpub.com` if you are having a problem with some aspect of the book, and we will do our best to address it.

1

Introducing Liferay for Your Intranet

This book will show you how to create a company Intranet with Liferay. In this chapter, we will look at:

- The features your Intranet will have by the time you reach the end of the book.
- Why Liferay is an excellent choice for building your Intranet.
- Some of the other things people are using Liferay for, besides Intranets.
- How to find more technical information about what Liferay is, and how it works.

So let's begin by looking at exactly which site we're going to build in the book.

What Are We Going to Build?

Over the course of this book, we're going to build a complete corporate Intranet using Liferay. Let's discuss some of the features your Intranet will have.

Hosted Discussions

Are you still using email for group discussions? Then it's time you found a better way. Running group discussions over email clogs up the team's inbox. Also, you have to choose your distribution list in advance, and it is hard for team members to 'opt in and out' of the discussion.

Using Liferay, we will build a range of discussion boards for discussion within and between teams. The discussions are archived in one place. So it's always possible to go back and refer to them later.

Furthermore, it's just more convenient to move an email discussion to a discussion forum designed for the purpose. Once the forum is in place, you will find that a more productive group discussion takes place than it ever did over email.

Collaborative Documents Using Wikis

Your company probably has guideline documents that should be updated regularly. But, they swiftly lose their relevance as practices and procedures change. Worse, each of your staff will know useful, productive tricks and techniques—but there's probably no easy way to record that knowledge in a way that is easy for others to find and use.

We will see how to host 'wikis' within Liferay. A wiki enables anybody to create and edit web pages, and link all of those web pages together. You can put your 'guideline' documents into a wiki, and as practices change, your frontline staff can quickly and effortlessly update the guideline documentation.

Wikis can also act as a shared notebook, enabling team members to collaborate and share both ideas and findings, and also work together on documents.

Team And Individual Blogs

Your company probably needs frequent, chronological publications of personal thoughts and Web links in the Intranet. In more detail, your company probably has teams and individual works on specific projects in order to share files and Blogs about project processes, and furthermore use HTML text editor to create or update files and Blogs, and provide RSS feeds.

We will see how teams and individuals share files and Blogs within Liferay. Blogs provide a straightforward Blogging solution with a lot of features such as RSS support, comments, categories, tags, labels, rating, and so on. Liferay RSS with subscription provides the ability to frequently read RSS feeds from within the portal framework.

At the same time, WYSIWGs (What You See Is What You Get editors) provides the ability to edit web content, including Blog content. Less technical persons can use WYSIWGs without sifting through complex code.

Shared Calendars

Your company may be required to provide and share calendar information among users from different departments. At the same time, it may be required to provide workflow ability so that normal users can submit requests, and the manager can take decisions on these requests. Moreover, it may also be required to publish third party contents in the intranet website.

We will see how to share a calendar within Liferay. Shared Calendar can satisfy basic business requirements incorporated in a featured business intranet such as scheduling meetings, sending meeting invitations, checking for attendees' availability and so on. Thus, you can provide an environment for users to manage events and share calendars.

In addition, you can also use workflows to manage workflow definitions, instances, and tasks. Furthermore, you can also employ WSRP proxy effectively, and other portlets such as web proxy, IFrame and flash smoothly. These portlets provide ability to publish third party contents in the intranet website.

Document Stores

You company may have a lot of images and documents, and you may need to manage all images and documents as well. Thus, you require the ability to manage a lot of web content and also publish web contents in the intranet.

We will see how to manage and publish web contents within Liferay. Liferay Journal does not only provide high availability to publish, manage, and maintain web content and documents, but it also separates content from layout.

In addition, within Image Gallery, you can add folders and sub folders for images, can manage folders and sub folders, add images in folders and manage images, can set up permission on folders and images. Within Document Library, you can add folders and sub folders for documents, and manage documents, and also publish documents.

And More...!

The Intranet will also arrange staff members into teams and communities, provide a way for real-time IM and chat, and give each user an appropriate level of 'access'—implying that they get access to all the information they need, edit and add content as necessary, but can't meddle with sensitive information that they have no reason to see.

Everything in One Place

All these features are useful on their own. But it gets better when you consider that all these features will combine in one, easy-to-use, searchable portal.

A user of the Intranet, for example, can search for a topic— say 'financial report'—and can find in one go:

- Any group discussions about financial reports
- Blog entries within the intranet concerning financial reports
- Documents and files—the financial reports themselves, perhaps
- Wiki entries with guidelines on preparing financial reports
- Calendar entries for meetings to discuss the financial report

Of course, users can also restrict their search to just one area, if they already know exactly what they are looking for.

Liferay provides other features, such as tagging, to make it easier to organize information across the whole Intranet. We will do all of this and more over the course of the book.

Introducing Palm Tree Publications

In this book we are going to build an example Intranet for a fictions company. By applying the instructions to your own business, you will be able to build an Intranet to meet your own company's needs.

Palm Tree Publications needs an Intranet of its own, which we will call book.com.

The enterprise's global headquarters is in the United States. It has several departments: editorial, website, engineering, marketing, executive and human resources.

Each department has staff either in the United States, or in Germany, or both.

The intranet site provides a community called "Book Lovers",consisting of users who have an interest in reading books. The enterprise needs to integrate collaboration tools such as Wikis, Blogs, discussion forms, instant messaging, mail, RSS, shared calendars, tagging, and so on.

Palm Tree Publications has some more advanced needs too: a workflow to edit, approve and publish books. Furthermore, the enterprise has a lot of contents such as books stored and managed in Alfresco, currently. Now, it wants to publish the contents of Alfresco in the Intranet website.

In order to build the intranet site, the following functionalities should be considered:

- Installing the portal, experiencing the portal and portlets, customizing personal web pages.

- Bringing users to the portal—enabling document sharing, calendar sharing, and other collaboration within a business.

- Discussion forums—Employees discuss book idea and proposals.

- Wikis—keeping track of information about editorial guidance and other resources that require frequent editing.

- Distribution of knowledge via Blogs—small teams working on specific projects share files and Blogs about project process.

- Sharing calendar among employees and using workflow to manage (edit, approve, publish) pages within web contents among employees.

- Document repository—using effective content management systems (CMS), a natural fit for a portal for secure access, permissions, and distinct roles (writer, editor, designer, administrator).

- Collaborative chat and Instant Messaging.

- Managing a community named "Book Lovers", which consists of users who have similar interests in reading books.

- Federated search for Discussion forum entries, Blog posts, Wiki articles, users at Directory, and contents at both Document Library and Alfresco, Search by tags and so on.

- Integrating back-of-the-house software applications, such as Alfresco, Orbeon Forms, and BI/Reporting Pentaho, strong authentication and authorization with LDAP, single-authentication to access various company sites besides the Intranet site.

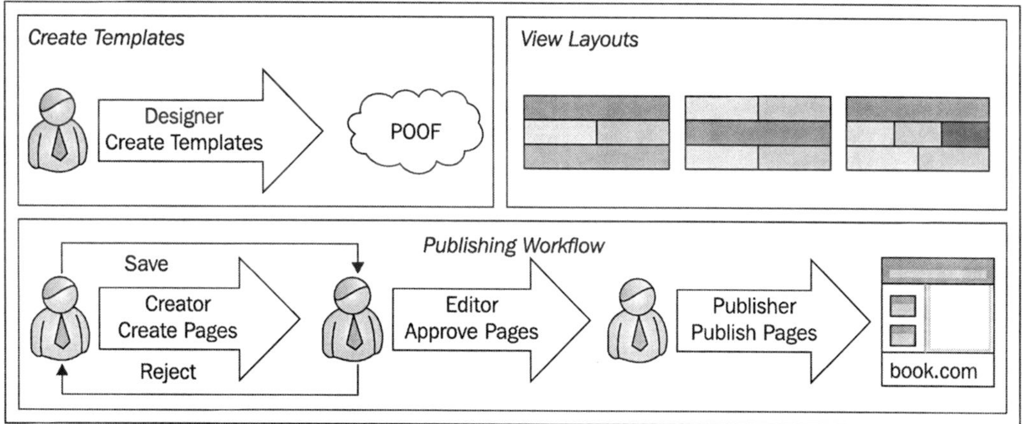

The enterprise may have the following groups of people:

- **Admin**: Installs Systems, Manages Membership, Users, User Groups, Organizations, Roles and Permissions, Security on resources, Workflow, servers and instances, and Integrates with third-party systems.
- **Executives**: Executive Management handles approvals.
- **Marketing**: Handles Web Site, Company Brochures, Marketing Campaign, Projects, and Digital Assets.
- **Sales**: Presentations, Contracts, Documents and Reports.
- **Website Editors**: Manage pages of the intranet; Write articles, Review articles, Design layout of articles, Publish articles.
- **Book Editors**: Write books, Review books, and Publish books.
- **Human Resources**: Manages Corporate Policy Documents.
- **Finance**: Manages Account Documents, Scanned Invoices and Checks, Notifications.
- **Corporate Communications**: Manages External Public Relations, Internal News Releases, and Syndication.
- **Engineering**: Sets up development environment, collaborates on Engineering Projects and Presentation Templates.

Why Use Liferay To Build An Intranet?

Of course, there are lots of ways to build a company Intranet. What makes Liferay such a good choice?

It's Got The Features We Need

All the features we have outlined for our Intranet come built into Liferay; discussions, wikis, calendars, blogs and so on, are part of what Liferay is designed to do.

It is also designed to tie all these features together into one searchable 'portal'. So, we won't be dealing with lots of separate components when we build and use our Intranet. All parts will work together.

It's Easy To Set up and Use

Liferay has an intuitive interface that uses icons, clear labels, drag and drop to make it easy to configure and use for the Intranet.

Setting up the Intranet will require a bit more work than using it, of course. But you will be pleasantly surprised by how simple it is—no programming is required to get your Intranet up and running.

It's Free And Open Source

How much does Liferay cost? Nothing! It's a free, open source tool.

This means that you can go to Liferay's web site, and download it without paying anything. You can then go ahead, install it, and use it.

The Liferay company makes its money by providing additional services, including training. But the standard use of Liferay is completely free. Now that you've bought this book, you probably won't have to pay another penny to get your Intranet working.

Being open source means that the program code that makes Liferay work is available for anybody to look at and change. Even if you're not a programmer, this is still good for you:

- If you need Liferay to do something new, then you can hire a programmer to modify Liferay so that it does this new thing.
- There are a lot of developers studying the source code, looking for ways to make it better. A lot of improvements get incorporated into Liferay's main code.
- Developers are always working to create 'plugins' — programs that work together with Liferay to add new features.

Probably for now, the big deal here is that it costs zero dollars. But as you use Liferay more, you will come to understand the other benefits of Open Source for you.

It Will Grow with You

Liferay is designed in a way so that it can work with thousands and thousands of users at once. No matter how big your business is, or how much it grows, Liferay will still work and handle all of the information you throw at it.

It also has features especially suited for large international businesses. Opening offices up in non-English speaking countries? No problem! Liferay has internationalization features tailored to suit many of the world's popular languages.

It Works with Other Tools

Liferay is designed to work with other software tools, ones that you're already using, and ones that you might use in the future. For example:

- You can hook Liferay up to your LDAP directory server so that users' details and login credentials are added to Liferay automatically.
- Liferay can work with Alfresco, a popular and powerful Enterprise CMS system (used to provide extremely advance document management capabilities — far beyond what Liferay does on its own).

It Is Based on "Standards"

This is a more technical benefit, but a very useful one, if you ever want to use Liferay in a more specialized way.

Liferay is based on standard technologies that are popular with developers and other IT experts. These include:

- **Built using Java**—a very popular programming language that can run on just about any computer. There are millions of Java programmers in the world. So it won't be too hard to find developers who can customize Liferay.

- **Based on tried and tested components**. With any tool, there's a danger of bugs. Liferay uses lots of well known, widely tested components to minimize the likelihood of bugs creeping in. If you are interested, here are some of the well known components and technologies Liferay uses: Apache ServiceMix, Mule, Ehcache, Hibernate, ICEfaces, Java J2EE/JEE, jBPM, Intalio | BPMS, JGroups, jQuery, Lucene, PHP, Ruby, Seam, Spring and AOP, Struts and Tiles, Tapestry, Velocity, and FreeMarker.

- **Uses standard ways to communicate with other software**. There are various standards established for sharing data between pieces of software. Liferay uses these so that you can easily put information from Liferay into other systems. The standards implemented by Liferay include: AJAX, iCalendar and Micro-format, JSR-168, JSR-127, JSR-170, JSR-286 (Portlet 2.0) and JSF-314 (JSF 2.0) in the future roadmap, OpenSearch, Open platform with support for web services (including: JSON, Hessian, Burlap, REST, RMI, WSRP), and WebDAV.

Many of these standards are things that you will never need to know much about. So don't worry if you've never heard of them. Liferay is better for using them, but mostly you won't even know that they are there.

What Else Can Liferay Do?

Liferay isn't just for Intranets! Users and developers are building all kinds of different web sites and systems based on Liferay.

Corporate Extranets

An Intranet is great for collaboration and information sharing within a company. An Extranet extends this facility to suppliers and customers, who usually log in over the Internet.

In many ways, this is similar to an Intranet—there are few technical differences. The main difference is that you create user accounts for people who are not part of your company.

Collaborative Websites

Collaborative websites not only provide a secure and administrated framework, but also empower users with collaborative tools such as Blogs, instant email, message boards, instant messaging, shared calendar, and so on. Moreover, it encourages users to use other tools such as tags administration, fine-grained permissions, delegable administrator privileges, enterprise taxonomy, and ad-hoc user groups. By these tools, as an administrator, you can ultimately control what people can do and cannot do in Liferay.

In many ways, this is similar to an Intranet—there are few technical differences. The main difference is that you use collaborative tools such as Blogs, instant email, message boards, instant messaging, shared calendar, and so on.

Content Management & Web Publishing

You can also use Liferay to run your public company web site with content management and web publishing.

Content management and web publishing are useful in websites. It is a fact that the volume of digital content for any organization is increasing on a daily basis. Thus, an effective content management system (CMS) is a vital part of any organization. Meanwhile, document management is also useful and more effective when repositories have to be assigned to different departments and groups within the organization.

Content management and document management are effective in Liferay. Moreover, while managing and publishing contents, we may have to answer many questions, such as "who should be able to update and delete a document from the system". Fortunately, Liferay security and permission model can satisfy the needs for secure access and permissions, and distinct roles (for example, writer, editor, designer, and administrator). Furthermore, Liferay integrates with the workflow engine. Thus, users can follow a flow to edit, approve and publish contents in the website.

Content Management and Web Publishing are also similar to an Intranet—there are few technical differences. The main difference is that you can manage content and publish web contents smoothly.

Infrastructure Portals

Infrastructure portals integrate all possible functions stated above. It covers collaboration and information sharing within a company, collaborative tools, content management and web publishing. In the infrastructure portals, users can create a unified interface to work with contents, regardless of source via Content Interaction API. Furthermore, using the same API and the same interface as well as that of built-in content management system (CMS), users can also manage content and publish web contents from third-party systems such as Alfresco, Vignette, Magnolia, or Microsoft Share-Point, and so on.

Infrastructure portals are similar to an Intranet — there are a few technical differences. The main difference is that you can use collaborative tools, manage content, publish web contents and integrate other systems in one place.

Why do you need a portal? The main reason is that a portal can be served as a framework to aggregate content and applications. A portal normally provides a secure and manageable framework, where users can easily make new and existing enterprise applications available. In order to build an infrastructure portal smoothly, Liferay portal provides SOA-based framework to integrate third party systems.

Finding More Information

In this chapter, we have looked at what Liferay can do for your corporate Intranet, and briefly seen why it's a good choice.

If you want more background information on Liferay, the best place to start is the Liferay corporate web site (`http://www.liferay.com`) itself. You can find the latest news and events, various training programs offered world wide, presentations, demonstrations and hosted trails. More interestingly, Liferay corporate web site plus Forums and Blogs is built by the Liferay Portal itself. It is a real demo of the Liferay Portal.

 The Liferay site uses MediaWiki for its wiki and Atlassian JIRA for its issue tracking. That is, the Liferay site does not use its own Wiki system.

Liferay is 100% open source and all downloads are available from `sourceforge.net` website at `http://sourceforge.net/project/showfiles.php?group_id=49260`.

Liferay site Wiki (`http://wiki.liferay.com`) contains documentation such as tutorial, user guide, developer guide, administrator guide, roadmap and so on.

Liferay discussion forums (`http://www.liferay.com/web/guest/community/forums`), Blogs (`http://www.liferay.com/web/guest/community/blog`), Road Map (`http://www.liferay.com/web/guest/community/road_map`) and Community Plugins (`http://www.liferay.com/web/guest/community/community_plugins`) are the best places to share your thoughts, to get tips and tricks about Liferay implementation, to know road map, and to use and contribute community plugins.

If you would like to file a bug or know more details about the fixes in a specific release, you must visit the bug tracking system at `http://support.liferay.com` .

Summary

In this chapter, we have looked at what Liferay can offer your Intranet. In particular, we saw:

- That our final intranet will provide shared documents, discussions, collaborative wikis and more in a single, searchable portal.

- That Liferay makes a great choice for the Intranet, because it provides so many features; it's easy to use, it's free and open source, is extensible and is well integrated with other tools and standards.

- Other kinds of site that Liferay is good for: extranets, collaborative web sites, content management and web publishing, and infrastructure portals.

- The various pages on `Liferay.com` that can provide us with more background information.

In the next chapter, we're going to install Liferay and start the hands-on task of building the Intranet.

2
Set-up The Home Page And Navigation Structure for The Intranet

This chapter will assist administrators and normal users in the enterprise "Palm-Tree Publications" to experience the implementation of a portal page with portlets first. Then it will provide guidance to administrators to set up the portal, and direct administrators and normal users to build pages and customize their personal area. Finally, it will guide both administrators and normal users to navigate the structure of their intranet web site. In addition, it will provide guidance to administrators to configure the portals and moreover, set the extension environment in order to extend the functionality provided by Liferay.

By the end of this chapter you will have learned how to:

- Experience implementing a portal page with portlets.
- Set up the portal.
- Configure the home page and the intranet web site.
- Customize the personal area.
- Build the portal pages.
- Navigate the structure of the Intranet.
- Configure the portal.
- And set up extension environment.

Experiencing Liferay Portal

As an administrator at the Enterprise "**Palm-Tree Publications**", named "**Palm Tree**", you can first experience Liferay portal locally. Simply log in at your local Liferay portal, and you will see the portal page interface similar to the one shown in the following figure. Generally, a portal page is made up of a set of portlets, such as **Navigation**, **Language**, and so on. Liferay portal runs locally with URL: `http://localhost:8080/user/joebloggs/home`.

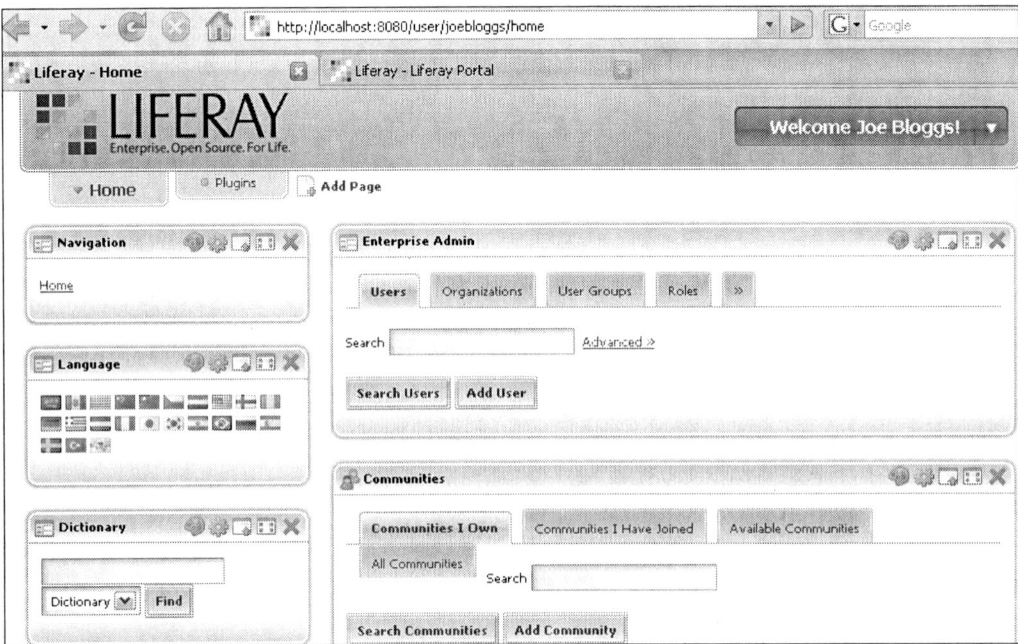

Quick Liferay Portal Installation

In order to get the previous portal page with portlets, let's install Liferays Portal in your local machine quickly, as follows:

Download Liferay Portal Bundled with Tomcat JDK 6.0 from Liferay official web site (`http://www.liferay.com`). It is a big file and you have to wait long to download it:

- Unzip the bundled file; run `$TOMCAT/bin/startup.bat` for Windows or `startup.sh` for Linux, UNIX, etc.
- Open your browser and go to `http://localhost:8080/user/joebloggs/home`.
- Log in as an administrator using the following data — User: **test@liferay.com** and **Password: test**.

Congratulations! You now have a running copy of Liferay. The remainder of this section will explain what a portal is, what a portlet is, and how to implement a portal page with a set of portlets, in general.

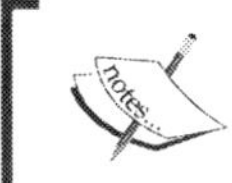 Does it work well? Make sure that you have installed JDK 6.0 or above in your local machine and set JAVA_HOME as well. This is the only one you need in order to install Liferay portal properly.

What's Happening Behind?

What you have seen previously is a portal page with the name, **Welcome**. The portal page **Welcome** has a logo, menu, header (that is, a list of page names), a set of portlets, and a footer. When you logged in, the portal generated this page. If you select another page name such as **Plugins**, the portal will generate another page.

An intranet website is made up of a set of pages, such as **Welcome** and **Plugins**. Liferay portals can be used to build and manage these pages flexibly.

To summarise, portals provide a lot of essential benefits: reduction in site running costs, greater customer satisfaction, and more efficient business processes.

Understanding Portlets

A portal page is made of a set of portlets. For example, the portal page such as **Welcome** contains portlets such as **Navigation**, **Language**, and so on And the portlet **Language** has icons (such as **Look and Feel**, **Configuration**, **Minimize**, **Maximize**, and **Remove**), title icon and title (such as **Language**), and a window which may contain contents (such as a set of language icons and links).

In a normal way, a portlet is an application that provides some content (such as information or service) that forms part of a portal page. A portlet container handles the portlets. A portlet container also processes requests and generates dynamic content. Actually, portals use portlets as pluggable user interface to provide a presentation layer information.

Loosely speaking, portlets are fragments of an HTML page, that is pieces of markup such as HTML, XHTML, WML, and so on (refer to JSR 286 specification). The content of a portlet is normally aggregated with the content of other portlets to form the portal page. The lifecycle of a portlet is managed by the portlet container. The content generated by a portlet may vary from one user to another, depending on the user configuration for the portlet.

Liferay Portal comes with several useful bundled portlets, and also supports the JSR-168 standard (and furthermore, JSR-286 standard) 100%, which allows the portal administrators to deploy any third party portlet developed according to this standard.

 Where can you find more details about JSR-168 and JSR-286? JSR-168 means Portlet Specification 1.0/1.1 and JSR-286 means Portlet Specification 2.0. You can find more details at `http://jcp.org/en/jsr/detail?id=168`, `http://jcp.org/en/jsr/detail?id=286`.

Using Portlet Container

The portlet **Language** runs in the portal page. It requires runtime environment, that is, a portlet container.

Generally, a portlet container provides portlets with persistent storage for preferences and required runtime environment (refer to JSR 286 specification). A portlet container manages portlet lifecycles and receives requests from the portal to execute requests on the portlets. A portlet container is the responsibility of the portal to handle the aggregation.

How Does A Portal Work?

The following is a typical sequence of events, initiated when you access the portal page such as **Welcome** (refer to JSR 286 specification):

- A client (e.g. the administrator "**Palm Tree**") after being authenticated makes an HTTP request to the portal.
- The request is received by the portal (for example, Liferay portal).
- The portal determines if the request contains an action targeted at the portlets such as **Language** associated with the portal page, **Welcome**.
- If there is an action targeted at a portlet such as **Language**, the portal requests the portlet container to invoke the portlet to process the action.
- A portal invokes portlets such as **Language, Navigation**, and so on through the portlet container.
- The portal aggregates the output of the portlets in the portal page to the client (for example the administrator "**Palm Tree**").

How Does A Portlet Work?

How does the portlet **Language** work? Let's focus on the portlet **Language** and press the language icon **Deutsch (Deutschland)**. You will see the language of portal page change as shown in the following figure:

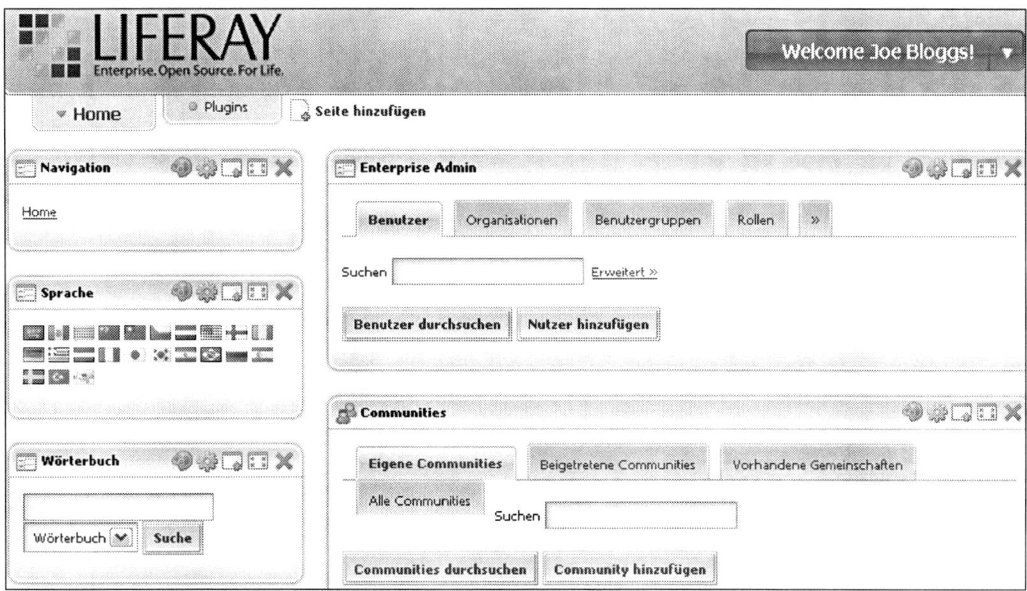

Further, let's do one more action on the portlet, **Language**. Simply click on the **Remove** icon at the top right of the portlet, and then click on the **OK** button. You will see the portlet **Language** disappear as shown in the following figure:

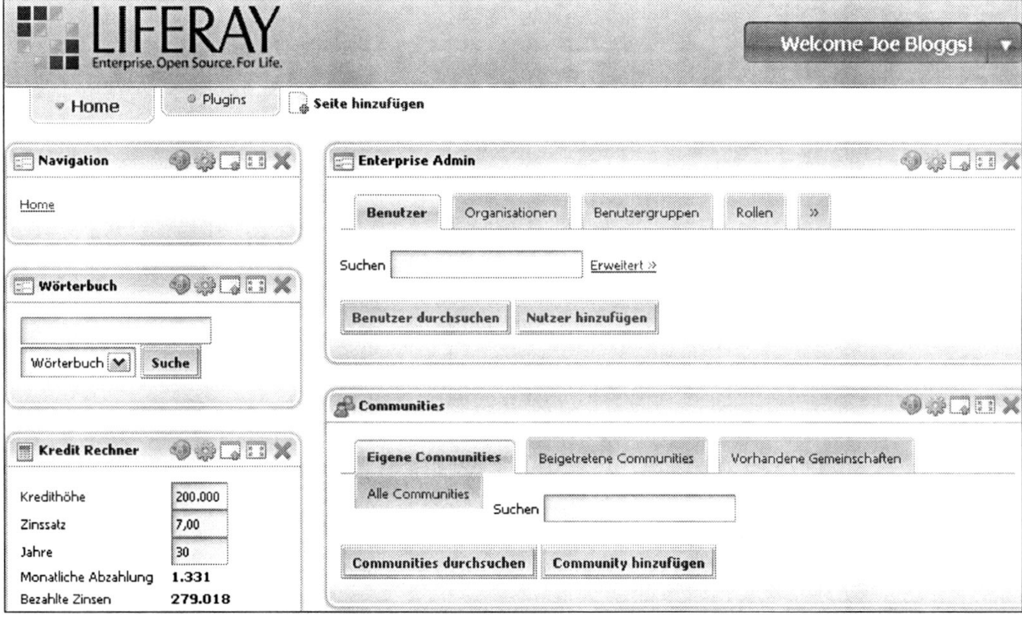

What the portal has done as stated before is related to portlet life cycle. You may need to read the following part (according to JSR-286 specification) if you are interested in the portlet life cycle. Otherwise, you can leave it for your future needs.

Applying Portlet Life-cycle

A portlet has a life-cycle defining how it is loaded, instantiated, and initialized, how requests from clients are handled, and how it is taken out of service (refer to JSR 286 specification). The lifecycle of a portlet includes the init, process-action, render and destroy methods of the portlet interface as shown in the following figure:

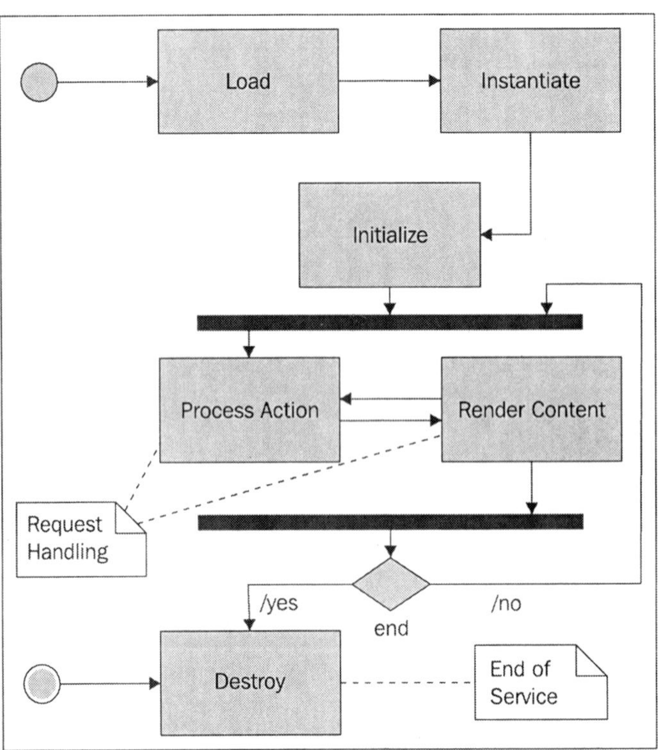

Loading and Instantiation — The loading and instantiation can happen when the portlet container starts loading the portlet applications. Or they can be delayed until the portlet container determines that request service is in need for the portlet.

Initialization — Portlets can initialize resources, and perform other one-time activities.

Request Handling — The portlet container may invoke the portlet to handle client requests. The portlet interface defines two methods for handling requests — the **Process Action** method and the **Render** method as shown in the following figure:

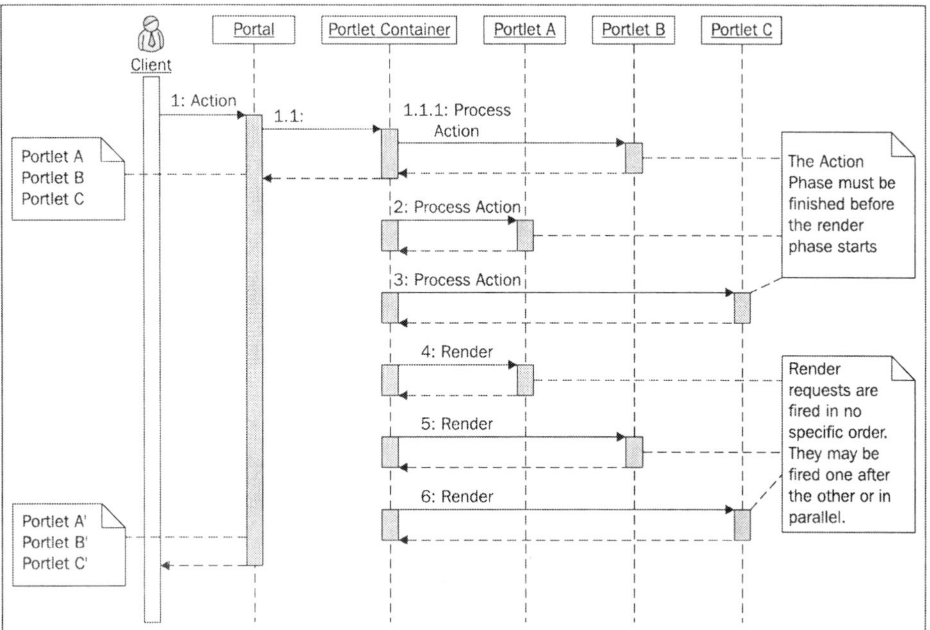

Generally, during a render request, portlets such as **Language**, **Navigation** and **Dictionary** generate content based on their current state.

End of Service—When the portlet container determines that a portlet would be removed from service, it will call the destroy method of the portlet interface in order to release any used resources and to save any persistent state.

Setting up Liferay Portal

As an administrator at the enterprise "**Palm-Tree Publications**", you need to undertake a lot of administration tasks, such as installing Liferay portal, installing and setting up databases, and so on.

You can install Liferay Portal through different ways, based on your specific needs. Normally, there are three main installation options:

- Using an open source bundle—It is the easiest and fastest installation method to install Liferay portal as a bundle. By using a Java SE runtime environment with an embedded database, you simply unzip and run the bundle as we have done in the beginning.

- Detailed installation procedure—You can install the portal in an existing application server. This option is available for all the supported application servers.

- Using the extension environment — You can use a full development environment to extend the functionality.

We will consider, partially, the second installation option "Detailed installation procedure" later (refer to Chapter 13 instructions). Meanwhile we will take up the third installation option "Using the extension environment" in the coming section.

In the previous section, we had used the first installation option "Using an open source bundle". Let's experience more details as follows:

Using Liferay Portal Bundled with Tomcat 5.5 in Windows

First let's consider one scenario when you, as an administrator, need to install Liferay portal in Windows with MySQL database, and your local Java version is JavaSE 5.0. Let's install Liferay portal bundled with Tomcat 5.5 in Windows as follows:

1. Download Liferay Portal bundled with Tomcat for JDK 5.0 from Liferay official web site.

   - Unzip the bundled file.

   - Set up MySQL database as follows:

2. Create a database and account in MySQL:

```
create database liferay;
grant all on liferay.* to 'liferay'@'localhost' identified by
'liferay' with grant option;
grant all on liferay.* to 'liferay'@'localhost.localdomain'
identified by 'liferay' with grant option;
```

3. Copy the MySQL JDBC driver `mysql.jar` to `$TOMCAT_DIR/lib/ext`;

4. Comment the Hypersonic data source (HSQL) configuration and uncomment MySQL configuration (`$TOMCAT_DIR/conf/Catalina/localhost/ROOT.xml`):

```
<!-- Hypersonic -->
<!--<Resource name="jdbc/LiferayPool" auth="Container"
type="javax.sql.DataSource" driverClassName="org.hsqldb.
jdbcDriver"
url="jdbc:hsqldb:lportal"
username="sa"
password=""
maxActive="20" /> -->

<!-- MySQL -->
```

```
<Resource name="jdbc/LiferayPool" auth="Container"
type="javax.sql.DataSource" driverClassName="com.mysql.jdbc.
    Driver"
url="jdbc:mysql://localhost/liferay?useUnicode=true&amp;characterE
    ncoding=UTF-8"
username="liferay"
password="liferay"
maxActive="20" />
```

5. Run `$TOMCAT_DIR /bin/startup.bat`.

6. Open your browser and go to `http://localhost:8080` (here we assume that it is a local installation, otherwise use the real host name or IP).

7. Login as an administrator — User: `test@liferay.com` and Password: `test`.

Note that the bundle comes with an embedded HSQL database loaded with sample data from the public website of Liferay. Do not use the Hypersonic in production.

Using Liferay Portal Bundled with Tomcat 6.x in Linux

Let's consider another scenario when you, as an administrator, need to install Liferay portal in Linux with MySQL database, and your local Java version is Java 6.0. Let's install Liferay portal bundled with Tomcat 6.0 in Linux as follows:

1. Download Liferay Portal bundled with Tomcat 6.0 from Liferay official web site.

2. Unzip the bundled file.

3. Create a database and account in MySQL (as stated before).

4. Run `$TOMCAT_DIR/bin/startup.sh`.

5. Open your browser and go to `http://localhost:8080` (assuming local installation; otherwise use the real host name or IP).

6. Log in as an administrator — User: *test@liferay.com* and Password: *test*.

Note that, Liferay Portal creates the tables it needs along with example data, the first time it starts. Furthermore, it is necessary to make the script executable by running **chmod +x filename.sh**. It is often necessary to run the executable from the directory where it resides.

Using More Options for Liferay Portal Installation

You can use one of the following options for Servlet containers and full Java EE application servers to install Liferay Portal:

- Geronimo + Tomcat
- Glassfish for AIX
- Glassfish for Linux
- Glassfish for OSX
- Glassfish for Solaris
- Glassfish for Solaris (x86)
- Glassfish for Windows
- JBoss + Jetty 4.0
- JBoss + Tomcat 4.0
- JBoss + Tomcat 4.2
- Jetty
- JOnAS + Jetty
- JOnAS + Tomcat
- Pramati
- Resin
- Tomcat 5.5 for JDK 1.4
- Tomcat 5.5 for JDK 5.0
- Tomcat 6.0

You can choose a preferred bundle according to your requirements and download it from the official download page directly. Simply go to the website http://www.liferay.com and click on **Downloads** page. This book uses the bundle Tomcat 6.0 to generate examples.

Flexible Deployment Matrix

As an administrator, you can install Liferay Portals on all major application servers, databases, and operating systems. There are over 700 ways to deploy Liferay Portal. Thus, you can reuse your existing resources, stick to your budget and get an immediate return on you investment that everyone can be happy with.

In general, you can install Liferay portal in Linux, UNIX and Windows with any one of the following application servers (or Servlet containers) and by selecting any one of the following database systems.

The applications servers (or Servlet containers) that Liferay Portal can run on, include:

- Borland ES 6.5
- Apache Geronimo 2.x
- Sun GlassFish 2 UR1
- JBoss 4.0.x, 4.2.x
- JOnAS 4.8.x
- JRun 4 Updater 3
- OracleAS 10.1.3.x
- Orion 2.0.7
- Pramati 5.0
- RexIP 2.5
- SUN JSAS 9.1
- WebLogic 8.1 SP4, 9.2, 10
- WebSphere 5.1, 6.0.x, 6.1.x
- Jetty 5.1.10
- Resin 3.0.19
- Tomcat 5.0.x/5.5.x/6.0.x

Databases that Liferay portal can run on include:

- Apache Derby
- IBM DB2
- Firebird
- Hypersonic
- Informix
- InterBase
- JDataStore
- MySQL
- Oracle
- PostgresSQL

- SAP
- SQL Server
- Sybase

Operating systems that Liferay portal can run on include:

- LINUX (Debian, RedHat, SUSE, Ubuntu, and so on.)
- UNIX (AIX, FreeBSD, HP-UX, OS X, Solaris, and so on.)
- WINDOWS
- MAC OS X

Customizing Personal Area

As an administrator such as "**Palm Tree**", at the enterprise of "Palm Tree Publications", you may expect to customize your personal area (that is, the default home page that you see when you sign in) in your own **Community** anytime. Normally, the personal area refers to both public pages and **Private Pages** at **My Community**. You can find it by clicking on the **Welcome, Palm Tree** first, then moving the mouse on **My Place** and furthermore, by clicking on **Private Pages** or **Public Pages**, under **My Community**.

Note that if there were no pages in **Private Pages**, under **My Community, My Account** would be used to add pages with **Page** tab selected. The page management at **My Account** is the same as that in **Manage Page** (refer to the next section). The difference is that **My Account** manages pages only in **My Community**, while **Manage Page** manages pages for any **Community**. For more details about **My Account**, refer to Chapter 3. For a change of logo , refer to the forthcoming section.

What's a **Private Page**? A **Private Page** is a page in a **Community** that can be accessed only by logged in users, who are part of the **Community**. If a user is not logged in (that is, the user is a guest), or if a user does not belong to your **Community**, then the user cannot access the **Private Page**.

What's a **Public Page**? A **Public Page** is a page in a **Community** that can be accessed by guests. As long as the guest has the appropriate URL, the guest can access any **Public Page**.

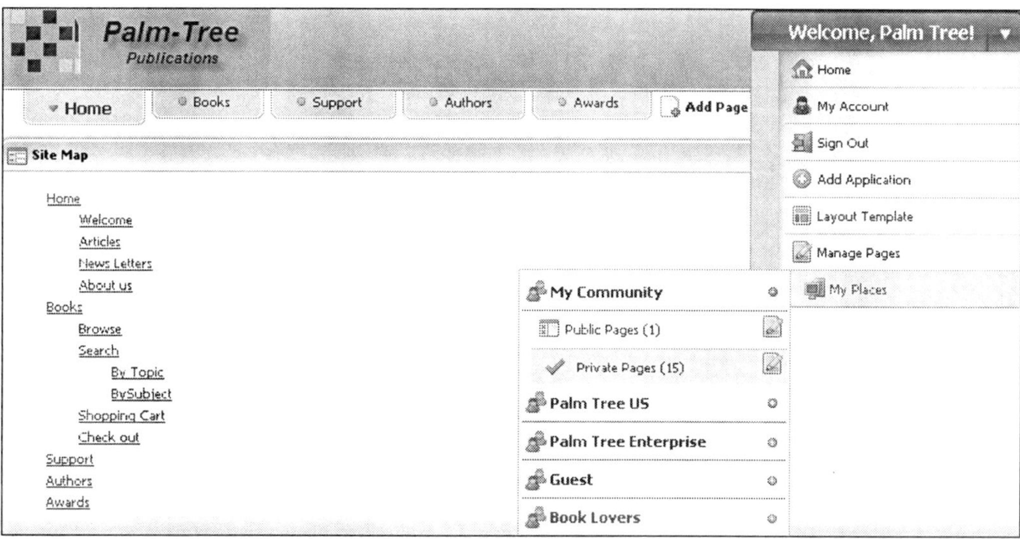

After logging in successfully, you are ready to customize the personal area at **Private Pages** for the following tasks:

- Add new pages including the home page, or remove existing pages, or update existing pages first, then add or remove portlets in the current page.

- Change the layout templates for the current page.

In general, registered users, who have the appropriate permission, will have a personal area, that is, the user's **Private Pages**. The personal area is organized in a set of pages as a hierarchy. The rest of this section shows how a user (such as an administrator) can customize his or her personal area.

Add Pages

You are ready to add two pages, **Home** and **Books** to your personal area. Let's add a page named **Home** as follows:

1. Click on **Add Page** icon and link.

2. Simply input the page name such as **Home** first, and then press the **Save** button next to the page name.

Similarly, you can add a page named **Books**. Let's do this as follows:

1. Click on **Add Page** icon and link.

2. Simply input the page name such as **Home** first, and then press the Save button.

 Note that the possibility of adding pages, depends on the theme, by default. With the theme, **Classic**, you can add page in the **Navigation** bar, but not with the theme, **Brochure**. In the theme **Classic**, you'll find in `navigation.vm: class="sort-pages modify-pages"`.

Of course, you can add as many pages as you want. After adding a set of pages, we can view them.

You may want to change the page name **Home** to **My Home**. It is simple to do this. Simply double click on the page name **Home**. Change the page name to **My Home** first, and then press the **Save** button next to the page name.

 How do you add children pages? To add children pages to first level pages, such as **Books**, you need to use **My Account** under the **Pages** tab to manage pages at your own **Community**. Especially, if you are at a **Community**, other than your own **Community**, such as **Guest Community**, you need to use **Manage Pages** with the **Children** tab to manage pages. For more details, refer to the next section.

Remove Pages

Suppose we do not require the page, **Home,** for some reason. We need to remove this page. Let's do it as follows:

1. Move the mouse to the page name, **Home**. If the page is not the current page, the **delete** icon will appear.

2. Click on the **delete** icon next to the page name. A message "**Are you sure you want to delete this page?**" with buttons **OK** and **Cancel** will appear.

3. Press the **OK** button if you want to remove the page.

Similarly, you can remove the other pages as well. It is simple and also dynamic to remove a page.

Note that there is no **delete** icon for the current page. If you want to delete the current page, you need to click other pages and make the current page a normal page first. Then you can delete it as stated before. Furthermore, any instances of portlets of the page would be removed, if the page is removed.

Add Portlets

It is time now to add portlets to your page. For example, we need to add portlet **Site Map** to the **Books** page. Let's do it as follows:

1. Click on the **Add Application** link. This will bring up **Add Application** panel on your screen.

2. Input portlet name **Site Map**; find the portlet "**Site Map**" from the menu.

3. Click on the **Add** button next to the right of the portlet name **Site Map**.

4. Click on the **Close** icon of the **Add Application** panel to close it.

You will see that the portlet has been added to the bottom of your page. Now you are ready to change the portlet placement. To do so, click on the title bar of the portlet and drag it to where you like. You can add as many portlets as you want in your pages.

Remove Portlets

Maybe you do not want the **Books** page to contain the portlet **Site Map** anymore. Therefore, we need to remove the portlet from the page. Let's do it as follows:

1. Locate the **Site Map** portlet.

2. Click on the **remove** icon at the upper right of the portlet.

3. A message "**Are you sure you want to remove this component?**" with buttons **OK** and **Cancel** will appear.

4. Click on the **OK** button.

Of course, you can remove any portlet from any page.

Note that everything related to the portlet in the page would be removed if the portlet is removed from the page. You cannot recover it after deletion.

Changing Layout Templates

You can also change the template for your page with the **Layout Template** button. Layout template allows you to arrange your portlets in one, two-two, or one-two-one columns as well as designate the width of the columns. You can add and arrange all the portlets that you would like on your page with the layout templates.

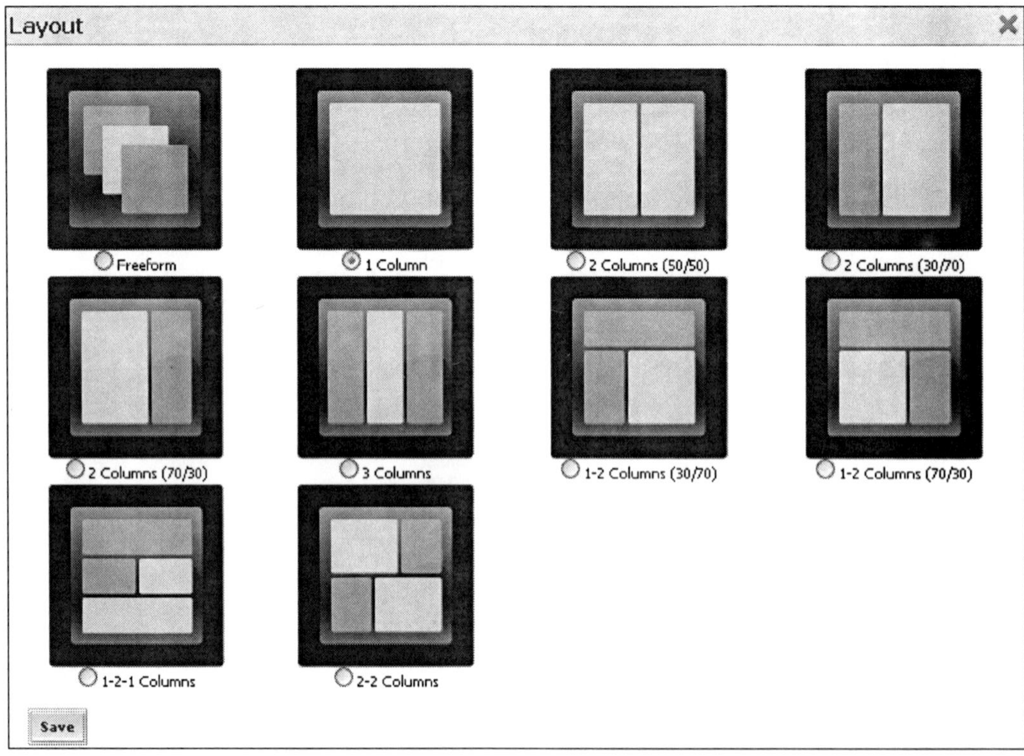

Generally speaking, layout templates define the areas where you can place the portlets in a page. By default, Liferay comes with several different layout templates as shown in the previous figure. Normal users of **Private Pages** or administrators of communities or public websites can choose the layout to use on each portlet page.

In most cases, the default layout templates would be suitable. But you may need a very specific portlet window organization, such as website games/videos/play-list landing pages. Thanks to Liferay, maximum flexibility is provided to portal administrators, to deploy extra layout templates developed either by you or by any third party.

Note that if the preloaded templates are insufficient for your needs, you can create your own deployable layouts, using a sample layout template, or using a **Community**-submitted one.

Setting up Portal Pages

We have discussed how to build the home page, that is, personal area. Now let's see how to set up normal pages. As an administrator or website editor, you are required to set up the pages of any **Community**. Suppose you want to set up both **Private Pages** and **Public Pages** of **My Community** "Palm Tree" with the following tasks:

1. Edit pages and add child pages to the current page such as "**Palm Tree**" **Private Page**. You can use the **Page** tab and the **Children** tab of **Manage Page**.

2. Change the logo and themes for "**Palm Tree**" **Private Page**. You can use the **Logo** tab and **Look and Feel** tab of **Manage Page**.

With **Manage Pages**, you can change the look and feel with one click, manage portal pages, insert JavaScript, sitemap protocol, and meta-data, and set friendly URLs.

Managing Pages

You can manage top pages by clicking the top page name on the left-hand side, such as **Palm Tree**. Under managing the top page, you can add child pages, change the logo for all **Private Pages**, and change the look and feel of public or **Private Pages**.

Add A Child Page

Suppose you need to add a child page, **Awards** under **Palm Tree**. You can add this page as follows:

1. Click the **Manage Pages** from your current page (**Private Pages**).
2. Click on the root **Palm Tree**.
3. Select the tab, **New Page,** after the tab, **Children,** is selected.
4. Input child page name, such as **Awards**.
5. Select a type, such as **Portlet**.
6. Check the **Hidden** box, if you want to hide the page.
7. Press the **Add Page** button when you are ready.

Of course, you may add more child pages if you wish. The root page, and all children pages form a hierarchy tree, as shown in the following figure:

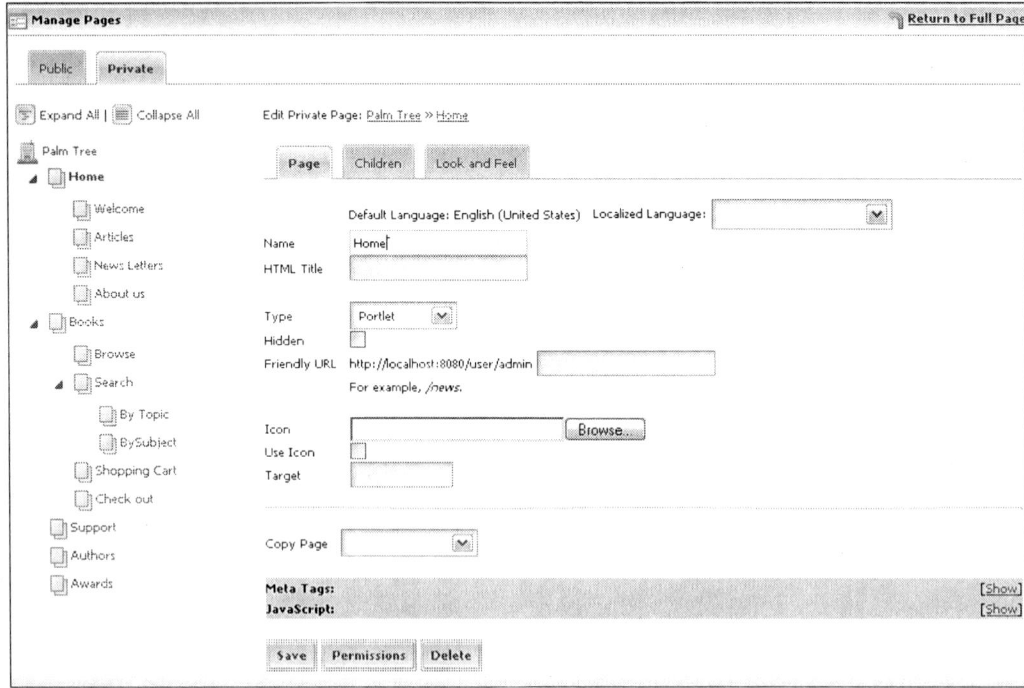

Change Display Order

You can change the display order of the child pages under **Managing Top Page**, as follows:

1. Select the tab, **Display Order**.

2. Click on a child page, such as **Books**; then click the **Move Up** button to move up the selected page; or click the **Move Down** button to move down the selected page; or click the **Remove** button to delete the selected page.

3. Press the **Update Display Order** button when you are ready.

Merge Pages

You can configure the top level pages of this public website to merge with the top level pages of the public **Guest Community**. Users can then navigate between the two sites seamlessly.

First, you can select a **Community** other than **Guest Community**. Then click on the **Manage Page** link and select the top of **Public** or **Private Pages**. By default, the **Children** tab is selected.

To enable merging the **Guest Public Pages**, simply select the tab, **Merge Pages**, and check the box, **Merge Guest Public Pages**. To disable merging pages, simply uncheck the **Merge Guest Public Pages** box. Press the **Save** button when you are ready.

Change The Logo

You can change the logo from the default enterprise logo. For example, you have seen the logo of "Palm Tree Publications" in the previous figures. How do we get it? Let's do it as follows:

1. Select **My Places** link and also select a **Community** (such as **My Community**, and, **Public pages** or **Private pages**).

2. Select **Manage Page** and further, select the top of the **public** or **Private Pages**, such as **Palm Tree**.

3. Press the **Logo** tab and upload a logo say, `"palmtree_logo.png"`.

In general, you can upload a logo for the public or **Private Pages** that will be used instead of the default enterprise logo.

Edit A Page

You can edit the pages such as **Awards** under **Manage Pages**. For example, if you want to replace the page title **Awards** with "Our Awards":

1. Find the page you want to edit in the left-hand tree structure.

2. Click on the **Awards** page.

3. Click on the **Page** tab.

4. Input the **HTML Title** of the page with the value "**Our Awards**".

5. Click on the **Save** button when you are ready.

You also have the option to rename the current page, change the display language of the current page, again change the HTML title, change the type of the current page, and change the option whether the current page should be hidden or not.

You can also provide a **Friendly URL** for this page. For example, you can create a URL for the page "**Awards**" as `"http://localhost:8080/user/admin/awards"`.

If many parameters are passed in, through the URL, the portal URL becomes very long and difficult to read. However, you can give your page a **Friendly URL** to make it easier to read and access.

Liferay portal also provides a **Friendly URL** for each **Community**. Thus you could just put in a **Friendly URL** for your page (it must also start with "/") such as "/awards". If there is no duplication, you can now access your page using the following URL pattern:

```
http://server-name/community-friendly-url/page-friendly-url
```

You can also upload an icon for the current page and decide whether the icon is used or not. For instance, you can upload "reference.gif" as the icon for the **Awards** page.

You already have the **Awards** page in your **Community**, and further, you could set up another page, **Others** exactly like the **Awards** page. For this, you can use the **Copy Page** function. Just select the **Awards** page that you want to copy from the drop-down next to **the Copy Page** and click the **Save** button while editing the **Others** page. Your current page, **Others**, will be an exact copy of the **Awards** page you have selected except for the page's name.

Furthermore, you can insert the **Meta Tags**, **Java Scripts**, and **Sitemap protocol** for this page.

Delete A Page

If you do not want the page **Awards** for some reason, you can delete it. You can delete the pages under **Manage Pages**:

1. Locate the page you want to delete in the left-hand tree structure.
2. Click the **Awards** page.
3. Click the **Page** tab.
4. Click the **Delete** button.
5. A screen will appear asking if you want to delete the selected page. Click the **OK** button to confirm.

Note that if a page such as the root page, **Palm Tree** is the only one page in the **My Community**, you cannot delete it under **Manage Pages**. Moreover, deleting a page will delete all child pages related to this page and remove all portlet instances that this page owns.

Changing Themes

At this point, you may have all the portlets that you expect to have in your pages. You can now change the look and feel of your portal. Liferay Portal provides different themes by default that you may apply to your page. As an administrator in the portal, you may want to configure additional themes.

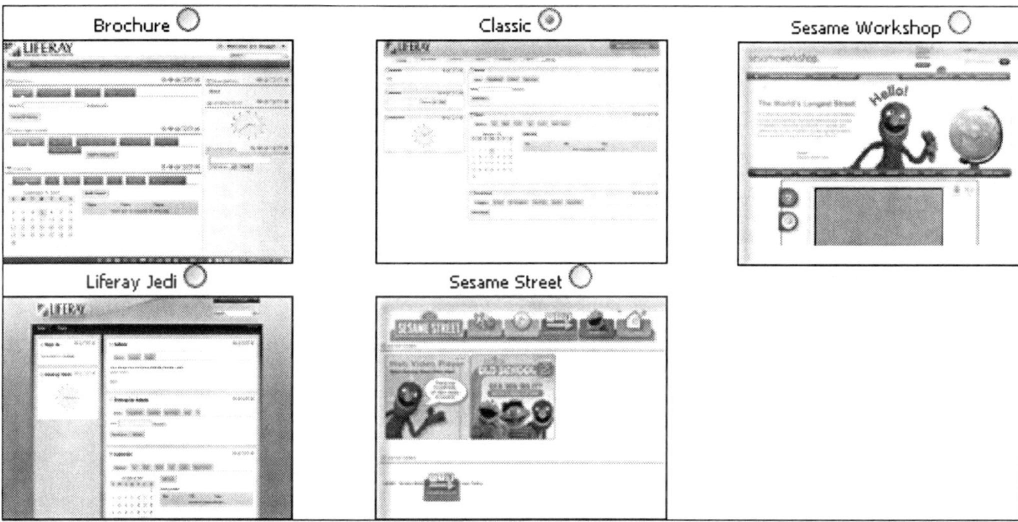

To change the theme you can refer to the following instructions:

1. Click on the **Manage Pages** link at the top-right of your page.

2. Select the page you would like to change the theme for, on the left hand side. Note that, by default, all children pages will inherit the theme from the parent. If you want to inherit the **Look and Feel** from the root node, select **Yes** for the "**Inherit look and feel from the private root node?**" box. Otherwise, select **No**.

3. Select the **Look and Feel** tab for that page.

4. You will see a number of bundled themes that are available. Choose your theme and color scheme. You can experiment with it as much as you like until you find a theme that pleases you.

Themes customize the overall look and feel. Liferay Portal groups themes are divided into two categories: regular browsers and mobile devices. By default, regular browser themes are further divided into three sub groups: Themes, Color Schemes and CSS (Cascading Style Sheets). You can insert custom CSS that will be loaded after the theme. In addition, Liferay portal provides WAP (Wireless Application Protocol) theme that is designed to run on mobile devices. If you had WAP clients, WAP theme would be an ideal look and feel.

By using themes, you can easily switch among different presentational layers. As a designer or developer, you can deliver an integrated package of JSP (or Velocity), JavaScript, image and configuration files (that is, a WAR file) that will control all presentation logic and design attributes for a portal **Community**.

How do you get the previous additional themes (**Sesame Street** and **Sesame Workshop**)? Just put the files: `themeStreet.war` and `themeWorkshop.war` in the folder `$USER_HOME/liferay/deploy`.

How Do You Customize Portlets ?

As an administrator or a normal user from website editorial department at "**Palm-Tree Publications**", you have added a set of portlets to your pages. Now you are ready to customize the portlets of the portal page. Suppose you are using the **Site Map** portlet and you want to customize it:

- Change the Background Color, Font and Text size.

- Change the **Title** and hide the border.

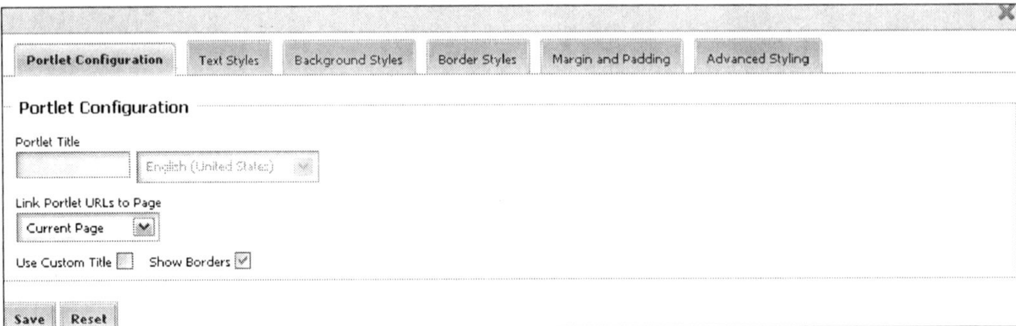

To change the Background Color, the Font and Text size of the portlet, you can simply click on the **Look and Feel** icon that appears in the portlet, **Site Map** first. On clicking, portlet customization screen will appear. Then by selecting tab **Background Style**, you can change the background color. By selecting the **Text Style** tab, you can change the font and text size. Press **Save** button when you are ready, click the **remove** icon if you want to cancel the changes, or press the **Reset** button if you want to reset.

To change the title of the portlet and hiding the border of the portlet, you can simply click on the **Look and Feel** icon that appears in the Portlet **Site Map** first. Then you simply input a title, select a language, select the checkbox, **Use Custom Title**, and uncheck the **Show Borders** box. Press **Save** button when you are ready.

Liferay portal provides the ability to change the look and feel of portlets dynamically with the following possibilities:

- **Portlet configuration**: for using custom title, showing borders, selecting languages for title, and so on.
- **Text Style**: for font, size, color, alignment, text decoration, word spacing, line height, letter spacing, and so on.
- **Background Style**: for background color, and so on.
- **Border Style**: for border width, border style, border color etc.
- **Margin and Padding**: for padding, margin, and so on.
- **Advanced Styling**: for entering in your custom CSS.

How Do You Navigate The Structure of Intranet Site?

As an administrator or a normal user from the website editorial department at the "**Palm-Tree Publications**" enterprise, you have customized the pages in the portal. Now it is ready for you to navigate the structure of the website. Suppose, your current page is **Search** and you want to provide the following tasks:

1. Show the structured directory of links to all pages in the portal. You simply add the **Site Map** portlet in the page if the portlet is not there.
2. Display a directory of links reflecting the portal's page structure, with drill down into the current page. You can add the **Navigation** portlet in the page.
3. Displays a trail of parent pages for the current page. You just add the **Breadcrumb** portlet in the page.

The Breadcrumb portlet provides ability to show a trail of parent pages for the current page. It can be placed on public portal pages as a navigational aid to publish websites. It helps the user visualize the structure of the site and quickly move from a page to a broader grouping of information.

The Navigation portlet provides a directory of links to reflect the portal's page structure, with drill down into the current page. Style and appearances are adjustable. The **Navigation** portlet displays links to other pages outside the current page's trail of parent pages. It helps the user visualize the structure of the site and provides links to move from page to page quickly. Further, it displays more information about the current page.

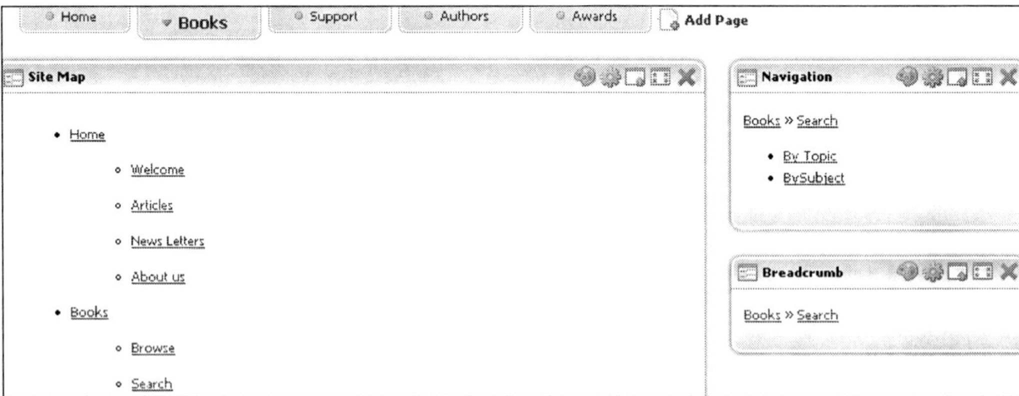

The **Site map** portlet provides the ability to display a structured directory of links to all the pages in the portal. It is used to navigate directly to any page on the site. Furthermore, it can be configured to display the entire site or a sub-section of pages.

When do you use these portlets? To display a trail of parent pages such as **Books.** for the current page such as **Search** only, use **Breadcrumb** portlet. To display both a trail of parent page, **Books** for the current page, **Search** and the page structure of the current page, use the **Navigation** portlet. To display a structured directory of links to all pages in the portal, use the **Site Map** portlet.

How to Configure Liferay Portal?

As an administrator at "**Palm-Tree Publications**", you may need to customize the Liferay portal through configuration files in order to satisfy your own requirements.

Let's see an example of how to customize Liferay Portal's configuration. In this example, Liferay Portal has been installed using the Tomcat bundle and then a custom theme called "**Sesame Street**" has been deployed as a WAR. As an administrator at the "**Palm-Tree Publications**" enterprise, you want this theme to be used by default in any newly created desktop or **Community**. To achieve that, you look in `portal.properties` and find that the property `default.regular.theme.id` can be used to set the default theme, so that you can create the file `portal-ext.properties` in `$TOMCAT_DIR/webapps/ROOT/WEB-INFO/classes` with the following values:

```
default.regular.theme.id=street1.0
```

After a server reboot, these properties are applied to the portal automatically. When your pages (with names **HOME, GAMES, VIDEOS, SESAME PLAYLISTS, MUPPETS**, and **MYSTREET**) use the theme, "**Sesame Street**" as **Look and Feel**, you will get the following figure:

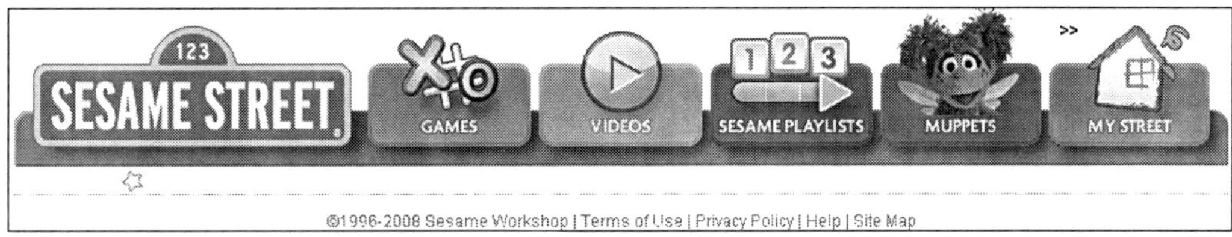

Liferay provides high customizability through the web, and through configuration files. Let's see how to customize mail servers and other configurations.

Customizing Mail Servers

Suppose that the Enterprise "Palm Tree Publications" has a mail server with the "`exg3.exghost.com`" domain. As an administrator, you need to integrate this mail server with Liferay portal by default. Let's do it as follows:

1. Find the file `ROOT.xml` in `$TOMCAT_DIR/conf/Catalina/localhost`.

2. Find the mail configuration.

3. And then configure it as follows:

```
<!-- Mail -->
<Resource name="mail/MailSession" auth="Container"
                       type="javax.mail.Session"
mail.imap.host="exg3.exghost.com"
mail.pop3.host="exg3.exghost.com"
mail.smtp.host="exg3.exghost.com"
mail.store.protocol="imap"
mail.transport.protocol="smtp"/>
```

Of course, you can integrate with Washington IMAP+Sendmail, Cyrus IMAP+Postfix, and Dovecot+Postfix, Microsoft Exchange, as well as other IMAP servers. For more details, refer to Chapter 9.

Configuring Portal Paths

There are two files which are used to configure portal paths: `portal.properties` and `system.properties`. You should not modify `portal.properties` and `system.properties` directly. You should just create two files named `portal-ext.properties` and `system-ext.properties`, and write in only the properties whose values you want to override. These two files can be placed with the original one, or in the global classpath of the application server. These two extended files are located at `$TOMCAT_DIR/webapps/ROOT/WEB-INFO/classes`.

Before customizing the configuration, it is better to review and update the values of the following properties;

- `auto.deploy.deploy.dir=${user.home}/liferay/deploy`: enable auto-deploy.
- `lucene.dir=${user.home}/liferay/lucene/`: for search to work.
- `jcr.jackrabbit.repository.root=${user.home}/liferay/jackrabbit`: for the document library.

Customizing Configuration

We can override the properties of configuration files. Let's configure the portal through the `portal-ext.properties` and `system-ext.properties` files that can be created and stored in any place in the class-path. When the extension development environment is used, you will find that these files are already present in the directory `ext/ext-impl/WEB-INF/classes`. Otherwise, they are stored in the global class-path of the application server. For example:

- Tomcat: Place them in `$TOMCAT_DIR/webapps/ROOT/WEB-INFO/classes`.
- JBoss: Place them in `$JBOSS_DIR/server/default/conf`.
- Other application servers: Read the documentation provided with them.

Liferay uses EasyConf to read `portal.properties`, so that all functionalities provided by this library are also available.

The main configuration file is `portal.properties`, which contains a detailed explanation of the properties that it defines. To change the value of any of its properties, do it through a file called `portal-ext.properties`.

The `system.properties` file is provided as a convenient way to set all properties for the JVM machine and related system settings. Start your application server with the system property *system.properties.load* set to true to load it. When the server starts, the portal will load the `system.properties` file and then the `system-ext.properties file`.

 What's EasyConf? EasyConf is a library to access the configuration of software components and applications. It defines simple conventions to make it easier to use.

Setting up Extension Environment

As an administrator or a developer from engineering department at the enterprise, **"Palm-Tree Publications"**, you may want to develop an engineering project (for example, collaborating on alfresco contents by Web services) on top of the Liferay portal, like a platform, without having to worry about upgrading in future. You can follow these instructions to set it up:

- Requirements: Java 1.4 or Java 5.0 or Java 6.0 or a later version; Ant 1.7 or a later version; Liferay Portal source code; Web Server (Tomcat, Resin, and so on).

- Set JAVA_HOME to your Java directory. Set ANT_HOME to your Ant directory. Add `JAVA_HOME/bin` and `ANT_HOME/bin` to System Path.

- Configuring your compiler (`build.${user.name}.properties`):

```
## javac.compiler
## classic (the standard compiler of JDK 1.1/1.2).
## modern (the standard compiler of JDK 1.3/1.4/1.5/1.6).
## jikes (the Jikes compiler).
## jvc (Microsoft's SDK for Java/Visual J++ ).
## kjc (the kopi compiler).
## gcj (the gcj compiler from gcc).
## sj (Symantec java compiler).
## extJavac (run either modern or classic in a JVM of its own).
javac.compiler=mordern
javac.debug=on
javac.deprecation=off
javac.fork=true
javac.memoryMaximumSize=256m
javac.nowarn=on
jsp.precompile=off
```

- Configuring your release properties.

- Ant clean start build-ext.

- Configuring your application server properties.

- Ant build.

- Developing your new portlets.

You now can develop and deploy your own custom portlets, themes, and applications.

Furthermore let's consider another scenario. Suppose that you, as an administrator or a developer from an engineering group, want to base your extensions on top of the latest sources of Liferay Portal, instead of using the stable release, you can follow these instructions to set it up:

1. Download and install Subversion and/or a subversion client such as SmartSVN, TortoiseSVN or those provided by IDE environments.

2. Configure the client to use the https protocol to connect to **lportal.svn.sourceforge.net**.

3. Check out the portal.

The extension environment is a complete development environment that eases customizing Liferay Portal to suit your own needs. It combines many Liferay tools that can probably be used to build your portlets and portals, such as Struts-Portlet, Spring MVC Portlet and Service Builder.

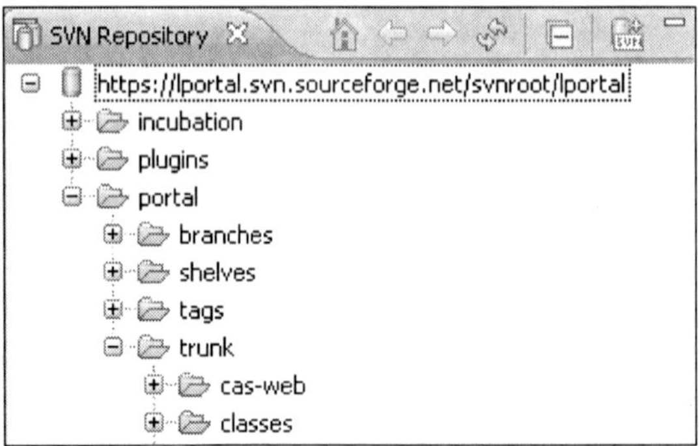

Note that for some projects in which there isn't a need to customize the portal extensively and there is only a need to develop new portlets and themes, you can use the Plugins SDK instead of the extension environment. It is also possible to use both environments at the same time for different needs. Refer to Chapter 10.

Summary

This chapter discussed how to experience implementing a portal page with portlets, understand portals, portlet containers, and portlets according to the JSR-286 specification. This chapter also discussed how to set up the portal, including installation options and deployment matrix, how to configure the home page and all other pages of the intranet web site. Then it introduced the concepts of how to customize the personal area, build the portal pages, and to navigate the structure of the Intranet via portlets such as **Site Map**, **Breadcrumb**, and **Navigation**. Finally, it provided guidance to configure the portal based on the `system-ext.properties` and `portal-ext.properties files`, and set up extension environment in order to extend functionality briefly.

3

Bringing In Users

Liferay Portal provides a powerful and yet highly configurable full security model for controlling **Users**, resources, workflow, search and policies. The full security model incorporates a fine-grained permission system to give administrators full control over access and privileges to portlets and objects within the portal. By this model, **Users** can assign **Permissions** to other **Users**, **Communities**, **Organizations**, **Locations**, and **User Groups** on a per portlet basis, and also, control **Permissions** all the way down to the object level.

This chapter begins with my account management, discusses bringing in **Users**, and all the ways to assign **Permissions** to **Users**. Finally, it gives a high-level overview of all the entities involved in the security model. In addition, this chapter introduces configurable authentications related to out-of-the-box managed accounts, LDAP (Lightweight Directory Access Protocol), SSO (Single Sign-On) CAS and OpenID.

By the end of this chapter, you would have learnt how to:

- Update the profile in **My Account.**
- Administrate **Users**, **User Groups**, **Organizations**, and **Locations.**
- Integrate with LDAP and SSO.
- Manage **Roles** and **Permissions**.
- Apply full access control security model.

Managing My Account

As an administrator at the enterprise "**Palm-Tree Publications**", you need to access the portal first, and then log into the portal. More interestingly, you can update your profile using your real personal information, such as name, password, language, time zone, icon, etc. The following sections show how to access the portal, log into the portal, and change the profile.

Accessing The Portal

By default, there are two ways to access Liferay portal: a regular connection (HTTP), and a secured connection (HTTPS). A default bundle installation supports HTTP only. The URL is `http://book.com:8080`. You can change the port number such as 80, and use a security connection by un-commenting the port number 433 at Tomcat.

 For more details about HTTP and HTTPS, refer to the Chapter 13.

Logging into The Portal

You can get the login page by clicking on a link "**Sign in,**" in the upper right corner that takes you to the login page. If it is not available in the default installation, you can go directly to the login page, by using the URL: `http://book.com/c/portal/login`.

In the login page, you are asked for the following information:

- Login name (as an e-mail address) `test@liferay.com`
- Password `test`

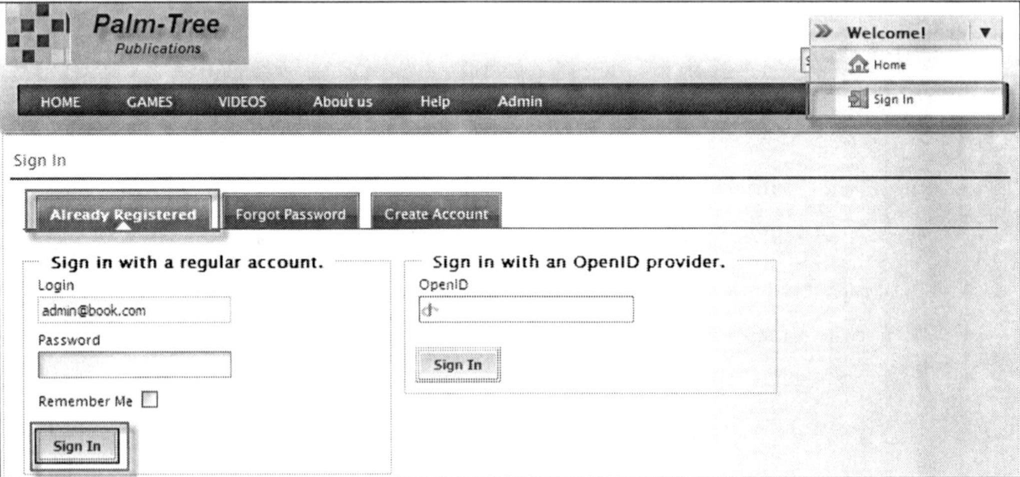

Updating Your Profile

As an administrator, you are running Liferay portal now, and you'll see a set of portlets in the default page. It is ready for you to update your profile anytime, such as **Screen Name, Email Address, First Name, Last Name, Icon, Language, Greeting Message**, and so on.

To update the profile, you simply use the **My Account** link first. Then you just update name, **Email Address, Language, Time Zone, Greetings, Password, Phone,** SMS messenger ID, comments, and so on, as you want. For example, if you want to display your icon in other portlets, such as discussion forums, you need to upload your own image by clicking on the **Change** link. Finally, press the **Save** button to save the changes. If you do not want to change anything, simply click on the **Cancel** button.

Note that, if you change your email address and password, you need to memorize your update. You have to use the updated email address and password for your login, next time.

In a nutshell, Liferay portal provides the ability to update the **User's** profile and also the **User's** own **Community** pages (such as **Public Pages** and **Private Pages**) dynamically, by using **My Account** link. It is useful for any **User** in the enterprise "Palm Tree Publications" after logging in, and using **My Account** link to update the profile.

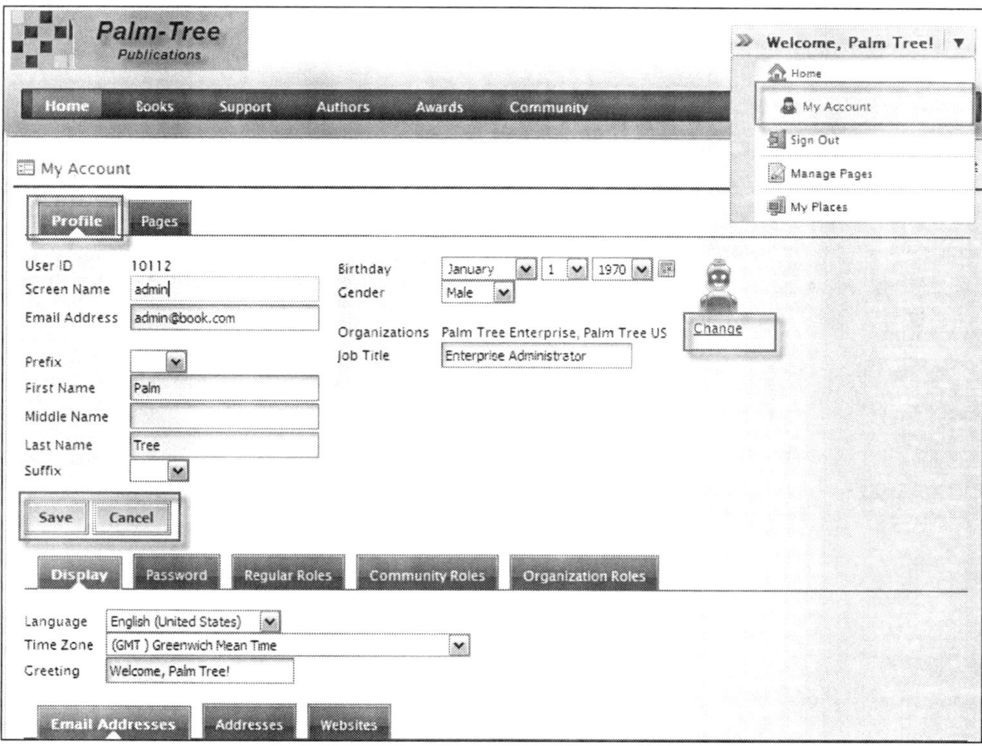

Adding and Managing Users

The enterprise "Palm Tree Publications" with its global headquarters in US, has several departments such as editorial, engineering, marketing, and so on. Each department has staff in the United States, or in Germany, or both.

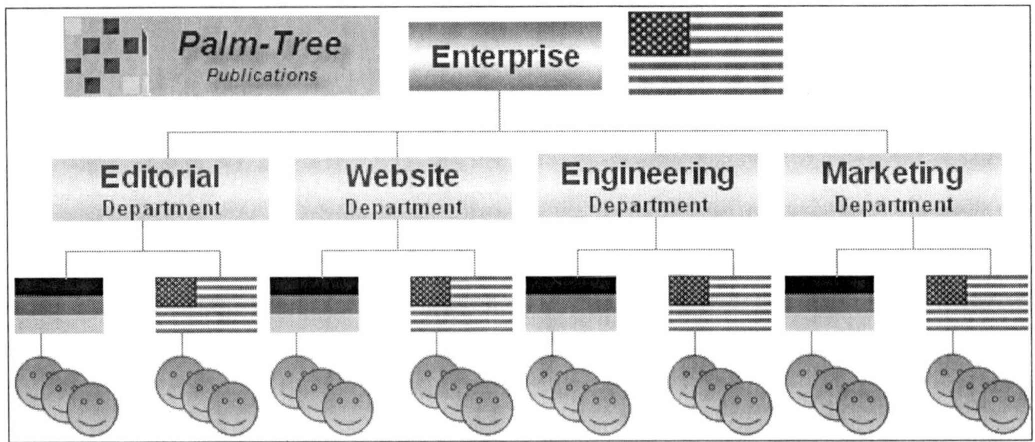

We are planning to bring in the following **Users** into the Portal. A **User** is an individual, who performs tasks using the portal.

Full Name	Screen Name	Email	Organization	Location
Palm Tree	Admin	**admin@book.com**	Enterprise	US
David Berger	David	**david@book.com**	Editorial	US
Lotti Stein	Lotti	**lotti@book.com**	Editorial	US
Rolf Hess	Rolf	**rolf@book.com**	Editorial	US
Julia Maurer	Julia	**julia@book.com**	Editorial	Germany
Martin Gall	Martin	**martin@book.com**	Editorial	Germany
James Masse	James	**james@book.com**	Website	US
Raja Fuchs	Raja	**raja@book.com**	Engineering	Germany
John Stucki	John	**john@book.com**	Marketing	Germany

Suppose that, as an administrator of "Palm Tree Publications", you plan to create a page called "**Admin**" at **Book Lovers Community**. Moreover, you plan to create a page called "**Users**" under the page "**Admin**," for administration tasks.

Working with Organizations

We can use **Organizations** to represent "Palm Tree Publications" and its departmental hierarchies.

Adding A Top-level Organization

First of all, we need to create a "top-level" **Organization** (that is, the enterprise) for the whole company — in this case, "Palm Tree Publications". Let's do it now:

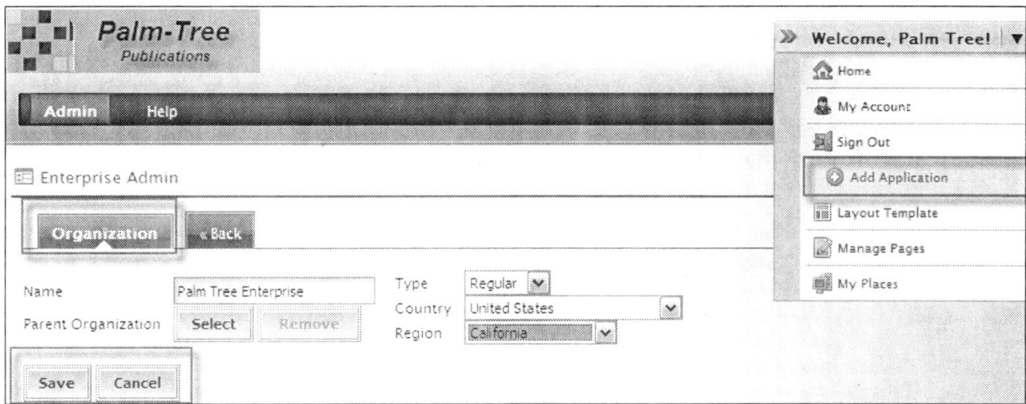

1. Log into the Portal as an administrator (using user email and password, you have updated by **My Account** in the previous section).

2. Add a page named "**Admin**" to **Book Lovers Community Private Pages**. Moreover, add a child page called "**Users**" under the page, "**Admin**".

3. Add **Enterprise Admin** portlet in the page "**Users,**" if the portlet is not there. (To achieve this, move the mouse on the links at the top right and find a link named **Add Application** first. Then click on the link, **Add Application**. In the popup **Add Application**, find **Enterprise Admin** through search or navigation under the **Admin** catalogue. Finally, click on the portlet **Enterprise Admin** to add the application, and click on the icon **Remove,** to close the popup.)

4. Click on the **Organizations** tab in the **Enterprise Admin** Portlet first. Then, click the button **Add Organization**.

5. Enter enterprise information in the **Name** input field such as "**Palm Tree Enterprise**", and select a value from the **Country** menu such as "**United States**", a value from the **Region** menu such as "**California**".

6. Select or Remove **Parent Organization**; here we maintain the default value.

7. Select **Type** with value, "**Regular**".

> Note that the Enterprise is the top level **Organization**. It has no parent **Organization**. At the same time, it is an **Organization**, which will have a set of sub **Organizations**. Thus, it is a regular **Organization** with type value "**Regular**".

8. Click the **Save** button to save the inputs.

So we've created a top-level **Organization**. Now we need to create **Organizations** for the main departments in the company.

Managing Organizations

Organizations can contain other **Organizations** such as sub **Organizations**. This is useful in large companies where each department might almost be a separate company, with little interaction among them.

Add Child Organizations

Let's create two departments within "Palm Tree Publications", Editorial and Marketing as follows:

1. Click on the **Organizations** tab in the **Enterprise Admin** portlet first, then click the button, **Add Organization**.

2. Enter enterprise information in the **Name** input field such as "**Editorial Department**" and select an option from the **Country** menu such as "**United States**", an option from the **Region** menu such as "**California**".

3. Click on the **Select** button to select the **Parent Organization**. In the **Organization** selection page, choose "**Palm Tree Enterprise**".

4. Select **Type** with value, "**Regular**".

5. Click the **Save** button to save the inputs.

Similarly, let's add a child **Organization** called "**Marketing department**" as follows:

1. Click on the **Organizations** tab in the **Enterprise Admin** Portlet first; then click the button **Add Organization**.

2. Enter enterprise information in the **Name** input field, such as, "**Marketing department**" and select a value from the **Country** menu, such as "**United States**", and a value from the **Region** menu such as "**California**".

3. Select **Type** with value, "**Regular**".

4. Click on the **Select** button to select the **Parent Organization**. In the **Organization** selection page, choose "**Palm Tree Enterprise**".

5. Click the **Save** button to save the inputs.

Of course, you can create other departments in most **Organizations** similarly. After adding child **Organizations** such as "**Engineering**" and "**Website**", we can view **Organizations**:

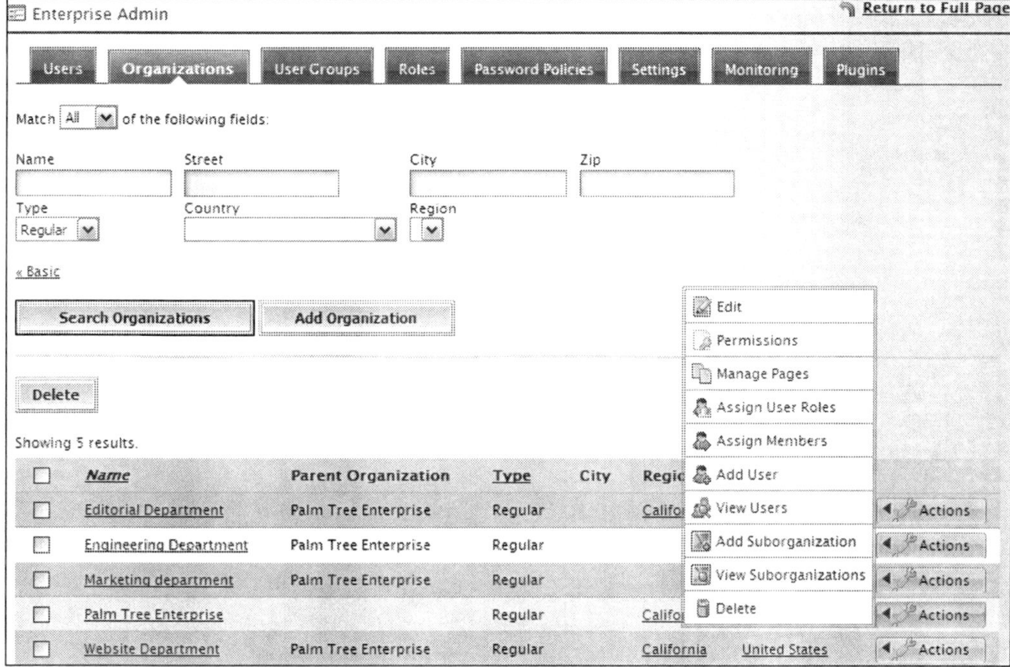

View Organizations

Similar to adding child **Organizations**, viewing **Organizations** is also simple, as follows:

1. Click on the **Organizations** tab in the **Enterprise Admin** Portlet to display the **Organizations** screen. A listing of **Organizations** appears at the bottom of the **Organizations** screen.

2. Locate an **Organization** such as "**Editorial Department**" that you want to view first, and then click on the **Organization** link such as "**Editorial Department**".

3. Or click the **View Sub-organizations** icon from **Actions** (next to **Organization)**, if you want to view sub **Organizations** of a given **Organization** "Palm Tree Enterprise".

Search Organizations

You can find **Organizations** by doing a basic search or an advanced search. To search **Organizations**, click on the **Organizations** tab in the **Enterprise Admin** portlet first. Then input search criterion for basic search, or input **Organization** information in the input fields and select **Type** value "**Regular**" for advanced search, and click the button, **Search Organizations**. A listing of **Organizations** based on search appears at the bottom of the **Organizations** screen.

Basic search will search both **Organizations** and **Locations**. Using advanced search, you may search **Organizations** (with type value "**Regular**") or **Locations** (with type value "**Locations**") or both (with type value "**Any**").

Edit An Organization

After adding **Organizations**, we are ready to manage **Organizations** now. For example, we want to update the **Organization's** information of "Website department", such as changing name and parent **Organizations**, and adding email addresses and comments. Let's do it as follows:

1. Click on the **Organizations** tab in the **Enterprise Admin** portlet. Locate **Organization** such as "**Website department**" with type value "**Regular**", which you want to edit.

2. Click the **Edit** icon from **Actions** next to the right of **Organization,** or click on any links of the **Organization,** say "**Website department**".

3. Type changes in the **Name** input field and select value from the **Country** and **Region**, or add **Email Addresses, Addresses, Website** and **Phone Numbers**, and furthermore, add **Services** and **Comments**.

4. Click **Save** to save the changes.

Delete An Organization

For some reasons, a department such as "**Website**", may not be wanted anymore. We need to delete this **Organization** from the Portal. Let's delete the **Organization** "**Website**" as follows:

1. Click on the **Organizations** tab in the **Enterprise Admin** Portlet.

2. Locate an **Organization** such as "**Website department**" that you want to delete.

3. Click the **Delete** icon from the **Actions** next to the right of the **Organization,** or select checkbox to the left of the **Organization,** and press the **Delete** button.

4. A screen will appear asking if you want to delete the selected **Organizations**. Click the **OK** button to confirm, or the **Cancel** button to cancel.

Note that you cannot delete an **Organization** which has child **Organizations** or **Locations** or **Users**. In order to delete this **Organization**, you need to remove sub **Organizations** or **Locations** or **Users** from this **Organization** first.

Using Organizations Effectively

Organizations represent the enterprise's departments hierarchy. Each **Organization** has a set of basic properties, such as name, parent **Organization** (not for top-level **Organizations**), status, country, and so on. It may also have a set of optional properties, such as email addresses, addresses, websites, phone numbers, services, comments, and so on.

An **Organization** can represent a parent corporation. An example would be the enterprise, "Palm Tree Publications".

An **Organization** that is a child **Organization** of top-level **Organization** can also represent departments of a parent corporation. Examples would be "Editorial department", "Marketing department", and so on.

Logically, **Users** can be members of more than one **Organization**. As a best practice, it is better to make a **User** belong to only one **Organization**. So make sure your **Organizations** don't overlap. For example, if you have a department called "marketing" and another called "engineering", then the marketing manager can be in one department or the other but not both.

This might seem limiting, but there is an answer to this in **User Groups**. A **User** can be a member of any number of **User Groups**, and "managers" is a common **User Group**. We'll see how to work with them later.

Working with Locations

Just like many departments, a company might have several **Locations**. "Palm Tree Publications" has one **Location** in San Jose, United States, and one in Berlin, Germany. Let's go ahead and create them.

Adding A Location for The Enterprise

First of all, we need to add a **Location** for the enterprise "Palm Tree Publications", that is the **Organization** "Palm Tree US". Let's do that now:

1. Click on the **Organizations** tab in the **Enterprise Admin** Portlet first, then click the button **Add Organization**.

2. Enter enterprise information, "**Palm Tree US**", in the **Name** input field and select a value such as "**United States**" from the **Country** menu, a value such as "**California**"from the **Region** menu.

3. Click on the **Select** button to select the **Parent Organization**. In the **Organization** selection page, choose "**Palm Tree Enterprise**".

4. Select **Type** with value "**Location**".

5. Click the **Save** button to save the inputs.

So we've added a **Location** for a top-level **Organization**. Now we need to create **Locations** for the department "Editorial".

Managing Locations

Generally speaking, a **Location** is a special **Organization**, which associates with a parent **Organization**. More importantly, **Locations** cannot have any associated child **Organizations**. **Location** is mostly distinguished by its geographic position. An **Organization** may have any number of sub organizations and **Locations**. Obviously, **Locations** are leaves of **organizations**.

Add Locations for Main Organizations

Let's create a **Location** called "**Editorial US**" for the department "Editorial",
as follows:

1. Click on the **Organizations** tab in the **Enterprise Admin** portlet first, then click the button **Add Organization**.

2. Enter enterprise information in the **Name** input field, "**Editorial US**" and select a value from the **Country** menu, "**United States**", a value from the **Region** menu, "**California**".

3. Click on the **Select** button to select the **Parent Organization**. In the **Organization** selection page, choose "**Editorial department**".

4. Select **Type** with the value "**Location**".

5. Click the **Save** button to save the inputs.

Similarly, we can add another **Location** called "Editorial Germany" for the department, "Editorial". Optionally, we can add the **Location** "Editorial Germany" from the **Organization** "Editorial department" directly:

1. Click on the **Organizations** tab in the **Enterprise Admin** portlet. Locate the **Organization**, "Editorial department".

2. Click the **Add Sub Organization** icon from **Actions,** to the right of the **Organization**.

3. Enter enterprise information in the **Name** input field, "**Editorial Germany**" and select a value from the **Country** menu, "**Germany**". Keep the default value for the **Region** menu.

4. Select **Type** with value, "**Location**".

5. Keep default value for the **Parent Organization.**

6. Click the **Save** button to save the inputs.

Of course, you can create other **Locations** for most **Organizations** similarly. After adding **Locations** for departments such as "Engineering" and "Website", we can view **Locations**.

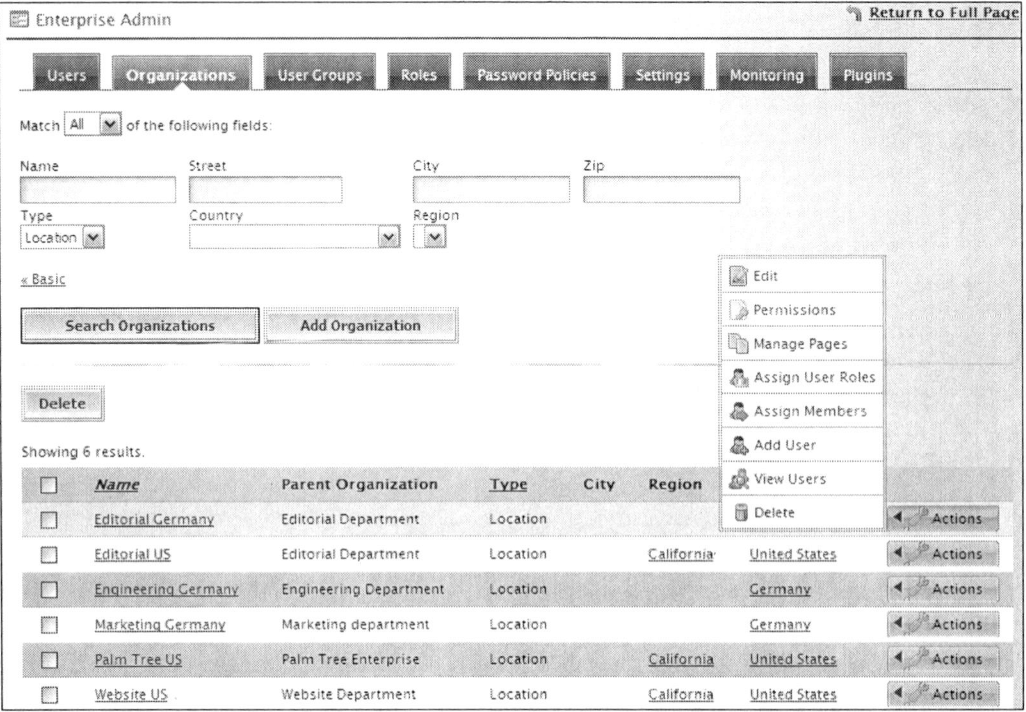

View Locations

Just like adding **Locations**, viewing **Organizations** is also simple:

1. Click on the **Organizations** tab in the **Enterprise Admin** portlet to view the **Organizations** screen. A listing of **Locations** appears at the bottom of the **Organizations** screen.

2. Locate an **Organization** with type value "**Location**" that you want to view first, and then click on the **Organization**.

Optionally, we can view **Locations** for a given **Organization**. To view **Locations** that belong to a specific **Organization**:

1. Click on the **Organizations** tab in the **Enterprise Admin** Portlet and locate an **Organization** first.

2. Then click on the **View Sub Organizations** icon from the **Actions** next to the organization on its right. A screen will appear showing all organizations that belong to the specific organization.

3. Locate an **Organization** with type value "**Location**" that you want to view first, and then click on the **Organization** name link.

Search Locations

Locations are searchable only by advanced search. To search **Locations**, simply click on the **Organizations** tab in the **Enterprise Admin** first. Then input **Organization** information in the input fields, and select **Type** value "**Location**" in advanced search, and click the button **Search Organizations**.

Edit A Location

After adding **Locations**, we are ready to manage **Locations** now. For example, we want to update the **Location** information of "**Website US**", such as name and parent **Organizations**, and add email addresses and comments. Let's do it as follows:

1. Click on the **Organizations** tab in the **Enterprise Admin** portlet. Locate the **Location, "Website US"** with type value "**Location**", which you want to edit.

2. Click the **Edit** icon from the **Actions** to the right of the **Location,** or click on any of the links under **Location** such as the name, "**Website US**".

3. Then in the edit page, type changes in the **Name** input field and select values from the **Country** and **Region** menus to make changes. Or add **Email Addresses, Addresses, Website** and **Phone Numbers**, and also **Services** and **Comments**.

4. Click **Save** button to save the changes.

Delete A Location

In some instances a **Location, say** "**Website US**" may not be wanted anymore. We need to delete this **Location** in the Portal. Let's delete the **Location "Website US"** as follows:

1. Click on the **Organizations** tab in the **Enterprise Admin** Portlet.

2. Locate the **Location** you want to delete such as "**Website US**".

3. Click the **Delete** icon from the **Actions** to the right of the **Location,** or select the checkbox to the left of the **Location** and press the **Delete** button.

4. A screen appears asking if you want to delete the selected **Locations**. Click the **OK** button to confirm.

Note that you can not delete a **Location** which has **Users**. In order to delete this **Location**, you need to remove **Users** from this **Location** first.

Using Locations Effectively

Locations are special **Organizations** associated with a parent **Organization** and having no child **Organizations**. A **Location** can be used to represent a child corporation of an **Organization**, distinguished mostly by its geographical location. An **Organization** can have any number of sub organizations and **Locations**, while a **Location** must belong to one and only one **Organization**. Examples would be "**Editorial US**", "**Editorial Germany**", and so on.

Each **Location** has a set of basic properties, such as name, parent **Organization**, country, and so on. As a special **Organization**, each **Location** may also have a set of optional properties, such as email addresses, addresses, websites, phone numbers, services, comments, and so on.

Bringing in Users

Finally, with the company, departments, **Organizations and Locations** in place, we can add some **Users**.

Adding Users

A **User** is an individual who performs tasks using the portal. **Users** can belong to any **Organization** (or a special **Organization—Location**) or **User Group**.

First of all, let's add "Martin Gall". He's an editorial guy in the Germany office:

1. Click on the **Users** tab in the **Enterprise Admin**.

2. Then click **Add Users** button.

3. Enter **Users** information in the input field and select values from the pull down menus. Normally, you can select an **Organization** (with type value "**Location**") such as "**Editorial Germany**" that the new **User** belongs to. More importantly, **Screen Name**, such as "**martin**", and **Email Address**, such as "**martin@book.com**" are required, since both act as a unique identifier for this **User**. When this **User** logs in, the screen name or email address or user ID will be used as login ID.

4. Click **Save** button to save the inputs.

What Just Happened?

We added our first **User** to Liferay. When we created the new account, Liferay sent an email to the specified email address, notifying the **User** that they could log in and start using the portal.

> The email will send successfully, only if you have specified an SMTP server for Liferay to use. Refer to Chapter 2 for detailed instructions.

Here's the example email Martin will receive:

Dear Martin,

Welcome! You recently created an account at `http://book.com/`. Your password is **your password**. Enjoy!

Sincerely,

Palm Tree

admin@book.com

`http://book.com`

When "Martin Gall" clicks the link, he'll be taken to a page that displays a regular account for signing in. After inputting his email address and password and clicking the **Sign in** button, he'll be taken to a page that displays terms and conditions.

> To change the email notification, such as account created notification and password changed notification, refer to Chapter 13 instructions.

Add More Users

Now go ahead and add a few more **Users**. We can add two more **Users, "David Berger"** and **"Lotti Stein"** in the same way as mentioned earlier. Both are editorial guys in the US offices.

Fortunately, there are two more options to add **Users**: to add a **User** for a given **Organization,** and to add a **User** from scratch as stated earlier.

Let's add the **User "David Berger"** from scratch as follows:

1. Click on the **Users** tab in the **Enterprise Admin.**
2. Click **Add Users** button.
3. Enter **User's** information in the input fields and select **values** from the pull down menus, and select an **Organization** (with type value "**Location**") such as, "**Editorial US**".
4. Click the **Save** button to save.

Let's add the **User "Lotti Stein"** through a given **Organization** as follows:

1. Click on the **Organizations** tab in the **Enterprise Admin.**
2. Locate an **Organization** say "**Editorial US**", to which you want to add a new **User.**
3. Click on the **Add User** icon from **Actions** located to the right of the **Organization** you want to add a **User** to. You will see that the given **Organization** has been selected by default.
4. Enter **Users** information in the input fields and select values from the pull down menus.
5. Click the **Save** button to save.

Add Users in Bulk

It won't take long before you're bored of manually adding **Users**. Fortunately, you don't need to type them all in one at a time. There are several options for adding **Users** in bulk:

- LDAP—Lightweight Directory Access Protocol.
- Single Sign-On (SSO)—a method of access control that enables a **User** to authenticate once and gain access to the resources of multiple software systems.
- OpenID—a decentralized single sign-on system.

Create Account on Fly

As an administrator at "Palm Tree Publications", you can set up the portal and allow **Users** to create accounts on fly. For example, "Rolf Hess" accesses the portal login page and clicks on the tab **Create Account**. He inputs **User's** information and text verification, and furthermore, presses the **Save** button.

The portal system will create an account for the **User** "Rolf Hess", and send an email to him with a new password.

Note that there is no **Organization** or no **Location** selected for the new account created on fly. In order to set proper **Organization** and **Location** for the new account, administrators have to update this account in the portal.

When The Password Is Forgotten

If a **User** such as "**Rolf Hess**" forgot his password, he can access the portal login page, and click on the tab, **Forgot Password**. He can input email address and text verification, and furthermore, press the **Send New Password** button.

The portal system will create a new password for the **User** "Rolf Hess", and send an email to him with this new password.

Managing Users

Of course, you can similarly add **Users** of other departments in most **Organizations**. After adding more **Users**, we can view **Users**.

View Users

Users could be active or inactive in the portal. It is simple to view active **Users**. Click on the **Users** tab in the **Enterprise Admin**. A list of **Users** appears at the bottom of the **Users** screen. Locate a **User** whom you want to view first. Then click on the **User** name such as "**Rolf Hess**".

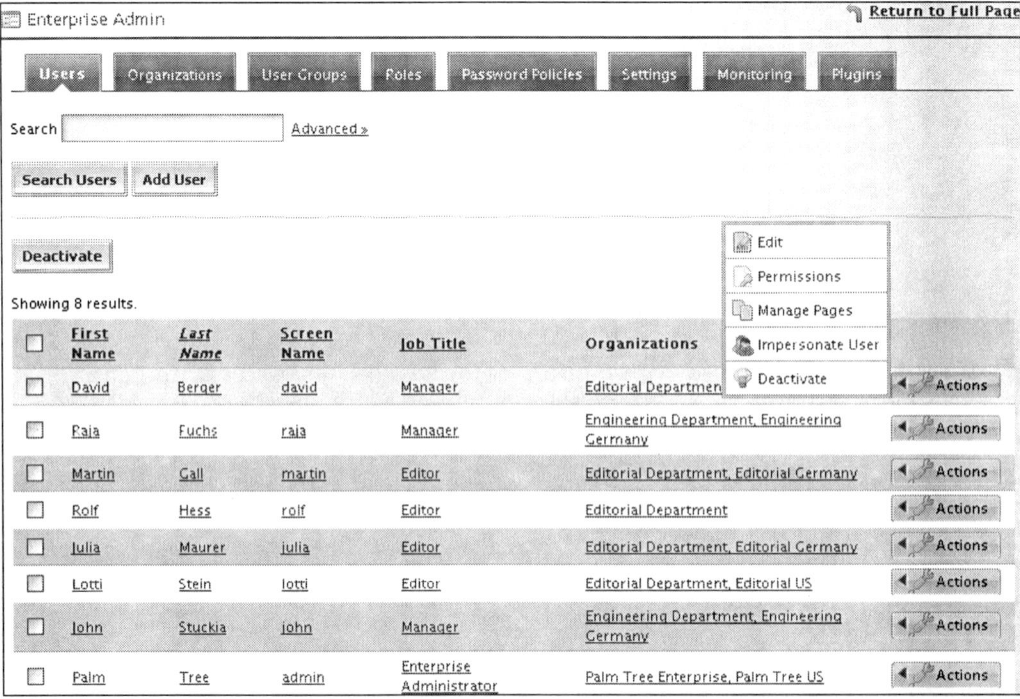

To view deactivated **Users**, click on the **Active** menu from the advanced search, and select **No** item. Click **Search Users** button to display a list of deactivated **Users**.

Optionally, we can view **Users** for a specific **Organization**. To view **Users** that belong to a specific **Organization**, simply click on the **Organizations** tab. Then click the **View Users** icon from the **Actions** located to the right of an **Organization**. You may view a **User** by locating it and clicking on it.

Similarly, you may view **Users** who belong to a specific **User Group** by clicking on the **User Groups** tab, and by clicking on the **View Users** icon from **Actions** located to the right of a **User Group**. Most interestingly, you may view **Users** associated with a specific **Role,** by clicking on the **Roles** tab, and clicking **View Users** icon from the **Actions** located to the right of the **Role**.

Search Users

Users are searchable. First you can search **Users** by clicking on the **Users** tab in the **Enterprise Admin**. Then, input search criterion for basic search, or input **User's** information in the input fields and select a value ("**Yes**" or "**No**") from the **Active** menu options for advanced search, and finally click on the **Search Users** button. A listing of **Users** based on the required search appears at the bottom of the **Users** screen.

Note that basic search is only useful for active **Users**. You cannot find inactive **Users** through basic search. To find inactive **Users**, you have to use advanced search, and select the value "**No**" from the **Active** menu options.

Edit A User

After adding **Users**, we are ready to manage **Users** now. For example, we want to update the **Users** information of "**Lotti Stein**", by changing name and parent **Organizations**, and adding email addresses and comments. Let's do it as follows:

1. Click on the **Users** tab in the **Enterprise Admin**.

2. Locate a **User** such as "**Lotti Stein**" whose information you want to update, and click on the **User**.

3. Click the **Edit** icon from **Actions** next to the right of the **User** or click any of the **User** links, or select the check box to the left of the **User**.

4. A screen appears displaying the **Users** information. Type changes in the **First Name**, **Middle Name**, **Last Name**, **Email**, and **Job Title** input fields, and select from the **Prefix**, **Suffix**, **Birthday**, **Gender** and **Organization** menus to make changes.

5. Optionally, you can change the icon, display language, time zone and greeting, password, **Roles**, and also update email addresses, addresses, comments, and so on.

6. Click the **Save** button to save changes.

The functions of editing a **User** are the same as that of updating the profile in **My Account**. Using **My Account**, you can only update your own information. By editing a **User**, you can update any **Users** information, if you have the **Permissions** to do so.

Deactivate A User

Suppose a **User** such as "**Lotti Stein**" has to be made inactive in the portal, we need to deactivate it. To deactivate a **User,** do the following:

1. Click on the **Users** tab in the **Enterprise Admin** first.
2. Locate the **User,** say "**Lotti Stein**", which you want to deactivate.
3. Then click on the box located next to the **User** you want to deactivate and click the **Deactivate** button. You can also deactivate a **User,** by clicking the **Deactivate** icon from **Actions** next to a **User**.

To deactivate all **Users** listed on a page, click the box located next to the **Name** column, and click the **Deactivate** button. A screen will appear asking if you want to deactivate the selected **Users**. Click **OK** to deactivate them. Click **Cancel** if you do not want to deactivate the selected **Users**.

Activate A User

In case we want to make an inactive **User**, "**Lotti Stein**" here, become active in the portal, we need to restore or activate it. To restore a **User** you can do the following:

1. Click on the **Users** tab in the **Enterprise Admin**.
2. Click on the **Active** menu in **advanced search**, and select **No**. Then click the **Search Users** button to display a listing of deactivated **Users**.
3. Click on the box located next to the **User** you want to reactivate and further click the **Restore** button.
4. You can also reactivate a **User** by clicking the **Activate** icon from **Actions,** to the right of the **User**.

To restore all **Users** listed in a page, click in the box located next to the **Name** column. Click **Restore** button.

Delete A User

In case a **User** such as "**Lotti Stein**" is not wanted any more, we need to delete it from the portal as follows:

1. To delete a **User** such as "**Lotti Stein**", you need to first deactivate the **User**.
2. Then click on the **Users** tab in the **Enterprise Admin**.
3. Click on the **Active** menu in advanced search, and select the item, **No**. Click **Search Users** to display a list of deactivated **Users**.
4. Click on the box located next to the **User** you want to delete, and click the **Delete** button. You can also delete a **User** by clicking the **Delete** icon from **Actions,** to the right of the **User**.

To delete all **Users** listed in a page, click the box located next to the **Name** column. Click the **Delete** button. A screen will appear asking if you want to permanently delete the selected **Users**. Click the **OK** button to delete. Click **Cancel** button if you do not want to delete the selected **User**.

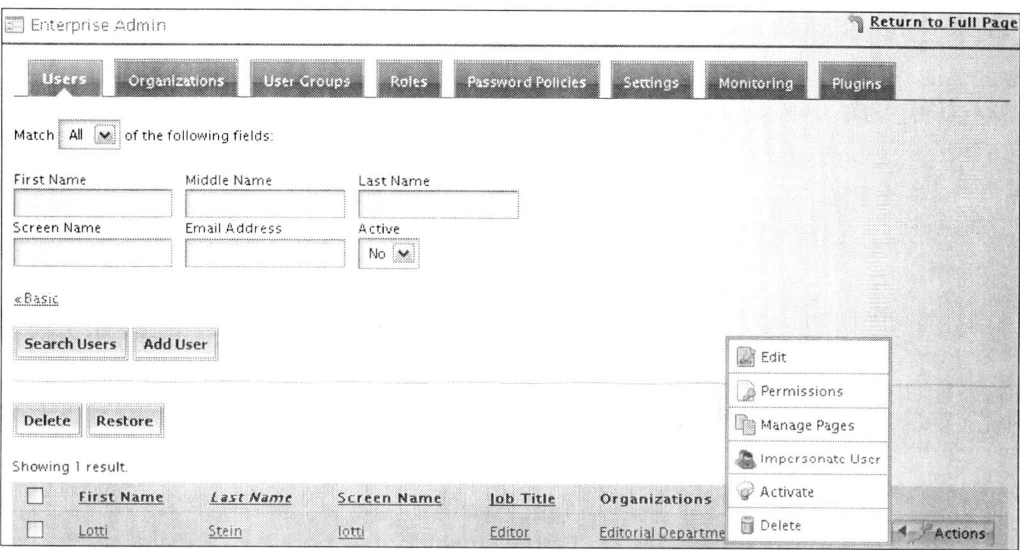

Impersonate A User

Administrators and normal **Users** can conveniently review updates performed for other **Users** with the **Impersonate** function. For example, the administrator gives **Permissions** to the **User** such as "**Lotti Stein**", to edit all **Users** in the "Palm Tree Publications" US **Location**. To verify whether the **Permission** has been correctly given, the administrator can sign in as **User** "**Lotti Stein**" or he or she can search for "**Lotti Stein**" in the **Enterprise Admin** portlet and click the **Impersonate** icon from **Actions** next to the **User**. By using the **Impersonate** function, the administrator can impersonate "**Lotti Stein**" to review updates without having to sign in as "**Lotti Stein**".

User Groups And Communities

Actually, **Communities** are special groups, which have a set of **Users**. That is, a **Community** may have a set of associated **Users**. Normally, a **Community** is used to present a set of **Users** who share common interests.

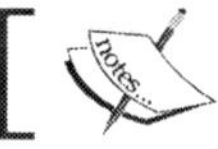 For more details about **Communities**, refer to Chapter 11.

As is the case with many departments, a company may have several **User Groups**. "Palm Tree Publications" has these **Users**: Raja Fuchs, an engineering manager in a Germany office; John Stucki, a marketing manager also in a Germany office. Both are managers, but belong to different departments. Thanks to the **User Group** called "**Managers**", we can include a number of **Users** belonging to different departments. Let's go ahead and create them.

Adding A User Group

First of all, let's create a **User Group** "**Managers**" which contains **Users** "**Raja Fuchs**" and "**John Stucki**" as follows:

1. Click on the **User Groups** tab in the **Enterprise Admin** first.

2. Then click **Add User Group** button.

3. Enter a name for the **User Group** in the **Name** input field such as "**Managers**".

4. Click the **Save** button to save the input.

5. Then click on the **Assign Members** icon from **Actions** to the right of the **User Group** "**Managers**".

6. Click on the **Available** tab to display a list of all available **Users** in the system. Check the checkboxes to the left of the desired **Users** such as "**Raja Fuchs**" and "**John Stucki**".

7. Click the **Update Associations** button to assign **Users** to a **User Group**. Optionally, to confirm whether the desired **Users** were successfully associated with the **User Group**, click on the **Current** tab.

Of course, you can create other **User Groups** similarly. After adding one more **User Group**, "**Developers**", we can view the **User Groups**.

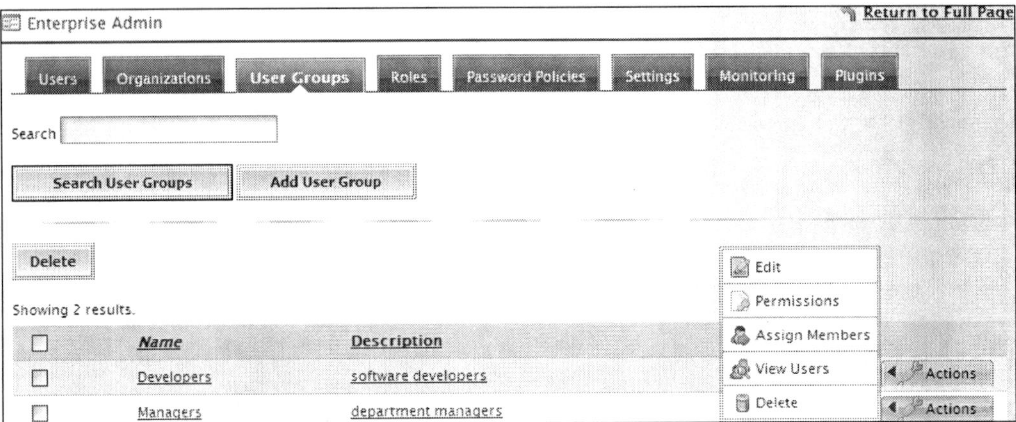

Managing User Groups

A **User Group** can hold a number of **Users**. In fact, a **User Group** is also a special group which may have a set of associated **Users**. **User Groups** are different from both **Organizations** and **Communities**, since they have no context associated with them.

View User Groups

To view **User Groups**, click on the **User Groups** tab in the **Enterprise Admin** first. A list of **User Groups** appears at the bottom of the screen. Click on a **User Group, say** "**Managers**", that you want to view. Normally, clicking on a **User Group** will only display the name of the **User Group**. To actually view the **Users** associated with the **User Group**, click on the **View Users** icon from **Actions** to the right of the **User Group**.

Search User Groups

User Groups are also searchable. To search **User Groups**, click on the **User Groups** tab in the **Enterprise Admin** first. Then type a **User Group** name as search keywords, and click **Search User Groups** button.

Edit A User Group

You may need to change the **User Group,** "**Managers**". Click on the **User Groups** tab in the **Enterprise Admin** first. Then locate the **User Group** you want to edit. Click the Edit icon from the **Actions** to the right of the **User Group**, or click any of the **links** in **User Group**. In the edit page, type changes in the **New Name** input field and the **Description** input field. Then click the **Save** button to save the changes.

Delete User Groups

For some particular reasons, a User Group, say "**Developers**", may not be wanted anymore. We need to delete this **User Group** in the Portal. Let's delete the **User Group** "**Developers**" as follows:

- Click on the **User Groups** tab in the **Enterprise Admin** first.
- Locate a **User Group,** "**Developers**", which you want to delete.
- Then click on the **Delete** icon from **Actions** to the right of the **User Group**, or check the box on the left of the **User Group** and click the **Delete** button.
- A screen will appear asking if you want to permanently delete the selected **User Groups**. Click **OK** button to delete the **User Group**.

Similarly, you can delete multiple **User Groups** by checking the boxes located to the left of the **User Groups** you want to delete, and then clicking the **Delete** button. Verily, you can delete all **User Groups** listed on a page, by checking the box located next to the **Name** column, and then clicking the **Delete** button. A screen will appear asking if you want to permanently delete the selected **User Groups**. Click the **OK** button to delete or the **Cancel** button if you do not want to delete the selected **User Groups**.

Assign A User Group

You can assign **Users** to a **User Group**. First, click on the **User Groups** tab in the **Enterprise Admin**. Then click on the **Assign Members** icon from **Actions** to the right of the **User Group**. Click on the **Available** tab to display a list of all available **Users** in the system. Search for the desired **Users** using the search form (through basic search or advanced search). Check the boxes to the left of the desired **Users**. If you would like to select all the **Users** on the page, check the box next to the **Name** column. Finally, click the **Update Associations** button to assign **Users** to a **User Group**. Optionally, to confirm whether the desired **Users** were successfully associated with the **User Group**, click on the **Current** tab.

Adding More Administrators

As mentioned before, "**Palm Tree**" is an administrator at the enterprise. We need to add more administrators at the department level and **Location** level. "**David Berger**" acts as an administrator in the "Editorial" department. Let's add it as follows:

1. Click on the **Organizations** tab in the **Enterprise Admin** portlet.

2. Locate an **Organization** such as "**Editorial department**" to which you want to add an admin.

3. Click on the **Permissions** icon from the **Actions** next to the **Organization**. By default, the **User** tab and **Current** sub-tab are selected.

4. Click on the **Available** tab if the **User, "David Berger"** is not there.

5. Locate the **User** "**David Berger**". Check the **User** "**David Berger**" checkbox, and click on the **Update Permissions** button.

6. Select all permissions from the **Available** select box, and click on the right arrow to add them to the **Current** select box.

7. Click on the **Finished** button if you are ready.

Similarly, "**Raja Fuchs**" acts as an administrator at the department, "**Engineering**", in the Germany office. Let's add it as follows:

1. Click on the **Organizations** tab in the **Enterprise Admin** portlet.

2. Locate an **Organization** (a **Location**), say "**Engineering**", to which you want to add an admin.

3. Click on the **Permissions** icons from **Actions** next to the **Location**. By default, the **User** tab and **Current** sub-tab are selected.

4. Click on the **Available** tab if the **User** "**Raja Fuchs**" is not there.

5. Locate the **User** "**Raja Fuchs**". Check the **User** "**Raja Fuchs**" checkbox, and click on the **Update Permissions** button.

6. Select all permissions from the **Available** select box, and click on the right arrow to add them to the **Current** select box.

7. Click on the **Finished** button if you are ready.

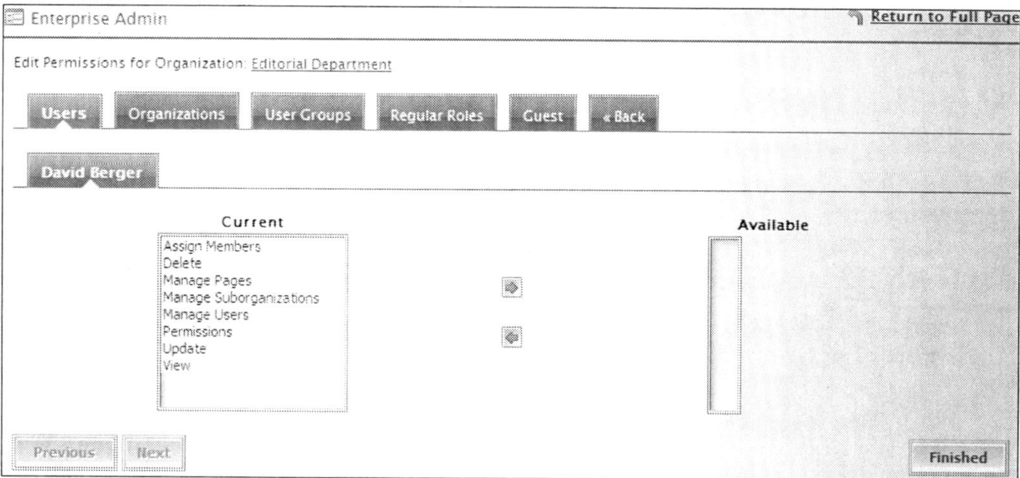

Of course, we can add more administrators at the enterprise level, department level and **Location** level.

Liferay provides two portlets for **User** administration: **Enterprise Admin** and **Organization Admin**. The two portlets provide different scopes of administration. The **Enterprise Admin** has the highest level of administrative functions. It has access to all **Organizations, Locations, User Groups, Users,** and **Roles**. The **Organization Admin** can access its own **Organization** information and information of any sub organization, **Locations** and **Users** of this **Organization.**

Enterprise Admin

As we have mentioned earlier, **Enterprise Admin** has access to all **Organizations** (sub **Organizations** and **Locations**), **User Groups**, **Users** and **Roles**, with the highest level of administrative functions. Additionally, **Enterprise Admin** provides the management of password policies, settings, monitoring, plug-ins, and so on.

Organization Admin

Various functions can be performed to your **Organization**, especially to **Location** and **Users** that belong to your **Organization** via **Organization Admin. You can**:

- View and edit an **Organization**.
- View, search, add, and edit **Locations** or sub organizations that belong to an **Organization**.
- View, search, add, edit, and deactivate **Users** that belong to an **Organization**.
- View, search, edit, delete, and assign **User Groups**.

Authentication Methods

As mentioned before, you don't need to type in **Users** all in one at a time. You can add **Users** in bulk by using LDAP server.

Working with LDAP Server

The enterprise "Palm Tree Publications" has **Users** in LDAP server. Suppose the LDAP server has the following information.

```
Base Provider URL: ldap://docs.cignex.com:10389

Base DN: ou=book, ou=system

Principal: uid=admin,ou=system

Credentials: secret

Encryption algorithm: SHA

Server Type: Apache Directory Server
```

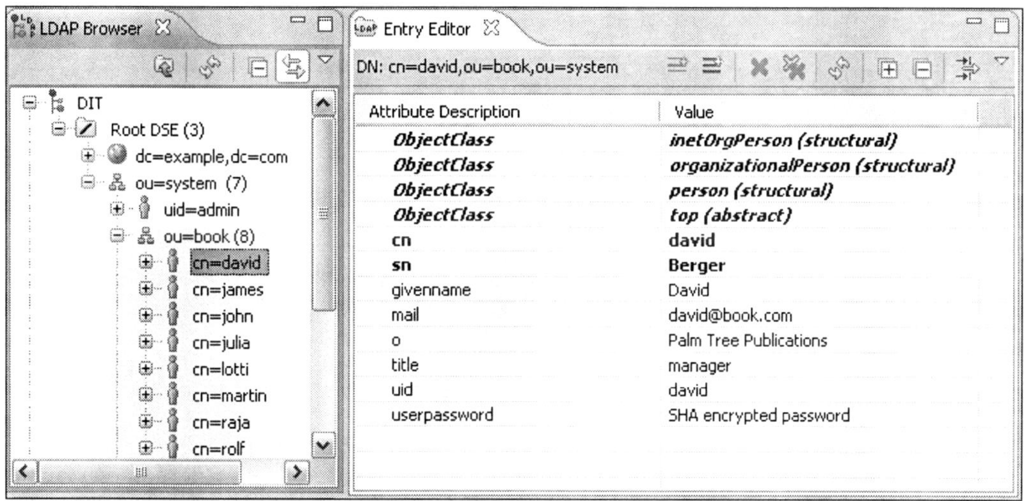

Thus, you can set authentication through the LDAP server. Let's do it as follows:

1. Click on the **Settings** tab in the **Enterprise Admin** portlet.
2. Click on the **Authentication** tab and **LDAP** tab.
3. In connection settings, select the checkboxes "**Enabled**" and "**Required**".
4. Input **Base Provider URL**: `ldap://docs.cignex.com:10389`, **Base DN: ou=book, ou=system**, **Principal: uid=admin,ou=system**, **Credentials: secret**.
5. Enter the encryption algorithm: **SHA**.
6. Enter server type: **Apache Directory Server.**
7. Select the checkbox "**Import Enabled**", if you want to import **Users** in bulk.

8. Click on the **Save** button when you are ready.

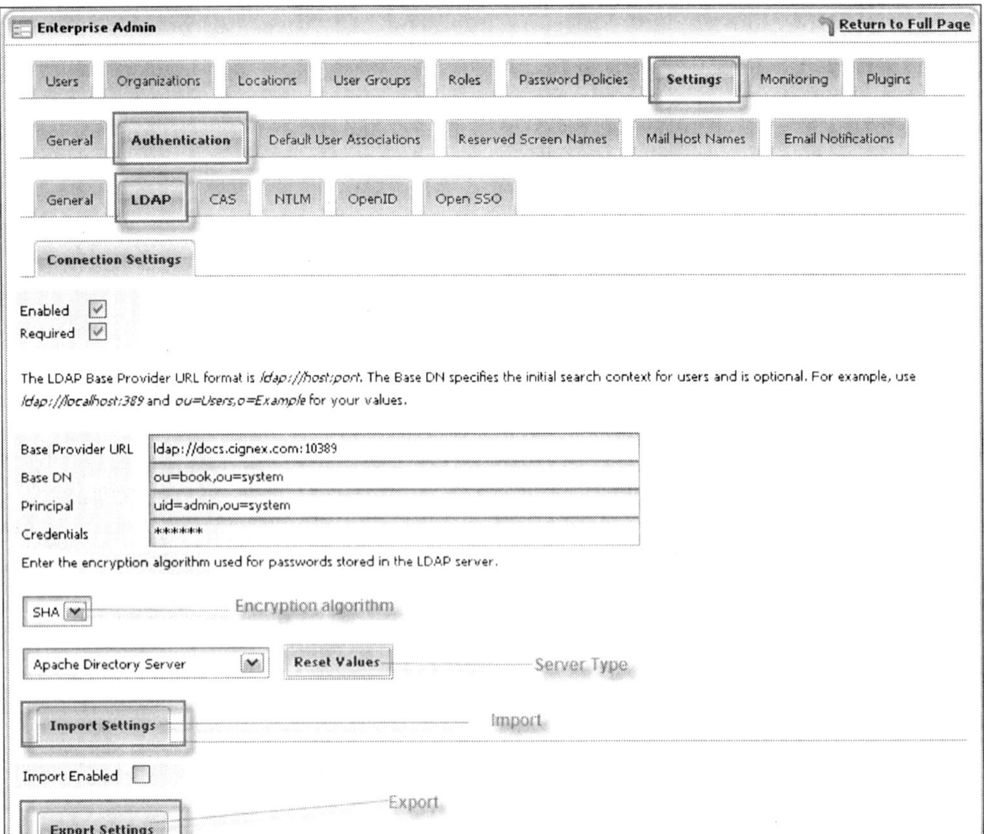

 LDAP (Lightweight Directory Access Protocol) is an application protocol for querying and modifying directory services running over TCP/IP. A Directory Information Tree (DIT) is data represented in a hierarchical tree-like structure consisting of the distinguished names (DNs) of the directory entries. URL: `http://www.ietf.org/rfc/rfc2251.txt`.

What Happens Next?

We connect Liferay with a LDAP server. Next time, when **Users** log in the portal, Liferay will authenticate them with the LDAP server.

 How to log in, if integration is broken? The enterprise admin such as **"Palm Tree"** is allowed to log in, even if the integration with LDAP is broken. This allows the administrator account to fix the problem.

Liferay provides out-of-the-box support for Apache, Directory Server, Microsoft Active Directory Server, Novell eDirectory, OpenLDAP, and so on.

Use LDAP Effectively

It is very important to choose a suitable security model at the beginning of the Liferay implementation. The authentication mechanism, the storage for **User** data, the security settings and the business rules and so on are based on the security model you choose.

Liferay imposes authentication through user login ID (email address or user ID) and password. This is where you choose a security model such as Liferay managed accounts, SSO (Single Sign-On) and LDAP.

Liferay imposes authorization, by assigning a **Role** or **Permission** to a specific **User** of a specific group. This is going to be the same irrespective of which model you choose.

The security model you choose, either Liferay out-of-the-box or external systems such as LDAP or SSO (such as, CAS, NTLM, OpenID, and Open SSO) will be based on the requirements of your enterprise.

General Configurations

Generally, authentication is configurable for **User** login functionalities in Liferay. **Users** can authenticate by email addresses, screen names or user IDs; allowing **Users** to automatically login; allowing **Users** to request forgotten passwords; allowing strangers to create accounts; allowing strangers to create accounts with a company email address; and requiring strangers to verify their email address?

By default, Liferay supports integration with LDAP, CAS, NTLM, OpenID, Open SSO, and so on. Of course, besides authentications, you can use out-of-the-box Managed Accounts. Liferay out-of-the-box security includes the following functionalities:

- **Users** and user management.
- Provision for personal information about **users**.
- **User** authentication.
- **User Groups** and **User Group** management.
- **Organizations** and **Locations** management.
- **Community** management.
- **Permissions** and permission management.
- **Roles** and role management

- Default settings.

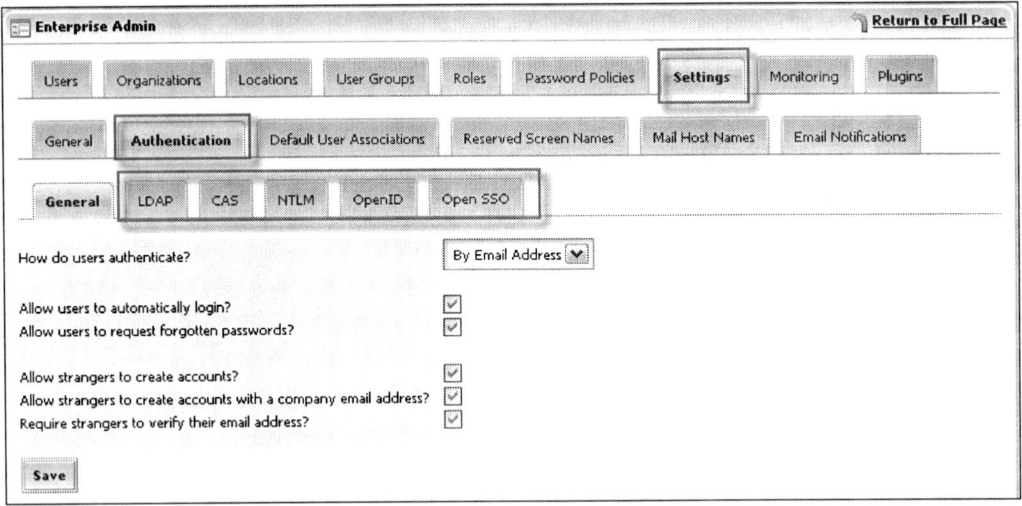

Working with SSO CAS

The enterprise "Palm Tree Publications" has SSO CAS server with URL "`https://docs.cignex.com`". You can set authentication through the SSO CAS server directly. Let's do it as follows:

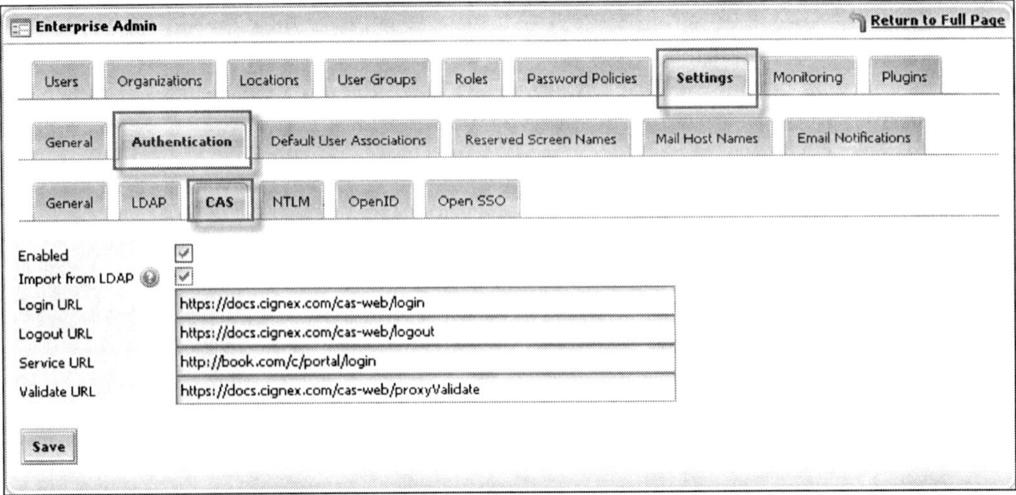

1. Click on the **Settings** tab in the **Enterprise Admin** portlet.

2. Click on the **Authentication** tab and **CAS** tab further.

3. Select the checkbox, "**Enabled**"; Select checkbox "**Import from LDAP**".

4. Input **Login URL:** `https://docs.cignex.com/cas-web/login`, **Logout URL:** `https://docs.cignex.com/cas-web/logout`, **Validate URL:** `https://docs.cignex.com/cas-web/proxyValidate`, **Service URL:** `http://book.com/c/portal/login`.

5. Click on the **Save** button when you are ready.

6. Now you are ready to use SSO CAS. Similarly, you can use NTLM and Open SSO.

What Happens Next?

The next time the **Users** log in to the portal, they will be redirected to the CAS server's login screen, if everything is set up correctly.

Liferay Portal integrates CAS Server to set up single sign on (SSO) between Liferay and an existing web application.

The JA-SIG Central Authentication Service (CAS) is an open single sign-on service that provides web applications the ability to defer all authentications to a trusted central server or servers. Refer to URL: `http://www.ja-sig.org/`.

Working with OpenID

We can also use OpenID as authentication. Let's first enable OpenID authentication as follows:

1. Click on the **Settings** tab in the **Enterprise Admin** portlet.

2. Click on the **Authentication** tab and **OpenID** tab further.

3. Select check box to enable OpenID.

4. Click **Save** to save the changes.

Now it is ready for **Users** to log in through OpenID.

OpenID is a decentralized single sign-on system. URL: `http://openid.net/`.

Working with Roles

Before playing with **Roles**, we need to create **Roles**. The enterprise "Palm Tree Publications" needs **Roles** for **Users** to handle the **Message Board** portlet in their page. Let us name these **Roles**, "MB Topic Admin " and "**MB Category Admin**".

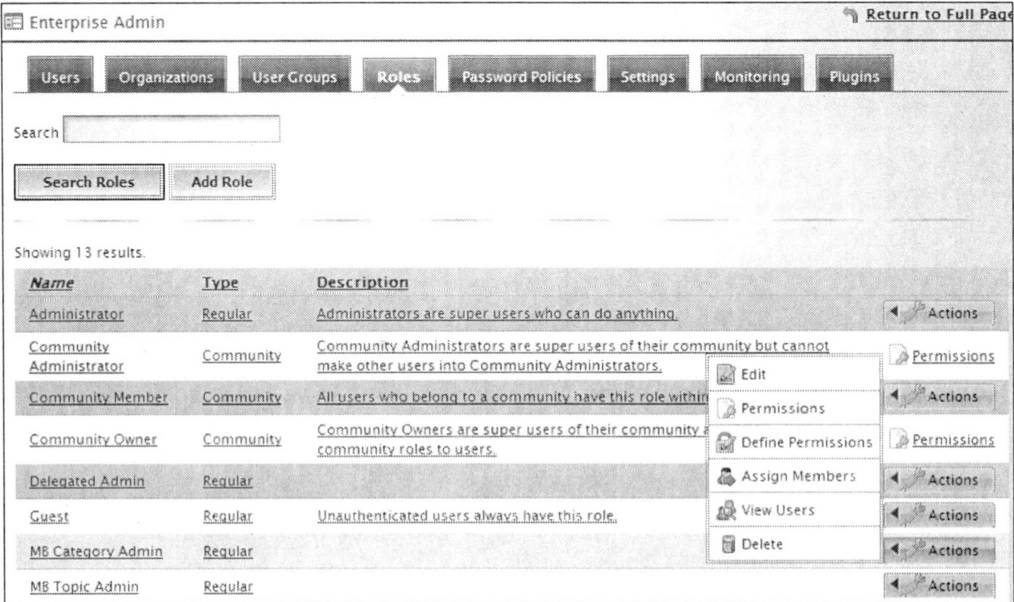

Adding a Role

First of all, we need to create a **Role** called "**MB Topic Admin**". Let's do that now:

1. Click on the **Roles** tab at the **Enterprise Admin** portlet.

2. Click on the **Add Role** button.

3. Enter value " **MB Topic Admin** " in the **Name** input field.

4. Select a type (with values: "**Regular**", "**Organization**" and "**Community**") such as "**Regular**".

5. Click the **Save** button if you are ready.

Of course, you can create other **Roles** in a similarl fashion. After adding **Roles** such as "**MB Topic Admin**", "**MB Category Admin**", and "**Delegated Admin**", we can view **Roles**.

Managing Roles

A **Role** is a collection of **Permissions**. There are system **Roles** and customized **Roles**.

System **Roles** are specified by default, and the required **Roles** are Administrator, Guest, Power User, and **User**. You cannot edit them or delete them at the UI level. Optionally, system **Roles** could be renamed at the system level. Customized **Roles** are built by **Users**, which can be edited and deleted.

View Roles

Besides creating **Roles**, you can view also them by :

1. Click on the **Roles** tab in the **Enterprise Admin** portlet to display the **Role** screen. A listing of **Roles** appears at the bottom of the **Roles** screen.

2. Locate a **Role** that you want to view, and then click on the **Role** link.

Search Roles

Roles are searchable. Click on the **Roles** tab in the **Enterprise Admin** first. Then type a **Role** name in the search keywords field. Click the **Search Roles** button.

Edit A Role

To edit a **Role**, click on the **Roles** tab in the **Enterprise Admin** first. Then locate the **Role** that you want to edit. Click the **Edit** icon from **Actions** to the right of the **Role**, or click any of the **Role** links. In the edit page, type changes in the **Name** input field and **Description** input field. Click the **Save** button to save the changes.

Note that you can update customized **Roles** only. You cannot edit or delete system **Roles**.

Delete Roles

It may happen that, a **Role** such as "**MB Category Admin**" is not wanted anymore. We need to delete this **Role** in the Portal. Let's delete the **Role** "**MB Category Admin**" as follows:

1. Click on the **Roles** tab in the **Enterprise Admin**.

2. Locate a **Role** such as "**MB Category Admin**" which you want to delete.

3. Then click on the **Delete** icon from **Actions** to the right of the **Role**.

4. A screen will appear asking if you want to permanently delete the selected **Roles**.

5. Click the **OK** button when you are ready.

Assign Enterprise Permissions to A Role

We need to assign **Permissions** to the "**MB Topic Admin**" **Role** that allows **Users** to view any **Message Board Category** in "Palm Tree Publications" (that is, action: *View*, resource: *Message Board Category*, scope: *Enterprise*). Let's do it as follows:

1. Select the **Roles** tab in the **Enterprise Admin**.

2. Click on the **Define Permissions** icon from **Actions** next to the "**MB Topic Admin**" **Role**.

3. Click on the **Message Boards** link. There are two options: **Add portlet permissions** and **Add portal permissions**. Every object in the portal is contained within a portlet. Therefore, the administrator must find the parent portlet of the object in question. Since the **Message Boards Category** resource is to be acted upon, the administrator must first find the **Message Board portlet.**

4. Then click on the **Message Boards Category** link. There are two lists for **Message Boards**: One presents a list of the actions that can be performed on the portlet itself while the other represents a list of the "Resources" (that is, objects) that are contained within the portlet.

5. **Slick on the Scope** drop-down menu next to the **View** action, and select "**Enterprise**".

6. Click on the **Next** button to return to the **Role** list under the **Roles** tab.

Similarly, we can assign **Community Permissions** to a **Role**.

Assign Roles

In some cases, we may need to assign the "**MB Topic Admin**" **Role** to the **User** "**Lotti Stein**". Let do it as follows:

1. Select the **Roles** tab in the **Enterprise Admin** portlet.

2. Click on the **Assign Members** icon from the **Actions** next to the "**MB Topic Admin**" **Role**.

3. Since the **Current** tab is selected by default, there are no **Users** associated with this **Role**. Therefore, click on the **Available** tab in order to search for the **User** "**Lotti Stein**".

4. Check the checkbox next to the **User,** "Lotti Stein".

5. Click the **Update Associations** button. If needed, click on the **Current** tab to confirm whether the association was successful.

6. It is clear that the association was successfully created. If you want to discard this association, you can uncheck the checkbox next to the **User's** name first and then click the **Update Associations** button.

Similarly, we can assign **Roles** to other entities, such as **Community, Organization, Location,** or **User Group,** by just repeating the previous steps. In fact, the same results could have been achieved by associating the "**MB Topic Admin**" **Role** with the appropriate **Community, Organization, Location,** or **User Group,** instead of associating directly to the **User,** "Lotti Stein".

Using Roles Effectively

There are three types of **Roles**: **regular, Organization** and **Community** as shown in the following table. **Community Roles** allow administration of **Roles** scoped to a specific **Community**. The objective is to create a new type of **Role** that is associated with a **Community,** when it is assigned to a **User**:

- **Community** Owner: This **Role** is automatically given to the creator of a **Community** and gives him total control over the **Community** management including website configuration and content management.

- **Community** Administrator: **Users** with this **Role** can administer the **Community** but cannot assign new **Users** or edit existing ones. They can create new content in the **Community** portlets, but cannot manage the content created by others.

- **Community** Member: It's a **Role** that is automatically given to **Users** when they are assigned to a **Community**. It does not give any special right by default, but can be edited by the portal administrator to add privileges that might be desirable in certain situations.

Name	Type	Possible Actions on Roles					
		Edit	Permissions	Define Permissions	Assign Members	View Users	Delete
Administrator	Regular		X		X	X	
Community Administrator	**Community**		X			X	
Community Member	**Community**		X	X		X	
Community Owner	**Community**		X			X	
Organization Administrator	**Organization**		X			X	
Organization Member	**Organization**		X	X		X	
Organization Owner	**Organization**		X			X	
Guest	Regular		X	X	X	X	
Power User	Regular		X	X	X	X	
User	Regular		X	X	X	X	
Customized Role	Regular	X	X	X	X	X	X

Organization Roles are administrative **Roles** scoped to a specific **Organization**. An **Organization Role** is a **Role** associated with an **Organization** when it is assigned to a **User**:

- **Organization** Owner: specifies the super **Users** of their **Organization** but cannot make other **Users, Organization** Administrators.

- **Organization** Administrator: specifies that all **Users** who belong to an **Organization** have this **Role** within that **Organization**.

- **Organization** Member: specifies super **Users** of their **Organization,** and a super **User** who can assign **Organization Roles** to **Users**.

Working with Permissions

Finally, we can work with **Permissions** after having **Organizations, User Groups,** and **Roles**. We will work with assigning **Permissions** and delegating **Permissions**.

In order to work with **Permissions**, we have the following assumptions. Assume we have added a **Message Board** portlet in the page "**Admin**", at the **Book Lovers** Community **Private Pages**. A category called "**Book Category**" has been created and this category contains three categories — "**Book Category A**," "**Book Category B**," and "**Book Category C**". By default, all categories are viewable by **Users** in the **Book Lovers** Community. The **Permission** to view "**Book Category C**" has been removed for the **Users** of Book Lovers Community. Also assume that "**Book Category C**" contains a single thread.

For comparison purposes, assume the **User** "Lotti Stein" who belongs to the **Book Lovers** Community also logs in and views the **Message Board** portlet. When compared with the Administrator's view, it is clear that Lotti Stein's view is much more limited in functionality. **Lotti Stein** is missing several buttons and icons that the administrator has.

 How to create a **Community** "Book Lovers"? Refer to Chapter 11 for instructions.

Assign Individual Portlet Permissions

Assume that the **User**, "Lotti Stein", does not have **Permission** to add a root category to the **Message Boards** portlet in the **Book Lovers** Community.

As an administrator, "**Palm Tree**", you may need to assign the "**Add Category**" portlet **Permission** to the **User** "Lotti Stein". Let's do it as follows:

1. Log in to the portal as an Administrator, "**Palm Tree**", and go to the **Book Lovers** Community located in the **My Places** menu. Click on the **Configuration** icon in the upper-right corner of the **Message Boards** portlet.

2. Click on the **Permissions** tab.

3. The **User** tab and **Current** sub-tab are selected. This means that the current **Users** who have portlet **Permissions** assigned to them are being displayed. Obviously, there are no **Users** who have portlet **Permissions** for this particular portlet.

4. Click on the **Available** tab.

5. Locate the **User**, "Lotti Stein".

6. Check the **User**, "Lotti Stein" checkbox, and click on the **Update Permissions** button.

7. Select **Add Category** from the **Available** select box and click on the right arrow to add it to the **Current** select box.

8. Click the **Finished** button.

Alternatively, you can assign individual portlet **Permissions** for the **Organizations, User Groups, Community, Regular Roles, Community roles** or use **Guest** tab for assigning portlet **Permissions** to each of these entities.

Portlet **Permissions** are only applicable to the portlet instance for which they were configured. For example, "**Lotti Stein**" can only add root categories to the **Message Board** in the **Book Lovers** Community. "**Lotti Stein**" would not be able to add root categories to the message boards in other **Communities** unless they were specifically configured as such.

Assign Default Permissions

As an administrator, "**Palm Tree**", you may need to create a new **Message Board Category** in the **Book Lovers** Community's message board and assign default **Permissions** to it. Let's do it as follows:

1. Log in to the portal as an administrator, and go to the **Book Lovers** Community. Click on the "**Book Category**" link in the Message Boards portlet, and then click on the **Add Category** button.

2. To set **Permissions** for the category, click **Configure**.

3. All actions under **Community** are checked and the **Guest View** option is checked. By default, a new **Message Board Category** allows **Community** members (in this case, **Book Lovers** Community members) to view it, subscribe to it, and add messages to it, and also allows guests to view it.

4. Keep the default **Permissions** checkboxes checked. Enter "**Book Category D**" into the **Name** field, input the text verification code.

5. Click the **Save** button if you are ready.

If the **User Lotti Stein** were to click on the "**Book Category**" link now, the **User** would see the new "**Book Category D**" topic and would be able to view the contents of the topic and post a new thread (that is, message) to the category because of the **Community** default **Permissions**.

Assign Individual Permissions

As an administrator "**Palm Tree**", you may need to assign a **Permission** to **User** "**Lotti Stein**" to delete the "**Book Category D**" topic in the **Book Lovers** community's **Message Boards** portlet. Let's do it as follows:

1. Go to the page "**Admin**" at **Book Lovers** Community **Private Pages**, click on the "**Book Category**" link in the Message Boards portlet, and then click on the **Permissions** icon from the **Actions** next to the "**Book Category D**".

2. The **Users** tab and the **Current** sub-tab are selected. This means that the current **Users** who have **Permissions** for the "**Book Category D**" topic are being displayed. Currently, only the Administrator has **Permissions** for this category. Go to the **Available** tab, find the **User** "Lotti Stein", check the **User's** checkbox, and click on the **Update Permissions** button.

3. Select the **Delete** action from the **Available** select box and click on the left arrow to add it to the **Current** select box.

4. Click the **Finished** button when you are ready.

The **User** "Lotti Stein" has been updated with the "**Delete**" **Permission**. To see this **Permission** in effect, log in to the portal as "**Lotti Stein**", go to the **Book Lovers** Community **Private Pages**, and click on the "**Book Category**" link in the **Message** Boards portlet. The "**Book Category D**" topic now has a **Delete** icon from **Actions** next to it.

Alternatively, you can assign **Permissions** to the **Organizations**, **User Groups**, **Community**, or use **Guest** tab for assigning individual **Permissions** to each of these entities.

> Note that there is a special case for assigning individual Permissions to Locations that requires a slightly different use case. Refer to the following part.

It should also be noted that very fine-grained **Permission** allotments can be obtained through using individual **Permissions**. As this use case showed, administrators have the power to control objects within a portlet at a very micro level. For example, take the four topics in "**Book Category**." An administrator could easily decide that all **Users** in the department "Editorial" can post messages to "**Book Category A**," but only members of the **Book Lovers** Community can view the messages in "**Book Category B**". In addition, only "**Lotti Stein**" can update "**Book Category C**," while anyone in the "**Editorial Germany**" **Location** can update "**Book Category D**." The possibilities are endless.

Delegate Permissions

Assume the administrator has created a **Role** called "**Delegated Admin**" and assigned it to the **User** "Lotti Stein", and the **Communities** portlet have been added in the page "**Admin**" at the **Book Lovers** Community. Moreover, assume the **User** "Lotti Stein" has **Permissions** (view in fact) on the **Enterprise Admin** portlet.

As an Administrator, "**Palm Tree**", you may need to delegate **Permissions** to **Users** which allow them to have certain administrative rights as well. For example, you may assign the **User** "**Lotti Stein**" **Permissions** to add **Communities** to the system as follows:

- Log in to the portal as "**Lotti Stein**" and go to the **Book Lovers** Community. Click on the **Current** tab in the **Communities** portlet. The **User** "**Lotti Stein**" can't add new **Community** to the system.

- Log in to the portal as an Administrator "**Palm Tree**". Go to the **Book Lovers** Community and click on the **Roles** tab in the **Enterprise Admin** portlet. Click on the **Define Permissions** icon from the **Actions** next to the "**Delegated Admin**" Role.

- Select the **Add Portal Permissions** button.

- Choose "**Enterprise**" from the **Scope** drop-down next to the **Add Community** action. Click the **Next** button.

- The result of these steps is that any **User** with the "**Delegated Admin**" **Role** can now add **Communities** to the system. To confirm this, go back to "**Lotti Stein**" and refresh the **Current** tab in the **Communities** portlet. Notice that there is an **Add Community** button now.

Similarly, we can enable any **User** with the "**Delegated Admin**" **Role** to have **Permission** to add **Organizations, Roles, Users**, and **User Groups** to the system. Just go back to the Administrator and perform the mentioned steps. But this time, choose "**Enterprise**" from the **Scope** drop-down next to the "**Add Organization**" ("**Add Role**" or "**Add User**" or "**Add User Group**") action.

Logically, you can delegate **Permissions** which includes portals **Permissions, Community Permissions**, page **Permissions**, portlet **Permissions**, and **Role Permissions**. Besides the above mentioned portal **Permissions** delegation, you can do the following:

- Delegate **Permissions** to **Users** so that they will be able to manage **Roles**.

- Delegate **Permissions** to **Users** so that they will be able to manage portlets within pages.

- Delegate **Permissions** to **Users** so that they will be able to manage pages within their **Communities**.

- Delegate **Permissions** to the members of the **Community**.

Using Permissions Effectively

Permission is an action on a resource. Liferay provides exclusive **Permissions** mechanism.

Assume the delete **Permission** for "**Book Category A**" is added to the "**Editorial Germany**" **Location**. As expected, the **User** "Lotti Stein" receives the delete **Permission**. Then, the delete **Permission** for "**Book Category A**" is added to the "**Editorial US**" **Location**. Though an explicit check is not made, it is assumed that this allows all members of the "**Editorial US**" **Location** to also have delete **Permission**. In other words, any member of either "**Editorial US**" or "**Editorial Germany**" has delete **Permission** for "**Book Category A**".

However, when the value of the "**Permission exclusive to members of current location and community?**" was changed from "**No**" to "**Yes**" for "**Editorial Germany**", suddenly "**Lotti Stein**" lost the delete **Permission**.

In other words, in order to have the delete **Permission** on "**Book Category A**," a **User** had to be a member of both the "**Editorial US**" **Location** and the **Book Lovers** Community. Since "**Lotti Stein**" was *only* a member of the **Book Lovers** Community, and *not* a member of the "**Editorial Germany**" **Location**, "Lotti Stein" did not meet the criteria and was excluded from receiving the delete **Permission**.

Exclusive **Permissions** take precedence over all other **Permissions** except **Permissions** assigned directly to a **User**. Therefore, even if the delete **Permission** had been assigned to the "**Editorial US**" **Location** and the **Book Lovers** Community, or if the delete **Permission** had enterprise scope and had been assigned to a **Role** that was assigned to "Lotti Stein", it wouldn't have mattered. The exclusive **Permission** would still have taken precedence, and "**Lotti Stein**" would not have received the delete **Permission**. However, if the delete **Permission** had been assigned directly to the **User** "Lotti Stein", "Lotti Stein" would have received the **Permission**.

Although exclusive **Permissions** are not additive with other **Permissions**, they are additive among themselves. In other words, if the "**Permission exclusive to members of current location and community?**" was changed from "**No**" to "**Yes**" for "**Editorial US**" as well, "**Lotti Stein**" would receive the delete **Permission** once again. However, it should be noted that only "**Editorial US**" and "**Editorial Germany**" **Users** would receive the **Permission**, even if the delete **Permission** was assigned to other **Users** through other entities (such as, **Organization**, **Community**, **Role**, and so on).

Applying Full Access Control Security Model

Traditional membership models address two basic criteria, Authentication (who can access) and Authorization (what they can do):

- Authentication is the process of determining whether someone is what it is declared to be or not.

- Authorization is the process of finding out where the person, once identified, has permissions on the resource or not.

Liferay extends the security model by resources, **Users, Organizations, Locations, User Groups**, and **Communities, Roles, Permissions**, and so on. Liferay provides a fine-grained permission security model, which is a full access control security model. At the same time, Liferay also provides a set of administrative tools to configure and control the membership.

The remainder of this section will explore these concepts and relationships among the mentioned terms. It would be useful to provide a big picture on how to bring in **Users**. For example, as a **User** in the engineering department, you may plan to develop a number of portlets to satisfy the current and even future requirements of "Palm Tree Publications". Thus it is important to have a big picture on how to bring in **Users** anytime.

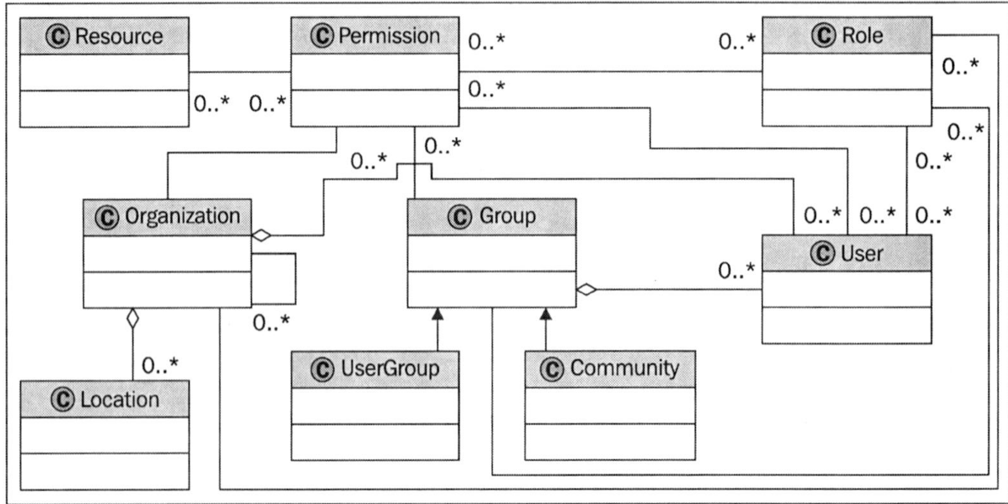

As shown in the previous figure, a **Resource** is a base object. It can be a portlet (such as, Message Boards, Calendar, Document Library, and so on), a Java class (for example, Message Board Topics, Calendar Event, Document Library Folder, and so on), or a file (such as, documents, images, applications, and so on). Resources are scoped into enterprise, **Community** and individual.

Then **Permission** is an action on a resource. Enterprise and **Community** scoped **Permissions** can only be assigned to entities (for example, **Users**, **Communities** and **Organizations**) via **Roles**. Individual scoped **Permissions** can be assigned to a **User**, **Community**, **Organization**, or **Guest**.

A **Role** is a collection of **Permissions**. **Roles** can be assigned to a **User**, **Community**, or **Organization**. If a **Role** is assigned to a **Community**, **Organization**, or **Location**, then all the **users** who are members of that entity receive the **Role**.

A **User** is an individual. Depending on what **Permissions** and **Roles** have been assigned, the **User** either has **Permission** or does not have **Permission** to perform certain tasks.

Organizations represent the enterprise and departments hierarchy. **Organizations** can contain other **Organizations**. Moreover, an **Organization** acting as a child **Organization** of a top-level **Organization** can also represent departments of a parent corporation.

A **Location** is a special **Organization** with one and only one associated parent **Organization,** and without any associated child **Organization**. **Organizations** can have any number of **Locations** and sub organizations. Both **Roles** and individual **Permissions** can be assigned to **Organizations** (**Locations** or sub **Organizations**). By default, **Locations** and sub organizations inherit **Permissions** from their parent **Organization**.

A **Community** is a special group. It may hold a number of **Users** who share common interests. Both **Roles** and individual **Permissions** can be assigned to **Communities**.

Finally, a **User Group** is a special group with no context, which may hold a number of **Users**. Both **Roles** and individual **Permissions** can be assigned to **User Groups**, and every **User** that belongs to that **User Group** will receive the **Role** or **Permission**.

Summary

This chapter introduced how to update the profile with **My Account**; how to create **Organization** and **Locations**; how to add **Users** and manage (such as view, search, update, deactivate, restore, delete and impersonate) **Users**; how to add **User Groups** and manage (such as view, search, update, delete and assign) **User Groups**; and how to add more administrators at the enterprise level, department level and **Location** level. Then it discussed how to integrate with different authentication servers: LDAP, CAS, NTLM, OpenID, Open SSO, and so on. Furthermore, it also discussed how to manage **Permissions**, and how to add **Roles** and manage (for example, view, search, update, delete and assign) **Roles**. Finally, it provided a big picture about fine-grained permission security model via a conceptual diagram.

Discussion Forums And Tags

4

In the intranet website "book.com" of "Palm Tree Publications", it is required that an environment for employees is provided to discuss book ideas and proposals, and to share important and interesting contents with other users inside or outside of the intranet website. Liferay **Message Boards** provides a full-featured discussion forums solution, while Liferay Meta **Tags** provide a way of organizing and aggregating contents. This chapter will introduce both Liferay **Message Boards** and Liferay Meta **Tags**.

By the end of this chapter, you will have learned how to:

- Add categories and sub-categories for **Message Boards**.
- Add **Threads** and **Posts** for a given category.
- Manage (view, add, update, delete, and feed) **Categories**, **Threads** and **Posts**.
- Use **Permissions** for **Message Boards**, **Categories** and **Threads**.
- Add a **Tag**, manage (add, delete, and change category) **Tags**.
- Tag contents.
- Display tagged contents.

Working with Message Boards

In order to provide an environment for employees to discuss book ideas and proposals, we should use **Message Boards** portlet at the **Book Lovers** Community (**Public Pages**). In the previous chapter, we assumed we have added a **Message Board** portlet to the **Book Lovers** Community. A **Category** called "Book Category" has been created, and the **Category** contains four **Categories** — "Book Category A," "Book Category B," "Book Category C" and "Book Category D".

As an administrator of "**Palm-Tree Publications**", you need to create a page called "**Forums**" under the page "**Community**", at **Book Lovers** Community and further add **Message Boards** portlet in the page "**Forums**". Then you are ready to create a **Category** called "**Book Category**", and further, add four sub-categories for the Category "**Book Category**", which are "**Book Category A**", "**Book Category B**", "**Book Category C**", and "**Book Category D**".

Adding And Managing Categories

As an administrator of "**Palm-Tree Publications**", you need to create a category "**Book Category**" and sub categories "**Book Category A**", "**Book Category B**", "**Book Category C**", and "**Book Category D**". These sub categories will hold messages related to book ideas and proposals.

Adding Categories

First of all, we need to create a **Category** called "**Book Category**". Let's do it now:

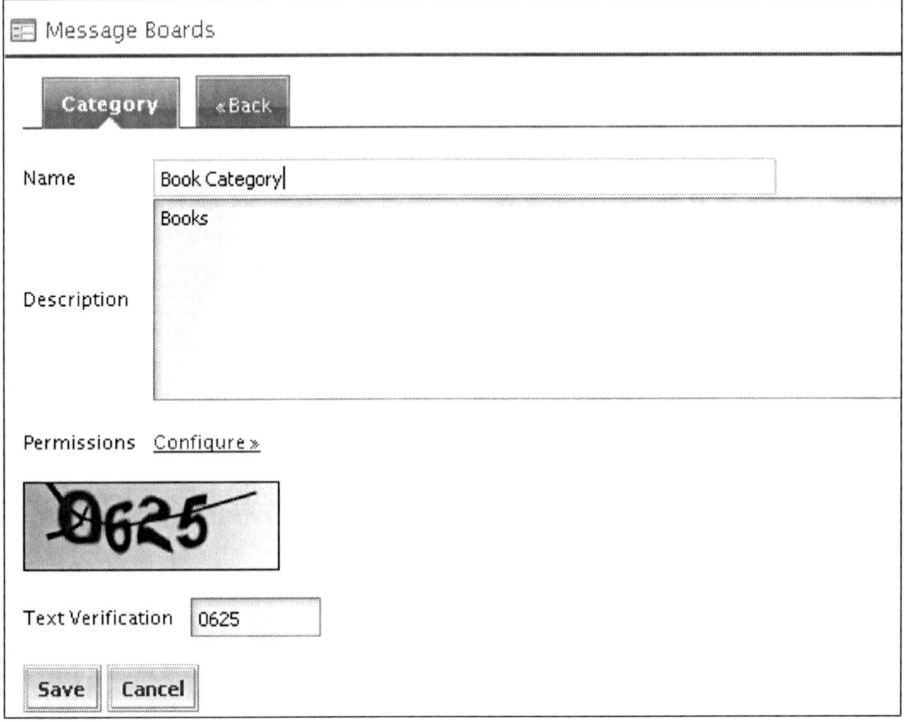

1. Add a page called "**Community**" at the **Book Lovers** Community **Public Pages,** if the page is not there. Add a child page called "**Forums**" of the page "**Community**".

2. If **Message Boards** Portlet is not there, add **Message Boards** Portlet in the page "**Forums**" of the **Book Lovers** Community where you want to publish forums.

3. Click on **Add Category** button.

4. Enter a name "**Book Category**" and a description "**Books**".

5. Set **Permissions** by clicking on **Configure** link. To configure additional **Permissions**, click on the **More** link. Here, we just use default settings.

6. Enter the **Text Verification** code.

7. Click on the **Save** button to save the inputs.

Do you find different themes used for this portlet? By default, there are a set of themes available, such as "**Brochure**", "**Classic**", "**Desktop**", "**Genesis**", and "**Liferay Noir**", "**liferay jedi**", and so on and a set of themes from the community. In this chapter, we try to use the theme "**Brochure**" mainly. Liferay makes it easy to use any theme, and instructions in this book are intended to work with any theme.

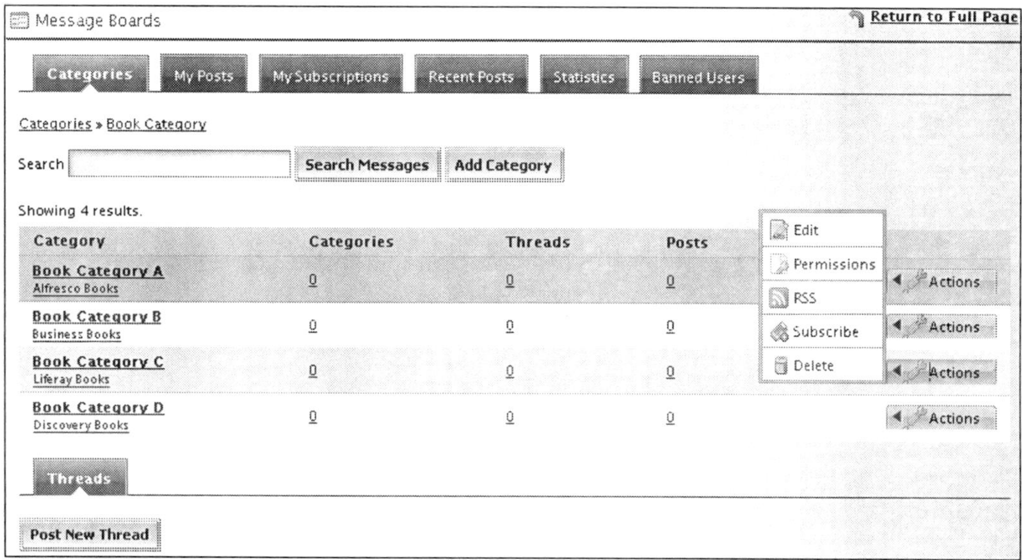

You can also definitely add other **Categories**. Normally, a forum may have many **Categories**, and each **Category** may have many **Categories** called sub-categories. For example, the **Category** "Book Category" contains four **Categories**: "Book Category A", "Book Category B", "Book Category C", and "Book Category D". Let's create the category "Book Category A" as follows:

1. Click on the newly created category "**Book Category**".
2. Click the **Add Category** button.
3. Enter a name "**Book Category A**" and a description "**Alfresco Books**".
4. Set permissions by clicking on the **Configure** link. To configure additional permissions, click on the **More** link. Here again, we just use the default settings.
5. Enter the **Text Verification** code.
6. Click on the **Save** button to save the inputs.

Of course, you can add as many **Categories** or sub-categories as you want. After creating the sub categories "**Book Category B**", "**Book Category C**", and "**Book Category D**", we can view the **Category** and its sub-categories. **Categories** "**Book Category B**" and "**Book Category D**" used the default permission setting, while **Category** "**Book Category C**" uses only "**View**" permission in the **Community** column.

Managing Categories

Categories or sub-categories are editable. For example, you may need to change the description of the **Category** "Book Category" from "Books" to "Books discussion category". Let's do is as follows:

1. Locate the category, "**Book Category**", which you want to edit.
2. Click on the **Edit** icon from the **Actions** located next to the category.
3. Maintain the value of name, and update the description of the selected **Category** "Book Category" with the value "**Books discussion category**".
4. Click on the **Save** button to save the changes.

You can update the name as well. For example, we can update the name "**Book Category**" with the value "**Books**". Similarly, we can edit sub-category such as "**Book Category C**" by updating the name with value "**Liferay Books**".

Alternatively, you can change the parent **Category** by selecting a **Category** as the parent **Category** of the **Category** or sub-category, or merging **Categories** with the parent **Category**, or removing the parent **Category**. If you remove the parent **Category**, the current **Category** will become a **Category** at the root level.

Categories or sub-categories are removable. For example, the sub-category "**Book Category B**" is not wanted anymore; you can remove it. Let's do it as follows:

1. Click on the category, "**Books**", in order to list its sub-categories.

2. Locate the sub-category, "**Book Category B**", which you want to delete.

3. Then click on the **Delete** icon from the **Actions** located next to the category.

4. A screen will appear asking if you want to delete this. Click **OK** to confirm deletion.

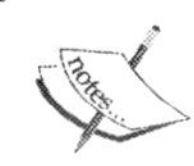

Note that deleting the **Category** will delete all related sub-categories, **Threads** and **Posts** which belong to this category.

View RSS Feeds

You can view **RSS** feeds of **Categories** or sub-categories. Suppose that you need to view the **RSS** feeds of the **Category** "**Books**". Let's do it as follows:

1. Locate the category "**Books**".

2. Click on the **RSS** icon from the **Actions** located next to the category.

3. Follow the browser's instructions to subscribe if you want to subscribe RSS Feeds.

What's **RSS**? Refer to Chapter 6 for instructions.

Adding And Managing Threads

Now, we are ready to post new **Threads**. Normally, a forum may have many **Categories**, and each **Category** may have many sub-categories and **Threads**.

Adding Threads

Let's suppose we want to post a new **Thread** "Let's discuss book Liferay" under the category "**Liferay Books**". Let's do it as follows:

1. Select a **Category** "Books" and find sub-category "**Liferay Books**".
2. Select the sub-category "**Liferay Books**" where you want to add a thread by clicking on the sub-category name.
3. Click on the **Post New Thread** button.
4. Enter a **Subject** "Let's discuss book Liferay" and **Body** "**It is time now to discuss Liferay book**" via an editor.
5. Check/uncheck the box, **Anonymous**.
6. Select one of the priorities (**none, urgent, sticky** and **announcement**) such as "**urgent**".
7. Input **Tags** or select **Tags** from existing **Tags**.
8. Set **Permissions** by clicking on the **Configure** link; to configure additional **Permissions**, click on the **More** link; here we just use the default settings.
9. Enter the **Text Verification** code.
10. Click on the **Save** button to save the inputs.

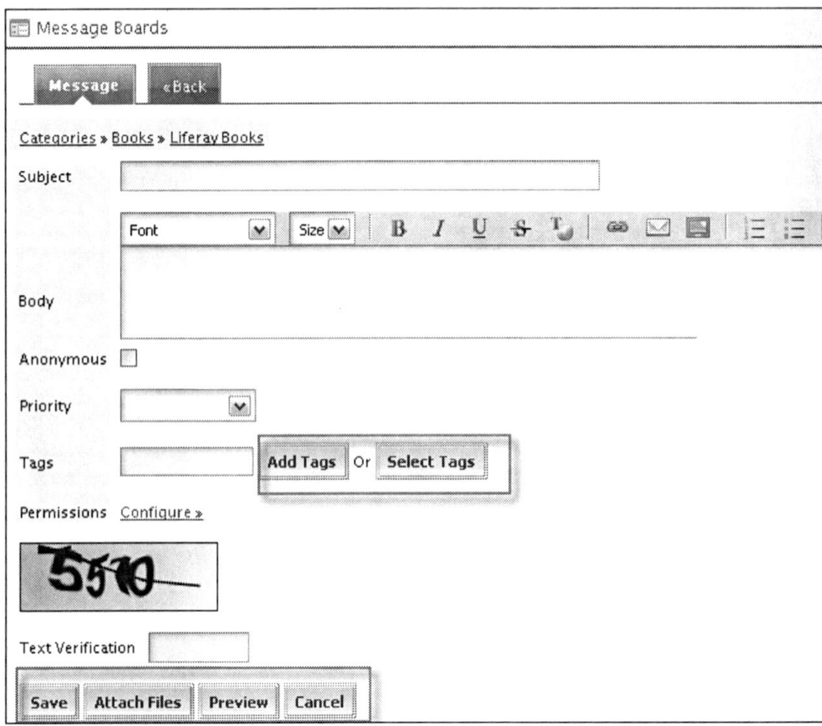

In addition, we can attach files by clicking on the **Attach Files** button and upload files further. Similarly, we can preview the **Thread** by clicking on the **Preview** button.

Adding a new **Thread** with a **Subject** such as "**Let's discuss book Liferay**" will add a **Post** automatically with the same **Subject** as that of the **Thread**.

 What are **Tags**? Refer to instructions in the next section of this chapter.

Likewise, we can add other **Threads**. After adding a **Thread** "**Where is the outline of Liferay Book?**", we can view **Threads**.

Managing Threads

Threads are also editable. For example, you may need to change the **Subject** of the **Thread** "**Where is the outline of Liferay Book?**" into "**Do you find the outline of Liferay Book?**" Let's do it as follows:

1. Locate the **Thread** "**Where is the outline of Liferay Book?**", which you want to edit.

2. Click on the **Edit** icon from the **Actions** located next to the thread.

3. Update the **Subject** of the selected category "**Where is the outline of Liferay Book?**" with the value "**Do you find the outline of Liferay Book?**".

4. Click on the **Save** button to save the changes.

You can update the **Body** and **Priority** as well. Alternatively, you can change the **Category** by selecting another **Category** as the **Category** of the **Thread**.

Updating the **Subject** of the **Thread,** such as **"Let's discuss book Liferay?"**, will automatically update the **Subject** of the top-level **Post** with the same **Subject** as that of the **Thread**.

Threads are also removable. For example, if the **Thread "Where is the outline of Liferay Book?"** is not wanted anymore, you can remove it. Let's do it as follows:

1. Locate the **Thread "Where is the outline of Liferay Book?"**, which you want to delete.
2. Then click on the **Delete** icon from the **Actions** located next to the thread.
3. A screen will appear asking if you want to delete this. Click **OK** to confirm deletion.

 Note that deleting a **Thread** will delete all related **Posts** that belong to this thread.

View RSS Feeds

You can view the **RSS** feeds of **Threads** as well as that of **Categories**. Suppose that you need to view the **RSS** feeds of the **Thread "Let's discuss book Liferay"**. Let's do it as follows:

1. Navigate to the category **"Books"** and the sub-category **"Liferay Books"**.
2. Locate the **Thread "Let's discuss book Liferay"**.
3. Click on the **RSS** icon from the **Actions** located next to the thread.
4. Follow the browser's instructions to subscribe if you want to subscribe **RSS** Feeds.

Adding And Managing Posts

Finally, we are ready to add more **Posts**. Normally, a forum may have many **Categories**, and each **Category** may have many sub-categories and **Threads**, and each **Thread** may have a lot of **Posts**.

Adding Posts

We can reply to the **Thread "Let's discuss book Liferay"** with the message "OK". Let's do it as follows:

1. Select category **"Books"** and sub-category **"Liferay Books"**.

2. Click on the **Thread** with the name "**Let's discuss book Liferay**".

3. Locate the post ("**Let's discuss book Liferay**") to which you want to reply first.

4. Then click on **Reply** icon at the top right of the post.

5. Maintain the default **Subject** "**Re: Let's discuss book Liferay**", **Body** as (via an editor) "**OK**" and select **Tags** or input **Tags**.

6. Set **Permissions** by clicking on the **Configure** link; to configure additional **Permissions**, click on the **More** link; here we just use the default settings.

7. Check/uncheck the **Anonymous**; and select **Priority**.

8. Click on the **Reply** button to save the inputs.

In addition, you can attach a file by clicking on the **Attach Files** button; and preview the **Post** or **Reply** by clicking on the **Preview** button. Moreover, you can reply with quote by clicking on **Reply with Quote** icon at the top right of the post.

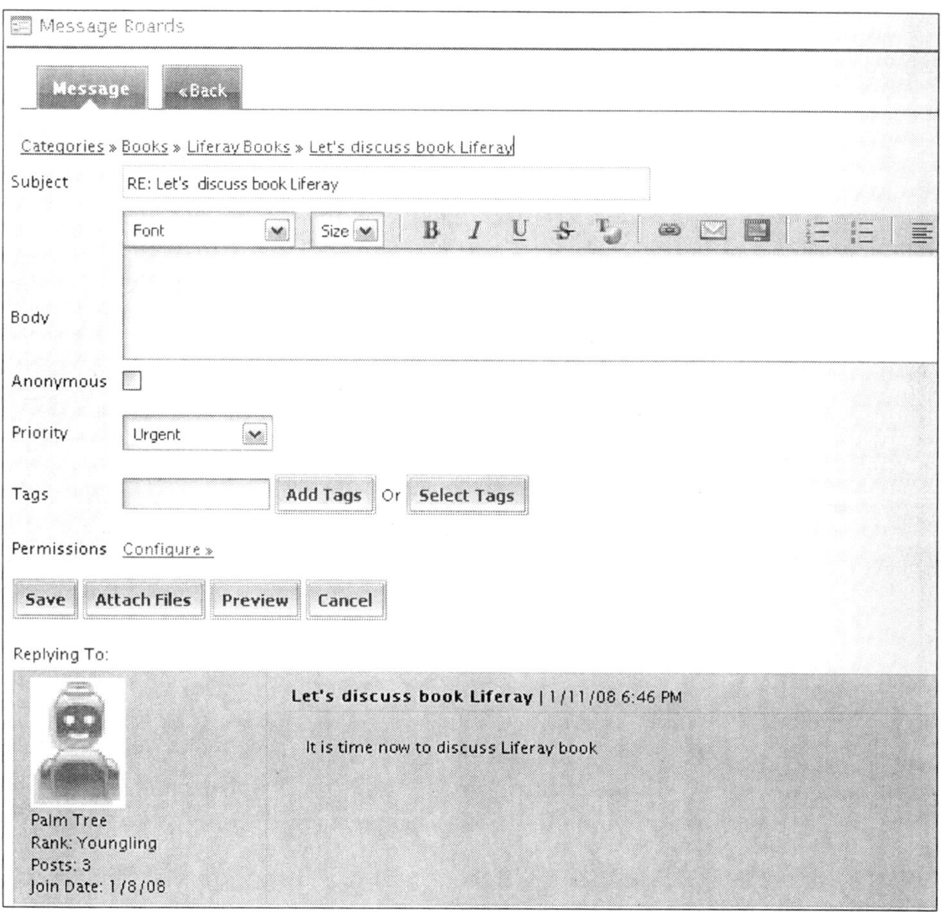

Of course, you can reply to other posts to discuss your ideas or proposals.

Managing Posts

You can manage posts easily through: editing post, replying post, deleting posts and viewing posts, and so on. Let's manage post as follows.

Edit Posts

Posts are editable. To edit a post, click on the **Edit** icon at the bottom right of the post. You can change the **Category, Subject, Body** (via an editor), **Priority** and **Tags**. Then you simply click on the **Save** button to save the changes or click on the **Cancel** button to cancel.

Alternatively, you can attach a file by clicking on **Attach Files** button, or preview the **Post** by clicking on the **Preview** button.

Updating the **Subject** of the top-level **Post** such as "**Let's discuss book Liferay**" will automatically update the **Subject** of the **Thread** (which the top-level **Post** belongs to) with the same **Subject** as that of the top-level **Post**.

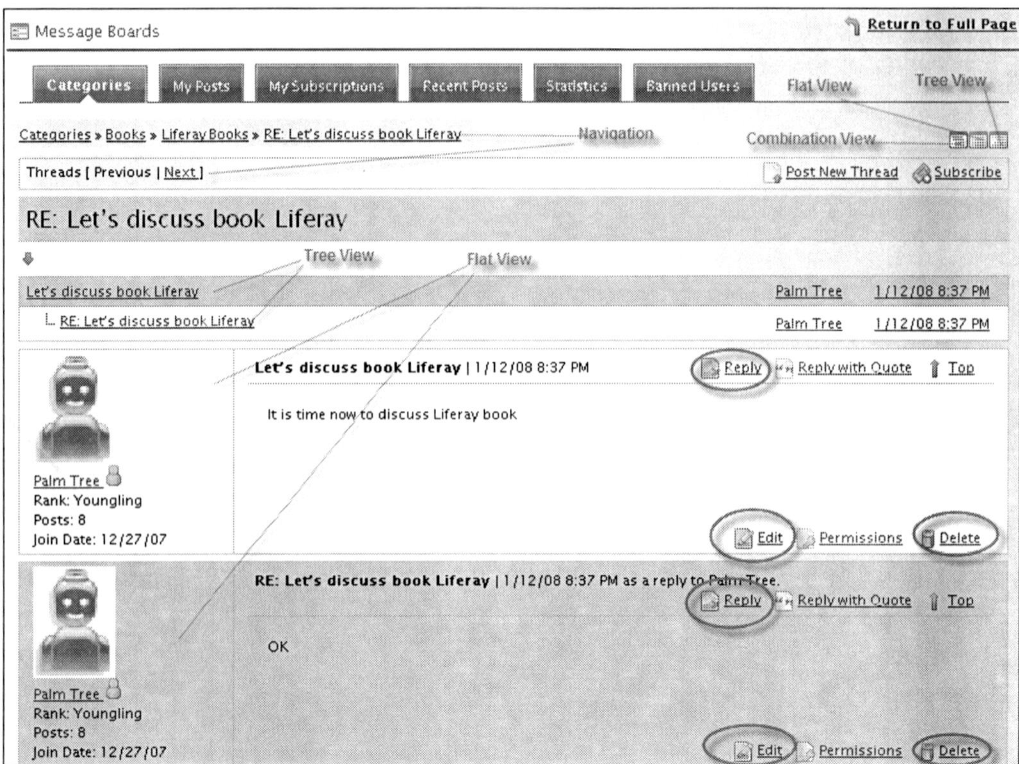

Ban Users

In addition, you can ban a user if you have proper **Permissions**. Let's suppose that "Lotti Stein" has a post "**Alfresco Books - discussion**" under the category "**Book Category A**". As an administrator, you will see the icon (**Ban this User**), under the user "Lotti Stein" image. If you need to ban this user, simply click on the icon (**Ban this User**). Then you will see that the **Ban this User** icon becomes the **Un-ban this User** icon.

When the user "**Lotti Stein**" logs in, she will see a message at the **Message Board**: "**You have been banned by the moderator**".

As an administrator, you can un-ban the user "**Lotti Stein**", by simply clicking on the icon, **Un-ban this User**. Then you will see that the icon, **Un-ban this User** becomes the icon, **Ban this User**.

Delete Posts

Posts are also removable. For example, if the **Post** "**Re: Let's discuss book Liferay**" is not required anymore, you can remove it. Let's do it as follows:

1. Locate the post "**Re: Let's discuss book Liferay**", which you want to delete.
2. Click on the **Delete** icon at the bottom right of the post.
3. A screen will appear asking if you want to delete this. Click **OK** to confirm deletion or Cancel to cancel deletion.

More interestingly, if the top-level **Post**, "**Let's discuss book Liferay**" was deleted, the **Thread** which the top-level **Post** belongs to will link to the low-level **Post**, "**Re: Let's discuss book Liferay**". If the top-level **Post** , "**Let's discuss book Liferay**", was the only **Post** in the **Thread**, and it was deleted, then the **Thread** which the top-level **Post** belongs to will also be deleted.

Note that only the current **Post** has been deleted. The low level **Posts** related to the current **Post** will have a link to the top-level **Post** of the current **Post**.

View Posts

All **Posts** of a given **Thread** may have different views: **Combination View, Flat View** or **Tree View**. For example, the default view mode is **Combination View**. To change current view mode to **Flat View**, simply click on the **Flat View** button next to the navigation. Of course, you can use **Tree View** model.

You can also change the **Thread** by clicking on the "**Previous**" or "**Next**" buttons next to **Threads**. Moreover, you can change the **Categories** by clicking on the **Category** name on the navigation line.

Search Messages

We can easily find messages by search. For instance, in order to search messages which contain "**book**" in **Message Boards**, simply input the message keyword, "**book**", and then click on the **Search Messages** button. A list of **Categories** which contain the keywords in messages appears with columns: **Categories**, **Messages** (thread subject), **Thread Posts**, **Thread Vies** and **Score**.

Search is scoped by **Category**. For example, if you just need to search messages which contain "**book**" in the **Category** "**Categories->Books->Liferay Books**", simply navigate to the **Category** "**Liferay Books**" first, and then input message keyword such as "**book**", and, click on the **Search Messages** button.

What are messages in search? Messages here refer to the contents of **Threads** and **Posts**. They contain the **Subject** and **Body** of **Threads** and **Posts**.

View My Posts

You can view your own **Posts** by clicking the **My Posts** tab of the **Message Boards**. A list of your **Posts** will appear with **Thread, Started By, Posts, Views, Last Post** and **Actions** with a set of icons (**Edit, Permissions, RSS, Subscribe/Unsubscribe, Delete**, and so forth).

View Recent Posts

Similarly, you can view recent posts, by clicking the **Recent Posts** tab of the **Message Boards**. A list of recent postings will appear with **Thread, Started By, Posts, Views, Last Post** and **Actions** with a set of icons (**Edit, Permissions, RSS, Subscribe/ Unsubscribe and Delete**).

View Statistics

Furthermore, you can view general statistics by clicking the **Statistics** tab of the **Message Boards**. By this, statistics data such as **Number of Categories, Number of Posts** and **Participants** will appear. In addition, click the **Top Posters** sub tab to see a list of most active users.

View Banned Users

You can view banned users if you have proper **Permissions**. You may simply click on the **Banned Users** tab of the **Message Boards**. A list of banned users will appear with **Name, Ban Date, Un-ban Date**, and icon (**Un-ban this User**). To un-ban this user, just click on the icon, **Un-ban this User,** next to the **Un-ban Date**.

Subscribing Categories And Threads

As users of the **Message Boards**, you may be interested in changes in messages in specific **Categories** and **Threads**. For example, the administrator "Palm Tree" is interested in the messages in **Category** "Book Category A". You want to watch for any changes of the messages in this category. You can certainly use subscription function on the category, "**Book Category A**". Let's do it as follows:

1. Locate the category "**Book Category A**".

2. Click on the **Subscribe** icon from the **Actions** located next to the category. The **Subscribe** icon will change to **Unsubscribe,** for this category.

Of course, you can **Subscribe** to other **Categories**. You may be interested in the message of the thread "**Let's discuss book Liferay**". Thus you can **Subscribe** to it as follows:

1. Locate the category "**Liferay Books**" and locate the thread "**Let's discuss book Liferay**".

2. Click on the **Subscribe** icon from the **Actions** located next to the thread. The **Subscribe** icon will change to **Unsubscribe,** for this thread.

It's worth mentioning that you can **Subscribe** to other **Threads**. In addition, you can view your **Subscriptions** by a click on the **My Subscriptions** tab. You will find lists of **Categories** and **Threads** to which you have subscribed.

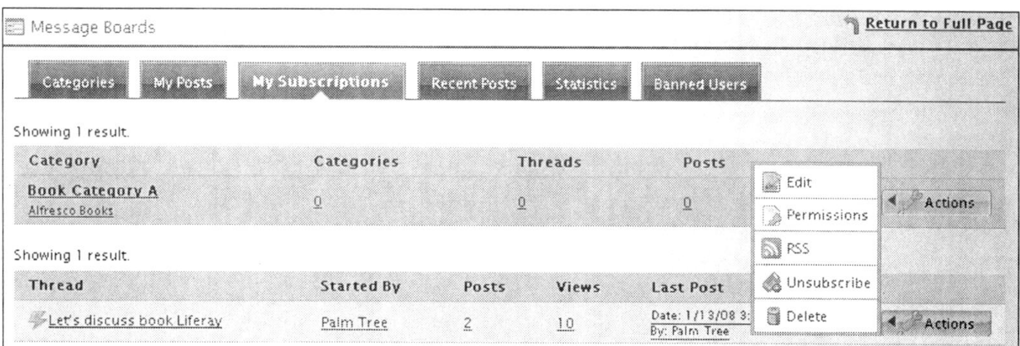

Unsubscribe Categories And Threads

In addition, you can **Unsubscribe** to **Categories,** or sub-categories, or **Threads,** if they have been subscribed to already. For example, you may need to **Unsubscribe** to the **Thread, "Let's discuss book Liferay"**. Let's do it as follows:

1. Click on the **My Subscriptions** tab in the **Message Boards**.

2. Locate the thread "**Let's discuss book Liferay**".

3. Click on the **Unsubscribe** icon from the **Actions** located next to the thread. The thread "**Let's discuss book Liferay**" will disappear from the view of **My Subscriptions**.

Or you can **Unsubscribe** to the **Thread "Let's discuss book Liferay"** from the view of **Categories** as follows:

1. Locate the **Category "Liferay Books"** and locate the **Thread, "Let's discuss book Liferay"**.

2. Click on the **Unsubscribe** icon from the **Actions** located next to the thread. The **Unsubscribe** icon will change to **Subscribe,** for this **Thread**.

What Happens Next?

If you have some **Categories** or **Threads** to which you have subscribed, and the messages of the subscribed to **Categories** or **Threads** have changed, you will receive notifications for these changes.

Subscription is, generally speaking, an agreement to receive electronic texts or services, especially over the Internet. The **Thread** subscription provides a useful function, that of notifying through email, when a new message has been posted or updated. On the one hand, you can subscribe to a **Thread** for a given **Category** or sub-category. Whenever a new message has been posted or updated, you will be notified through email. On the other hand, you can also unsubscribe to a **Thread** for a given **Category** or sub-category if it has been subscribed to already. Henceforth, you will not be notified through email; even if a message has been posted or updated.

Moreover, **Category** subscription provides a useful function, that is, to to notify through email, when a **Category** has been updated. Similar to the **Thread** subscription, you can subscribe to a **Category** or sub-category. Whenever **Category** or sub-category is updated, you will be notified through email.

How to set up mail notifications? Just refer to the following section.

Setting up Message Boards

As an administrator of "**Palm-Tree Publications**", you can set up **Message Boards**. For example, you can configure subscription emails.

To configure the subscription function, click on the **Configuration** icon on **Message Boards**. When the **Setup** tab is selected, there are six sub-tabs that appear: **Email From**, **Message Added Email**, **Message Updated Email**, **Thread Priorities**, **User Ranks, RSS**, and **Anonymous Posting**.

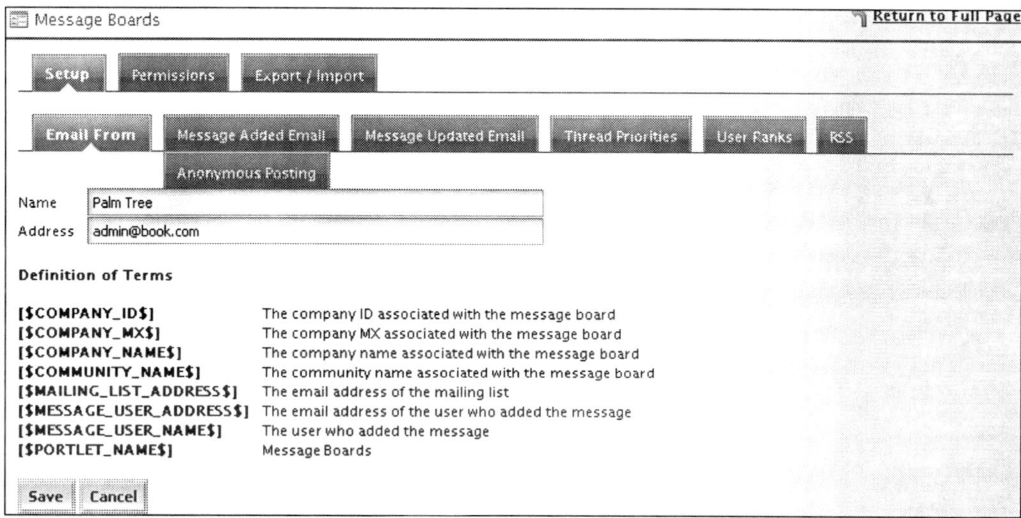

Selecting the **Email From** tab, you can change the names and addresses of the automatically sent emails.

The **Message Added Email** tab allows the Administrator to edit the email that is sent whenever a posting is added. To disable email alerts, uncheck the **Enabled** box. Click the **Save** button after making the changes.

Similarly, the **Message Updated Email** tab allows the Administrator to edit the email that is sent whenever a posting is updated. To disable email alerts, uncheck the **Enabled** box. Click the **Save** button after making the changes.

With the **Thread Priorities** tab selected, the Administrator can manage the **Thread Priorities** profiles. The following table depicts the default settings. The Administrator can change the **Name, Image**, and **Priority** requirements by making changes directly, and clicking the **Save** button.

Name	Image	Priority	Description
Urgent	`/message_boards` `/priority_` `urgent.png`	3.0	Enter the name, image, and priority level in descending order. **Threads** with a higher priority are displayed ahead of **Threads** with a lower priority. The name is the display name of the priority. The image is the display image of the priority and can either be a complete URL or a path relative to the theme.
Sticky	`/message_boards` `/priority_` `sticky.png`	2.0	
Announcement	`/message_boards` `/priority_` `announcement.` `png`	1.0	

Selecting the **User Ranks** tab, the Administrator can manage the ranking profiles. The following table shows the default settings. The Administrator can change the ranking names and posting number requirements by making changes directly, and clicking the **Save** button.

Rank	Minimum Posts	Description
Youngling	0	Enter rank and minimum post pairs per line. **Users** will be displayed with a rank based on their number of **Posts**.
Padawan	25	
Jedi Knight	100	
Jedi Master	250	
Jedi Council Member	500	
Yoda	1000	

Note that it is also possible to activate the Liferay SMTP events, to allow users to respond to mails sent by the **Message Boards**. In order to avoid HTML problems while posting replies, the mails are now sent in plain text.

Selecting the **RSS** tab, the administrator can manage the RSS settings. The administrator can change the '**Maximum Items to Display**', "**Display Style**", and "**Format**", and then click on the **Save** button.

In addition, selecting the **Anonymous Posting** tab, the administrator can enable or disable the checkbox, "**Allow Anonymous Posting**".

Using Permissions

We have used the default settings for **Message Boards** portlet in the page, "Forums" of the page "**Community**", under the **Book Lovers** Community. When the administrator "**Palm Tree**" logs in, he will see the button "**Add Category**" in the **Message Boards**. As we know that the user "Lotti Stein" is also a member of the **Book Lovers** community, try logging in as "Lotti Stein", and you will find that there is no button "**Add Category**" in the **Message Boards**.

What's happening? This is something related to **Permissions**. There are three levels of **Permissions**: Portlet Permissions, Permissions on Category and **Permissions on Thread**.

Working with Portlet Permissions

The following table shows the various **Permissions** of the **Message Boards** portlet. A **Community** user may set up all the **Permissions** (marked 'X'): **Add Category, Ban User,** and **Configuration,** and **View** while a **Guest User** has only one possibility , **View** (marked as 'X'). By default, a **Community** has the actions (marked as '*'):**View** and so does the **Guest**.

Action	Description	Community	Guest
Add Category	Adds top-level **Category** in the portlet	X	
Ban User	Bans **Users** in the **Message Boards**	X	
Configuration	Configures the portlet	X	
View	Views the details of the portlet	X, *	X, *

Obviously, as a user of the **Book Lovers** community, "**Lotti Stein**" has only the **View Permission** on the portlet, **Message Boards,** by default. Since the **Book Lovers** community has no **Permission** "Add Category", "Lotti Stein" also has no **Permission** "Add Category".

Working with Permissions on Category

The following table shows the **Permissions** for a forum and **Categories**. A **Community** user may set up all **Permissions** (marked 'X'): **Add Category, Add File, Add Message, Reply to Message, Delete, Permissions, Subscribe, Update, Update Thread Priority,** and **View**. A **Guest** user has only the possibility to set up **Add Message, Delete, Permissions,** and **View** (marked 'X'). By default, a **Community** has the actions (marked '*'): **Add File, Add Message, Subscribe** and **View**; while a **Guest** has only one action (marked '*'): **View**.

Action	Description	Community	Guest
Add Category	Adds **Category** to the portlet	X	
Add File	Adds a file (sub-category) to the **Category**	X, *	
Add Messages	Adds message to the **Category**	X, *	X
Reply to Messages	Replies to messages	X, *	X
Delete	Deletes the sub-category and its **Threads**	X	X
Permissions	Controls the permissions for the **Category**	X	X
Subscribe	Subscribes the **Category**	X, *	
Update	Updates the **Category**	X	
Update Thread Priority	Updates the **Thread** priority of the **Category**	X	
View	Views the details of the **Category**	X, *	X, *

Obviously, as a **User** of **Book Lovers** community, "**Lotti Stein**" has only **View, Add File, Add Message, Reply to Message** and **Subscribe Permissions** on the sub categories "**Book Category A**", "**Book Category B**" and "**Book Category D**" (since we have added them by community default setting). "**Lotti Stein**" has only **View Permission** on "**Liferay Books**", since we have added it with **View Permission** only for community.

As an administrator, you may need to set up the community, **Users,** having default **Permissions** setting (**View, Add File, Add Message, Reply to Messages** and **Subscribe**) on the **Category,** "**Liferay Books**". That is, you need to add **Permissions** (**Add File, Add Message, Reply to Messages** and **Subscribe**) on the **Category** "**Liferay Books**" for **Book Lovers** community. Let's do it as follows:

1. Click on the parent **Category,** "**Books**" in order to list its sub-categories.
2. Locate the sub-category "**Liferay Books**" for which you want to change **Permissions**.
3. Then click on the **Permissions icon** from the **Actions** located next to the category.
4. Select the **Community** tab.
5. Select **Permissions: Add File, Add Message, Reply to Message** and **Subscribe** in **Available** box.
6. Click on the **Add** arrow.
7. Click on the **Save** button, if you are ready.

Now, as a user of the **Book Lovers** Community, "**Lotti Stein**" has **View**, **Add File**, **Add Message**, **Reply to Messages** and **Subscribe Permissions** on the sub-category "**Liferay Books**" finally.

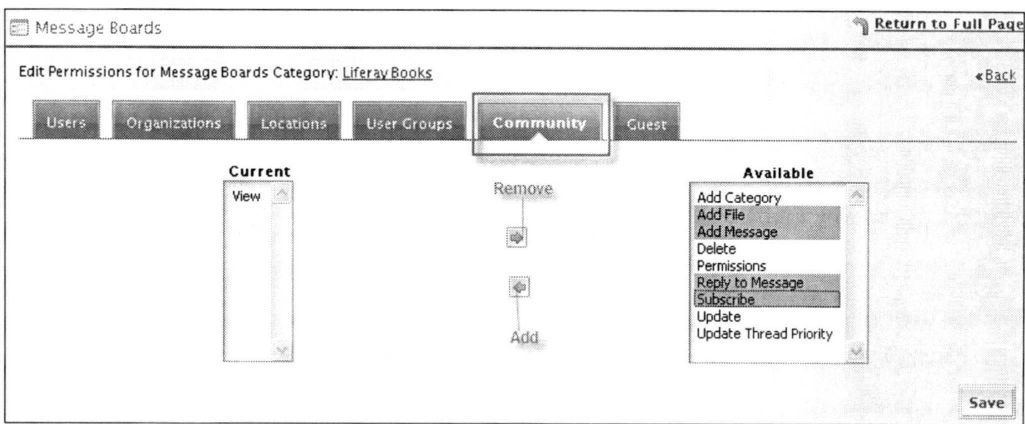

Of course, you assign **Permissions** to **Users**, **User Groups**, **Organizations** and **Locations**.

Working with Permissions on Thread

The following table shows **Permissions** for a **Thread**. A **Community** may set up all **Permissions** (marked 'X'): **Delete**, **Permissions**, **Subscribe**, **Update**, and **View**. A **Guest** has **Permissions** only to set up **Delete**, **Permissions**, and **View** (marked 'X'). By default, a **Community** has actions (marked '*'): **Subscribe** and **View**; while a **Guest** has only action (marked '*'): **View**.

Action	Description	Community	Guest
Delete	Deletes the **Thread** and its **Posts**	X	X
Permissions	Controls the **Permissions** for the **Thread**	X	X
Subscribe	Subscribes the **Thread**	X, *	
Update	Updates the **Thread**	X	
View	Views the details of the **Thread**	X, *	X, *

Using Message Boards Effectively

The following figure depicts a forum structure overview of **Liferay Message Boards**. A forum is made up of a set of **Categories**. Each **Category** may have many sub-categories and **Threads**. And furthermore, each **Thread** may have many **Posts** (or called reply). The **Thread** refers to the collection of messages. The messages may be displayed in flat chronological order by the date of posting, or in a question-answer order. The latter is a **Thread** of one question followed by all answers in a hierarchy. Actually, **Threads** can be regarded as the root level **Posts** (or called replies). Sub-posts are also supported, which enable comments in one of the replies to start another **Thread** that remains linked to the original.

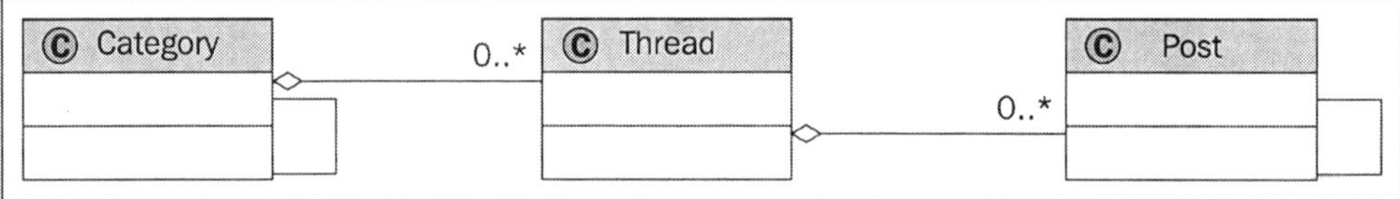

Working with Tags

Sooner or later, we will have a lot of **Posts** in the **Message Boards**. It would be useful to allow **Users** to generate content **Post** and classify that content **Post** in their own unique way. Let's first experience tagging contents first.

Tagging Contents

As an administrator at "**Palm-Tree Publications**", you may need to add **Tags** "Liferay" and "Book" in the **Post** "**RE: Let's discuss book Liferay**". Let's do it as follows:

1. In your post updating page, find the **Tag** box.

2. In the **Tag** text box, simply start typing the **Tag,** and a list of **Tags** will appear. As shown in the following figure, "**li**" is typed into the text box and a list of the available **Tags** is populated. Select the **Tag** ("**Liferay**") you want, and the **Tag** should show up adjacent to the box.

3. Similarly, "**bo**" can be typed into the text box and a list of the available **Tags** is populated. Select the tag ("**Book**") you want, and the tag should show up adjacent to the box.

4. Click on the **Save** button when you are ready.

For some reason, you need to remove a **Tag** "**Book**" from the **Tag** list. To remove a **Tag** "**Book**", simply click on the mark "**[x]**" located next to the **Tag** first, and then click on the **Save** button when you are ready.

Similarly, you can **Tag** contents including **Bookmarks entries, Blogs entries, Document Library documents, Image Gallery images, Wiki articles, Journal articles**, and **Message Board threads**.

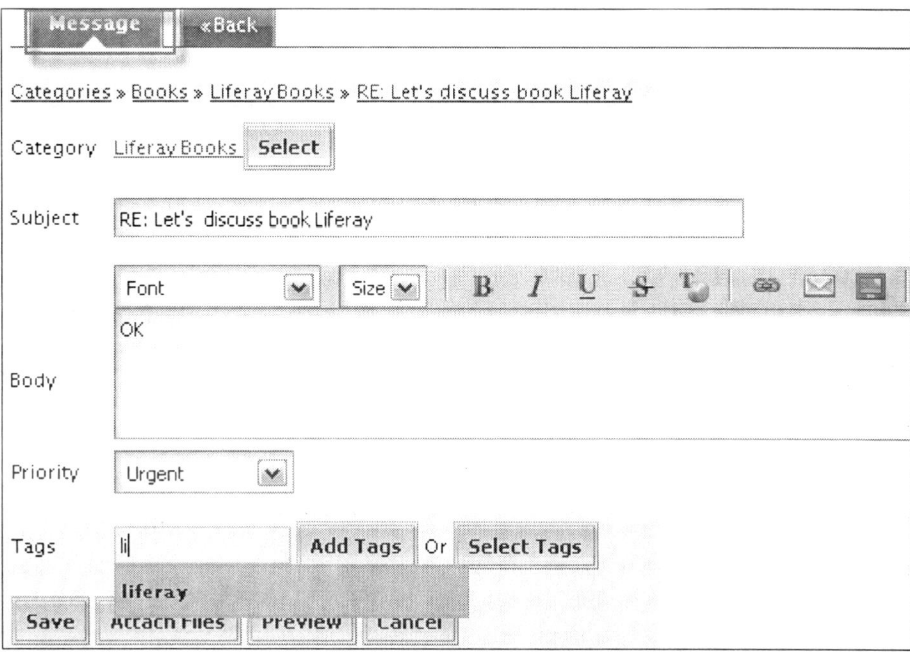

In a word, Liferay provides Meta **Tags**, that is, a tagging system, which allows you to tag web content, documents, message board threads and more, and dynamically publish content by using **Tags**.

Managing Tags

The following is a summary of the **Tag** related portlets in Liferay.

Administrate **Tags**:

- **Tags Admin**

Tag different types of content in Liferay:

- **Bookmarks entries**
- **Blogs entries**

- **Wiki articles**
- **Document Library documents**
- **Image Gallery images**
- **Journal articles** and
- **Message Board threads**

Aggregate Content:

- **Asset Publisher**

Users can choose **Tags** from a dictionary list at the **Tags Admin** portlet, while tagging content.

Tags Admin

By **Tags Admin** portlet, you can add **Tags and** organize **them** into **Categories**. As shown in the following figure, **Tags Admin** portlet provides three groups of functionalities to manage tags: **Search Tag**, **Edit Tag** and **Add Tag**.

To search for a **Tag** in **Search Tag** group, select a **Category**: "**all**" or "**no category**" or a specific one. Once you input a search criterion, search results will appear dynamically.

To edit a tag, click the **Tag** by edit links. In **Edit Tag** group, **Tag Value** and **Properties** are displayed. To delete a property of a given **Tag**, click on the property first, and then click on the **Delete** button. Or click on the **Delete** button at the right of the property, for all properties other than the "**category**" property. Deleting '**category**' property will delete the **Tag** to which the property belongs. Deleting a property other than the '**category**' property will delete only that property. To add a property of a given tag, just click on the **Add Property** button first. Then simply input **Name** and **Value**. Click the **Save** button to save the inputs or **Cancel** to cancel the inputs.

To delete a **Tag**, click on the mark "[x]" located next to the tag.

To add a tag, simply input tag name in **Add Tag** group, and select a **Category**. Then click the **Save** button to save the inputs. If the **Tag** doesn't exist in the current **Category**, the **Tag** will be added to the current **Category**.

If you select a **Category** '(new)', a **Category** name is required to be input, and the tag will be added to the current inputted **Category**. If you select a **Category** '(no)', the tag will be added to a special **Category** named "**no category**". All **Tags** will be displayed well and grouped by **Categories**.

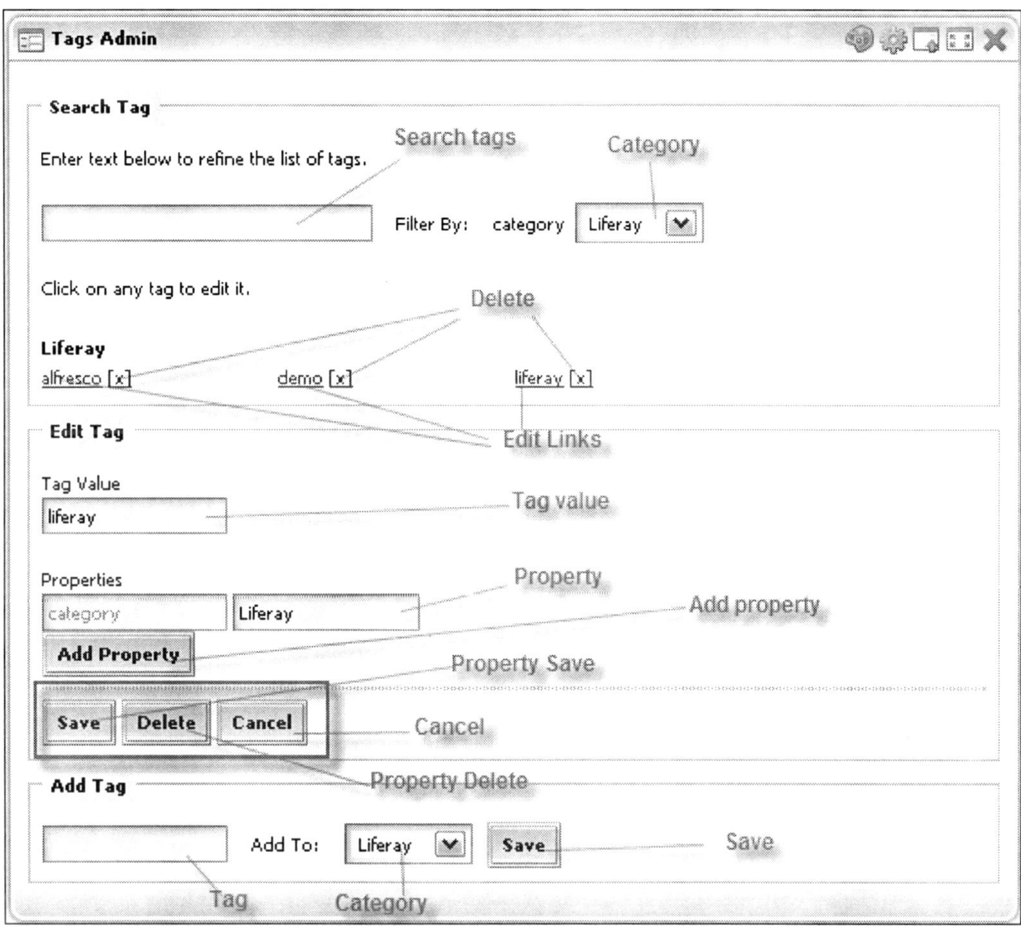

Display Tagged Contents

As an administrator at "**Palm-Tree Publications**", you may need to display contents with specific **Tags** "**Liferay**" and "**Book**". Let's do it as follows:

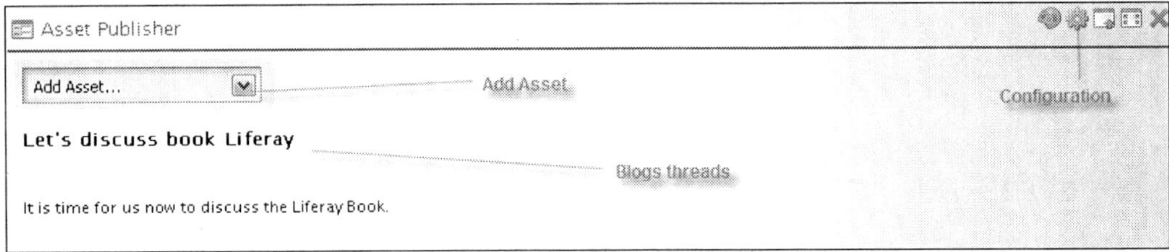

- Add **Asset Publisher** portlet in the page where you want to display contents with specific **Tags**.

1. Configure **Asset Publisher** portlet to display content "tagged" with specific **Tags,** and click on the **Configuration** icon at the upper right.

2. With "**Setup**" selected as default, input tags "**Liferay**" and "**Book**" which displayed content must contain, and simply start typing the **Tag,** and a list of **Tags** will appear. Pick up a **Tag** which the displayed content must contain. The selected **Tags** will appear to the right of input box.

3. Click on the **Save** button to save and press the arrow **Return to full page.** You will see your tagged contents in the **Asset Publisher** portlet.

Set up Asset Publisher

It is configurable to set up the view of tagged contents via the **Asset Publisher** portlet. You can set the choice of asset selection, as either **Dynamic** or **Manual**. For **Manual** selection, you will have a chance to select the assets directly. The **Dynamic** selection allows you to select tagged contents by specific **Tags**.

Before selecting specific **Tags**, you can select a specific **Tags** category. The default **Tags** category is "**None**".

To input **Tags** which the displayed content must contain, simply start typing the **Tag** and a list of **Tags** will appear. Pick up a **Tag** which the displayed content must contain. The selected **Tags** will appear to the right of input box. To remove a **Tag,** click on the mark "**[x]**" located next to the tag.

Similarly, to input **Tags** which displayed content must not contain, just start typing the **Tag,** and a list of **Tags** will appear. Pick up a tag which must not contain the displayed content. The selected **Tags** will appear to the right of input box also.

You can narrow down the search results by setting up **Search Operator**. There are two search operators: "**and**" and "**or**". The "**and**" means **that all the conditions** (must contain certain **Tag**, must not contain certain **Tag**) must be satisfied, while the "**or**" means that at least one of the conditions (must contain certain **Tag**, must not contain certain **Tag**) must be satisfied.

Click the **Save** button to save the changes if you are ready, or click the **Cancel** button to cancel the changes.

Tagged content display settings are also configurable. To change the display settings, click on the **Display Settings** tab first, and then select one of the display styles: **full content/abstract**. Check/uncheck the boxes "**Show Query Logic**" and "**Show Available Locales**". Click the **Save** button to save the changes, or the **Cancel** button to cancel the changes.

The Asset Publisher portlet provides a way to display tagged contents: **Bookmarks entries**, **Blogs entries**, **Document Library documents**, **Image Gallery images**, **Wiki articles**, **Journal articles**, and **Message Board threads**. Given a set of **Tags**, the contents "tagged" with specific **Tags** will be shown in this portlet.

In addition, you can easily add assets (such as **Bookmarks entries**, **Blogs entries**, **Document Library documents**, **Image Gallery images**, and **Journal articles**) via this portlet.

For **Bookmarks entries**, **Blogs entries**, **Document Library documents**, **Image Gallery images**, **Wiki articles**, and **Journal articles**, refer to the forthcoming chapters.

What Makes Tags Important?

Tags are so important that users can generate content and classify that content in their own unique way.

For example (refer to Folksonomies at `http://www.uie.com/articles/folksonomies/`), suppose that you have a photo-sharing site, where users can **Tag** their humorous pictures from a vacation. Some pictures, they may tag "**hawaii**" only, others they may tag "**funny**" only. A number of pictures they may tag both "**funny**" and "**hawaii**". Later, when they want to view their pictures from Hawaii, they simply select "**hawaii**". If they want to view all their funny pictures, they would select "**funny**". If they want to view only their funny pictures from Hawaii, they would simply select both "**hawaii**" and "**funny**".

Let's consider another example (refer to Tags & Folksonomies at `http://www.threadwatch.org/node/1206`). Suppose that you have a website on hobbies and you have lots of users who like fishing. Thus when users input data, photos, reviews or anything you might dream up, they will invariably tag their posts with "**Fishing**". Some of the users will tag their posts with "**Angling**", and others may use two or more tags such as "**Fishing Vacation**" or "**Holiday Fishing**".

Then you can generate a web site with the following data:

- **Fishing** — 100 posts
- **Angling** — 200 posts
- **Fishing Vacation** — 300 posts
- **Holiday Fishing** — 400 posts

Imagine creating menus and pages based on these categories.

Using Tags Effectively

Liferay tagging system allows you to tag web content, documents, message board threads and more, and dynamically publish content by tags. **Tags** provide a way of organizing and aggregating content. Basically the tag admin determines which **Tags** are available for usage. The users use these **Tags** on their content. Any content that is tagged can be grouped or aggregated.

The following figure depicts an overview of **Tags** and **Contents**. A **Tag** may belong to a **Category**. That is, a **Category** may have many **Tags**. When you create a **Tag**, a predefined **Category** or dynamically created **Category** will be assigned to it. In a word, **Tags** are managed and grouped by **Categories.**

A **Tag** may have many properties. Each **Property** is made up of a name and a value.

A **Tag** may be associated with **Content**. By **Tags**, you can tag almost anything: **Bookmarks Entries, Blogs Entries, Wiki Articles, Document Library documents, Image Gallery Images, Journal articles** and **Message Board threads,** and so on. You can also use these **Tags** to pull content with **Asset Publisher** portlet.

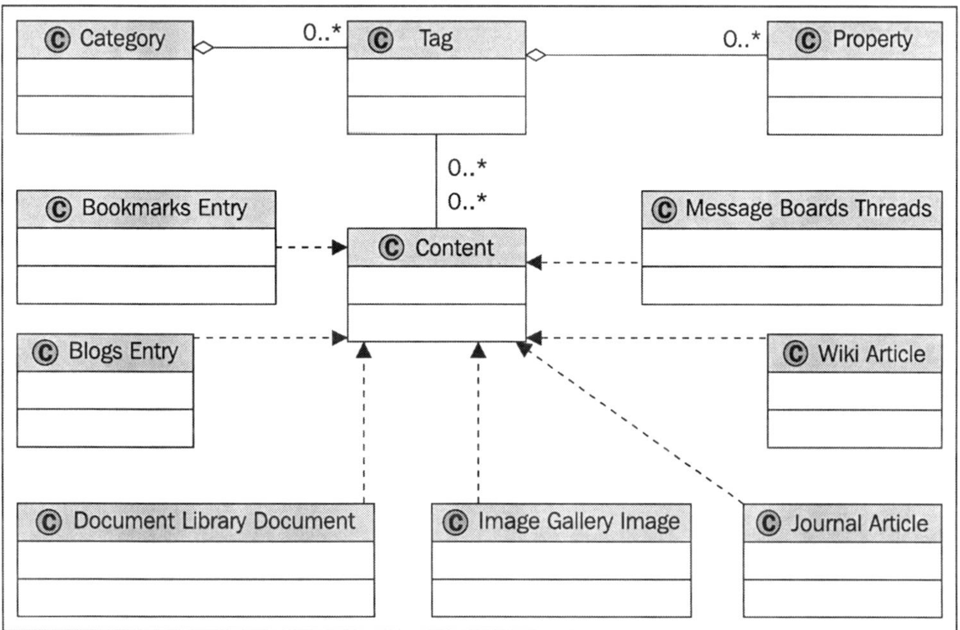

 Do Meta **Tags** work for educatinal purposes? The answer is clearly no. Meta **Tags** allow users to generate **Content** and classify that **Content** in their own unique way. If educating **Tags** was in need, you could add these **Tags'** properties of **Contents** in your content model.

Summary

This chapter discussed how to add **Categories** and sub-categories for **Message Boards**; how to add **Threads** and **Posts** for a given **Category**; how to manage (view, add, update, delete, and feed) **Categories**, **Threads** and **Posts**; and how to set **Permissions** of **Message Boards**, **Categories** and **Threads**. Then it discussed how to add a **Tag** and manage (add, delete, and change category) **Tags**; and how to **Tag** contents and display tagged contents.

Wikis, Web Form And Polls

5

In the intranet website "book.com" of "Palm Tree Publications", it is required that a track of information is kept about editorial guidance and other resources that require frequent editing, It is also required that a track of **Votes** is kept on the topic, "**Is Liferay Book a proper book**", and moreover, collect suggestions on the subjects such as "**Liferay Book**" and "**Alfresco Book**". Liferay **Wiki** provides a straightforward **Wiki** solution. Liferay **Web Form** provides a way to collect **Users**' suggestions and **Polls,** and provides survey to assess public opinions. This chapter will introduce you to Liferay **Wikis**, **Web Form** and **Polls**.

By the end of this chapter, you will have learned how to:

- Add **Node** and manage (view, update and delete) **Nodes** of **Wikis.**
- Add **Pages** at the nodes in **Wikis.**
- Manage (view, update, delete and search) **Pages** of a given **Node** in **Wikis.**
- Use **Permissions** on **Wikis nodes.**
- Publish **Wiki** articles.
- Set up **Web Form** portlet.
- Configure **Polls** portlet.
- Display **Polls.**

Working with Wikis

In order to provide an environment for employees at "Palm Tree Publications" to keep track of information about editorial guidance and other resources that require frequent editing, we can use Liferay **Wikis** portlet at the **Book Lovers** Community (**Public Pages**).

As an administrator of "Palm Tree Publications", you need to create a page called "**Wikis**" under the **Page** "**Community**" at the **Book Lovers** Community and further, add the **Wikis** portlet in the page "**Wikis**". Then you are ready to create **Nodes** called "**Liferay**" and "**Alfresco**".

Adding And Managing Nodes

As an administrator of "Palm Tree Publications", you need to create **Nodes** called "**Liferay**" and "**Alfresco**".

Adding Nodes

First of all, we need to create a **Node** called "Liferay". Let's create a **Node** as follows:

1. Add a child **Page** called "Wikis" of the **Page** "Community" at the **Book Lovers** Community **Public Pages**.

2. If **Wiki** Portlet is not already present, add **Wiki** portlet in the **Page** "Wikis" under the **Page** "Community" at the **Book Lovers** Community where you want to manage Wiki articles.

3. By default, the **Node** "**Main**" is created. Click on the "**Administer Nodes**" icon from the **Actions** below the **FrontPage**.

4. Click on **Add Node** button.

5. Enter a **Name** "Liferay", and a **Description,** "Liferay root".

6. Set **Permissions** by clicking on the **Configure** link. To configure additional **Permissions**, click on the **More** link. Here, we just use default settings.

7. Click on the **Save** button to save the inputs.

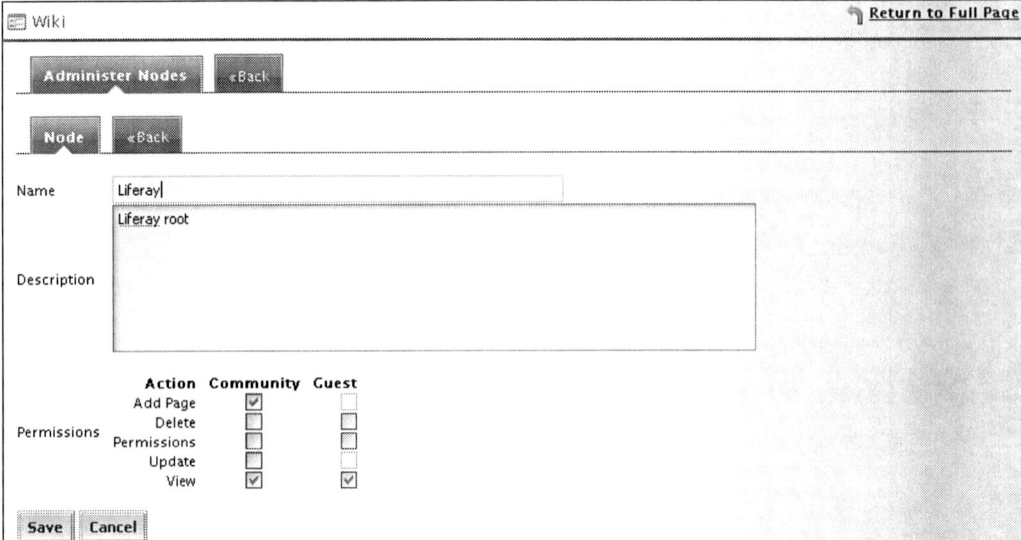

Note that we have created a **Page** called "**Community**" at the **Book Lovers** community **Public Pages** in the previous chapter. We also added a **Page** called "**Forums**". The **Page** "**Wikis**" here is a sibling **Page** of the **Page** "**Forums**". In the next chapter, we will create another **Page** called "**Blogs**" as a sibling **Page** of the **Page** "**Wikis**".

Of course, you can add other **Nodes** that you want. After creating the **Node** called "**Alfresco**", we can view **Wikis Nodes**. **Nodes** are displayed as **Node** name, **number of Pages, Last Post Date** and **Actions** with a set of icons (such as, **Edit, Permissions** and **Delete**).

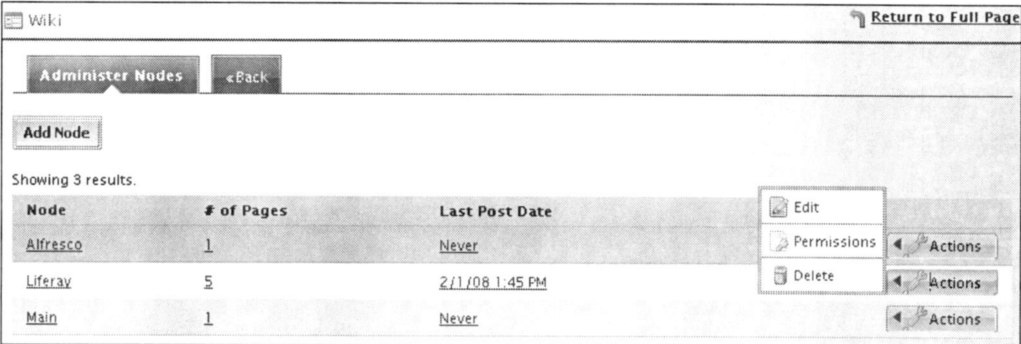

In short, we can create a **Node** by clicking on the **Add Node** button, and filling the **Name,** and optionally, the **Description**. An initial **Page** called **FrontPage** (called a Wiki Article) is created automatically, when a **Node** is created.

Managing Nodes

Generally speaking, a set of **Pages** in groups is called **Nodes**. Each **Node** acts as a whole **Wiki**. **Nodes** may have their own set of **Permissions, Recent Changes** list and listing of **All Pages**. After creating **Nodes**, we can manage **Wikis Nodes** easily.

Edit A Node

Nodes are editable. For example, we plan to change the description of **Node** "**Liferay**" from value "**Liferay root**" to value "**Liferay Wikis Root**". Let's do it as follows:

1. Locate the **Node "Liferay"**.

2. Click on the **Edit** icon from the **Actions** next to the node.

3. Update the description with value "**Liferay Wikis Root**".

4. Click the **Save** button to save the inputs.

Delete A Node

Nodes are removable. For instance, the **Node** "**Alfresco**" is not wanted anymore. We have to remove this from the **Wiki** portlet. Let's delete it as follows:

1. Locate the **Node** "Alfresco", which you want to delete.
2. Click on the **Delete** icon from the **Actions** located next to the node.
3. A screen will appear asking if you want to delete this. Click **OK** to confirm deletion.

> Note that deleting a **Node** will delete all related **Pages** which belong to this **Node**. Moreover, any **Comments** related to the **Pages** of the **Node** will be deleted too.

Adding Pages

As an administrator of "Palm Tree Publications", you may need to add more **Pages**, such as "**LiferayAlfrescoIntegration**" and "**AlfrescoBook**", under the node "**Liferay**". Let's do it as follows:

1. Locate the **Node** "Liferay" tab.
2. Click on the name of the **Node** "**Liferay**".
3. Click on the icon **Edit** from the **Actions** below the **Page** "FrontPage".
3. Select a **Format** such as "**Classic Wiki**".
4. In the editing **Page**, input "**LiferayAlfrescoIntegration**" and "**AlfrescoBook**".
5. If you need to add **Tags**, press the button **Select Tags**, or input tag and press the button, **Add Tags**,.
6. Click on the **Save** button when you are ready.

Of course, you can add a **Page** directly. Let's suppose you want to add a **Page** "**MyPage**" under the **Node** "**Liferay**". Let's do it as follows:

1. Locate the **Node** "Liferay" tab.
2. Click on the name of the **Node**, "**Liferay**".
3. Click on the icon, **Add Page**, from the **Actions** below the **Page** "FrontPage".
4. Input the **Page** name as "**MyPage**".
5. Click on the **OK** button to save.

Note that the **Page** name must follow the CamelCase syntax. CamelCase is a naming convention in which the words are joined without spaces and are capitalized within the compound.

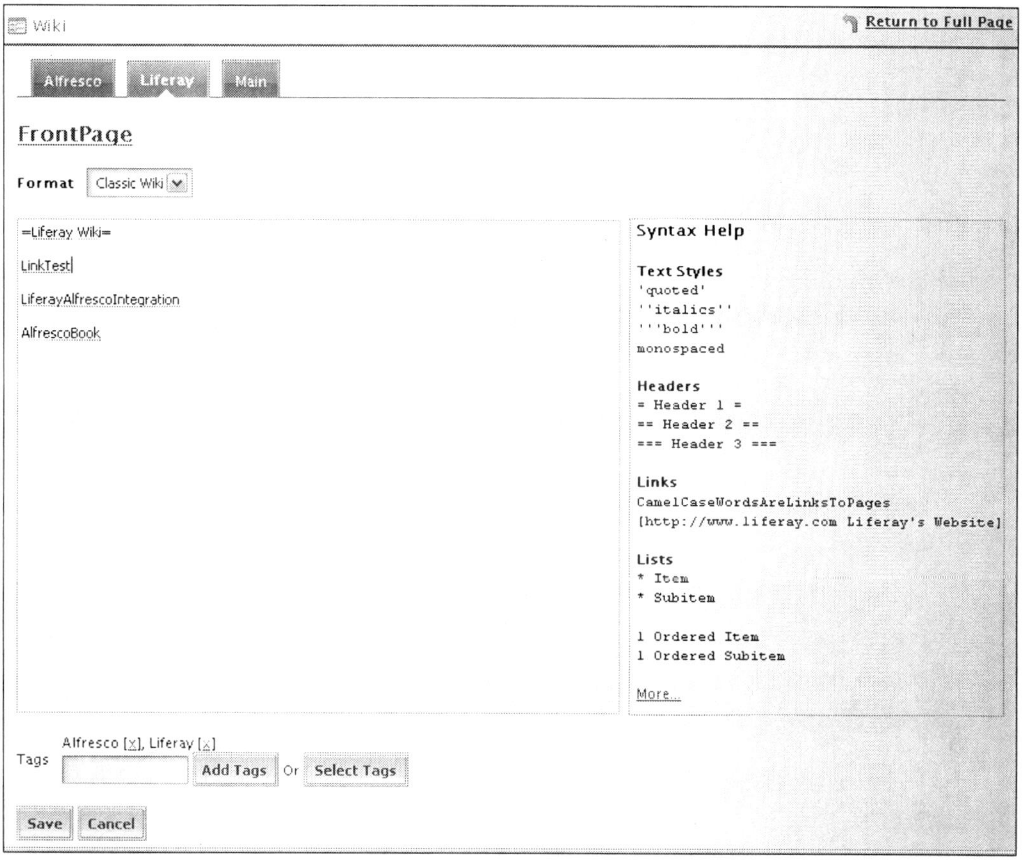

As mentioned previously, there are three editing modes, that is, **Formats,** to edit **Wiki Pages**: **Classic Wiki,** HTML and **Plain Text.** Select one of editing modes. By default, **Classic Wiki** editing mode is selected. You can follow Liferay Wiki classic mode syntax to edit Wiki **Pages**. For example, you can represent internal links by putting two or more words together (without spaces between them), and uppercasing the first letter of each of the words. You can represent external Links by beginning with a bracket ([), then including URL, space, display name, and ending with a bracket (]); or beginning with a double quotation mark ("), and then including display name, and double quotation mark ("), following URL.

 For more details about **Classic Wiki**, please refer to the forthcoming section.

You can simply start typing the **Tag** in the tag text box, and you will see a list of **Tags**. Just select the tag you want. You will see the **Tag** showing up adjacent to the box. You can remove a **Tag** by clicking on the mark "**[x]**" located next to the tag. To save the inputs, just click the **Save** button; to cancel all actions, just click the **Cancel** button.

 For more details about **Tags**, refer to Chapter 4.

Of course, you can create other **Pages** as you wish. Let's suppose we need to add a **Page** called "**AlfrescoWiki**" under the **Page** "**AlfrescoBook**". We can do it as follows:

1. Locate the **Node** "**Liferay**".
2. Click on the name of the **Node, "Liferay"**.
3. Find the link "**AlfrescoBook**", and click on the name, "**AlfrescoBook**".
4. Click on the icon, **Edit,** from the **Actions** for the **Page** "**AlfrescoBook**".
5. Select **Format** such as "**Classic Wiki**".
6. In the editing **Page**, input "**AlfrescoWiki**".
7. Press button **Select Tags** or input tag and press button **Add Tags** if you need to add tags.
8. Click on the **Save** button when you are ready.

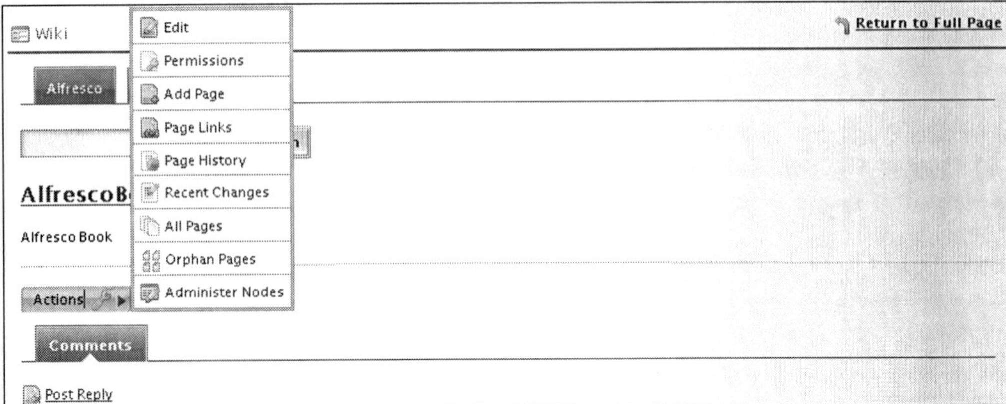

To create new **Pages** (Wiki Article), you have to edit an existing **Page,** and use the syntax as described next to create a link to the new **Page**. When the **Page** is created, instead of being displayed as a link, the name of the new **Page** is identified by two or more words together without spaces between them and uppercasing the first letter of each of the words. When you click on the name, the portlet will create the **Page** automatically. Further, once the **Page** is created, you can also edit it regularly. At the same time, the name of the **Page** on the original **Page** will be converted to a link.

Managing Pages

You may need to view **Page Links** of the **Page** "AlfrescoBook". You can do it as follows:

1. Locate the **Node** "**Liferay**".

2. Click on the name of the **Node** "**Liferay**".

3. Find the link "**AlfrescoBook**" and click on the name "**AlfrescoBook**".

3. Click on **Page Links**. A list of pages with links will appear.

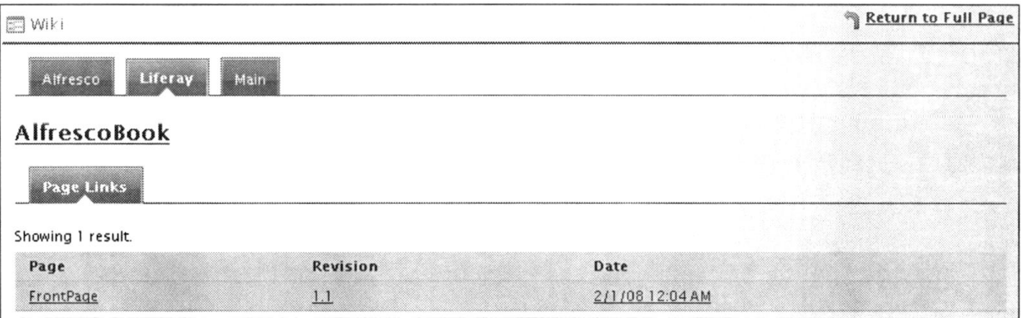

You may need to view **Page History** of the **Page** "**AlfrescoBook**". You can do it as follows:

1. Locate the **Node, "Liferay"**. Click on the name of the **Node, "Liferay"**.
2. Find the link "**AlfrescoBook**" and click on the name "**AlfrescoBook**".
3. Click on **Page History**. A list of pages with history will appear.

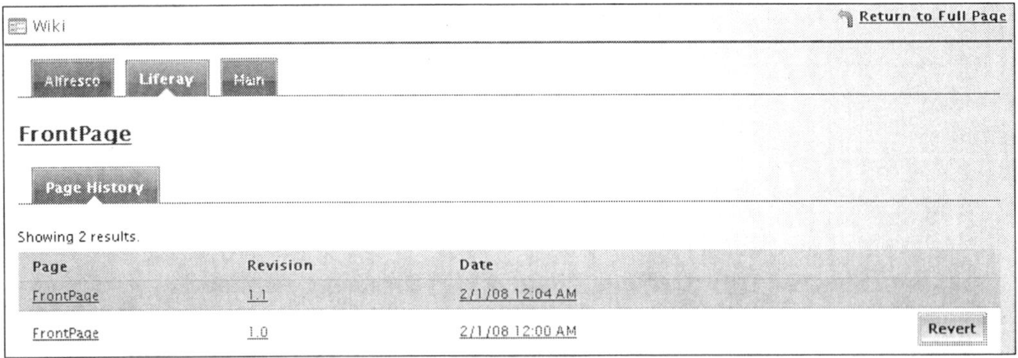

Similarly to view recent changes, simply click on **Recent Changes**. To view all the pages or only orphan pages, simply click on **All Pages** or **Orphan Pages**.

Add Comments

As stated before, the administrator has created a **Page** called "**AlfrescoBook**". As a **User** of "Palm Tree Publications" such as "**Lotti Stein**", you may want to review this page and add **Comments, say,**"**This is a good book**". You can do it as follows:

1. Log in as "**Lotti Stein**".
2. Navigate to the **Book Lovers** community and select **Public Pages**.
3. Navigate to the "**Community**" **Page** and further to the "**Wikis**" **Page**.
3. Locate the **Node, "Liferay"**.
4. Click on the name of the **Node, "Liferay"**.
5. Find the link "**AlfrescoBook**", and click on it.
6. Find the **Comment** tab at the bottom of the **Page**.
7. Click on the **Post Reply** icon.
8. Input **Comment, "This is a good book"**.
9. Finally, click on the **Reply** button to save the inputs.

As an administrator, you can view **Comments** from "**Lotti Stein**" for the **Page** "**AlfrescoBook**" as follows:

1. Locate the **Node, "Liferay"**. Click on the name of the **Node "Liferay"**.
2. Find the link, "**AlfrescoBook**", and click on it.

To reply to a **Comment**, locate the comment to which you **want** to reply first. Then, click on the **Post Reply** icon at the bottom left of the comment. Input comments, and then click on the **Reply** button to save the inputs, or the **Cancel** button to cancel.

To edit a **Comment**, click on the **Edit** icon at the bottom left of the comment. You can change the subject and body. Then, click on the **Update** button to save the changes, or the **Cancel** button, to cancel the changes.

To delete a **Comment**, click on the **Delete** icon at the bottom left of the comment. A screen will appear asking if you want to delete this. Click **OK** to confirm deletion or **Cancel** to cancel deletion.

Note that only the current **Comment** has been deleted. The low level **Comments** related to the current **Comment** will have a link to its parent **Comment**.

To go to the top of the **Comments**, simply click on the **Top** button at the bottom left of any comment.

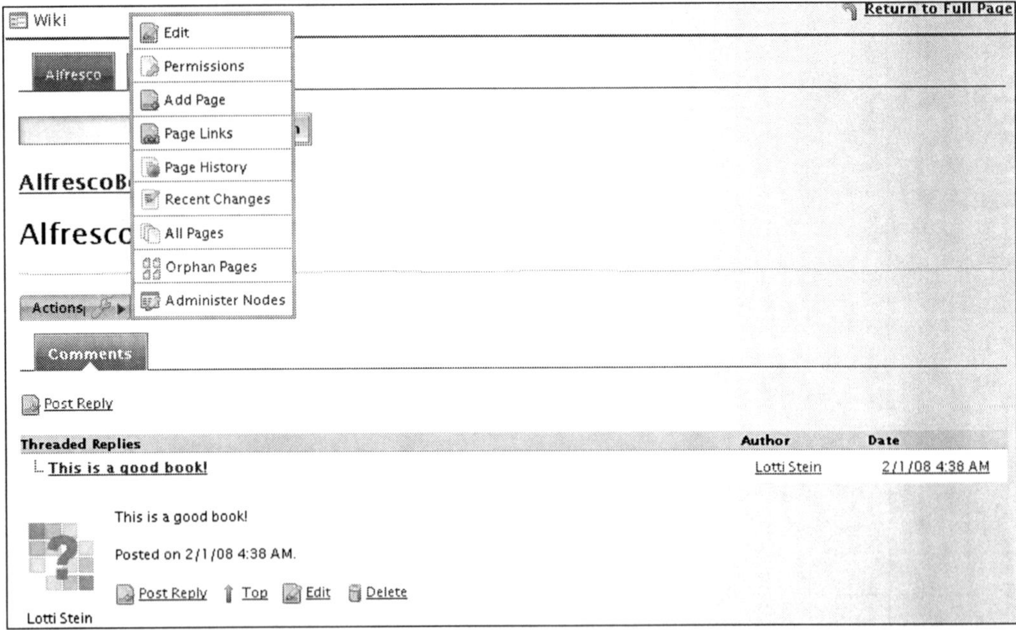

Generally, to add a discussion for the current page, simply click on **Post Reply** at the bottom of the **Page**. Then input the comments. Finally click on the **Reply** button to save the comments, or the **Cancel** button to cancel the comments.

Additionally, to edit a comment, simply click on the **Edit** icon at the bottom of the **Post** first. Then, change the comments of the post. Further, click on the **Update** button to save the changes, or the **Cancel** button to cancel the changes.

Using Permissions

We have used default settings for the **Wikis** portlet in the page "**Wikis**", of the page "**Community**", under the **Book Lovers** Community. As mentioned before, when the administrator "**Palm Tree**" logs in, he will see the button "**Add Node**" in the **Wikis**. As we know, the user "**Lotti Stein**" is also a member of the **Book Lovers** community. Try to log in as "**Lotti Stein**", you will see that the button "**Add Node**" is not there in the **Wikis**. Further, you will also see that the **Node** "**Liferay**" does not have **Actions**.

What's happening? This is something related to **Permissions**. There are three levels of **Permissions**: Portlet **Permissions**, **Permissions** on **Nodes** and **Permissions** on **Pages**.

Update Portlet Permissions

The following table shows **Permissions** for the **Wiki** portlet. A **Community User** may set up all **Permissions** (marked 'X'): **View**, **Add Node**, and **Configuration**. A **Guest User** on the other hand may set up **Permissions**: **View** and **Configuration**. By default, a **Community** has the **Permission View** (marked '*'), and so does a **Guest User**.

Action	Description	Community	Guest
View	Views this portlet	X, *	X, *
Configuration	Configures this portlet	X	X
Add Node	Adds a **Node** to the portlet	X	

Obviously, as a **User** of the **Book Lovers** Community, "**Lotti Stein**" has only the **View Permissions** on the portlet, **Wikis,** by default. Since the **Book Lovers** community has no **Permission** to "**Add Node**", "**Lotti Stein**" too has no **Permission** to "**Add Node**".

Set up Permissions on Nodes

The following table shows the **Permissions** for a **Node** in the **Wiki** portlet. A **Community User** may set up the **Permissions** (marked 'X'), **View**, **Delete**, **Permissions**, **Update**, and **Add Page**, while a **Guest User** may set up the **Permissions**, **View**, **Delete**, and **Permissions**. By default, a **Community User** has **Permission** (marked '*') **View**, **Update** and **Add Page**, while a **Guest User** has **Permission View** only.

Action	Description	Community	Guest
View	Views the **Node**	X, *	X, *
Delete	Deletes the **Node**	X	X
Permissions	Configures **Permissions** for the **Node**	X	X
Update	Updates the **Node**	X, *	
Add Page	Adds a page for the **Node**	X, *	

Obviously, as a **User** of the **Book Lovers** Community, "**Lotti Stein**" has **Permissions**, **View** and **Add Page** only on the **Node**, "**Liferay**", since we have added them by **Community** default setting. The **User** does not have the **Permissions, Delete, Permissions** and **Update** and will see no actions on the **Node** "**Liferay**".

As an administrator, you may need to set up the **Community Users** having **Permissions,Update** as well as **Permissions, View** and **Add Page** on the **Node, "Liferay"**. So, you need to add the **Permission, Update,** on the **Node, "Liferay"** for the **Book Lovers** community. Let's do it as follows:

1. Click on the icon, "**Administer Nodes**" from the **Actions** below the **FrontPage** of the "**Liferay**" tab.

2. Locate the **Node, "Liferay"**, for which you want to change **Permissions**.

3. Then click on the **Permissions** icon from the **Actions** located next to the node.

4. Select the **Community** tab.

5. Select the **Permission, Update** in the **Available** box.

6. Click on the **Add** arrow, and

7. Click on the **Save** button if you are ready.

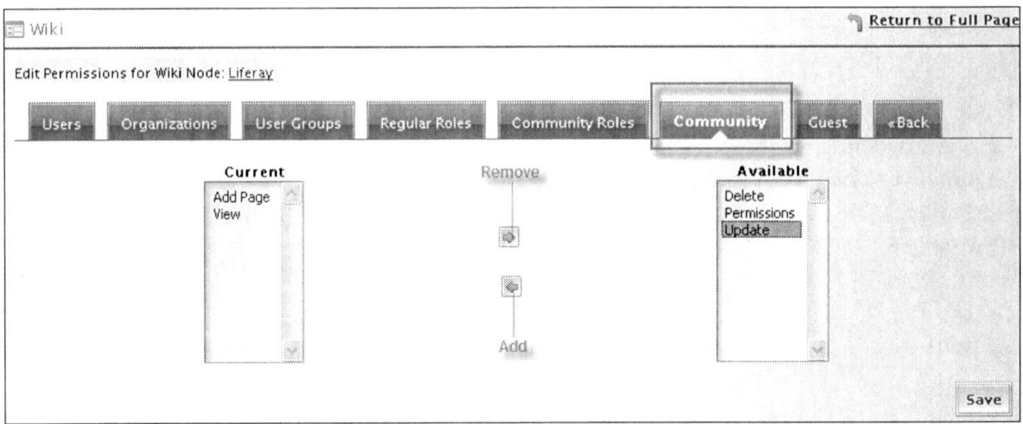

Now, as a **User** of **Book Lovers** Community, "**Lotti Stein**" has **View**, **Add Page** and **Update Permissions** on the **Node, "Liferay"**, finally. Try to log in as "**Lotti Stein**" and you will see the **Node, "Liferay"**, with an action icon, "**Edit**".

Update Permissions on Pages

The following table shows **Permissions** for the **Pages** of a given **Node**. A **Community User** may set up **Permissions** (marked 'X'): **View, Delete, Permissions, Update,** and **Add Discussion**, while a **Guest User** may set up **Permissions** with **View, Delete,** and **Permissions**. By default, a **Community User** has **Permission** actions (marked '*'): **View, Update** and **Add Discussion**, while a **Guest User** has only **Permission, View**.

Action	Description	Community	Guest
View	View the **Pages**	X, *	X, *
Delete	Delete the **Page**	X	X
Permissions	Configure **Permissions** of the **Page**	X	X
Update	Update **Pages**	X, *	
Add Discussion	Add discussions (**Comments**) for the **Page**	X, *	

Obviously, as a **User** of the **Book Lovers** Community, "**Lotti Stein**" has **Permissions** only to **View**, **Update**, and **Add Discussion** on the Pages, since the **Pages** under the **Node** "Liferay" have been added by **Community** default setting. She does not have the **Permissions**, Delete and Permissions.

Using Wikis Effectively

Wiki was originally described as a simple online database. Actually, a **Wiki** (refer to Wikipedia) is a Web-based collaboration platform that lets any user write, place pictures and post links, anywhere on any **Page**. That is, anyone can edit anything on any **Page**. You can do it through the web interface without the need for additional software. Surely, you don't want to learn HTML, or wait for a designated webmaster to upload your files !

Characteristics

You can write the **Wiki** documents collaboratively, in a simple mark-up language via a web browser (refer to Wikipedia). Here a single **Page** in **Wiki** is called a **Wiki Page** while the entire body of **Pages**, which are usually highly interconnected via hyperlinks, is called the **Wiki**. Loosely speaking, a **Wiki** is a database used to create, browse and search for information.

Wiki Pages can be created and updated easily. But there is no review, before modifications are accepted for a **Wiki Page**. Some **Wikis** may be open to the general public without the need to register any user account. In order to acquire a Wiki-signature cookie for auto signing edits, session log-in may be requested. However, many edits on a **Wiki Page** can be made in real-time, and almost appear instantaneously online. This may lead to an abuse of the system. On the other hand, private **Wiki Pages** require users' authentication to edit **Pages**, to add new **Pages**, and even to read **Pages**.

Design Principles

Wiki design principles involve the following items (refer to Wiki Design Principles at `http://c2.com/cgi/wiki?WikiDesignPrinciples`):

1. Open—a **Page** should be incomplete or poorly organized, any reader can edit it as he wants.

2. Cross-referencing—**Pages** can cite other **Pages** that may have not been written yet.

3. Organic—it is open to edit and evolve the structure and text content of the web site.

4. Secular—a small number of text conventions provide access to the most useful page markup.

5. Universal—any writer is automatically an editor and an organizer. Editing and organizing **Wiki Pages** is the same as writing a **Wikis Page**.

6. Manifest— the formatted output will suggest the input required to reproduce **Wikis Pages**.

7. Unified—no additional context is required to interpret **Pages**, since **Page** names are drawn from a flat space.

8. Precise—in order to avoid most name clashes, **Pages** are titled with sufficient precision, typically, by forming noun phrases.

9. Tolerant—interpretable behavior is preferred to error messages.

10. Observable—any other visitor can watch and review activity within the site.

11. Convergent—remove duplication by finding and citing similar or related content.

Wiki Text

Wiki-Text language is a mark-up language, alternative to HTML, to write **Wikis pages** (refer to Wikipedia). Unfortunately, there is no commonly accepted standard Wiki-text language, since the grammar, structure, features and keywords of the Wiki-text language are dependent on the particular **Wiki** software used on the particular website.

The following figure depicts an overview of the **Wiki** article search and creation. Initially, you enter the search criterion. If you do not find the articles, you can think of another term, and search again. If you find the articles, then you just display them. Further, if you find related terms, you can create a redirection; otherwise you just create a new article. Wiki text are used as tools to create new article and redirection.

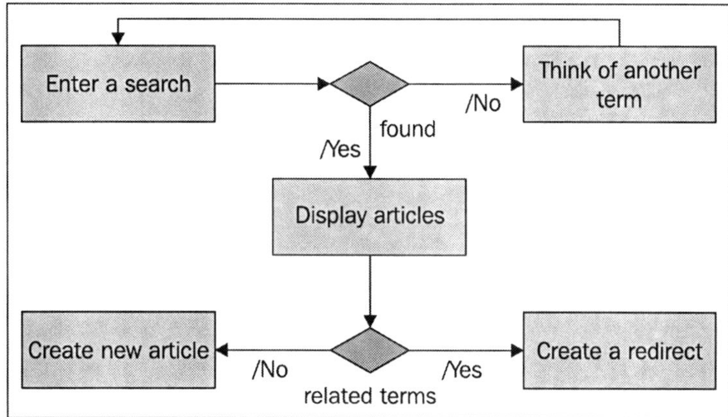

Pros And Cons

Wikis have their own advantages and disadvantages. Some advantages of **Wikis** are:

1. There is no need to install HTML authoring tools.
2. Minimal training is needed.
3. It can help develop a culture of sharing and working together.
4. It is useful for joint working, when there are agreed shared goals.

Some disadvantages of **Wikis** are:

1. The success of one **Wiki** (such as Wikipedia) may not necessarily be replicated elsewhere.
2. There is no standard lightweight Wiki mark-up language available as yet.
3. A collaborative **Wiki** may suffer from the lack of a strong vision.
4. There may be copyright and other legal issues regarding collaborative content.
5. It can be ineffective, when there is a lack of consensus.

Wikipedia is the biggest multilingual free-content encyclopedia on the Internet. URL: `http://www.wikipedia.org/`

What Can Wikis Be Used for?

Wikis are useful for a number of purposes. Here, we just list some of them:

1. **Wikis** enable users to contribute information on public web sites easily.

2. They provide an opportunity to learn about team working and trust for teaching.

3. They make it easier to develop collaborative documents for researchers.

4. They have the ability to manage departmental content on intranets for departmental administrators with minimal HTML experience.

5. **Wikis** are useful at events for note-taking in discussion groups.

Using Liferay Wikis

Liferay **Wikis** allows the creation of contents in collaboration style. It is based on Friki with the following features in addition to those commonly found in good **Wikis**:

1. Content parsing.
2. ACL (access control list) security style.
3. Easy to use macros.
4. Easy to adapt security, content, parsing and versioning.
5. Manage all content and security by console tools.

[ What's Friki? Friki is a Wiki engine developed in Java.]

Pages are designed in groups, called **Nodes** in Liferay. Each **Node** can act as a whole **Wiki**. It has its own set of **Permissions, Recent Changes** list and listing of **All Pages**, that is, Wiki articles, and so on. The **Wiki** in Liferay has a very powerful functionality with a robust security model. For example, users can use the **Wiki** in the traditional way (open to public), or users can use the **Wiki** as a tool to organize private information for certain **Organizations** or **User Groups** of people.

The following diagram depicts Liferay **Wiki** structure overview. Liferay **Wikis** is made up of a set of **Nodes**. Each **Node** may have many **Pages**. Each **Node** has at least one **Page** called "**Front Page**" by default. Each **Page** may have many **Comments**.

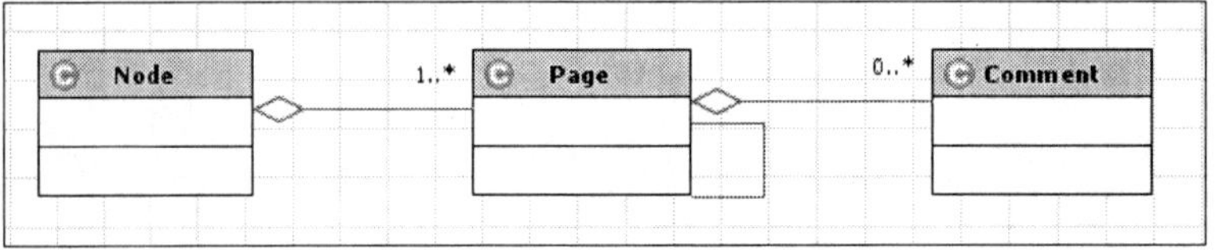

Liferay **Wiki** comes with three editing modes: **Classic**, **HTML** and **Plain Text**.

Classic Mode

The classic editing mode uses text conventions to format **the** text. The text is later converted to HTML which will be presented by the Friki engine.

Liferay **Wiki** uses the forthcoming syntax (refer to Liferay Wiki):

- Text styles: at the beginning and at the end of the text:
    - Sole single-quote (') for quote.
    - Double single-quotes ('') for emphasis, usually italics.
    - Triple single-quotes (''') for strong emphasis, usually bold.
    - Quadruple single-quotes ('''') for strong emphasis, usually bold and italics.
- Lists:
    - Tab * (or 8 spaces and *), for first level; tab-tab * for second level, and so forth.
    - * for bullet lists, '1.'. For numbered lists (mix at will) — always use '1.'; it will be renumbered automatically.
- Headers:
    - Single equal-sign (=) for header 1.
    - Double equal-sign (==) for header 2.
    - Triple equal-sign (===) for header 3, and so on.
- Embedded and formatted RAW HTML: also HTML table tags.
- Horizontal rule: four or more hyphens (----) at the beginning of a line make a horizontal rule.
- Mono spaced indent: a blank or more spaces (not 8 spaces) at the beginning of the line.
- Internal Links: two or more words together, without spaces between them, and uppercasing the first letter of each of the words.
- External Links:
    - Beginning with a bracket ([), then including URL, space, display name, and ending with a bracket (]).
    - Beginning with a double quotation mark ("), then including display name, and double quotation mark ("), followed by the URL.

- Definitions: starting with tab, then term; following with colon and tab; finally the definition.
- Indented paragraphs: tab plus space at the beginning of the paragraph.

HTML Mode

The text area incorporates an embedded HTML text editor in the HTML mode. HTML mode allows the user to write the document in a WYSIWYG editor, which is similar to working in MS Word or Open Office.

[ What's HTML text editor? How to use WYSIWYG editor? Refer Chapter 6.]

Plain Text Mode

The text area incorporates pure plain text in **Plain Text** mode, as well as in **Classic** mode with no rules and syntax. It is the same as editing source in HTML text editor.

Publishing Wiki Articles

We have discussed how to create **Node** and how to add **Pages** in order to keep track of information about editorial guidance and other resources that require frequent editing. As the administrator of Palm Tree Publication", you have created the Node, "**Liferay**". Now you can publish Wiki articles for the Node, "**Liferay**". Let's do it as follows:

1. If **Wiki Display** is not already present, add the **Wiki Display** portlet in the page "**Wikis**" of the **Book Lovers** Community where you want to publish Wiki articles.
2. Click on the **Configuration** icon on the upper right of the **Wiki Display** portlet.
3. With the **Setup** tab selected, a **Node** selection list appears. Select the **Node** named, "**Liferay**", which you want to publish as a **Wiki** in your **Page** first.
4. Then, click on the **Save** button to save the changes. If needed, click on the arrow **Return to Full Page** to return.

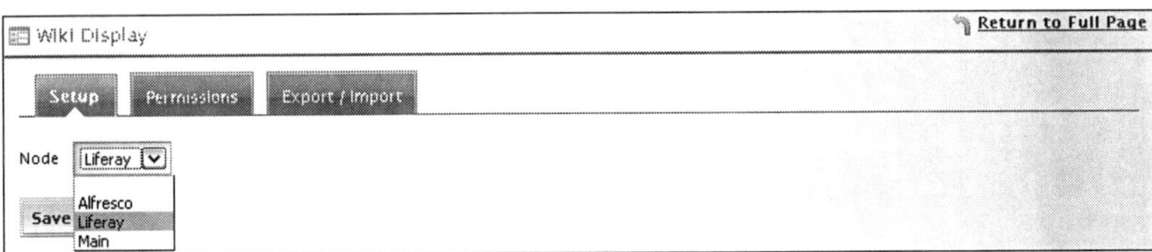

Liferay **Wiki Display** portlet provides a way to publish **Wiki** articles in a given **Page** of a **Community**. The following figure depicts **Wiki Display** portlet with a **Wiki Page**.

As an administrator, say "**Palm Tree**", you have proper permission to edit the current **Wiki Page** and add **Comments** on the current **Wiki** page, and also change the **Page Permissions** since you have proper access right to do so.

As a **User** of "Palm Tree Publications", such as "**Lotti Stein**", you have proper **Permission** to edit the current **Wiki** page and add **Comments** on the current **Wiki** page. But you cannot change **Page Permissions** since you have proper access to do so.

What's happening? This is something related to **Permissions**.

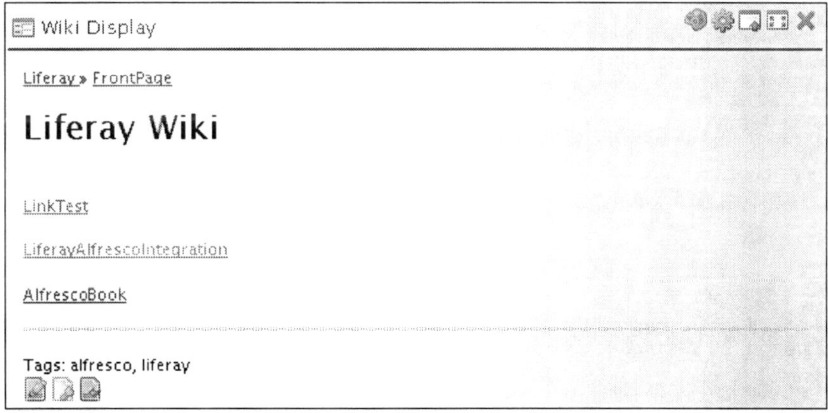

The following table shows the **Permissions** for the **Page**, "**FrontPage**", of a given **Node**, "**Liferay**" in the **Wiki Display** portlet. A **Community User** may set up **Permissions** (marked 'X'): **View, Delete, Permissions, Update**, and **Add Discussion**, while a **Guest User** may set up **Permissions** with **View, Delete**, and **Permissions**. By default, a **Community User** has **Permission** actions (marked '*'): **View, Update** and **Add Discussion**, while a **Guest User** has the **Permission** to **View** only.

Action	Description	Community	Guest
View	Views the **Pages**	X, *	X, *
Delete	Deletes the **Page**	X	X
Permissions	Configures **Permissions** of the **Page**	X	X
Update	Updates Pages	X, *	
Add Discussion	Adds discussions (**Comments**) for the page	X, *	

Obviously, as a **User** of the **Book Lovers** Community, "**Lotti Stein**" has only the **Permissions** to **View**, **Update**, **Add Discussion** on the **Pages**, since the **Pages** under "**Liferay**" was added by **Community** default setting. She does not have the **Permissions**, **Delete** and **Permissions**.

As an administrator, you may need to set up the **Community Users** having **Permissions** to **View** and **Update** on the **Page**, "**FrontPage**", of the **Node**, "**Liferay**". That is, you have to remove the **Permissions**, **Add Discussion** on the **Page**, "**FrontPage**", of the **Node**, "**Liferay**", for the **Book Lovers** community. Let's do it as follows:

1. Click on the **Permissions** icon at the bottom of the **Page, "FrontPage"**.
2. Select the **Community** tab.
3. Select **Permission, Add Discussion,** in the **Current** box.
4. Click on the **Remove** arrow.
5. Click on the **Save** button, if you are ready.

Now, as a **User** of the **Book Lovers** Community, "**Lotti Stein**" has the **View** and **Update Permissions** on the **Page**, "**FrontPage**", of the **Node**, "**Liferay**", finally. Try to log in as "**Lotti Stein**" and you will see the **Page "FrontPage"** of the **Node, "Liferay"** without an action icon, "**Comments**".

Working with Web Form

Do you want to collect suggestions on the "**Liferay Book**" and "**Alfresco Book**"? Do you want to collect **Comments** on other topics? The **Web Form** portlet would be a useful tool.

The **Web Form** portlet allows a web administrator to define a form to be published in the website. Users who visit the website can then fill the form, which is then sent to a configured email address.

There are two modes for the **Web Form** portlet: view mode and edit mode.

Using View Mode

The following figure depicts the view mode of the **Web Form** portlet. As an administrator, you may need to add the **Web Form** portlet in the page, "**Web Form**", of the page "**Community**. Let's do it as follows:

1. Add a child page called "**Web Form**" of the page "**Community**", at the **Book Lovers** Community **Public Pages**.

2. If **Web Form** Portlet is not already present, add the **Web Form** portlet in the page, "Web Form", of **Community** where you want to fill the form.

As a normal **User,** say "Lotti Stein", you may plan to submit your **Comments** on the "**Liferay Book**". You can do it as follows:

1. Log in as "Lotti Stein".

2. Navigate to the **Book Lovers** community and select **Public Pages**.

3. Navigate to the "**Community**" **Page** and further to the "**Web Form**" **Page**.

4. Input **Name** "Liferay Book", under **Suggestions** (message: "**Your input is valuable to us. Please send us your suggestions.**").

5. **Select a Rating from a select box (Excellent, Good, Satisfactory, Poor), say "Good".**

6. **Input Comments if possible.**

7. Click on the **Send** button when you are ready to send the form.

What will happen next? The portal will send email according to the configuration which you have set up.

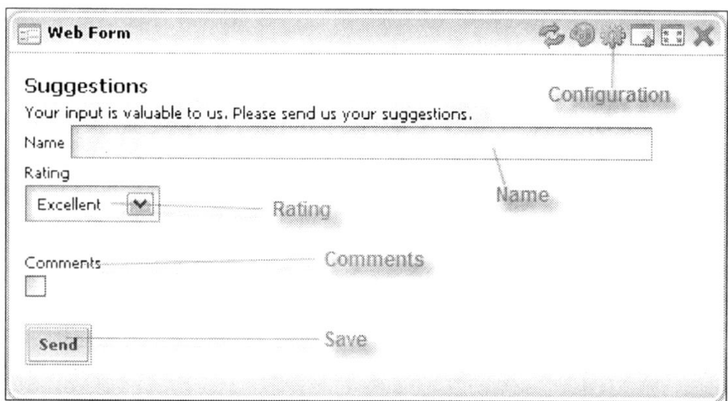

Using Edit Mode

As an administrator, you can view the edit mode of the **Web Form** portlet. You simply click on the **Configuration** icon at the upper right of the **Web Form** portlet. The following figure depicts the edit mode of the **Web Form** portlet. You can set up a form to be published in the website and configure **Permissions**, if you have proper access.

There are only two **Permission** actions for the portlet, **View** and **Configuration**:

1. With the **View Permission**, users can **View** and fill the form, which is then sent to a configured email address.

2. With **Configuration Permission**, users can set up a form to be published in the website and configure **Permissions**, such as reassign **Permissions** and delegate **Permissions** for **Users, User Groups, Organizations, Community** and **Guest**.

In general, the **Web Form** portlet (in edit mode) has the following features:

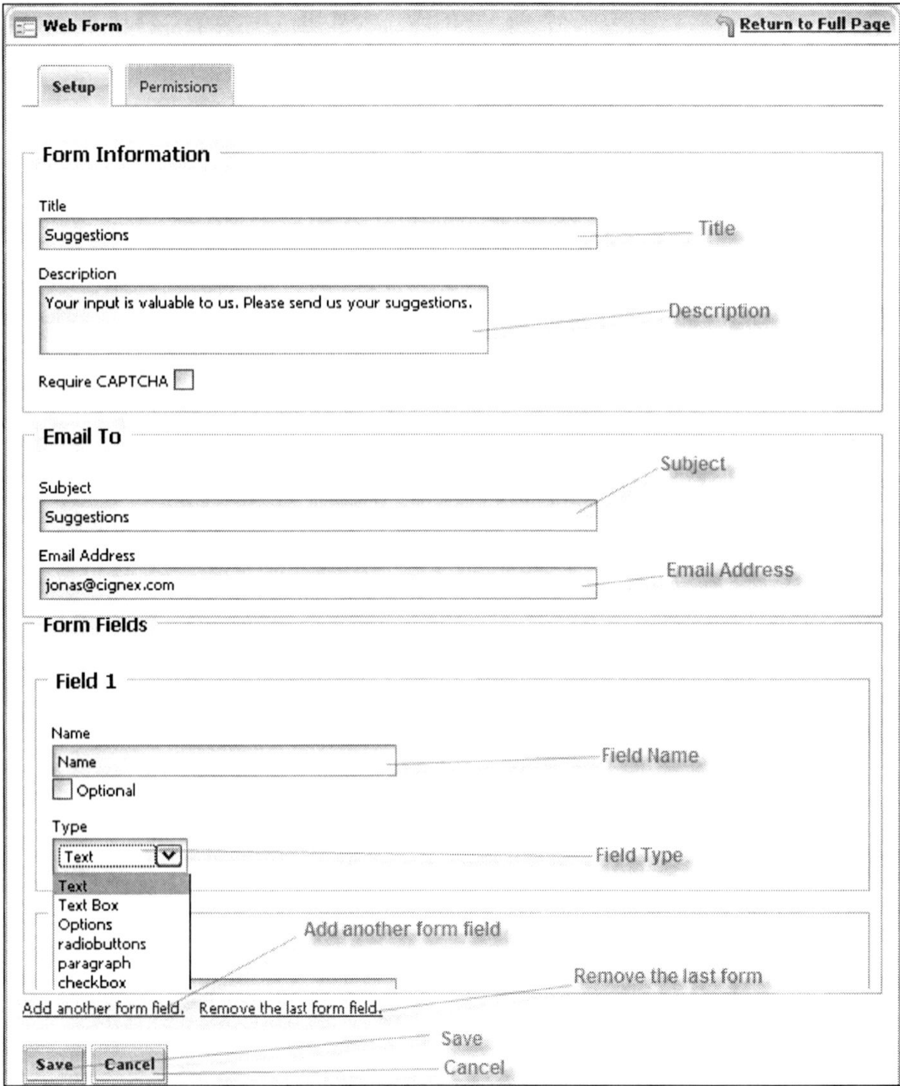

1. The **Title** and introductory **Description** of the form shown to the users are configurable.

2. The **Email Address** and **Subject** of the email is also configurable per form.

3. It is possible to have as many different forms per website and **Page,** as desired.

4. It supports many types of fields: **Text, Text Box, Options** (separated by commas), **radiobuttons, paragraph** and **checkbox.**

5. To add a new **Form Field**, simply click on the link "**Add another form field**"; to remove the last form field, simply click on the link "**Remove the last form field**". Click **Save** to save the changes, or **Cancel** to cancel the changes.

Working with Polls

Do you want to keep track of the votes on "**Is Liferay Book a proper book**"? The **Polls** portlet and **Polls Display** portlet are useful tools.

Using Polls Portlet

First of all, we plan to add questions. As an administrator, you may need to create a page "**Polls**" under the page "**Community**" first. Then you need to create a lot of questions for polls such as, "**Is Liferay Book a proper book**" or "**Do you plan to buy alfresco book next month**". To do this we should:

1. Add a child page called "**Polls**" of the **page** "**Community**" at the **Book Lovers** Community **Public Pages**.

2. Add the **Polls** Portlet in the page, "**Polls**" of **Community,** where you want to manage questions, if **Polls** Portlet is not already present.

3. Click on the button "**Add Question**".

4. Input the name, "**Is Liferay Book a proper book**", Description "Votes", **Choices** "**Yes**" and "**No**".

5. Add choice by clicking on the **Add Choice** button. After clicking on the **Add Choice** button, you can delete a choice by clicking on the **Delete** button located next to the choice name input box.

6. Check/uncheck **Never Expire** box or set the **Expiration Date**.

7. Set **Permissions** by clicking on the **Configure** link. To configure additional **Permissions,** click on the **More** link. Here, we just use default settings.

8. Click on the **Save** button to save the inputs.

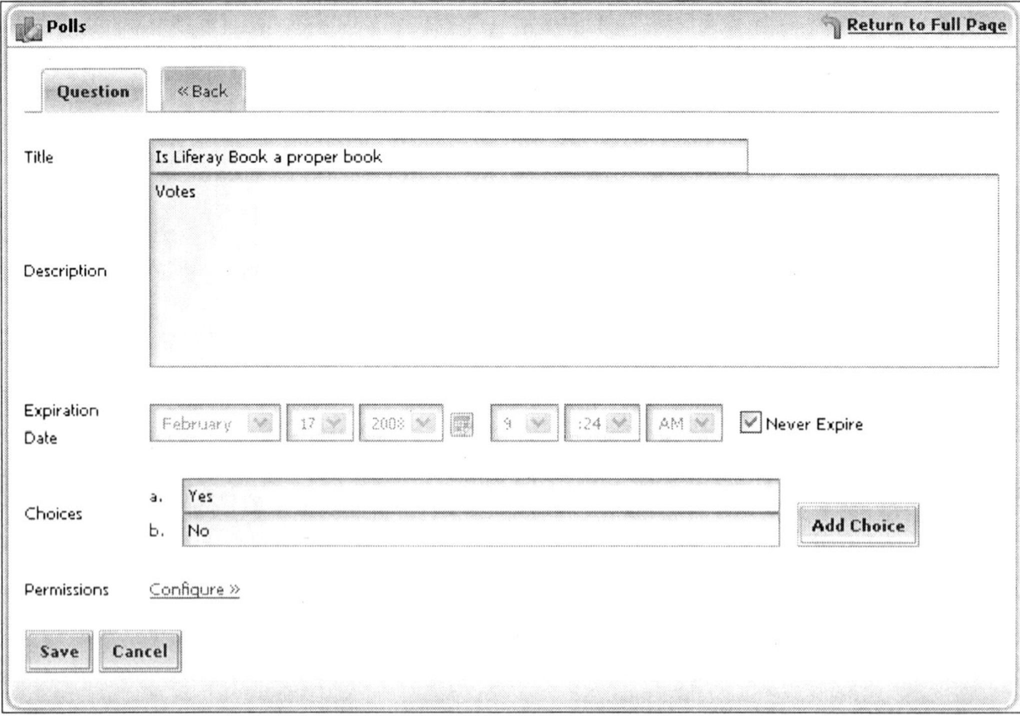

Of course, you can add other **Questions**. After adding **Question "Do you plan to buy alfresco book next month"**, we can view the **Questions**.

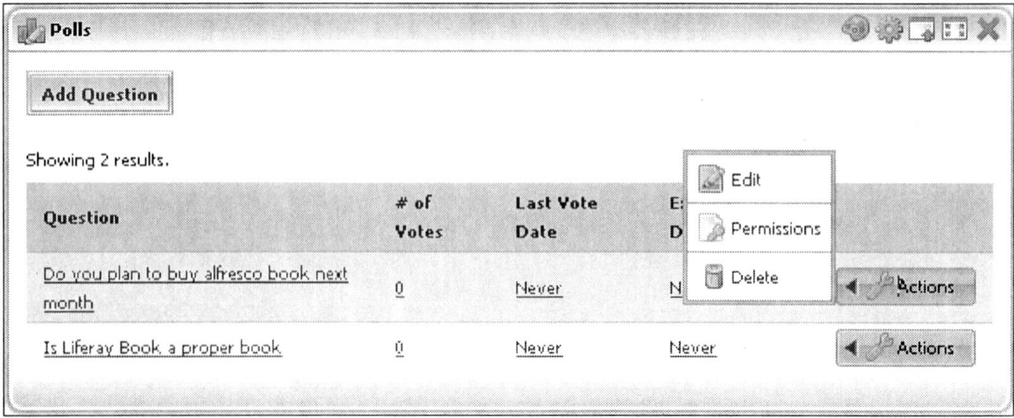

Managing Questions

Polls questions are displayed as question name, **number of Votes**, **Last Vote Date**, **Expiration Date**, and **Actions**, with the set of icons: **Edit**, **Permissions**, and **Delete**. By default, this portlet will display all **Questions** for the current **User** who has proper **Permissions**.

Edit a Question

Let's suppose that we want to change the **Description** of the question, "**Do you plan to buy alfresco book next month**" from "**alfresco book**" to "**vote for alfresco book**". We need to edit and update it. Let's do it as follows:

1. Locate the question "**Do you plan to buy alfresco book next month**" in the **Polls** portlet, and click on the **Edit** icon from the **Actions** next to the question.

2. Update the **Description** with the value "**vote for alfresco book**".

3. Click **Save** button to save the inputs.

Delete a Question

Suppose that the **Question** "Do you plan to buy alfresco book next month" is not wanted anymore, we need to delete it. Let's delete it as follows:

1. Locate a **Question** ("**Do you plan to buy alfresco book next month**") that you want to delete.

2. Click on the **Delete** icon from the **Actions** located next to the question.

3. A screen will appear asking if you want to delete this.

4. Click **OK** button to confirm deletion.

Note that deleting a **Question** will delete all related votes which belong to this **Question**.

Set Up Permissions

As a **User** at "Palm Tree Publications", such as "**Lotti Stein**", you have proper **Permissions** to **View** and **Add Vote** on the **Question, "Is Liferay Book a proper book**". But you do not have **Permissions** to **Update** and **Delete**.

What's happening? The following table shows the **Permissions** for the **Polls Questions**. A **Community User** may have **Permissions** (marked 'X'): **View**, **Delete**, **Permissions**, **Update**, and **Add Vote**, while a **Guest User** may have the **Permissions**, **View**, **Add Vote**, **Delete**, and **Permissions**. By default, a **Community User** has the **Permission** actions (marked '*'), **View** and **Add Vote**, while a guest user only has **Permission** to **View**.

Action	Description	Community	Guest
View	Views **Polls Questions**	X, *	X, *
Delete	Deletes **Polls Questions**	X	X
Permissions	Configures **Permissions** of **Polls Questions**	X	X
Update	Updates **Polls Questions**	X	
Add Vote	Adds vote for the **Question**	X, *	X

Obviously, as a **User** of the **Book Lovers** Community, "**Lotti Stein**" has only **Permissions** to **View** and **Add Vote** on the **Question**.

As an administrator, you may need to set up the **Community Users** having **Permissions** to **View**, **Add Vote**, **Delete** and **Update** on the **Question**, "**Is Liferay Book a proper book**". Let's do it as follows:

1. Click on the **Permissions** icon from the **Actions** next to the **Question**, "**Is Liferay Book a proper book**".
2. Select the **Community** tab.
3. Select **Permissions**, **Delete** and **Update** in the **Available** box.
4. Click on the **Add** arrow.
5. Click on the **Save** button if you are ready.

Now, as a **User** of the **Book Lovers** Community, "**Lotti Stein**" has **Permissions** to **View**, **Add Vote**, **Update** and **Delete** on the **Question**, "**Is Liferay Book a proper book**" finally. Try to log in as "**Lotti Stein**" and you will see the **Actions** with icons **Edit** and **Delete** next to the **Question**, "**Is Liferay Book a proper book**".

View Votes

Suppose that you want to view **Votes** for the **Question**, "**Do you plan to buy alfresco book next month**" in different ways. You can simply click on the name of the **Question**. You will see the **Votes** in percentage, or other **Charts** (such as **Area**, **Horizontal Bar**, **Line**, **Pie** and **Vertical Bar**). Further, you can also view the actual voters if you have proper **Permissions**.

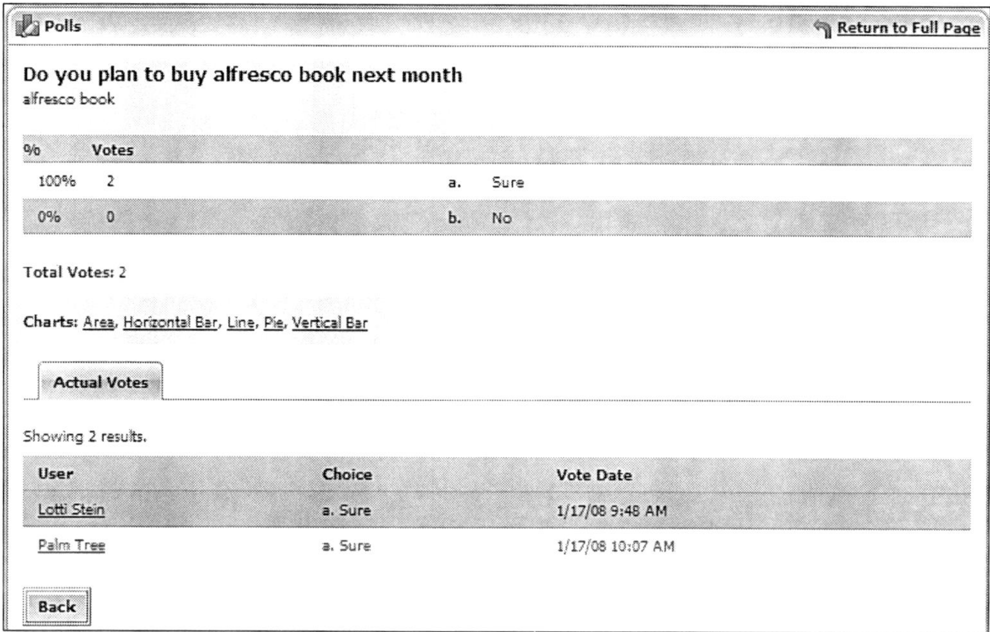

Using Polls Display Portlet

Do you want to display a specific poll's results in the Intranet? The **Polls display** portlet would be a useful tool for that.

In the **Polls display** portlet, the **Poll Votes** for the given **Question, "Is Liferay Book a proper book"**, are displayed as **Percentage, Number of Votes, Last Vote Date**, and **Choice** names. The selected **Question** name is shown at the upper left and the total **Votes** are shown at the bottom left. By default, this portlet will display all the **Votes** for a given **Poll Question,** for a current **User** who has proper **Permissions**.

You can select different **Poll Questions** by simply clicking on the **Configuration** icon at the upper right of the **Polls Display** portlet. Then, you can select a **Question** from a list of **Poll Questions** to be published in the website by selecting the **Setup** tab. Furthermore, you can also configure **Permissions,** if you have proper access, by selecting **Permissions** tab.

There are only two **Permission** actions for the portlet: **View** and **Configuration**:

1. With **View Permission,** users can view the **Poll** results.

2. With **Configuration Permission,** users can update the **Poll Questions** to be published in the website and configure **Permissions,** such as reassign **Permissions** and delegate **Permissions** for **Users, User Groups, Organizations, Community** and **Guest.**

Using Polls Effectively

Generally speaking, **Users** (who have proper **Permissions**) or administrators can create multiple choice **Polls** that keep track of **Votes** and display results on the **Page** in the **Polls** portlet. On the one hand, the **Polls** portlet can manage several separate **Polls**. On the other hand, a separate portlet such as the **Polls Display** portlet can be configured to display a specific poll's results.

Actually, the **Polls** portlet acts as a voting application in order to take the public opinions. It provides users with scientifically sampled survey to assess public opinions. Meanwhile, it effectively uses the portal's customization and personalization features, and furthermore, allows an end user to customize the results shown.

As **Poll** administrators, you can easily add and delete the **Poll** topics. You can customize the portlet through actions such as changing the result title, reordering the **Poll** options and specifying whether the user can select multiple options.

In theory, **Polls** are scheduled to open and close at given times. As **Poll** administrator, you may view previous **Poll** results if you want to make use of this information for your statistical analysis. At the same time, you may configure portlet instance to determine which **Poll** is to be shown in the portlet.

However, there are some differences between survey and **Poll**. A survey is a multiple pages survey questionnaire, while a **Poll** is a one page questionnaire and is replaced by **Poll** results after voting., **Polls** consists of straightforward lists relating to questions and potential responses, either in the form of multiple choices or text. When information gathering requirements are simple, and you do not require the identification of the respondents, you can use **Polls**. Otherwise, you have to use survey.

Summary

This chapter instructed us, how to add and manage (view, update and delete) **Nodes** of **Wikis**, add **Pages** at the **Nodes** in **Wikis**, manage (view, update, delete and search) **Pages** for a given node in **Wikis**, use **permissions** for **Wikis** portlet and **Permissions** on **Nodes**, and publish **Wiki** articles in the intranet first. Then it discussed how to set up **Web Form** in order to collect **Users'** suggestions, to configure **Polls** and to display a survey in order to assess public opinion.

Internal Bloggings And RSS

In the intranet website "book.com", of "Palm Tree Publications", it is required to let small teams work on specific projects, share files and Blogs about project process, use HTML text editor to create or update files and Blogs, and employ RSS feeds. Liferay Blogs provide a straightforward Blog solution with features such as RSS support, **User** and **Guest Comments**, browseable categories, **Tags** and labels, and an entry rating system. Liferay RSS with subscription provides the ability to frequently read RSS feeds from within the portal framework. At the same time, Liferay WYSIWGs (What You See Is What You Get editors) provides ability to edit web content, including Blogs' content. Less technical persons can use WYSIWGs without sifting through complex code. This chapter will introduce us to working with Blogs, publishing them, building Blog content and working with RSS.

By the end of this chapter, you would have learnt how to:

- Add entries of Blogs.
- Manage (view, update and delete) entries of Blogs.
- Add comments for a given entry of Blogs.
- Use **Permission** on the Blogs portlet and entries of Blogs.
- Publish Blogs by Recent Bloggers portlet and Blogs Aggregator portlet.
- Build Blogs with WYSIWGs editor.
- Use RSS including RSS portlet, News Portlets and Weather portlet.

Working with Blogs

In order to let small teams working on specific projects share files and Blogs about project process, we should use Liferay Blogs at **Book Lovers** Community **Public Pages**.

As an administrator of the enterprise "Palm Tree Publications", you need to create a **Page** called "**Blogs**" under the page "**Community**", at the **Book Lovers** Community and moreover, add **Blogs** portlet in the **Page, "Blogs"**. Then you are ready to create **Blogs** such as, "How to write computer book" and "Is your book sellable?".

Adding Entries

First of all, we need to create an **Entry** called "**How to write computer book**". Let's create the **Entry** now as follows:

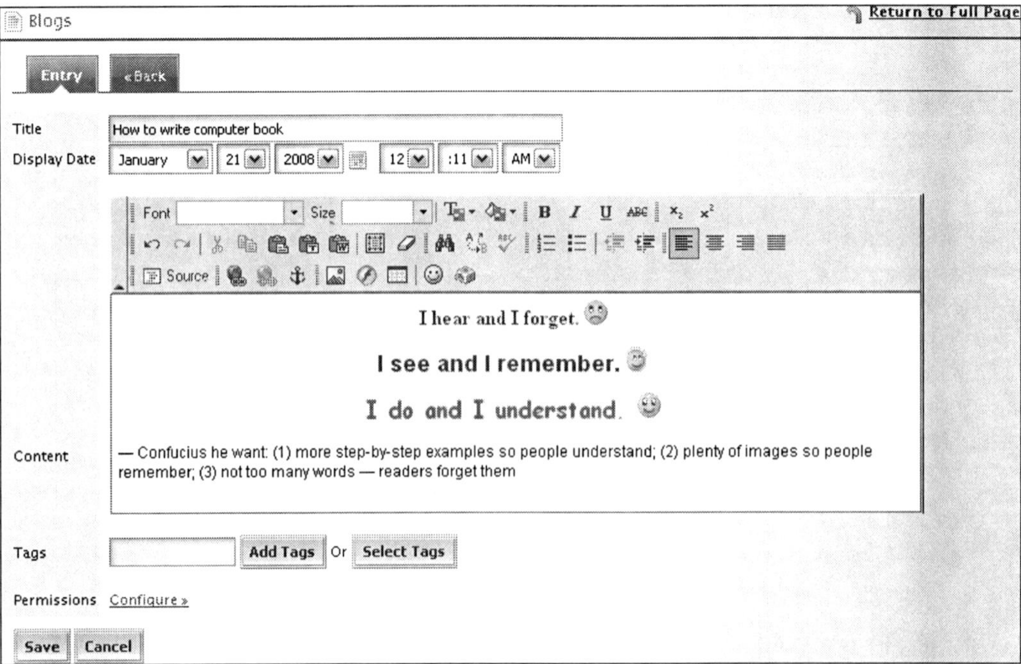

1. Add a child page called "**Blogs**" of the **Page "Community"** in the **Book Lovers** Community, **Public Pages**.

2. If the **Blogs** portlet is not already present, add it in the **page "Blogs"** of the **Book Lovers** Community, where you have to manage the **Blogs** entries.

3. Click on the **Add Entry** button.

4. Input title, "**How to write computer book**", which could be duplicated.

5. Input **Display Date** — default date and time are current.

6. Input **Content** — text, graphics and any links — by HTML Text editor.

7. Press the button, **Select Tags,** or input tag and press the button **Add Tags,** if you need to add tags.

8. Set **Permissions** by clicking on the **Configure** link. To configure additional **Permissions**, click on the **More** link. Here, we just use the default settings.

9. Save inputs by pressing the **Save** button.

10. Return to the original page, by clicking the **Return to Full Page** arrow.

Of course, you can create other **Entries** that you may want. After creating the **Entry, "Is your book sellable?"**, we can view **Entries**.

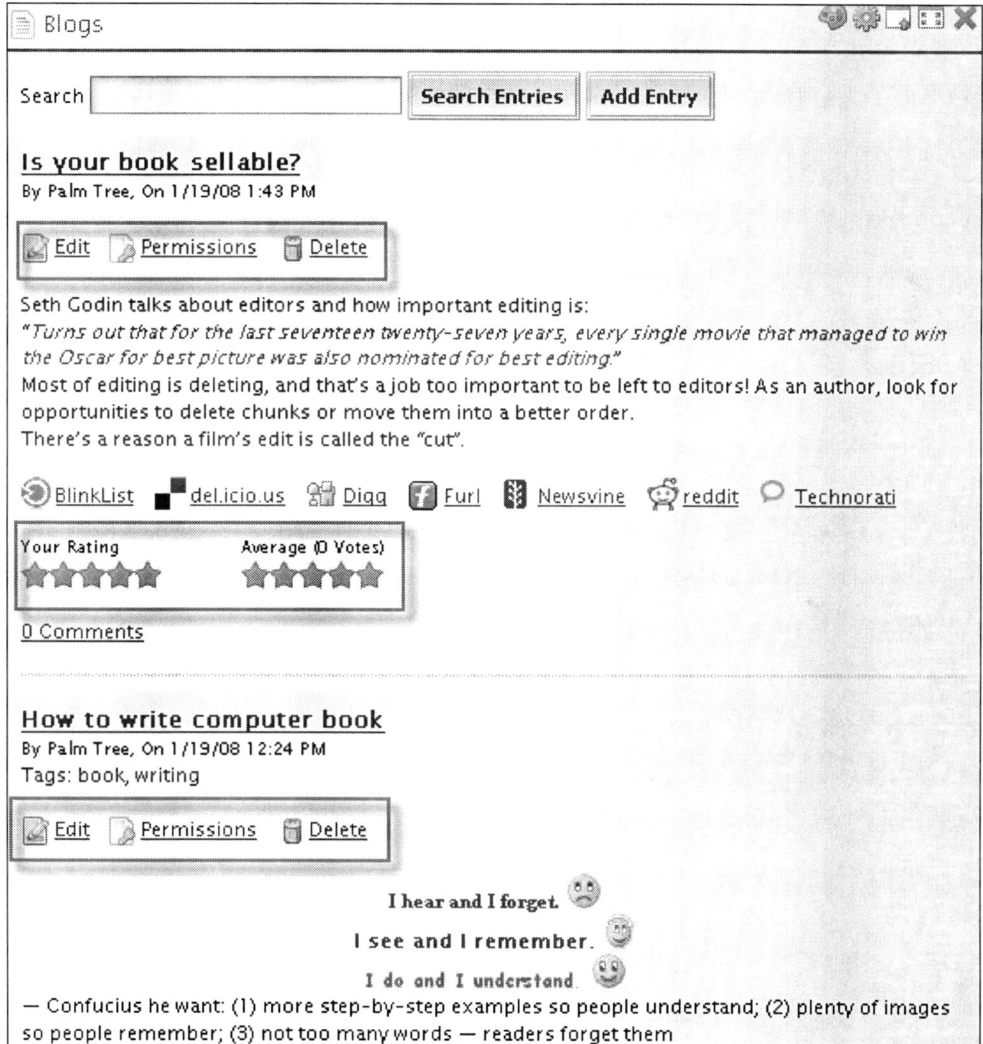

Managing Entries

After creating **Entries**, we can manage them easily.

Edit Entries

Entries are editable. For example, we need to change the title of the **Entry, "Is your book sellable?"** from value "**Is your book sellable?**", to the value "**How to write sellable book**". Let's do it as follows:

1. Locate the **Entry "Is your book sellable?"** that you want to edit.
2. Click on the **Edit** icon below the title, "**Is your book sellable?**".
3. Update the title, "**Is your book sellable?**", with new value, "**How to write sellable book?**".
4. Retain the values of **Display Date, Content**, and **Tags**.
5. Save inputs by pressing the **Save** button.

Delete Entries

Entries are removable. For instance, the **Entry, "How to write sellable book?"**, is not wanted anymore. We have to remove this from the **Blogs** portlet. Let's delete it as follows:

1. Locate the **Entry, "How to write sellable book?"**, that you want to delete.
2. Click on the **Delete** icon below the title, "**How to write sellable book?**".
3. A screen will appear asking if you want to delete this.
4. Click the **OK** button to confirm deletion.

Note that deleting an **Entry** will delete all related **Comments** which belong to this **Entry**.

Search Entries

The **Contents** of **Entries** are searchable. Suppose that as an administrator, you want to search **Entries** by the keyword "**them**". Let's search it as follows:

1. Find the button, **Search Entries** in the **Blogs** portlet.
2. Input the search criterion (that is keyword), "**them**".
3. Click on the **Search Entries** button.

4. A list of **Entries** appears at the bottom of the **Blogs** portlet. **Entries** are listed by **number**, **Entry** and **Score**. Obviously, **Entries** are displayed in the descending order of the **Score**.

Surely, you can search entries using any keyword. There is only one condition that you need to have proper **Permissions** (view) on the **Entries**. In other words, if you have no proper **Permissions** (view) on the **Entries**, you cannot view them by **Search**.

For example, as an administrator, you can simply change the **Permissions** on the **Entry**, "**How to write sellable book?**". For example, let the **Community User** have no **Permissions** (view) on this **Entry**. Now,try to log in as "**Lotti Stein**". You just input the search criterion, "**them**", and click on the button, "**Search Entries**". You will see the **Entry**, "**How to write sellable book?**". But when you click on its title, you will receive the message, "**You do not have the required permissions**".

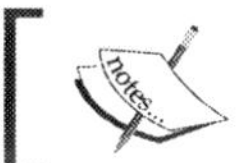 What's happening? This is something related to **Permissions** on the **Entries**. Refer to the section *"Using Permissions"*.

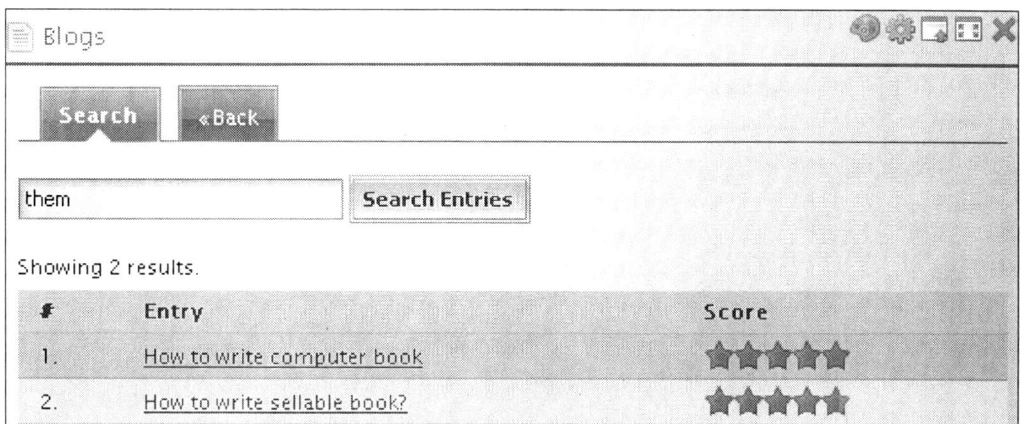

Giving Your Rating

You can give your own rating for any **Entries**, if you have proper **Permissions** to view them. For instance, as an administrator, you have read the **Entry**, "**How to write computer book**" and want to give your rating as two stars. You simply click on the second star under "**Your Rating**" of the **Entry**, "**How to write computer book**".

Try to log in as "**Lotti Stein**", who can also read the **Entry** "**How to write computer book**" and wants to give her rating as three stars. You simply click on the third star under "**Your Rating**" of the **Entry** "**How to write computer book**". Now you will find that the average is two and half stars with the message, "**2 Votes**".

Employing RSS Feeds

You can export **Blogs** as RSS feeds. Let's do it as follows:

1. Click on the **RSS Feed** icon ("Subscribe to this blog") at the bottom of the **Entries**.
2. **RSS Feeds Page** appears. All **Entries** are displayed with a brief content.
3. You can subscribe to the feed using different applications.
4. Locate the **Entry** (by title) that you want to view, and click on the link.
5. You will return to the **Entry** view **Page**.

Adding Comments

As stated above, the administrator has created an **Entry** called "**How to write computer book**". As a **User** of "Palm Tree Publications", "**Lotti Stein**" wants to review the **Entry** and add her **Comments, "Cool!"** Let's do it as follows:

1. Log in as "**Lotti Stein**".
2. Navigate to the **Book Lovers** community and select **Public Pages**; navigate to the **Community Page** and further to the **Blogs Page**.
3. Locate an **Entry** (by page up or page down) that you want to view; and click on the **Entry** (by title), "**How to write computer book**".
4. Under the **Comments** tab, click on the **Post Reply** link, if you want to add a new topic (or subject).
5. Or below **Subject**, click on the **Post Reply** link, if you want to add new sub topic or **Subject**.
6. Input text "**Cool!**".
7. Click the **Reply** button to save the input.

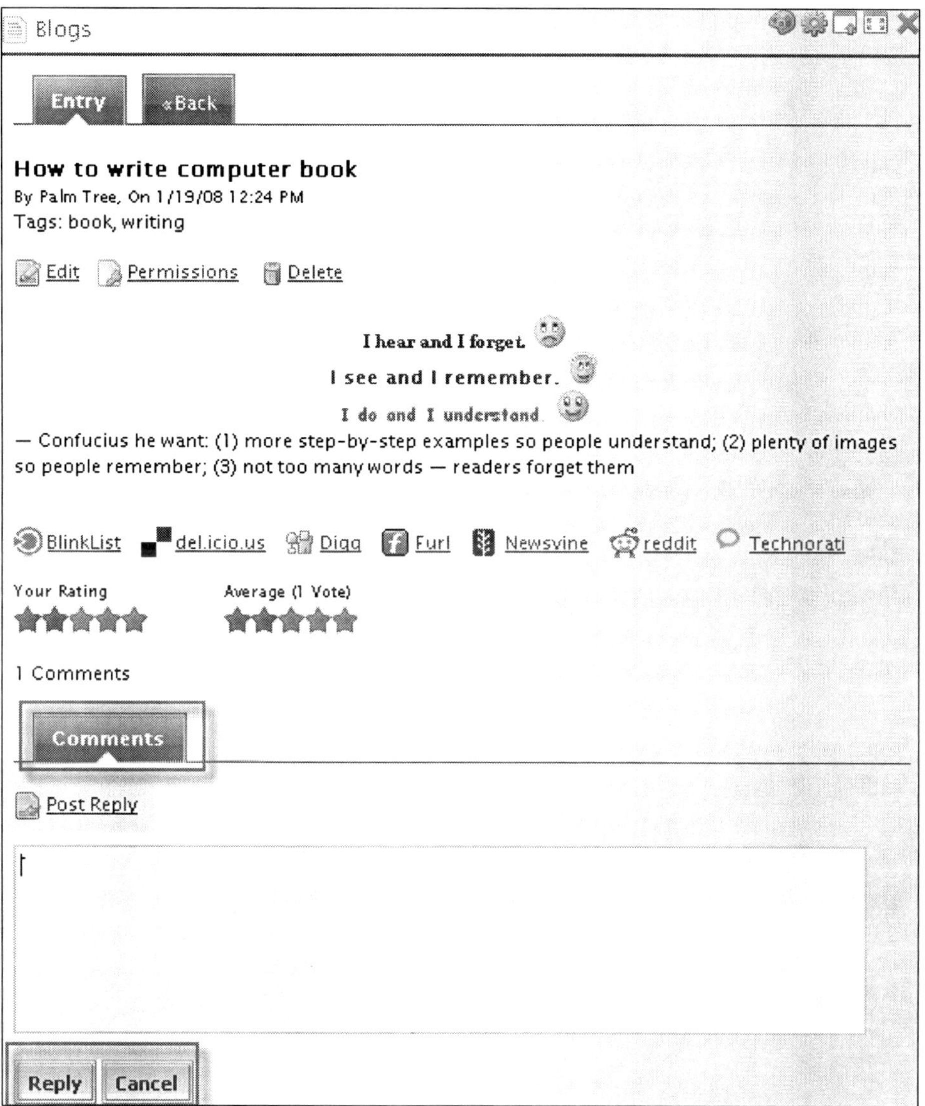

Blogs
Entry
«Back
How to write computer book
By Palm Tree, On 1/19/08 12:24 PM
Tags: book, writing
Edit   Permissions   Delete
I hear and I forget.
I see and I remember.
I do and I understand.
— Confucius he want: (1) more step-by-step examples so people understand; (2) plenty of images so people remember; (3) not too many words — readers forget them
BlinkList   del.icio.us   Digg   Furl   Newsvine   reddit   Technorati
Your Rating
Average (1 Vote)
1 Comments
Comments
Post Reply
Reply   Cancel

As an administrator, you can view **Comments** from "**Lotti Stein**", for the **Entry**, "**How to write computer book**" as follows:

1. Locate the **Entry**, "How to write computer book".

2. Click on the title of the **Entry**, "**How to write computer book**".

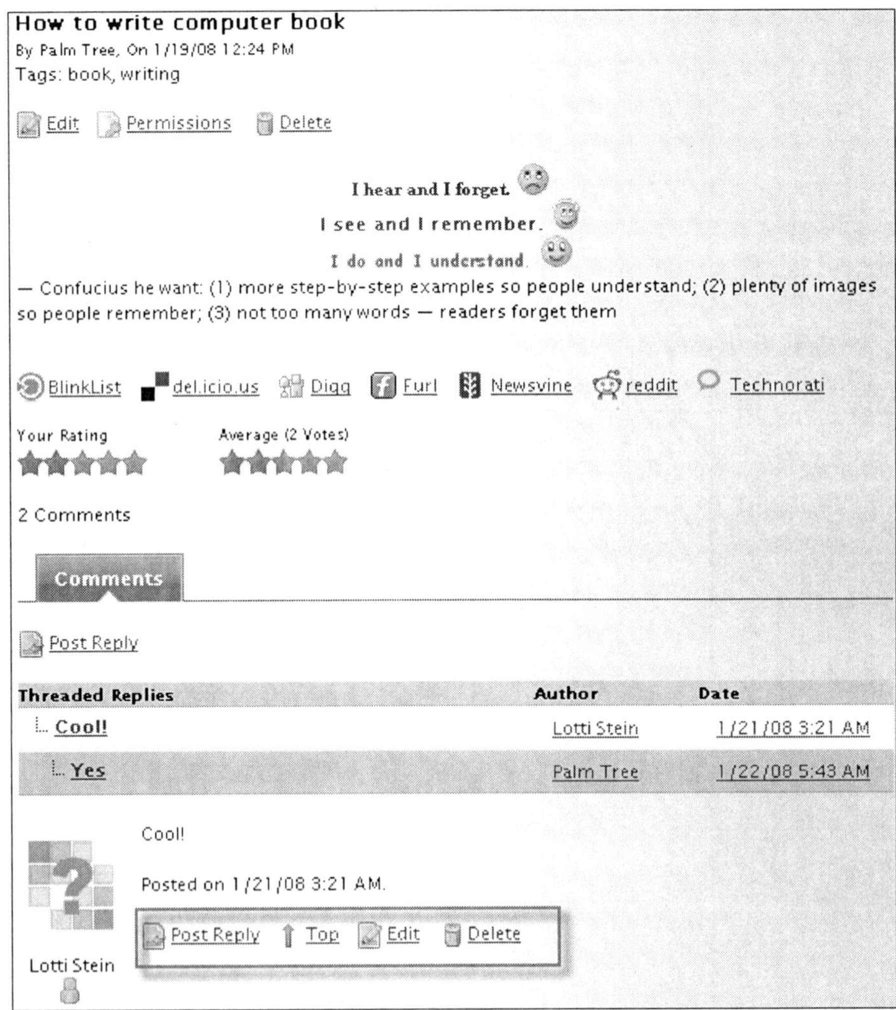

Moreover, you can also reply to a **Comment**. You locate the **Comment** to which you want to reply first. Then, click on the **Post Reply** icon at the bottom left of the **Comment**. Input **Comments**, and then click on the **Reply** button to save the inputs, or the **Cancel** button to cancel.

Furthermore, you can also edit a **Comment**. You click on the **Edit** icon at the bottom left of the **Comment**. You can change the **Subject** and the **Body**. Then, click on the **Update** button to save the changes, or the **Cancel** button to cancel the changes.

You can also delete a **Comment**. You click on the **Delete** icon at the bottom left of the **Comment**. A screen will appear asking if you want to delete this. Click **OK** to confirm deletion or **Cancel** to cancel deletion.

Note that only the current **Comment** has been deleted on action. The low level **Comments** related to the current **Comment** will have a link to its parent **Comment**.

Finally, in order to go to the top of the **Comments**, simply click on the **Top** button at the bottom left of any **Comment**.

Using Permissions

We have used default settings for the **Blogs** portlet in the **Page, "Blogs"** of the **Page "Community"** under the **Book Lovers** Community. As mentioned earlier, when the administrator "Palm Tree" logs in, he/she will see the button, "**Add Entry**" in the **Blogs**. As we know, the **User** "**Lotti Stein**" is also a member of the **Book Lovers** community. Try to log in as "**Lotti Stein**", and you will see that there is no "**Add Entry**" button in the **Blogs**. Furthermore, you see the **entry, "How to write computer book"**, without the **Action** icons (**Edit, Permissions** and **Delete**).

What's happening? This is something related to **Permissions**. There are two levels of **Permissions**: **Portlet Permissions** and **Permissions on Entries**.

Update Portlet Permissions

The following table shows **Permissions** related to the **Blogs** portlet. A **Community User** may set up all **Permissions** (marked 'X'), **View, Add Entry**, and **Configuration**, while a **Guest User** may set up **Permissions, View** and **Configuration**. By default, a **Community** has the **Permission** action **View** (marked '*'), and so does a guest user.

Action	Description	Community	Guest
View	Views this portlet	X, *	X, *
Configuration	Configures this portlet	X	X
Add Entry	Adds an **Entry** to the portlet	X	

Obviously, as a **User** of the **Book Lovers** Community, "**Lotti Stein**" has only **View Permission** on the portlet, **Blogs,** by default. Since the **Book Lovers** community has no "**Add Entry**" **Permission**, "**Lotti Stein**" also has no "**Add Entry**" **Permission**.

As an administrator, you may need to set up the **Community Users** having **Add Entry Permission,** as well as **View Permission** on the **Blogs** portlet. That is, you need to add the **Add Entry Permission** on the **Blogs** portlet at the **Book Lovers** community. Let's do it as follows:

1. Click on the **Configuration** icon at the top right of the **Blogs** portlet.

2. Then click on the **Permissions** icon from the **Actions** located next to the node.

3. Select the **Community** tab.

4. Select **Permission, Add Entry** in the **Available** box.

5. Click on the **Add** arrow.

6. Click on the **Save** button if you are ready.

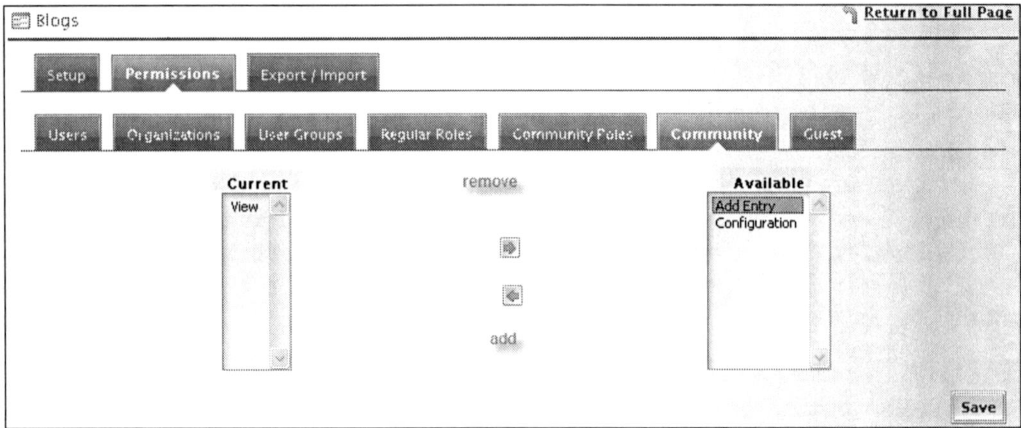

Try to log in as "**Lotti Stein**", and you will see that there is a button, "**Add Entry**", next to the button, "**Search Entries**", in the **Blogs**. Furthermore, you can view **Entries** without any **Actions** icons (such as **Edit, Permissions** and **Delete**). You can also view and add discussions, but you still can not delete and update discussion (that is **Comment**). Let's change **Permissions** on the **Entry,** "**How to write computer book**", at the **Book Lovers** community.

Set up Permissions on Entries

The following table shows **Permissions** for the **Blogs Entries**. A **Community User** may set up all **Permissions** (marked 'X'): **View, Update, Delete, Permissions, Add Discussion, Delete Discussion,** and **Update Discussions**. A **Guest User** may set up the **Permission, View**. By default, a **Community** has **Permission** actions such as **View** and **Add Discussion** (marked '*'), while a **Guest User** has **Permission** action **View** only.

Action	Description	Community	Guest
View	Views the details of the **Entry**	X, *	X, *
Update	Updates the **Entry**	X	
Delete	Deletes the **Entry**	X	
Permissions	Controls the **Permissions** for the **Entry**	X	
Add Discussion	Adds the discussion for the **Entry**	X, *	
Delete Discussion	Deletes the discussion for the **Entry**	X	
Update Discussion	Updates the discussion for the **Entry**	X	

Obviously, as a **User** of the **Book Lovers** Community, "**Lotti Stein**" has only **Permissions, View** and **Add Discussion** on the **Entry,** by default. Since the **Book Lovers** community has no **Permissions** (such as **Update, Delete, Permissions, Delete Discussion** and **Update Discussion**), "**Lotti Stein**" has no **Permissions** (for example, **Update, Delete, Permissions, Delete Discussion** and **Update Discussion**) too. Thus, "**Lotti Stein**" cannot see the **Action** icons (**Edit, Permission,** and **Delete**) on the **Entries**. And also "**Lotti Stein**" does not have the **Actions** icons (such as, **Delete Discussion** and **Update Discussion**) on the **Comments**.

As an administrator, you may need to set up the **Community Users** having **Permissions,** (such as up **Update Discussion** and **Delete Discussion**) on the **Entry, "How to write computer book"**. This means that you have to add **Permissions** (**Update Discussion** and **Delete Discussion**) on the **Entry,** "How to write computer book". Let's do it as follows:

1. Locate the entry "**How to write computer book**".
2. Click on the **Permissions** icon under the entry title.
3. Select the **Community** tab.
4. Select **Permissions**: **Delete Discussion** and **Update Discussion** in the **Available** box.
5. Click on the **Add** arrow, and
6. Click on the **Save** button if you are ready.

Try to log in as "**Lotti Stein**", and you can view **Entries** with no **Actions** (**Update**, **Delete** and **Permissions**). You can also view, add, delete and update discussion (**Comment**).

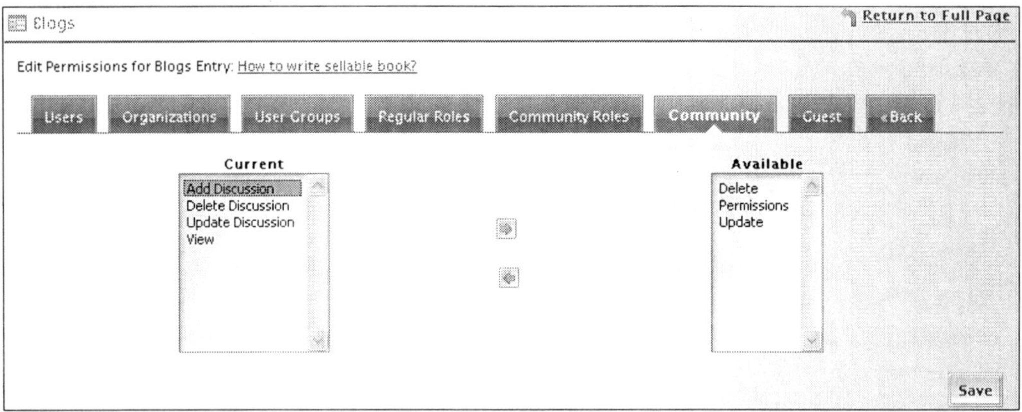

Similarly, as an administrator, you can set up the **Community Users** having **Permissions** (such as up **Update**, **Delete** and **Permissions**) on the **Entry**, "**How to write computer book**". Now, try to log in as "**Lotti Stein**", and you can view the **Entry**, "**How to write computer book**" with the **Actions** icons (such as **Edit**, **Permissions** and **Delete**).

Using Blogs Effectively

Generally speaking, a **Blog** (short for web-log) is a personal online content that is frequently updated for general public consumption. **Blogs** are a series of **Entries** posted to a single page in reverse-chronological order. Generally, they represent the author's personality or reflect the purpose to host the **Blog** at the Web site. Topics of blogs could be brief philosophical musings, links to other sites the author favors, and commentary on Internet and other social issues, and so on. A **Blog** content could include anything, from what is happening in a person's life, to what is happening on the Web, a kind of hybrid diary or guide site, and so on.

The author of a **Blog** is called a Blogger. Bloggers can syndicate their **Blog** content to subscribers using RSS. In general, blogs are frequent, chronological publications of personal thoughts and Web links.

Blog Types

There are various types of **Blogs** such as v-log, link-log, photo log, and so on. And each of them is different in the way the content is delivered and written.

Blogs can be classified by media type, such as a v-log (one comprising videos), a link-log (one comprising links), a sketch-blog (a site containing a portfolio of sketches), a photo-blog (one comprising photos), tumble-logs, art-log (a form of art sharing and publishing), and so on.

In addition, **Blogs** can be classified by devices, such as, a mo-blog (written by a mobile device like a mobile phone or a PDA).

Liferay Blogs Portlet

The Blogs portlet can help you publish information easily on the web. It helps in the rapid development of your community, and furthermore, gives your enterprise a platform to easily share information among different departments.

The Blogs portlet allows the users of the enterprise to manage web-log entries in a portal page. You can create, edit, and delete web-log entries, and change **Permissions** on **Entries**. In addition, it provides a simplified interface for creating web-logs and publishing them as RSS feed.

Liferay **Blogs** portlet has the following features:

- RSS feed capability for each **Blog** and all **Blogs** combined.
- Ability to view the list of all available **Blogs**.
- Calendar view for **Blog Entries**.
- Ability to navigate directly to "My Blog".
- Comments capability.
- A direct link for each **Blog Entry** and each **User Blog**.
- **Tags** and labels ability.
- An **Entry** rating system.

The following figure depicts the Liferay **Blogs** structure overview. Liferay **Blogs** is made up of a set of **Entries**. Each **Entry** may have many comments.

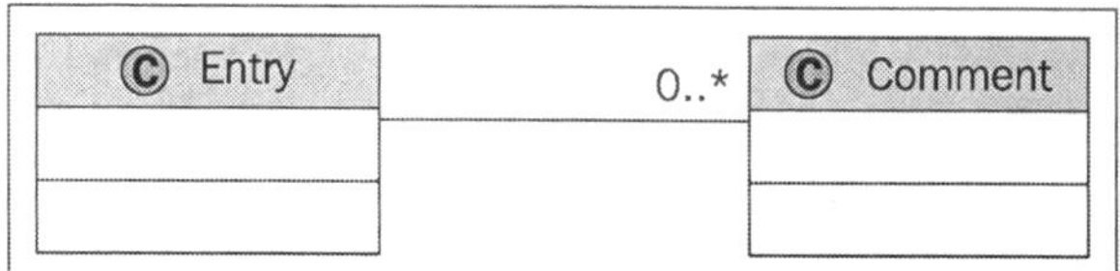

Publishing Blogs

We have discussed how to create **Entries** in order to let small teams working on specific projects share files and **Blogs** about project process. As the **User** at "Palm Tree Publication", you may have created a lot of **Entries**. You may be required to show a list of the latest **Users** from a given department, and show the latest **Posts** for a given department.

Using Recent Bloggers Portlet

Do you want to show a list of the latest **Users** from the **Editorial Department** of the **Book Lovers** community? Let's do it as follows:

1. Add the **Recent Bloggers** portlet in the page, "**Blogs**", of the **Book Lovers** Community where you want to show a list of users, if the **Recent Bloggers** portlet is not already present.

2. Click on the **Configuration** icon of the portlet.

3. By default, the tab, "**Setup**", is selected. You can select an organization such as the "**Editorial Department**".

4. Select the **Display Style**, such as, "**User Name and Image**".

5. Select **Maximum Bloggers to display**, such as "**20**".

6. Click on the **Save** button when you are ready.

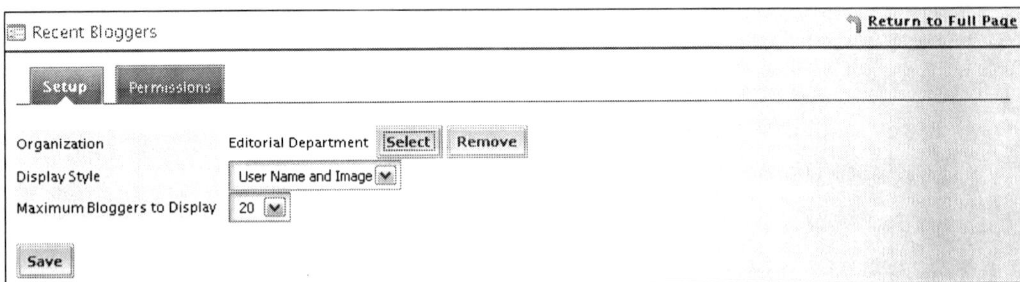

Of course, you can select another **Organization** such as "**Engineering Department**". The **Recent Bloggers** portlet will show a list of the latest users from the **Engineering Department** at the **Book Lovers** community. Also, you can remove the **Organization** if need be. In this case, the portlet will show a list of the latest users from any department at the **Book Lovers** community.

The **Recent Bloggers** portlet allows showing a list of the latest **users** of the portal who have written the post, **Entry**.

Using Blogs Aggregator Portlet

Do you want to show the latest posts from the **Editorial Department** at the **Book Lovers** community? Let's do it as follows:

1. If **Blogs Aggregator** portlet is not already present, add the **Blogs Aggregator** portlet in the page, "**Blogs**", of the **Book Lovers** Community where you want to show the latest posts.

2. Click on the **Configuration** icon of the portlet.

3. By default, the "**Setup**" tab is selected. You can select an **Organization** such as the "**Editorial Department**".

4. Select the **Display Style**, such as "**Abstract**". Other **Display Styles** are also available: "**Body and Image**", "**Body**", "**Abstract and Image**", "**Title**".

5. Select **Maximum Items to Display**, say,"**20**".

6. Click on the **Save** button when you are ready.

Surely, you can select other **Organizations** such as the "**Engineering Department**". The **Blogs Aggregator** portlet will show the latest posts from all the posts of the **Engineering Department** at the **Book Lovers** community. You can also remove the **Organization,** if needed. In this case, the portlet will show the latest posts from all the posts of any department at the **Book Lovers** community.

In general, the **Blogs Aggregator** portlet shows the latest posts from all the posts of any department at the **Book Lovers** community, and moreover, it exposes an aggregated RSS feed.

Building Blogs

We have discussed how to create an **Entry** such as "**How to write computer book**". The content of the **Entry** is simple but contains image and text with centre alignment. How do we align text, insert image and so on? These functions are related to the HTML text editor.

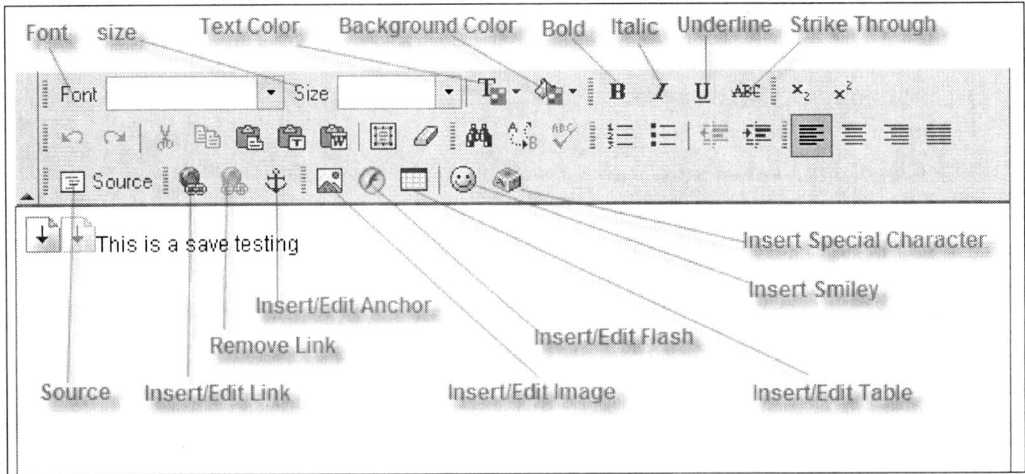

Liferay integrates FCKeditor as the default HTML text editor. Of course, it is possible that as an administrator, you can integrate other HTML editors in Liferay. Here, we just use FCKeditor as an example to build the contents of the **Blogs' Entries**.

FCKeditor is a web-based HTML text editor with powerful formatting capabilities. It brings to the web much of the power of desktop editors such as MS Word. Moreover, it's lightweight and doesn't require any kind of installation on the client computer. URL: `http://www.fckeditor.net/`.

Let's consider the following use cases about HTML text editor:

- Use general functions on text: **Font, size**, alignment, **Color, Background Color**, copy, paste, list, and so on. You can use them easily.
- Insert an image.
- Insert links.
- Insert **Flash, Table, Smiley** and **Special Characters**.
- Edit **Source** directly.

Inserting Image

You can insert an image, either as an internal image (from Image Gallery) or as an external image (an URL outside of Liferay Portals). For example, if you want to insert an image with URL "`http://liferay.cignex.com/cignex-logo.png`" in the **Entry, "How to write computer book**", do the following:

1. Click on the **Edit** icon below the title, "**How to write computer book**".

2. Locate the position where you want to insert an image.

3. Click the **Insert/Edit** image in HTML Text Editor.

4. Enter a URL (External Image, by inputting URL and properties), say "`http://liferay.cignex.com/cignex-logo.png`".

5. Click the **OK** button when you are ready.

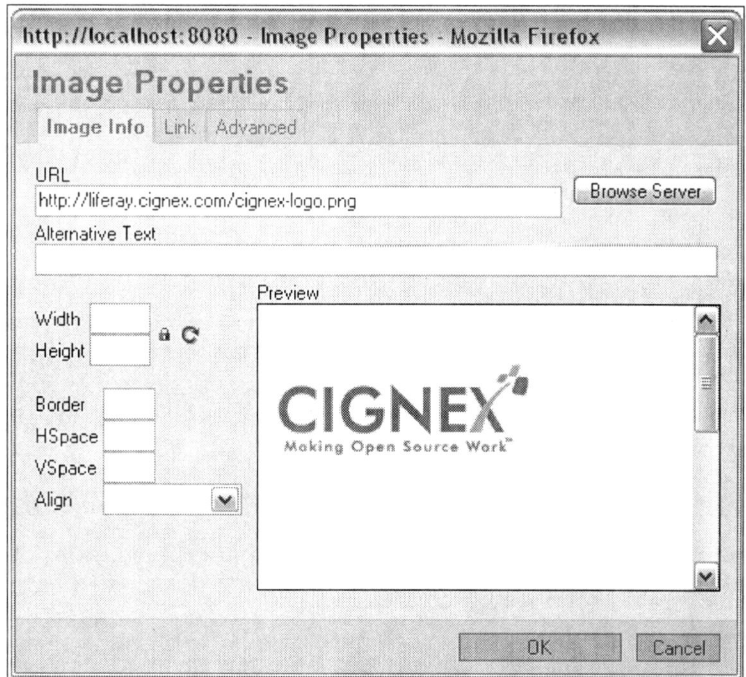

You can also insert an image, which is an internal image (from the Image Gallery) as follows:

1. Click on the **Edit** icon below the title "**How to write computer book**".

2. Locate the position where you want to insert an image.

3. Click the **Insert/Edit** image in HTML Text Editor.

4. Click the **Browse Server** (Internal Image) button.

5. Click the **Create New Folder** to add folder under the current folder.

Any folders or images that are added here will be placed in the Image Gallery. The Image Gallery provides a centralized repository for images to be stored and it also provides a unique URL for each image.

1. Type the name of the new folder and click **OK**.

2. Click on the newly created folder to add an image to it.

3. Click the **Browse** button and select an image.

4. Click the **Upload** button to add the image to the folder.

5. Click on the image and click **OK** to add the image to the document.

6. Click **Save** button to save the updates.

In addition, you can insert an image or a flash or a document link from alfresco repository. It is called full RESTful integration between Liferay and Alfresco. In this case, Alfresco is used as a repository of Liferay. For more details, refer to Chapter 13.

Inserting Links

You can also insert internal links and external links. For example, if you want to insert a link with URL "`http://liferay.cignex.com/cignex/Liferay-Full-Integration.doc`" in the **Entry, "How to write computer book"**, you can do the following:

1. Click on the **Edit** icon below the title, "**How to write computer book**".

2. Locate the position where you want to insert a link.

3. Select text and click **Insert/Edit** link.

4. You can add an URL directly (for external links) such as `http://liferay.cignex.com/cignex/Liferay-Full-Integration.doc`.

5. Click on the **OK** button if you are ready.

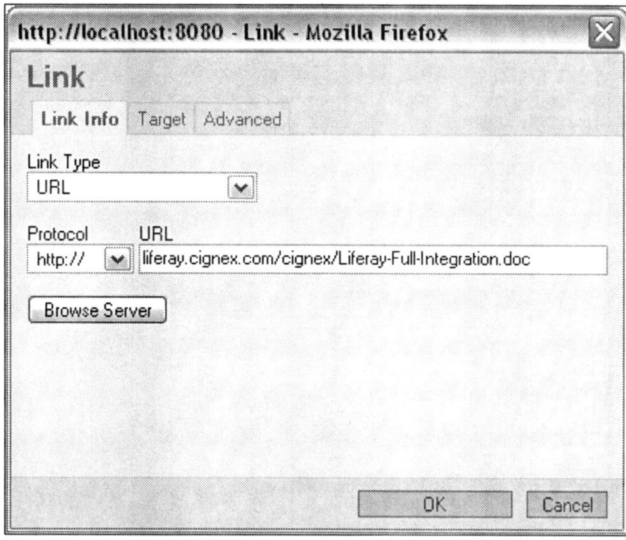

The internal links refer to any links in Liferay Portals, such as images in Image Gallery, documents in Document Library and pages. There are three types of resources related to internal links: document, image, and page. The external links refer to any links outside of Liferay Portals, where link types are URL, Link to anchor in the text, and Email. Protocols would be http, https, news, ftp, and others (internal URL, such as "/c/ document_library/get_file?folderId=10955&name=DLFE-109.gif") if link type is URL.

Link to A Document

If you need to link to a document, do the following:

1. In the **Resource Type** menu, select **Document**.

2. To link to a new document, select a **Community** in which the document will be stored.

3. Click **Create New Folder**. Any documents added here will be placed in the Document Library.

4. Enter the name of the new folder.

5. Click on the newly created folder to add a document to it. Click the **Browse** button and locate the document.

6. Click the **Upload** button to add the document to the folder.

7. Click on the document and click the **OK** button to link the document with the selected text.

Link to A Page

You may need to link to a page, say "**web/guest/home**". You can do it as follows:

1. In the **Resource Type** menu, select **Page**.
2. Select the Community where the page is located.
3. Click on the page that you want to link the selected text to, such as "**web/guest/home**".
4. Click **OK** to link the page with the selected text.

Link to An Image

You may need to link to an image. You can do it as follows:

1. In the **Resource Type** menu, select **Image**.
2. Select the **Community** either where the image is located, or where it will be stored.
3. If the image is stored in the system, click on the image to link with the selected text and click **OK**.
4. To link to a new image, select a folder to upload the image to, or click **Create New Folder** to add a new folder to place the image in. Any images added here will be placed in the Document Library.
5. If you are using an existing folder, skip to step **Upload.**
6. Enter the name of the new folder.
7. Click on the newly created folder to add an image to it.
8. Click **Browse** and locate the image.
9. Click **Upload** to add the image to the folder.
10. Click on the image and click **OK** to link the image with the selected text.

Insert Flashes, Tables, Smiley And Special Characters

You can insert/edit a flash as follows:

1. Locate the position where the flash will be inserted.
2. Click **Insert/Edit Flash** in HTML Text Editor.
3. Enter a URL (of flash, by inputting URL and properties) at the **Info** tab; optionally, enter details at the **Advanced** tab. The HTML Text Editor will transfer data from the related URL.

4. To edit a flash, locate the flash first. Then right click to open **Flash Properties**.

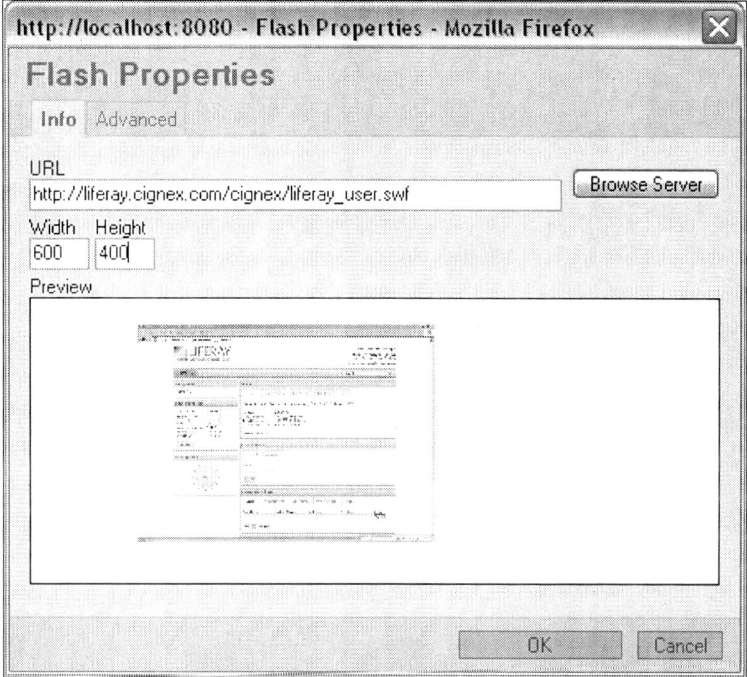

Similarly, you can insert/edit a table as follows:

1. Locate the position where the table will be inserted.
2. Click **Insert/Edit Table** in HTML Text Editor.
3. To edit a table locate the table first. Then, right click to open **Table Properties**.

In addition, you can **Insert/Edit Smiley**, which is a set of icons, as follows:

1. Locate the position where the smiley will be inserted.
2. Click **Insert/Edit Smiley** in HTML Text Editor.
3. To edit smiley, locate **Smiley** icon first. Then, right click to open **Image Properties**.

You can insert/edit special character as follows:

1. Locate the position where the special character will be inserted.
2. Click **Insert Special Character** in HTML Text Editor.
3. To edit the special character, locate the table first. Then cut, copy, or paste it.

What is flash? Flash here refers to SWF, which is a proprietary vector graphics file format.

Editing Source

For advanced users, you can edit HTML source. To edit source directly, you simply click on the **Source** button. The following table shows possible HTML tags and examples for editing **Source** manually.

Action	HTML Tag	Examples
Insert Image	`<img>`	`<img src="/image/image_gallery?img_id=11138"/>`
Link to a document	`<a>`	`<a href="/c/document_library/get_file?folderId=10955&name=DLFE-109.gif" />`
Link to an image	`<a>`	`<a href="/image/image_gallery?img_id=11138" />`
Link to a page	`<a>`	`<a href ="/web/guest/home" />`
Insert Flash	`<embed>`	`<embed width="600" height="400" type="application/x-shockwave-flash" pluginspage="http://www.macromedia.com/go/getflashplayer" src="http://liferay.cignex.com/cignex/liferay_user.swf" play="true" loop="true" menu="true"></embed>`
Insert Smiley	`<img>`	`<img src="/html/js/editor/fckeditor/editor/images/smiley/msn/regular_smile.gif" />`
Insert Table	`<table>`	`<table width="200" cellspacing="1" cellpadding="1" border="1"><tbody> <tr><td> </td><td> </td></tr></tbody></table>`
Insert Special Character	none	`"@"`

Working with RSS

As an administrator, you may need to include formatted data (news) from external Really Simple Syndication (**RSS**) feeds. For example, you want to add **CNN** news feed (such as, `http://rss.cnn.com/rss/cnn_world.rss`) and **BBC** news feeds (such as, `http://newsrss.bbc.co.uk/rss/newsonline_world_edition/front_page/rss.xml`) in the page "**News**" under the **Page** "**Community**" at the **Book Lovers** Community. Whenever that RSS XML file is updated on the remote site, the page will reflect those updates on the next portal page reload.

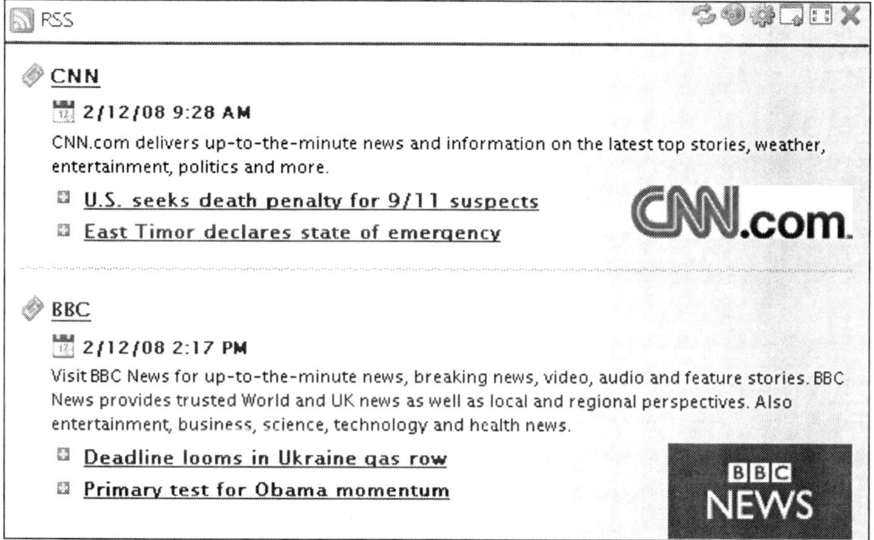

Let's add the **RSS** portlet at the page "**News**" first:

1. Add a child **Page** called "**News**" of the **Page** "**Community**" at the **Book Lovers** Community **Public Pages**.

2. Add the **RSS** portlet in the page "**News**" of the **Book Lovers** Community where you want to manage RSS feeds, if **RSS** portlet is not already present.

How to get the displayed news? You need to configure the **RSS** portlet as follows:

1. To set the feeds that you want displayed, click on the **Configuration** icon first at the top of the **RSS** portlet.

2. By default, the tab **Setup** is selected.

3. To add a feed, click on the **Add** icon first, then input title such as "CNN" and URL such as "`http://rss.cnn.com/rss/cnn_world.rss`".

4. To add another feed, click on the **Add** icon first; then input title such as "**BBC**" and URL such as `"http://newsrss.bbc.co.uk/rss/newsonline_world_edition/front_page/rss.xml"`.

5. To delete a feed, locate the feed and click on the **Delete** icon to the right of the feed.

6. To edit a feed, locate the feed, and click on the title and/or URL; change the title and URL as you want.

7. Select the **number of Entries Per Feed,** say "**4**" that you want displayed.

8. Click on the **Save** button to save the changes, and click on **Return to Full Page** arrow to return.

Of course, you can use other news feeds. In a word, to add a feed, simply click on **Add** icon first; then input the title and the URL.

Using News Portlet

As an administrator of "Palm Tree Publication", you may need to retrieve RSS news feed, such as "**International relations**" and "**Top stories**". Let's do it as follows:

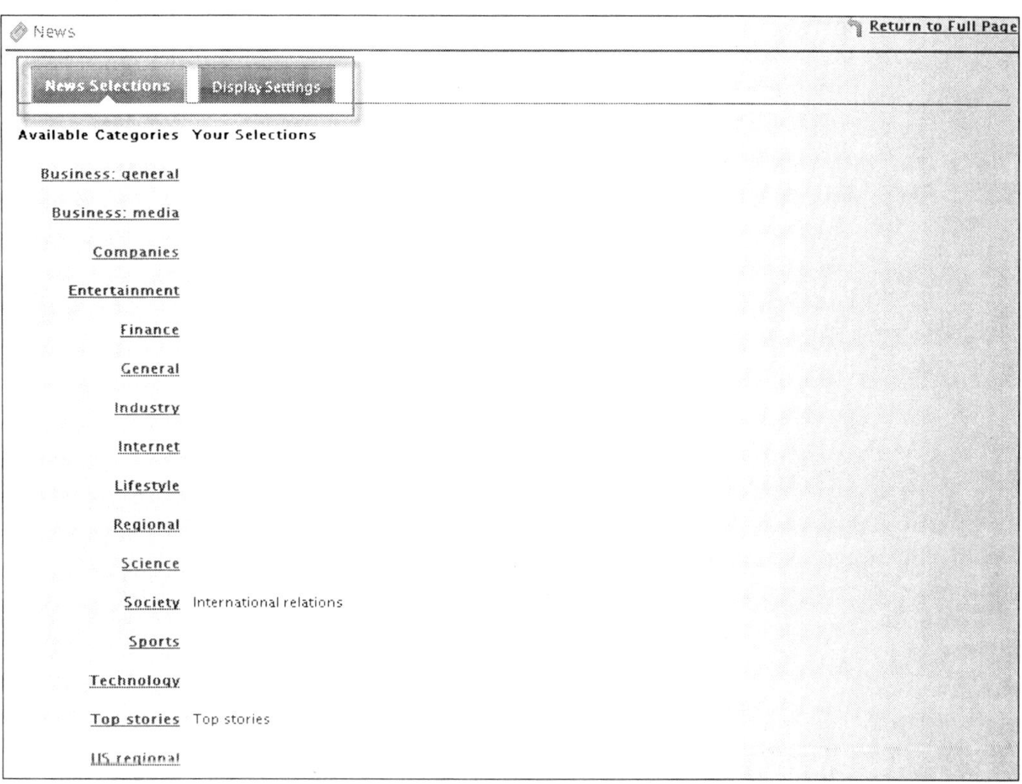

1. If **News** portlet is not already present, add the **News** portlet to the **Page** "News", under the page "**Community**" where you need it.

2. To set the news that you want displayed in the **News** portlet, click on the **Preferences** icon first.

3. To select news, click one of the available categories such as "**Society**", and select multiple items such as "**International relations**" at the **News Selection** tab.

4. To select other news, click one of the available categories such as "**Top stories**", and select multiple items such as "**Top stories**", at the **News Selection** tab.

5. Click on the **Save** button to save the changes, and click on **Return to Full Page** arrow, to return.

6. To remove a selection, locate the selection under the **Display Setting** tab, and click on the **Delete** icon to the right of the box.

7. To change the order of selections, locate the selection under the **Display Setting** tab, and click on the **Move Up** or **Move Down** icon to the right of the box.

8. Select the **number of Entries Per Feed** under the **Display Setting** tab.

9. Click on the **Save** button to save the changes, and click on **Back** arrow to return.

The **News** Portlet retrieves a RSS news feed, based on a URL, and displays it as HTML to the user. By default, Moreover Technologies is used as the news provider.

Moreover Technologies is the premier provider of real-time news, current awareness and business information—pioneering the way online news is gathered, refined, categorized and delivered. URL: `http://w.moreover.com/categories/category_list.tsv2`.

Using Weather Portlet

As an administrator at "Palm Tree Publication", you may need to show the latest weather message in the **page, "News"** under the **page, "Community"**. Since the enterprise has two locations: US (San Jose city) and Germany (Frankfurt/main city), the latest weather message about both US (San Jose city) and Germany (Frankfurt/main city) is required in the page, "**News**". At same time, we want to know the latest weather message about other cities, such as Rome (Italy), Zurich (Switzerland) and Beijing (China). Let's do it as follows:

1. If the **Weather** portlet is not already present, add the **Weather** portlet to the page, "**News**" under the **page, "Community"** where you need it.

2. To set the city or zip code that you want displayed in the portlet, click on the **Preferences icon.**

3. Enter one city or zip code per line. For example, 94043; Frankfurt/main Germany; Rome, Italy; Zurich, Switzerland; and Beijing, China.

4. Select temperature format, such as **Fahrenheit** and **Celsius**. Here, we select **Fahrenheit** which is default.

5. Click on the **Save** button to save the changes and finally, click on **Return to Full Page** arrow to return.

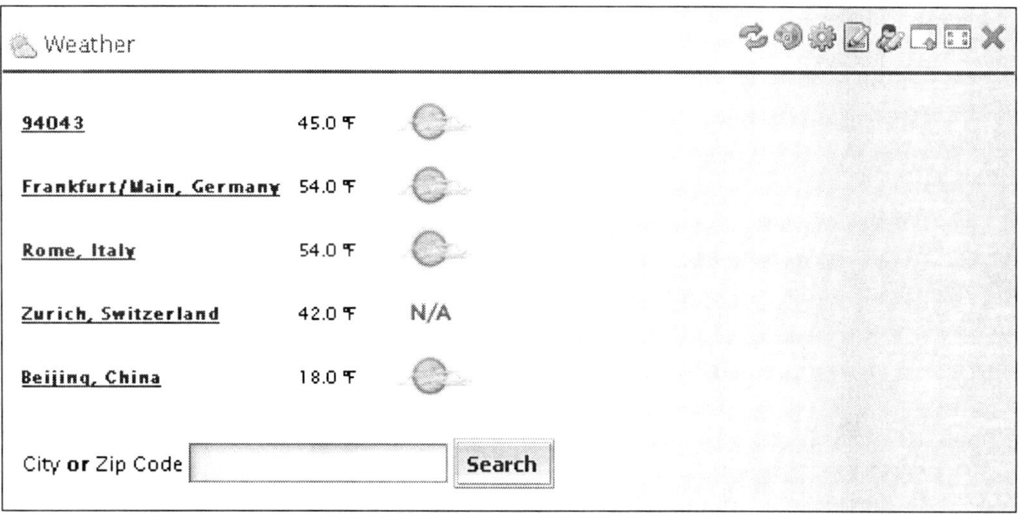

Of course, you can show the latest weather message about other cities around the World. Liferay **Weather** Portlet provides the ability to display the temperature and weather on a portal page. **Weather** portlet displays temperature and weather information for a given zip code or city. **Users** may also query temperatures and weather for alternate zip codes or city without any customization. By default, the Weather Channel is used as a weather message provider to bring the breaking weather to its viewers and users.

The Weather Channel (also TWC) is a U.S. cable and satellite television network that broadcasts weather forecasts and weather-related news 24 hours a day. URL: **http://weather.com**.

Using RSS Effectively

Generally speaking, a web feed is a XML-based document containing content items with web links to longer versions. For example, common sources for web feeds may include news websites, blogs, and structured information such as weather data, "top ten" lists of hit tunes to search results, and so on. **RSS** and **Atom** are two main web-feed formats.

The Atom applies to two standards (refer to RSS Specification at `http://www.rss-specifications.com`). The Atom Syndication Format (ASF) is an XML language used for web feeds and the Atom Publishing Protocol (APP) is a HTTP-based protocol for creating and updating Web resources.

In general, RSS is used to refer to the following formats:

- Really Simple Syndication (RSS 2.0)
- RDF Site Summary (RSS 1.0 and RSS 0.90)
- Rich Site Summary (RSS 0.91)

There are three formats of syndication that have emerged: RSS 2.0, RSS 1.0, and Atom. Which feed format do we choose? In general, the three formats are for three different goals:

- RSS 2.0 — This is the simplest format (although extensible) available, to display links on articles of a site.
- RSS 1.0 — to get information on the feed.
- Atom — requires special software to process, and has more requirements about format of data.

In short, RSS is a XML-based web content syndication format, compliant to the XML 1.0 specification.

RSS Specification

RSS, not a perfect format, is very popular and widely supported. Here, we briefly introduce RSS 2.0 specification.

For more details related RSS specification, refer to the URL `http://www.rss-specifications.com/rss-specifications.htm`.

A RSS document has an element `<rss>` with an attribute version at the top level. The attribute version specifies the version of RSS that the document conforms to. Subordinate to the **<rss>** element is a single element **<channel>**, which contains information about the channel and its contents.

The following table depicts a list of the required channel elements, each with a brief description (refer to RSS Specification at `http://www.rss-specifications.com/`):

Element	Description
Title	The name of the channel.
Link	The URL link to the website corresponding to the channel.
Description	Phrase or sentence describing the channel.
Item	One item tag at least, for the content.

For example,

```
<rss version="2.0">
<channel>
    <title>Integration</title>
    <link>http://liferay.cignex.com/</link>
    <description>LDAP, SSO, Liferay and Alfresco Full integration
</description>
    <item>
    </item>
</channel>
</rss>
```

A channel may contain any number of items. An item represents content. The description is a synopsis of the content, while the link points to the full content.

For example:

```
<item>
        <title>Liferay and Alfresco - RESTFul Integration</title>
        <link>http://liferay.cignex.com/sesame</link>
        <description>Integration based on REST</description>
</item>
```

How It Works

Suppose there are web pages, which we want other websites to display. The set of pages is the RSS feed. The RSS system, which publishes articles and news, over the web, works as follows:

- An XML file defines the RSS feed, which holds URL, title and summary of each page to display.

- A **User**, who wants to read the feed on his computer, uses an RSS reader or its browser, and just adds the feed with the proper command of its software.

- Or a **User** displays the feed in a website — loading the RSS file from the provider, by extracting the URL of pages, and displaying titles and summaries.

- On visiting the website of the receiver, the script is launched first; it recalls the RSS file from the provider's website and displays a list of news from the extracted data.

- Visitors display a page from the provider by clicking on the title of the list.

Summary

This chapter has introduced to us how **Entries** in **Blogs**, are added, how they are managed (for example, view, update and delete), and how **Comments** are added on a given **Entry** of **Blogs**. Then it discussed how to use **Permission** on the **Blogs** portlet and **Entries** in **Blogs**. It also introduced ways to publish **Blogs** by **Recent Bloggers** and using **Blogs Aggregator** portlets, and to build **Blogs** with WYSIWGs editor. Finally, it discussed **RSS** and related portlets such as **RSS**, **News** and **Weather** portlets.

7
Shared Calendars, WSRP And Workflow

In the intranet website "book.com" of "Palm Tree Publications", we are required to provide calendar information to **Users** and share calendar among **Users** from different departments. At the same time, we are also required to provide workflow ability so that normal **Users** can submit requests, and the manager can take decisions based on these requests. Moreover, we are required to publish third party contents in the intranet website.

This chapter introduces calendar portlet to create, manage and search events, and to share calendar. Furthermore, it introduces workflow integration, WSRP (Web Services for Remote Portlets) proxy and other portlets.

By the end of this chapter, you will have learnt how to:

- Create, manage, and search events in calendar
- Share calendar by iCalendar
- Deploy workflows
- Manage workflow definitions
- Manage instances and tasks
- Employ WSRP
- Use other portlets such as web proxy, IFrame and flash

Working with Calendar

As an administrator at "Palm Tree Publications", you need to satisfy the basic business requirements incorporated in a featured business intranet such as scheduling meetings, sending meeting invitations, checking for attendees' availability and so on. Thus, you may need to provide an environment for **Users** to manage events, and share calendar at the **Page "Calendar"** under the **Page "Community"** of the **Book Lovers** community.

Adding Events

First of all, let's add an **Event**, "**Monday Meeting**", at the **Book Lovers** community as follows:

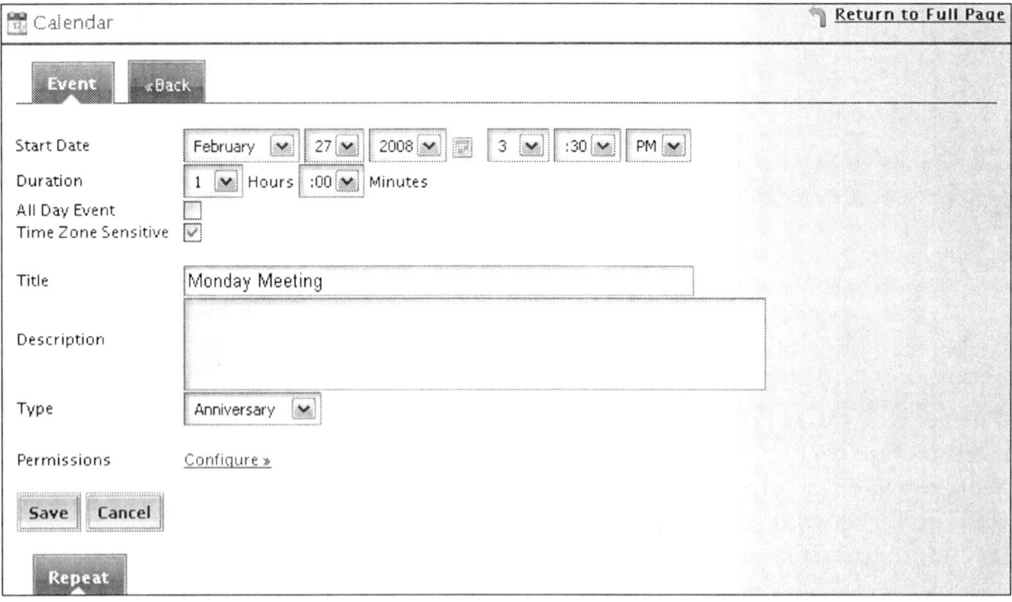

1. Add a **Page** named "**Calendar**" under the **Page, "Community"**, of the **Book Lovers** community.

2. Add the **Calendar** portlet in the **Page, "Calendar"**, of the **Book Lovers** Community where you want to manage **Events** and share **Calendar**, if **Calendar** portlet is not already present.

3. Click on the **Add Event** button.

4. Enter **Title** such as "**Monday Meeting**", **Description** such as "**First Meeting**", **Start Date, Duration, Type** such as "**Meeting**", and so on.

5. Set **Permissions** by clicking on the **Configure icon**.

6. To configure additional **Permissions**, click on the **More link**.

7. Select **Repeat Style** and **Reminder Style**.

8. Click the **Save** button to save the inputs.

9. The **Repeat Style** could be **Never (Do not repeat this event), Daily, Weekly, Monthly and Yearly.**

10. You can set up reminding style as, remind me, 15 minutes and again 5 minutes before the event by using any of the following: **Do not send a reminder, Email Address** (such as **admin@book.com**), **SMS, AIM, ICQ, MSN,** and **YM**. The minutes are configurable, say 30 minutes and again 15 minutes before the event.

Default **Event** Types include: **Anniversary, Appointment, Bill Payment, Birthday, Breakfast, Call, Chat, Class, Club-Event, Concert, Dinner, Event, Graduation, Happy-hour, Holiday, Interview, Lunch, Meeting, Movie, Net-event, Other, Party, Performance, Press-release, Reunion, Sports-event, Travel, TV show, Vacation, Wedding,** and so on. The **Types** of **Events** are configurable.

To reset the list of **Event Types**, simply change the portal properties directly as follows. Note that the display text of each of the **Event Types** is set in content language properties.

```
calendar.event.types = anniversary, etc.
```

Of course, you can add other **Events**. After adding an **Event "Having Fun Party"**, you can view **Events** as shown in the following figure.

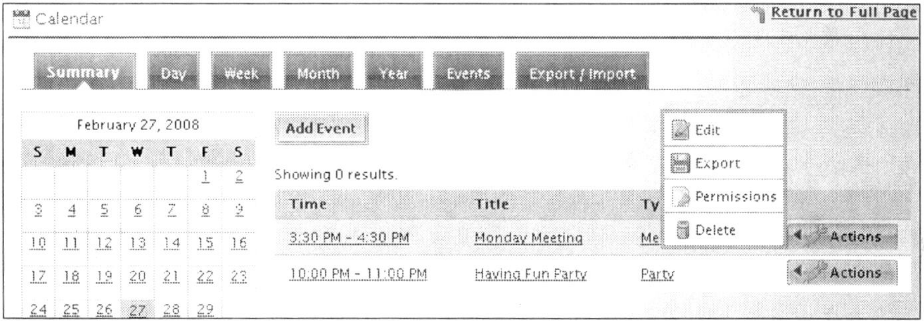

Managing Events

The Calendar portlet helps the portal users manage **Events** easily on the web. It helps in the rapid development of your **Community,** and gives your enterprise a platform to easily manage **Calendar Events** and shared calendar.

View Events

Events are viewable in various ways. **Calendar Events** are displayed by **Summary** view as **Event Time, Title, Type,** and a set of icons: **Edit, Export, Permissions,** and **Delete.** By default, this portlet will display all **Events,** which belong to the current day for current **User** having proper **Permissions.** The current month calendar is displayed on the left side and the current day is highlighted.

Normally, to view all **Events**, simply click on the **Events** tab as shown in the following figure. This portlet will display all **Events** for the current **User** having proper **Permissions**.

Similarly, to view **Events** by day, simple click on the **Day** tab. This portlet will display day-based events of the current week for the current **User** having proper **Permissions**. You can filter the **Events** by **Types**: **All Events** or one type such as **Meeting**. Or change **Day** by clicking on the left-arrow to decrease day or right-arrow to increase day.

Again, to view events by week, simply click on the **Week** tab as shown in the following figure. This portlet will display week-based events of the current month for the current **User** having proper **Permissions**. You can also filter the **Events** by **Types**: **All Events** or one **Type** such as **Party**. Or change **Week** by clicking on the left-arrow to decrease week period, or right-arrow to increase week period.

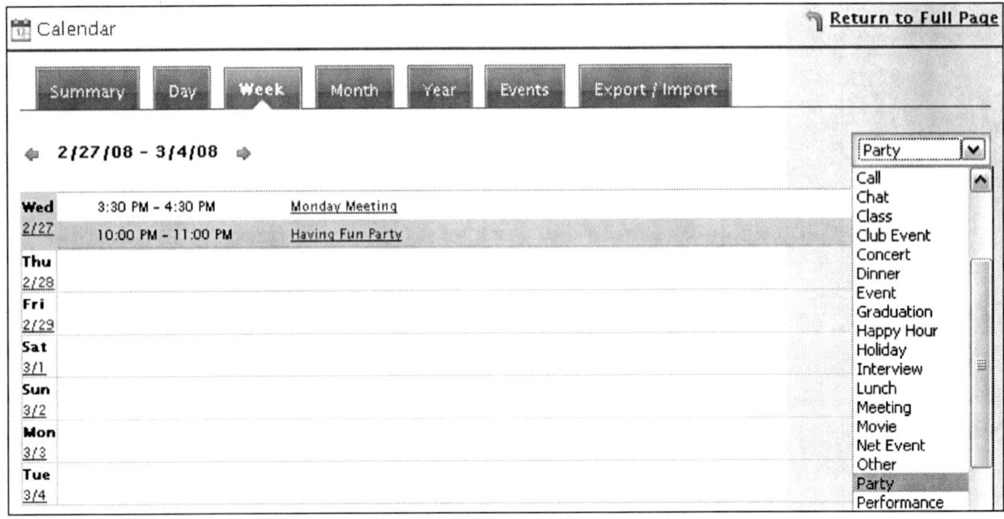

Once more, to view events by month, simply click on the **Month** tab. This portlet will display month-based events of the current year for the current **User** having proper **Permissions**. To change the **Month**, click on the left-arrow to decrease month number, or the right-arrow to increase month number.

To view events by the year, simply click on the **Year** tab. This portlet will display year-based events for the current **User** having proper **Permissions**. To change **Year**, click on the left-arrow to decrease year number, or the right-arrow to increase year number.

Edit An Event

Events are updatable. We have an **Event** called "**Having Fun Party**" currently. But now, we want to change the **Description** from "**a party**" to "**This is a special party for Lotti Stein**". Let's do it as follows:

1. Select the **Events** tab in the **Calendar** portlet.
2. Locate an **Event** such as "**Having Fun Party**" in the **Calendar** portlet, and click on the **Edit** icon from the **Actions** next to the event.
3. Update **Description** with value "**This is a special party for Lotti Stein**".
4. Maintain other values.
5. Click **Save** button to save the inputs.

Delete An Event

Events are removable. We have an **Event** called "**Having Fun Party**" currently. But for some reason, this **Event** is not wanted anymore. We have to delete this **Event**. Let's delete this **Event** as follows:

1. Locate an **Event** such as "**Having Fun Party**" that you want to delete.
2. Click the **Delete** icon from the **Actions** located next to the event.
3. A screen will appear asking if you want to delete this.
4. Click the **OK** button to confirm delete action.

Note that deleting an **Event** will delete all related information that belongs to this **Event**.

Export/Import Events

Events are importable and exportable. As an administrator, you may have to import and export **Events** in the **Calendar** portlet. Let's do it as follows (see the following figure):

1. Select the **Export/Import** tab.

2. Input the **Export** file name.

3. Click the **Export** button to export **Events** to the given file.

4. Input a file name for importing, or click the **Browse ...** button to upload a file from the local machine.

5. Click the **Import** button to import **Events** to the portlet.

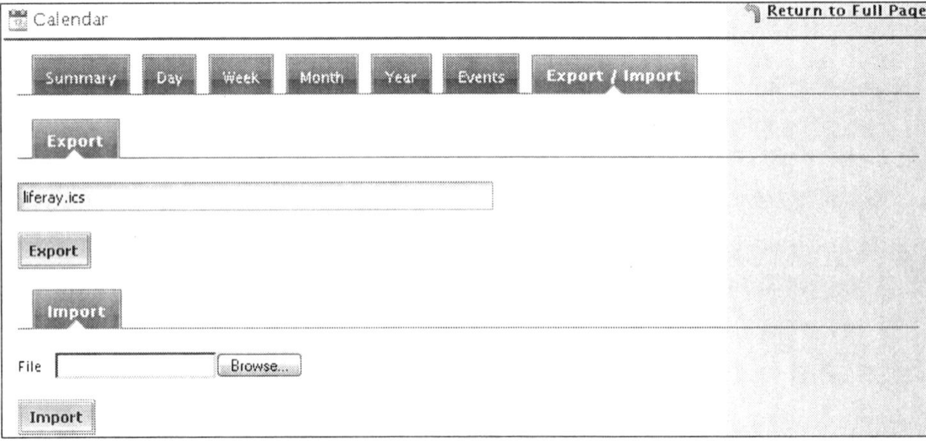

Liferay provides the ability to **Import** and **Export Events** from the **Calendar** portlet.

Setting up Email

As stated earlier, the system can remind you 15 minutes and again 5 minutes before the **Event** through email. As an administrator, you can change the email setting such as **Email From** and the **Event Reminder Email**. Let's do it as follows:

1. Click the **Configuration** icon on the upper right of the calendar portlet.

2. With the **Setup** tab selected, the **Name** and **Address** boxes appear under the tab, **Email From**. Change **Name** and **Address** that you want to update such as **Palm Tree** and **admin@book.com**.

3. Click the **Save** button to save the changes.

4. Select the **Event Reminder Email** tab to change the **Event** reminder email.

5. Click the **Save** button to save the changes.

6. If in need, click on the arrow, **Return to Full Page,** to return.

Your **Event Reminder Email** may have the following format:

Dear [TO_NAME],

This is an autogenerated email for the [$PORTLET_NAME$] portlet.

Your event with the title [$EVENT_TITLE$] will start at [$EVENT_START_DATE$].

Sincerely,

[$FROM_NAME$]

[$FROM_ADDRESS$]

http://[$PORTAL_URL$]

Sharing Calendar

We have used default setting for the **Calendar** portlet in the **Page**, "Calendar", under the **Page** "Community" at the **Book Lovers** Community. When the administrator,"**Palm Tree**", logs in, he/she will see the button, **Add Event**, as mentioned earlier. As we know, the **User** "**Lotti Stein**" is also a member of the **Book Lovers** community. Try to log in as "**Lotti Stein**", and you will see that there is no button, **Add Event**. Furthermore, you see the **Events** with one action icon, **Export**.

What's happening? This is something related to **Permissions**. In order to share **Calendar**, we have to consider two levels of **Permissions**, **Permissions** portlet and **Permissions** on Events.

Use Portlet Permissions

The following table shows **Permissions** for the **Calendar** portlet. A **Community User** may set up all **Permissions** (marked 'X'), **View**, **Configuration**, **Add Event** and **Export All Events**, whereas a **Guest User** may have **Permissions**, **View**, **Configuration** and **Export All Events**. By default, a **Community** has **View** action (marked '*'), and so does a **Guest User**.

Action	Description	Community	Guest
View	Views this portlet	X, *	X, *
Configuration	Configures **Permissions** for this portlet	X	X
Add Event	Adds an **Event** in this portlet	X	
Export All Events	Exports all **Events** from this portlet	X	X

Obviously, as a **User** of **Book Lovers** Community, "**Lotti Stein**" has only **View** **Permissions** on the **Calendar** portlet, by default. Since the **Book Lovers** community has no **Permission, Add Event,** "**Lotti Stein**" too has no **Permission, Add Event.**

As an administrator, you may need to set up the **Community Users** having **Permission, Add Event,** as well as **Permission, View,** on the **Calendar** portlet. That is, you need to add **Permission,Add Event,** on the **Calendar** portlet at the **Book Lovers** community. Let's do it as follows:

1. Click on the **Configuration** icon to the top-right of the **Calendar** portlet.
2. Then click on the **Permissions** tab.
3. Select the **Community** tab.
4. Select **Permission Add Event,** in the **Available** box.
5. Click on the **Add** arrow.
6. Click on the **Save** button if you are ready.

Permissions On Events

The following table shows **Permissions** for an **Event**. A **Community User** may set up **Permissions** (marked 'X'), **View, Delete, Permissions,** and **Update,** while a **Guest User** may set up **Permissions, View, Delete,** and **Permissions.** By default, a **Community User** has the **Permission** action (marked '*') **View,** and so does a **Guest User:**

Action	Description	Community	Guest
View	View the **event**	X, *	X, *
Delete	Delete the **event**	X	X
Permissions	Configure **permissions** for the **event**	X	X
Update	Update the **event**	X	

Obviously, as a **User** of the **Book Lovers** Community, "**Lotti Stein**" has only **View** **Permissions** on the **Events,** by default. Since the **Book Lovers** community has only the **Permission, View,** "**Lotti Stein**" too has only the **Permission,View.**

As an administrator, you may need to set up the **Community Users** having **Permission, Update,** as well as **Permission, View,** on the **Event, "Monday Meeting"**. That is, you need to add **Permission, Update,** on the **Event**. Let's do it as follows:

1. With the **Events** Tab selected, locate the **Event Monday Meeting**.

2. Then click the **Permissions** icon from the **Actions** next to the event.

3. Select the **Community** tab.

4. Select **Permissions Update,** in the **Available** box.

5. Click on the **Add** arrow.

6. Click on the **Save** button, if you are ready.

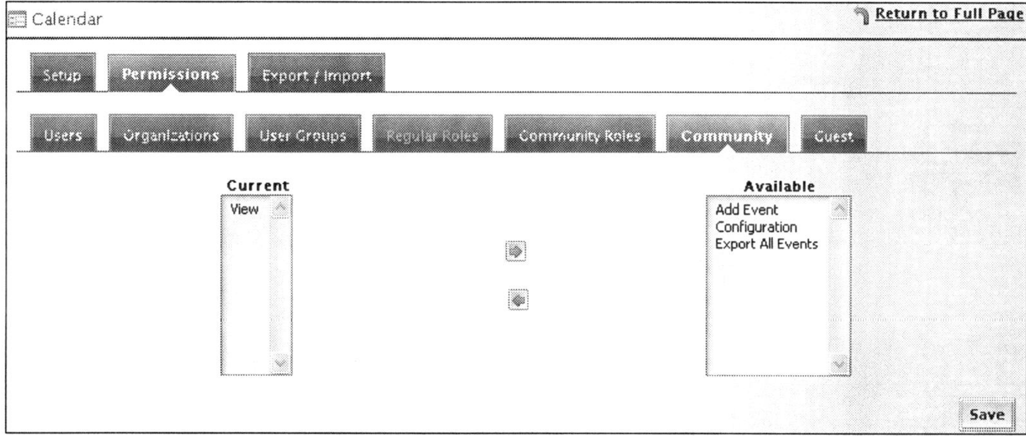

Now as a **User** of **Book Lovers** Community, "**Lotti Stein**" has **Permissions, Update** and **Export,** on the **Event, "Monday Meeting"**. Try to log in as "**Lotti Stein**", and you will see the **Actions** button with icons (**Edit** and **Export**) next to the **Event, "Monday Meeting"**. But you see only one icon, "**Export**", next to the **Event, "Having Fun Party"**, since the **Permissions** have been set up by default settings (only **Permission "View"**).

Using iCalendar Effectively

Liferay **Calendar** portlet provides the ability to display calendar information and allows **Users** to create, manage, and search for **Events**. By this portlet, we can share **Events** across **Communities**, and set up event reminders to alert **Users** of upcoming **Events** through email, IM, or SMS (refer to more details at `http://www.wirelessdevnet.com/channels/sms/features/sms.html`). Liferay **Calendar** portlet has the following features:

- Support shared calendar—you can keep track of group-based events.

- Support Micro-format—you can transfer your calendar and **User** information via Web 2.0 standards. Data in micro-formats (hCard, hCalendar, and so on) could be easily used by and integrated with third-party applications.

- Support Calendaring—both iCal and Exchange, providing flexible import and export of **Events**.

hCalendar is a simple, open, distributed calendaring and **Events** format, based on the iCalendar standard (RFC2445), suitable for embedding in XHTML, Atom, RSS, and arbitrary XML; while hCard is a simple, open, distributed format for representing people, companies, organizations, and places, using a 1:1 representation of vCard (RFC2426) properties and values in semantic XHTML, also suitable for embedding in XHTML, Atom, RSS, and arbitrary XML.

Liferay Calendar portlet supports iCalendar Standards. iCalendar is a standard (Requests for Comments—RFC 2445) for calendar data exchange. By this, **Users** can send event-based requests and tasks to other **Users** through email, while recipients of the iCalendar email can respond to the sender easily.

With a common data format, we can use iCalendar standard to store information about calendar-specific data such as to-do lists, appointments, events, and so on. Most of the popular calendaring tools, such as Lotus Notes, Outlook, Google Calendar, Zimbra and Apple's iCal also support the iCalendar standard.

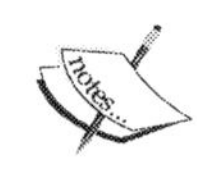

Request for Comments (RFC) documents are a series of memoranda encompassing new research, innovations, and methodologies applicable to Internet technologies. Refer to URL `http://www.rfc-editor.org/`

Use Core Object

In iCalendar, the core object (or called top-level object) is a collection of calendaring and scheduling information (refer to RFC2445 at `http://www.ietf.org/rfc/rfc2445.txt`. Normally, this information consists of a single iCalendar object. But it is possible to group multiple iCalendar objects together.

It must start with "`BEGIN: VCALENDAR`", and end with "`END: VCALENDAR`". The contents are called the "`i-cal-body`", consisting of a sequence of calendar properties, and one or more calendar components. The calendar properties (that is, attributes) apply to the calendar as a whole. The calendar components refer to collections of properties expressing a particular calendar semantic. For instance, a calendar component may specify an event, or free/busy time information, or an alarm, or a to-do list, and so on.

Here is a simple example:

```
BEGIN:VCALENDAR
VERSION:2.0
PRODID:-//PALM TREE PUBLICATIONS//EN
BEGIN:VEVENT
DTSTART:20081014T170000Z
DTEND:20081015T035959Z
SUMMARY: Day Editorial Party
END:VEVENT
END:VCALENDAR
```

There are many different types of components defined in the standard as described in the following table (refer to RFC2445 at `http://www.ietf.org/rfc/rfc2445.txt`).

Object	Names	Description
VEVENT	Events	Describes an event that represents a scheduled amount of time on a calendar.
VTODO	To-do	Describes a to-do item, that is, an action-item or assignment.
VJOURNAL	Journal entry	Describes a journal entry.
VFREEBUSY	Free/busy time	Describes either a request for free/busy time, a response to a request, or describes a published set of busy time.
VTIMEZONE	Time zone	Defines time zones.
VALARM	Alarms	Defines alarms.

Note that some components may include other components (VALARM is often included in other components), and some components are often defined to support other components defined after them (VTIMEZONE is often used this way).

Especially, under the VTODO, the UID field facilitates distribution of updates, that is, a scheduled event change. A type of globally unique identifier (UID) is generated when the event is generated first. If a later event is distributed with the same UID, it means the original one is replaced. An example UID might be **"Y2008S3C121M4@book.com"**, for the 4th meeting of class 121 in semester 3 at "Palm Tree Publications".

Exchange Data

The iCalendar format describes calendar-based data such as **Events**. But it does not describe what to do with that data. Thus, other protocols are in need to implement actions to be done with this data. In general, the iCalendar format supports interoperability of calendar data, while the features are widely supported by iCalendar implementations.

iCalendar Transport-Independent Interoperability (I-TIP) (RFC 2446) defines a protocol to exchange iCalendar objects for the purposes of group calendaring, and scheduling between "Calendar Users" (CUs). It defines a set of methods such as PUBLISH, REQUEST, REPLY, ADD, CANCEL, REFRESH, COUNTER and DECLINE-COUNTER (negotiate/decline the counter-proposal).

iCalendar Message-based Interoperability Protocol — IMIP (RFC 2447) defines a method to implement I-TIP on standard Internet email-based transports.

Working with Workflow

As an administrator, you may need to provide an environment for **Users** to manage workflows at the **Page, "Workflow"**, under the **Page, "Community"**, of the **Book Lovers** community. For example, the **User, "Lotti Stein"**, at the Editorial department submits a request, "request-holiday", and the manager, **"David Berger"**, at the Editorial department reviews/approves/rejects the request via a workflow. First, let's set up workflow as follows:

1. Add a **Page** named **"Workflow"** under the **Page, "Community"**, of the **Book Lovers** community.

2. If the **Workflow** portlet is not already present, add **it** in the **Page, "Workflow"**, of the **Book Lovers** Community, where you want to let **Users** manage workflows by other portals.

Now, you are ready to deploy a workflow.

Deploying Workflow

Suppose that a workflow, **"holiday"**, was used for the above example. Let's deploy this workflow as follows:

1. Navigate to the **Page, "Workflow"**, under the **Page, "Community"**, at the **Book Lovers** community.

2. Locate the **Workflow** portlet.

3. By default, the **Definitions** tab is selected as shown in the following figure. The **Workflow** portlet displays all the workflows that have been deployed in the system.

4. To deploy a workflow, say "**holiday**", click on the **Add Definition** button.

5. At this point, you can paste the contents of a definition XML.

6. Click the **Save New Version** button.

7. An error message will be displayed, if the input is invalid. A success message will be displayed, if the input is valid.

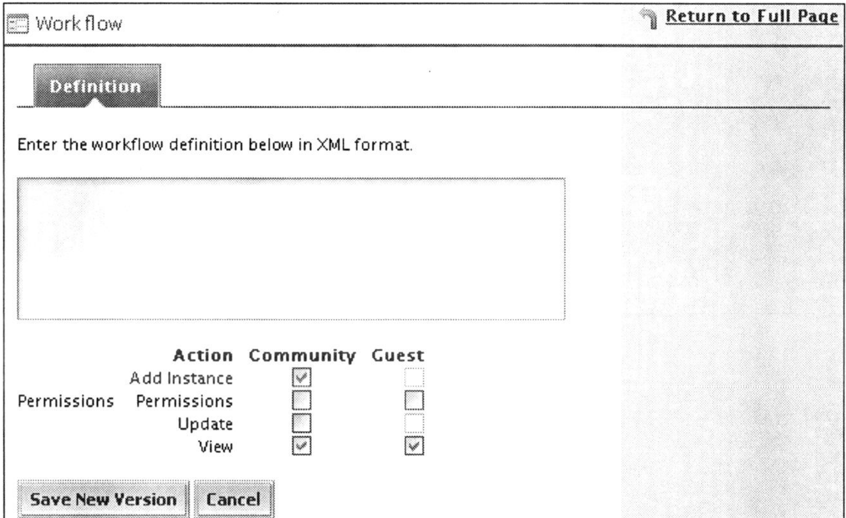

In order to make **Workflow** work well, you have to deploy jbpm-web (WAR) and mule-web (WAR) or Servicemix-web (WAR) first. Refer to Chapter 10 to know how to deploy portlets. The **Workflow** portlet works well in version 4.3.4. Staging enhancement and Workflow is available in version 5.x. For more details, refer to Chapter 13.

Of course, you can deploy other workflow definitions, such as "**Websale**" and "**Datatypes**". After deploying workflow definitions "**Websale**" and "**Datatypes**", you can view workflows.

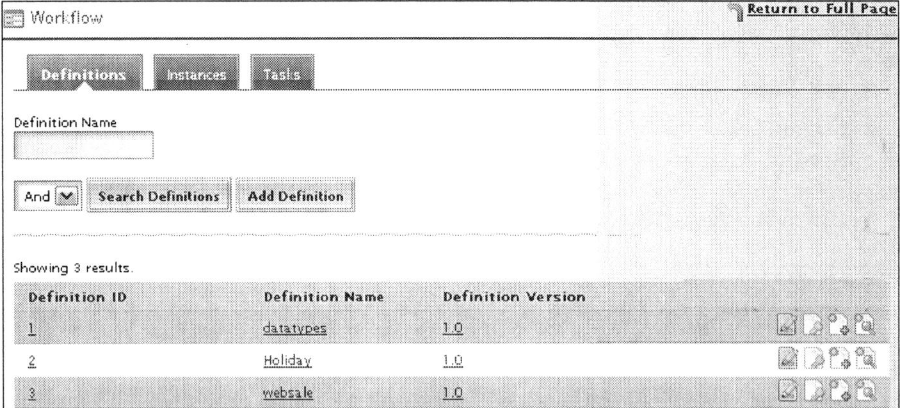

Managing Definitions

Since business processes may change over time, we have to manage every version of **Workflows**. To edit an existing **Workflow** version, simply click on the **Edit** icon located next to the definition name (or from the **Actions** next to the definition name). Update the XML in the text area first, and then click the **Save New Version** button.

The new version number will be incremented by one from the previous version number. For example, the current version of **Workflow**, "datatypes", is **1.0**. Then the new version number of **Workflow**, "datatypes", would be **2.0**.

Managing Instances

Now a **Definition**, "Holiday", is deployed. We are ready to add a new **Instance** of a **Workflow Definition**. "Holiday". Let's do as follows:

1. By default, the **Definitions** tab is selected.

2. Locate the **Workflow Definition**,"Holiday", and simply click on the **Add Instance** icon.

3. A new instance will appear on the **Instances** tab.

Now, a **Definition** "Holiday" was deployed and an **Instance** of that **Definition** was started. It is up to the **User** to manage the life cycle of the **Instance**. **Instance** management is controlled from the **Instances** tab with an icon, "**Manage**".

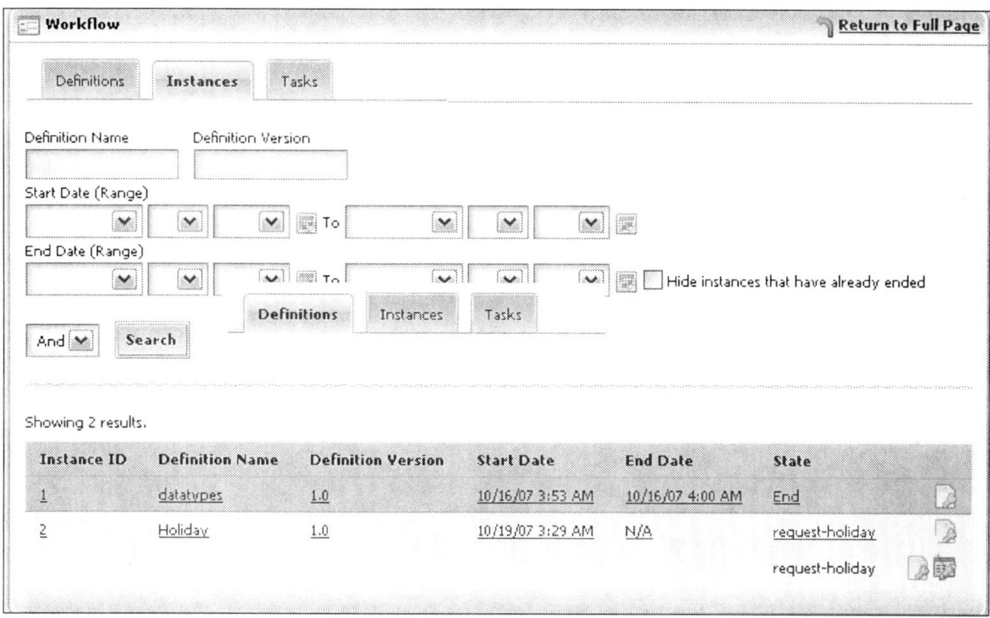

You can view all **Instances** of a **Workflow Definition**. To view all the **Instances** of a particular **Definition**, click the **View Instances** icon. Finally, you can also search for a **Definition** by name using the **Definition Name** and **Definition Version** input boxes.

The **Instances** tab displays every **instance** of every version of every **Workflow** deployed in the system. They are listed alphabetically by **Definition Name** followed by **Definition Version, Start Date, End Date, State** and set of actions in descending order.

The **Instances** of **Workflow Definitions** are searchable. You can search **Instances** by **Definition Name** and **Definition Version**. The **Search** form at the top of the screen allows you to find specific **Instances** to manage. You display only active, running **Instances** by checking the box, **Hide instances that have already ended** checkbox. The date ranges also allow you to search by **Start Date** and/or **End Date**. In addition, you will see the first row for a given **Instance** that describes the state of the **Instance**, and following rows for a given **Instance** specify tasks that are associated with the current state. Frequently, the current state and current task have the same name.

You can play with the given **Instance** in its current state by the **Actions** in the right-most column in the results table. The **actions** will either be blank or appear with the **Manage** icon, and/or the **Permissions** icon.

Managing Tasks

As a **User** at the Editorial department, "**Lotti Stein**" plans to use **Workflow** by sending a holiday request to the manager,"**David Berger"**, for approval. Suppose that "Lotti Stein" has proper **Permissions to do so**:

1. Log in as "**Lotti Stein**".

2. Navigate to the **Page, "Workflow"**, under the **Page, "Community"**, at the **Book Lovers** community.

3. Locate the **Workflow** portlet.

4. Select the **Tasks** tab. You will find **Task Name, "request-holiday"**, with an action icon, **Manage**.

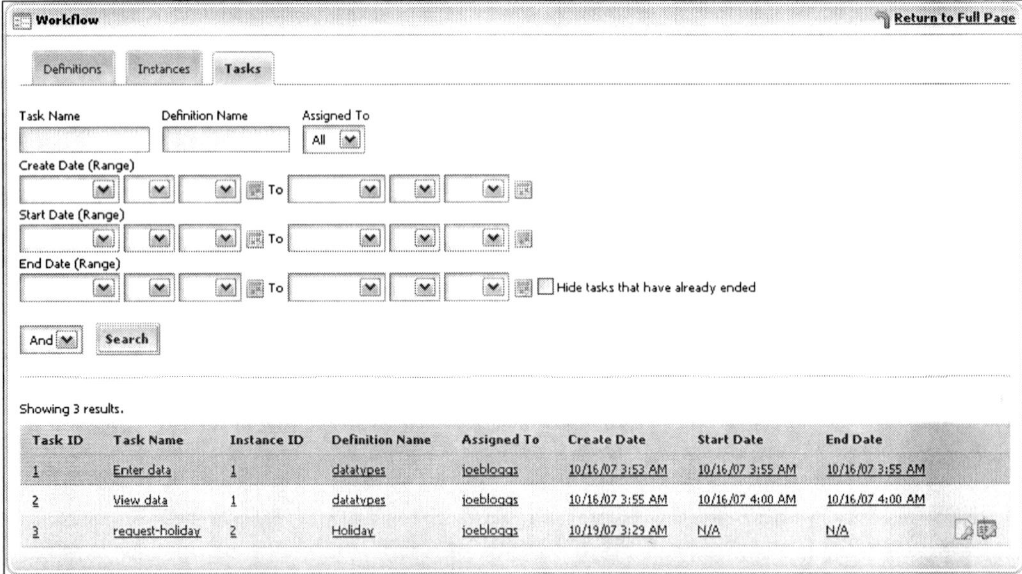

5. Locate the **Task, "request-holiday"**.

6. Click on the icon **Manage**.

7. Input the start day as say **Feb. 11, 2008**.

8. Input the end day as say **Feb.15, 2008**.

9. Click on the **Save** button when you are ready.

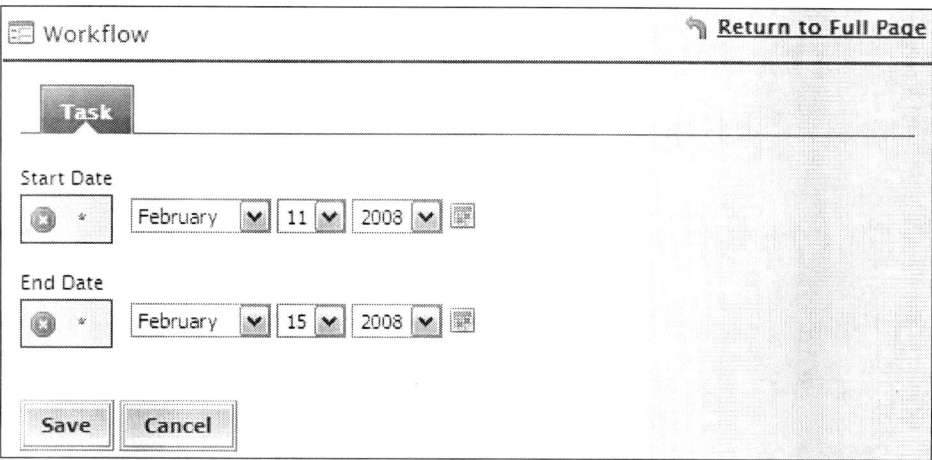

As a **User** of the Editorial department, "**Lotti Stein**" has sent a holiday request to the manager. Now it is up to the manager "**David Berger**", to **Approve** or **Reject** the request, or send the request back to the requester for review. As a manager at the Editorial department, "**David Berger**" has to take decisions based on the request:

1. Log in as "**David Berger**".

2. Navigate to the **Page, "Workflow"**, under the **Page, "Community"**, at the **Book Lovers** community.

3. Locate the **Workflow** portlet.

4. Select the **Instances** tab. You will find the **Task Name, "request-holiday"**, with an action icon, **Manage**.

5. You can view the request **Start Date** and **End Date**.

6. Input your **Comments** as "**This is my comments**", as shown in the following figure:

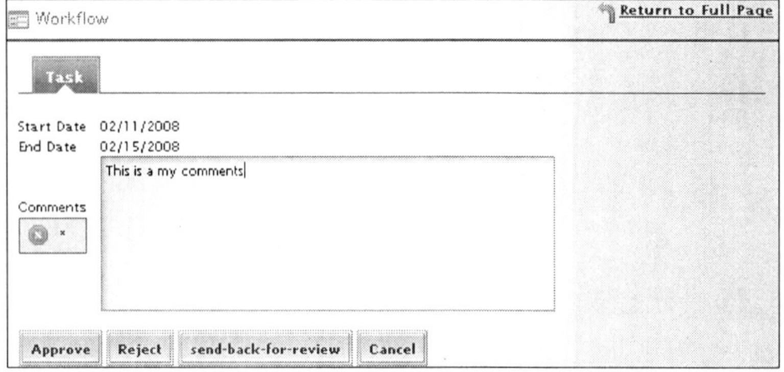

7. Click the **Approve** button if you want to approve it, or click the **Reject** button if you want to reject the request. Click the **send-back-for-review** button, if you want to send it back for review.

Here, we only use the **Workflow, "Holiday"**, as an example for tasks management and instances management. Of course, you can use other **Workflows** such as "**datatypes**", "**websale**", and your own workflows.

Using Permissions

We have used a default setting for the **Workflow** portlet in the **Page, "Workflow"**, of the **Page, "Community"**, under the **Book Lovers** Community. When the administrator "**Palm Tree**" logs in, he/she will see the button, **Add Definition**, as mentioned earlier. We know that the **User "Lotti Stein"** is also a member of the **Book Lovers** community. Try to log in as "**Lotti Stein**", and you will see that there is no **Add Definition** button. Further, you will also see the **Instances** without the **Action** icons,**Signal**, **Permissions** and **Manage**.

Why are the two cases different? This is something related to **Permissions**. There are four levels of **Permissions**: portlet **Permissions**, **Permissions** on **Definitions**, **Instances** and **Tasks**.

Portlet Permissions

The following table shows **Permissions** related to the **Workflow** portlet. A **Community User** may set up all **Permissions**, (marked 'X'): **View**, **Add Definition**, and **Configuration**, while a **Guest User** may set up **Permissions**, **View** and **Configuration**. By default, a **Community** has the **Permission** action **View** (marked '*') and so does a **Guest User**.

Action	Description	Community	Guest
View	Views this portlet	X, *	X, *
Configuration	Configures this portlet	X	X
Add Definition	Adds a **Definition** to the portlet	X	

Obviously, as a **User** of the **Book Lovers** Community, "**Lotti Stein**" has only **View Permissions** on the **Workflow** portlet, by default. Since the **Book Lovers** community has no **Add Definition Permission**, "**Lotti Stein**" too has no **Add Definition Permission**.

Permissions on Definitions

The following table shows **Permissions** related to the **Definitions** on the **Workflow** portlet. A **Community User** may set up all **Permissions** (marked 'X'), **View**, **Add Instance**, **Update**, and **Permissions**, while a **Guest User** may set up **Permissions**, **View** and **Permissions**. By default, a **Community** has **Permission** action **View** (marked '*') and so does a **Guest User**.

Action	Description	Community	Guest
View	Views this **Definition**	X, *	X, *
Update	Updates this **Definition**	X	
Permissions	Changes **Permissions** on this **Definition**	X	X
Add Instance	Adds an **Instance** to this **Definition**	X	

Obviously, as a **User** of the **Book Lovers** Community, "**Lotti Stein**" has only **View Permissions** on the **Definition,** by default. Since the **Book Lovers** community has no **Permission**, "**Add Instance**", "**Lotti Stein**" too has no **Permission, "Add Instance"**.

Permissions on Instances

The following table shows **Permissions** related to the **Instances** on the **Workflow** portlet. A **Community User** may set up all **Permissions** (marked 'X'), **Manage**, **Signal** and **Permissions**, while a **Guest User** may set up **Permissions, Permissions**. By default, neither a **Community** nor a **Guest User** has a **Permission** action.

Action	Description	Community	Guest
Manage	Manages the **Instance**	X	
Signal	Signals the **Instance**	X	
Permissions	Changes permissions on this **Instances**	X	X

Permissions on Tasks

The following table shows **Permissions** related to the **Tasks** on the **Workflow** portlet. A **Community User** may set up all **Permissions** (marked 'X'), **Manage** and **Permissions**, while a **Guest User** may set up **Permission, Permissions**. By default, neither a **Community** nor a **Guest User** has a **Permission** action.

Action	Description	Community	Guest
Manage	Manage this **Task**	X	
Permissions	Change permissions on this **Task**	X	X

Using Workflow Effectively

In the case where a portal is used as the foundation of a website, the **Users** are responsible for using the tools provided by the portal for laying out a website, its **Pages**, the contents of each **Page**, assigning layouts, themes, friendly URLs and so on. **Workflow** provides the ability to take what is essentially a working copy of a layout (that is portal **Page**) and its associated assets called the process assets, and send them through a process. Throughout the **Workflow,** the process assets should be previewed. **Workflow** could be different across **Organizations,** and thus any solution should provide the opportunity for an **Organization** to define its workflow.

The **Workflow** portlet provides the ability to manage the **Workflows** at the presentation layer. Further, it allows the **Users** to create and edit **Workflows** using a simple drag and drop style interface.

The Workflow portlet works based on ESB (Enterprise Service Bus), a switching station between services. The portal also needs a **Workflow** service. Although there are several different **Workflow** engines that would satisfy the needs, you have high flexibility in choosing the one you want to use. Therefore, the portal will directly access the ESB, and the ESB will then decide on which **Workflow** component to use, to access the **Workflow** service. Thus, no matter how many ways the **Workflow** service changes, the portal would never be directly impacted. The ESB provides a mechanism to plug in services, and you can therefore update services easily with little or no impact to the portal configuration. Currently both Service-Mix and Mule are useful for these purposes.

> Service-Mix is truer to the traditional definition of an ESB (it adheres to the Java Business Integration (JBI) JSR-208 specification), whereas Mule is based on ESB (it doesn't adhere to the specification) and is more flexible. In short, Mule is a bit easier to configure and set up and running. However, Service-Mix has a smaller footprint than Mule has.

Define Business Process

The following figure depicts a business process example called holiday. The **Start State** is called "**request-holiday**", followed by the "**Task Node**", "**evaluate-holiday-request**". Then the following could apply to the **Task** "**send-back-for-review**", "**resubmit**", "**approve**" and "**reject**". Finally, there is an **End State,** "**End**".

Business processes in jBPM are defined by XML documents (called process definitions) written in jBPM Process Definition Language (JPDL). These XML specify the following:

- The entities such as the process roles known as swim-lanes, the various states such as "**Start State**" known as **Nodes**

- The **Tasks** such as "**evaluate-holiday-request**" associated with each **Node** such as "**notify-requestor-of-approval**"

- The transitions from one **Node** to the next

- The variables associated with each **Task's** form

- The **Roles** associated with each **Task**

- The external actions executed on entry or exit of a **Node**

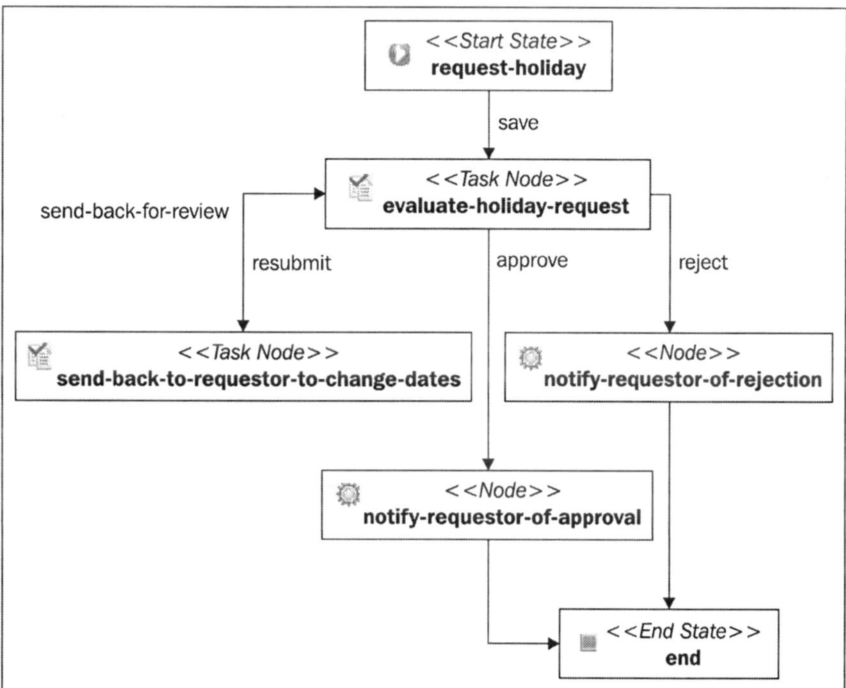

JBoss jBPM is a workflow and BPM (Business Process Management) engine that enables the creation of business processes that coordinate between people, applications and services. With its modular architecture, jBPM combines easy development of workflow applications with a flexible and scalable process engine. The jBPM process designer graphically represents the business process steps in order to facilitate a strong link between the business analyst and the technical developer.

Integrate with Users, Groups And Roles

Workflow can be integrated with **Users**, groups, and **Roles**. You can use process roles named swim-lanes associated with **Users**, groups, and **Roles** In JPDL.

```
<swimlane name="approver">
  <assignment class="*" config-type="field">
    <type>user</type>
    <companyId>book.com</companyId>
    <id>10838</id>
  </assignment>
</swimlane>
```

As shown, the `"approver"` `swimlane` is associated with the `user`, "**David Berger**" who has a User ID `"10838"`, and belongs to a Company ID,`"book.com"`. That is, "**David Berger**" is acting as an approver.

Similar to associating a `user` with User ID, you can also associate a `user` such as "**David Berger**" with a `swimlane` by email address, such as `"david@book.com"`, as shown in the following XML snippet.

```
<swimlane name="approver">
    <assignment class="*" config-type="field">
      <type>user</type>
      <companyId>book.com</companyId>
      <name>david@book.com</name>
    </assignment>
  </swimlane>
```

As shown in the previous XML, the `"approver"` `swimlane` is associated with the `user`, "**David Berger**", who has an email address, `"david@book.com"`, and belongs to a Company ID, `"book.com."`

```
<swimlane name="approver">
    <assignment class="*" config-type="field">
      <type>group</type>
      <companyId>book.com</companyId>
```

```
      <id>1116</id>
    </assignment>
  </swimlane>
```

In the previous XML, the "approver" swimlane is associated with any user that belongs to a group with the Group ID, "1116" (which defaults to the **Book Lovers** community), and Company ID, "book.com". In other words, the "approver" swimlane is assigned to the pool of "**Book Lovers**" Users. If one of the "**Book Lovers**" **Users** were to manage an approver task, this **User** would automatically be assigned to all other approver **Tasks** in the **Workflow**.

```
<swimlane name="approver">
  <assignment class="*" config-type="field">
    <type>group</type>
    <companyId>book.com</companyId>
    <name>Book Lovers</name>
  </assignment>
</swimlane>
```

The previous XML shows an alternative way to associate the "approver" swimlane with the Book Lovers community using the actual **Community's** name. Again, as the **Community** names must be unique per Company ID, this format accomplishes the same results as the previous XML.

```
<swimlane name="approver">
  <assignment class="*" config-type="field">
    <type>role</type>
    <companyId>book.com</companyId>
    <id>11123</id>
  </assignment>
</swimlane>
<swimlane name="approver">
  <assignment class="*" config-type="field">
    <type>role</type>
    <companyId>book.com</companyId>
    <name>MB Topic Admin</name>
  </assignment>
</swimlane>
```

As shown above, the two XML snippets are very similar to the Group XML snippets. But both of them associate their swimlanes with a role, the first XML uses the Role ID, "11123", and the second XML uses the role's unique name, "MB Topic Admin".

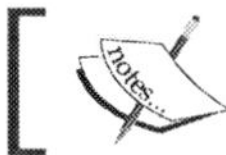

For more details about jPDL, refer to jPDL specification at http://docs.jboss.com/jbpm/v3/userguide/jpdl.html

Working with WSRP

As an administrator, you may need to access portlets' contents published by other portals such as "`http://portalstandards.oracle.com:80/portletapp/portlets`" across the Internet using Web Services at the **Page, "Media"**, under the **Page, "Community"**, of the **Book Lovers** community. Let's do it as follows:

1. Add a **Page** named "**Media**" under the **Page, "Community"**, of the **Book Lovers** community.

2. Add the **WSRP Proxy** portlet in the **Page, "Media"**, of the **Book Lovers** Community where you want to access portlets' contents published by other portals, if the **WSRP Proxy** portlet is not there.

3. By default, you will see the contents as shown in the following figure.

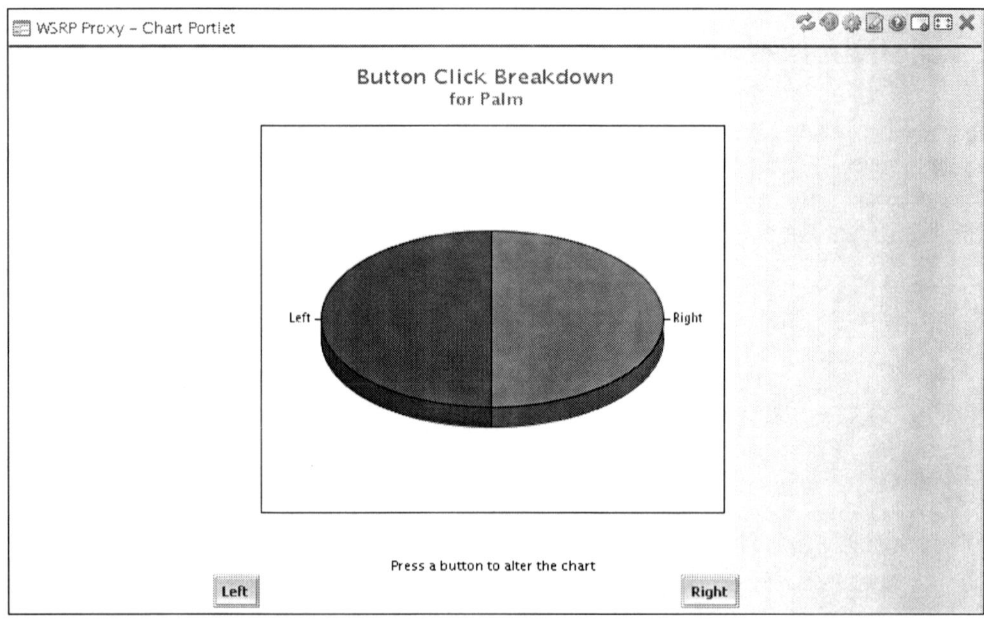

How do you get it? Here are the options to change **Permissions,** and change the portlets and their contents as follows:

1. Click the **Configuration icon to the upper right, to change Permissions if you have proper access right.**

2. Click the **Preferences icon to the upper right to edit local and remote preferences.**

3. **Press the Edit Local Preferences link.**

The following figure depicts how to use **Edit Local Preference**.

1. Edit **WSRP Service URL, Markup Endpoint, Service Description Endpoint, Registration Endpoint, Portlet Management Endpoint**.

2. Further, select a portlet such as **Chart Portlet** from the **Portlet** list.

3. Press **Save** button to save the changes.

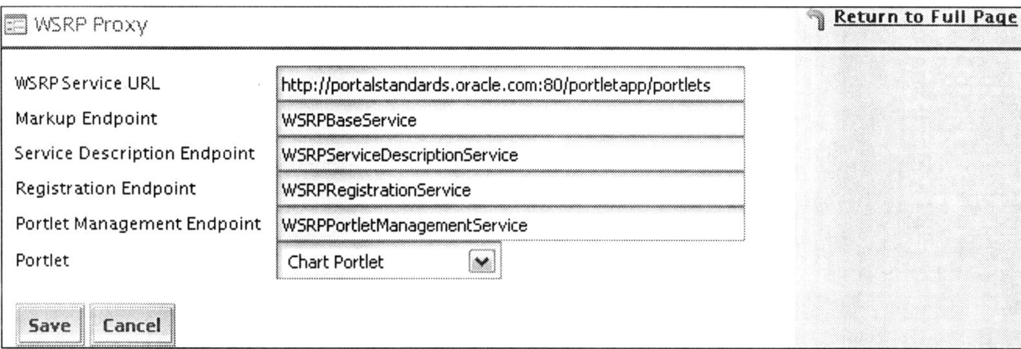

In addition, you can use **Edit Remote Preference**. For a given producer, you can change title, and then press the **OK** button to keep the current setup, or press the **Apply** button to apply the changes.

Using WSRP Effectively

WSRP (Web Services for Remote Portlets), as an OASIS-approved network protocol standard, is employed for communications with remote portlets. The WSRP specification defines a web-service interface to interact with presentation-oriented web services.

The WSRP specification defines ways to plug remote web services as portlets into the pages of online portals and other user-facing applications. Here is a simple flow: First, portal or application owners embed a web service from a third party into a portlet easily; then interactive content and services, which are updated from the provider's servers, are displayed in the portlet dynamically.

OASIS (Organization for the Advancement of Structured Information Standards) is a not-for-profit consortium that drives the development, convergence and adoption of open standards for the global information society. URL: `http://www.oasis-open.org/`

Why Use WSRP?

There are a set of scenarios that motivate WSRP functionality. Here, we just list some of them as follows:

- Aggregation engines use content hosts (such as portal servers) to provide portlets as presentation-oriented web services.
- Portal uses content aggregator (such as portal servers) to consume presentation-oriented web services and integrate them into a portal framework.

WSRP is also useful for web development. It involves the following features:

- It decouples the deployment and delivery of applications.
- It delivers both the data and its presentation logic.
- It requires little or no programming for implementation.

In addition, WSRP provides a lot of additional benefits, such as interoperability and portability. Normally, Liferay can act as both a consumer and producer of WSRP. But, some disadvantages of WSRP are its slowness, its lack of wide adoption, and so on.

How Does It Work?

WSRP involves two integral components:

- The remote application, called a WSRP producer, implements standards-based Web Services using the SOAP (Simple Object Access Protocol) specification over HTTP. Producers are normally created by third-party implementations of WSRP.
- A WSRP consumer acts as a portal application. Typically, the consumer application refers to the producer's WSDL (Web Services Description Language). The consumer directly accesses the producer when the portal is active.

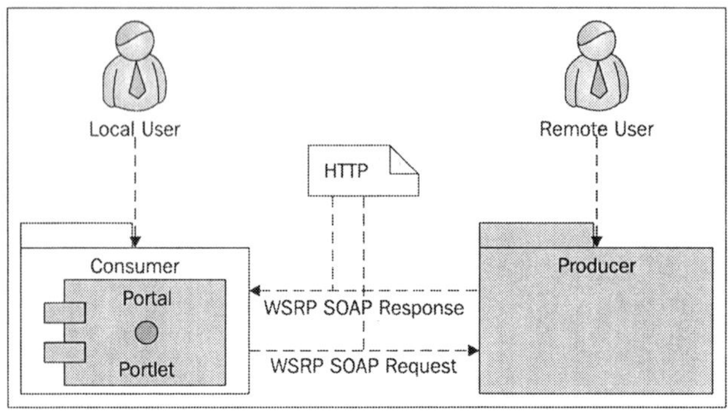

In short, the WSRP defines a collection of Web services and data objects that enable remote consumption of portlets. WSRP allows the Consumer to get UIs exported from a remote portal server ("Producer"). It is different from traditional paradigm which constructs local UI widgets that connect to remote server components. WSRP defines four Web service interfaces briefly:

- Service Description Service — a registry of portlets, available to a portlet consumer.

- Markup Service — generating portlet markup and executing actions, in order to change the portlet state.

- Portlet Management Service — cloning producer portlets in order to reflect consumer-specific states, destroying portlets, and getting portlet metadata, and so on.

- Registration Service — if the producer supports on-line registration, it lets consumers register themselves.

For more details about WSRP, refer to WSRP specification at `http://www.oasis-open.org/committees/tc_home.php?wg_abbrev=wsrp`.

Using Web Proxy Portlet

As an administrator, you may need to bring in content from external sites into the portal such as "`http://liferay.cignex.com`" at the **Page, "Media"**, under the **Page, "Community"**, of the **Book Lovers** community. Let's do it as follows:

1. Add **Web Proxy** portlet in the **Page, "Media"**, of the **Book Lovers** Community where you want to bring content from external sites into the portal, if **Web Proxy** portlet is not already present.

2. Click on the **Configuration** icon to the top-right of the portlet.

3. By default, **Setup** tab is selected. Input value "`http://liferay.cignex.com`" for URL.

4. Keep default values for others.

5. Click on the **Save** button when you are ready.

6. Click on the **Return to full Page** arrow icon to return to the main view.

Of course, you can input another URL. After inputting the value `"http://liferay.cignex.com"` as URL, you can view your **Page** with content from external sites.

The Web Proxy portlet allows **Users** to bring in content from external sites, supporting various authentication schemes, and using XSL to rewrite content from external sites. In fact, **Web Proxy** is a JSR 168 compliant portlet for a downstream web site. By default, the **Web Proxy** portlet displays only the content of the tag `<BODY>`, while we can use custom XSLT to transform the data from the downstream site.

The **Web Proxy** portlet provides ability to seamlessly integrate with web-based services regardless of the implementation technology. In addition, **Web Proxy** provides abilities for authentication (such as NTLM), clipping, content caching, for passing user-specific information to the back-end application, and so on.

Using IFrame Portlet

As an administrator, you may need to create an inline frame that contains another document or website such as `"http://sesamestreet.cignex.com"` at the **Page, "Media"**, under the **Page, "Community"**, of the **Book Lovers** community. Let's do it as follows:

1. Add the **IFrame** portlet in the **Page, "Media"**, of the **Book Lovers** Community where you want to create an inline frame that contains another document, if the **IFrame** portlet is not already present.

2. Click on the **Configuration** icon to the top-right of the portlet.

3. By default, the **Setup** tab is selected. Input value `"http://sesamestreet.cignex.com"` for Source URL.

4. Keep default values for others.

5. Click on the **Save** button when you are ready.

6. Click on **Return to full Page** arrow icon to return to main view.

Of course, you can input another URL. After inputting the value
"`http://sesamestreet.cignex.com`" source URL, you can view your **Page** with an
inline frame that contains another document or website.

What Are The Differences Between IFrame And Web Proxy?

There are several differences between the **IFrame** and **Web Proxy** portlets. The
IFrame portlet is simpler than the **Web Proxy** portlet. The downstream site via the
IFrame portlet is often more faithfully rendered.

The **Web Proxy** portlet however has several advantages. An **IFrame** is like a window
onto another site, while the **Web Proxy** portlet behaves more like a portlet, providing
a block of HTML in your portal page. The following are the main differences
between **IFrame** and **Web Proxy**:

- **IFrame** doesn't resize easily to accommodate the size of the downstream
  content, while **Web Proxy** portlet does the same by putting a fixed size `<div>`
  into the XSLT around the content.

- **The IFrame** URLs take you out of the portal. This is often not the behavior
  you'd expect from a portlet.The **Web Proxy** portlet can be configured either
  way using the "scope" preference.

- **IFrame** exposes the whole downstream site to the public.

- The content of **IFrame** is unchangeable. It means that while it looks exactly like
  the downstream site, it may not look like the rest of the portal. However, the
  Web Proxy portlet allows you to modify the XSLT that transforms the content.

- **IFrame** shows everything from the downstream site, while the **Web Proxy Portlet** allows for "web clipping" using custom XSLT. This means you get only what you want.

- Finally, **IFrame** works on most browsers, except the ones with XHTML specification. Web proxy would probably be a better choice under most circumstances.

Using Flash Portlet

As an administrator, you may need to show a **Flash** movie clock such as "/flash/analogclock.swf" at the **Page**,"Media", under the **Page, "Community"**, of the **Book Lovers** community. Let's add the flash movie as follows:

1. Add **Flash** portlet in the **Page, "Media"**, of the **Book Lovers** Community where you want to show a flash movie, if the **Flash** portlet is not already present.

2. Click on the **Configuration** icon to the top-right of the portlet.

3. By default, the **Setup** tab is selected. Input value "/flash/analogclock.swf" for Movie.

4. Keep default values for other flash attributes and flash variables.

5. Click on the **Save** button when you are ready.

6. Click on **Return to full Page** arrow icon to return to main view.

Of course, you can input other flash movies. After inputting flash movie "/flash/analogclock.swf", you can view your page with a flash movie-clock as shown in the following figure:

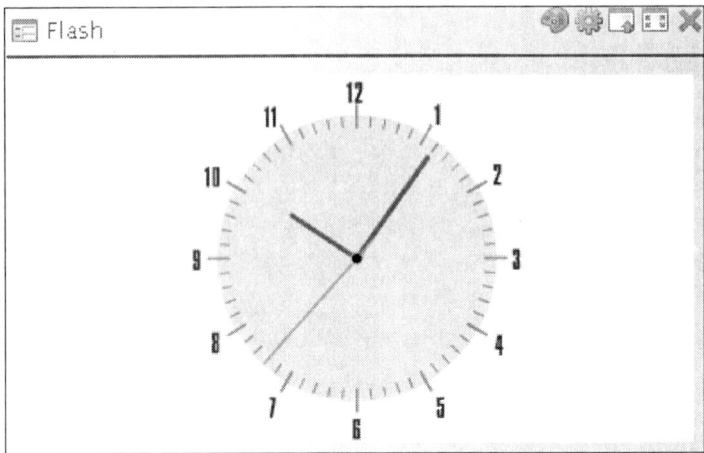

In general, Liferay provides a set of portlets to incorporate other technologies with it at the presentation layer. Besides the portlets such as **Flash, IFrame** and **Web Proxy,** Liferay also provides support for Laszlo, Velocity, JSP, Struts, PHP, Perl, Spring MVC, and so on.

Summary

First, this chapter discussed how to create, manage (edit, delete, add, view), and search **Events** in a **Calendar,** and how to share calendar using iCalendar. Then,it discussed how to deploy **Workflows** and how to manage **Workflow Definitions, Instances** and **Tasks.** Finally it showed us how to employ WSRP proxy effectively, and other portlets such as **Web Proxy, IFrame** and **Flash,** smoothly.

8

Content Management and Publishing

In the intranet website "book.com" of "Palm Tree Publications", a lot of web contents are required to be managed and published. Liferay Journal not only provides high availability to publish, manage, and maintain web content and documents, but also separates content from layout. This chapter will introduce us to managing and publishing images first. Then, it will discuss how to manage and publish documents. Finally, it will focus on the articles' creation, management and publishing.

By the end of this chapter, you will have learned how to:

- Add folders and sub folders for images.
- Manage (view, search, edit, delete) folders and sub folders.
- Add images in folders and manage (view, search, edit, delete) images.
- Set up permissions on folders and images.
- Add folders and sub folders for documents.
- Manage (view, search, edit, delete) documents, add **Comments**, give your rating, view version history.
- Set up **Permissions** on folders and documents.
- Publish documents.
- Manage (view, search, edit, delete) structures.
- Manage (view, search, edit, delete) template.
- Manage (view, search, edit, delete, approve, preview) articles.
- Set up **Permissions** on Journal, articles, templates and structures.
- Publish articles.
- Employ other CMS tools.

Working with Image Gallery

In order to let small teams manage web contents and publish web contents easily, we should use Liferay Journal. Before creating web contents, we have to prepare a set of images and documents. Let's see how to manage images first.

As an administrator of "Palm Tree Publications", you need to create a page called "**Images**" under the page "**Admin**" at the **Book Lovers** Community and moreover, add the **Image Gallery** portlet in the page, "**Images**". Further, you need to create folders such as "**Home**" and "**Liferay**", and sub folders such as "**Book**", in order to hold a set of images. At the same time, you need to group all images into different folders for easy use and management.

Adding A Folder

First of all, we need to create a folder called "**Home**", which contains a number of images. Let's do it as follows:

1. Add a page called "**Image**" under the **Page** "**Admin**" at the **Book Lovers** Community **Private Pages**, if the page is not already present.

2. Add the **Image Gallery** portlet in the **Page** "**Images**" of the **Book Lovers** Community where you want to manage images, if the **Image Gallery** portlet is not already present.

3. Click the **Add Folder** button.

4. Enter a **Name**, "**Home**", and a **Description**, "**Images Folder for Book Lovers Community**", as shown in the following screenshot.

5. Set **Permissions** by clicking on the **Configure** link. To configure additional **Permissions**, click the **More** link. Here, we just use default settings.

6. Click the **Save** button to save the inputs.

Adding A Sub Folder

Suppose that we need to create a **Subfolder** named "**Book**" under the folder, "**Home**", which will contain a set of images for "Liferay Book". Let's do it as follows:

1. Locate the **Folder, "Home"**; click the link of the **Folder, "Home"**.

2. Click the **Add Subfolder** button.

3. Enter a **Name** such as "Book" and a **Description** such as "Images folder for book".

4. Set **Permissions** by clicking the **Configure** link. To configure additional **Permissions**, click the **More** link. Here, we just use default settings.

5. Click the **Save** button to save the inputs.

Of course, you can create other **Folders** as siblings of the **Folder, "Home"**. After adding a **Folder, "Liferay"**, we can view **Folders** as shown in the following figure.

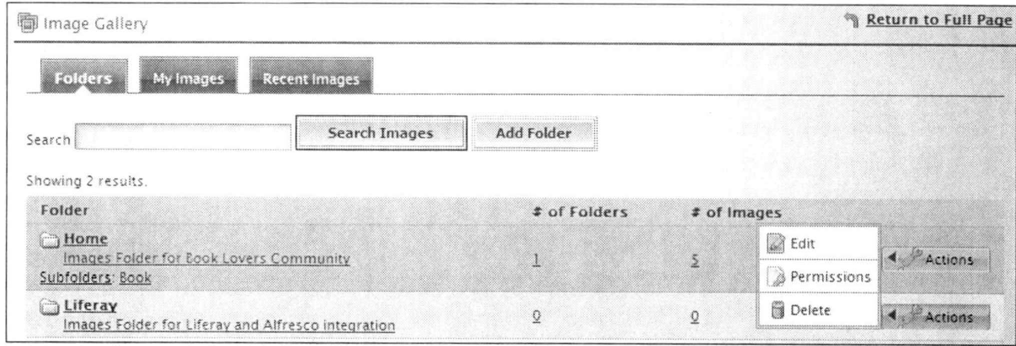

Obviously, all **Folders** or **Subfolders** names form a folder tree. The names of **Folders** or **Subfolders** must be unique at the same level in the folder tree. The names could be the same at different levels.

Adding An Image

Finally, we can add an image in a given **Folder**. Suppose that we need to add a logo of "Palm Tree Publications" in the folder "**Home**". Let's do it as follows:

1. Locate the folder "**Home**"; click on the link of the **Folder "Home"**.

2. Click the **Add Image** button.

3. Click the **Browse** icon to find an **Image, "PalmTree_logo.png"**, in the local machine. Should you wish, you can browse multiple files, such as "**United_States.png**" and "**Germany.png**" as shown in the following figure.

4. Click the **Upload Files** icon to upload files.

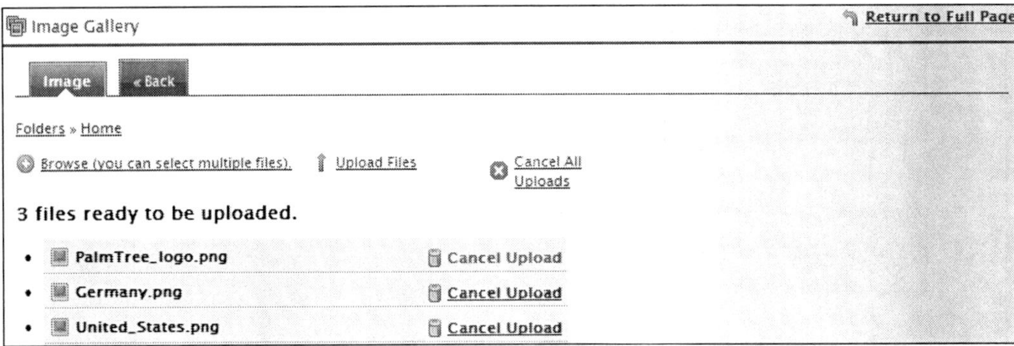

Of course, you can add other **Images**. After adding **Images** "`liferay_logo.png`" and "`alfresco_logo.png`", we can view all images under the folder "**Home**" as shown in the following figure.

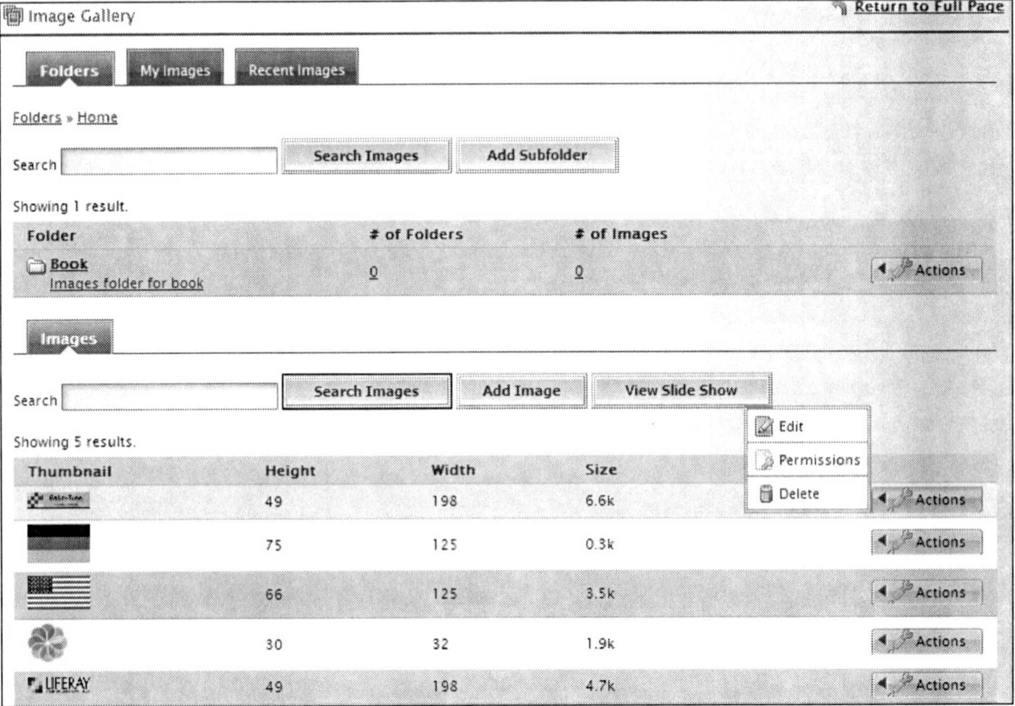

Managing Folders

Folders and **Subfolders** are editable. For example, you may need to change the description of the **Folder, "Liferay"**, from "**Images Folder for Liferay and Alfresco integration**" to "**Images Folder for Integration**". Let's do is as follows:

1. Locate the **folder "Liferay"** that you want to edit.

2. Click the **Edit** icon from the **Actions** located next to the folder.

3. Maintain the value of **Name** and update the **Description** of the selected **Folder "Images Folder for Liferay and Alfresco integration"** with the value "**Images Folder for Integration**".

4. Click the **Save** button to save the changes.

You can update the **Name** as well. For example, we can update the **Name "Liferay"** with the value "**Liferay-Alfresco**".

Optionally, you can change the parent **Folder** by selecting a **Folder** as the parent **Folder** of the **Folder** or **Subfolder**, or merging the **Folder** with the parent **Folder**, or removing the parent **Folder**. If you remove the parent **Folder**, the current **Folder** will become a **Folder** at the root level.

Folders or **Subfolders** are removable. For example, if the **Folder "Liferay-Alfresco"** is not wanted anymore, you can remove it. Let's do it as follows:

1. Locate the **Folder "Liferay-Alfresco"** that you want to delete.

2. Click the **Delete** icon from the **Actions** located next to the folder.

3. A screen will appear asking if you want to delete this. Click **OK** to confirm deletion.

Note that deleting a **Folder** will delete all related **Subfolders** and **Images** which belong to this folder.

Managing Images

After adding **Folders** and **Images**, you can manage **Images** easily. You can view **Images** as a slideshow, search images, edit images and delete images.

View Images as a Slideshow

Images are viewable. To view an **Image**, simply click on the link of an **Image**. For example, you want to view the **Image**, "PalmTree_logo.png" under the **Folder**, "**Home**". You can just click the link of the **Folder** "**Home**" first, and then locate the **Image**, "PalmTree_logo.png. Finally, click the link of the **Image**. A new window will appear showing a full-size image of "**PalmTree_logo.png**".

Optionally, you can view your own **Images**, by clicking the tab **My Images** in the **Image Gallery** portlet and you can also view the recent **Images** by clicking the tab **Recent Images**, in the **Image Gallery** portlet.

All **Images** from a folder can be viewed as a slideshow. For example, if you want to view all **Images** under the **Folder**, "**Home**" as a slideshow, click the **Folder** "**Home**" first, and then click the **View Slide Show** button. A new window will appear showing a full-size **Image** and a set of commands such as **previous**, **play**, **pause**, **next**, and **speed selection**, and so forth.

Search Images

Images are searchable. There are three options to search **Images**. You can search **Images** from the root, search **Images** from the current folder only, or search **Images** both in the **current Folder** and its **Subfolders**.

Suppose that there is an **Image**, "**Sesame Street Logo**", under the **Folder**, "**Book**", which is **Subfolder** of the **Folder**, "**Home**", and there is also an **Image**, "**Sesame Workshop Logo**" under the **Folder**, "**Liferay-Alfresco**".

First, let's search **Images** from the root. In **Image Gallery**, simply input the keyword such as "**logo**", and click the **Search Images** button. A list of **Images** will appear including the above two **Images**.

Then, let's search **Image** from the **Folder**, "**Home**" and its **Subfolders**. In **Image Gallery**, locate the **Folder**, "**Home**", and click on the link of the **Folder** "**Home**". Simply input the keyword, "**logo**", and click the **Search Images** button below the **Folder** navigation **Folders » Home**. A list of **Images** will appear, except the **Image**, "**Sesame Workshop Logo**".

Finally, let's search **Image** from the **Folder**, "**Home**", only. Simply input the keyword, "**logo**", and click the **Search Images** button under the tab **Images**. A list of **Images** will appear, except the **Images**, "**Sesame Workshop Logo**" and "**Sesame Street Logo**".

Edit An Image

Images are editable. For example, you may need to change the **Description** of the Image, "PalmTree_logo.png", under the **Folder, "Home"**, from "**PalmTree_logo.png**" to "**Palm Tree Publications Logo**". Let's do is as follows:

1. Click the folder "**Home**".

2. Locate the "**PalmTree_logo.png**" **Image** that you want to edit.

3. Click on the **Edit** icon from the **Actions** located next to the **Image**.

4. Update the **Description** of the selected **Image**, "**PalmTree_logo.png**", with value, "**Palm Tree Publications Logo**".

5. Click the **Save** button to save the changes.

Optionally, you can change the **Folder** by selecting a **Folder** as shown in the following figure. At the same time, you can change the content of the **Image** by uploading another **Image** file. Furthermore, you can find a URL for the **Image** and reference the **Image** by this URL. For instance, you can refer an **Image** in an article. We'll see how to work with URLs, later.

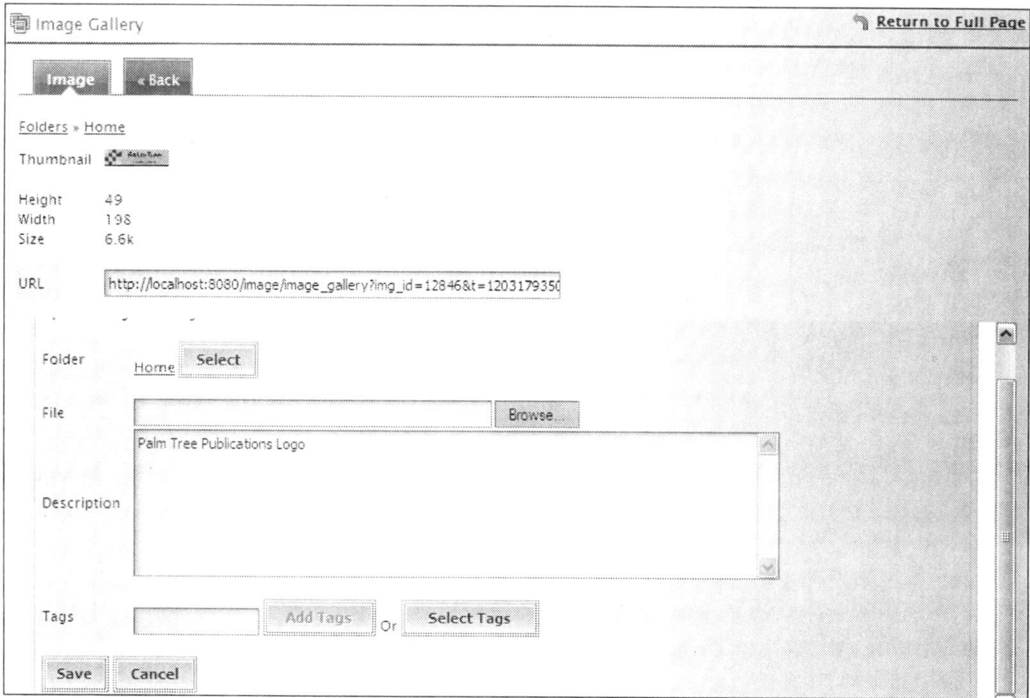

Delete An Image

Images are removable. For example, the **Image, "alfresco-logo.png"**, is not wanted anymore, and can be removed. Let's do it as follows:

1. Locate the **Image, "alfresco-logo.png"** that you want to delete.

2. Then click the **Delete** icon from the **Actions** located next to the image.

3. A screen will appear asking if you want to delete this. Click **OK** to confirm deletion.

Set up Permissions

We have used default settings for the **Image Gallery** portlet in the **Page, "Images"**, of the **Page "Admin"** under the **Book Lovers** Community. As mentioned earlier, when the administrator **"Palm Tree"** logs in, he will see the button, **Add Folder**. As we know, the **User "Lotti Stein"** is also a member of the **Book Lovers** community. Try to log in as **"Lotti Stein"**, and you will see that the **Add Folder** button is not there. Furthermore, you will also see that the **Folders, "Home"** and **"Liferay-Alfresco"** have no **Actions** icons.

Why? Different **Users** have different actions in the **Image Gallery** because of **Permissions**. Normally, there are three levels of **Permissions**: **Permissions** on portlet, **Permissions** on **folders** and **Permissions** on **Images**.

Use Permissions on Portlet

The following table shows **Permissions** on the **Image Gallery** portlet. A **Community User** may set up all **Permissions** (marked 'X'), **View**, **Add Folder**, and **Configuration**, while a **Guest User** may set up **Permissions**, **View** and **Configuration**. By default, a **Community** has **Permission** action **View** (marked '*'), and so does a **Guest User**.

Action	Description	Community	Guest
View	Views this portlet	X, *	X, *
Configuration	Configures this portlet	X	X
Add Folder	Adds a **Folder** to the portlet	X	

Obviously, as a **User** of the **Book Lovers** Community, **"Lotti Stein"** has only the **View Permissions** on the portlet **Image Gallery,** by default. Since the **Users** of the **Book Lovers** community have no **Add Folder Permission**, **"Lotti Stein"** also has no **Add Folder Permission**.

Use Permissions on Folders

The following table shows **Permissions** on **Folders**. A **Community User** may set up all **Permissions** (marked 'X'), **View, Add image, Add Subfolder, Delete, Permissions**, and **Update**, while a **Guest User** may set up **Permissions, View, Delete** and **Permissions**. By default, a **Community** has **Permissions, View** and **Add Image** (marked '*'), while a **Guest User** has only **View Permission**.

Action	Description	Community	Guest
View	Views this **Folder**	X, *	X, *
Add Image	Adds an **image** to the **Folder**	X, *	
Add Subfolder	Adds a **Subfolder** to the **Folder**	X	
Delete	Deletes the **Folder**	X	X
Permissions	Assigns **Permissions** on the **Folder**	X	X
Update	Updates the **Folder**	X	

Obviously, as a **User** of **Book Lovers** Community, "**Lotti Stein**" has only **View** and **Add Image Permissions** on **Folders,** by default.

Use Permissions on Images

Similarly, a **Community User** may set up all **Permissions** on **Images** (marked 'X'), **View, Delete, Permissions**, and **Update**, while a **Guest User** may set up **Permissions, View, Delete** and **Permissions**. By default, a **Community** has **Permission View** (marked '*'), and so does a **Guest User**.

Action	Description	Community	Guest
View	Views this Image	X, *	X, *
Delete	Deletes the Image	X	X
Permissions	Assigns permissions on the Image	X	X
Update	Updates the Image	X	

Using Images Effectively

An Image Gallery provides the ability to manage **Images**. Generally speaking, **Image Gallery** is a central repository of **Images** used via a unique URL.

The following diagram depicts an overview of an **Image Gallery,** conceptually. **Image Gallery** has a set of **Folders** associated with it. Each **Folder** may have many **Subfolders** associated with it. Each **Folder** (or **Subfolder**) may have a set of **Images**. And each **Image** has a unique **URL** to be referred.

ⓒ Folder	0..1	0..*	ⓒ Image	0..1	0..1	ⓒ URL

Working with Document Library

In order to let small teams manage web contents and publish web contents, we need not only a set of images, but also a set of documents.

Thus, as an administrator of "Palm Tree Publications", you need to create a page called "**Documents**" under the **page,** "**Admin**" at the **Book Lovers** Community and moreover, add the **Document Library** portlet in the **Page,** "**Documents**". Furthermore, you need to create **Folders** such as "**Books**" and "**Integration**", and **Subfolders** such as "**Chapters**", in order to hold a set of documents. As with the **Image Gallery**, you can group all documents into different folders for easy use and management.

Adding A Folder

Before adding a document, we need to create a **Folder** called "**Books**", which contains a lot of documents. Let's do it as follows:

1. Add a page called "**Documents**" under the page "**Admin**" at the **Book Lovers** Community private pages, if the page is not already present.

2. If the **Document Library** portlet is not already present, add it in the page "**Documents**", of the **Book Lovers** Community where you want to manage documents.

3. Click the **Add Folder** button.

4. Enter a **Name,** "Books" and a **Description, "Documents Folder for Books"**as shown in the following figure.

5. Set **Permissions** by clicking on the **Configure** link. To configure additional **Permissions,** click on the **More** link. Here, we just use default settings.

6. Click the **Save** button to save the inputs.

Adding A Subfolder

Suppose that we need to create a **Subfolder** named "Chapters" under the **Folder,** "Books", in which will be contained a set of documents for "**Liferay Book**". Let's do it as follows:

1. Locate the **Folder** "Books" and click on the link of the **Folder, "Books"**.

2. Click the **Add Subfolder** button.

3. Enter a **Name** such as "Chapters", and a **Description** such as "**Documents folder for chapters**".

4. Set **Permissions** by clicking on the **Configure** link. To configure additional **Permissions,** click on the **More** link. Here we just use default settings.

5. Click the **Save** button to save the inputs.

Similarly, you can create other **Folders** as siblings of the "**Books**" Folder. After adding a **Folder, "Integrations"**, we can view **Folders** as shown in the following figure. Specially, WebDAV URL is available for the root of the **Document Library**.

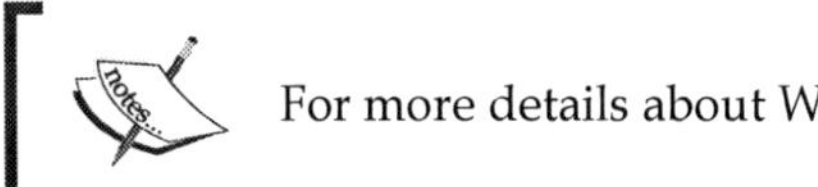

For more details about WebDAV, refer to Chapter 10.

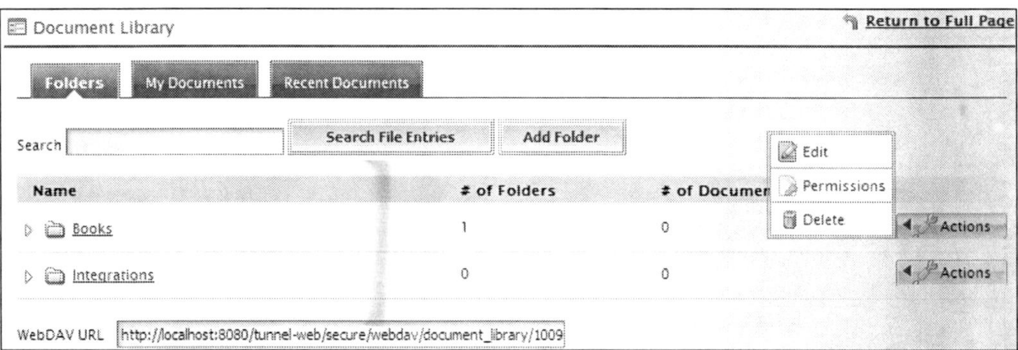

Adding A Document

Finally, we can add **Files** for a given **Folder** as we have added **Images**. Suppose that we need to add a **File, "Liferay Book Chapter 1"**, under the **Folder, "Books"**. Let's do it as follows:

1. Locate the **Folder "Books"**, and click on the link of the **Folder "Books"**.
2. Click the **Add Document** button.
3. Click the **Browse** icon to find a **File, "Liferay Book Chapter 1"**, (PDF) in the local machine. You can now browse multiple **Files**, such as "**Full RESTful integration of Liferay and Alfresco**" (text) and "**Full Integration of LDAP, SSO, Liferay and Alfresco**" (text).
4. Click the **Upload Files** icon to upload **Files**.

Add A Shortcut

You can create a **Shortcut** to any document that you have read access for, by clicking the **Add Shortcut** button, where you can select specific **Community** and **Document**. The **Permissions** set on the **Shortcut** enable others to access the original **Document** through the **Shortcut**. Suppose that we need to add a **Shortcut** under the **Folder, "Books"**, for the **Document, "Liferay Book Chapter 1"**. Let's do it as follows:

1. Locate a **Folder** such as "**Books**", and click on the "**Books**" link.

2. Click the **Add Shortcut** button.

3. Select the **Community** such as "**Book Lovers**".

4. Select the **Document** such as "**Liferay Book Chapter 1**" as shown in the following figure.

5. Set **Permissions** by clicking on the **Configure** link. To configure additional **Permissions**, click on the **More** link. Here, we just use default settings.

6. Click the **Save** button to save the inputs.

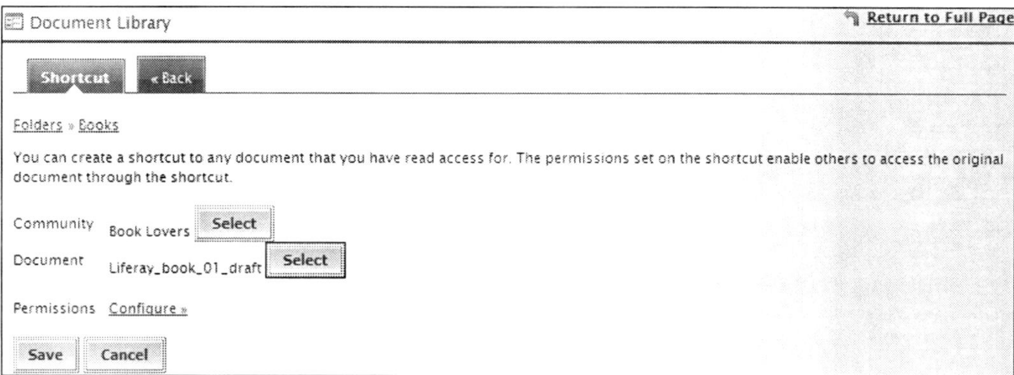

Managing Folders And Documents

The functions of managing **Folders** in **Document Library** are the same as that of managing **Folders** in **Image Gallery**. The **Folders** and **Subfolders** are editable and removable. For more details, you can refer to the previous section.

View Documents

Documents are viewable. Suppose that you want to view the **Document** "**Full RESTful integration of Liferay and Alfresco**" under the **Folder, "Books"**. Let's do it as follows:

1. Click the **Folder** "**Books**".

2. Locate the **Document** "**Full RESTful integration of Liferay and Alfresco**" that you want to view.

3. Click the **View** icon from the **Actions** located next to the document.

Optionally, you can view your own **Documents** by clicking the tab, **My Documents**, of the **Document Library** portlet. Moreover, you can also view the recent documents by clicking the tab, **Recent Documents**, of the **Document Library** portlet.

Search Documents

Documents are searchable, like **Images**. There are three options to search **Documents**. You can search **Documents** from the root, search **Documents** from the current folder only, or search **Documents** both in the current **Folder** and its **Subfolders**. For more details, refer to the previous section.

Edit A Document

Documents are editable, similar to **Images**. For example, you may need to change the **Description** of the **Document**, "**Full RESTful integration of Liferay and Alfresco**" under the **Folder**, "**Books**" to the value, "**Full RESTful integration**". Let's do it as follows:

1. Click the **Folder** "**Books**".

2. Locate the **document, "Full RESTful integration of Liferay and Alfresco"** that you want to edit.

3. Click the **Edit** icon from the **Actions** located next to the document.

4. Update the **description** of the selected **document**, "Full RESTful integration of Liferay and Alfresco", with the value "**Full RESTful integration**".

5. Click the **Save** button when you are ready.

Optionally, you can change the **Folder** by selecting a **Folder**. At the same time, you can change the contents of the **Document** by uploading another **File**. As shown in the previous figure, updating the content of the **Document** will create a new **Version** of the **Document**. Furthermore, you can find a URL for the **Document**. You can reference the **Document** by this URL in an article.

Delete a Document

Documents are removable, just like **Images**. For example, the **Document**, "Full RESTful Integration", is not wanted anymore. So, you can remove it as follows:

1. Locate the **Document, "Full RESTful integration"** that you want to delete.

2. Then click the **Delete** icon from the **Actions** located next to the document.

3. A screen will appear asking if you want to delete this. Click **OK** to confirm deletion.

View Version History

Whenever the contents of the **Document** changes, a new **Version** of the **Document** is generated. To view **Versions**, first view the **Document** and then click on the **Version History** tab. For example, we want to view **Version History** of the document, "**Full RESTful integration**". Let's do it as follows:

1. Locate the **Document** "**Full RESTful integration**" that you want to view.

2. Then click the **View** icon from the **Actions** located next to the document.

3. By default, the **Version History** tab is selected, and all **Versions** of the document will appear below the button, **Compare Versions**.

4. Check the checkbox to the right of the **Version, say** "**1.0**", and then click on the **Compare Versions** button. A comparative result appears, such as, "**There are no differences between 1.0 and 1.1**".

Give Your Rating

As for an **Entry** of **Blogs**, you can give your own rating for any **Document**. For example, as an administrator, you can read the document "**Full Integration of LDAP, SSO, Liferay and Alfresco**" and give your rating, say two stars. You simply click the second star under "**Your Rating**" of the **Document**.

Log in as "**Lotti Stein**", and you can read the **Document, "Full Integration of LDAP, SSO, Liferay and Alfresco**" and can also give **Your Rating,** say four stars, by simply clicking on the fourth star under "**Your Rating**" of the **Document**. Now you will find the average is three stars, with a message, "**2 Votes**".

Add Comments

As stated above, the administrator has created a **Document** called "**Full Integration of LDAP, SSO, Liferay** and **Alfresco**". As a **User** of "Palm Tree Publications", "**Lotti Stein**" wants to review the **Document** and add **Comments** such as "**Need more details**". Similar to adding **Comments** on an **Entry** of **Blogs**, "**Lotti Stein**" can also add **Comments** on **Documents**.

Setup Permissions

Similar to the **Permissions** on the **Image Gallery**, there are three levels **Permissions** for the **Document Library**: **Permissions** on portlet, **Permissions** on **Folders** and **Permissions** on **Documents**.

Permissions on the **Documents Library** portlet are the same as those on the **Image Gallery**. For more details, refer to the previous section.

Use Permissions on Folders

The following table shows **Permissions** on **Folders**. A **Community User** may set up all **Permissions** (marked 'X'), **View, Add Document, Add Shortcut, Add Subfolder, Delete, Permissions,** and **Update**, while a **Guest User** may set up **Permissions, View, Delete** and **Permissions**. By default, a **Community** has **Permission** actions **View, Add Document, Add Shortcut,** and **Add Subfolder** (marked '*'), while a **Guest User** has only the **View** permission action.

Action	Description	Community	Guest
View	Views this **Folder**	X, *	X, *
Add Document	Adds a **Document** to the **Folder**	X, *	
Add Shortcut	Adds a **Shortcut** to the **Folder**	X, *	
Add Subfolder	Adds a **Subfolder** to the **Folder**	X, *	
Delete	Deletes the **Folder**	X	X
Permissions	Assigns **Permissions** on the **Folder**	X	X
Update	Updates the **Folder**	X	

Use Permissions on Document

Similarly, a **Community User** may set up all **Permissions** on **Document** (marked 'X'), **View, Add Discussion, Delete, Permissions,** and **Update**, while a **Guest User** may set up permissions, **View, Delete** and **Permissions**. By default, a **Community** has **Permission View** (marked '*'), as does a **Guest User**.

Action	Description	Community	Guest
View	Views this **Document**	X, *	X, *
Add Discussion	Adds discussion on the **Document**	X, *	
Delete	Deletes the **Document**	X	X
Permissions	Assigns permissions on the **Document**	X	X
Update	Updates the **Document**	X	

Publishing Documents

As stated before, we have discussed how to create **Folders** and how to add **Documents**. As an administrator at the enterprise, "Palm Tree Publication", you can publish documents in the page "**Documents**" under the **Page** "**Community**" at the **Book Lovers** Community **Public Pages**. At present, there are two ways to publish **Documents**: **Recent Documents** and **Document Library Display**.

First let's publish **Documents** using **Recent Documents** as follows:

1. Add a page named "**Documents**" under the page "**Community**" of the **Book Lovers** community.

2. Add the **Recent Documents** portlet in the **Page, "Documents"**, of the **Book Lovers** Community.

3. A set of recent **Documents** will appear in this portlet.

Then let's publish **Documents** using **Document Library Display** as follows:

1. Add **Document Library Display** portlet in the page, "**Documents**", of the **Book Lovers** Community.

2. A set of **Folders** with **Documents** will appear in this portlet. You can navigate the **Documents** by clicking on the **Folders'** names.

Using Documents Effectively

Document Library acts as a centralized repository with versioning and library services such as check-in, check-out, and so on. It is backed by a JCR-170 compliant Java Content Repository (Jackrabbit).

Apache Jackrabbit is a fully conforming implementation of the Content Repository for Java Technology API (JCR). URL: `http://jackrabbit.apache.org/`

Using OpenOffice, documents can be converted automatically to multiple formats. For example, the **Document "Full RESTful integration of Liferay and Alfresco"** is in plain text format. Thus we can download it as text file. At the same time, it has been converted into DOC, ODT, PDF, RTF, SXW, and so on. What's happening? The following table shows possible formats for automatic conversion via OpenOffice. Obviously, the plain text of the above document has been converted into **Portable Document Format, OpenDocument Text, OpenOffice.org 1.0 Text, Rich Text Format, Microsoft Word,** and so on.

Category	From	To
Text Formats	OpenDocument Text (`*.odt`)	Portable Document Format (`*.pdf`)
	OpenOffice.org 1.0 Text (`*.sxw`)	OpenDocument Text (`*.odt`)
	Rich Text Format (`*.rtf`)	OpenOffice.org 1.0 Text (`*.sxw`)
	Microsoft Word (`*.doc`)	Rich Text Format (`*.rtf`)
	WordPerfect (`*.wpd`)	Microsoft Word (`*.doc`)
	Plain Text (`*.txt`)	Plain Text (`*.txt`)
Spreadsheet Formats	OpenDocument Spreadsheet (`*.ods`)	Portable Document Format (`*.pdf`)
	OpenOffice.org 1.0 Spreadsheet (`*.sxc`)	OpenDocument Spreadsheet (`*.ods`)
	Microsoft Excel (`*.xls`)	OpenOffice.org 1.0 Spreadsheet (`*.sxc`)
	Comma-Separated Values (`*.csv`)	Microsoft Excel (`*.xls`)
	Tab-Separated Values (`*.tsv`)	Comma-Separated Values (`*.csv`)
		Tab-Separated Values (`*.tsv`)
Presentation Formats	OpenDocument Presentation (`*.odp`)	Portable Document Format (`*.pdf`)
	OpenOffice.org 1.0 Presentation (`*.sxi`)	Macromedia Flash (`*.swf`)
	Microsoft PowerPoint (`*.ppt`)	OpenDocument Presentation (`*.odp`)
		OpenOffice.org 1.0 Presentation (`*.sxi`)
		Microsoft PowerPoint (`*.ppt`)
Drawing Formats	OpenDocument Drawing (`*.odg`)	Scalable Vector Graphics (`*.svg`)
		Macromedia Flash (`*.swf`)

How to get it? In the **Admin** portlet, you can select the **Server** tab, and then the **OpenOffice** tab. Then, you simply click the checkbox **Enable**. If OpenOffice was installed in a remote machine, just change the host and port accordingly. Finally, click the **Save** button when you are ready. That's it!

> OpenOffice.org is a multiplatform and multilingual office suite and an open-source project. URL: `http://www.openoffice.org/`

More interestingly, you can easily export and then import **Documents** (and other content such as **Images**, articles, **Message Boards**, **Wiki**, and so on to another server. How to do it? Simply click the **Configuration** icon of the portlet first. Then, select the **Export/Import** tab. Following the processes, you can export and import contents smoothly.

The following diagram depicts a conceptual overview of the **Document Library**. The **Document Library** has a set of **Folders**. Each **Folder** may have many **Subfolders** associated with it. Each **Folder** (or **Subfolder**) may have a set of **Documents**. Each **Document** has a unique referred **URL**. Each **Document** may have a number of **Comments** (that is, **Posts** and **Replies**) and **Ratings** associated, and each **Document** may have a list of **Versions**.

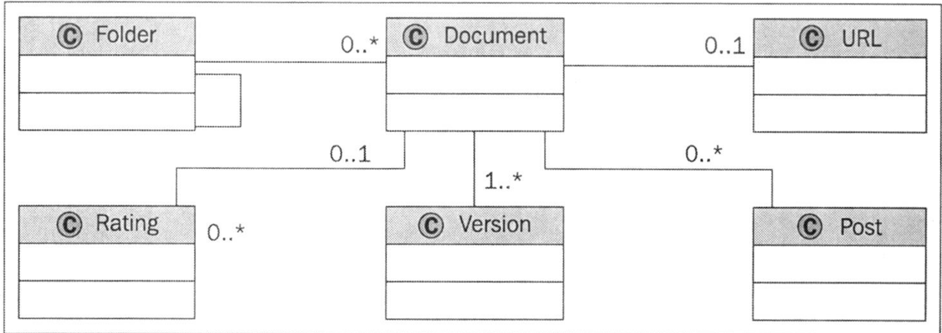

Adding And Managing Articles

Finally, we are ready to create an article based on the above **Images** and **Documents**. For example, we need to create an article called "About us" with **Texts**, **Images** and **Links** to **Documents** as shown in the following figure (named as **Original Required View**). Obviously, Liferay Journal would be very useful for this purpose.

Thus, as an administrator of the enterprise "Palm Tree Publications", you need to create a **Page** called "**Articles**", under the **Page** "**Admin**" at the **Book Lovers** Community and moreover, add the **Journal** portlet in the page, "**Articles**" first. Let's build this article.

Adding A Structure

First of all, we need to create a structure for the above article. A **Structure**, named "**Structure About us**", defines the dynamic parts of the article "About us". Let us create the **Structure** as follows:

1. Add a page named "**Articles**" under the **Page** "**Admin**" of the **Book Lovers** community.

2. Add the **Journal** portlet in the **Page**, "**Articles**", of the **Book Lovers** Community.

3. Click the **Structures** tab.

4. Click the **Add Structures** button.

5. Check the box **Auto Generate ID**, input **Name** "**Structure About us**", description "**Structure for About us**".

6. Set **Permissions** by clicking on the **Configure** link. To configure additional **Permissions**, click on the **More** link. Here, we just use default settings.

7. Add a row such as "**Title**", by clicking on the **Add Row** button, and select the type of the row, such as **Text**.

8. Add more rows such as "**Caption**", "**image_caption**" and so on.

9. Optionally, you can click the **Up** icon and the **Down** icon next to the row, to change the order of rows; or click the **Add** icon next to the row to add a sub row; or click the **Remove** icon next to the row to delete the current row.

10. Click the **Save** button when you are ready.

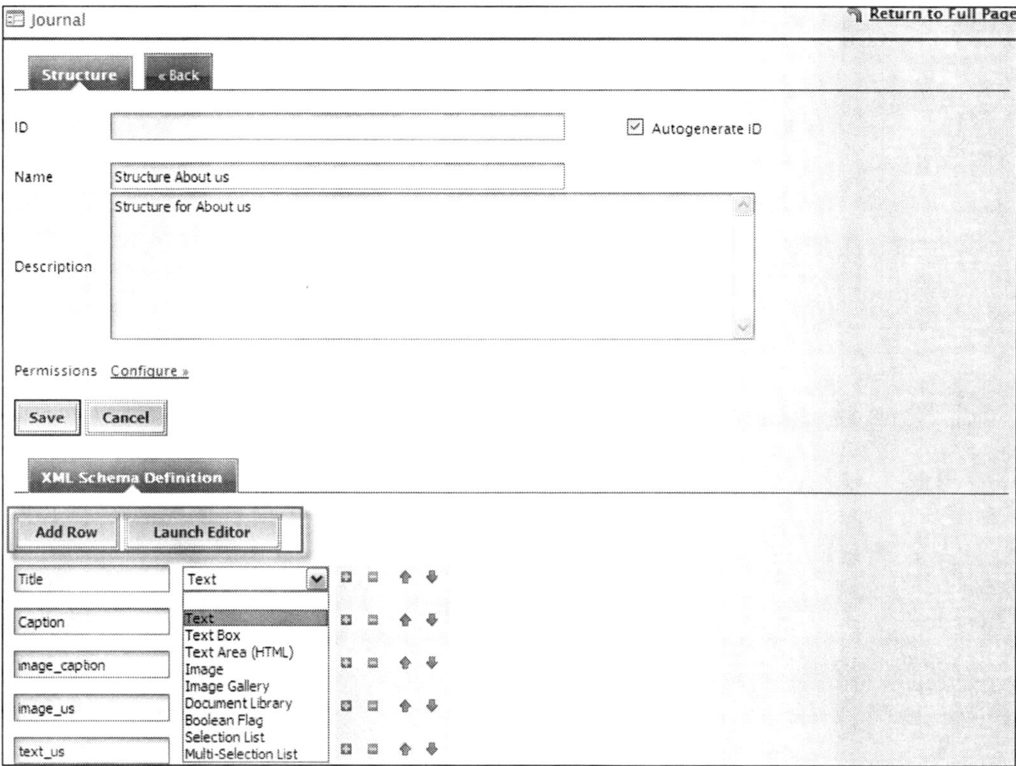

Of course, you can add other **Structures** as well. After adding a **Structure, "one image"**, we can view **Structures**.

Managing Structures

When **Structures** are created, it is simple to manage them. You can either edit a **Structure** or delete a **Structure**. Each **Structure** has a unique referred URL.

View Structures

By clicking the **Structures** tab in the **Journal** portlet, you can view **Structures** with paginations. You can view the **Templates** for a given **Structure** by clicking the **View Templates** icon. Or you can add **Templates** for a given structure by clicking the **Add Templates** icon. Furthermore, you can view the **Articles** related to a given structure by clicking the **View Articles** icon, or you can add **Articles** associated to a given **Structure** by clicking the **Add Article** icon.

More interestingly, you can download the **Structure,** and back it up in the local machine. For example, we need to download the **Structure, "one image"**. Let's do it as follows:

1. Locate the **Structure "one image"** that you want to update.

2. Then click the **Edit** icon from the **Actions** located next to the **Structure**.

3. Click the **Download** button. The **Structure** in XML schema will appear in your browser. Just save it as XML schema in your local machine, if you want. Actually, the unique URL of the structure is used for reference.

In addition, you can find structures either through basic **Search,** or **Advanced Search**. To **Search Structures,** simply click the **Search Structures** button for both basic **Search** and **Advanced Search**. You can switch the basic **Search** interface into **Advanced Search** interface by clicking the **Advanced >>** link, or you can switch the **Advanced Search** interface into **Basic Search** interface by clicking the **>> Basic** link.

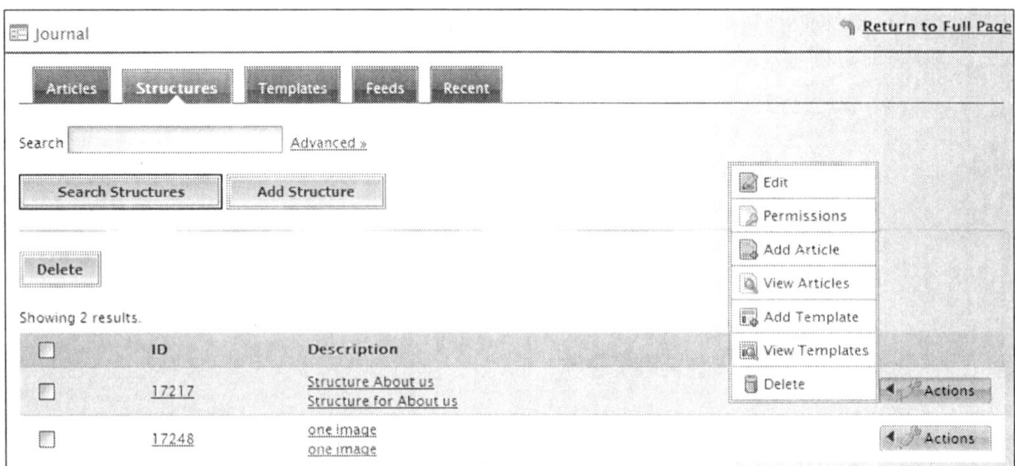

Edit A Structure

Structures are editable just like documents and images. For example, you may need to add a row of the structure, "one image", with the name, "Title". Let's do is as follows:

1. Locate the **Structure** "**one image**" that you want to update.

2. Then click the **Edit** icon from the **Actions** located next to the structure.

3. Add a row such as "**Title**", by clicking on the **Add Row** button; and select the type of the row such as **Text**.

4. Optionally, you can launch an editor to update the rows directly, if you know XML schema, by clicking the **Launch Editor** button first. Then you can use either **Plain** or **Rich** editor types, to update the XML schema. Finally, click the **Update** button.

5. Click the **Save** button when you are ready.

Delete a Structure

Structures are removable just like **Documents** and **Images**. Suppose that the **Structure** "one image" is not wanted anymore, you can delete it as follows:

1. Locate the **Structure** "**one image**" that you want to delete.

2. Then click on the **Delete** icon from the **Actions** located next to the structure.

3. A screen will appear asking if you want to delete this. Click **OK** to confirm deletion.

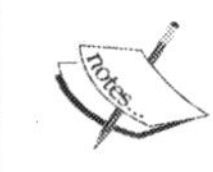

Note that you cannot delete a **Structure** which is used by **Templates**. In order to delete this **Structure**, you need to edit the **Templates** and remove the **Structure** association first. Then, you can delete the **Structure**.

Adding A Template

Next, we need to create a **Template** for the above **Article**. A **Template**, named "Template About us", is a pattern to rapidly generate the **Article "About us"**. Let's create the **Template** as follows:

1. Click the **Templates** tab.

2. Click the **Add Templates** button.

3. Check the box, **Auto Generate ID**, input **Name, "Template About us"**, description "**Template for About us**".

4. Select **Structure** such as "**Structure About us**", by clicking the **Select** button next to the **Structure**.

5. Select the **Language Type,** such as "**VM**" (that is, Velocity Macro).

6. Upload a **Template** script file, such as "**template.vm**" from the local machine, by clicking the **Browse...** button next to the **Script**.

7. Upload a small image such as "**template.png**", from the local machine by clicking the **Browse...** button, next to the **Small Image**.

8. Check the checkbox, **Use Small Image**.

9. Set **Permissions** by clicking on the **Configure** link. To configure additional **Permissions**, click on the **More** link. Here, we just use default settings.

10. Click on the **Save** button when you are ready.

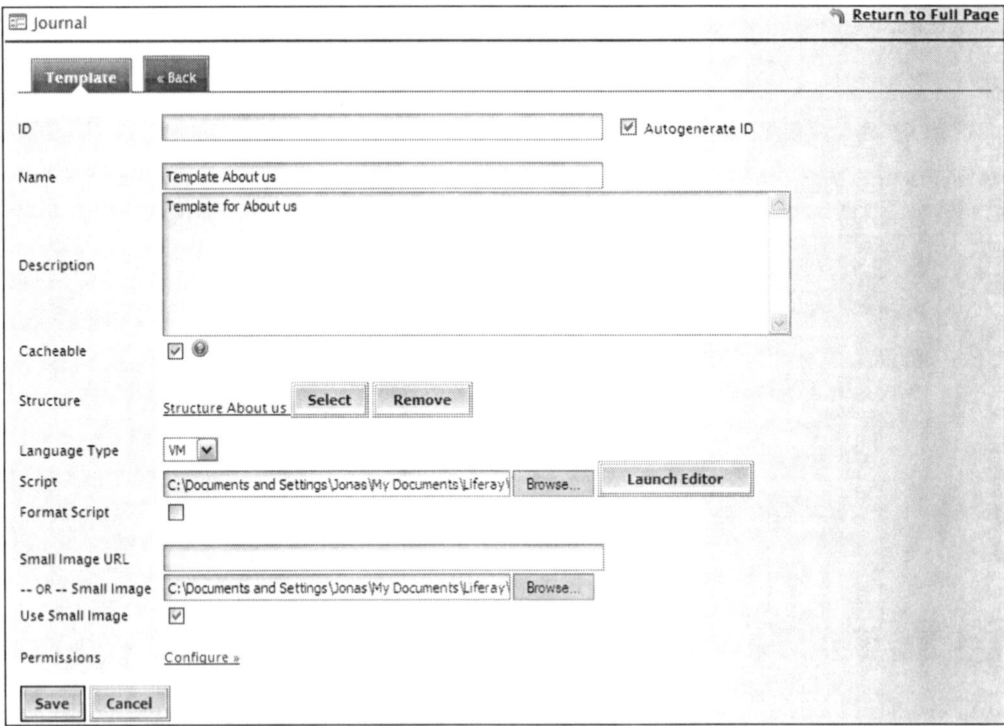

Surely, you can add other **Templates** that you want. After adding a **Template, "Template one image"**, associated with the **Structure, "one image"**, we can view **Templates**.

Managing Templates

Similar to managing **Structures**, you can either edit a **Template** or delete a **Template**. Each **Template** may have a structure associated with it and moreover, it has a unique URL to be referred.

View Templates

By clicking the **Templates** tab in the **Journal** portlet, you can view **Templates** with paginations. You can edit the **Structure** associated with a given **Template** by clicking the **Edit Structure** icon. Furthermore, you can view **Articles** related to a given **Template,** by clicking the **Views Articles** icon or you can add an article associated with a given **Template** by clicking the **Add Article** icon.

Similarly, you can download the **Template** via the unique URL, and backup it in local machine like **Structure**.

In addition, you can query **Templates** either through basic **Search,** or **Advanced Search,** as in **Structures**.

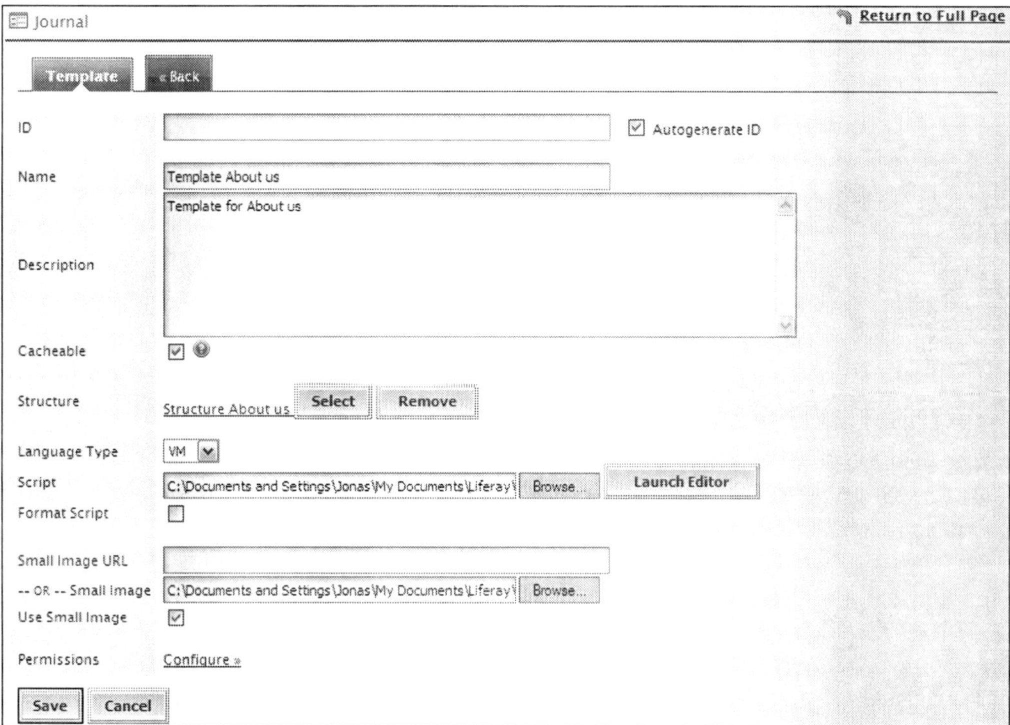

Edit A Template

Similar to Structures, Templates are also editable. For example, you may need to change the expression of the **Template, "Template one image"**, with a new item, **"Title"**, according to the structure, **"one image"**. Let's do it as follows:

1. Locate the **Template, "Template one image"** that you want to update.

2. Then click the **Edit** icon from the **Actions** located next to the **Template**.

3. Launch an editor to update the content of the **Template,** by clicking the **Launch Editor** button first. Then you can use either **Plain** or **Rich** editor types to update the content such as, adding the new item according to the **Structure "one image"**. Finally, click the **Update** button.

4. Click the **Save** button when you are ready.

Delete A Template

Similar to Structures, Templates are also removable. Suppose the **Template, "Template one image"**, is not wanted anymore ,we can delete it as follows:

1. Locate the **Template, "Template one image"** that you want to delete.

2. Then click on the **Delete** icon from the **Actions** located next to the template.

3. A screen will appear asking if you want to delete this. Click **OK** to confirm deletion.

Note that you cannot delete a **Template** which is used by **Articles**. In order to delete this **Template**, you need to edit **Articles** and remove the **Template** association first. Then, you can delete the **Template**.

Adding An Article

When **Structures** and **Templates** are ready, we can create the **Article, "About us"**, now. An **Article** is the actual content of the web **Page**, which may be associated with a **Template** and a **Structure**. Let's create the **Article** as follows:

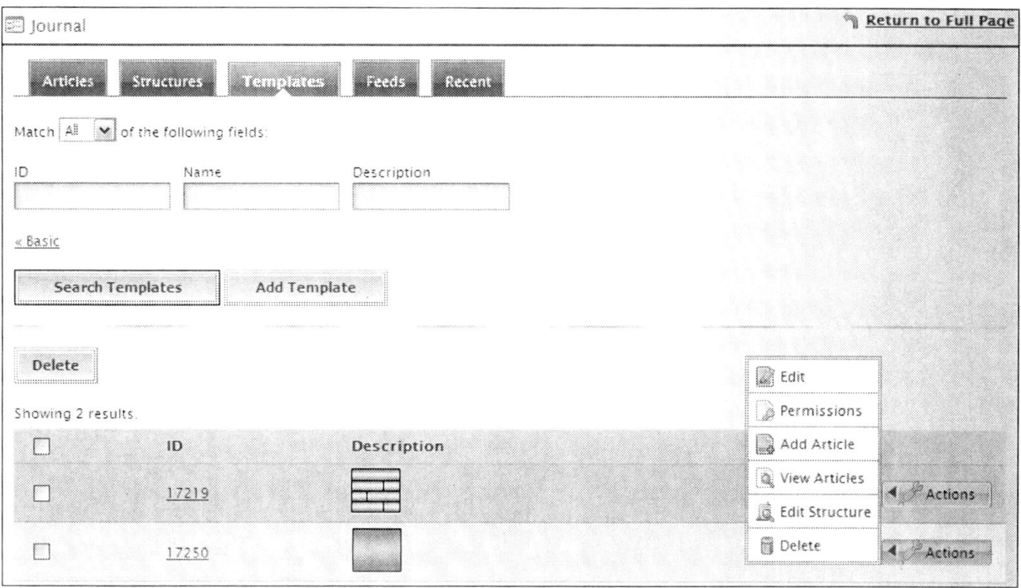

1. Click the **Articles** tab.

2. Click the **Add Article** button.

3. Use **Auto Generate ID**; input a **Name** such as "**About us**", a **Description** such as "**Article for About us**".

4. First, select a **Structure** such as, "**Structure About us**", by clicking on the **Select** button next to the **Structure**. Then, select a **Template** such as "**Template About us**".

5. Alternatively, select the **Template** such as "**Template About us**", by clicking the **Select** button next to the **Template**. The content pieces will change, following the **Structure** and **Template**.

6. Set **Permissions** by clicking on the **Configure** link. To configure additional **Permissions**, click on the **More** link. Here, we just use default settings.

7. Optionally, you can input an **Abstract** for this **Article**. Input a **Description** such as "**Article About us for a page**"; upload a small **Image** such as "**article. png**", from a local machine by clicking the **Browse...** button next to the **Small Image**. Check the checkbox, **Use Small Image**.

8. In addition, you can set up the **Schedule**, such as **Display Date**, **Expiration Date**, and **Review Date**.

9. Or click the button, **Select Tags,** if you want to select existing tags or click the button, **Add Tags,** if you need to add new **Tags**.

10. Click on the **Save** button when you just want to save it, or click on the **Save and Continue** button, when you want to save and continue the current work. Or click on the **Save and Approve** button when you want to save it and moreover, approve it. Here, we click on the **Save and Approve button.**

 Note that an **Article** can be approved or not approved. Only approved **Articles** can be used in the **Pages**.

Of course, you can add other **Articles** that you want. After adding an **Article** such as "**Article one image**", associated with the **Template** "**Template one image**", we can view **Articles**.

Managing Articles

Each **Article** may have a **Template** and a **Structure** associated. After adding a set of **Articles**, you can edit, delete, preview, search and approve **Articles**. Moreover, you can make **Articles,** expired or restore an expired **Article,** or create new versions of **Articles**.

View Articles

By clicking the **Articles** tab in the **Journal** portlet, you can view **Articles** with paginations (if there are a lot of **Articles**). You can edit the **Article** by clicking the **Edit** icon from the **Actions** next to the article.

To view recent **Articles**, **Structures** and **Templates** that you can access, simply click the **Recent** tab in the **Journal** portlet. Moreover, you can also add feeds (**RSS**) and manage feeds in the **Journal** portlet. RSS types such as **Atom 1.0** and **RSS 2.0,** are supported as well.

Meanwhile, you can preview an **Article**. Suppose that you want to preview the **Article** "**About us**". Let's do it as follows:

1. Locate the **Article** "**About us**" that you want to update.

2. Then click the **Preview** icon from the **Actions** located next to the article.

In addition, you can query **Articles** either through basic **Search** or **Advanced Search** as in **Structures** and **Templates**. You can search by **Version, Content, Type** and **Status** in **Advanced Search,** as shown in following figure.

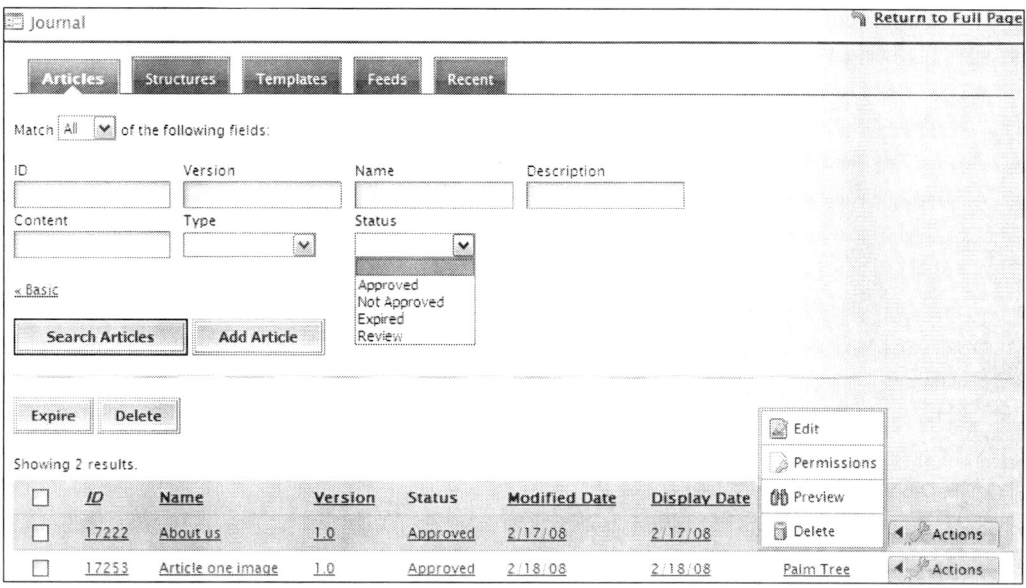

Edit An Article

Similar to Structures and **Templates, Articles** are also editable. For example, you may need to change the contents of the **Article, "Article one image"** with the other **Image, "PalmTree_logo.png"** according to the structure, **"one image"**. Let's do it as follows:

1. Locate the "**Article one image**" that you want to update.

2. Then click the **Edit** icon from the **Actions** located next to the article.

3. Upload the **Image, "PalmTree_logo.png"**, by clicking the **Select** button above the content piece **Image**.

3. Click the **Save** button when you are ready.

An **Article** may have a list of **Versions**. Suppose that the **Article, "Article one image" Abstract Description,** is updated with value ,"**Palm Tree Logo**", in a new **Version**. Let's do it as follows:

1. Locate the "**Article one image**" that you want to update.

2. Then click the **Edit** icon from the **Actions** located next to the article.

3. Update the **Abstract Description** with the value, "**Palm Tree Logo**".

4. Select the checkbox, **Increment Version on Save,** under the **Workflow**.

5. Click on the **Save and Approve** button when you are ready.

In addition, you can expire an **Article, or** restore an expired **Article**. Suppose that the Article "**Article one image**" has to be made expired. Let's do it as follows:

1. Locate the "**Article one image**" that you want to update.

2. Then click the **Edit** icon from the **Actions** located next to the article.

3. Click the **Expire** button under the **Workflow**.

Later, we may want to restore the **Article, "Article one image"**, and also update it for other purposes. Let's restore it as follows:

1. Select the checkbox, **Never Auto Expire**.

2. Click the **Save and Approve** button.

Delete An Article

Articles are also removable just like **Structures** and **Templates**. Suppose that the Article, "**Article one image**", is not wanted anymore. Let's delete it as follows:

1. Locate the **Article** "**Article one image**" that you want to delete.

2. Then click on the **Delete** icon from the **Actions** located next to the article.

3. A screen will appear asking if you want to delete this. Click **OK** to confirm deletion.

Note that after an **Article** has been deleted, you cannot restore it. If you do not want to delete it actually, you can just make it expired. Sooner or later, when you want to reuse this **Article**, you can restore it easily.

Setting up Journal

As an administrator of the enterprise, "Palm Tree Publications", you can set up **Journal**. You can configure **Email From**.

To configure the **Email From**, click the **Configuration** icon on **Journal**. On selecting the **Setup** tab, the following five sub-tabs appear: **Email From, Article Denied Email, Article Granted Email, Article Requested Email**, and **Article Review Email**.

With the **Email From** tab selected, you can change the name and address of the automatically sent emails.

The **Article Denied Email** tab allows the Administrator to edit the email that is sent whenever an article is denied. To disable email notification, uncheck the **Enabled** box. Click the **Save** button after making any changes.

Similarly, as an administrator, you can set up **Article Granted Email**, **Article Requested Email**, and **Article Review Email** as you want.

Updating Permissions

Suppose that "**David Berger**" is a content designer who can create **Structures** and **Templates**; "**Lotti Stein**" is a content writer who can write **Articles**; "**Rolf Hess**" is a content editor who can edit and approve **Articles**. Let's see what **Permissions** are present by default.

The following table shows **Permissions** on **Journal**. A **Community User** may set up all **Permissions** (marked 'X'), **View, Add Article, Add Feed, Add Structure, Add Template, Approve Article** and **Configuration**, while a **Guest User** may set up **Permissions, View** and **Configuration**. By default, a **Community** has the **View Permission** (marked '*'), as does a **Guest User**.

Action	Description	Community	Guest
View	Views this portlet	X, *	X, *
Add Article	Adds an **Article** to the portlet	X	
Add Feed	Adds a feed to the portlet	X	
Add Structure	Adds a **Structure** to the portlet	X	
Add Template	Adds a **Template** to the portlet	X	
Approve Article	Approves an **Article** on the portlet	X	
Configuration	Configures this portlet	X	X

As members of the **Book Lovers** community, "**David Berger**", "**Lotti Stein**" and "**Rolf Hess**" have only the **View Permission** on the **Journal** portlet, by default. How to implement the above requirements? Let's do it as follows:

1. Create a user group named **Content Designers**; and assign "**David Berger**" as its member.
2. Create a user group named **Content Writers**; and assign "**Lotti Stein**" as its member.
3. Create a user group named **Content Editors**; and assign "**Rolf Hess**" as its member.
4. Click the **Configuration** icon in the **Journal** portlet.
5. Select the **Permissions** tab, and furthermore, select the **User Group** tab.
6. Update **Permissions** on **Content Designers** with **Add Article, Add Feed, Add Structure, Add Template, Approve Article,** and **View**.
7. Update **Permissions** on **Content Writer** with **Add Article** and **View**.
8. Update **Permissions** on **Content Editors** with **Add Article, Approve Article** and **View**.

Thus, as a content designer, "**David Berger**" can create **Structures** and **Templates**; as a content writer, "**Lotti Stein**" can write **Articles**; as a content editor, "**Rolf Hess**" can edit and approve **Articles**. Try to log in as "**David Berger**", "**Lotti Stein**", or "**Rolf Hess**". You will have different **Permission** actions on the **Journal** portlet.

Using Permissions on Articles

We can set up **Permissions** based on individual **Articles**. The following table shows **Permissions** on **Articles**. A **Community User** may set up all **Permissions** (marked 'X'), **View, Add Discussion, Delete, Expire, Permissions,** and **Update**, while a **Guest User** may set up **Permissions, View, Add Discussion, Delete,** and **Permissions**. By default, a **Community** has **View** and **Add Discussion** (marked '*') **Permissions**, while a **Guest User** has only **View Permission**.

Action	Description	Community	Guest
View	Views this **Article**	X, *	X, *
Add Discussion	Adds an **Article** to the **Article**	X, *	X
Delete	Deletes this **Article**	X	X
Expire	Makes this **Article** expired	X	
Permissions	Assigns **Permission** on this **Article**	X	X
Update	Edits this **Article**	X	

Using Permissions on Structures And Templates

We can set up **Permissions** based on individual **Structures** or **Templates**. The following table shows **Permissions** on **Structures** and **Templates**. A **Community User** may set up all **Permissions** (marked 'X'), **View, Delete, Permissions,** and **Update**, while a **Guest User** may set up **Permissions, View, Delete,** and **Permissions**. By default, a **Community** has **Permission** action, **View** (marked '*'), and so does a **Guest User**.

Action	Description	Community	Guest
View	Views this **Structure** or **Template**	X, *	X, *
Delete	Deletes this **Structure** or **Template**	X	X
Permissions	Assigns **Permission** on this **Structure** or **Template**	X	X
Update	Edits this **Structure** or **Template**	X	

Using Articles Effectively

The following diagram depicts the conceptual relationships between **Article**, **Template** and **Structure**. Normally, an **Article** may have one **Template** associated with it. It is possible that an **Article** may not use any **Template**, while a **Template** may serve many **Articles**. This is the reason why we can view **Articles** by a given **Template**. Each **Article** may have a number of **Comments** (that is, **Posts** and **Replies**) and **Ratings** associated, and each **Article** may have a list of **Versions**. More interestingly, each **Article** has different status: approved or not approved, expired, or reviewed.

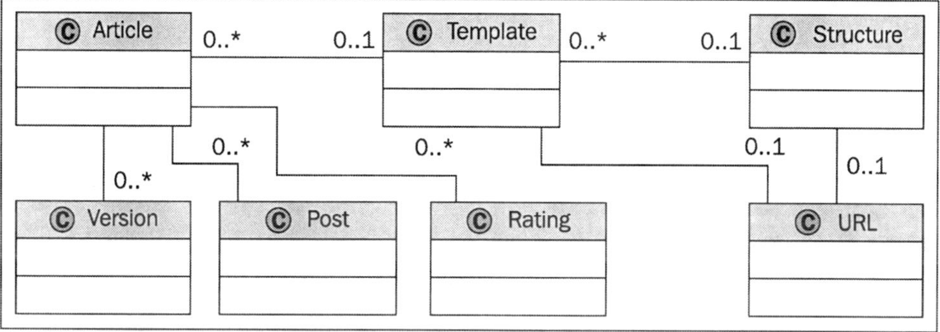

Similarly, a **Template** may have one **Structure** associated, or a **Template** does not employ any **Structure**. Meanwhile, a **Structure** may serve many **Templates**. Thus, on the one hand, we can edit **Structure** by a given **Template**. On the other hand, we can view **Templates** and **Articles** by a given **Structure**. Each **Template** and **Structure** has a unique **URL** to be referred.

Build A Structure

Structure is an XML (Extensible Mark-up Language) definition of the dynamic parts of the **Article**. These parts may be text, a text box, a text Area (HTML), an **Image**, **Image Gallery**, **Document Library**, a Boolean flag (true or false), a selection list, multiple selection list etc. Actually, the **Structure** is a specific XML schema.

By **Structures**, we can unify the **Articles** with the same numbers and types of items. For example, the **Page** "**About us**" of "Palm Tree Publications" may have five **Articles**, each requiring a title, a caption and an **Image** for the headquarters, an **Image** and a text area for the US office, a text area and an **Image** for the Germany office. A **Structure** would be created with three **Images**, two texts, and two text areas, each named accordingly. This allows writers to create the individual **Articles** and other texts without needing to recreate the **Page Structure** for each **Article**.

Based on the example (**Original Required View**), the **Structure** lists out the eight content pieces:

- One text element named "Title" (1).

- One text box element named "Caption" (2).

- Two text area elements named "text_us" (5) and "text_de" (6); and a link to a **Document** "Open Source project" (8).

- Three image elements named "image_caption" (3), "image_us" (4), and "image_de"(7).

Below are real codes of **Structure** "**Structure About us**".

```
<root>
<dynamic-element name='Title' type='text'></dynamic-element>
<dynamic-element name='Caption' type='text_box'></dynamic-element>
<dynamic-element name='image_caption' type='image_gallery'></dynamic-
element>
<dynamic-element name='image_us' type='image_gallery'></dynamic-
element>
<dynamic-element name='text_us' type='text_area'></dynamic-element>
<dynamic-element name='text_de' type='text_area'></dynamic-element>
<dynamic-element name='image_de' type='image_gallery'></dynamic-
element>
</root>
```

Create A Template

Template (Web Template) is a pattern to rapidly generate and mass-produce web pages, associated to a **Structure**. A **Template** defines the layout of the **Article**, and determines how the content items will be arranged.

Templates used for creating **Articles** can be created in XSL, Velocity (VM), CSS and FreeMarker, and so on. You can create many **Templates** for one **Structure**. Or you can give the writers the discretion to decide the best layout.

The following are the real codes of the **Template, "Template About us"** in VM.

```
<html>
<head><title>$reserved-article-id.getData()</title></head>
<body>
  <table><tr><td align="center"><h1>$Title.getData()</h1></td></tr>
    <tr>
            <td width="60%"><font size="3" color="#0000A0">$Caption.
                    getData()</font></td>
            <td width="40%" align="center"><img src="$image_caption.
```

```
getData()"/></td>
    </tr>
  </table>
  <table>
    <tr>
            <td width="30%" align="center"><img src="$image_
                                    us.getData()"/></td>
            <td width="70%">$text_us.getData()</td>
    </tr>
  </table>
  <table>
    <tr>
            <td width="70%">$text_de.getData()</td>
            <td width="30%" align="center"><img src="$image_
                                    de.getData()"/></td>
    </tr>
  </table>
</body>
</html>
```

Construct An Article

Article is the actual content of the web page, associated with a **Structure** and a
Template. Each content piece is populated with actual texts and **Images**. Each
Article is integrated with two status of **Workflow**, either approved or not approved.
Meanwhile, each **Article** may have a set of dates associated, such as display date,
expiration date, and review date, and so on.

There are three kinds of **Users** involved in **Article** lifecycle: designers, writers and
editors. Typically, designers create **Structures** and **Templates** first. Then, **Articles**
are written normally by writers, and editors edit and approve the **Articles**. Finally,
Articles are displayed or expired by designers.

By default, **Article** types include **Announcements, Blogs, News, General, Press
release** and **Test**.

Type Name	Description
Announcements	Publications for making known publicly.
Blogs	Frequent and chronological publications of personal thoughts and Web links.
News	Information about recent events or happenings.
General	General publications / information.
Press release	News that is sent out or released by the company making the news.
Test	Testing information.

It should be noted that these **Article** types are configurable. For example, you can configure **Articles** types in `portal-ext.properties` by removing **Test** as follows:

```
journal.article.types=announcements,blogs,general,news,press-release
```

Publishing Articles

We have used the **Journal** portlet to create contents (**Articles**) stored in CMS. Now, we are ready to publish contents to portal **Users** and **Guests**.

Suppose that there are two **Pages**, "**Articles**" and "**About us**", under the **Page, "Home"** at the **Book Lovers** Community **Public Pages**. The **Page, "Articles"**, will display all **Articles,** and **Users** can navigate these **Articles**, while the **Page, "About us"**, will display the **Article, "About us"** only. Thanks to **Journal Content** and **Journal Articles**, these are very useful for these two scenarios.

Using Journal Content

As an administrator of "Palm Tree Publications", you need to create a **Page** called "**About us**" under the **Page "Home"** at the **Book Lovers** Community, and also add the **Journal Content** portlet in the **Page, "About us"**. Finally, publish the **Article, "About us"**, in the **Page, "About us"**. Let's publish the **Article** as follows:

1. Add a **Page** called "**About us**" under the **Page, "Home"**, at the **Book Lovers** Community **Public Pages,** if the **Page** is not already present.

2. Change the layout with the value "1-Column" by clicking the link **Layout Templates**.

3. If the **Journal Content** portlet is not present, add it in the page, "**About us**", of the **Book Lovers** Community where you want to publish the **Article**.

4. Select an **Article** by clicking the **Select Article** icon in the **Journal Content** portlet.

5. Locate the **Article "About us"**, and select the **Article** by clicking the link **Name**.

6. Optionally, check the checkbox, **Enable Ratings,** if you want to enable **Ratings;** check the checkbox, **Enable Comments,** if you want to enable **Comments**. Here, we just use default settings.

7. Click the **Return to Full Page** arrow when you are ready.

8. Optionally, remove the border of the portlet by clicking the **Look and Feel** icon and unselecting the checkbox, **Show Border**. Click the **Save** button and click the **Remove** icon to return.

9. Open a new browser such as "Opera", and input URL with the value "`http://localhost:8080/web/booklovers/aboutus`", and you will see the page "**About us**", as shown in following figure.

Do you find any difference between this **Page,** and the **Original Required View**? Of course, all content pieces are the same as that of **Original Required View**, such as **Images,** texts and links. But the look and feel is slightly different. As stated earlier, the content designer can update the **Template, "Template About us"**, with CSS to provide the best layout. In short, you can provide the best layout that you can imagine through **Templates** and CSS.

Using Journal Articles

As an administrator of "Palm Tree Publications", you need to create a **Page** called "**Articles**" under the **Page, "Home"**, at the **Book Lovers** Community. You also have to and add the **Journal Articles** portlet in the **Page, "Articles"**, and finally publish **Articles** in the **Page, "Articles"**. Let's do it as follows:

1. Add a **Page** called "**Articles**" under the **Page, "Home"**, at the **Book Lovers** Community **Public Pages,** if the **Page** is not present.

2. Change the layout with value "1-Column" by clicking on the link **Layout Templates**.

3. Add the **Journal Articles** portlet in the page, "**Articles**", of the **Book Lovers** Community where you want to publish **Articles**, if **Journal Articles** portlet is not present.

4. Click the **Configuration** link to modify the properties of the portlet.

5. Choose the **Community** such as "**Book Lovers**", **Article Type** such as "**General**", **Display URL, Display per Page, Order by Column**, and **Order by Type** as well.

6. Click the **Save** button.

7. Click on the **Return to Full Page** arrow when you are ready.

Do you find a list of **Articles** in the **Page** "**Articles**"? One of them is the **Article** "**About us**".

Note that only approved **Articles** will appear in the **Journal Articles** portlet. You cannot see the **Articles** which are not approved or the ones which have expired.

Using Other CMS Tools

There are some other CMS tools, which are useful for web content publishing. Here, we just list some of them as follows:

- XML content: provides ability to publish XML-based content.

- Asset publisher: a generic front end to several content types and sources such as **Blogs Entry**, Bookmarks Entry, **Document Library Document, Image Gallery Image, Journal Article**, and last but not the least, Tagged Content.

- Nested portlets: holds one or more portlets inside. It provides nested portlets layout, that is, portlets within portlets.

Summary

This chapter covered how to add **Folders** and **Subfolders** for **Images**; how to manage **Folders** and **Subfolders**; how to add **Images** in **Folders** and manage **Images**; and how to set up **Permission** on **Folders** and **Images**. It also discussed how to add **Folders** and **Subfolders** for **Documents**; how to manage **Documents**, how to add **Comments**, how to give your **Rating** and view **Versions**; how to set up **Permission** on **Folders** and **Documents** and how to publish **Documents**. Further, it also introduced us to **Structure** management, **Template** management and **Article** management. It emphasised on how to build **Articles** based on **Structures** and **Templates**, and how to set up **Permissions** on **Journal**, **Articles**, **Templates** and **Structures**. Finally, it discussed how to publish **Articles** and to employ other CMS tools. In short, Liferay Journal does not only provides high availability to publish, manage, and maintain web contents and documents, but also separates contents from the layout.

9

Chat and Instant Messaging

In the intranet website book.com of "Palm Tree Publications", as an administrator, you are required to provide an environment for employees to enjoy chatting, instant messaging, mailing, and SMS text messaging with others. This chapter will introduce to us, how to enjoy instant messaging. Then, it will discuss how to manage emails. Finally, it will focus on SMS text messenger.

By the end of this chapter, you will have learnt how to:

- Add a participant for chatting.
- Manage (view and delete) participants in the chat portlet.
- Start chatting.
- Set up chat portlet.
- Manage (check, delete, forward, reply, search) mails.
- Set up mail portlet.
- Manage SMS text messenger portlet.

Working with Chat Portlet

In order to let employees enjoy chatting and instant messaging with others, we should use the Liferay **Chat** portlet. Let's experience how to enjoy chatting and instant messaging first.

As an administrator of "Palm Tree Publications", you need to create a **Page** called "**Instant Messaging**" under the **Page**, "**Community**", at the **Book Lovers** Community and also add the **Chat** portlet in the **Page**, "**Instant Messaging**".

Adding a Participant

First of all, log in as "**Palm Tree**" and do the following:

1. Add a **Page** called "**Instant Messaging**" under the **Page**, "**Community**" at the **Book Lovers** Community **Public Pages**, if the **Page** is not already present.

2. Add the **Chat** portlet in the **Page**, "**Instant Messaging**" of the **Book Lovers** Community where you want to set up chatting and an instant messaging environment, if **Chat** portlet is not already present.

After adding the **Chat** portlet, you can view it as shown in the following figure.

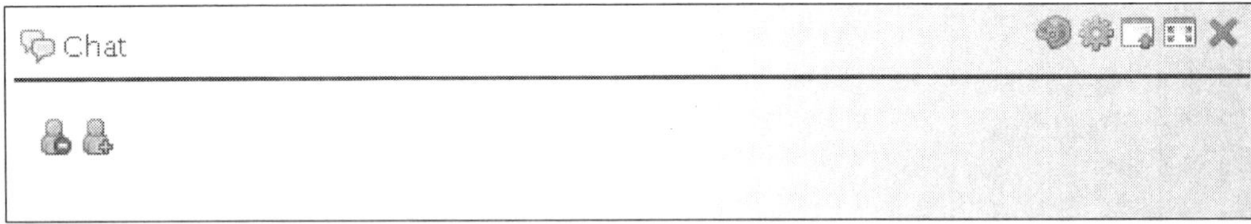

Then, we need to add a participant in the **Chat** portlet. As an editor at the Editorial department, "**Lotti Stein**" wants to ping the manager, "**David Berger**", online and further share some comments about Liferay books. Let's do it as follows:

1. Login as "**Lotti Stein**" first.

2. Go to the **Page**, "**Instant Messaging**", " under the **Page**, "**Community**", at the **Book Lovers** Community **Public Pages**.

3. Click on the **Add** icon.

4. Input a participant's email address, such as "**david@book.com**".

5. Press the **Enter** key.

You will see the participant's full name appear, such as "**David Berger**". After adding more participants, such as "**John Stuckia**" and "**Rolf Hess**", you can view all participants as shown in the following figure.

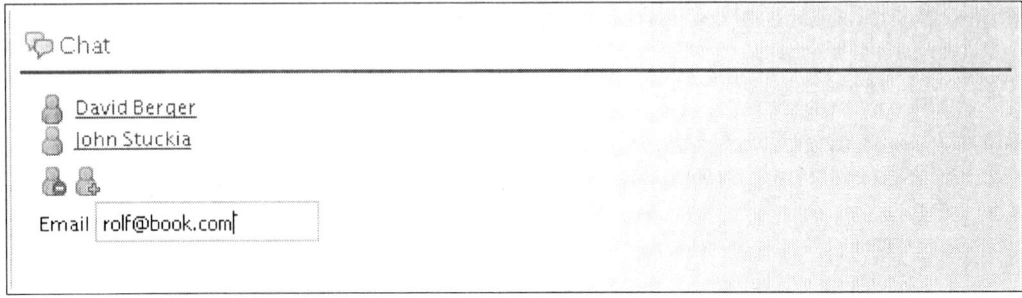

Managing Participants

All the **Users** you've invited will appear as a list of participants. If the **User** "**David Berger**" is online ,then the icon to the left of the **User** name becomes light blue. Otherwise, it remains light gray; for example, **User** "John Stuckia". As shown in the following figure, only two **Users** ("**David Berger**" and "**Lotti Stein**") are online in the server. For details about **OpenFire**, refer to the forthcoming section.

The participants are removable. For example, "**Lotti Stein**" wants to remove a participant "**Rolf Hess**", from the list of participants. Let's do it as follows:

1. Locate the participant, such as "**Rolf Hess**".

2. Click on the icon to the left of the **User** name, such as "**Rolf Hess**". You will see that the participant "**Rolf Hess**" is highlighted.

3. Click the **Remove** icon. This participant will be removed from the list of participants.

In short, to remove a **User** from the list of participants, simply locate the **User** you want to remove by clicking on the icon to the left of the **User** name. Then, click the **Remove** icon. The selected **User** name will be removed from the list of participants.

Starting Chatting

Irrespective of whether the participants are online or not, you can begin to **Chat** with them. For example, as an editor of editorial department, "**Lotti Stein**" wants to start chatting with the manager, "**David Berger**". Let's do it as follows:

1. Locate the participant, "**David Berger**".
2. Click the **User** name, ,"**David Berger**".
3. A **Chat** box will appear.
4. Input the message, "**David, how are you**?"
5. Press the **Enter** key. Your messages will appear starting with the keyword, **Me,** in the message box (as shown in the following figure).

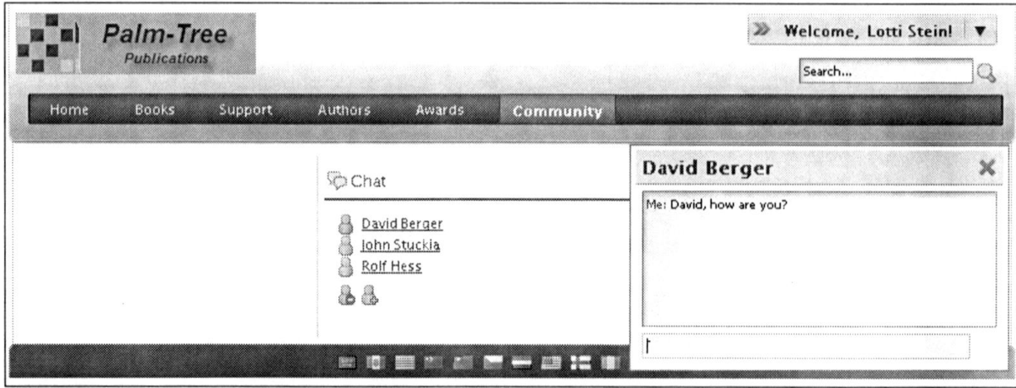

As a manager of the editorial department, "**David Berger**" will have to do the following, to receive the messages from "**Lotti Stein**":

1. Login as "**David Berger**" in new browser.
2. Go to the **Page**, "**Instant Messaging**" under the **Page**, "**Community**" at the **Book Lovers** Community **Public Pages**.
3. Locate the participant, "**Lotti Stein**".
4. Click the **User** name, "**Lotti Stein**".
5. A chat box will appear with the messages from "**Lotti Stein**".
6. Input the message, "**I am fine, and you?**"

7. Press the **Enter** key. Your messages will appear starting with the keyword "**Me:**" in the message box and the messages sent by the other **User, Lotti Stein**" here, will appear starting with the **User's** name as shown in the following figure:

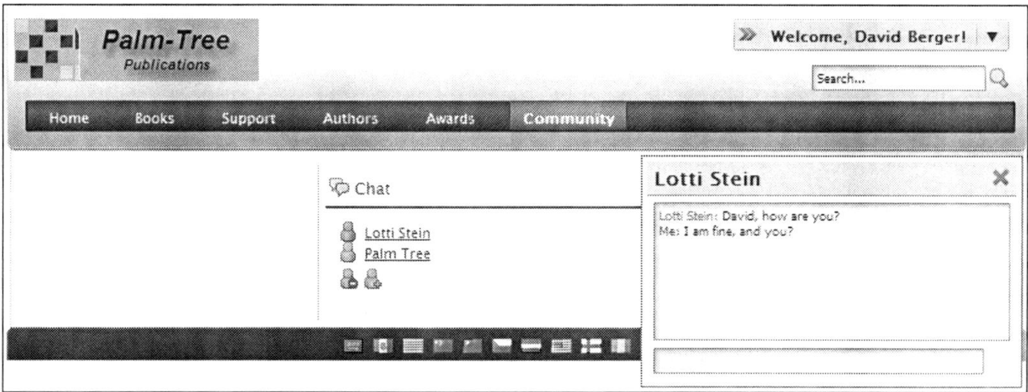

Generally, to start chat, locate the **User** you want to chat with, by the **User** name first. Click on the **User** name link. A **Chat** box will appear. You can chat with many **Users** at the same time. To do this, just click on the **Users'** name link. Each **Chat** box is only for one unique **User**.

The **Chat** box contains the **User's** name on the upper left. You can close the current **Chat** box by clicking on the mark **X** to the upper right.

> Note that the **Chat** box is hidden in your current **Page** initiatively. Whenever a new message comes from the **User,** you are chatting with, the **Chat** box will pop up with the new message and possible previous messages.

To send messages, simply input your messages in the message input box first, and then press the **Enter** key. Your messages will appear starting with the keyword, **Me,** in the message box, and the messages sent by the other **Users** will appear starting with their **User** names.

How Does It Work?

Liferay **Chat** portlet (AJAX Instant Messaging) allows **Users** to automatically chat over XMPP (Jabber) protocol with other **Users**. Instant Messaging lets members interact with other members in real time. A private room may exists for customers which could give them access to others.

Liferay **Chat** portlet integrates with a Jabber server, that is, OpenFire. This session will introduce Instant Messaging, AJAX, and Jabber (OpenFire).

OpenFire (previously known as Wildfire Server) is a real-time collaboration (RTC) server, adopted open protocol for instant messaging, XMPP (also called Jabber). URL: http://www.jivesoftware.com/products/openfire/.

Use Instant Messaging

Instant messaging (IM) acts as a form of real-time communication among **Users,** based on typed text. It allows easy collaboration. In contrast to email, the participants know whether the peer is available. Conversations by instant messaging can be saved for later reference.

One of the Instant Messaging protocols is Extensible Messaging and Presence Protocol (XMPP).

XMPP is an open, XML-inspired protocol for near-real-time, extensible instant messaging (IM) and presence information. It is the core protocol of the Jabber Instant Messaging and Presence technology. URL: http://www.xmpp.org/.

On the one hand, XMPP is based on open standards, different from other instant messaging protocols. Similar to email, XMPP is an open system where a **User** having a domain name and a suitable Internet connection can run a Jabber server, and talk to others on other servers.

On the other hand, another useful feature of the XMPP system is, transports, also called gateways. Through this, **Users** can access networks using other protocols. These protocols can be other instant messaging protocols, such as SMS or Email. The case is different from multi-protocol clients, as **Users** can access XMPP server at the server level. That is, it communicates with other servers through gateway services, which are running on a remote server.

Another interesting feature of XMPP is the HTTP binding behind restricted firewalls.

For instance, **Community A User** wants to chat with **Community B User**. **Community A User** and **Community B User** have accounts on the Jabber Server and the Third Part Server respectively. When **Community A User** types in and sends his/her message, a sequence of events is set in action, as shown in the following figure:

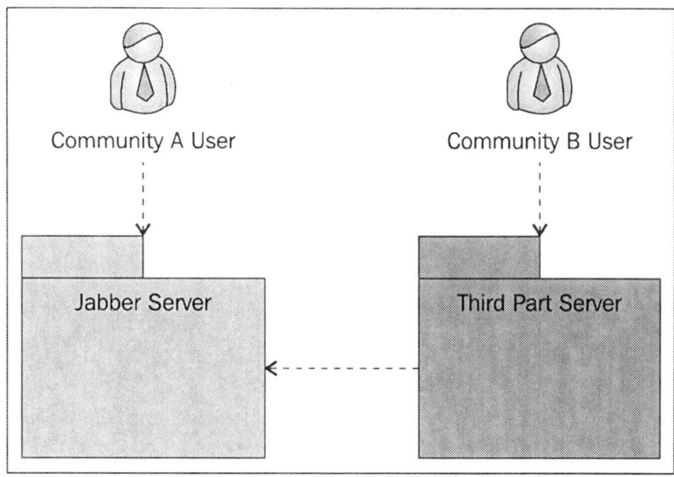

- **Community A User's** client sends his/her message to the Jabber Server.
  - If **Third Part Server** is blocked on Jabber Server, the message is dropped.

- The **Jabber Server** opens a connection to the Third Part Server.

- The Jabber server delivers the message to **Community B User**.
  - If **Jabber Server** is blocked on **Third Part Server**, the message is dropped.

- If **Community B User** is not currently connected, the message is stored for later delivery.

Jabber is the Linux of instant messaging—an open, secure, ad-free alternative to consumer IM services. URL: `http://www.jabber.org/`

Employ AJAX

AJAX is Asynchronous JavaScript and XML. In short, AJAX makes portal **Pages** feel more responsive, by exchanging minimum amounts of data with the server. Thus, the entire portal **Page** does not have to be reloaded, when the **User** requests a change. You can use AJAX to increase the portal **Page's** interactivity, usability, functionality and speed.

In other words, AJAX acts as an asynchronous data transfer mechanism, that is, HTTP requests, between the browser and the portal server, allowing portal **Pages** to request a few bits of information from the server, instead of whole portal **Pages**. The AJAX makes portal applications smaller, faster and more user-friendly as shown in the following figure:

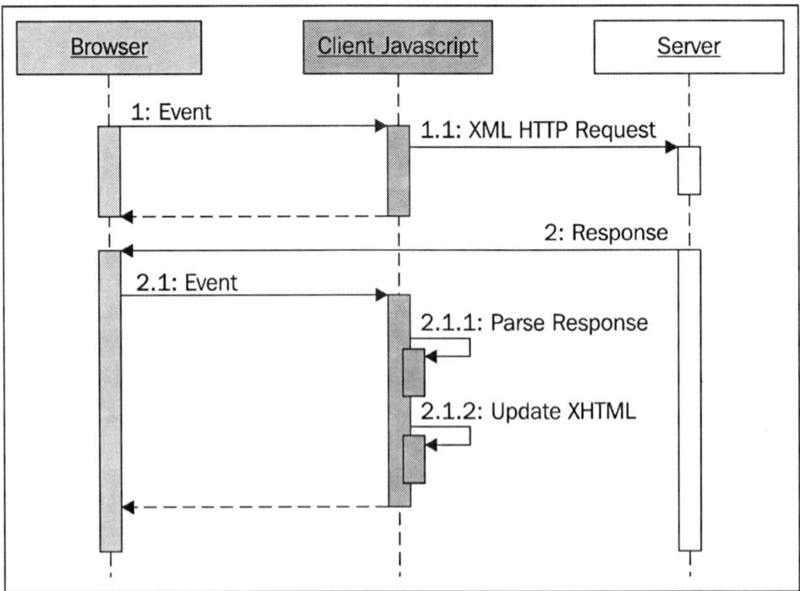

In general, AJAX is based on the following standards:

- JavaScript — Scripting language of the Web
- XML — Extensible Markup Language
- XHTML (or HTML) — Extensible Hypertext Markup Language
- CSS — Cascading Style Sheets

AJAX follows web standards supported by all major browsers. Thus, AJAX applications are browser and platform independent. The main advantage of AJAX is the separation of data, format, style, and function.

Using Chat Portlet Effectively

The **Chat** portlet allows **Users** to chat over XMPP protocol with other logged-in **Users** automatically. In order to use the **Chat** portlet effectively, let's set up an XMPP server and configure Liferay.

Set up XMPP Server

First, we have to set up a XMPP (Jabber) server. Suppose that we use **OpenFire** as an XMPP (Jabber) server. Here are the steps to set up **OpenFire** as follows:

1. Create a folder, and name it **OpenFire.**

2. Download the **OpenFire.**

3. Extract the file to the **OpenFire** folder.

4. Open the **OpenFire** folder and furthermore, `bin`.

5. Click on `openfire_x_x_x.exe` or unzip `openfire_x_x_x.tar.gz`.

6. Click **Launch Admin**.

7. Proceed with configuring **OpenFire** based on your requirements, as shown in the following figure.

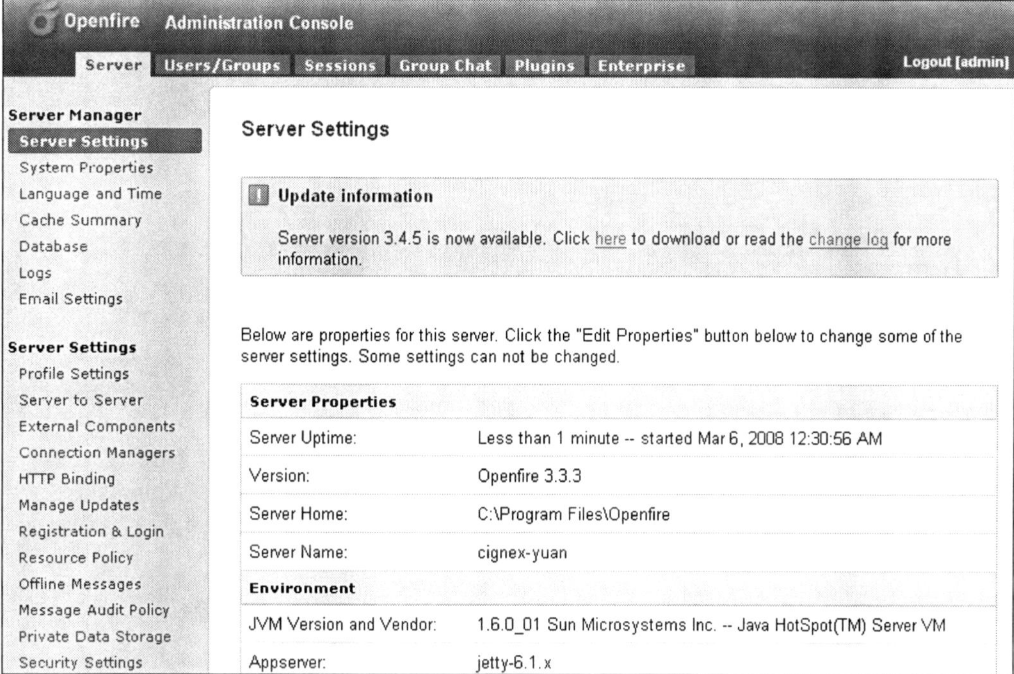

Configure Liferay

Then, you need to configure the XMPP server (such as **OpenFire**) with Liferay. You can simply open `portal-ext.properties` at `$LIFERAY_ROOT/webapps/Root/WEB-INF/classes`.

You just enter the following lines (Suppose that **OpenFire** and Liferay are on the same server):

```
jabber.xmpp.server.enabled=true
reverse.ajax.enabled=true
```

If you want to configure the integration by default settings, here are some options. The following is the complete set of properties related to the setup of XMPP server.

```
jabber.xmpp.server.enabled=false
jabber.xmpp.server.address=localhost
jabber.xmpp.server.name=localhost
jabber.xmpp.server.port=5222
jabber.xmpp.user.password=admin
```

You can also configure the **Chat** portlet when XMPP server is on a separate server. The following lines are a real example.

```
jabber.xmpp.server.enabled=true
reverse.ajax.enabled=true
jabber.xmpp.server.address=liferay.cignex.com
jabber.xmpp.server.name=liferay-cignex
jabber.xmpp.server.port=5222
jabber.xmpp.user.password=admin
```

 Note that you have to turn firewall off in Windows for the **Chat** Portlet to run properly.

Working with Mail Portlet

In order to let employees manage their emails, we can use the Liferay **Mail** portlet. As an administrator of "Palm Tree Publications", you need to create a **Page** called "**Mail**" under the **Page**, "**Community**" at the **Book Lovers** Community **Public Pages** and also add the **Mail** portlet in the **Page, "Mail"**.

Experiencing Mail Management

First of all, login as "**Palm Tree**". Then, let's do the above as follows:

1. Add a **Page** called "**Mail**" under the **Page** "**Community**" at the **Book Lovers** Community **Public Pages**, if the **Page** is not already present.

2. If the **Mail** portlet is not already present, add it in the **Page, "Mail"** of the **Book Lovers** Community where you want to manage mails. You will see the **Mail** portlet as shown in the following figure.

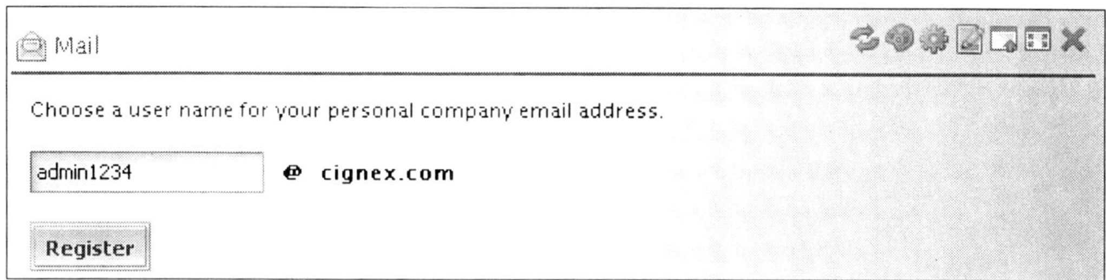

Let's assume that we set up the mail domain as "**cignex.com**" in the **Enterprise Admin** portlet for testing purposes, as we have a mail engine with this mail domain already. Of course, you could set up the mail domain as "**book.com**", or something else, if you had a mail engine with this mail domain in your hand.

As an editor of the editorial department, "**Lotti Stein**", you may want to manage your mails in the mail domain, "**cignex.com**". You can first **choose a user name for your personal company** the **email address**, say "**admin1234**" and register. Let's do it as follows:

1. Login as "**Lotti Stein**".
2. Go to the **Page "Mail"** under the **Page, "Community"**, at the **Book Lovers** community **Public Pages**.
3. Locate the **Mail** portlet.
4. Input the value for **User** name as "**admin1234**".
5. Click the **Register** button.

Your new email address is "admin1234@cignex.com". This email address will also serve as your login, as shown in the following figure.

You can now check for new messages in your inbox, by clicking the **Inbox** link first. Then, you can view the **Unread messages**, and either **Check Mail** or create a **New** mail, as shown in the following figure:

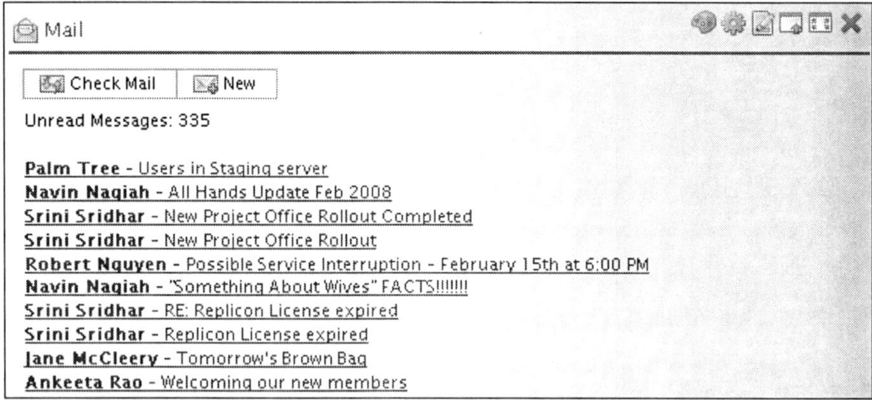

You can go to the **Page** of **Mail** management by clicking on any link of **Unread Messages**, or **Check Mail** button or **New** button. Further, you can manage emails through the **Mail** portlet of your current account. Email management includes the following features (as shown in the following figure):

- Create a **New** email.
- **Check Mail**.
- **Reply to** an email.
- **Reply All** emails.
- **Forward** emails.
- **Delete** emails.
- **Print** emails, and
- Search.

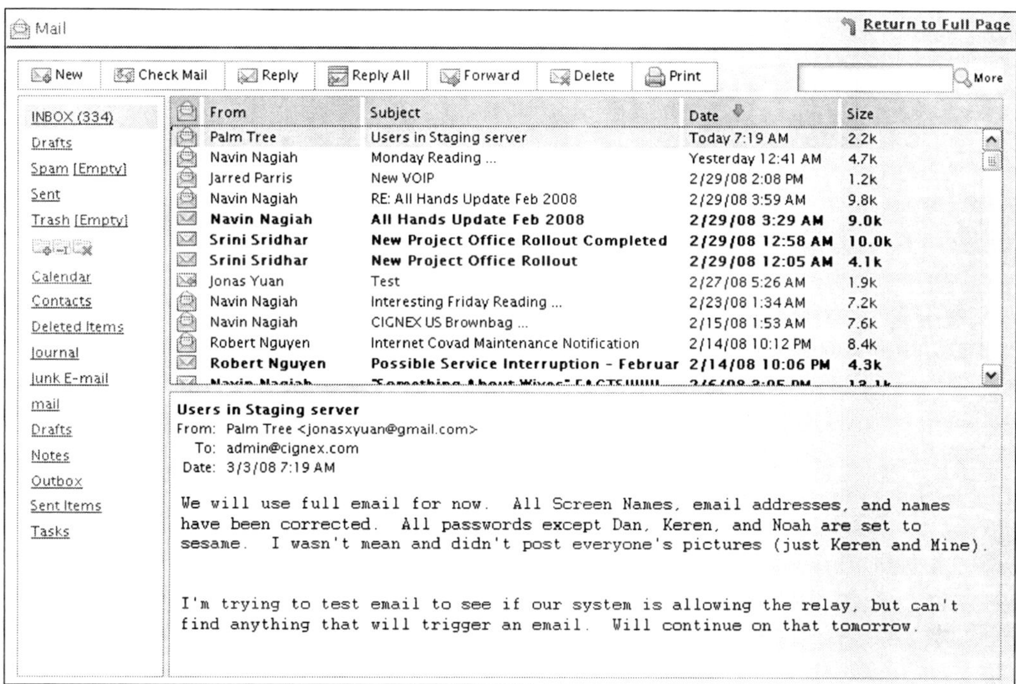

Note that the first email with the subject, "**Users in Staging server**", is sent through the **SMS Text Messenger** portlet. For more details, refer to the forthcoming section.

How to Set up Mail Server?

In order to make the **Mail** portlet work, we have to set up a mail server with IMAP, POP and SMTP protocols. Suppose that the Enterprise "Palm Tree Publications" has a mail server with the domain "`exg3.exghost.com`", an account "`admin@cignex.com/admin1234`", and protocol IMAP, POP and SMTP. As an administrator, you need to integrate this mail server with **IMAP**, **POP** and **SMTP** protocol in Liferay. Let's do it as follows:

1. Find the file `ROOT.xml` in `$TOMCAT_DIR/conf/Catalina/localhost`.

2. Find the mail configuration first.

3. Then configure it as follows:

```
<!-- Mail -->
<Resource
name="mail/MailSession"
```

```
auth="Container"
type="javax.mail.Session"
mail.imap.host="exg3.exghost.com"
mail.imap.port="143"
mail.pop.host="exg3.exghost.com"
mail.pop.port="110"
mail.store.protocol="imap"
mail.transport.protocol="smtp"
mail.smtp.host="exg3.exghost.com"
mail.smtp.port="2525"
mail.smtp.auth="true"
mail.smtp.starttls.enable="true"
mail.smtp.user="admin@cignex.com"
password="admin1234"
mail.smtp.socketFactory.class="javax.net.ssl.SSLSocketFactory"
/>
```

In short, a **Mail** portlet is an AJAX web-mail client. We can configure it to work with any mail server. It reduces page refreshes, since it displays message previews and message lists in a dual pane window.

How to Set up Mail Portlet?

If you have proper **Permissions**, you can change the preferences of the **Mail** portlet. To change the preferences, you can simply click the **Preferences** icon to the upper right of the **Mail** portlet.

With the **Recipients** tab selected, you can find potential recipients from the **Directory** (**Enabled** or **Disabled**) and the **Organization** (**My Organization** or **All Available**). Click the **Save** button after making any changes.

Using the **Filters** tab, you can set the values to filter emails associated with an email address to a **Folder**. Click the **Save** button after making any changes.

Note that the maximum number of email addresses is ten. This number is also configurable at the `portal-ext.properties`

Similarly, the **Forward Address** tab allows all emails to be forwarded to the email address you want. Enter one email address **Per Line**. Remove all entries to disable email forwarding. Select **Yes** to leave, or **No** to not leave a copy of the forwarded message. Click the **Save** button after making any changes.

Further, the **Signature** tab also allows you to set up your signature using HTML text editor. The signature you have set up will be added to each outgoing message. Click the **Save** button after making any changes.

The **Vacation Message** tab allows you to set up vacation messages using HTML text editor. **The vacation message notifies others of your absence** (as shown in the following figure). Click the **Save** button after making any changes.

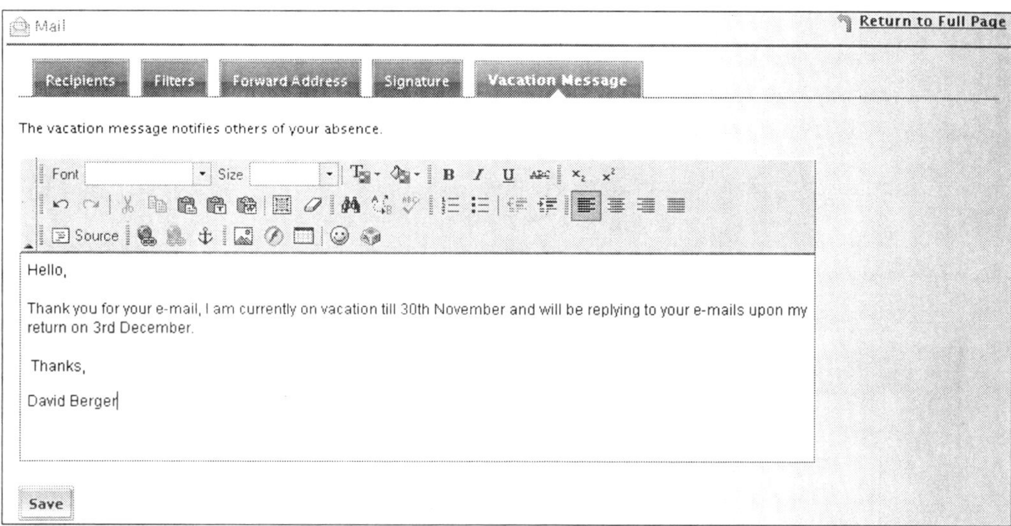

Using Permissions

The following table shows **Permissions** for the **Mail** portlet. A **Community User** can set up all **Permissions** (marked 'X') while a **Guest User has** the **View, Configuration** and **Preferences Permissions**. By default, a **Community** (marked '*') as well as a **Guest User** has **View** action.

Action	Description	Community	Guest
View	Views this portlet	X, *	X, *
Configuration	Configures **Permissions** of this portlet	X	X
Preferences	Configures mail setting of this portlet	X	X

Obviously, as a **User** of the **Book Lovers** Community, "**Lotti Stein**" has only **View Permissions** on the **Mail** portlet, by default. Since the **Book Lovers** community has no **Permission** "Preferences", it follows that "**Lotti Stein**" too has no "**Preferences**" Permission.

As an administrator, you may need to set up the **Community Users** having **Permissions, Preference** as well as **View,** on the **Mail** portlet. Thus, the **Community User** can set up mail settings. That is, you need to add **Permissions (Preference)** on the **Mail** portlet at the **Book Lovers** community. Let's do it as follows (see the following figure):

1. Click on the **Configuration** icon to the top right of the **Mail** portlet.
2. Then click on the **Permissions** tab.
3. Select the **Community** tab.
4. Select **Permission, Preferences,** in the **Available** box.
5. Click on the **Add** arrow, and
6. Click on the **Save** button if you are ready.

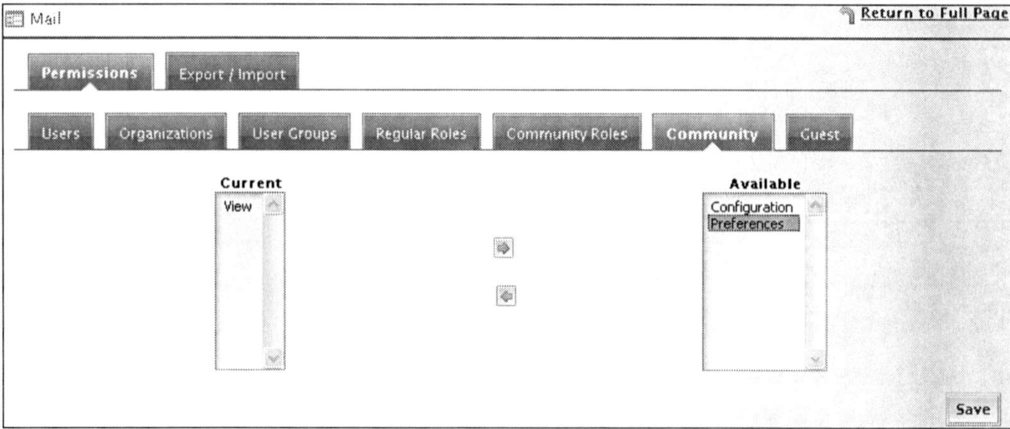

Using Mail Portlet effectively

Liferay Portal can integrate with Washington IMAP + Sendmail, Cyrus IMAP + Postfix, and Dovecot + Postfix, as well as with Microsoft Exchange and other IMAP servers. As stated above, the mail server "exg3.exghost.com" is Microsoft Exchange server.

You can access your email through an IMAP server. If access is on IMAP, the portal does not have to know where to persist the mail.

 IMAP stands for Internet Message Access Protocol. URL: `http://www.imap.org/`.

One of the popular protocols used for email is IMAP, an application layer Internet protocol. IMAP operates on port 143 that allows a local client to access email on a remote server.

IMAP supports both connected and disconnected modes of operation. Until the **User** explicitly deletes them, email IMAP clients generally leave messages on the server. Moreover, IMAP offers access to the mail store.

IMAP has a lot of advantages. Here, we have listed just some of them:

- Use connected and disconnected modes of operation.
- **Users** can connect to the same mailbox simultaneously.
- **Users** have access to MIME message parts and partial fetch.
- Has message state information.
- Supports multiple mailboxes on the server.
- Provides ability for search on the server-side.
- Has a built-in extension mechanism.

Working with SMS Text Messenger

In order to let employees send text message to others, anytime, we can use the Liferay **SMS Text Messenger** portlet. As an administrator of "Palm Tree Publications", you need to create a **Page** called "SMS" under the **Page** "Community" at the **Book Lovers** Community and add the **SMS Text Messenger** portlet in the **Page, "SMS"**.

Using SMS Text Messenger

First of all, login as "**Palm Tree**". Then, let's do the above action as follows:

1. Add a **Page** called "**SMS**" under the **Page** "**Community**" at the **Book Lovers** Community **Public Pages**, if the **Page** is not already present.

2. Add the **SMS Text Messenger** portlet in the **Page**, "**SMS**" of the **Book Lovers** Community where you want to set up **SMS Text Messenger** (if this portlet is not already present). You will see the **SMS Text Messenger** portlet as shown in the following figure:

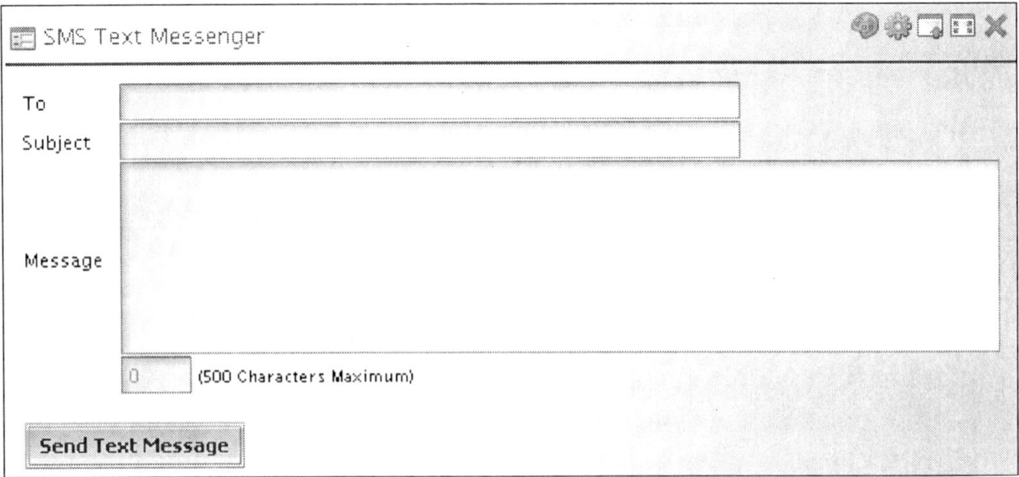

As an editor of the editorial department, "**Lotti Stein**" wants to send a **Message,** say "**Users in Staging server**", to a person, say"**admin@cignex.com**". Let's do it as follows:

1. Login as "**Lotti Stein**".

2. Go to the **Page** "**SMS**" under the **Page** "**Community**" at the **Book Lovers** community **Public Page**.

3. Locate the **SMS Text Messenger**.

4. Input value for **To** as "**admin@cignex.com**", **Subject** as "**Users in Staging server**" and a **Message**.

5. Click the **Send Text Message** button.

The **User** "**admin@cignex.com**" will receive this email sooner or later, as we have described in the previous section.

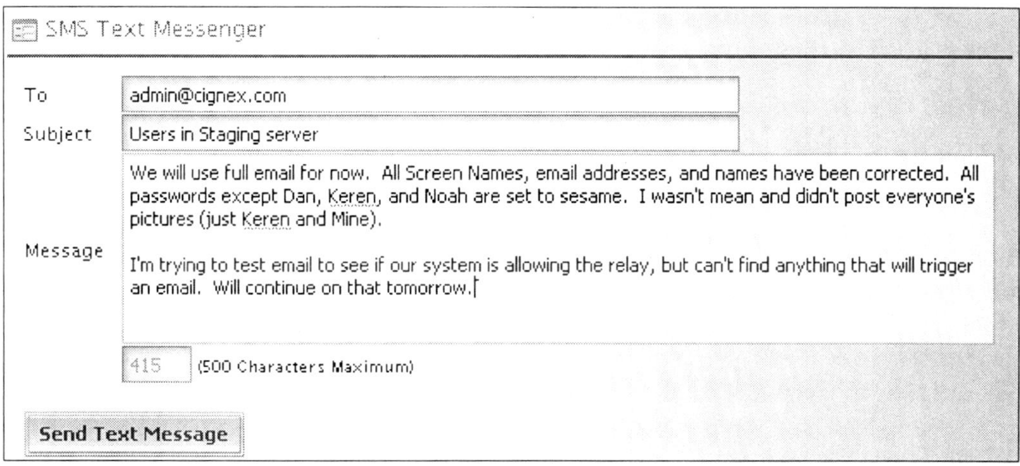

How to Set up SMTP?

In order to make **SMS Text Messenger** work well, we have to set up the mail server with SMTP protocol. Suppose that the Enterprise "Palm Tree Publications" has a mail server with a domain `"smtp.gmail.com"`, an account `"jonasxyuan/jonas1234"`, and a protocol, SMTP. As an administrator, you need to integrate this mail server with SMTP protocol in Liferay. Let's do it as follows:

1. Find the file `ROOT.xml` in `$TOMCAT_DIR/conf/Catalina/localhost`.

2. Find the mail configuration first.

3. Then, configure it as follows:

```
<Resource
name="mail/MailSession"
auth="Container"
type="javax.mail.Session"
mail.imap.host="smtp.gmail.com"
mail.pop.host="smtp.gmail.com"
mail.store.protocol="imap"
mail.transport.protocol="smtp"
mail.smtp.host="smtp.gmail.com"
mail.smtp.port="465"
mail.smtp.auth="true"
mail.smtp.starttls.enable="true"
mail.smtp.user="jonasxyuan"
password="jonas123456"
mail.smtp.socketFactory.class="javax.net.ssl.SSLSocketFactory"
/>
```

In short, the **SMS Text Messenger** portlet allows you to send SMS text messages from your portal page anytime.

Using SMS Effectively

The Short Message Service (SMS), called text messaging, is used to send short messages to and from mobile phones. It provides a mechanism for the delivery of short text messages over mobile networks, in order to transmit messages to and from mobiles. The text message from the sender can be stored in a central short message center, which then forwards it to the recipient. If the recipient is not available, the short message is stored temporally and will be sent later. SMS provides return receipts. Thus, the sender gets a brief message notification if the short message is delivered to the recipient.

You may need to read the following part, if you are interested in the organization of network elements for supporting SMS. Otherwise, you can leave it for your future needs. The following figure shows a typical organization of network elements in a network supporting SMS (refer to more details at `http://www.wirelessdevnet.com/channels/sms/features/sms.html`).

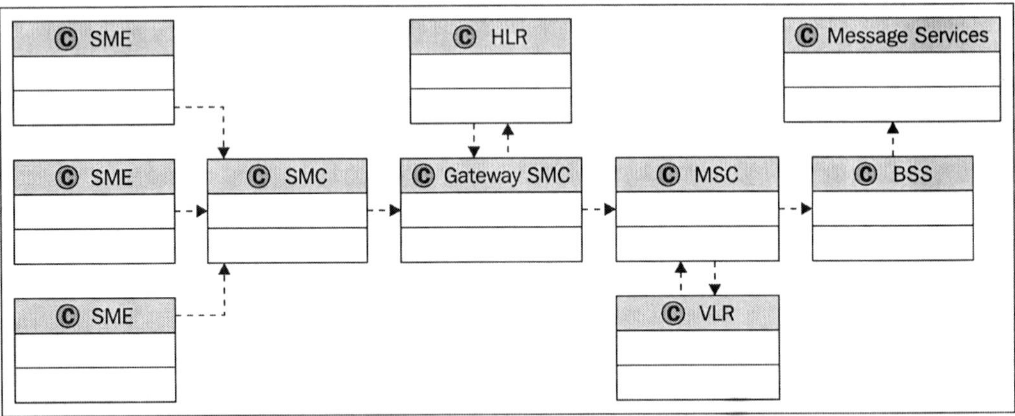

The **SMC** (Short Message Center) stores and forwards messages, to and from the message station. The **SME** (Short Message Entity) receives and sends short messages.

The SMS GWMS (SMS gateway **MSC**), a gateway **MSC**, can receive short messages. After receiving the short message from the message center, GMSC employs the SS7 (Signaling System #7) network to interrogate the current position of the mobile station from the **HLR** (home location register).

HLR, as a main database, holds information about the subscription profile of the mobile. It also maintains the routing information for the subscriber where the mobile is currently situated. The GMSC thus passes on the short message to the correct **MSC**.

MSC (Mobile Switching Center) switches connections between mobile stations.

A **VLR** (Visitor Location Register) communicates with each **MSC** and contains temporary information about the mobile. **MSC** switches the short message to the corresponding **BSS** (Base Station System), which transmits the short message to the mobile. The **BSS** is made up of transceivers, which send and receive information over the air interface, to and from the mobile station. The short message is passed over signaling channels, so that the recipient (for example, mobile) can receive this short piece of information, even if a data call or a voice call is going on.

Summary

This chapter discussed how to add a participant for chatting, how to manage (view and delete) participants in the **Chat** portlet, how to start chatting, and how to set up the **Chat** portlet first. Then it discussed how to manage (check, delete, add, reply, forward, search) emails and also to set up the **Mail** portlet properly. Finally, it discussed how to manage the **SMS Text Messenger** portlet and send SMS text messages.

10

Help Desk/Customer Support

The enterprise "Palm Tree Publications" may often provide help desk support to its customers via a toll-free number, website and/or e-mail. But in the intranet website "book.com", of "Palm Tree Publications", it is required to provide help desk and customer support—an information and assistance resource that troubleshoots problems related to websites. Liferay packages facilities that will help "Palm Tree Publications" design, develop, deploy, and support the websites. It offers unbeatable out-of-the-box functionality with over 60 JSR-168 / JSR-286 compliant portlets. With these portlets, we can easily build help desk assistances and customer support information on the web site of "Palm Tree Publications".

This chapter mainly discusses how to use a set of portlets in order to provide an information and assistance resource that troubleshoots specific requirements. Furthermore, it also introduces us to multilingual support and the usage of WebDAV. Finally, it provides brief guidance on how to develop new portlets to deal with specific requirements, in order to provide help desk assistances and customer support information efficiently.

By the end of this chapter you will have learnt how to:

- Use financial tools.
- Work with Google portlets.
- Employ religion tools.
- Use additional tools.
- Employ shopping portlets in the portal.
- Play with entertainment portlets in the website.
- Play with multiple languages.
- Use WebDAV.
- Develop your own portlets.

Working with Financial Portlets

In order to provide help desk and customer support related to financial tools, we should use a lot of portlets. Let's see how to provide help desk and customer support for financial purposes in the intranet first.

As an administrator of "Palm Tree Publications", first you need to create a **Page** called "**Financial**" under the the **Page**, "**Community**", at the **Book Lovers** Community **Public Pages**, and then add the required portlets in the **Page**, "**Financial**".

First of all, log in as "**Palm Tree**" and create a **Page** called "**Financial**" under the **Page**, "**Community**", at the **Book Lovers** Community. Let's do it as follows:

- Add a **Page** called "**Financial**" under the page "**Community**" at the **Book Lovers** Community **Public Pages** (if the **Page** is not already present).

Now you are ready to add portlets in the **Page** "**Financial**".

As an administrator at "Palm Tree Publications", you may need to build the **Financial Page** with following features:

- Perform pricing calculations.
- Use loan & mortgage payment calculations.
- Display the company's ticker symbol with stock price; and
- Perform foreign exchange rate calculations on the Intranet.

In order to provide the ability to perform pricing calculations and loan & mortgage payment calculations in the **Financial Page**, simply add the **Calculator** portlet and **Load it**. Now, normal **Users** from financial groups can use the **Calculator** portlet for performing pricing calculations, and moreover, use **the Loan Calculator** for loan & mortgage payment calculations on the **Financial Page**.

Similarly, in order to provide the ability to display the company's ticker symbol with stock price and to perform foreign exchange rate calculations in your page, simply add **the Currency Converter** and **Stocks** portlets in the **Financial Page**. Now, normal **Users** from financial group can use **Currency Converter** portlet for performing foreign exchange rate calculations and furthermore, use **the Stocks** portlet for displaying the company's ticker symbol with stock price on the **Financial Page**.

Using Calculator And Load Calculator

The Calculator portlet provides a basic calculator to perform mathematical calculations. Simply enter the numbers and operands, and the **Calculator** will perform pricing calculations and display the results dynamically as shown in the following figure.

The Loan Calculator refers to the loan & mortgage payment calculator. The **Loan Calculator** portlet provides the ability to determine what your monthly payments will be, and how much you'll owe when the loan is up and the payment falls due.

The Loan Calculator portlet also determines the monthly payments for any fixed-rate loan. Just enter the **Loan Amount, Interest Rate** and **Years**, and the **Loan Calculator** will do the rest. Click on the **Calculate** button to see how much interest you'll pay each month and over the lifetime of the loan. The **Loan Calculator** will also show extra **Interest Paid** and **Total Paid** as shown in the following figure.

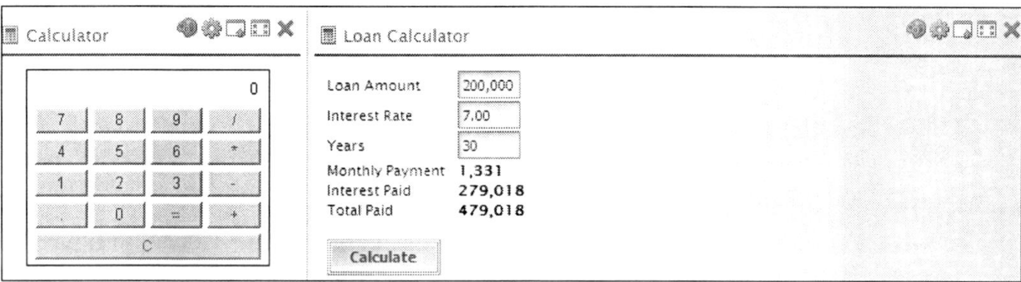

Using Currency Converter

It is pretty easy to use the **Currency Converter** portlet. Input the **Number, and** select the **from-symbol** and the **to-symbol** from the list first. Then, you can press the **Convert** button. The portlet will display foreign exchange rates as shown in the following figure.

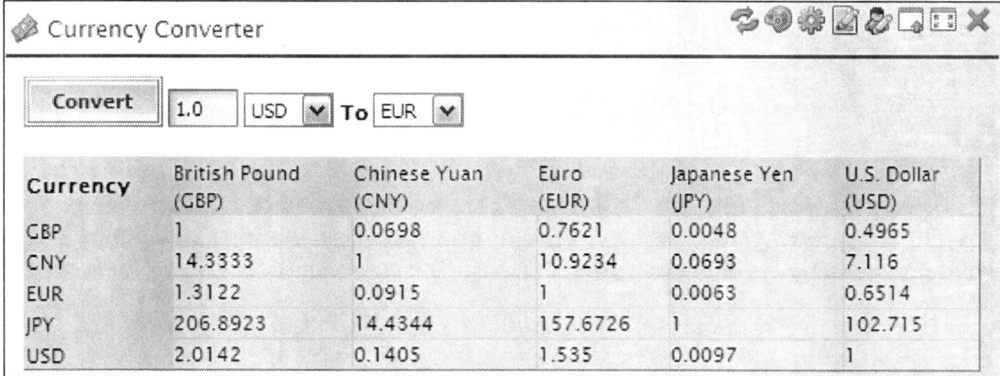

Currency	British Pound (GBP)	Chinese Yuan (CNY)	Euro (EUR)	Japanese Yen (JPY)	U.S. Dollar (USD)
GBP	1	0.0698	0.7621	0.0048	0.4965
CNY	14.3333	1	10.9234	0.0693	7.116
EUR	1.3122	0.0915	1	0.0063	0.6514
JPY	206.8923	14.4344	157.6726	1	102.715
USD	2.0142	0.1405	1.535	0.0097	1

You can also change current **Currency** by updating preferences, such as **GBP, CNY, EUR, JPY** and **USD**. Let's do it as follows:

1. Click the **Preferences** icon. There are two boxes for currencies. The **Current** box contains current currencies and the **Available** box contains available currencies which you may use.

2. You can change the order of currencies by selecting a currency such as "**Euro**" first, and then press the **Move Up** button to move up or press the **Move Down** button to move down.

3. You can remove a currency from the **Current** box. You simply select the currency such as "**Japanese Yen**" in the **Current** box, and then press the **Remove** button to the right.

4. Similarly, you can add a currency from the **Available** box to the **Current** box. You simply select the currency such as "**Chinese Yuan**" in the **Available** box, and then press the **Add** button to the left.

5. Click the **Save** button when you are ready as shown in the following figure.

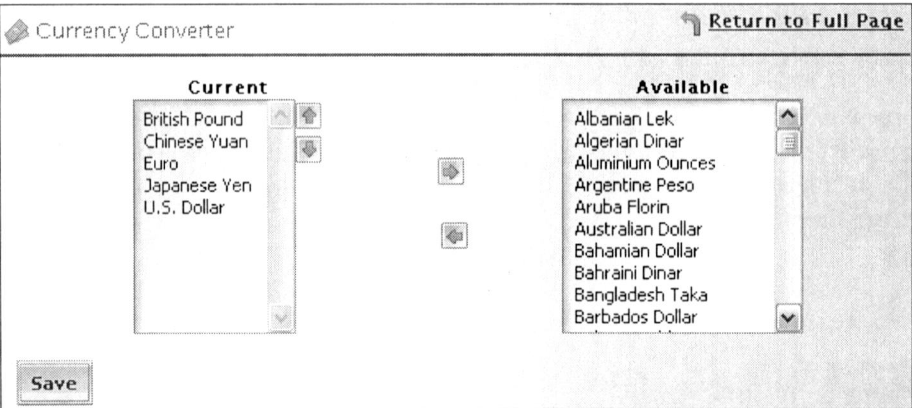

The Currency Converter portlet allows you to perform foreign exchange rate calculations on the Intranet, using up-to-the-minute currency rates. More than 147 currencies are supported at present.

By default, **Yahoo Financial** is used as Service provider with the following URL access.

```
http://finance.yahoo.com/d/quotes.csv?s=symbols=X&f=sl1d1t1c1ohgv&
e=.csv
```

An example of the symbol would be **USD, GBP, EUR, JPY, CNY**, and so on.

Employing Stocks Portlet

The Stocks portlet provides personalized stock quotes in the portal. It allows access to global market indices. You can select the companies and indices to monitor and their order of appearance in the portlet. You can also view price and volume charts.

For example, you can allow normal users to customize their **Stock** portlets with their own portfolio of **Stocks** as shown in the following figure:

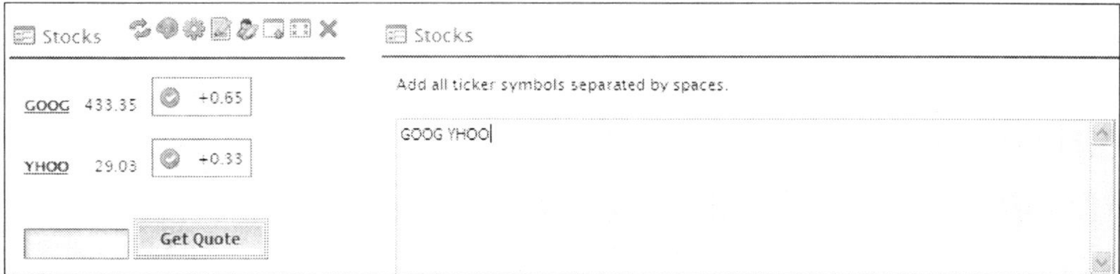

You can also change default ticker symbols. Let's do it as follows:

1. Click the **Preferences** icon of the **Stocks** portlet.
2. Input all ticker symbols, separated by spaces as in "GOOG, YHOO".
3. Click the **Save** button when you are ready.

By default, Yahoo Financial is used as Service provider with the following URL access:

```
http://finance.yahoo.com/d/quotes.csv?s=symbol&f=sl1d1t1c1ohgv&e=.csv
```

An example of the symbol could be **YHOO**, **GOOG**, and so on.

You can view **Stock** information such as "GOOG". Let's do it as follows:

1. Input the **Stock** symbol such as "GOOG" first.
2. Then, click the **Get Quote** button.

3. The stock portlet delivers stock information including **intra-day/week chart, last price, net change, percent change, Open, Day High, Day Low,** and **Volume** as shown in the following figure.

4. Optionally, you change the chart by selecting **Days, Months** and **Years**.

Using Stocks Portlet Effectively

Moreover, Liferay provides the ability to configure the **Stocks** portlet application parameters. You can change the **Stocks** portlet application parameters, `<preferences-unique-per-layout>` and `<preferences-owned-by-group>` as follows:

 `Liferay-portlet.xml` at the `$TOMCAT_DIR/ROOT/WEB-INF` is the DTD for the Portlet Application parameters that are specific to Liferay Portal.

Preferences-Unique-Per-Layout

If the preferences for the **Stocks** portlet are unique across all pages, you should set up the `preferences-unique-per-layout` with the value, "`true`". If the preferences for the portlet has to be shared across all pages, you should set up the `preferences-unique-per-layout` with the value, "`false`". By default, we set the value to `true`.

Preferences-Owned-By-Group

If the group owns the preferences of the **Stocks** portlet in a group page, then you can set up `preferences-owned-by-group` with the value, "`true`". Otherwise, you can set up the `preferences-owned-by-group` with the value, "`false`". That is, the **Users** own the preferences at all times. By default, we just set the value to `true`.

If the **Stocks** portlet has `preferences-unique-per-layout` with the value, "`true`", and `preferences-owned-by-group` with the value, "`false`", then you can set up a different list of stocks for either a personal **Page** or a **Community Page**.

If the **Stocks** portlet has both `preferences-unique-per-layout` and `preferences-owned-by-group` with the values, "`false`", then you can set up a list of stocks shared across the personal **Pages** and a **Community's** set of **Pages**.

If the **Stocks** portlet has both `preferences-unique-per-layout` and `preferences-owned-by-group` with the value, "`true`", then you can set up a different list of stocks at a personal **Page**. Furthermore, if you are administrators, you can set a different list of stocks in this case for a **Community Page**, shared by all **Users** within a **Community**.

If the **Stocks** portlet has `preferences-unique-per-layout` with the value "`false`" and `preferences-owned-by-group` with the value, "`true`", then you can set up a list of stocks shared across personal **Pages**. In this case, if you are administrators, you can set up the portlet preferences for all the **Users** in a **Community Page**, and a list of stocks shared by all **Users** across a **Community's** set of **Pages**.

Working with Google Portlets

As an administrator of the enterprise, "Palm Tree Publications", you may need to create a **Page** called "**Help**" under the **Page** "**Community**" at the **Book Lovers** Community **Public Pages** and moreover, add the required portlets in the page, "**Help**". Let's do it as follows:

- Add a **Page** called "**Help**" under the **Page**, "**Community**" at the **Book Lovers** Community, **Public Pages,** if the **Page** is not already present.

As an administrator at "Palm Tree Publications", you may need to build an advertising **Page** with the following features:

- Show locations for a given IP address.

- Show world clocks for locations, for example, US (California), Hong Kong, Germany, and Canada (Ontario).

- Enable text, image and video advertisements on the page, "**Help**".

Using Google Gadgets

For the first two features, the **Google Gadgets** portlet would be helpful:

1. **Set up**: Add **Plugin Installer** portlet in the **Page**, "Admin", and install **Google Gadget** portlet.

2. Add **Google Gadget** portlet in the page, "**Help**".

3. Customize **Google Gadget**: To customize the **Google Gadget** portlet, use the **Configuration** icon on the portlet window. Once the **Setup** options are accessed, **Permissions** for the portlet can be changed.

4. Choose "**Geo IP Tool**" from the list of recommended **Google gadgets**. Press the **Save** button when you are ready, as shown in the following figure.

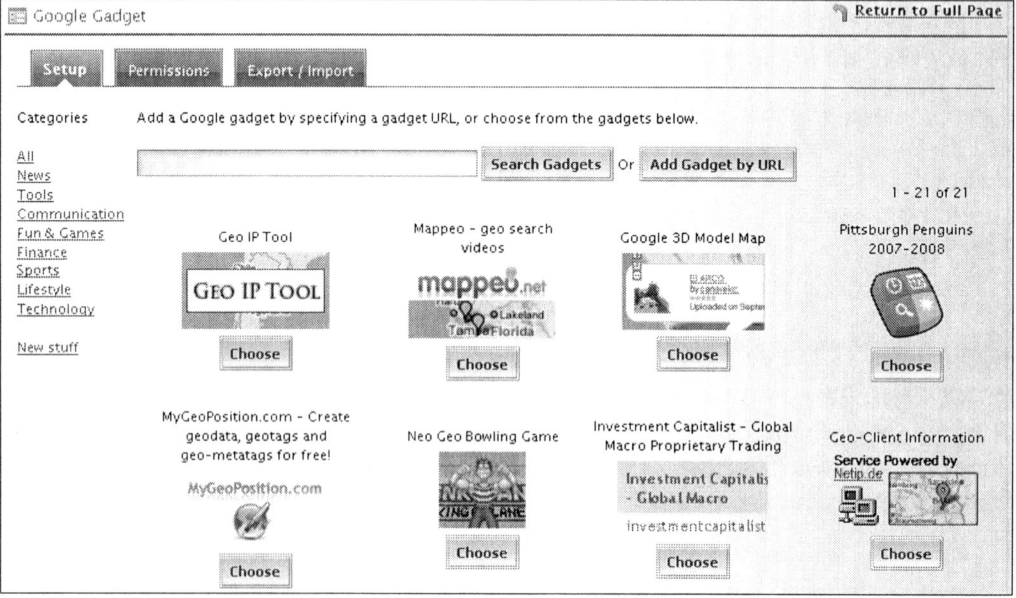

5. To create world clocks for the locations, **US California, Hong Kong, Germany**, and **CA Ontario** in the website, "Google Gadgets for Your Webpage", generate the code and copy it.

6. Choose "**obtain the Google Gadget code directly and paste it below**" and paste the code into the box as instructed.

7. Press the **Save** button when you are ready.

That's it! You got your custom **Google gadget**! **Google Gadget** portlet allows easy integration with Google Gadgets as shown in the following figure.

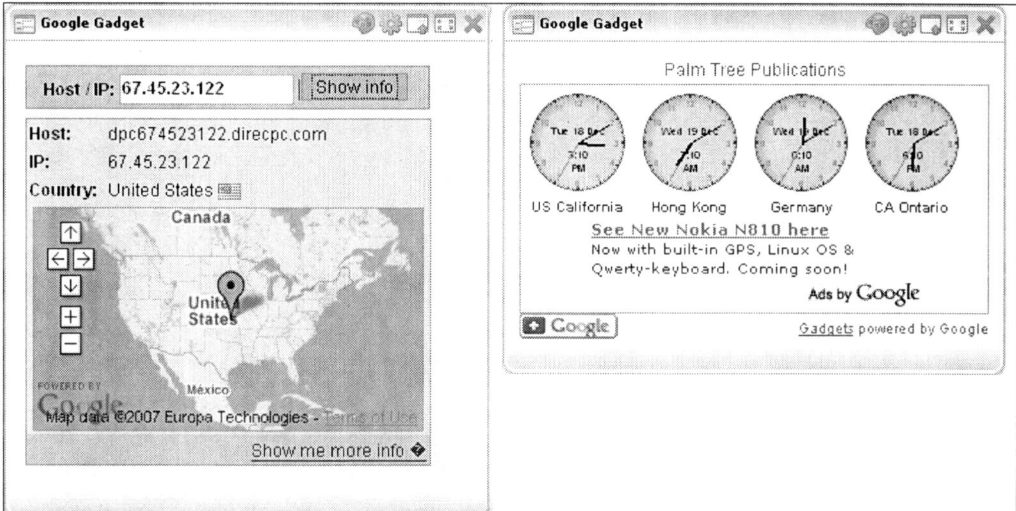

Gadget World Clock could be used for the intranet that displays multiple analog or digital clocks at the times in the selected time zones, or countries, or cities. You can synchronize the world clocks with the server to always display the correct time.

Google Gadgets act as mini-applications built using HTML, with JavaScript, Flash, or Silver-light for dynamic behaviors. URL:
`http://www.google.com/ig/directory?synd=open`

Employing Google AdSense

For the third feature, the **Google AdSense** portlet would be useful:

1. **Set up**: Open **Plugin Installer** Portlet in the **Page, "Admin"**, and install the **Google AdSense** portlet.

2. Add the **Google AdSense** portlet in your page.

3. Customize Google AdSense: Customize the **Google AdSense** portlet using the **Configuration** icon on the portlet window. Once the **Setup** options are accessed, **Permissions** for the portlet can be changed.

4. Input the **Ad Client, Ad Channel, Ad Type, Ad Format**, and so on.

5. Press the **Save** button when you are ready.

That's it! You got your custom **Google AdSense! Google AdSense** portlet provides ability to allow easy integration with Google AdSense as shown in the following figure.

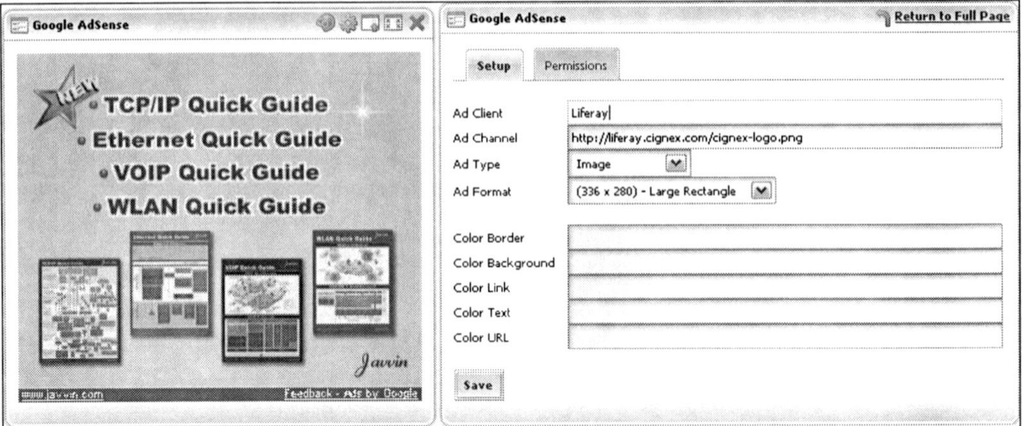

The AdSense API enables users to programmatically generate ad code snippets for insertion into a **User's** web **Pages**.

Google AdSense, commonly just AdSense, acts as an ad serving program run by Google. The Website owners may enroll to enable text, image and, more recently, video advertisements on their sites. URL: `www.google.com/adsense`

Working with Religion Portlets

As a normal **User** at "Palm Tree Publications", you may need to build a personal religion **Page** with following features:

- Show a situation or concern, for which one can pray, in the **Page**.

- Show message about **Today in Christian History** in the **Page**.

As an administrator of "Palm Tree Publications", you may need to create a **Page** called "**Religion**" under the **Page** "**Community**" at the **Book Lovers** Community **Public Pages** and further, add the required portlets in the **Page, "Religion"**. Let's do it as follows:

- Add a **Page** called "**Religion**" under the **Page** "**Community**" at **Book** Lovers Community **Public Pages,** if the **Page** is not already present.

To show a situation or concern on which to pray, you simply add the **Global Prayer Digest** portlet in the **Page, "Religion"**, and you will see the situation or concern for which one can pray, as shown in the following figure.

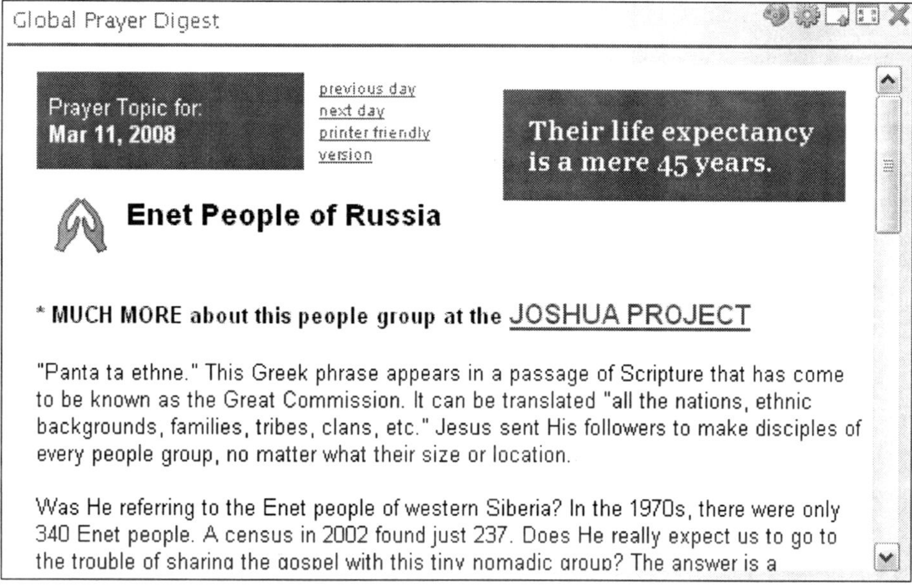

The Global Prayer Digest portlet provides the ability to allow simple integration with Global Prayer Digest.

The Global Prayer Digest is a daily prayer guide for those groups of people, who have not had the opportunity to encounter Christianity around the world, and the missionaries who serve the religion. The Prayer Digest gives a glimpse of what God is doing around the world each day, and what still remains to be done. The Adopt-A-People movement focuses on daily prayer for the unfinished tasks. It also gives biblical challenges, urgent reports, condensed missionary stories, exciting descriptions of un-reached people groups, and so on. More interestingly, it encourages people to provide a digest of a rich fuel of prayer for the world.

The Global Prayer Digest acts as a key tool in a movement to help fulfill Christ's commission to make disciples of all the people on the earth, involving a daily discipline of learning, praying, and giving, to help reach the world's nearly 9,000 un-reached people groups. Un-reached people groups refer to groups which do not have churches in their own cultural or social setting. URL: `http://www.global-prayer-digest.org/`

To show a message about **Today in Christian History** in the **Page**, you simply add the **Today in Christian History** portlet in the **Page, "Religion"**. You will see a story of **Today in Christian History** as shown in the following figure.

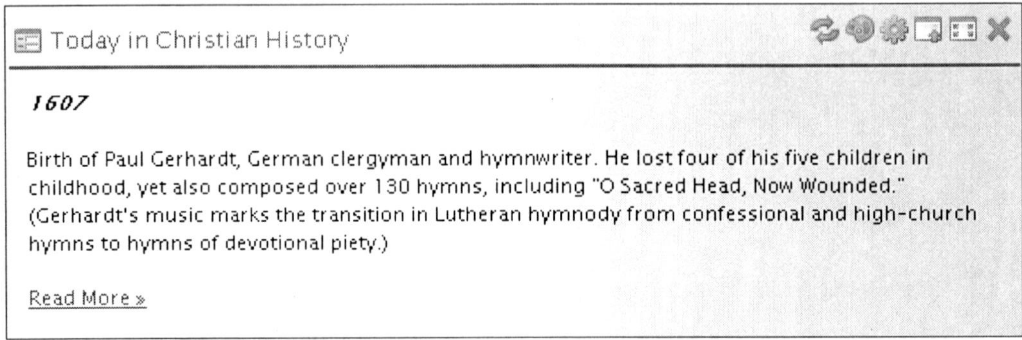

The Today in Christian History portlet allows simple integration with Today in Christian History.

For more details about Today in Christian History, check URL:
`http://www.studylight.org/his/tich`

Christians have been making history for over 2,000 years, founding a country or burning it for the sake of their beliefs. Until this day in Christian History, you can wow the visitors with interesting tidbits of history, every day of the year. To add this resource, you just cut and paste the following codes to the desired page:

```
<script language="Javascript" src="http://www.studylight.org/jscripts/
tichcode.cgi"></script>
```

Using Religion Portlets Effectively

Several portlets dealing with religious or spiritual topics are available. You can use them as prototypes for other similar portlets, including a scripture reference tool, a guide to prayer for the current world events, a daily historical events portlet, and so on.

Besides the above portlets, Liferay also provides other portlets dealing with religious or spiritual topics as follows:

- **The Bible Gateway** portlet allows linked integration with Bible Gateway.

The Bible Gateway acts as a tool for reading and researching scripture online. It supports most Bible versions in the language or translation. Moreover, it provides advanced search capabilities, which allow readers to find and compare particular passages in scriptures, based on keywords, phrases, or scripture reference. URL: `http://www.biblegateway.com/`

- **The Gospel for Asia** portlet allows easy integration with Gospel for Asia.

Gospel for Asia (GFA), a Christian missionary organization, spreads the Gospel to India and the surrounding countries, through native missionaries. It sets up churches among the world's most un-reached people groups - those who have never heard the Good News of Jesus Christ. URL: `http://www.gfa.org/`

- The **Random Bible Verse** portlet picks a verse number at random from a pre-selected list of verses.

The pre-selected list of verse numbers was statically specified in the file: `random-bible-verse.xml`. Flexibly the language of the random Bible verse is configurable by clicking on the **Preferences** icon. Once a verse number (and furthermore, the language) is selected, this portlet uses the service of Bible Gateway to reach the verse as follows.

```
http://www.biblegateway.com/passage/?search=*&version=*
```

If you want to add more verses, simply update the file: `random-bible-verse.xml`.

- **The Westminster Catechism** portlet provides the ability to view both Westminster larger catechism and Westminster shorter Catechism.

Westminster Catechism was statically specified in the file: `westminster-catechism.xml`. If you want to update Westminster (larger/shorter) catechism, simply update the file: `westminster-catechism.xml`.

Playing with Additional Tools

As a normal user at "Palm Tree Publications", you may need to build a specific **Page** with the following features:

- Resolve a hostname to the IP address in the **Page**.
- Add a quick note in the **Page**.
- Translate a text from English to German.
- Generate random password online.

The Network Utilities portlet would be helpful in resolving a hostname to an IP address in the **Page**. To use the Network Utilities, simply add the portlet in your **Page**, as shown in the following figure. With this portlet, you can resolve hostnames to IP addresses via DNS by inputting hostnames under the **DNS Lookup** tab and pressing the **Search** button, when you are ready. Moreover, you can lookup information in any WHOIS database by inputting hostnames under the **Whois** tab and pressing the **Search** button.

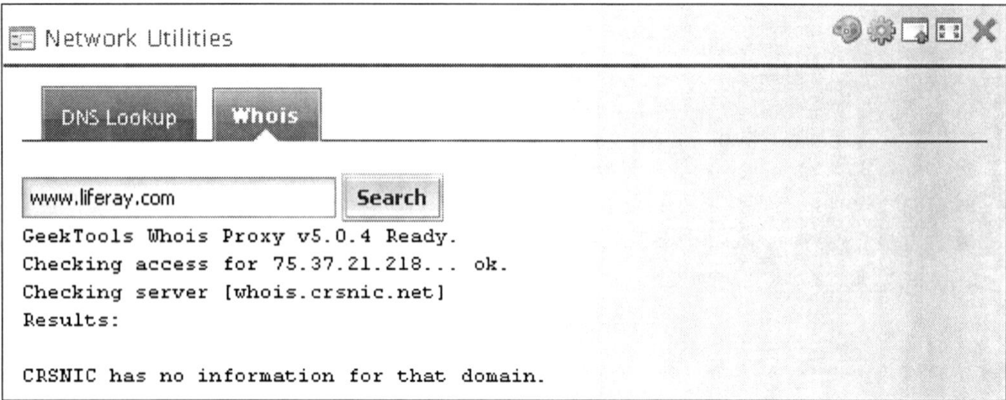

The Quick Note portlet would be useful in adding a quick note in the **Page**. To make a quick note, simply add th eQuick Note portlet in your **Page,** as shown in the following figure. With this portlet, you can input your quick note in the page, and choose a background color.

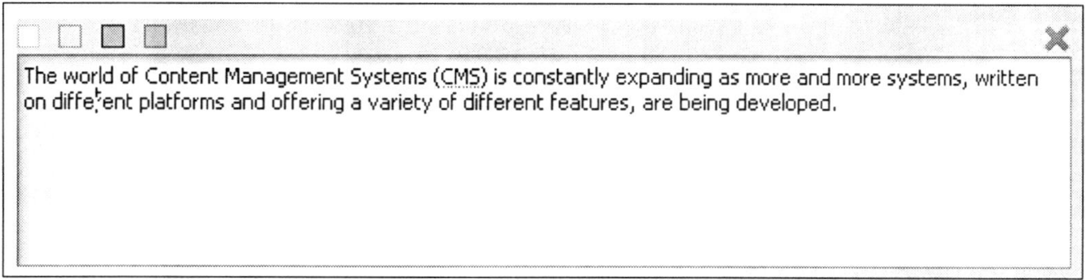

To translate a text, you can use the **Translator** portlet. To translate any text from English to German, first add the **Translator** portlet in the **Page**. Then input text in English such as "**Good Morning!**" and select the **English to German**. Press the **Translate** button when you are ready. The portlet will translate the text and furthermore, display the result, say "**Guten Morgen!**"

The Translator portlet allows easy integration with language translator, as shown in the following figure:

By default, Altavista Babel Fish Translation is used as Service provider with the following URL access.

```
http://babelfish.altavista.com/babelfish/tr?doit=done&urltext=Text
&lp=*
```

To set the default languages to translate a given text, simply update the following line at `portal-ext.properties`.

```
translator.default.languages=en_es
```

AltaVista Babel Fish Translation provides a useful tool to communicate with non-English speaking or bilingual customers. It can be used to translate words, phrases, or entire web pages into more than 19 languages, including to and from English, Chinese, French, German, Italian, Japanese, Korean, Portuguese, and Spanish. URL: `http://babelfish.altavista.com/`

To generate a random password online, you can use the **Password Generator** portlet. To generate random password online, add the **Password Generator** portlet in your **Page** first. Then select options, such as, whether using **Numbers** or not, enabling **Lower Case Letters** and **Upper Case Letters**, and selecting the **Length** of password. Press the **Generate** button when you are ready.

The Password Generator portlet allows you to generate good, secure and random passwords easily, as shown in the following figure:

To summarize, Password Generator provides the ability to create passwords that are highly secure and extremely difficult to crack, since it uses an optional combination of **Lower** and **Upper Case Letters**, and **Numbers**.

In addition, Liferay provides a set of built-in useful portlets as additional tools:

- **The Analog Clock** portlet allows the display of analog clocks. Since "Palm Tree Publications" has geographically distributed teams in both US and Germany, coordination among teams is critical. It can be of tremendous help to have a clock that shows the time in both US and Germany, especially while trying to schedule meetings and events, or to know when employees would arrive to their desks.

- **The Dictionary** portlet links to Dictionary.com.

 Dictionary.com provides online dictionary search, translator, word of the day, crossword puzzles and word games, and vocabulary learning resources for many languages. URL: `http://dictionary.reference.com/`.

- **The Unit Converter** portlet provides the ability to convert area, length, mass, temperature and volume online.

- **The Sign In** portlet provides the ability to sign in, if you registered already, to deal with forgotten password issue, and to create new accounts.

- **The OpenID Sign In** portlet provides the ability to sign in via OpenID, if you have an OpenID already.

Experiencing Shopping Tools

Let's consider a scenario. As an administrator at "Palm-Tree publications", you may need to build a specific **Page** called "**Shopping**" for online shopping with the following functions:

- Ability to find rankings about a book, before buying it.

- Ability to manage online shopping—manage SKU (Stock Keeping Unit), pricing, descriptions, stock quantities, shipping and tax calculation, a shopping cart, order management, coupon management, checkout with credit card payments.

As an administrator of "Palm Tree Publications", you may need to create a **Page** called "**Shopping**" under the **Page** "**Community**" at the **Book Lovers** Community **Public Pages,** and add the required portlets in the **Page, "Shopping"**. Let's do it as follows:

- Add a **Page** called "**Shopping**" under the **Page** "**Community**" at the **Book Lovers** Community **Public Pages,** if the **Page** is not already present.

To find rankings about a given book, the **Amazon Rankings** portlet would be useful:

1. First, add the following line into the file `portal-ext.properties`:

   `amazon.license.0=0F8PF7VK38NX3T19QE02`

2. Shutdown Liferay portal, if it is running.

3. Restart Liferay system, and login as an administrator, say "**Palm Tree**".

4. Add the **Amazon Rankings** portlet in the page where you want to show online shopping.

5. Configure the portlet by clicking the **Configuration** icon, and add all ISBN numbers separated by spaces as in "**1847190979 184719270X 1904811175**".

6. You will see the rankings of books as shown in the following figure.

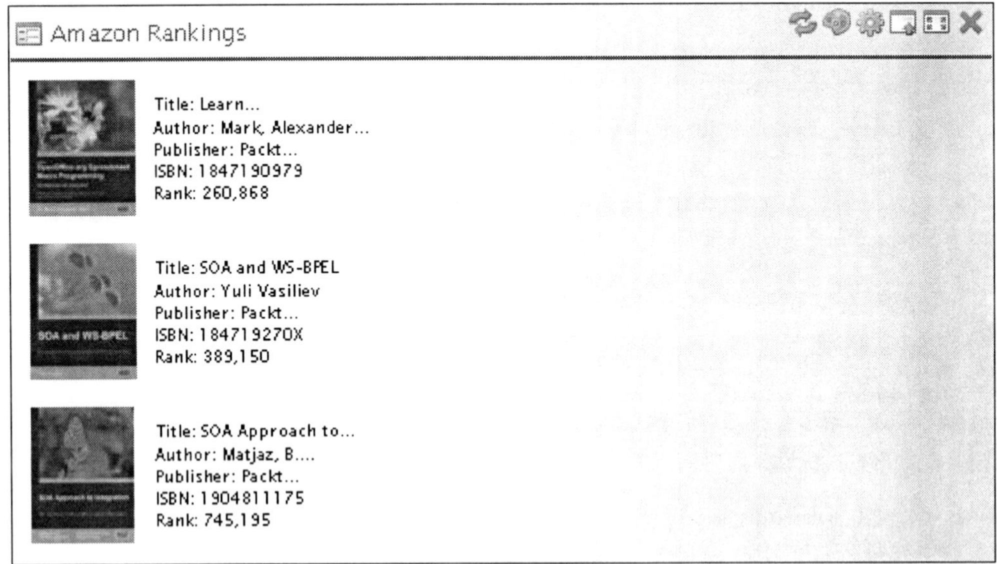

Note that you can enter a list of valid Amazon license keys. You can configure additional keys by incrementing the last number. The keys are used following a Round-Robin algorithm.

The Amazon Rankings portlet provides the ability to display Amazon sales information on any number of items. You can use it as a prototype to collect Amazon data with other proprietary data or web services.

For shopping online, the **Shopping** portlet shown in the following figure, would be useful:

- First, add the following line into the file: `portal-ext.properties`:

If cart quantities have to be in multiples of the item's minimum quantity, you can set the following to true:

```
shopping.cart.min.qty.multiple=true
```

In order to forward a User to the **Cart Page,** when he or she adds an item from the **Category Page,** set the following to true. The item may have dynamic fields, and all items with dynamic fields will have to be forwarded to the item's details page, regardless of the following setting.

```
shopping.category.forward.to.cart=true
```

In order to show special items when you browse a category, set the following to true:

```
shopping.category.show.special.items=true
```

In order to show the availability of an item, you can set the following to true:

```
shopping.item.show.availability=true
```

1. Shutdown Liferay portal, if it is running.
2. Re-startup Liferay system, and log in as an administrator say, "**Palm Tree**".
3. Add the **Shopping** portlet in the **Page** where you want to show online shopping.
4. Manage **SKU**, a shopping cart, order, coupon, checkout with credit card payments.

To summarize, the **Shopping** portlet offers inventory management including SKU (Stock Keeping Unit), pricing, descriptions, stock quantities, shipping and tax calculation, a shopping cart, order management, coupon management, checkout with credit card payments and more.

Enjoying Entertainment Tools

As an administrator at "Palm Tree Publication", you may need to include **Reverend Fun** in your web page. You can simply add the **Reverend Fun** portlet in the **Page** where you want to show **Reverend Fun**.

Reverend Fun is daily humor for people as shown in the following figure. Through this portlet, website **Users** can view daily humor or view some other day's humor, by clicking on the link **Previous** or **Next**.

Liferay offers unbeatable out-of-the-box functionality with over 60 JSR-168 / 286 compliant portlets, including entertainment tools. Besides the above mentioned **Reverend Fun** portlet, it also provides a lot of entertainment tools. Here, we list some of them as follows:

- **The Games** portlet provides the ability to show a campy rendition of **Hangman** and **Windows Classic**, **Minesweeper**, and so on.

- **The Words** portlet provides the ability to display lists of words that can be formed from the letters of any input.

Working with Multiple Languages

"Palm Tree Publications" needs the ability to accommodate global business environment with multilingual support. For example, you may be required to configure the website in German, since the enterprise has an office in Germany. Thus, as an administrator, you may have to configure the intranet with German language support.

It is quite easy to configure the web site with multilingual support. You can simply add the **Language** portlet to any **Page** and allow end-users to quickly select a different localization with one click. Let's do it as follows:

1. To change the current language into German language, you simply click on the icon, "**Deutsch (Deutschland)**", in the **Language** portlet.

2. The whole web site will appear in German language, and a sample is shown in the following figure.

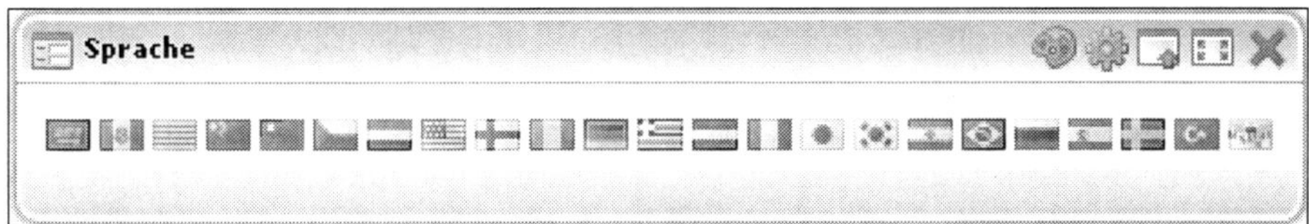

Liferay provides the ability to handle many languages. You can pull out all language-specific texts, and store them in the `language.properties` file. When a **Page, say** "Help", is loaded, the portal will detect the language first, and then pull up the corresponding language file, and finally display the text in the correct language.

With this, you can do a lot of work as follows:

- Easily support as many languages as you can imagine.
- Have a central location for multiple languages.
- Change the way a certain word is translated. If you want, you could effectively rename the portlet, such as **Message Boards,** as **Forums**. Then the title will be translated according to the language you choose.

In short, there are many properties, including languages, which you can configure in order to customize the portal.

Removing an Unwanted Language

By default, Liferay supports all the following languages.

```
locales=ar_SA,ca_AD,ca_ES,zh_CN,zh_TW,cs_CZ,nl_NL,en_US,fi_FI,fr_
FR,de_DE,el_GR,hu_HU,it_IT,ja_JP,ko_KR,fa_IR,pt_BR,ru_RU,es_ES,sv_
SE,tr_TR,vi_VN
```

If you want to support English, German and Chinese only, you can simply remove the unwanted locales, and your locales value looks like this:

```
locales=en_US,de_DE,zh_CN
```

Priority of Language Files

Liferay provides many language files and every language file overwrites another language file. What is the priority of these language files?

There are three simple rules:

- `-ext` versions such as `language-ext_ de_DE.properties`, `language-ext_ de.properties` and `language-ext.properties` take precedence over the non `-ext` versions.
- language-specific versions, such as `Language_ de_DE.properties` take precedence over the non-language-specific versions, such as `Language-ext_ de.properties`.
- location-specific versions, such as `language_de.properties` take precedence over the non-location-specific versions, such as `Language-ext. properties`.

For German, here is a ranking:

- `Language-ext_ de_DE.properties`
- `Language_ de_DE.properties`
- `Language-ext_de.properties`
- `Language_de.properties`
- `Language-ext.properties`
- `Language.properties`

> Note that, you may find the entry in "`Language.properties`". So you may think that you just need to override the value by editing "`Language-ext.properties`". However, this will not change anything, since all values in "`Language.properties`" are also in "`Language_ de.properties`" and locale-specific definitions take precedence. Therefore, "`Language_de.properties`" will override any changes you have made in "`Language-ext.properties`". That is why, you edited the "`Language-ext_en.properties`" file.

You can edit the same files to change **Language Settings, Portlet Titles, Category Titles, Action Names, Messages** and any other text that is language dependant.

Using WebDAV

As an employee of "Palm Tree Publications", you may want to view articles from Journal and contents in the Document Library using WebDAV. Thus, as an administrator, you need to configure WebDAV.

For example, in the **Document Library** portlet, navigate to the specific **Folder,** such as "**Books**", and edit it by clicking the **Edit** button to the right of the **Folder, "Books"**. There, you will see the direct WebDAV URL for that location. In the **Journal** portlet, navigate to the specific **Journal Template** and edit it. You should see the direct WebDAV URL for that **Template**.

Each WebDAV accessible resource has an associated URL. Let's use the WebDAV as follows:

1. Copy the WebDAV URL of the folder "**Books**"—`http://localhost:8080/ tunnel-web/secure/webdav/document_library/10095/11116/Books`.

2. Paste the URL in the address of the browser.

3. You will be asked to authenticate with your user ID and password.

 WebDAV, Web-based Distributed Authoring and Versioning, refers to the set of extensions to the Hypertext Transfer Protocol (HTTP). It allows the **Users** to collaboratively edit and manage files on remote World Wide Web servers, and offers functionality to create, change and move documents on a remote server.

WebDAV Support in Liferay Portal includes:

- Users can productively manage portal content with familiar operating system conventions for **Folders** and **Documents**.
- Full support for OS such as Windows and Linux.

Both **Document Library** and **Journal** portlets support the WebDAV protocol. Thus, **Users** can upload and organize resources from both a web interface and the file explorer of their desktop operating system.

To summarize, Liferay Portal allows WebDAV URL connections from any server using HTTP or HTTPS by default. You can also have a more secure configuration through the properties in `portal-ext.properties` as follows:

```
webdav.servlet.hosts.allowed=
webdav.servlet.https.required=false
```

Developing Portlets

Liferay built-in portlets and community plugins (portlets) may not satisfy your specific requirements related to your website building. Fortunately, you can develop new portlets to reach your own specific needs. The remaining section will describe the portlet development briefly.

Developing a Java Portlet is similar to developing a Servlet based web application. Existing web application development frameworks such as Struts, JSF, Webwork, and so on. can be used through the use of bridges. Existing frameworks may be adapted directly, without the need of a bridge, such as the Spring Portlet MVC (Model-View-Controller) framework.

Here is an example of **Spring MVC** Portlets for Liferay Plugin-SDK:

1. Download plugins-SDK with **Spring MVC** portlets from `http://liferay.cignex.com/sesame/plugins-sdk.zip`.
2. Unzip `plugins-sdk.zip`; find `build.Jonas.properties`.
3. Rename `build.Jonas.properties` as `build.${username}.properties`.

4. Update entry (`app.server.dir`) in `build.${username}.properties`. Let it point to the Liferay Tomcat directory. For instance: `app.server.dir=C:/training/tomcat`.

5. Drop "`build.xml`" at `/portlets` to **Ant** view.

6. Develop and run **Deploy** at **Ant** view if you are ready.

7. Test portlets at Liferay runtime....

In short, it is possible to use Liferay Service Builder or Plugin-SDK to develop your portlets, using the same service oriented architecture that Liferay Portal is based on.

Summary

This chapter discussed how to use a set of portlets to provide an information and assistance resource that troubleshoots specific requirements. Further, it also discussed multilingual support, and the usage of WebDAV. Finally, it provided guidance on how to develop new portlets to deal with specific requirements, in order to provide help desk assistances and customer support information efficiently.

11
Roll Out To Other Teams

The intranet website "book.com" of "Palm Tree Publications" is required to have the ability to build a **Community**, such as **Book Lovers**, where employees can share interests, and roll out to other teams. Liferay Communities provide the ability to create and manage **Communities** and their **Users**. A **Community** in Liferay has its own set of **Pages**, content management systems and **Permissions** management.

This chapter will provide a reference for administering **Communities**. It will include a discussion on how to create and manage **Communities**, as well as how to create and manage the **Pages** and **Users** within a **Community**. Moreover, it will introduce portal staging and publishing, manage staging workflow, community virtual hosting, and, in addition, a set of community tools - portlets.

By the end of this chapter, you will have learnt how to:

- Add a **Community.**
- Manage (edit, delete, search, join, leave) **Communities.**
- Add and manage the **Pages** and **Users** within a **Community.**
- Employ **Community** virtual hosting.
- Stage, preview and publish a web site.
- Manage staging workflow.
- Use **Community** tools, such as bookmarks, page comments, and so on.

Working with Communities

As an administrator at "Palm Tree Publications", you would need to provide an environment to roll out to other teams. Thus, you may need to provide an environment for **Users** to manage **Communities** at the page, "**Home**", of **My Community Private Pages**.

Adding A Community

First of all, we need to add the portlet, **Communities,** in the **Page,** "Home", and create a **Community,** "**Book Lovers**". Let's do it as follows:

1. Log in as an administrator, "**Palm Tree**".

2. Add a **Page** named "**Home**" of the **Book Lovers** community **Private Pages**.

3. Add the **Communities** portlet in the **Page,** "Home", of the **Book Lovers** Community where you want to manage **Communities,** if the **Communities** portlet is not already present.

4. Enter a **Name** for the **Community** such as "Book Lovers" in the **Name** input field, as shown in the following figure:

5. Optionally, enter a description for the **Community** such as "**A community for Book Lovers**" in the **Description** text area.

6. Select the **Open** value, if you want users to be able to join and leave this **Community** on their own. There are other values such as **Restricted** and **Private**.

7. Check the **Active** checkbox, if you want to activate this **Community** directly.

8. Click the **Save** button if you want to save the inputs.

Of course, you can create other **Communities**. After adding the **Communities,** such as "**Sesame Street**", and "**Sesame Workshop**", you can view all **Communities** as shown in the following figure:

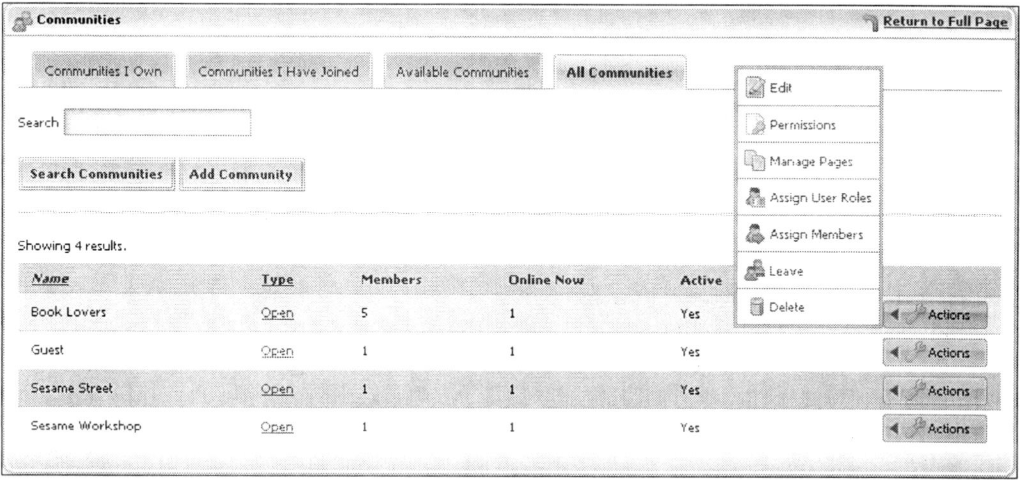

Managing Communities

After having **Communities** ready, you can manage them easily. You can view **Communities**, search, edit and delete **Communities** as well.

View Communities

The **Communities** portlet will display related **Communities** in different ways as follows:

- **Communities** I Own.

- **Communities** I Have Joined.

- Available **Communities**.

- All **Communities**.

To view all communities, simply click on the **All Communities** tab in the **Communities** portlet, as shown in the following figure. **Communities** will appear with **Name**, **Type**, number of **Members**, number of members **Online Now**, and a set of icons, such as **Edit**, **Permissions**, **Configure Pages**, **Assign Members**, **Assign User Role**, **Join/Leave**, **Delete**, and so on.

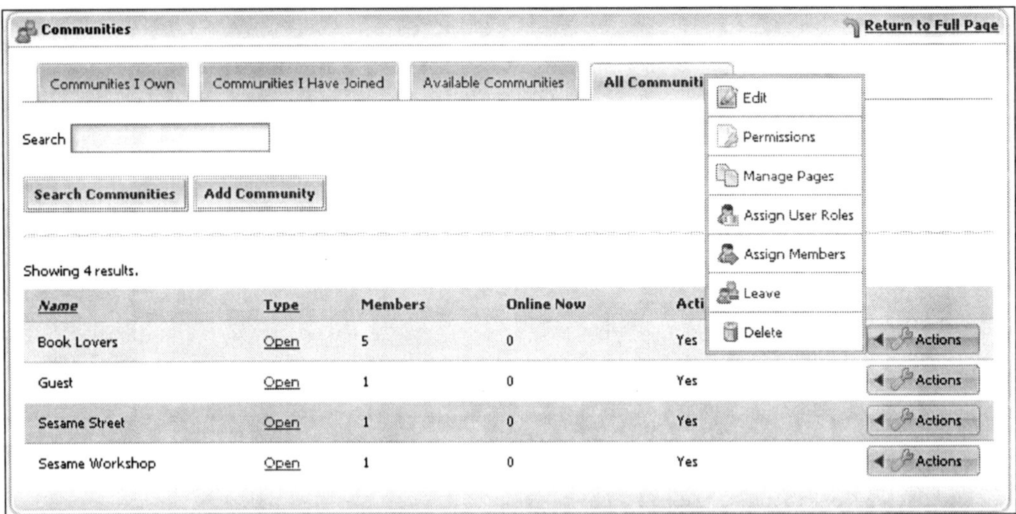

Similarly, you can view the **Communities** that you own, by clicking on the **Communities I Own** tab; view the **Communities** which you have joined by clicking on the **Communities I Have Joined** tab; and view the open available **Communities** by clicking on the **Available Communities** tab.

Search Communities

To search **Communities** on any tab, simply type the search criterion in the **Search** input field first. Then, click the **Search Communities** button. The portlet will list the search results, that is, a list of **Communities**.

Edit A Community

Suppose that you want to update the **Description** of the **Community**, "Sesame Street", from "a community of Sesame Street" to "an example community". The following is a simple set of steps to edit the **Community** in the **Communities** portlet:

1. Locate the **Community** you want to edit on the **All Communities** tab.

2. Click the **Edit** icon from the **Action** to the right of the **Community**, "Sesame Street".

3. Type changes such as "**an example community**", in the **Description** input field.

4. Optionally, make changes in the **Name** text field, the **Type** selection and the **Active** checkbox.

5. Click the **Save** button if you want to save the changes, or click the **Cancel** button if you want to cancel these actions.

Similarly, you can edit a **Community** on the tabs: **Communities I Own, Communities I Have Joined** and **Open Communities**.

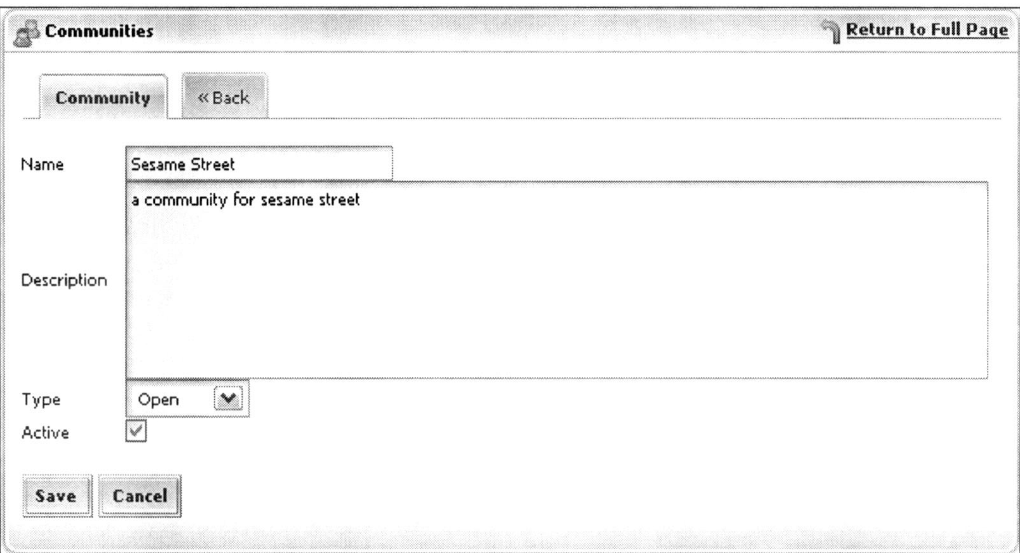

Delete A Community

Suppose that the **Community "Sesame Street"** is not wanted anymore. We can delete it following these simple steps:

1. On the **All Communities** tab, locate the **Community** you want to delete.

2. Click the **Delete** icon from the **Action** to the right of the **Community, "Sesame Street"**.

3. A screen will appear asking if you want to delete the selected **Community**. Click **OK** to delete. Click the **Cancel** if you do not want to delete the selected **Community**.

Similarly, you can delete a **Community** on the tabs **Communities I Own, Communities I Have Joined** and **Available Communities**.

Note that deleting a **Community** will delete all **Pages** that belong to this **Community**. At the same time, the links of all the **Users** assigned to this **Community** will be released.

Managing Pages

A **Community** is just a shell which can contain a set of **Pages**. Through the **Communities** portlet you can manage **Pages** of a given **Community**.

View Pages

To view the **Pages** of a **Community**, first locate a **Community**, such as the "**Book Lovers**" community. Then click on the **Manage Pages** icon from the **Actions** to the right of the community.

The **Pages** that belong to the **Book Lovers** community are displayed in a tree structure on the left. Every **Page** can have child **Pages** as shown in the following **Pages**. To actually view these **Pages** in the portal, use the **View Pages** button.

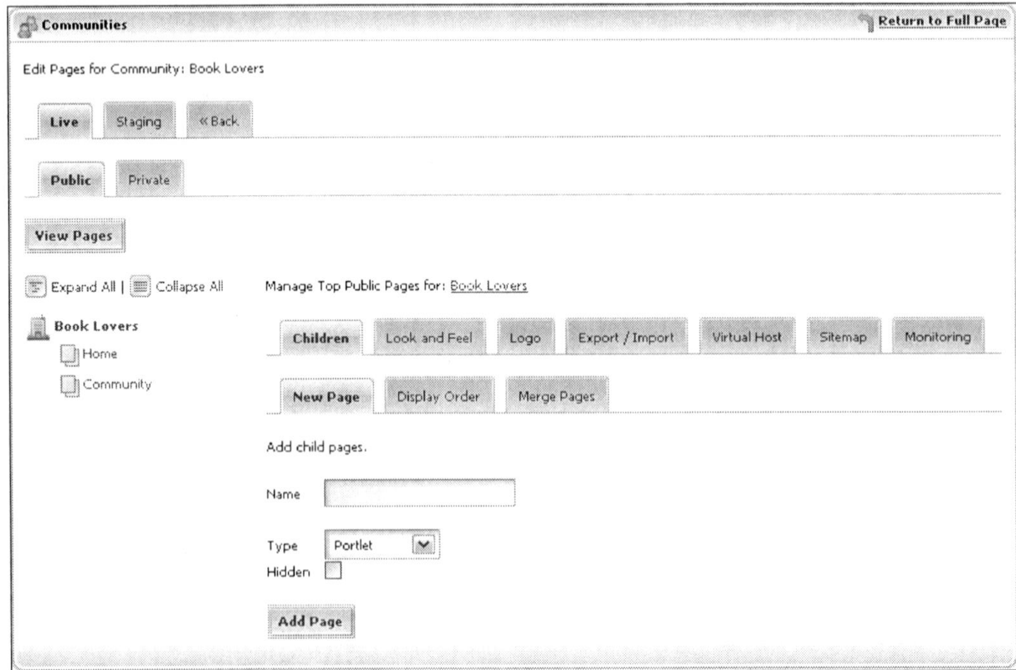

To view all **Pages** in the tree structure, simply click on the **Expand All** button. To view only the top level **Pages**, and the root node, that is, **Community** name, in the tree structure, simply click on the **Collapse All** button.

To view all **Pages** in the **Public**, simply click on the **Public** tab; or click on the **Private** tab to view all **Pages** in the **Private**.

Further, you can also add, edit, delete the pages, as stated in Chapter 2.

Import And Export Pages

You can also import and export **Pages** in a given **Community,** such as "Book Lovers", as follows:

1. In the **Communities** portlet, click on the **Configure Pages** icon to the right of the community for which you want to import/export **Pages**.

2. Click on the **Import / Export** tab.

3. If you click on the **Export** button, it will export all the **Pages**, their layouts, their configurations, their look and feel, and their **Permissions** to a LAR file (Liferay Archive). After you click the **Export** button, you will be prompted with a dialog window asking where to save the file.

4. You can also import a LAR file into your current **Community**.

5. To import a LAR file, click on the **Browse** button, find the LAR file on your hard drive, and click the **Import** button.

LAR file is a Liferay Archive. It includes all the **Pages**, their layouts, their configurations, their look and feel, and their **Permissions**.

Note that importing an LAR file will overwrite any existing **Pages** with the **Pages** configured in the LAR file.

Monitor Pages

Suppose that you want to use Google Analytics (GA) to generate detailed statistics about the visitors to a website. Let's do it as follows:

1. In the **Communities** portlet, click on the **Manage Pages** icon to the right of the community for which you want to monitor **Pages**.

2. Click on the **Monitoring** tab.

3. Set the **Google Analytics ID** that will be used for this set of pages.

4. Click on the **Save** button to save the inputs.

Assigning Users to A Community

You can assign **Users** to a **Community** directly. You can assign **Users** "David Berger" and "Lotti Stein" to the **Community, "Book Lovers"** as follows:

1. Go to the **Communities** portlet.

2. Click on the **Assign Members** icon from the **Action** to the right of the **Community,** such as "**Book Lovers**", for which you want to assign **Users**.

3. When a **Community** is first created by "**Palm Tree**", only the **User** "**Palm Tree**" is assigned to it.

4. Click on the **Available** tab.

5. Use the **Search** form to search for the **Users,** such as "**David Berger**" and "**Lotti Stein**", whom you want to assign to this **Community,** directly.

6. Check the boxes to the left of the **Users,** "**David Berger**" and "**Lotti Stein**", whom you want to assign to this **Community,** directly.

7. Click the **Update Associations** button as shown in the following figure.

8. Alternatively, **Users** can assign themselves directly to the available **Communities** by joining them.

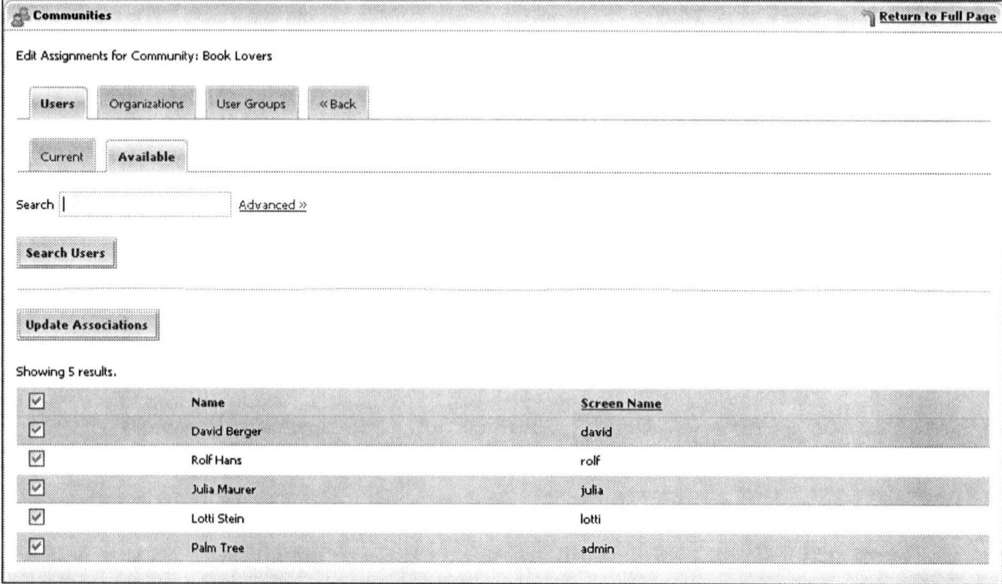

You can also assign **Users** to a **Community** indirectly through **Organizations** and **User Groups**. Suppose that you need to assign **Users** to the **Community, "Book Lovers"**, by the **User Group, "Managers"**. Let's do as follows:

1. Go to the **Communities** portlet.

2. Click on the **Assign Members** icon from the **Actions** to the right of the **Community** for which you want to assign **Users**.

3. Click on the **Available** tab.

4. Click on the **Organizations** or **User Groups** tabs.

5. In short, you can use the **Search** form to search for the **User Groups** that you want to assign to this **Community**. All the members of your selected **User Groups** will be assigned indirectly to this **Community,** via a link. However, for all intents and purposes, the **Users** will function as members of the **Community**.

6. Check the boxes to the left of the **User Groups that** you want to assign to this community.

7. Click the **Update Associations** button.

Similarly, you can assign **Users** to a **Community** indirectly, through **User Group**.

You can also assign **Users** indirectly to a **Community** by assigning **User Roles**. You can assign **User Role, "Content Creator"** to a **Community** through the following steps:

1. Go to the **Communities** portlet.

2. Click on the **Assign User Roles** icon from the **Actions** to the right of the community for which you want to assign users.

3. Click on the **Available** tab.

4. Use the **Search** form to search for the **Users** such as **"David Berger"** and **"Lotti Stein"**, whom you want to directly assign to this **Community**.

5. Check the boxes to the left of the **User Group "Content Creator"** that you want to directly assign to this **Community**.

6. Click the **Update Associations** button.

Joining An Open Community

As **User** "**Lotti Stein**" of "**Palm Tree Publications**", suppose that you want to join the **Community,** "**Sesame Street**":

1. Go to the **Communities** portlet, and select the **Available Communities** tab. Locate a **Community,** such as "**Sesame Street**", which you want to join.

2. Click on the **Join** icon to the right of the community.

3. Assuming that **Community** already has **Pages** configured for it, the **My Places** menu will now have an entry for the **Community** you have just joined. Click on that **Community's** name, and you will be able to navigate to it.

Leaving An Open Community

As **User** "**Lotti Stein**" of "**Palm Tree Publications**", suppose that you want to leave the **Community,** "**Sesame Street**":

1. Go to the **Communities** portlet, and select the **Available Communities** tab.

2. Locate the **Community** such as "**Sesame Street**" which you want to leave.

3. Click on the **Leave** icon to the right of the community.

4. The **Community** you just left will no longer appear in the **My Places** menu, and you will no longer have access to it.

Updating Permissions

Suppose that as an administrator, "**Palm Tree**", of "Palm Tree Publications", you want to give the **User,** "**Lotti Stein**", **Permission** to manage the **Pages** in the **Community,** "**Book Lovers**". Let's do it as follows:

1. Go to the **Communities** portlet.

2. Locate the community "**Book Lovers**", where you want to change **Permissions**.

3. Then click on the **Permissions** icon from the **Actions** located next to the community.

4. Select the **Users** tab.

5. Find **User** "**Lotti Stein**"in the **Available** box.

6. Click on the **Update Permissions** button.

7. Select **Permissions**: **Manage Pages** in the **Available** box.

8. Click on the **Add** arrow.

9. Click on the **Finished** button, if you are ready, as shown in the following figure.

Now, as a **User** of the **Book Lovers** Community, "**Lotti Stein**" has the **Permission, "Manage Pages"**, on the **Community, "Book Lovers"** finally.

Similarly, you can update **Permissions** by **Organizations, User Groups** such as "**Managers**", **Regular Role** such as "**User**", and **Guest**, as shown in the following figure:

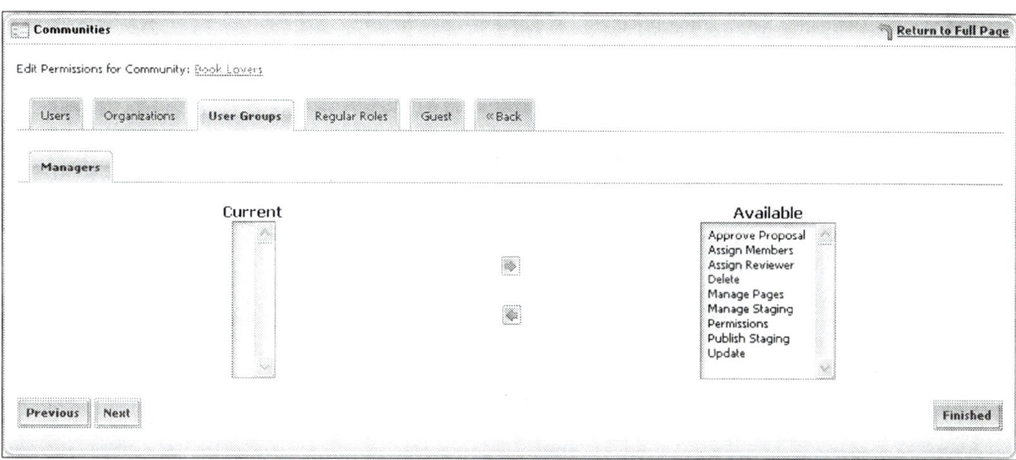

The following table shows **Permissions** for a **Community**. A regular **User** may set up all **Permissions** (marked 'X'), **Approve Proposal, Assign Members, Assign Reviewer, Delete, Manage Pages, Manage Staging, Permissions, Publish Staging,** and **Update**, while a **Guest User** can set up only **Approve Proposal, Assign Reviewer**, and **Publish Staging** (marked 'X') **Permissions**.

Action	Description	Regular User	Guest
Approve Proposal	Approves proposal	X	X
Assign Members	Assigns members	X	
Assign Reviewer	Assigns reviewers	X	X
Delete	Deletes the **Community**	X	
Manage Pages	Manages pages	X	
Manage Staging	Manages staging **Pages**	X	
Permissions	Changes the **Permission** of the community	X	
Publish Staging	Pusblishes the staging **Pages**	X	X
Update	Updates the **Community**	X	

Working with Community Virtual Hosting

Suppose that you have a domain name, booklovers.com, and you want to set up virtual hosting for the **Community, "Book Lovers"**, on this domain. That is, end **Users** can visit all the **Pages** of the "Book Lovers" **Community** in the domain name.

Let's configure **Community** virtual hosting as follows:

1. Go back to the **Communities** portlet, and click on the "**Available Communities**" tab to list open **Communities**.

2. Locate the **Community, "Book Lovers"**.

3. Click on the **Manage Pages** icon from the **Actions** to the right of the community for which you want to configure virtual hosting.

4. Click on the **Virtual Host** tab.

5. In the **Virtual Host** tab, enter the **Public Virtual Host** such as "**booklovers. com**", that will map to the public friendly URL.

6. Enter the friendly URL such as "**booklovers**" that will be used by **Public Pages,** as shown in the following figure.

7. Click on the **Save** button to save the changes when you are ready.

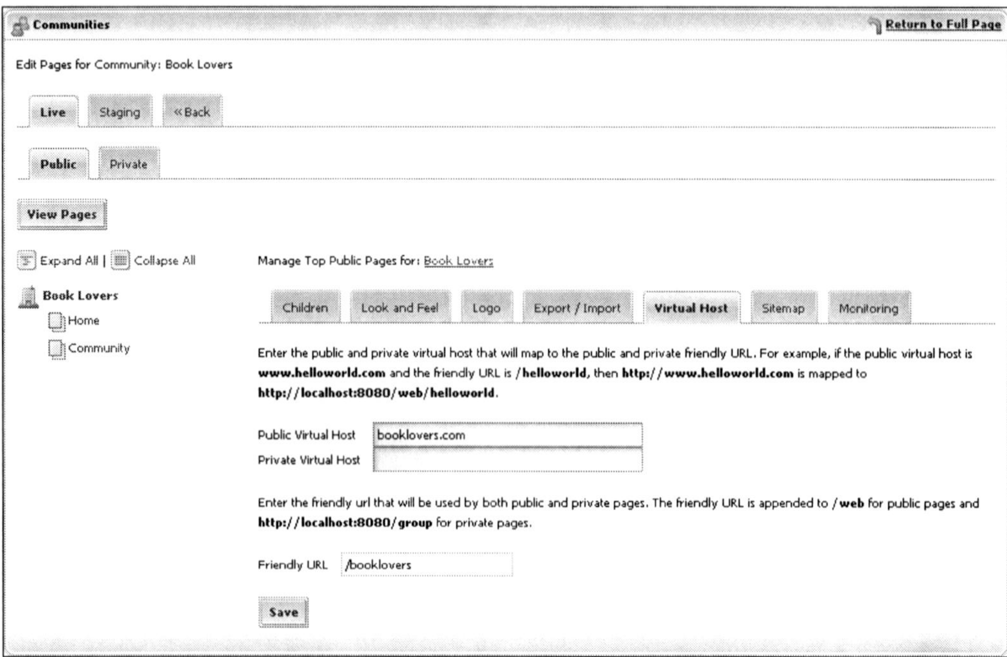

Using Virtual Hosting Effectively

Virtual hosting means to host more than one domain name on the same computer, mostly on the same IP address. There are two basic methods to fulfill virtual hosting: name-based, and IP address based or IP-based. Name-based virtual hosts are used with multiple host names in order to share the same web server IP address, while in IP-based virtual hosting, each site will point to a unique IP address. You can configure the web server with multiple physical network interfaces, virtual network interfaces on the same physical interface, or multiple IP addresses on one interface.

Liferay Community Virtual Hosting is an extension of the friendly URL functionality. It allows one or more **Communities** in a single portal instance, identified by separate and unique host names. End users only input the name of the host they expect to visit, into the address bar in the browser. Although, it appears to the users that they are visiting different web sites, they are in fact being directed to a single web server. In fact, based on the host name, the server determines the **Community** to be presented to the **User**.

Setup Virtual Hosting

There are two steps to set up virtual hosting. The first step is to ensure that a Domain Name Server (DNS) entry exists for each virtual host you want, and that every one of them points to the IP address of the server.

Next, set up a virtual host filter at `system.properties` as follows.

```
com.liferay.portal.servlet.filters.virtualhost.
VirtualHostFilter=true
```

Note that, the virtual host filter maps hosts to both the **Public** and **Private pages**.

Working with Community Staging & Publishing

It is a basic requirement for the **Users** to have the capability to stage their work. That is, they need the ability to work on a working copy of the website first. At the same time, they need to manipulate this working copy and preview it, as if it were the web site. Moreover, they need the capability to have many "working copies" in progress at any point in time. More interestingly, **Users** should be able to preview a working copy at any time, without disrupting the live **Pages**.

Meanwhile, it also is required to manage staging properly. Let's consider one scenario. Here, we have the content creator who can create the pages in the staging, content producer who can approve the **Pages** or reject the **Pages** and return to the content creator. We have the content reviewer who can approve the **Pages** or reject the **Pages** and return it to the content producer. Ultimately we have the content editor who can either reject the **Pages** and return it to the content producer, or publish the **Pages**.

Let's implement these requirements as follows:

Using Community Staging

First of all, let's activate the staging as follows:

1. To access Staging, use the **Communities** portlet to go to the **Available Communities** tab.

2. Locate a **Community** first. Then click on the **Manage Pages** icon from the **Actions** to the right of the community.

3. There, you will see the **Live** tab and **Staging** tab. If you choose **Staging,** and activate it, the **Page** changes to show you how to copy the live branch into the staging branch, or vice versa.

4. It will create a copy of the site as a new virtual **Community,** which you can see and navigate, before pushing content as shown in the following figure.

To preview the **Pages** in the staging branch, simple click on the **View Pages** button under the buttons **Staging** and **Public**. The **Pages** in the staging server appear in a highlighted background color. You can view the pages in the staging branch and also add and remove portlets (that is, contents) of the pages.

Publishing Pages

Publishing is an ability to push one or more assets from staging to a live environment. Publishing should include the following features (as shown in the following figure):

- Publishing should include the capability to publish to local and remote systems.

- Publishing should be as simple as the push of a button, or it should be included as a step in a workflow.

- Publishing should not disrupt the production environment except to effect the published change.

To publish the **Pages** in the **Staging Branch**, simply click on the **Publish to Live** button next to the button, **View Pages**. Portal will copy the **Staging Branch** into the **Live Branch**.

 Note that, the **Pages** in the **Live Branch** will be overwritten by the **Pages** in the **Staging Branch**.

To copy from the **Live Branch** to the **Staging Branch**, simply click on the button, **Copy from Live,** next to the **View Pages** and **Publish to Live** buttons. The following figure depicts how to **Activate Staging, Copy from live** to staging, publish from staging to live.

 Note that, the **Pages** in the **Staging Branch** will be overwritten by the **Pages** in the **Live Branch**.

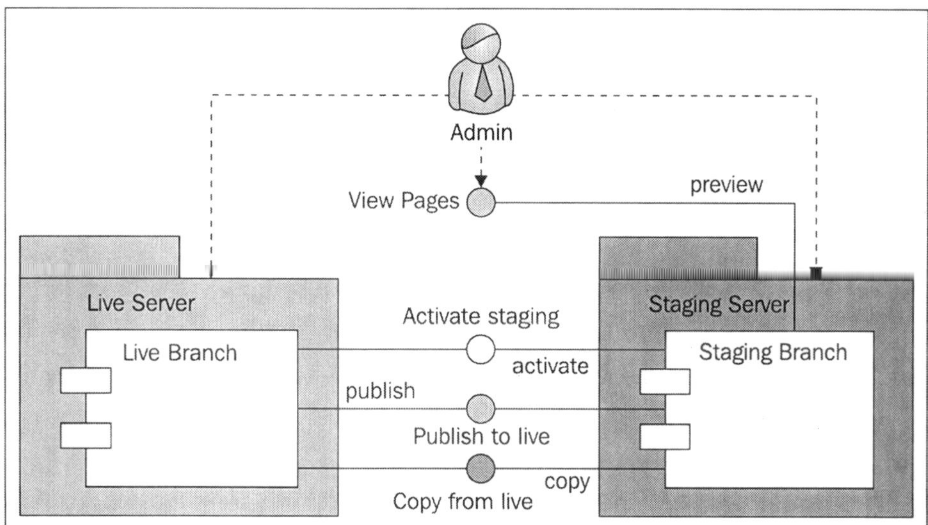

Manage Staging with Workflow

Let's implement the previously mentioned scenario. First of all, let's create a set of **Roles** as follows:

1. Create a **Role, "Content Creator"**, in the **Enterprise Admin** portlet.
2. Add a **User, "Lotti Stein"** with the **Permissions, View, Update and Delete** in the **"Content Creator"**.
3. At the same time, define **Permission, "Manage Pages"**, for the **Role, "Content Creator"**, with the **Communities** portlet.
4. Create a **Role, "Content Producer"** in the **Enterprise Admin** portlet.
5. Add a **User, "Rolf Hans"**, with the **Permissions, View, Update and Delete** in the **"Content Producer"**.
6. At the same time, define the **Permissions, "Manage Pages"**, **"Assign Reviewer"** and **"Approve Proposal"** for the **Role, "Content Producer"** with the **Communities** portlet.
7. Create a **Role, "Content Reviewer"** in the **Enterprise Admin** portlet.
8. Add a **User, "Julia Maurer"**, with the **Permissions, View, Update and Delete** in the **"Content Reviewer"**.
9. At the same time, define **Permission, "Approve Proposal"**, for the **Role, "Content Reviewer"** with the **Communities** portlet.
10. Create a **Role "Content Editor"** in the **Enterprise Admin** portlet.
11. Add a **User, "David Berger"**, with the **Permissions, View, Update and Delete** in the **"Content Editor"**.
12. At the same time, define the **Permissions, "Approve Proposal"**, **"Manage Pages"**, **"Manage Staging"** and **"Publish Staging"** for the **Role, "Content Reviewer"** with the **Communities** portlet.

When **User Roles** are ready, we can configure managed staging workflow. Let's do it as follows:

- To access **Staging**, use the **Communities'** portlet and go to the **Available Communities** tab.

Now, we are ready to **Activate Managed Staging**. Let's use the **Community Roles** and set up staging and publishing workflow, as shown in the following figure:

1. Activate managed stages by checking on the checkbox.
2. Select the **Number of Approval Stages**, such as "4".
3. Select value of **"Content Creator"** for **Stage "1"**.

4. Select value of "**Content Producer**" for **Stage** "**2**".

5. Select value of "**Content Reviewer**" for **Stage** "**3**".

6. Select value of "**Content Editor**" for **Stage** "**4**".

7. Click on the **Save** button when you are ready.

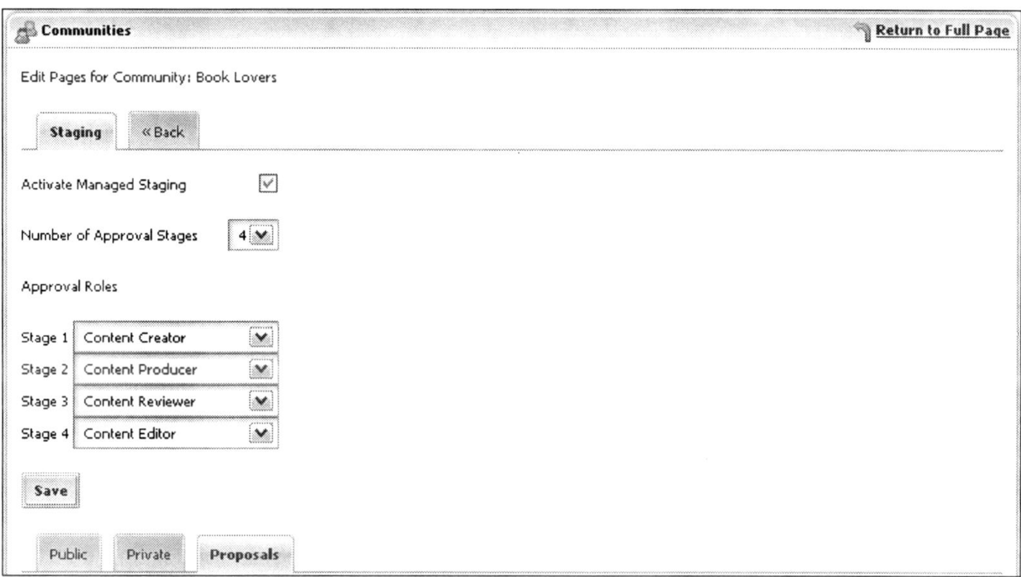

Now we have **Staging** and publishing workflow ready. Let's do it as follows:

1. Log in as a **Content Creator,** say "**Lotti Stein**".

2. Create a **Page,** such as "**Test**", with contents such as Bookmarks.

3. Input **Proposal** publication and assign **Reviewer,** such as "**Rolf Hans**".

4. Click the **Save** button when you are ready.

5. Log in as a **Content Producer,** such as "**Rolf Hans**".

6. You can view **Proposals** to either approve or reject.

7. You can also assign **Reviewer,** such as "**Julia Maurer**".

8. Log in as a **Content Producer,** say "**Julia Maurer**".

9. You can view **Proposals** to either approve or reject.

10. You can also assign **Reviewer,** such as "**David Berger**".

11. Then Log in as a **Content Producer,** such as "**David Berger**".

12. You can view **Proposals** and reject it.

13. Or you can publish it to **Live**.

Employing Community Tools

There are a set of portlets related to the community, such as bookmarks, directory, enterprise announcements, community announcements, invitations, communities, page comments and page rating. This section mainly introduces portlets including bookmarks, directory, announcements, invitation, page comments and page rating.

Using Announcements

Announcement is a brief message (typically ten seconds) that advertises a product or service or offers public service information. It is used mainly in the interval between **Pages** to capture the attention of the audience of both **Pages**.

The announcement portlets (either an enterprise such as "Palm Tree publications", or a **Community** such as "**Book Lovers**") display each specific announcement. They enable users to create, modify, delete and post announcements for the enterprise, "Palm Tree publications", or the **Community, "Book Lovers"**.

The following are a set of simple steps for setting up the Announcement for "Palm Tree Publications":

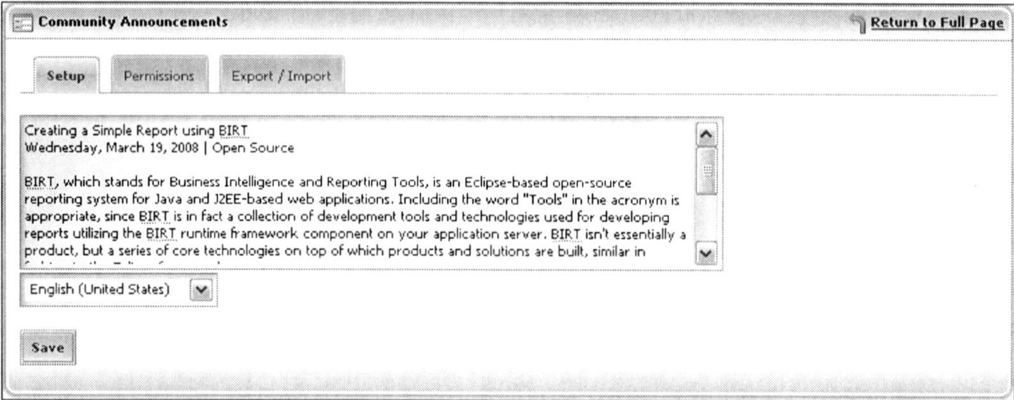

1. Add the **Company Announcement** portlet to the **Page, Community,** if the **Company Announcements** portlet is not already present.

2. To set up the announcement that you want to display in the portlet, click on the **Configuration** icon as shown in the previous figure.

3. Select the **Setup** tab and input the announcement, such as "**Creating a Simple Report using BIRT … **".

4. Click on the **Save** button to save the changes, and further, click on the **Back** arrow to return.

Working with Bookmarks Portlet

Bookmarks are retrievable names and URLs (that is, web page locations). Their primary purpose is to catalog and easily access web pages that **Users** have visited, either by name or by URL.

The **Bookmarks** portlet provides the ability for the **Users** to keep track of URLs in the portal. An administrator can use **Bookmarks** to publish relevant links to a group of **Users**.

To add a bookmark to the **Bookmarks** portlet, simply follow these steps in sequence:

1. Add the **Bookmarks** portlet to the **Page, "Home"**, of the **Guest Community** where you want to show bookmarks, if the portlet is not already present.
2. To add a bookmark (called an entry) to an empty **Bookmarks** portlet, you should first add a **Folder**.
3. Click the **Add Folder** button.
4. Give a **Name** such as, "**My Home**", and **Description** such as, "**This is a bookmark for My Home**" for the **Folder**. The **Permissions** for the **Folder** determine what **Users** can do. To change the **Permissions**, simply click on the **Configuration** link. To change all **Permissions**, click on the **More** link.
5. Click the **Save button.**

Then you can view the Folder, as shown in the following figure. The **Folders** will appear with name, description, number of sub folders, **number of Entries**, and a set of **Actions**, such as **Edit**, **Permissions** and **Delete**.

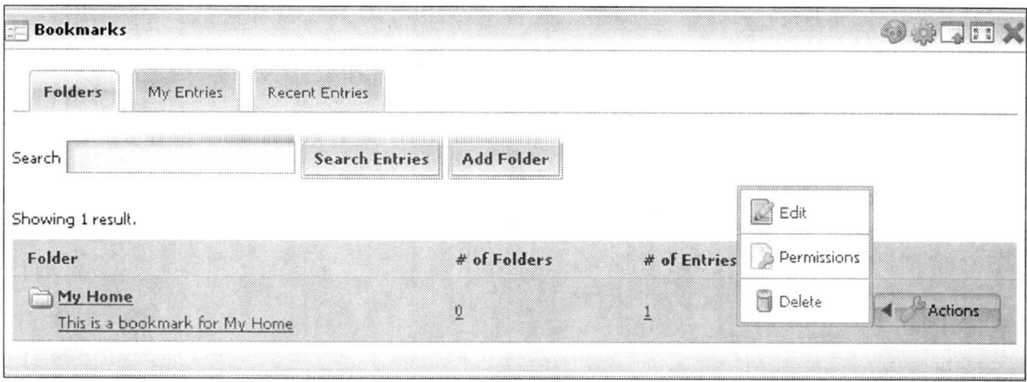

1. To add a bookmark to the **Folder, "My Home"**, click on the **Folder** name such as "**My Home**".

2. You can either add more **Folders** to further divide your bookmarks into more specific categories, or you can add a bookmark to the current folder. Click the **Add Entry** button.

3. Give a **Name** such as "**SSO, LDAP, Liferay and Alfresco**", URL such as "`http://liferay.cignex.com`", and **Description** such as "**Full integration of SSO, LDAP, Liferay and Alfresco**" to the bookmark. The **Permissions** for the bookmark determine what **Users** can do.

4. Click the **Save button** when you are ready.

Then you can view the **bookmarks** under the **Folder,** as shown in the following figure.

In short, the **Bookmarks** portlet provides a way for **Users** to store the names and URLs of Web sites. After a bookmark is created, you can click the link to open the site in a new browser window.

To view recent entries, you can simply click the **Recent Entries** tab. Similarly, to view entries which you have created, simply click the **My Entries** tab. The bookmarks will appear with entry name, URL, number of **Visits**, number of **Priority**, **Modified Date** and a set of **Actions,** such as **Edit, Permissions** and **Delete**. More interestingly, the number of visits will be updated dynamically when the site has been visited through the URL link in the **Bookmarks** portlet.

Using Directory Portlet

The **Directory** portlet provides the ability to display a list of **Users** registered on the portal. The **Directory** portlet displays personal information for individual **Users** and also gives listings of available **Organizations** and **User Groups**.

You can find **Users** through basic **Search,** as shown in the following figure. You just input the search criterion and click the **Search Users** button. Similarly, you can find **Users** through **Advanced Search**. You just click on the **Advanced** link first, and then input **Search** criterions for advanced search, and then click on the **Search Users** button. Moreover, you can find **Users,** by available **Organizations** as well as **User Groups**.

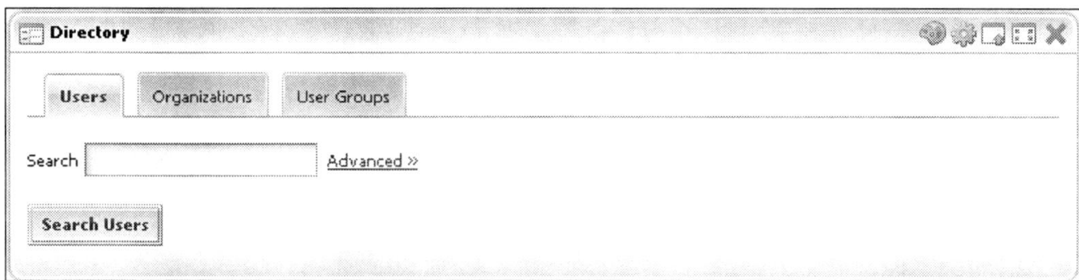

Working with Invitation Portlet

The **Invitation** portlet allows you to invite friends to come and see your web sites, or portal pages. The following are a simple set of steps to invite friends using the **Invitation** Portlet (as shown in the following figure):

1. Add the **Invitation** portlet in the page, "**Home**", of the **Guest Community** where you want to invite friends, if the portlet is not already present.

2. Click on the **Invite Friends** link.

3. **Enter up to 20 email addresses of friends** whom **you would like to invite. Enter one email address per line** as shown in the following figure.

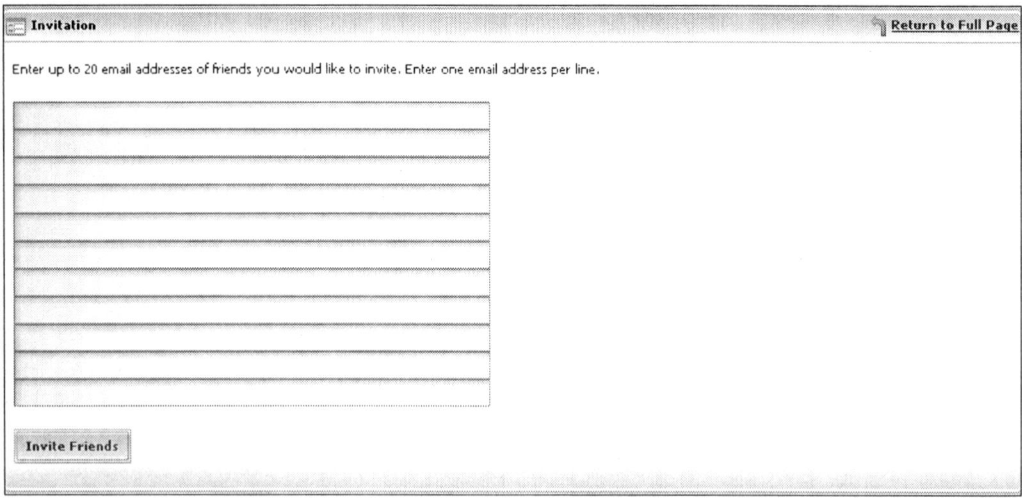

4. Click on the **Invite Friends** button when you are ready.

5. **To change the email setup and Permissions for Users, simply click on the Configuration icon at the top right of the portlet.**

The number of email addresses of friends you would like to invite is configurable. You can change the number of recipients (at `system-ext.properties`) as follows:

```
invitation.email.max.recipients=20
```

Using Page Comments Portlet

The **Page Comments** portlet allows you to add page comments easily in your portal page. Using this portlet, you can easily add, or edit, or delete **Page Comments**. Let's do is as follows:

1. Add the **Page Comments** portlet in the **Page, "Home"**, of the **Guest community** where you want to add **Page Comments**, if the portlet is not already present.

2. Click the **Post Reply** link, if you want to add **Page Comments**.

3. Input your **Page Comments**. Click the **Reply** button to save the inputs, or the **Cancel** button to cancel the inputs.

4. You can edit **Page Comments** by clicking on the **Edit** icon first. Then, update the **Comments**. Click the **Update** button to save the changes, or the **Cancel** button to cancel the changes, as shown in the following figure.

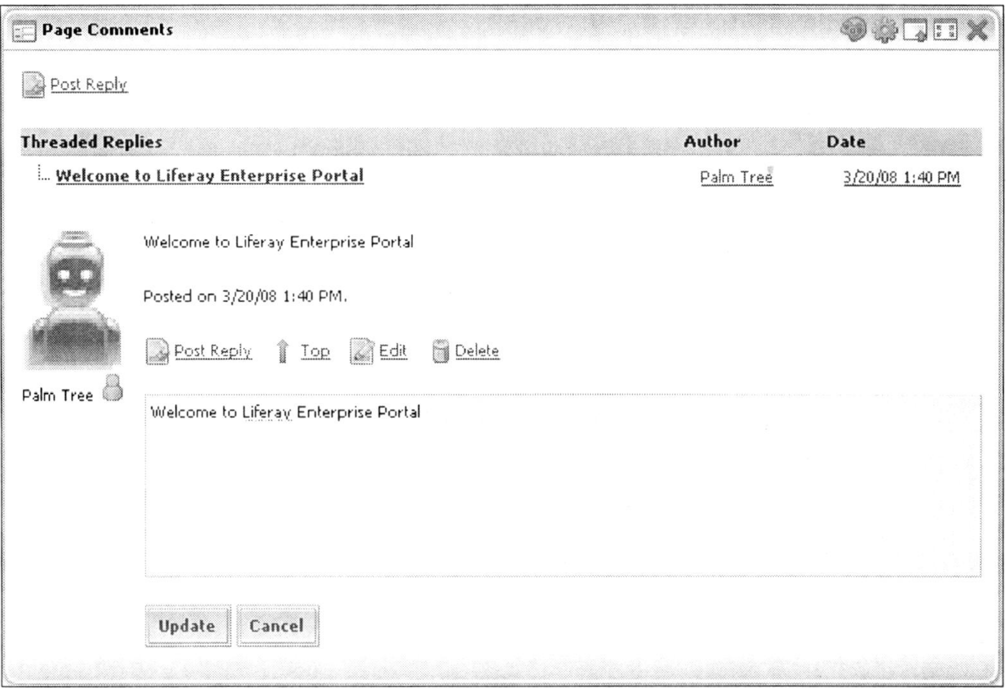

5. Alternatively, you can delete **Page Comments** by clicking on the **Delete** icon. A screen will appear asking if you want to delete this. Click **OK** to confirm deletion, or **Cancel** to cancel deletion.

6. If there are a lot of **Page Comments,** and you are not at the top of the portlet, you can go to the top, by clicking on the **Top** icon.

Working with Page Rating Portlet

The **Page Ratings** portlet allows you to add page rating in your portal page. This allows you to change page rating. Let's do it as follows:

1. Log in as the administrator, "**Palm Tree**".

2. Add the **Page Ratings** portlet in the page, "**Home**", of the **Guest Community Public Pages** where you want to change the **Page Rating** (if the portlet is not already present).

3. Click on the star to change **Your Rating,** such as three stars. The number of votes, such as only one, will appear. If you move your mouse to the stars below **Average,** you will find three stars.

4. Log in as **User, "Lotti Stein"**.

5. Click on the star to change **Your Rating to say,** two stars. The number of votes will appear as two now. If you move your mouse to the stars below **Average,** the number of stars will appear, as say two and half, as shown in the following figure.

Summary

This chapter first introduced us to the **Communities** portlet, and discussed how to add a **Community,** and how to manage (edit, delete, search, join, leave) **communities**. Then it discussed how to add and manage the **Pages** and **Users** within a **Community** and how to employ **Community** virtual hosting . Further, it also discussed how to use stage, preview and publish a web site, and manage **Staging** workflow. Finally, it also discussed how to use **Community** tools, such as **Bookmarks, Page Comments,** and so on.

12
Search

In the intranet website "book.com" of "Palm Tree Publications", we are required to query **Message Boards** entries, **Blogs** posts, **Wikis Articles**, **Users** at Directory and contents at **Document Library**, bookmarks entries, **Images** at **Image Gallery**, and so on. Furthermore, a lot of contents are stored and managed in the alfresco server. Thus, it is also required to search alfresco contents in the intranet websites. Meanwhile, it would be very helpful to provide maps search and CSZ (City, State, and Zip code) search in the intranet websites as well as Google Maps and Google Search.

This chapter first will introduce a federated search for **Message Boards** entries, **Blogs** posts, **Wikis Articles**, **users** of Directory and the contents at **Document Library**, **Bookmarks** entries, and alfresco contents. Then, it will describe a CSZ search, maps search, Google Maps and Google search portlets. Further, it will also discuss the OpenSearch concept and the Journal content search portlet, in detail. Finally, this chapter will discuss how to use the sitemap for search engines, and how to deploy and manage search portlets.

By the end of this chapter, you will have learnt how to:

- Employ federated search.
- Integrate search against alfresco contents.
- Use CSZ search and map search.
- Employ Google search and Google maps.
- Understand OpenSearch within alfresco content portlet.
- Use Journal Content search.
- Configure sitemap for search engines.
- Deploy search portlets
- Manage search portlets.

Working with Federated Search

It is very useful to provide federated search abilities, such as search for alfresco contents, **Blogs** entries, **Users**, **Bookmarks** entries, **Documents**, **Wiki Articles**, journal articles, and so on. in "book.com". Thanks to Liferay, there are a set of search portlets available for this requirement. In this section, let's work with these portlets.

Using Search Portlet

The **Search** Portlet is a JSR-168 compliant portlet that can be used for federated search. By default, Liferay itself is a search provider.

As shown in the following figure, the **Search** Portlet provides a federated search against **alfresco** content, **Blogs** entries, **Users**, **Bookmarks** entries, **Documents**, **Wiki Articles**, journal articles, and so on.

The following is a simple set of steps to use the **Search** portlet:

1. Add the **Search** portlet in the page, "**Home**", of the **Book Lovers** Community where you want to search, if the search portlet is not already present.
2. Input the **Search** criterion, "**Alfresco**".
3. Click the **Search icon.**
4. Optionally, you can set **Permissions** by clicking the **Configure icon to the upper right of the portlet.**

Liferay provides many portlets to support OpenSearch, such as **Message Boards**, **Blogs, Wikis**, Directory and **Document Library**, and so on. In addition, the **Alfresco Content** portlet also supports OpenSearch. Normally, these portlets have the following configuration:

```
<open-search-class>class-name</open-search-class>
```

The following figure depicts the **Search** results with the **Search** criterion, "**alfresco**". The search results include **alfresco** contents, **Message Boards** entries, **Blogs** posts, **Wikis Articles, Users** at Directory and contents at the **Document Library**, and so on.

How do we get the following results related to **alfresco** contents? Let's do it as follows:

1. Deploy alfresco web client application "`alfresco.war`" (for example alfresco version 2.1.1 enterprise version) to the **Folder.** `$TOMCAT_DIR/webapps/`.

2. Download the **Alfresco Content** portlet from community plugins.

3. Copy the plugin `WAR` file manually to the auto deploy configured directory `$USER_HOME/liferay/deploy`.

4. Copy Open search interface from `webapps/alfresco-content-portlet/WEB-INF/classes` to `$TOMCAT_DIR /webapps/ROOT/WEB-INF/classes`.

5. Configure open search as shown in the next section.

6. Shutdown the Liferay server.

7. Restart the Liferay server.

8. Play with the **Search** portlet.

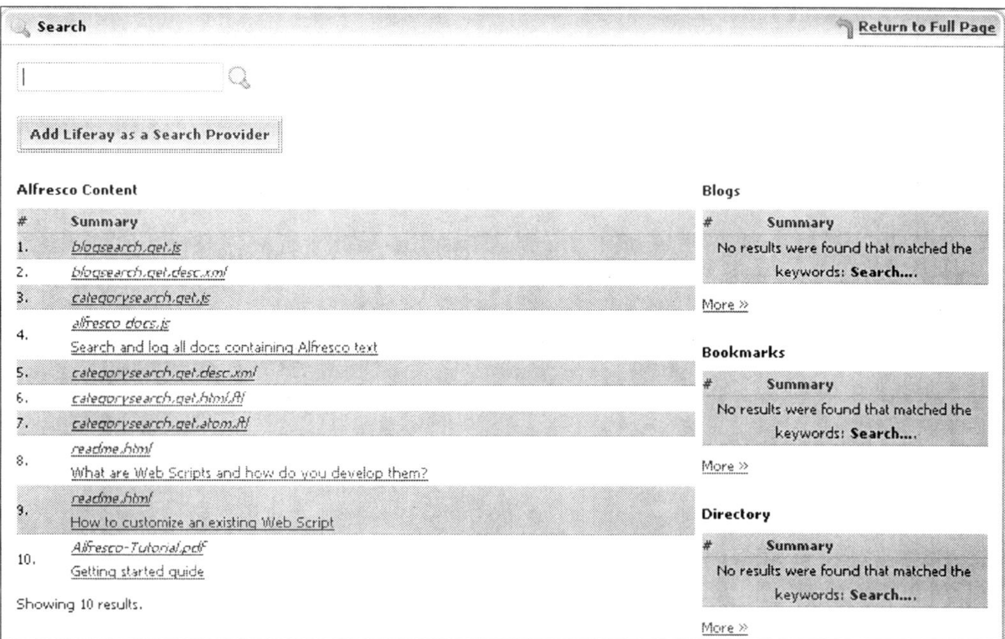

Query Alfresco Content via OpenSearch

Alfresco does not ony provide the ability to expose its search engines via OpenSearch, but it also provides an aggregate OpenSearch feature in the Alfresco Web Client. Moreover, **alfresco** keyword search mimics the keyword search of the Alfresco Web Client.

First, let's view the search URL template as follows:

```
http://<host>:<port>/alfresco/service/api/search/keyword?q={search
Terms}&p={startPage?}&c={count?}&l={language?}
```

where:

- searchTerms = keyword or keywords to search.
- startPage (optional) = the page number of search results desired by the client.
- count (optional) = the number of search results per page (default: 10).
- language (optional) = the locale to search with (XML 1.0 Language ID for example en-GB).

Then in order to let the **Alfresco Content** portlet support OpenSearch, we need to simply set the `open-search-class` value (at `liferay-portlet.xml`) as follows:

```
<open-search-class>com.liferay.portlet.alfrescocontent.util.
AlfrescoOpenSearchImpl</open-search-class>
```

Finally, in Liferay portal, we need to let the **Search** Portlet know that the **Alfresco Content** portlet supports OpenSearch, and sets the values used to query Alfresco via OpenSearch as follows:

```
open.search.enabled=true
open.search.protocol=http
open.search.host=localhost
open.search.port=8080
open.search.realm=Alfresco
open.search.username=admin
open.search.password=admin
open.search.path=/alfresco/service/search/keyword
```

If the domain for alfresco server was `sesame.cignex.com`, and port number was `80`, we can set the values used to query Alfresco via OpenSearch as follows:

```
open.search.enabled=true
open.search.protocol=http
open.search.host=sesame.cignex.com
open.search.port=80
```

```
open.search.realm=Alfresco
open.search.username=admin
open.search.password=admin
open.search.path=/alfresco/service/search/keyword
```

Using CSZ Search

Suppose that we want to find the zip codes for a city named "Mountain View" in the state of "California" in the USA. The CSZ search portlet would be very useful for doing this search.

1. Add the **CSZ Search** portlet in the **Page, "Home"**, of the **Book Lovers** Community where you want to search, if the **CSZ Search** portlet is not already present.

2. Input the **City, "Mountain View"** and the **State, "California"** first.

3. Then click the **Search** button.

4. **The Zip** codes associated with the given **City** and **State** will appear.

5. Alternatively, you could input the **Zip** code first.

6. Then press the **Search** button.

7. **The names of the City** and **State** associated with the given **Zip** will appear.

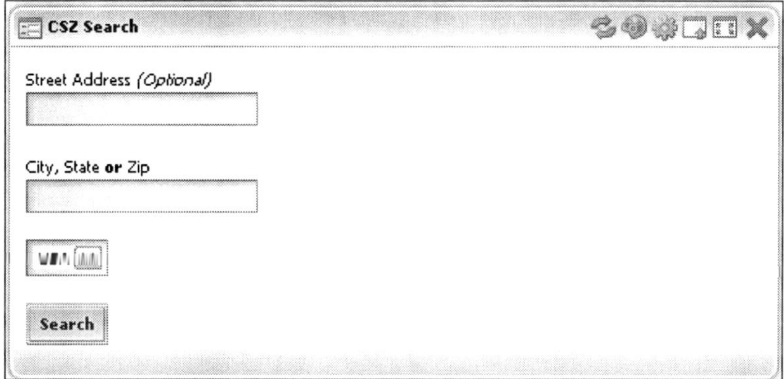

The following figure depicts the **CSZ Search** example and search results. It shows all the related **zip codes** for the **City**, "**Mountain View**" and **State, "California"** in the **USA**.

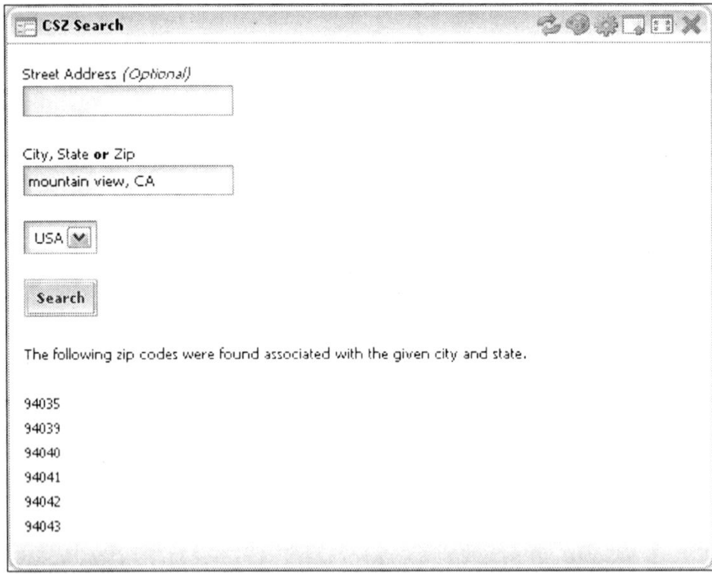

In general, the **CSZ** (**City, State** and **Zip**) search portlet provides a way to **Search Zip** codes by address, **City** and **State**, or to **Search City** and **State** by **Zip** code. USPS ZIP code lookup is used as a web service provider.

> USPS (U.S. Postal Service) provides services for ZIP code lookup, URL: `http://www.usps.com/zip4/`.

Using Maps Search

Suppose that we know the **City** name, say "**Mountain View**", and the **State** name, say such "**California**", in the **USA** and we want to find the related maps. The **Maps** portlet would be useful for this purpose.

1. Add the **Maps** portlet in the **Page, "Home"**, of the **Book Lovers** Community where you want to search for maps, if the **Maps** portlet is not already present.

2. Input the **Address, City** as "**Mountain View**", **State** as "**California**", the related **Zip** code and the country as "**USA**" first.

3. Then press the **Search** button as shown in following figure:

A **Map** associated with the given **Address**, **City**, **State**, **Zip** code and country will appear as shown in the following figure:

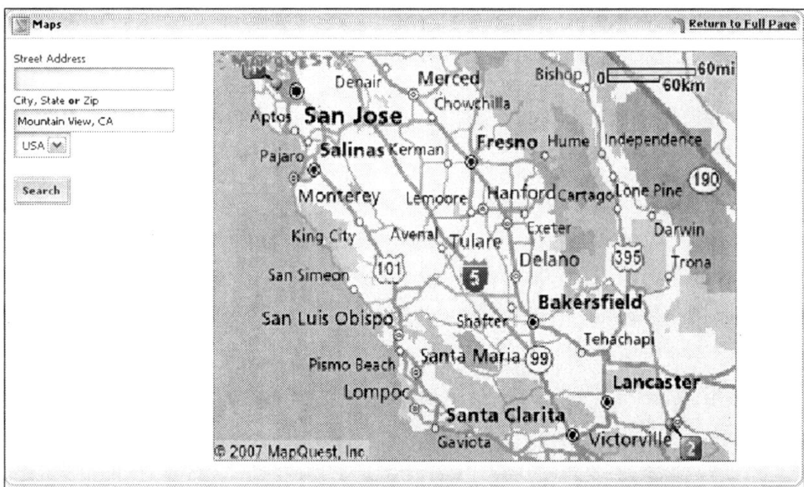

In short, the **Maps** portlet provides the ability to find **Maps** by **Address**, **City**, **State**, **Zip** code and country. MapQuest is used as a web service provider.

MapQuest is a map publisher and provides a free online Web mapping service. URL: `http://www.mapquest.com/`

Employing Google Search

The Google Search portlet allows easy integration with Google Search. Google Search is used as a web service provider. First, let's hot deploy the **Google** portlet as follows:

1. Add the **Plugin Installer** portlet in the **Page, "Home"**, of the **Book Lovers** Community where you want to manage plugins, if the **Plugin Installer** portlet is not already present.
2. Find the **Google Search** portlet either by browsing or through search.
3. Select the **Google Search** portlet by clicking on the related links.
4. After viewing the description of the portlet, click on the **Install** button.
5. The system will install the portlet which you have selected using the hot deploy mode.

Normally, there are two ways to install plugins portlets: auto deploy mode and hot deploy mode. For more on auto deploy mode, refer to the forthcoming section.

After deploying the **Google Search** portlet in the portal, we can configure the **Google Search** portlet as follows:

1. Add the **Google Search** portlet in the **Page, "Home"**, of the **Book Lovers** Community where you want to search, if the **Google Search** portlet is not already present.
2. **The Google Search** portlet appears with **Configuration** and **Preferences** icons.
3. Click on the **Configuration** icon to the upper right.
4. By default, the tab **Setup** is selected.
5. Input **Google License** such as "**ABQIAAAAQs-h8ZMuuqU5BHvxm9hw1hRnqZIGs9ll2RH1BN33yRy U5baSXRSHFVtqcOk8OCuiJXGCnAoXaRQUhw**"; Surely, you can get a key online.
6. Press the **Save** button.
7. Optionally, configure permissions by selecting the tab **Permissions**.

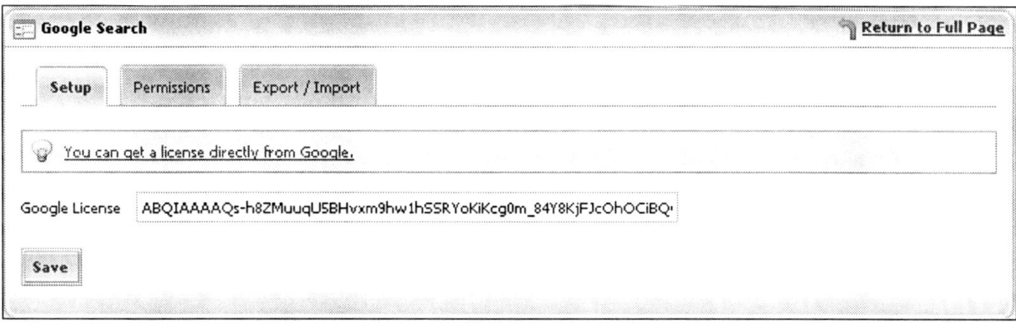

After configuring the **Google Search** portlet, we can search the contents now. The following figure shows the integration with Google search. Suppose that we want to search the keyword, "**Liferay**", using **Google Search**:

1. Input the **Search** criterion as "**Liferay**".
2. Select the type of **Search:** "**Search**" or "**Spell**".
3. Click the **Search** icon.

Actually, the **Search** portlet will use Google search services to search or check the spelling for a given keyword first. And then it will display the search results or spellcheck results.

You can also set up the preferences on the **Google Search** portlet as follows:

1. Click on the **Preferences** icon to the upper right of the portlet.
2. Then check the **Safe Search** checkbox as shown in the following figure.
3. Press the **Save** button.
4. Optionally, press the link **Return to full page** to return.

To summarize, the **Google Search** portlet provides an easy integration with Google Search.

Enjoying Google Maps

Suppose that we know the **Address,** say "**2675 Fayette Dr.**", the city name, say "**Mountain View**", the zip code say "**94040**", the state name, say"**California**" in the USA and we want to get related **Google Maps**. The **Google Maps** portlet would be useful for this purpose. First let's install **Google Maps** portlet by auto deployment as follows:

1. Download the **Google Maps** portlet from community plug-ins at the Liferay official website.

2. Rename the**Google Maps** portlet (WAR file) as "Google-Search.war".

3. Copy the WAR file to $USER_HOME/liferay/deploy.

After the **Google Maps** portlet is auto deployed, it is ready for use. Let's add it as follows:

*   Add the **Maps** portlet in the **Page, "Home"**, of the **Book Lovers** Community where you want to search maps, if te **Maps** portlet is not already present.

Before using the **Google Maps** portlet, we have to configure it. Let's set up the **Google Maps** portlet as follows:

1. Click on the **Configuration** icon to the upper right.

2. The default selected tab is **Setup**; input **Google License** such as "**ABQIAAAAQs-h8ZMuuqU5BHvxm9hw1hSSRYoKiKcg0m_84Y8KjFJcOhOCiBQOo96w2RkYDME8_7SMyZ4-opo3Yg**" as shown in the following figure.

3. Input **Map Address**, and check the **Map Input Enabled** checkbox.

4. Input **Directions Address** and check the **Directions Input Enabled** checkbox.

5. Input the value for **Height,** say "300".

6. Press the **Save** button when you are ready.

7. To configure permissions, you can select the tab, **Permissions**.

8. Optionally, press the link **Return to full page** to return.

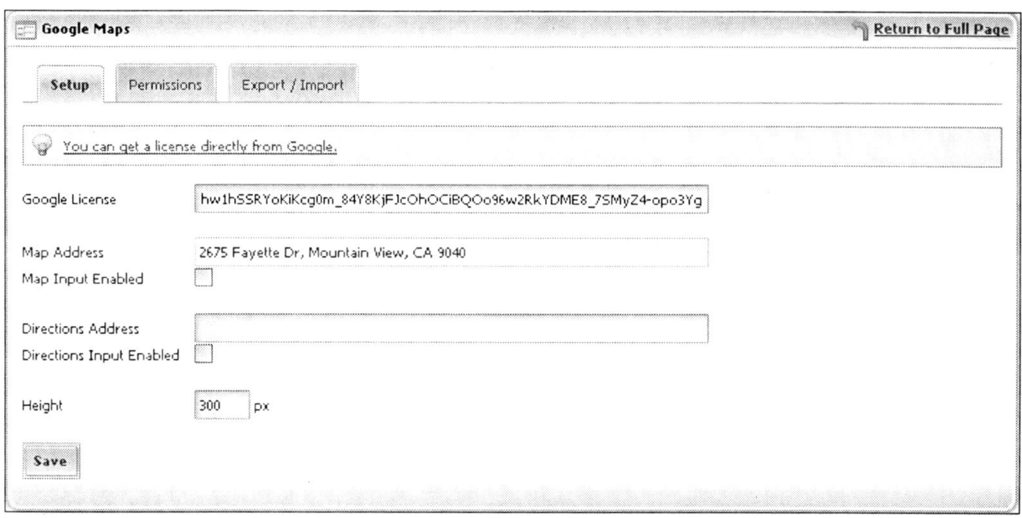

The following figure depicts the **Google Maps** portlet with an example of search results. It shows a map for the given **Address** ("**2675 Fayette Dr.**", in the city, "**Mountain View**", with the zip code, "**94040**", in the state of "**California**" in USA).

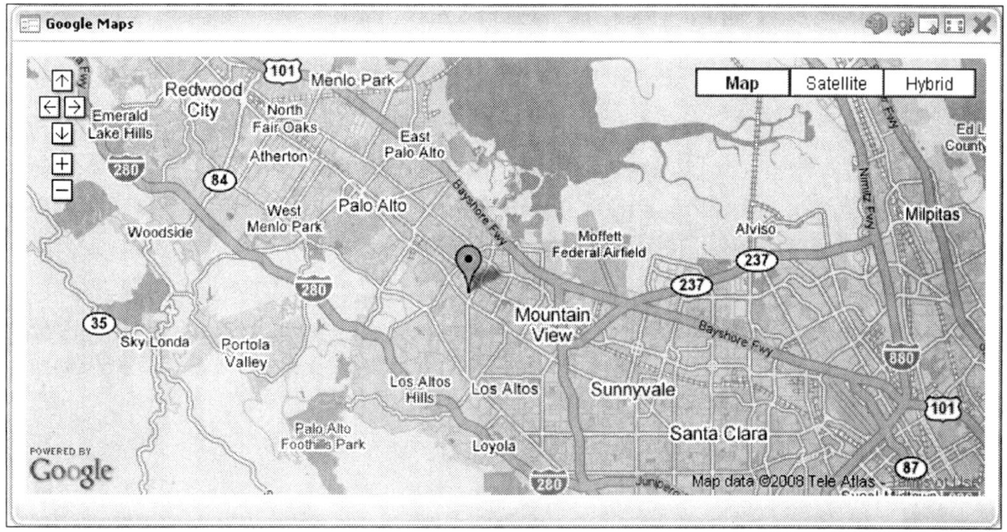

In short, the **Google Maps** portlet allows easy integration with Google Maps. Google Maps is used as a web service provider.

 Google Maps provide directions, interactive maps, and satellite/aerial imagery of the United States. URL: http:// maps.google.com.

Using OpenSearch Effectively

As stated before, we use OpenSearch to integrate alfresco contents in the **Alfresco Content** portlet. So, what's OpenSearch? Why is OpenSearch useful?

OpenSearch is a collection of simple formats, which enable the sharing of search results (refer to OpenSearch at http://www.opensearch.org). Generally speaking, OpenSearch allows the publishing of search results in a format for syndication and aggregation. It is a useful way for both websites and search engines to publish search results in a standard and accessible format.

Design Principles

OpenSearch consists of the following elements (refer to OpenSearch at http://www.opensearch.org):

- Description: XML files that identify and describe a search engine.
- Query Syntax: describes where to retrieve the search results.
- RSS or Response: format for providing open search results.
- Aggregators: Sites that can display OpenSearch results.
- Auto-discovery: signals the presence of a search plug-in link to the **User,** and the link embedded in the header of HTML pages.

OpenSearch Description lists search result or responses for the given website. It provides support for multiple responses in any format. Generally speaking, RSS and Atom are the only ones formally supported by OpenSearch aggregators. However, other types, such as HTML are perfectly acceptable.

OpenSearch Specification

OpenSearch description document defines three kinds of elements in general: the **OpenSearch Query** element, the **OpenSearch URL** template syntax, and the **OpenSearch Response** elements.

OpenSearch description documents are referred to, via the following type:

```
application/opensearchdescription+xml
```

The XML Namespaces URI for the XML data formats described in this specification by default is:

```
http://a9.com/-/spec/opensearch/1.1/
```

Example of a simple OpenSearch description document:

```xml
<?xml version="1.0" encoding="UTF-8"?>
 <OpenSearchDescription xmlns="http://a9.com/-/spec/opensearch/1.1/">
   <ShortName>Web Search</ShortName>
   <Description>Use Book.com to search the Web.</Description>
   <Tags>Book website</Tags>
   <Contact>admin@book.com</Contact>
   <Url type="application/rss+xml"          template="http://book.com/
?q={searchTerms}&amp;pw={startPage?}&amp;format=rss"/>
 </OpenSearchDescription>
```

As shown in the following table, the root node of the OpenSearch description document is **OpenSearchDescription**. We can use this table as a reference for OpenSearch specification (refer to `OpenSearch` at `http://www.opensearch.org`).

Element Name	Description
OpenSearchDescription	Is the root node of the OpenSearch description document.
ShortName	Contains a brief human-readable title that identifies this search.
Description	Contains a human-readable text description of the search engine.
URL	Describes an interface by which a search client can make search requests of the search engine.
Contact	Contains an email address at which the maintainer of the description document can be reached.
Tags	Contains a set of words that are used as keywords to identify and categorize this search content
LongName	Contains an extended human-readable title that identifies this search engine.
Image	Contains an image that identifies this search engine.
Query	Defines a search query that can be performed by search clients.
Developer	Contains the human-readable name or identifier of the creator or maintainer of the description document.
Attribution	Contains a list of all sources or entities that should be credited for the content contained in the search feed.
SyndicationRight	Contains a value that indicates the degree to which the search results provided by this search engine can be queried, displayed, and redistributed.

Element Name	Description
AdultContent	Contains a Boolean value that should be set to true, if the search results contain material intended only for adults.
Language	Contains a string, which indicates that the search engine supports search results in the specified language.
InputEncoding	Contains a string, which indicates that the search engine supports search requests encoded with the specified character encoding.
OutputEncoding	Contains a string, which indicates that the search engine supports search responses encoded with the specified character encoding.

Working with Journal Content Search

In the intranet "book.com", you will have lots of articles, sooner or later. In order to manage these articles easily, search functions become very important. The **Journal Content Search** portlet provides the ability to search for articles by types. Let's use the Journal content search as follows:

1. Add the **Journal Content Search** portlet in the **Page, "Home"**, of **Book Lovers** Community, where you want to search the content of journal CMS articles, if the **Journal Content Search** portlet is not already present.

2. Input keyword, **Search** criterion, "**alfresco**" first.

3. And then click on the **Search** icon as shown in the following figure:

Setting up Search

It is simple to configure the **Journal Content Search** portlet. Suppose that we need to search articles with the type, **General**. Let's do it as follows:

1. Click on the **Configuration** icon to the upper right of the portlet.

2. With the **Setup** and **Current** tabs selected, there is an articles type list. You can select the **Article Type, General,** that you would like to limit the search to, as shown in the following figure.

3. Select the checkbox if you want to only show the results for the articles.

4. Input **Target Portlet ID,** if needed.

5. To search articles in Archive, click the **Archived** tab.

6. And then click the **Save** button to save the changes.

7. If needed, click on the arrow **Return to Full Page,** to return.

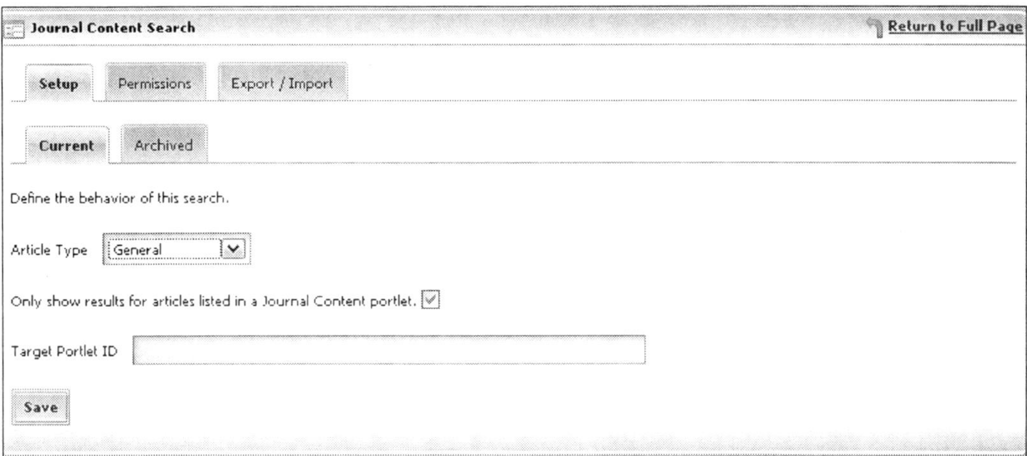

There are several default **Article Types: Announcements, Blogs, News, General, Press Release** and **Test**. As mentioned earlier, these types are configurable. If there is no type selected, this portlet will search any article within any type.

You can also change **Permissions** of the **Journal Content Search** portlet. You can simply click on the **Permissions** tab. You can change **Permissions** by **Users, Organizations, User Groups, Regular Roles** and **Guest**. Optionally, you can set up the features of exporting and importing.

Using Journal Content Search Effectively

Liferay provides search ability restricted to the content of Journal CMS articles. The portlet is called **Journal Content Search**, powered by the Apache Lucene search engine.

Apache Lucene acts as a high-performance and full-featured text search engine. It is a suitable for almost any application that requires full-text search, especially cross-platform. URL: http://lucene.apache.org/

The Apache Lucene search engine has the following features:

- Ranked searching - best results returned first.
- Many powerful query types: phrase queries, wildcard queries, proximity queries, range queries and more.
- Fielded searching (for example, title, author, contents).
- Date-range searching.
- Sorting by any field.
- Multiple-index searching with merged results, and
- Simultaneous update and searching.

Adding Sitemap for Search Engines

Liferay provides the ability to generate the sitemap XML automatically for all public websites. By sitemap, we can easily inform the search engines about pages on the sites that are available for crawling.

Using The Sitemap

Suppose that, as an administrator of "Palm Tree Publications", you want to use the sitemap for the **Book Lovers** Community. Let's do it as follows:

1. Add the **Communities** portlet in the page, "**Admin**", of **My Community**.
2. Click the **All Communities** tab.
3. Locate the **Community Book Lovers**.
4. Click on the **Manage Pages** icon from the **Actions** to the right of the community for which you want to use the sitemap.
5. Click on the **Settings** tab first.
6. Click on the **Sitemap** tab further as shown in the following figure.

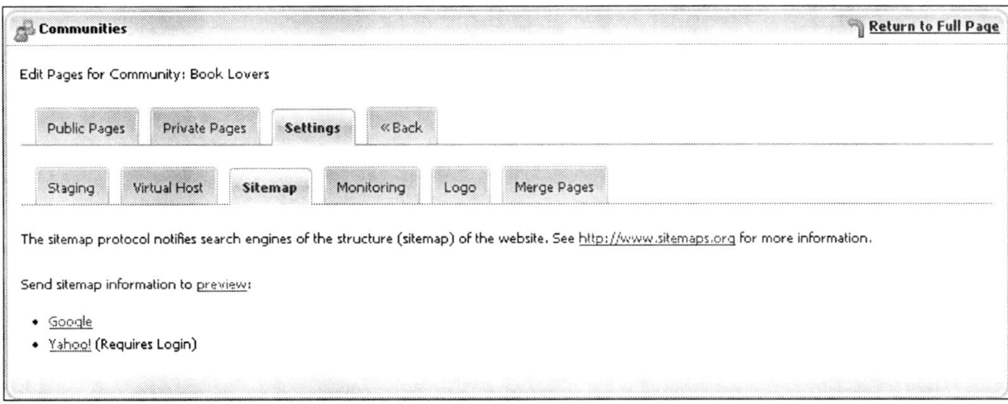

By clicking on the **Search Engine** links, the sitemap will be sent to them.

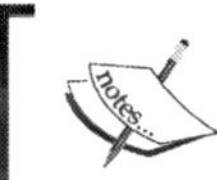
Note that it's only necessary to do this once per site. The search engine crawler will automatically ask for the sitemap again, ever so often.

If you want to see the generated XML, you can click the **Preview** link. By this link, you may view what is being sent to the search engines. Here is an example of the sitemap XML for the **Book Lovers** Community.

```
<urlset>
<url>
<loc>http://localhost:8080/c/portal/layout?p_l_id=10157</loc>
</url>
<url><loc>http://localhost:8080/c/portal/layout?p_l_id=10158</loc>
</url>
</urlset>
```

Customizing The Sitemap for Pages

Suppose that as an administrator of "Palm Tree Publications", you want to customize the sitemap for the **Page, "Home"**, of the **Book Lovers** Community **Public Pages**. Let's do it as follows:

1. Locate the **Community Book Lovers**.

2. Click on the **Manage Pages** icon from the **Actions** to the right of the community for which you want to customize the sitemap.

3. Select the page, **Home**.

4. Click on the **Page** tab.

5. Click on the **Show** next to the **Sitemap Protocol.**

6. **Change Frequency**: such as **Daily** from a list of **Always, Hourly, Daily, Weekly, Monthly, Yearly, Never**, and so on.

7. **Page Priority**: such as **3.0**. A number from **0.0** to **1.0** indicates the priority of the page relative to other pages of the website.

8. **Include**: such as **Yes**, from a list of **Yes** or **No,** as shown in the following figure:

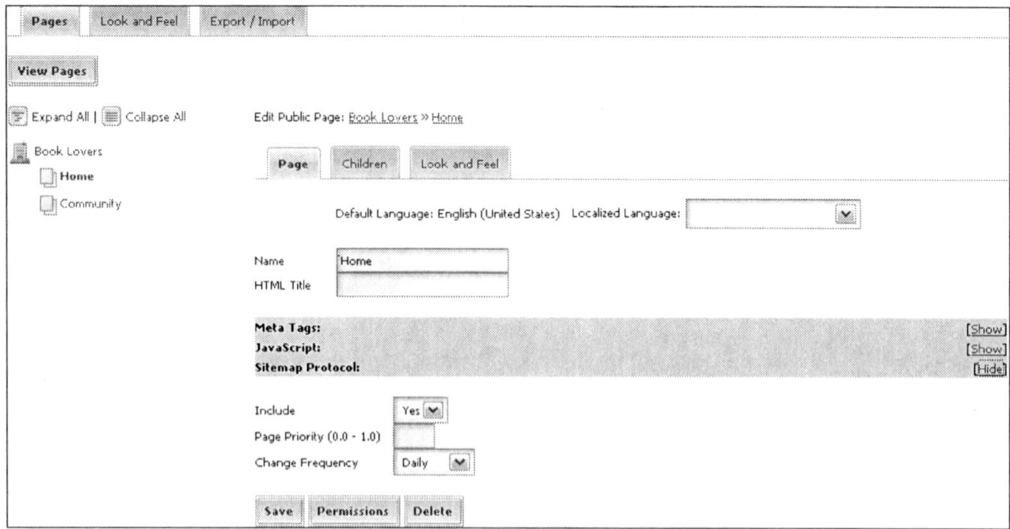

Using Sitemap Effectively

Simply, the sitemap protocol notifies the search engines of the structure (that is, sitemap) of the website (refer to Sitemaps at `http://www.sitemaps.org`). In short, the sitemap provides the ability to make newly added pages searchable by major search engines without additional configuration.

Sitemaps provides the ability to inform search engines about pages scrawling on their sites. We can benefit from Sitemaps in the following situations:

- Access all areas of a website through a browseable interface. Thus search engines can't find these pages with big contents such as "Archives" and "Database" easily.

- Use rich AJAX or Flash. Thus, search engines can't navigate through to get to the content.

We can generate a sitemap containing all accessible URLs on the site first. And then we can submit it to the search engines. Since search engines, such as Google, MSN, and Yahoo, support the same protocol, through a sitemap we could make the search engines having the updated **Pages** information.

Liferay sitemaps protocol makes any new **Pages** searchable by the major search engines, supporting automatically updating sitemap information, which is available for web-crawling.

XML Sitemap Format

You may be interested on the XML sitemap format. Here, we list some of the XML sitemap formats for reference. Otherwise, you can leave it for your future requirements.

The Sitemap protocol format consists of XML tags. All data values in a Sitemap must be entity-escaped. The file itself must be UTF-8 encoded.

The Sitemap must:

- Begin with an opening `<urlset>` tag, and end with a closing `</urlset>` tag.
- Specify the namespace (protocol standard) within the `<urlset>` tag.
- Include a `<url>` entry for each URL, as a parent XML tag.
- Include a `<loc>` child entry for each `<url>` parent tag.

As shown in the following table, other tags are optional. It is true that support for these optional tags may vary across search engines (refer to Sitemaps at `http://www.sitemaps.org`).

Attribute	Required	Description
urlset	Yes	Encapsulates the file and references the current protocol standard.
url	Yes	Parent tag for each URL entry. The remaining tags are children of this tag.
loc	Yes	URL of the page.
lastmod	No	The date of last modification of the file. This date should be in W3C Date-Time format. This format allows you to omit the time portion, if desired, and use YYYY-MM-DD.
changefreq	No	How frequently the page is likely to change. This value provides general information to search engines and may not correlate exactly to how often the page was crawled.
priority	No	The priority of this URL relative to other URLs on your site. Valid values range from 0.0 to 1.0.

Here is an example sitemap that contains just one URL and uses all optional tags, as shown here.

```
<urlset xmlns:xsi="http://www.w3.org/2001/XMLSchema-instance"
xsi:schemaLocation="http://www.sitemaps.org/schemas/sitemap/0.9
          http://www.sitemaps.org/schemas/sitemap/0.9/sitemap.xsd">
      <url>
              <loc>http://www.book.com</loc>
              <lastmod>2008-03-26</lastmod>
              <changefreq>daily</changefreq>
              <priority>0.8</priority>
      </url>
</urlset>
```

Deploying And Managing Search Portlets

As stated, we have used a lot of **Search** portlets. Before using these portlets, we need to deploy them in the portal first. There are several ways in which you can deploy **Search** portlets as follows:

- Hot deploy by **Plugin Installer** portlet.
- Update by **Update Manager** portlet.
- Manage by **Software Catalogue** portlet.

Using Plugin Installer for Hot Deploy

We can hot deploy the **Google Maps** portlet or other portlets via **Plugin Installer** portlet. **Plugin Installer** portlet allows portal administrators to administer and install plugins in the portal and pages. There are two ways to access the **Plugin Installer**:

- By adding the **Plugin Installer** portlet directly to a portal **Page,** say **Page "Admin"** of **Book Lovers** Community.
- By clicking the **Add more portlets** from the **Admin** or **Update Manager** portlets.

We have auto deployed **Google Maps** earlier. Here, let's hot deploy **Google Maps** portlet as follows:

1. Add the **Plugin Installer** portlet to a portal **Page,** say the **Page "Admin"**, of **Book Lovers** Community.

2. Click on the **Browse Repository** tab.

3. Input search criterion say, "**Google**".

4. Locate the **Google Maps** portlet.

5. Click the **Google Maps** portlet first.

6. Then click the **Install** button.

7. The **Plugin Installer** portlet will download the **Google Maps** portlet, and hot deploy it in the portal.

Similarly, you can upload the WAR file or download the WAR file via the **Plugin Installer** portlet. You can also set up the configuration for hot deployment. As shown in the following figure, you can enable the hot deploy, set up **Deploy Directory** and **Destination Directory**, and set the **Interval** such as **10 Seconds,** and **Blacklist Threshold** such as **10**, and so on.

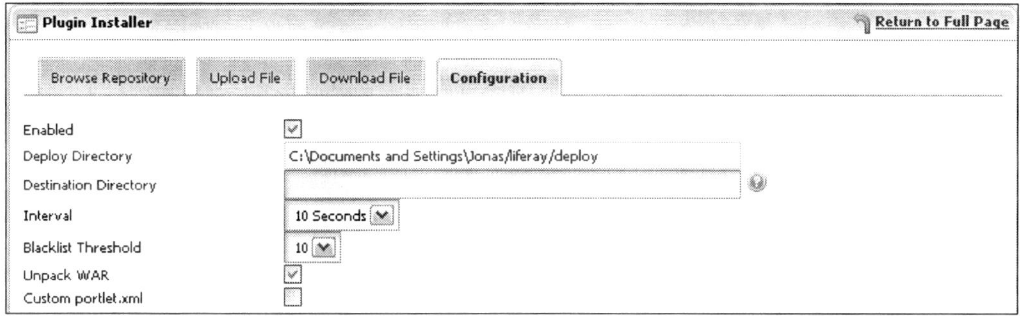

Using Update Manager

Suppose that you already have a **Search** portlet (that is, a **Sample Spring** portlet) in the portal (for example, version 4.3.6). Now you want to update the portlet to the current version (for instance version 4.4.2 or above). Let's do it as follows:

1. Add the **Update Manager** portlet to a portal **Page, say** "**Admin**" of **Book Lovers** Community.

2. Locate the portlet, "**Sample Spring Portlet**".

3. Click the **Update** icon from the **Actions** icon next to the portlet.

4. The **Update Manager** will search for the new version of the portlet first, and then it will update the portlet automatically.

Similarly, you can install more plugins by clicking the button, **Install More Plugins**, or you can ignore all updates by clicking the button, **Ignore All Updates**.

More interestingly, you can restore the update status of the portlet by clicking the **Unignore** icon from the **Actions,** next to the portlet. Thus, when the new version is ready, the **Update Manager** will show a message for updates. Or you can uninstall the portlet by clicking the **Uninstall** icon from the **Actions,** next to the portlet.

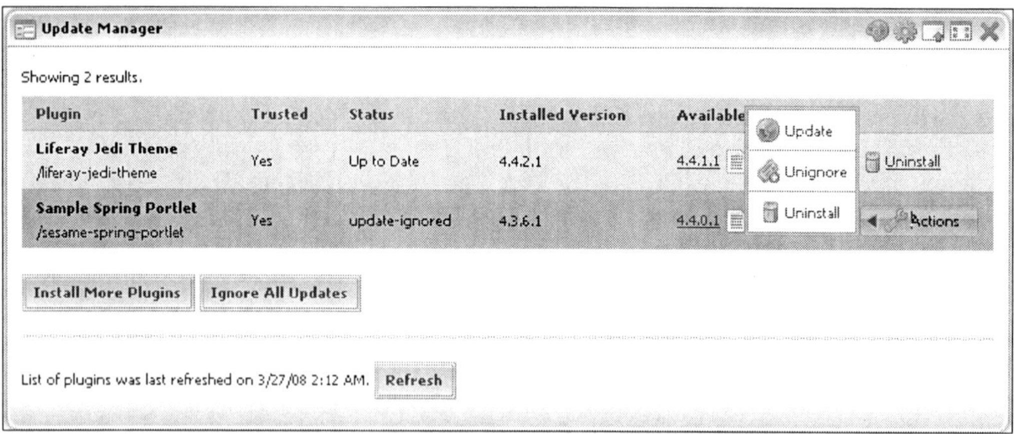

Using Auto Deployment

Besides the hot deploy, we can also use auto deployment. That is, we can perform a hot deploy through the file system, by copying the plugin WAR file manually to the auto deploy configured directory. Auto deployment is a very convenient way to access the file system, where portal is installed. It can also be used to automate the process, deploy to several servers in a cluster, and so on.

In order to use auto deployment, we need to configure auto deploy first. Let's do it as follows:

- Set the resource directory to scan for plugins to auto deploy.

```
auto.deploy.deploy.dir=${resource.repositories.root}/deploy
```

For example, the resource repositories root is /root/liferay, then auto deploy directory would be /root/liferay/deploy.

- Set the interval in milliseconds, for how often to scan the resource directory for updates.

```
auto.deploy.interval=10000
```

Managing Search Portlets via Software Catalogue

Suppose that you have a product called the **Scheduling Content** portlet (scheduling the contents of pages with publishing dates). You can use the **Software Catalogue** portlet. Let's do it as follows:

1. Add the **Software Catalogue** portlet to a portal **Page, say "Admin"** of **Book Lovers** Community.

2. Click the **Add Product** button, as shown in the following figure.

3. Input product information, such as **Name, Type, Licenses, Author, Page URL, Tags, Short Description, Long Description and Permissions**.

4. Click the **Save** button when you are ready.

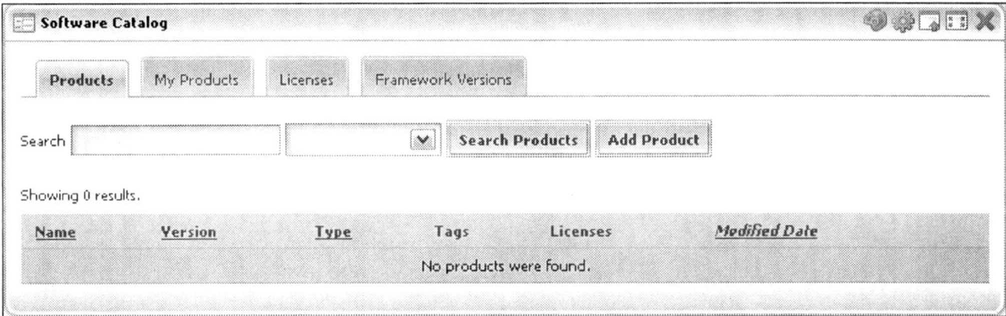

In addition, we can easily manage products using **Software Catalogue** portlet, such as **Search products**, view **My Products**, and manage **Licenses** and **Framework Versions**.

Note that these tools are not only useful to deploy and manage **Search** portlets, but are also suitable for any plugin's (portlets) deployment and management.

Summary

This chapter discussed how to employ federated search, and how to integrate search against **alfresco contents** first. Then it discussed how to use the **CSZ Search** and **Map Search** portlets. More interestingly, it depicted how to integrate Google search and Google maps in the portal pages.Then, it discussed the OpenSearch concept. It also discussed **Journal Content Search** and how to configure sitemap for search engines. Finally, it discussed how to deploy **Search** portlets, and how to manage **Search** portlets in the portal pages.

13

Ongoing Admin Tasks

In the intranet website "book.com" of "Palm Tree Publications", we are required to manage servers, instances, and plugins. Further, we are also required to use password policies, to update the website settings, and to monitor **Users'** activities. Moreover, we also have to publish contents, which are stored in Alfresco. Liferay provides **Admin** portlet to manage servers, instances and plugins, and **Enterprise Admin** portlet to manage password policies and enterprise information settings, and to monitor **Users'** activities.

This chapter will introduce how to manage a server, instances and plugins via **Admin** portlet first. Then it will discuss how to use password policies, how to update the system –level settings, and how to monitor **Users'** activities in **Enterprise Admin** portlet. More interestingly, it will explain how to integrate Liferay with Alfresco. Finally, it will introduce how to integrate other systems in Liferay such as Ad Sever (such as OpenX) and Orbeon Forms.

By the end of this chapter, you will have learnt how to:

- Manage servers and instances
- Manage plugins in Admin Portlet
- Use password policies and update settings
- Monitor **Users'** activities in **Enterprise Admin** portlet
- Integrate Liferay with Alfresco by web service and web scripts
- Integrate Liferay with Other Systems such as Ad Server and Orbeon Forms

Working with Admin Portlet

As an administrator "**Palm Tree**", at the enterprise "Palm-Tree Publications", you can handle a lot of administration tasks on the portal. The first admin tool you can use is the **Admin** portlet. **Admin** portlet provides the ability to view server information, to create and manage instances, to update and install available portlets, **Themes** and layout **Templates**, and so on. This section will mainly introduce server management, instances management and plugins management.

Managing Server

First of all, we have to add the **Admin** portlet in the **Private Pages, "Home"**. Let's do it as follows:

1. Log into the portal as an administrator, say "**Palm Tree**".

2. Add the **Admin** portlet in a **Page** named "**Home**" at **My Community Private Pages**.

3. **The Admin** portlet appears with a default view. You will see **Portal Version**, **Date** and **Uptime**.

4. Click the **More** link, and you will find more details such as memory usage related to portal administration tasks, as shown in the following figure.

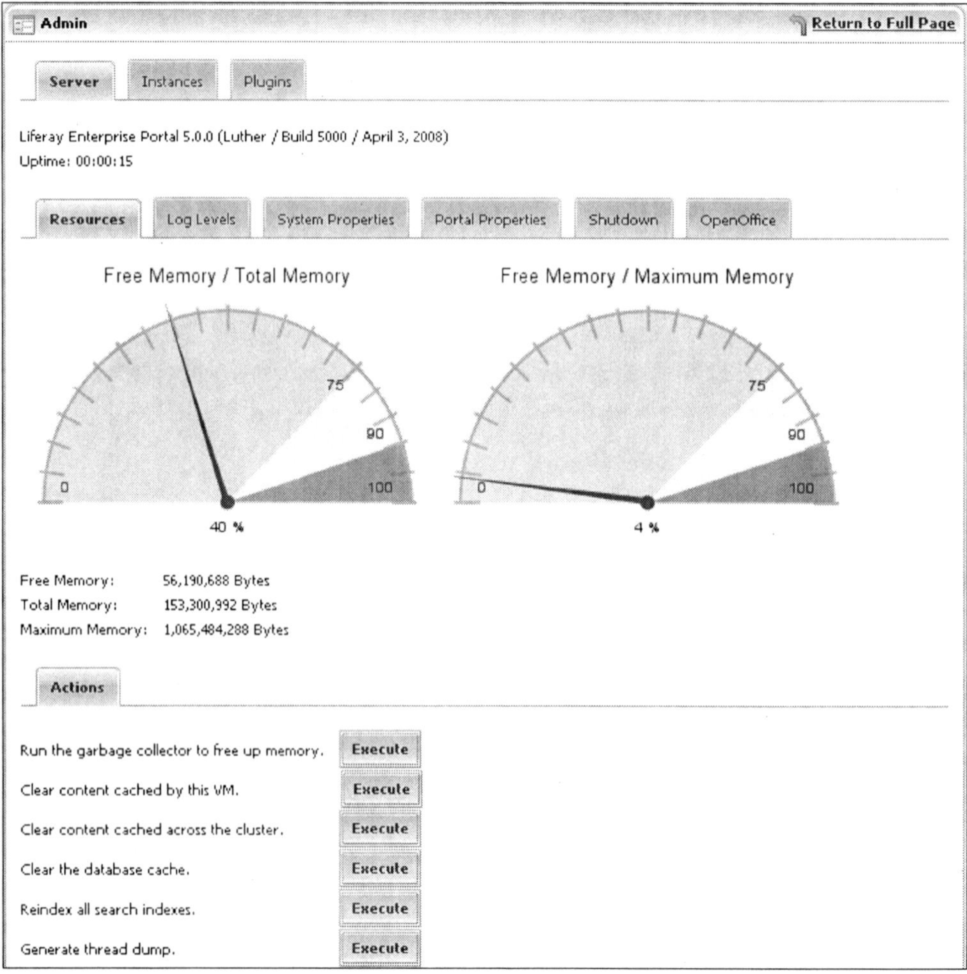

With the **Server** tab selected, you can also manage resources of the server, by clicking on the **Resources** tab, and then clicking the **Execute** button for the following tasks:

- **Run the garbage collector to free up memory**.
- **Clear content cached by this VM** (Virtual Machine).
- **Clear content cached across the cluster**.
- **Clear the database cache**.
- **Re-index all search indexes**.
- **Generate thread dump**.

With the **Server** tab selected, you can also shutdown the server as follows:

1. Click on the **Shutdown** tab.

2. Input the number of minutes, say "**5**", as the duration after which the server will be shut down in the **Number of Minutes** box.

3. Add notes such as "**shutdown server in 5 minutes**" in the **Custom Message** box.

4. Click the **Shutdown** button, as shown in the following figure.

5. Optionally, you can cancel the shutdown action. Enter the value "**0**" in the **Number of Minutes** box, and click the **Shutdown** button.

Moreover, with the **Server** tab selected, you can do the following jobs:

- Add category and update categories of logs by changing the levels (such as OFF, FATAL, ERROR, WARN, INFO, DEBUG, ALL, and so on) under the **Log Levels** tab.
- View system properties under the **System Properties** tab.
- Survey portal properties under the **Portal Properties** tab.
- Enable **OpenOffice** integration to provide document conversion functionality under the **OpenOffice** tab.

Managing Instances

The portal may have many instances. Fortunately, you can manage instances easily. Let's do it as follows:

1. Access the portal as the administrator, "**Palm Tree**".

2. Add the **Admin** portlet in the **Page, "Home"**, of **My Community,** if it's not already present.

3. Click the **Instances** tab as shown in the following figure:

    - A list of instances will appear with **Instance ID, Web ID, Virtual Host, Mail Domain** and **Number of Users.**

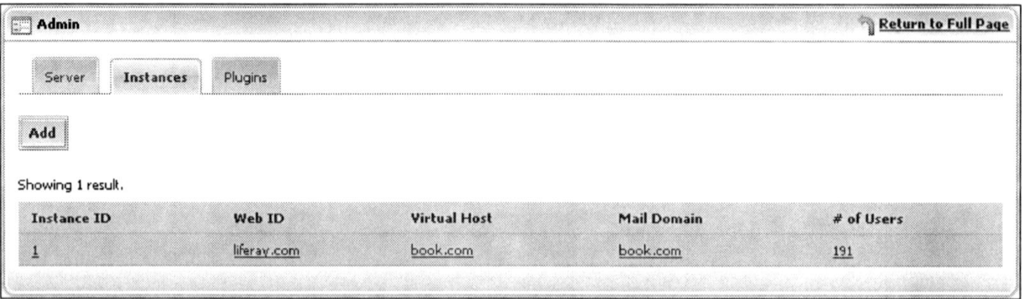

Instances are editable. Suppose that you want to edit the **Instance** with **Instance ID** "**1**" and reset the **Mail Domain** with value "**mail.book.com**". Let's do it as follows:

1. Locate the **Instance** with **Instance ID** "**1**".

2. Click the **Instance** name link such as **Instance ID, Web ID, Virtual Host, Mail Domain** and **Number of Users.**

3. Change the **Mail Domain** with the value, "**mail.book.com**".

4. Click the **Save** button, if you want to save your inputs.

5. Or click **Cancel** button, if you want to cancel your inputs.

You can also add a new **Instance**. Suppose that you want to add a new **Instance** with the domain name, "**staging.book.com**". Here are the steps necessary to create a new **Instance**:

1. Preparation: Use DNS configuration to assign a new domain to the server where Liferay is installed, such as "**staging.book.com**"; make sure all the necessary changes to external software (web servers, load balancers, firewalls, and so on) have also been done. Assume that the domain **staging. book.com** has been set up.

2. Access the portal as the administrator, "**Palm Tree**", and go to the **Admin** portlet. For example, add it to **My Community,** if it's not already present.

3. Click the **Instances** tab.

4. Click the **Add** button.

5. Fill the form fields as shown in the following figure:

    -   **Web ID**: This is the identifier that will be assigned to this **Instance**. The domain name should be used. For example, **staging.book.com**.

    -   **Virtual Host**: to access the portal instance. For example, staging.book.com.

    -   **Mail Domain**: to assign email addresses to the users of this instance. For example: staging.book.com.

6. Click the **Save** button, if you want to save to your inputs.

7. Or click the **Cancel** button, if you want to cancel your inputs.

8. Now, you can access the newly created **Instance** in a different browser window. In this example, you can do it through the URL `http://staging.book.com`, if the port number "80" was applied, or `http:// staging.book.com:8080`, if you are accessing tomcat directly and is running in its default port.

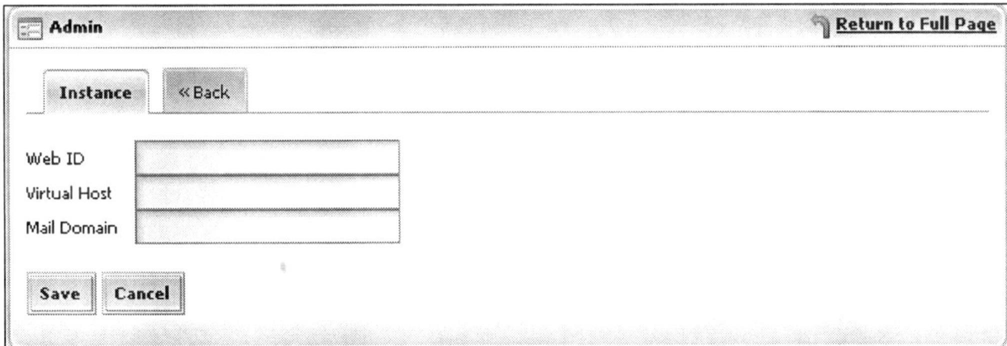

Liferay supports multiple portal **Instances** in a single installation in order to obtain a complete isolation of the **Users**, **Organizations**, **Communities** and any other data created through portlets. **Users** in one portal have no information about the other portal. The portals are separate by domains, and each portal exists in its own space identified by an ID (such as company's ID).

Liferay portal provides the ability to create new portal **Instances** directly from the web UI, with no need to restart the application server. More interestingly, this method works well with any application server. In a word, the creation and administration of portal **Instances** can be done by the **Admin** portlet.

Managing Plugins

The **Admin** portlet provides flexibility to manage **Plugins**, such as **Portlets**, **Themes** and **Layout Templates**. Through this portlet, you can not only view **Plugins** which have been installed, but also install more **Plugins** online, as shown in the following figure. This function is similar to that of the **Enterprise Admin** portlet, under the **Plugins** tab. The difference is that, in the **Enterprise Admin** portlet ,you can only view **Plugins and** not updates. But here, you can install more **Portlets** by clicking the **Install More Portlets** button.

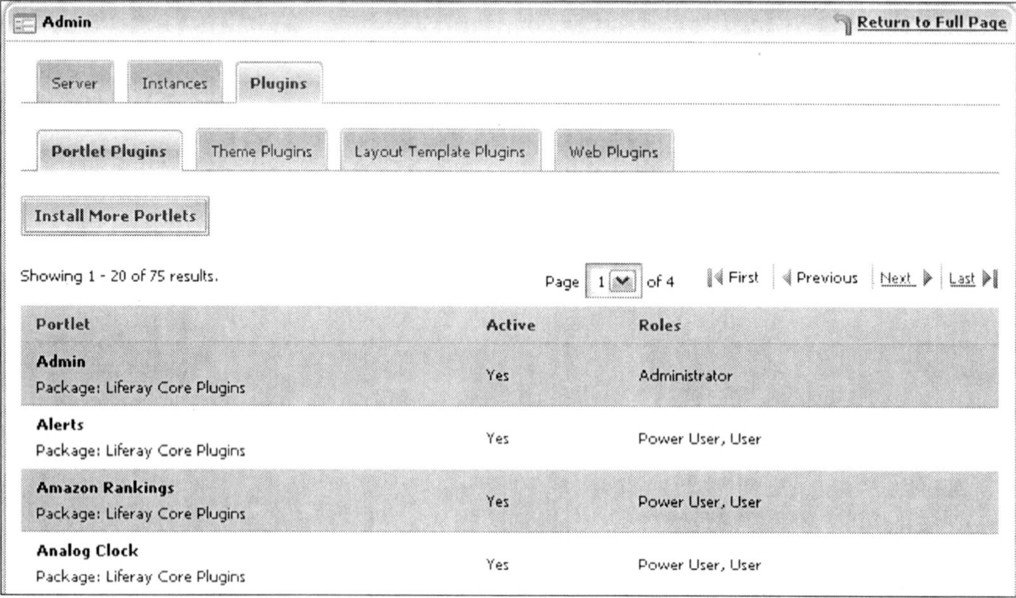

Working with Enterprise Admin Portlet

Enterprise Admin portlet provides administrative functions also. Using this portlet, we can not only access all **Organizations**, **Roles**, **User Groups** and **Users**, but also manage portal version information, enterprise information (such as **Organization** name, ticker symbol, address, logo, and so on), available **Portlets/Themes/Layout Templates**, current live sessions, authentication preferences, LDAP and SSO integration configuration, new **User** preferences, mail configuration, password policies, and more. We have discussed authentications in Chapter 3. This section will discuss password policies, enterprise information settings and current live sessions only.

Using Password Policies

As the administrator ,"**Palm Tree**", of "Palm Tree Publications", you may need to update the **Password Policies** and user account lockout. Let's do it as follows:

1. Log into the Portal as an administrator, say "**Palm Tree**".

2. Add the **Enterprise Admin** portlet in a **Page** named "**Home**" at **My Community Private Pages**, if the portlet is not already present.

3. Click the tab, **Password Policies**.

4. You can view the **Password Polices** with **Name**, **Description** and **Actions** with a set of icons (such as **Edit**, **Permissions** and **Assign Members**), as shown in the following figure:

You can either search the **Password Policies** by inputting the **Search** keyword and clicking the **Search Password Policies** button, or add the **Password Policies** by clicking the **Add Password Policy** button.

You can either update permissions by clicking the **Permissions** icon from the **Actions**, or change the members by clicking the **Assign Members** icon from the **Actions**.

Definitely, you can edit **Password Policies** by clicking the **Edit** icon from the **Actions** as shown in the following figure first. Then you can change the setting of **Password Policies** as follows:

You can use **Changeable** settings as follows:

- **Changeable**: Allow **User** to change his/her own password.
- **Change Required**: Requires the **User** to change his password when the **User** first logs in.
- **Minimum Age**: Determines how long a **User** must wait before changing his/her password again.

You can change **Password Syntax Checking** by clicking the checkbox, **Syntax Checking Enabled** first, and then configure the following items:

- **Syntax Checking Enabled**: Enable portal to check for certain words and length requirements.
- **Allow Dictionary Words**: Allow a dictionary word to be used as the password.
- **Minimum Length**: The minimum length of a password.

You can also change **Password History** by clicking the checkbox, **History Enabled,** first and then configure the following items:

- **History Enabled**: Enable tracking of password history, to prevent reuse of old passwords.
- **History Count**: The number of passwords to be kept in the history.

Similarly, you can update **Password Expiration** by clicking the checkbox, **Expiration Enabled,** and changing the following items:

- **Expiration Enabled**: Enable passwords to expire after a specified time.
- **Maximum Age**: The maximum time for which a password is valid, before it needs to be changed again.
- **Warning Time**: The duration, before a password expires, in which to warn the **User** of the upcoming password expiration.
- **Grace Limit**: The number of logins allowed after the password has expired.

To update User Account **Lockout,** you can click the checkbox, **Lockout Enabled,** and then configure the following items:

- **Lockout Enabled**: Enable **User** accounts to get locked out, after a specified number of failed logins.

- **Maximum Failure**: The maximum number of failed login attempts, before the account is locked out.

- **Reset Failure Count**: The duration before the "failed login count" is reset.

- **Lockout Duration**: The duration for which a User is locked out, preventing them from logging in.

In short, Liferay provides the ability to implement enterprise **Password Policies** and user account **Lockout**. **Password Policies** are managed internally from the **Enterprise Admin** Portlet.

Updating Settings

You can update enterprise information under the **Settings** tab, such as general configuration, authentication, default **User** associations, reversed screen names, mail host names and email notifications. The following figure depicts the main tabs which can be used to change the enterprise information in detail:

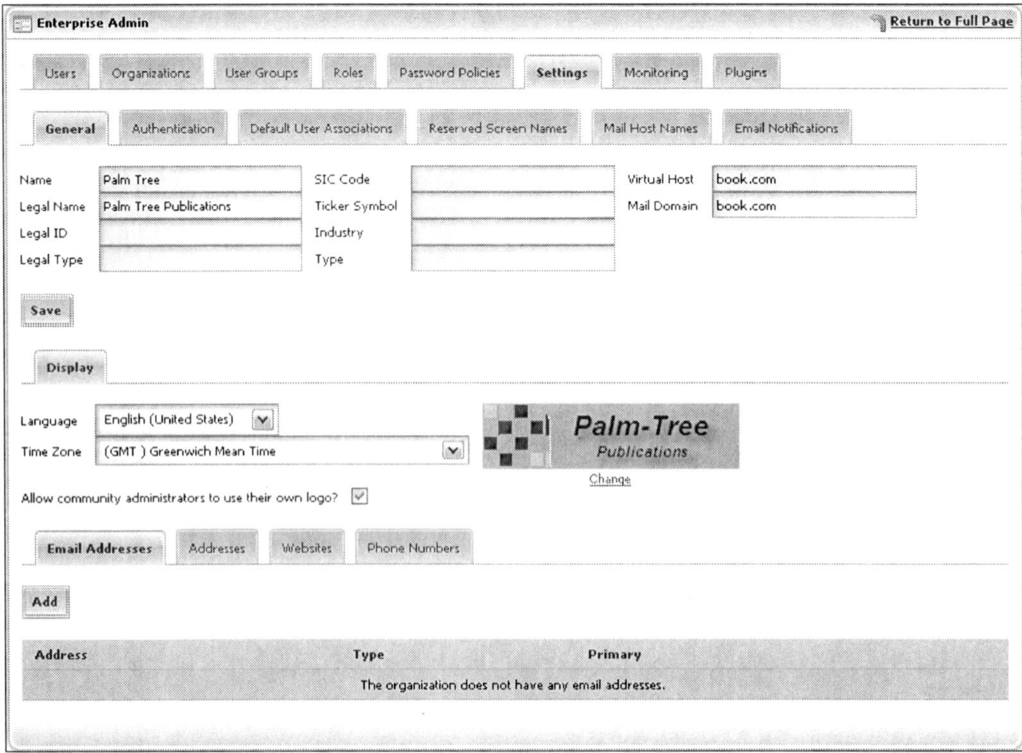

With the **General** tab selected, you can change the enterprise's information via the following steps:

1. An enterprise's information can be viewed or edited from the **General** tab. For example, the **Mail Domain** box contains the domain names that the server will recognize.

2. Click the **Save** button after making any changes.

3. The default **Language**, **Time Zone**, and logo image can also be changed in the **Display** section.

4. Check the box if you allow community administrators to use their own logo.

5. Select a tab, such as **Email Addresses, Addresses, Websites,** and **Phone Numbers.**

6. Click the **Add** button, if you want to add email addresses, addresses, websites, or phone numbers.

Set up Default User Associations

Under the **Default User Associations** tab, you can change the default associations with the newly created **Users** as shown in the following figure. The following are the main steps to set up **Default User Associations:**

1. You can enter the default community names per line that are associated with the newly created users.

2. You can also enter the default role names per line that are associated with newly created users.

3. You can also enter the default user group names per line that are associated with newly created users.

4. Click the **Save** button after making any changes.

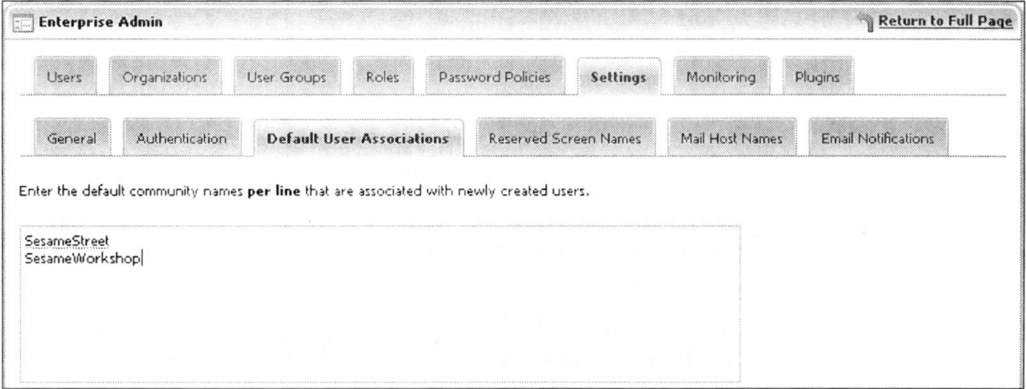

Update Reserved Screen Names

You can reserve the screen names under the **Reserved Screen Names** tab as follows:

1. You may enter one screen name per line to reserve the screen name.

2. You may also enter one user email address per line to reserve the user email address.

3. Click the **Save** button after making any changes.

Update Mail Host Names

Under the **Mail Host Names** tab, you can change all additional mail host names
as follows:

1. Enter one mail host name per line for all additional mail host names such as
   "**mail.book.com**".

2. Click the **Save** button after making any changes.

Update Email Notifications

Under the **Email Notifications** tab, you can change the configuration of email
notifications, as shown in the following figure. The following are the main steps to
update email notifications:

1. From the **General** tab, you can enter the **Name,** say "**Palm Tree**", and
   email **Address,** say "**admin@book.com**".

2. With the **Account Created Notification** tab selected, you can make changes
   to the default message that is automatically sent when accounts are created.

3. To disable new account emails, uncheck the **Enabled** box.

4. With the **Account Created Notification** tab selected, you can make changes
   to the default message that is automatically sent when a new password
   is created.

5. To disable new account emails, uncheck the **Enabled** box.

6. Click the **Save** button after making any changes.

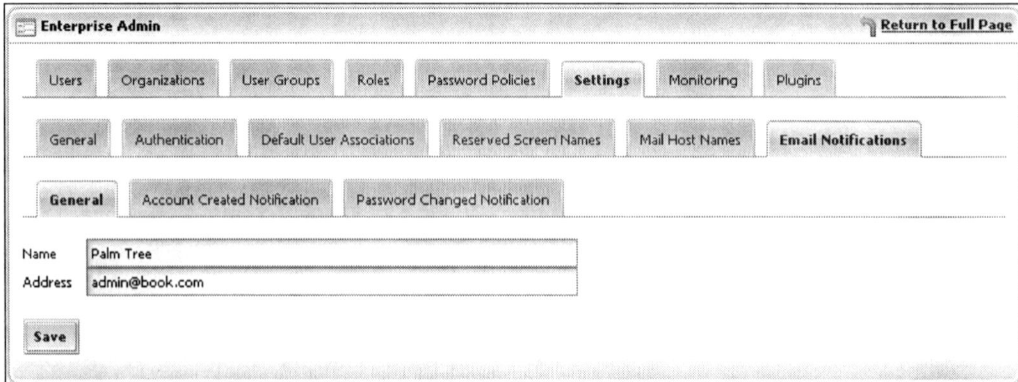

Monitoring Users' Activities

As an administrator, say "**Palm Tree**", at "Palm Tree Publications", you may need to monitor the **Users'** activities. Suppose that the **Users,** "**Lotti Stein**" and "**David Berger**", are online now. Let's monitor their activities as follows:

1. Log into the Portal as an administrator, say "**Palm Tree**".

2. Add the **Enterprise Admin** portlet in a **Page** named "**Home**" at **My Community Private Pages,** if the portlet is not already present.

3. Click the tab, **Monitoring**.

4. A set of live sessions will appear with **Session ID, User ID, Name, Screen Name, Last Request** and **Number of Hits** as shown in the following figure. For example, "**David Berger**" has **11** hits and "**Lotti Stein**" has **2** hits.

Session ID	User ID	Name	Screen Name	Last Request	# of Hits
9EB6D3ECD0A6083D12DB39AE144EAEC6	10112	Palm Tree	admin	4/1/08 4:02 PM	28
AE3A8E689535D600E8A0D9DC56542D9C	10838	David Berger	david	4/1/08 4:02 PM	11
B30B2E106447A3F2E46E8FD9D9FF0B9F	10844	Lotti Stein	lotti	4/1/08 4:00 PM	3

You can terminate a **User's** session. To end a **User's** session, select a session by clicking on the **User** name, "**Lotti Stein**", as a link first. Then in **Live Session,** click the **Kill Session** as shown in the following figure.

Note that you cannot kill your own session.

Integrating with Alfresco

Liferay provides the ability to fully integrate with Alfresco to take care of **Users**, **Communities** and **Permissions** synchronization so that **Users** can see Alfresco as a Liferay CMS and use it through Liferay portlets. These portlets include **Alfresco Client** and **Alfresco Content**.

Alfresco is the leading open source for enterprise content management. The open source model allows Alfresco to employ best-of-breed open source technologies and contributions from the open source. URL: http://www.alfresco.com/

Using Alfresco Web Client

You can use Alfresco Web Client as a portlet in Liferay. That is, you use Alfresco content management system inside Liferay. The following figure shows **Alfresco Client** as a portlet in Liferay.

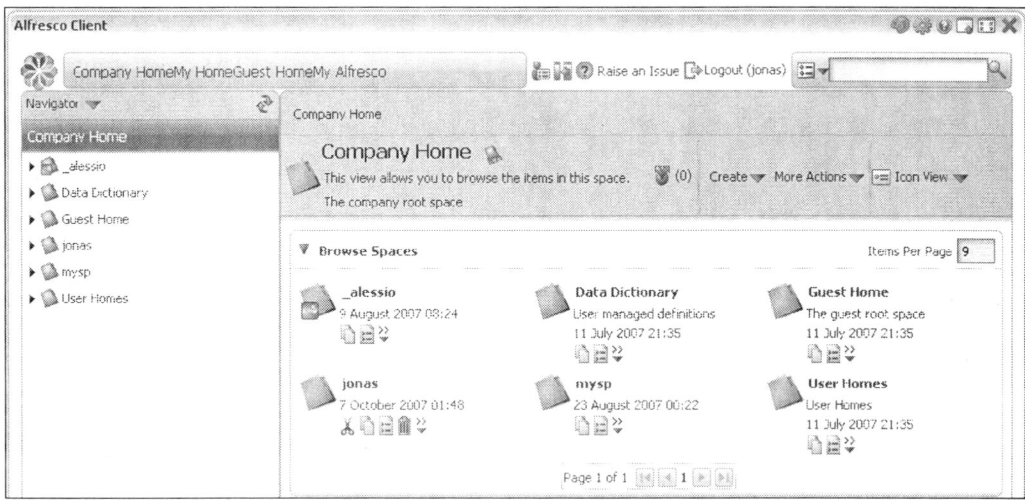

Liferay provides the ability to allow the publication of Alfresco contents through the portal. You can find **Alfresco Client** from the Liferay official web site, which provides an Alfresco package prepared for deployment:

1. Download the Alfresco Web Client war file. Rename the file as `alfresco.war`.

2. Increase the maximum memory. Edit to increase the memory size:

   ```
   SET JAVA_OPTS="-Xms1024m -Xmx1024m -XX:MaxPermSize=128m -
   Dfile.encoding=UTF8 -Duser.timezone=GMT -Djava.security.auth.
   login.config=$CATALINA_HOME/conf/jaas.config"
   ```

3. Startup Tomcat. Log in as the administrator.

4. In the **Plugin Installer** portlet, click on the **Upload** tab.

5. Click **Browse,** and locate the `alfresco.war` file.

6. Click **Deploy**.

7. You can now add the **Alfresco Client** to your page.

Using Alfresco Content

Alfresco web services support remote access and bindings to any client environment. Web Services—SOA is recognized as a way forward for integrating disparate systems including Content Management and building new enterprise-wide solutions. Furthermore, Alfresco Web Scripts are ideal for building data access and updating APIs, simple UI components such as portlets, and integration adaptors. Alfresco OpenSearch has been hosted as a series of Web Scripts. Within Liferay SOA framework, we can export Alfresco content in portlets via Web Services or Web Scripts.

Enjoy Web Services

Web services are applications designed to support interoperable interaction over a network. In fact, web services are just Web APIs accessed over a network, such as the Internet, and executed on a remote system that hosts the requested services.

Alfresco Web Services is provided by Alfresco Repository. It supports remote access and bindings to any client environment. For example, alfresco community is already using PHP, Ruby and Microsoft .NET. Numerous standards and integration efforts are focused around Web Services—SOA is recognized as a way forward for integrating disparate systems including Content Management and building new enterprise-wide solutions. BPEL (Business Process Execution Language) plays an important role in orchestrating all these services.

Alfresco web services API include the following core Services:

- Authentication
- Repository—query and model manipulation
- Content—content manipulation
- Authoring—collaborative content creation
- Access Control—**Users**, groups, **Roles** and **Permissions**
- Administration—environment, configuration, export and import
- Dictionary—model descriptions
- Content Rules—automate content management behavior
- Classification—apply classifications and categories

The following figure depicts an example for **Alfresco Content**—web services portlet. You can navigate contents, search contents by OpenSearch, and set up default access account. After selecting the content, the portlet will display the content directly in the Portal.

Employ Web Scripts

A Web Script provides a service on the web, where the service may perform any function. Web Scripts are suited for Content Management functions, as they are backed by the Alfresco Repository. Each Web Script is bound to a HTTP method and custom URL such as `http://sesame.cignex.com/cms_services/services?action=navigate`. A library of URLs may be built up to provide a complete (RESTful) HTTP API (for example, to download an image: `http://sesame.cignex.com/cms_services/services?action=download&uid=01232bda-f934-11dc-aef1-813a1994e4b0`).

Web Scripts allow us:

- to build custom URL-identified and HTTP accessible Content Management Web Services
- to turn your Alfresco Repository into a Content Management powered HTTP Server
- to easily access, manage and cross-link your content via a tailored RESTful API

The following figure depicts an example of the **Alfresco Content—Web Scripts** portlet. You can first navigate the contents dynamically by browse tree. After selecting content from the contents list, the portlet will display the content with its own format intelligently. For example, if content format is HTML, the portlet will display the content by HTML. If content format is PDF, the portlet will allow the **User** to download the content first, and then use local reader to open the content. Then, you can search the contents by keywords.

Finally, you can configure the Alfresco server connection, such as **Server URL**, **Default Account** for connection, and so on.

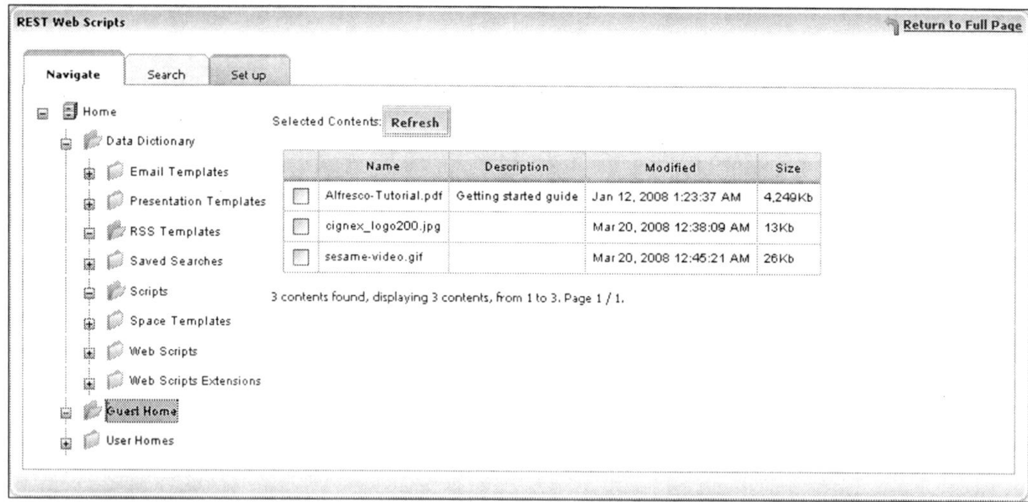

Use Alfresco as Liferay Direct Repository

Liferay has a wide range of portlets available freely for things such as **Blogs, Calendar, Document Library, Image Gallery, Mail, Message Boards, Polls, RSS Feeds, Wiki**, and many others. Liferay Portal also ships with Liferay Journal CMS (Content Management System), which provides basic ECMS (Enterprise Content Management Systems) features. If you want something beefier, then it will integrate with Alfresco.

When you integrate Alfresco with Liferay, you may need to consider the following questions:

- Do you want to integrate **Alfresco Contents** within Liferay articles?
- Do you want to use Alfresco document management as CMS repository of Liferay?
- Do you want to replace CMS in Liferay with Alfresco CMS in Liferay?

Here is a possible solution:

Alfresco CMS + Liferay Portal = Website

Let's use alfresco repository for Liferay repository as follows:

1. Add the **Journal** portlet in the current page.
2. Click the **Add Article** button.

3. In the editor, click the **Insert Image** icon next to the **Source** button and the **Insert Anchor** icon as shown in the following figure.

4. In the **Image Properties** windows, click the **Browse Server** button.

5. In the **Resources Browser** windows, you can browse folders (that is spaces in alfresco) and select files (such as image files) as shown in the following figure.

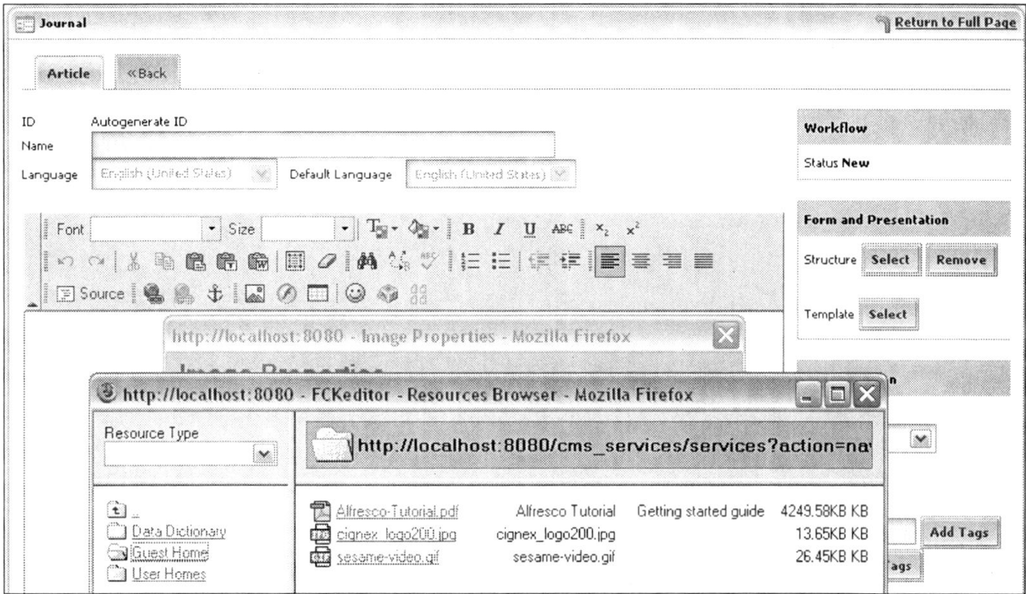

How does it work? Here are possible steps abstracted from the real website:

- Prepare web scripts in Alfresco server, such as search contents, update contents, get contents, download contents, and navigate spaces as folders.

- Prepare CMS services for searching contents, updating contents' metadata, getting contents' metadata, downloading contents and navigating spaces.

- In the editor, consume the CMS services replacing the Liferay **Image Gallery** services and **Document Library** services.

For example, you can get the bundled files and read-me messages from the web site `http://liferay.cignex.com/sesame/` and furthermore, you can play with it as a do-it-yourselfer.

Migrating Contents

Suppose that you already have contents stored in Liferay such as **Image Gallery** and **Document Library**. Now, you want to transfer these contents stored in Liferay into Alfresco. Let's do it as follows.

A portlet called **Alfresco Importer** provides services of content migration from Liferay Content Management repositories to alfresco repositories. Through Liferay services, the portlet gets all CMS contents with all communities; again by web services, the portlet writes all CMS contents into Alfresco repository, where the space names are created automatically by community's names. The following figure depicts the look and feel of the **Alfresco Importer** portlet.

You need to fill the following fields in the **Alfresco Importer** portlet:

1. **Alfresco username and password**: these fields will be used to connect to Alfresco through web services.

2. **Destination path**: this is the path of the Alfresco space in which the folders will be created, and the files imported. "Company Home" is the default root space.

3. You need to specify the **folders**' name that will be created for each CMS portlet. Then, three **folders** ("spaces" in alfresco terminology) will be created in Alfresco repository: one each for **Document Library, Journal Articles** and **Image Gallery**.

After you click on the **Import** button, the portlet will do the following steps:

- For each **community** in the current company, create a space in the root space (described in the second bullet step above). Each space's name will be the same as the **community's** name.

- Inside each **community's** space, create three folders with the names chosen (in third bullet step above).

- Import the files from **Document Library** and **Image Gallery**, keeping the same folder structure they have in these portlets. **Journal Articles** are imported to the same **Folder**, their content is merged with their **Templates** and the result is imported to Alfresco as HTML files.

Note that when importing contents from CMS in Liferay to Alfresco repository, links, images, CSS, and JavaScript references in HTML generated article may not resolve correctly.

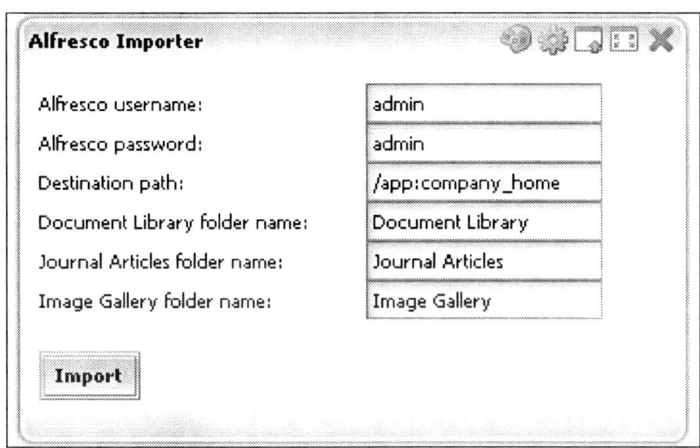

Integrating Liferay with LDAP, SSO And Alfresco

The following diagram shows full integration of **Liferay**, **Alfresco**, **LDAP** and **SSO** CAS. Here is a generic solution for full integration of **SSO** CAS and **LDAP** against Liferay Portal and **Alfresco Portlets**. Here is the generic solution of **SSO** CAS plus **LDAP** against:

- Alfresco Standalone Application — shown as **SSO 1**.

- **Liferay Portal** and, furthermore, **Alfresco** Portlets – shown as **SSO 2**, **SSO 3**, and **SSO 4"**.

To integrate **SSO** CAS plus **LDAP** with **Liferay Portal** and **Alfresco** Portlets such as **Alfresco Client** portlet and **Alfresco Content** portlet, simply follow these steps in sequence:

1. First configure the **Liferay Portal** authenticating with **LDAP**.

2. Then configure the **SSO** CAS server authenticating with **LDAP**.

3. Finally configure the **Alfresco** portlets (**Alfresco Client** and **Alfresco Content**) authenticating with **SSO**.

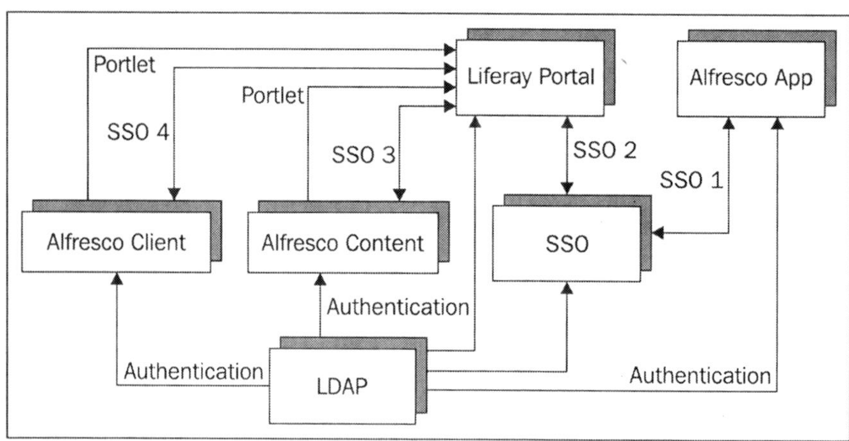

For example, you can first log in to Alfresco standalone application `http://liferay.cignex.com:8090/alfesco` by a **User** account. You are asked to input authentication information here. You will see Alfresco web client standalone application. Then, click Liferay portal `http://liferay.cignex.com:8092/c/portal/login`. You will see that you don't have to log in to the Liferay portal. You are logged into the **Alfresco Web Client** portlet automatically. That is, web applications (Alfresco standalone application, **Liferay Portal** and portlets) share the same access ticket— to defer all authentications to a trusted central server (**SSO** and **LDAP**).

The full integration involves two main functionalities: filters in action for **Liferay Portal** and Alfresco applications, and portlets in action for any portlet in **Liferay Portal**. The following are some general instructions to implement these two main functionalities: filters in action and portlets in action.

Filters in action involve the following steps:

- Enhanced SSO Filter
- Authenticating **SSO** CAS Server with **LDAP**
- Enhanced validating URL in **SSO** CAS Server
- Authenticating with **LDAP**
- Automatic login

Portlets in action involve the following steps:

- Loading portlet
- Tracing current **User** from filter
- Authenticating portlet with **LDAP**
- Automatic login

Integrating with Other Systems

As the world's leading open source portal platform, Liferay provides a unified web interface for data and tools scattered across many sources. Within Liferay portal, a portal interface is composed of a number of portlets — self contained interactive elements that are written to a particular standard. Since portlets are developed independently of the portal itself, and loosely coupled with the portal, they are apparently SOA (Service-Oriented Architecture). This section will discuss how to use SOA to integrate other systems.

Working with Ad Server—OpenX

The OpenX community has grown rapidly to become the web's largest ad space community. As a powerful ad serving solution, OpenX puts control over online advertising back in the hands of web publishers.

OpenX ad server gives site owners everything they need to generate revenue from their websites. Publishers can get complete control of banners and campaigns along with a tracking system, as shown in the following figure:

How do we integrate OpenX in Liferay? Here are some possible steps to do this:

- Consume web services from Ad Server in OpenX.
- Prepare **Ad** portlet to manage ads in Liferay.
- Prepare **Ad Display** portlet to publish **Ad Banners**.
- Deploy these two portlets (**Ad** portlet and **Ad Display** portlet) in Liferay.

The features are necessary in setting up the banners of the content of **Ads** portlet should include:

- Displaying ads (that is, banners) based on a specific day; for example, at Christmas, showing GUND's banner.
- Displaying ads based on a general day; for example, on Monday, display a Fisher-Price ad; on Tuesday, display a GUND ad.
- Displaying ads on percentage basis for the duration of a given day; for example, on Tuesday, display GUND 40%, and Fisher-Price 60%.

We can use ads server OpenX to manage information on companies including banners (called Ads repository), as well as the alfresco server for content repository. At the same time, we can get complete control of banners and campaigns along with a tracking system. Further, we can do more tasks such as these:

- Provide version feature for Ads in Liferay. Thus, we can see which ad version it was in the past.
- Separate **Ad Display** from **Ad** management in Liferay. In ads, **admin** will manage all possible ads with the above mentioned rules (similar to **Journal** portlet). **Ad Display** provides a way to display ads (similar to that of display articles in **Journal Content**) in any page.
- Schedule ads (that is, banners) in **Ad Display**, which is the same as that of articles in **Journal Content**. We can preview **Pages** on a specific date, say July 14th, including all updated **Pages**, home **Page**, and all scheduled articles and ads.

> OpenX is a hugely popular, free ad server for web publishers. It takes control, manages your advertising and makes more money from online advertising. URL: `http://www.openx.org/`

Working with Orbeon Forms

The Orbeon Forms WAR can be directly deployed into the Liferay portal through the following steps:

1. Download Orbeon Forms ZIP file.
2. Unzip Orbeon Forms ZIP file.
3. Drop `orbeon.war` into the Deploy Directory such as `$user-home/liferay/deploy`.
4. Create a new Liferay page called "Orbeon", and open that page.
5. Click the **Add Application** link from the drop-down menu.
6. You should see the **Orbeon Form** portlet appear in the menu.
7. Select **Add** to add the portlet to the page.
8. The portlet displays a welcome page with links to Orbeon Forms examples.
9. **Flickr Resize** example running in the portlet is shown in the following picture.
10. Enter one or more **Flickr tags** such as "**yellow stone**".
11. Press the **Find** button. You can then use the slider to resize the images returned.

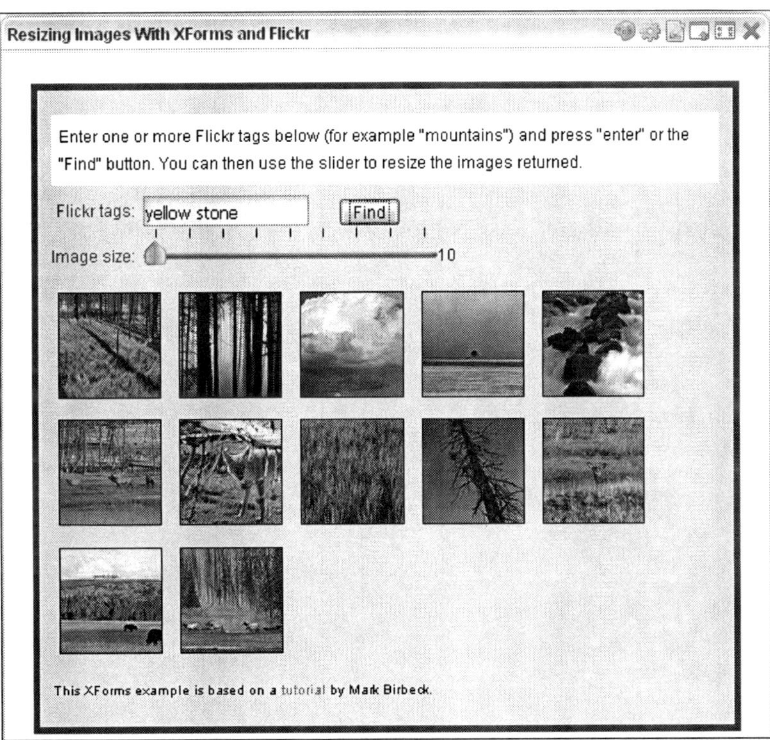

Orbeon Forms is an open source forms solution that handles the complexity of forms. URL: `http://www.orbeon.com/`

Working with Other Integrations

We can also integrate other applications such as Jasper Reports, Pentaho, Intalio, and so on. Here, we just discuss some of them.

Using Jasper Reports, we can easily integrate reporting tool in Liferay portal.

Jasper Reports is an open source reporting tool that can write to screen, to a printer or into PDF, HTML, Microsoft Excel, RTF, ODT, Comma-separated values and XML files. URL: `http://www.jasperforge.org/jaspersoft/opensource/business_intelligence/jasperreports/`

Using Pentaho, we can add ETL capabilities for Business Intelligence (BI) inside the Liferay portal.

Pentaho is an Open Source application software for reporting, analysis, dashboard, data mining, and workflow and Business Intelligence. URL: `http://www.pentaho.com`

Using Intalio | BPMS, we can integrate the BPMN and BELP inside the Liferay portal.

Intalio | BPMS is the BPMS to natively support the BPMN and BPEL industry standards. URL: `http://www.intalio.com/`.

Summary

This chapter first introduced us to the **Admin** portlet, which provides the ability to view server information, to create **Instances**, and to view available **Portlets, Themes** and **Layout Templates**. Then it discussed the **Enterprise Admin** portlet which not only allows **Users** with **Permissions** to manage **Users, Organizations, User Groups,** and **Roles**, but also shows portal settings information, **Password Policies** besides monitoring **Users'** activities. In addition, it discusses full integration with Alfresco through web services and web scripts. Further, it also discussed full integration of **LDAP, SSO** CAS, Liferay and Alfresco to take care of **Users, Communities** and **Permissions** synchronization so that **Users** can see Alfresco as a CMS in Liferay and use it through Liferay portlets. Finally, it discussed other forms of integration such as Ad Server, which includes OpenX, Orbeon Forms, and so on.

In general, we have introduced Liferay, including Portal, Journal CMS, Collaboration suite and various integrations with other systems such as Alfresco, **SSO** and **LDAP**. We tried to explain why Liferay is a better solution for building dynamic and interactive web sites with web content management and web content publishing. Moreover, we also tried to expound how Liferay satisfies the current and future requirements of your website.

Index

X

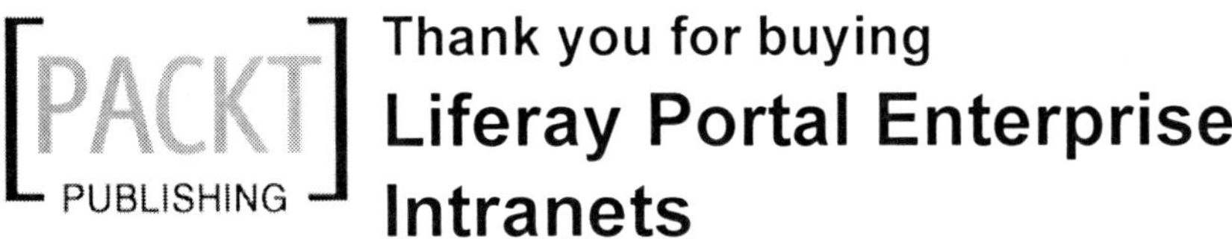

Thank you for buying
Liferay Portal Enterprise Intranets

Packt Open Source Project Royalties

When we sell a book written on an Open Source project, we pay a royalty directly to that project. Therefore by purchasing Liferay Portal Enterprise Intranets, Packt will have given some of the money received to the Liferay project.

In the long term, we see ourselves and you—customers and readers of our books—as part of the Open Source ecosystem, providing sustainable revenue for the projects we publish on. Our aim at Packt is to establish publishing royalties as an essential part of the service and support a business model that sustains Open Source.

If you're working with an Open Source project that you would like us to publish on, and subsequently pay royalties to, please get in touch with us.

Writing for Packt

We welcome all inquiries from people who are interested in authoring. Book proposals should be sent to authors@packtpub.com. If your book idea is still at an early stage and you would like to discuss it first before writing a formal book proposal, contact us; one of our commissioning editors will get in touch with you.

We're not just looking for published authors; if you have strong technical skills but no writing experience, our experienced editors can help you develop a writing career, or simply get some additional reward for your expertise.

About Packt Publishing

Packt, pronounced 'packed', published its first book "Mastering phpMyAdmin for Effective MySQL Management" in April 2004 and subsequently continued to specialize in publishing highly focused books on specific technologies and solutions.

Our books and publications share the experiences of your fellow IT professionals in adapting and customizing today's systems, applications, and frameworks. Our solution-based books give you the knowledge and power to customize the software and technologies you're using to get the job done. Packt books are more specific and less general than the IT books you have seen in the past. Our unique business model allows us to bring you more focused information, giving you more of what you need to know, and less of what you don't.

Packt is a modern, yet unique publishing company, which focuses on producing quality, cutting-edge books for communities of developers, administrators, and newbies alike. For more information, please visit our website: www.PacktPub.com.

Drupal

ISBN: 1-904811-80-9   Paperback: 267 pages

How to setup, configure and customise this powerful PHP/MySQL based Open Source CMS

1. Install, configure, administer, maintain and extend Drupal

2. Control access with users, roles and permissions

3. Structure your content using Drupal's powerful CMS features

4. Includes coverage of release 4.7

Building Websites with Joomla! v1.0

ISBN: 1-904811-94-9   Paperback: 250 pages

A step by step tutorial to getting your Joomla! CMS website up fast

1. Walk through each step in a friendly and accessible way

2. Customize and extend your Joomla! site

3. Get your Joomla! website up fast

Please check **www.PacktPub.com** for information on our titles

What's God Got to Do With It?

Also by *W.T. Jeffrey*

Literature:

The Earthist: Musings in Postmodern Pagan Thought

A Kentucky Tale

Music:

Rock Camp Blues

Available at
Glenreynie.com

What's God Got to Do with It?

By
W.T. Jeffrey

GLENREYNIE
Vanceburg, Kentucky

What's God Got to Do with It?
Copyright © 2014 by Williams Thomas Jeffrey

Printed in the United States of America

Library of Congress Control Number: 2014919651

ISBN: 978-0-9862994-0-7

Published by
Glenreynie
946 Rock Camp Branch Road
Vanceburg, Kentucky 41179
www.glenreynie.com

What's God Got to Do with It?
*…is dedicated to all who embrace reason, seek
evidence to inform their thoughts and actions, and place
faith in humanity's capacity to evolve toward a future
where superstition is no longer an acceptable ground for
discrimination, bigotry, hatred, and violence.*

CONTENTS

Introduction

My name is Williams Thomas Jeffrey. I am an atheist. I am not angry or disgruntled, nor do I feel jaded or betrayed by religion. Actually I am a happy atheist, and have discovered honesty in regard to religion, first to myself and then more broadly from a public stance, to be liberating and inspiring. To identify one's self as an atheist is really nothing more than a simple, sincere, though at times courageous, answer to a basic question. "Do you believe in god?" "No."

In the following chapters we will explore questions, answers, and the reasons it is important to embrace truth by facing reality with reason and integrity. First and foremost readers should understand that I am writing this book as a professional, a care giver, and as a pastor. Yes, as a pastor, and with a sense that a therapeutic approach rooted in compassion is required to achieve results. I am not simply interested in "stirring the pot," or "fanning flames." It is time, however, long overdue in fact, to see the end, or at least the transformation, of what has been one of the most divisive, delusional, hurtful, manipulative, and deceptive forces in the evolution of human civilization. Religion is that force.

This is a book to help readers embrace life without religion, and in so doing find joy and meaning through celebration and acceptance of the real universe in which we live. This book is certainly of interest to atheists, will be very insightful to those who identify themselves as agnostic, but has the potential to be the most liberating for those who rely upon religious ideology, Judeo-Christian-

Islamic ideologies in particular, as the basic ground for meaning in their lives.

By way of introduction I believe it is important to share a little bit more about myself, first to assure readers that the author has a genuine level of credibility, and second as an invitation for readers to think about their own life experiences and why they believe what they do. In the scientific community transparency is a cardinal value, and no less should be expected here.

Most colleagues would know me as Reverend Jeff Earwood. For over 25 years I served congregations in the Christian Church (Disciples of Christ) as their senior pastor or minister. I first served as a licensed minister under the review of a Commission on the Ministry while completing my academic studies at Western Kentucky University and Lexington Theological Seminary. I was then officially recognized and ordained with standing into the ministry. At WKU I majored in Sociology and Religion and graduated summa cum laude with honors. At LTS I was given the seminary's highest scholarship, earned a Master of Divinity degree, and graduated with awards in Biblical Languages, Old, and New Testament Studies.

Over the years I successfully served six congregations in four states, worked with ecumenical, interfaith, civic, and social justice groups, and was a respected leader in the communities I served. I was never fired or asked to leave a pastorate, nor was I ever censured for ethical violations by local or denominational officials. The congregations I served grew, and to my knowledge always felt a high degree of appreciation for my work. Over the years I worked with thousands of people, and knew hundreds of them personally. There were lots of

blessings of children, weddings, and funerals over those years, and of course more sessions than I could count that involved confidential aspects of pastoral care and counseling. The life a clergy person lives is in many respects a case study into some of the most deeply personal aspects of what it is to be human.

Today I go by W.T. Jeffrey, and whether you knew me then or now, "Jeff" is still the name that brings a sense of continuity to my evolving life. There's a bit of a story here that is actually pertinent to this introduction. I am a child of adoption. When I was born my very first name was simply "Williams," hence I use it now with affection for my patrilineal heritage. Actually it was more like "boy" Williams probably written on a little blue card, and later the name "John" was applied, as in "John Doe" for the official adoption process. "Thomas" I have incorporated into my public persona as a nod to my matrilineal heritage.

I have been fortunate over the years to develop a positive relationship with my biological family, but at six months of age I was adopted by a wonderful family and given the name Jeffrey Edward Earwood. For those who wondered why I write and perform as W.T. Jeffrey, the answer should now be transparent.

I grew up in a loving home with a class act family that was also very involved in their church. They were never religious conservatives, or liberals really, but moderates would be the fair assessment. I was socialized in Christian culture, and always found the idea of being accepted or adopted into the family of God as an appealing nuance given my context. Like many of us socialized in the predominantly Christian culture of the

United States, there never seemed to be a need to question the sacred tradition which nurtured my upbringing.

As time went on I decided to pursue ministry as a vocation, and began the decade long journey that meant serious academic study, an intense vetting process from church officials, and a sincere commitment to the communities I would serve. To be sure I was naïve, young, and entered my first student congregation with the same assumptions I had gleaned from being a lay person in the church. Like my parents I was mostly moderate in my views, but had no reason to question the teachings of the bible. These things we take for granted.

My first congregation was a fairly conservative group more closely aligned with the fundamentalist denomination known as the Independent Christian Churches and Churches of Christ in North America (not too awfully different from the Southern Baptist Convention) than the Disciple of Christ church I knew, but hey, the church is the church, right?

It didn't take long to begin dealing with the complex problems that emerge on personal, emotional, and social levels when having to reconcile church dogmas and biblical interpretations with the real world of living human beings in the church, their families, and the ever changing world beyond the pew. The role of women, the status of same gender oriented persons, the place of race, who gets to be in charge, and the slew of "rules" being pulled from words in the bible or church constitutions all become muddled questions when real flesh and blood is at the heart of it all.

The peer pressure of tradition is generally sufficient to appease the inner guilt one feels when being the

ambassador of a loving god requires one to discourage black children from being welcome at the white church, to assure women they're OK being subservient to men, or deal discretely with a church elder's gay child that attempted suicide. I was never so glad to learn a concept as the day I first heard the expression "cognitive dissonance" in a Sociology class.

The wet behind the ears of a young preacher begins to dry fast with the plethora of real life situations that fills the plate. The first visit to hold the hand of a terminally ill congregant or the first funeral quickly gives way to experience. Soon the congregation appreciates very deeply the one who has agreed to love them as they are, and all the more as the manner, style, and eloquence of the minister begins to mature.

For any of us that began the pursuit of a vocation in ministry serving a congregation at the onset of academic preparation, which I'm willing to wager, is most, especially if the congregation "loves" you, the thing one begins to hear quite frequently is the warnings about college and seminary. There is a significant clue here about the reason religion remains popular in the culture, and if you're catching it, then you know it doesn't have anything to do with religion. I'll address this later.

The warnings are always the same. Academic study will ruin you, make you turn liberal, cause you to question your faith, start using "context" when explaining the biblical passages we hold dear, etc., etc. The fear is unmistakable, because they know academic study will confront their minister with evidence. As in all things when evidence is examined, especially when current views are based on assumption, tradition, or surface level

considerations, the conclusions will change. In the same way DNA evidence can overturn a jury conviction, examining the languages, the sources, the history, and yes, the "contexts" of a sacred tradition can and will change everything.

In this respect what is understood to be truth, like knowledge, requires change. The more we learn, the more we are challenged to alter our conclusions, and at times abandon the traditional view for something new altogether. This can be one of the most exhilarating and exciting aspects of life, but it can also be one of the most disruptive and debilitating. Change can equal loss.

At this point in the introduction I have disclosed about all the personal information from my life journey and background that is necessary. I will add, however, one more important detail. I consider myself to be a person of faith. In fact I can state with utmost sincerity that as an atheist my "faith" has never been more vibrant, curious, alive, imaginative, and fulfilling as it is now without the constraints of religion or allegiance to primitive supernatural speculations.

I will clarify just a bit especially for atheist readers who are risking a seizure by my use of the "f" word. When I speak of faith I am referencing the human capacity to function on a subjective level. At no point in this book will I be using the word faith as a synonym for the word religion. Faith, as I understand it, is our capacity to look beyond into the unknown, a suspicion or even trust that something more or else is the case. In this respect faith is an open mind, an unfinished sentence, an emotive risk without guarantee.

Faith as a subjective experience is neither a good thing nor a bad thing. It is ambiguity, unsettling, at times nauseating precisely because it lacks clarity and is incapable of resolution. This subjective, personal energy within the human brain is always in tension with its more objective and analytical counterparts. Faith is an insatiable curiosity that doesn't bode well without knowing. It wants to die, to end, to be gratified, completed by an answer.

Faith and knowledge is never the same thing. They can lead to each other in a wonderful interplay between subjective and objective contexts. One can trust the air we breathe has stuff in it that makes us capable of living. Yet only by observing, testing, and experimenting through an objective or scientific method do we confirm or disconfirm the truth to any degree of certainty. Once the evidence is compelling that oxygen is in fact present, we are free to imagine what else there may be.

Faith is more appropriate as a verb than a noun, and always relates to speculative moments when we don't know. Faith is not about conclusions. I can say I know the universe is capable of producing the conditions for life to evolve after death because millions of stars died producing the elements we utilize for life. If I have faith there may be some reason for it, then that is a subjective notion that may or may not have merit.

Faith, properly understood, is a necessary component in the human cognitive and emotive process. In fact a healthy subjective or "faith claim" experience should lead to an objective examination based upon evidence. It is normal to presuppose, muse, speculate, assume, but then adjust or discard views accordingly, first in the face of contrary evidence, and second when the

notion at hand is clearly beyond objective consideration. I recently heard an "Old Wives' Tale" believed by some that a broody hen's eggs won't hatch after a thunderstorm. Some eggs are hatching and some are not. This "faith claim" is perhaps fodder for a light hearted conversation, but hardly warrants mention in the Department of Agriculture's manual on raising poultry.

Sometimes we get into semantic games when using words like faith or spirituality. There is no doubt that human beings have an innate capacity for intuition, imagination, philosophical contemplation, and that we are intrigued by the mysterious. These things help us feel a sense of meaning in our lives, yet there is no evidence that anything outside of our neural network is involved. In spite of this, faith, or subjective aspects of experiencing life, are often rewarding, challenge us to keep an open mind, and enable us to experience change without necessarily succumbing to fear and despair.

If atheists have become wary of the idea of faith due to its association with religion, then it might be well to point out that religious people are often equally unsettled. Faith, by definition is inherently agnostic. Folks in churches resist it almost as much as they do lengthy services that intrude upon the Sunday lunch hour. I would argue this dilemma is implicated in the steady decline of moderate to liberal mainline churches in the US. In these churches clergy, typically well educated clergy, raise "faith" questions, resist drawing conclusions, rarely use expressions like "And the word of God says," and are generally uncomfortable positing the absolutes congregants would like to have for assurance.

Authentic faith as a subjective condition demands trust without evidence. Two people in a marriage embrace their union as a faith claim even though the empirical evidence suggests more than half of all marriages end in divorce. Many church goers will publicly and emphatically tout their "faith," especially those who ally themselves with conservative, fundamentalist, and evangelical traditions, yet they resist the ambiguity entailed in the notion of "living by faith."The problem is that at some point our subjective claims require evidence in order to be verified objectively or discarded. If the object of one's faith fails to confirm the basis for trust, as with a wayward spouse, or more particularly, a god that doesn't actually exist, then there is no ground for faith. Cognitive dissonance ensues. Either one will accept the conclusion and move on, or bargain out some strategy to make the incongruity palatable. For many in the religious world this means creating the appearance of evidence.

The latter is the case for many if not most church goers today. Again this is especially true in conservative, evangelical, and fundamentalist type churches. If you are a religious person or have been on the fringe of a religious tradition, and you are reading this book, then you will probably catch this right off. One of the most common and popular assertions in church evangelism is to fuse faith and knowledge into a singular concept. "Do you know the Lord Jesus Christ as your personal savior?" is a common question.

This of course is cheating. At times it is a ploy used by church leaders to give parishioners a heightened level of confidence in the claims they are making. This shift from faith to something objective, concrete, and absolute is

convenient for political rhetoric and bolstering right wing social agendas, but ironically it's not really biblical. Even in the bible faith and knowledge are separate concepts. A good example is found in the way many preachers use John 3:16 and following verses. It is perhaps the best known passage in the New Testament and as such there is no obligation to quote it. It does however utilize the subjunctive mood, "should not perish," which is a form of speech that suggests conditionality, ambiguity, or a "shades of grey" kind of situation. Nevertheless this passage is quickly turned into an indicative mood filled with guarantees and absolute certainties by overzealous, frequently untrained, preachers who want it to be so. It is an effective tactic for bargaining away the dissonance between faith and knowledge.

Why we have the ability to convince ourselves that things we embrace as faith claims can be equivalent to objectively verified facts is a problem that neuroscientists are helping us solve. We have a way to go, and the question of what can be considered normal verses the basis for mental illness looms large on the horizon. How do we get from "having faith" to "knowing?" In some cases when this happens it is clear that a person is bordering on a very unhealthy set of conclusions and possibly a serious form of mental illness.

Frequently when a murder is committed it is considered a "crime of passion." Historically one of the most common of such crimes involves a spouse being caught in an act of infidelity. Faith has been broken, and the emotional stress triggers tremendous hostility for the one who feels violated. While juries may sympathize, the violence remains inexcusable. Religion generates similar

emotion, and the stakes can be equally severe where the need for human civilization to evolve beyond its mythical past is concerned. Some within religion are skeptical of evidence and indifferent to the need for change for a variety of reasons, but others become extremely emotional, distraught, and even violent when any challenge to them "knowing" God or Jesus or Allah is raised. Herein hides a significant clue, and perhaps the primary reason why scientific knowledge so frequently fails to convince religious adherents to embrace reason.

Change, as suggested earlier, often equals loss. In 1969 Elizabeth Kübler-Ross published her watershed book "On Death and Dying." Therein she outlined her theory of The Five Stages of Grief. Since that time Denial-Anger-Bargaining-Depression-Acceptance has been widely recognized as offering a relevant model for facing and coping with "grief" associated with loss. I use grief in quotes because much about her work is disputed. Numerous studies have been done over the years that call her conclusions into question. In summary the theory Kübler-Ross proposed specifically to explain grief in relation to one's shock in learning of terminal illness, and subsequently the process of dying, both for the individual and significant others, succumbs to many factors including her personal biases and struggles with grieving.

Kübler-Ross's "Grief Theory" fails on sociological grounds because not all cultures face or view death the same way. The way we are socialized plays a significant role in the way various human cultures place meaning on changing life situations, including death, so the model is not universal. The idea of grief itself was challenged by George Bonanno where he found resilience in the face of

death, rather than grief, was the more common outcome. This view is especially implicated where lengthy illnesses are the case. A family may feel a sense of relief that their loved one's suffering is over, and they are free to remember and celebrate the more meaningful and positive influences of their loved one's life.

Other research has found some evidence confirming parts of the theory, and some groups have tried to broaden the model to contain more stages. Nevertheless the Kübler-Ross model remains popular among care givers and professionals. It may be that her work is a better tool for observers providing a standard whereby certain types of behavior in the face of loss can be identified, and thus treated. Or more likely, what Kübler-Ross identified in her research wasn't a theory that explained stages of grief, but a more general pattern for how human beings deal with loss – the loss of anything. Since change, most any kind of change generally constitutes losing or replacing something, perhaps even the idea of loss is too narrow.

Are we hardwired genetically, through evolution, through adaptation, with a strategy that helps us successfully negotiate change? Kübler-Ross made a significant contribution toward answering that question. Continuing research will help us fine tune the answer to this question, but the evidence to date is quite compelling.

Any number of scenarios can be depicted as one begins to test the hypothesis, and it doesn't seem to matter whether the change related circumstance is perceived as positive or negative. Rather than using Kübler-Ross's grief specific stages we can broaden the pattern just a bit by suggesting the following: A change event occurs eliciting a shock/awakening experience followed by Denial –

Emotional Reaction – Bargaining/Negotiating Behavior – Emotional Reflection – Acceptance/Appropriation of Change.

If Mary wins the lottery her first response is shock, possibly ecstatic shock. She will look at the ticket in disbelief, perhaps check and recheck the numbers, maybe say "I can't believe I won." She will respond emotionally, perhaps tears, perhaps "Thank you Jesus," perhaps "Shit fire, and save the matches." She may return to denial for a moment, or even go back and forth several times between emotion and denial. She will begin to bargain or attempt to rationalize; perhaps as she says to herself "nothing will change," "I'm still the same old me," etc. Emotional reflection will set in as she realizes everything will change. She will likely have to move from her neighborhood, quit her job, put her children in a different school, and maybe even change her name. Eventually she will cash the ticket and move on with her life.

Since losing car keys or one's glasses have been used many times, how about the coin you put in your pocket for the parking meter on Main Street just outside the office where you have a 9:00 AM job interview? It's a beautiful morning, and you leave early for the interview with great confidence. You have thought of everything, and specifically placed a quarter in your right front pocket for the parking meter. You stop to get gas and a few things, but fail to realize that by taking your keys back out of your pocket the quarter fell out. You arrive, find the perfect parking spot, and park. With a confident smile you reach into your pocket for the coin, but are shocked to discover it is not there.

There is no rule that determines the duration of the change/loss cycle we go through in any particular situation. In five seconds you can discover the coin is lost, think "I can't believe I lost it," say "damn," negotiate your options, feel disappointed in yourself for losing the coin, accept that it is gone, quickly drive somewhere for some change, and make it back in time for the interview. Then again you might spend ten minutes going back and forth through the process until you finally accept the fact that the quarter is gone. You don't want it to be gone, but it is. How we reconcile what we want something to be, or the desire for something to remain the same, with reality is a persistent challenge.

Change, loss, the unexpected, the unintended, the "out of the blue" all exacerbate the vulnerabilities we pretend don't exist, and challenge the core assumptions we hold dear that allow us to believe we have some measure of control. We can be pathetically humorous especially when we are snagged going back and forth between bargaining and denial. How many times are you going to empty that pocket before accepting the coin is lost? Worse, how long are you going to spend searching all of your other pockets even though you know you put it in your front right pocket? How many times will you go back and forth searching the car seat, then your pockets again, how many expletives, and how long before your potential employer looks out to see a raving lunatic?

The Denial-Anger-Bargaining-Depression-Acceptance cycle first presented by Kübler-Ross doesn't provide a viable theory to explain the universal way human beings grieve, but it does reveal a typical pattern for the way human beings respond to change, particularly

change experienced as loss. It is not necessarily the only model that applies to how we process change or loss, but arguably it is the most common in western culture. Further it is not a given that people move through the cycle from start to finish. It is more a continuum with fluidity than an exact series of linear stages.

The DABDA cycle functions as an integrative strategy that allows emotional and cognitive aspects of experience to reconcile and conclude with resolution. But here lies a bit of a rub. If there is a "goal," even on a sub-conscious level, the first order of business is a defense mechanism; much like the "fight or flight" response that occurs when one perceives danger, the change/loss experience primarily requires interpretation followed by action. As long as the problem appears to be solved, the dissonance or disruption put into perspective, one is free to move on, at least temporarily.

In the film "The Edge" the three survivors of a plane crash encounter a bear. First they can't believe their eyes. Second is the emotional outbursts and subsequent running. Then, once a certain distance is reached, they stop confident they have escaped. They bargain their way back to denial – that all is well. Of course the bear returns. Only much later when bargaining is exhausted and the emotional reflection/angst of their impending doom experienced, do they face the bear and overcome.

DABDA as an emotive/cognitive process is engaged with the onset of experience perceived as a change, a loss, or an affront to some normative state. Best stated we can say if and when such an experience occurs it is likely that one will have a denial type reaction, followed by an emotional/feeling based experience, and then will begin to

bargain or negotiate a reasonable solution. If the consequences of the change event are undeniable and non-negotiable, then a period of emotional reflection will likely ensue. At this point acceptance offers the best hope toward integrating the change and moving on.

What becomes apparent is there is great ambiguity in the way human beings work through the reality of change. We generally follow identifiable patterns, like a modified DABDA, but there is a range of choices. One explanation is provided through various aspects of Exchange Theory first proposed in 1958 by sociologist George Homans.

Essentially we have the capacity to mediate our choices based upon the perceived advantages and disadvantages available. A lottery winner has a choice between long term payouts which will yield a larger sum of the total, or take the cash payout which immediately deducts the full amount of tax but provides instant wealth. A winner with well established finances will be more likely to consider the annuity option especially where the payments may continue to heirs through their estate than a lower income winner who "needs" the money now.

When notification strikes that a tragic accident has occurred, and a loved one is deceased, DABDA is quickly at work. Denial like a fog mingles with the numbing shock. Emotion as well overwhelms the senses. The drive to identify the body is fraught with pleas that a mistake has been made. The inevitable is faced and few choices are available. The cycle may repeat itself many times, or even indefinitely for some people. Eventually choices will be made after considering every conceivable option, though the standard view of acceptance may not be the conclusion.

Persons with a strong community of support are much more likely to demonstrate resilience, celebrate the deceased with a positive outlook, and continue on with a vibrant and healthy life. Contrast this with an elderly widow or widower, largely homebound with little contact with others. The old clothes will never come out of the closet. Two plates may always be set for dinner. And monologue imagined as conversation will continue as though the other is just in another room. Nevertheless this person may appear happy and well adjusted. This raises a formidable question. To what degree is it necessary for a person to embrace reality and still function within the parameters of a "normal," socially healthy life?

In some cases "denial" provides a more comfortable option. When a person is missing as due to abduction or kidnapping the worst is suspected. A family receives the shock, can't believe it happened, is profoundly angry, bargains profusely for a hopeful scenario, experiences very deep feelings of melancholy, depression, and guilt, but until a body is found or the person returns, denial becomes the default state. Even though the majority of cases are shown to have been homicides, occasionally the missing person turns out to be alive. "My loved one is still out there." "My loved one will be OK." In a case such as this, or even when it is a child suspected to have runaway or a soldier missing in action, the primary community of support is centered in the optimistic "maybes" that fluctuate between bargaining and denial. Those who would vie for accepting the more likely outcome that the missing person is deceased are regarded as cynical, unduly pessimistic, and even callous.

Much the same dilemma occurs when religion is challenged by reason. Scientific evidence is viewed with skepticism, and the defense mechanisms are legion. In reality there is much more at stake than individual persons accepting the fact that supernatural beings are not real. It is not as simple as acknowledging we were not created, but evolved, or that brain chemistry not holy spirits determines the feelings associated with what we experience. There are many exchanges involved, and as has so often been discovered, particularly by atheists, being "right" is a paltry exchange for "being accepted," "being connected," being in "the" community, or honoring "the tradition."

The course ahead is in some respects similar to facing the problem of a missing person, to facing the death of a loved one, but more accurately, coping with the loss of a persona, a public figure, an authority, a legend that has never existed in the real universe. Much like that moment when a child faces the reality that Santa Claus doesn't exist religion's day has come. Change is afoot. Yet not only is there a challenge for people of religion, equally, if not more so, there is a challenge for atheists and those who would see human civilization take a much needed step in its evolution. There are two sides of a coin here. Both sides need polishing, though for differing reasons, and to overlook this reality is, in fact, the epitome of denial.

What's God Got To Do With It?

Renowned singer Tina Turner thrilled fans with the song "What's Love Got to Do with It?" which also became the title of the film adapted from her memoir "I, Tina." The opening lyrics are:

You must understand
though the touch of your hand
Makes my pulse react
That it's only the thrill of boy meeting girl
Opposites attract
It's physical
Only logical
You must try to ignore
that it means more than that ….

In many respects a similar type context emerges when we ask of religion, "What's God got to do with it?" Christians, in particular, at this juncture, might want to give serious thought to this question.
Muslims and Jews are not exempt either.

There used to be a popular cliché asked by evangelicals a few years ago when calling their flocks to greater faithfulness that went something like this "If someone examined your life as a Christian, would the evidence convict you?" Another of my favorites came from the late Christian musician Keith Green who frequently argued that being a real Christian meant a radical commitment to mission work and discipleship. He would

say things like "Going to church makes you a Christian about like going to McDonalds makes you a hamburger," and "God can't cash out of state checks in heaven man, he needs you." These pastoral ploys from within Christianity highlight a truth most clergy know all too well. Many if not most Christians don't really believe the teachings attributed to Jesus apply to them.

Pastors are equally guilty, and in fact know if they don't make their congregations feel good about themselves they'll be out of a job. Statisticians would be amazed at the inordinate amount of time ministers spend preaching sermons explaining why congregants don't really have to sell all their possessions, stop for stranded motorists, or love people unconditionally. "God loves the sinner, but hates the sin." That is one of the most popular *non-biblical* justifications for not openly accepting everyone unconditionally, right up there with "The lord helps those who help themselves."

No, Jesus didn't really mean to love one's enemies, that one's forgiveness was predicated on reciprocity, that one had to sell possessions and give to the poor, deny one's self, or keep pious acts like praying and giving alms private. Jesus was obviously kidding when he said not to call any one on earth by prestigious titles like Father or Teacher. Granted there are some conservative denominations with a measure of humility that only use words like Elder or Brother or Sister for their leaders, but most congregations glory just a bit when they can boast about their Reverend, Right Reverend, His Immanence, Archbishop, Cardinal, and the most juicily sacrosanct of them all – Holy Father.

What's particularly damning in the evidence department is the rise over the last three decades of the mega church, televangelist centered, health and wealth preaching that features really rocking contemporary music and the core message that god wants you to be rich. "Sow seeds of faith," by way of dollars in the plate, and "God will bless you!" The fastest growing churches in the US fit this bill, and currently the Nigerian based Redeemed Christian Church of God is working the fraud into frenzy.

It is rather amazing how by any conservative evaluation this movement attributed to Jesus that would lead followers to embrace a socialist or even communist lifestyle has become for so many a path celebrating success, abundance, and individualistic values. This Jesus, who states before Pilate, though in a rather Gnostic context, that his kingdom is not of the earth, has somehow morphed into the evangelical and fundamentalist Christian mascot for the Republican political platform. Their Jesus is pro-gun, supports the death penalty, favors the wealthy, and works for the privatization of health care and social security. They want what they call a Christian America when it is clear they want an exclusivist America with the name of a divine to sanction their authority. Naturally this isn't the first time in history human beings have legitimized their political ambitions with the moniker of a god. It is however becoming painstakingly close to an overt crime against humanity.

The charade is evident to anyone who tests the claims of fundamentalists by actually reading scripture. They claim their notion of family values is the same as biblical family values. In the Old Testament the family was essentially an economic institution with privilege extended

to first born male heirs. The structure was patriarchal with polygamy being the accepted norm. Women were largely considered property. Unruly and disobedient children who dishonored their family were to be stoned to death. Slavery was normative, and the male patriarch had sexual rights over female concubines. In many cases God demanded the genocide of neighboring cultures including the slaughter of every man, woman, and child, even infants and pregnant mothers.

This type of family structure is actually still alive in today's world, though largely in Islamist nations. Ironically even conservative Christians seem to find such beliefs appalling. New Testament family values, at least from the Jewish perspective, do not negate traditions stemming from the Old Testament periods. What can be deduced about family values from various New Testament texts is hardly the nostalgic tip of the hat conservative Christians give to the Ozzie and Harriet, Father Knows Best, and Leave it to Beaver television families portrayed as "American" in the late 1950's and early 1960's.

What we know about early Christian like movements is that they were mostly Gnostic in terms of how they viewed the world. Jesus is quoted as saying in Luke 14:26ff "Whoever comes to me and does not hate father and mother, wife and children, brothers and sisters, yes, even life itself, cannot be my disciple." The material world was viewed as corrupt, temporary, and illusory. There were several "flavors" of Gnosticism that competed for primacy until Christianity was formally created under the authority of the Roman Emperor Constantine at the Council of Nicea in 325, but there were common threads. The flesh counted for little to nothing, as did worldly goods and

relationships, including family. The "faith" community was the family, and that's why leaders like Paul recommended people be celibate if possible, and not worry about marriage, etc. This style of approaching family values has been tried in modern times, as with the Shakers. They left behind nice museums.

Even liberal Christians miss this Gnostic connection in early Christianity. They celebrate passages like Galations 3:28 where Paul writes "There is no longer Jew or Greek, … slave or free, … male or female; for all of you are one in Christ Jesus," as being egalitarian. The Gnostic view eliminated gender on the spiritual plane while struggling to deal with normative social divisions on the physical. This certainly led to confusion and conflict where the roles of men and women were concerned. Another clear example and one where fundamentalist Christians exude ignorance is found in Ephesians. Here the model for family structure seems to be given quite clearly as husband over wife, father over children, and master over slave. Actually the structure of the passage is an allusion to Aristotle's book Politics. The writer of Ephesians places caveats between the traditional cultural views which engenders the very kind of spiritual mutuality shared by many Gnostic Christian groups of that day.

However one interprets the meaning of family in the New Testament it is hardly reconcilable to the "traditional family values" being promoted by fundamentalist Christians today. It is as though they are putting words into the mouth of God. Naturally it is not the first time people have done such a thing. This is a perplexing phenomenon to many people, because who would be so arrogant as to make something up and then say "God"

said it. Actually the book of Genesis provides us with just such a rude awakening.

Most everyone knows the story of Noah and the Ark which begins in Genesis 6. Yahweh chooses Noah, his three sons, and their wives to be the only humans to survive the great deluge Yahweh is preparing to bring as judgment upon all living things. They are to gather up two of every animal and bird, a male and female of each, and put them in the ark. As chapter 7 begins Yahweh bids Noah and his family to go into the ark. Perhaps your bible only says "The Lord," and you are wondering why Yahweh? Most bibles give this information in the introduction which will state that whenever YHWH (Yahweh) is used, the sacred name of god revealed to Moses, it will be rendered Lord with the "L" capitalized.

If you haven't thought about it before it is probably becoming apparent that this story has an editor, or perhaps even more than one. Why would the name given to Moses be used to tell a story that allegedly happened several hundred years prior? Obviously if the story of Noah existed prior to the time of Moses it must have used a different name for god which has been changed or discarded by the editor. This isn't so much of a problem really, though it is evidence of human revision. Fundamentalists will argue Moses wrote what god inspired him to write, and it only made sense to go back and use Yahweh for all of the old stories.

The real problem begins in 7:2 and recurs in 8:20 and 9:3. Yahweh in 7:2 says "Take with you seven pairs of all **clean** animals …; and a pair of the animals that are not clean …; and seven pairs of the birds of the air also." Really, Yahweh said that to Noah? In chapter 8 following

the flood verse 20 states "Then Noah built an altar to Yahweh, and took of every **clean** animal and of every **clean** bird, and offered burnt offerings on the altar." The problem is as obvious as it is contradictory. The law where Yahweh reveals which animals are clean and unclean doesn't come about until Leviticus, again, at best, hundreds of years later when the people of Israel are told what they can and cannot eat, use for offerings, etc. Further proving that human beings, most likely priestly editors of the time period after the Babylonian Exile (c. 400 BCE), put words into Yahweh's mouth is chapter 9:3 where god, now Elohim and not Yahweh, says to Noah "Every moving thing that lives shall be food for you; and just as I gave you the green plants, I give you everything."

As an aside it is worth pointing out that the next verse states "Only, you shall not eat flesh with its life, that is, its blood." This of course is the origin of the kosher food law, which by the way in Acts 21:25 is actually one of three requirements from Jewish law imposed on gentile Christians by James and the church elders in Jerusalem. There would be a lot fewer Christians if they knew they had to eat kosher meats **and** give up their possessions.

One can only muse at how confused Noah must have been, first to have to learn about "clean" animals, and then later once he has it, to be told "Go ahead you can eat anything." But the fact is clear, human beings from another time put words into god's mouth that were consistent with their beliefs at the time. Human beings have been appropriating legends and myths from previous cultures, reinterpreting them, and modifying them to suit the present agenda for millennia. It is no different today. The expression "God says" is a powerful tool for

communicating authority, and no one feels more comfortable using it than those entrusted with guarding and promoting a religious tradition.

Today when Christian evangelicals, conservatives, and fundamentalists seek to influence politics, pound the bully pulpit of family values, fight against women's rights, the right of same gender oriented persons to enjoy the full liberty of their inalienable rights, they speak for themselves and not for a god. They too put words in the mouth of god. Sometimes they go as far as to blaspheme the very religion they embrace. Nothing is more offensive and dishonest than when literalists, creationists, and fundamentalists refer to the bible as "The Word of God." They make extraordinary claims about a book, technically a collection of writings more akin to a library than a book, that no one text ever makes for itself. They hold extremist views that in general were never held by Jewish authorities who brought us the Old Testament, or the Roman Catholic Church that created the New Testament and the current arrangement of the modern bible. Even the reformers like Luther and Calvin, though placing high value on the authority of scripture never went to the extremes of modern fundamentalists.

It was the late nineteenth and early twentieth century when the modern fundamentalist movement began and this largely out of fear. Darwinian evolution and science on many fronts was reshaping the way we understood the world, the universe, and ourselves. At that time it was decided to assert and persist in asserting, regardless of evidence, like the child having a tantrum with closed eyes and covered ears, that the bible was the word of God,

inerrant, infallible, and from cover to cover, inspired by God.

This view took hold in spite of many passages in the bible itself that make such a view untenable and potentially idolatrous. For example, in the Gospel attributed to John, Jesus alone is called the Word. "The word became flesh…." In John 5:39 Jesus is depicted as rebuking Jewish leaders and contemporaries by saying "You search the scriptures because you think that in them you have eternal life…Yet you refuse to come to me to have life."Granted, John is the most Gnostic of the four canonical gospels, the only one where Jesus repeatedly claims to be divine, but for the point at hand, the bible, which didn't even exist in its present form until the fourth century is not the "Word of God."

Speaking of words, what about "god" as a word? Religious readers may already feel a little defensive, but in earnest, it is not necessary. Today's churches believe many things, and there is no dispute that most people believe in some type of higher power. We'll come to that, but given the evidence, and that "honesty is the best policy," it's time to wiggle a foot out of the closet. Yes, it is OK to admit it, you don't really believe in god, or at least not any of the gods mentioned in the bible.

The evidence; well thus far it is fair to suggest we have looked at a few pretty significant things, and there is a lot more. This author has been relatively generous concerning the teachings of Jesus, and hasn't even gotten into the really strict, nitpicky stuff. It suffices to suggest that we have by and large bargained ourselves into a view whereby we try to be good people, were baptized after all, and as a rule don't feel in danger of hellfire. We believe in

a heaven, not anything that will measure up to a biblical text, but an afterlife where we'll meet our loved ones, and probably receive rewards. This is the religion that comforts us. The underlying reason that so many churches and Christians feel no burden of consequences for reordering "God's" universe, and at times taking some really serious liberties, is because deep down, perhaps sub-consciously, we know gods don't really exist.

People do things, but god doesn't. God doesn't do any of the things attributed to Jesus. God doesn't heal, resurrect, ferment water into wine, or even mellow the hearts of believers into kind, gentle, peace loving folk. Prayers are prayed into the infinite silence, but no definitive response. I have genuine respect for those clergy who have the integrity to look at parishioners and say "I don't know." The preachers who pander denial by saying trite things like "God answers all prayers. Sometimes it's yes, sometimes it is no, and sometimes it's maybe" make fine marionettes. The ones who blame others, particularly those struggling with illness or hard times, for not having enough faith or not giving enough money are criminals who should be prosecuted for fraud.

Churches can be fine institutions, but "What's God got to do with it?" Almost all churches devote 80-90% of their budgets to themselves. Staff salaries, operational expenses, capital campaigns all cut quite deeply into the ethos of feeding the hungry, clothing the naked, sheltering the homeless, and caring for the sick and imprisoned. There's no guilt in it for leaders because success is the mark they are looking for. God language is the stamp of approval. It carries weight and has no measurable consequences. And when communities, even states, want

to protect themselves from change, from diversity, from immigrants, from scientists, educators who train children to think for themselves, then there is nothing more effective than rattling the god saber of fear and denial. But what does "god" have to do with it?

God is a word for winners. Both teams pray, but only one is giving god the glory for the victory. God is on their side and they get to dictate terms. Better yet they get to define the god, write the history books, and take liberties. But god is also the word for losers. The motif turns from the victor Almighty to the suffering servant, deliverer of the oppressed, hope of hopes, and the rising tide of recompense. Since gods never really weigh in, fight battles, take sides, set limits, call the shots, referee, opine, the lot falls to those who stand to gain the most by evoking the word – god.

"God" for all the intended specificity by those who claim to be believers in a god, is really one of the most ambiguous and generic words in most any language. Webster's dictionary defines the word "god" as "any of various beings conceived of as supernatural, immortal, and having special powers over the lives and affairs of people and the course of nature." In Greek the equivalent word is "theos," and of course is found in the studious word "theology." It is a word applicable to any god, but is not the specific name for a god. While it denotes a supernatural being it does not reveal any particular characteristic of the god in question.

The gods of antiquity had names, various attributes or powers, and stories about their origins. The list of gods from various cultures could itself make a rather lengthy book. Most people are not familiar with the names or the

roles the deities played in the cultures that venerated or worshipped them. Yet most of us do remember names like Zeus, Apollo, Poseidon, Ares, Athena, Aphrodite, Hera, or Isis, Ishtar, Horus, etc. In the bible the primary gods mentioned are El, Asherah, Baal, and Yahweh. There are a few others.

It is worth pointing out that the general view throughout the Old Testament isn't that "God" is the only god, but allegedly the most powerful god. Only quite late in the development of Jewish thought is Yahweh viewed as the only "true" god. In the older stories collected in the Hebrew Scriptures god is called El or most commonly by the plural form Elohim. There is a reality check that takes place on a psychological level for persons who read scripture if instead of using the generic words "God" and "Lord" that translators have created one uses the real names of El and Yahweh. For most "god" is an abstract concept that can mean the divine or higher power that one has been taught exists. The average person will feel a bit squeamish when looking into the mirror and saying "I believe in El/Elohim." The voice in the back of the head says "No I don't."

It is also worth pointing out that no real explanation is given in the biblical texts for the origin of heavenly beings like angels. While divine messengers visit mortals, and at times appear to even be the god, they are indistinguishable from humans. In the story where the three messengers come to Abraham they appear to be ordinary travelers. In the story of Jacob's name change the man he contends with turns out to be El. Jacob is blessed, given a bum hip, and named "Isra-El" meaning one who contends with El. He then names the place "Peniel"

because he saw El face to face and survived. How to construe the existence of heavenly beings became a real problem for the Jewish officials that created the Old Testament we have today. Their awkward revision of the stories left visible scars and evidence.

In the time period following the Babylonian Exile and the early canonization process of the Torah we begin to see the development of new forms of literature that attempt to address this problem. Apocalyptic writings like 1 Enoch expound upon the fight between good and evil, the eventual triumph of the righteous, and begin to offer an explanation for who and what is in heaven. After all if Yahweh were the only god, no wife, no children, he'd be pretty lonely. Revelation in the New Testament is also one of many writings in this tradition. So where did the "hosts of heaven" originate?

The answer to this question is fairly obvious, though quite shocking to most of us when we first realize the truth. I too felt the shockwave of reality, and the repercussion is more than sufficient to send one into a head spin back and forth between denial and bargaining for quite some time. The problem begins with being raised in a culture where the bible is the only book. It is the only "holy" book. The first time most of us see one as a child it is handled with sanctity and reverence. Our parents and grandparents point to it with authority. For westerners it is written in English, possibly Elizabethan English, and it has a very formal appearance complete with delicate paper and quality binding.

For some their first bible is the huge, oversized, coffee table version that has been passed down for generations. It has pictures of god, angels, prophets, and

Jesus, and in the middle is written the family genealogy that proves its sacred status. For every curse word, lie, act of mischief, or moment of rebellion, if it wasn't a trip straight to the woodshed, it was a finger pointed at that book that set one's course on an even keel. Sometimes the trip to the woodshed remained imminent which gave the book all the more power.

By the time I went to college I was fairly well read on a variety of world religions. I had read the Tau, thumbed through the Koran, read a few books on world religions, and had even read -- well looked at -- the Kama Sutra. Still as far as I knew the Holy Bible was the only viable book about god, and it stood apart as unique, the genuine chronicle of the one true god's interaction with humankind. The reality, and a reality that all too many have yet to face, is the "bible" is not the only book. In fact when families present the bible to their children as "God's Word," whether from an intentional bias or a reflection of their own lack of knowledge, it is equivalent to an act of censorship.

The simple fact is that long before the Israelites emerged Canaanites worshiped many gods, but the highest deity was El. There is an extensive mythology regarding El and the legends associated with him. El's primary consort or wife was Asherah, and he was depicted as a bull in carvings and idols. El reputedly fathered seventy or more children which were also gods but of lesser power. El/Elohim is clearly the god of early Israel, and the connection to the larger and more ancient Canaanite religions is unmistakable. Readers not interested in the grueling academics can simply Google "El" and read about him on Wikipedia.

The Old Testament however, when put in perspective, provides some of the most disturbing evidence. Everyone knows the saying "To the victors go the spoils," and according to the bible the southern tribes, primarily the Judean monarchy which was established in the capital city of Jerusalem was the last man standing. They came to place Yahweh over El, and in their bid to create a united kingdom under the authority of Jerusalem they attempted to force the other clans and tribal communities into the emerging religion of the Jerusalem temple cult.

What ensued was war and perpetual conflict. Frankly to this day the best scholarship we have cannot pinpoint with accuracy when Yahweh worship was established, or more particularly when Yahweh worship was combined with the Law of Moses. The best evidence suggests that what we now read as the Old Testament is formulated, edited, and established after the Babylonian exile during the Ezra/Nehemiah reform period. Contrary to what Christian fundamentalists like to argue about the divine inspiration of scripture, we know the editors of the bible used source material. We'll come to some of the Babylonian myths that influenced the Jewish revisionists to retell ancient stories for their culture, but the biblical texts themselves mention sources. We are told repetitively about the annals of the kings which no longer appear to exist, and there are the books "The Wars of Yahweh" (Nu. 21:14) and "Jashar" (Jos. 10:13, 2 Sam. 1:18) which have never been found.

What was believed and when remains a mystery. However we do know a few things. We know that El worship along with Asherah and other Canaanite deities

was widespread in the region long before Yahweh worship makes its appearance. We know, even from the bible, that the El/Baal traditions were rooted in traditional fertility religion. Further we can surmise that even where Yahweh worship was competing for primacy it did not necessarily mean the Law of Moses was in place or that the practice of traditional fertility religion was eliminated. One only has to read the good king bad king stories of 1 & 2 Kings to realize the conflict persisted until the Babylonians put an end to the southern kingdom of Judah in 587 B.C.E. Even wise Solomon who allegedly builds the great temple for Yahweh manages to keep the other gods and their traditions nearby.

If David was in fact an historical figure there is little doubt he was a devotee of Yahweh. But did he know the Law of Moses? Yes the traditions and legends of Moses appear connected to the rise of Yahweh worship, but they certainly don't appear to be known or observed by everyone. In fact the expanding codex of laws attributed to Moses during the wilderness days never seems to be implemented, at least not until the time of Ezra/Nehemiah.

It strains credulity to believe an intelligent god would command in Exodus 20:24ff after specifically stating not to make idols out of silver and gold "You need make for me only an altar of earth…but if you make for me an altar of stone, do not build it of hewn stones; for if you use a chisel on it you profane it," then in chapter 25 and following command just the opposite by detailing the lavish design of the ark, tabernacle, and creating an exclusive priesthood. Talk about out with the old and in

with the new! But that is exactly what's happening before the reader's eyes.

The older fertility religions with earthen altars on the high places are giving way to competitive and warring forces in the larger culture and the remnants of the struggles are reflected in these texts. By the time of the legendary warrior king David the battle between gods is being waged with human spears and swords. Laws are being established as a fledgling nation struggles to be born. This isn't unusual and in fact Israelite laws reflected in the Torah are very similar to the laws that were established for centuries throughout Mesopotamia. One only has to read Hammurabi's Code to see the similarities.

Still in spite of the idea that The Law of Moses stemmed from antiquity the people are governed by prophets, seers, judges, and the clans with the greatest might. If a code of laws is actually in place, then why is there the need for charismatic leadership? David for all the Psalms attributed to him never sings one specifically about the Ten Commandments. If the people knew and agreed about the authority of these laws, why wouldn't there be a psalm for the "big ten?"

In the story of David and Bathsheba, David, Yahweh's faithful servant, really pushes the limit. He covets his neighbor's wife, commits adultery, causes the murder of one of his greatest soldiers, and essentially lies about it in the attempt to cover it up. At least two of these violations require the death penalty. There is no provision exempting a king from Yahweh's laws. In fact Saul lost his anointing as king for not killing Agag the Amalekite king and keeping some of the booty when Yahweh through the prophet Samuel had commanded absolute genocide. The

only punishment David and Bathsheba received was that Yahweh takes the life of the illicit unwanted child. This biblical story is a real slap in the face to Christian conservatives who argue that "pro-life" is the biblical standard.

David takes Bathsheba as his wife and she eventually gives birth to Solomon who gets to be king in place of his older brothers. Clearly the Law of Moses as it appears today was not in place then, and the religion of Yahweh continued to supersede that of El by the might of victors whose stories managed to survive the trail of blood through the ages. Yet these are not the only stories that have survived.

In 1868 The Moabite Stone was discovered which tells of successes and victories of Mesha the Moabite king in the 9th century B.C.E. His god was Chemosh and the following is a quote from the stone translated by W.F. Albright:

And Chemosh said to me, "Go, take Nebo from Israel!" So I went by night and fought against it from break of dawn until noon, taking it and slaying all, seven thousand men, boys, women, girls and maid-servants, for I had devoted them to destruction for (the god) Ashtar-Chemosh. And I took from there the […] of Yahweh, dragging them before Chemosh…And the king of Israel… Chemosh drove him out before me….

The point is simple, and indicative of most every culture. The gods did nothing, but they were honored by the mortal powers that did. El, Baal, Yahweh, Chemosh, etc. waxed and waned with the cultures that revered their names.

The biblical stories are not unique when viewed over and against the rather expansive literature that has survived from the ancient Near East. The stories of El incorporated and glossed over by the stories of Yahweh, collected, revised, and passed down through the remnant culture of ancient Israel that survives in today's Jewish community may be the most polished and best known, but they exist in direct relation to many cultures that did not survive. Even so the biblical stories owe a debt of gratitude to their predecessors.

El was the Canaanite god of creation and the father of many lesser gods. Literally translated the Hebrew bible begins with this phrase "When Elohim began to create." What proceeds is an expansion of what happens during the primordial week resulting in the creation of the Sabbath day. Most scholars recognize this story as an etiology, a story that explains an origin, and creation, already the popular role of El, is not the point. What is fascinating about this story is the way its pattern connects with older Canaanite myths. For example, consider this text from the Ras Shamra-Ugarit excavations where El has reluctantly approved the building of a temple for his son/grandson Baal:

Lo, a [d]ay and a second, Fire feeds upon the house; Flame upon the palace: A third, a fourth day …A fifth, a sixth day… There, on the seventh day, the fire dies down in the house, the flame in the palace. The silver turns into blocks, the gold is turned into bricks. Puissant Baal exults: "My house have I builded of silver; my palace, indeed, of gold." The seven day pattern occurs in other parts of the mythical poetry as well.

That modern day Creationists and Christian fundamentalists insist on taking the biblical text literally, even to the point of supplanting science, is as untenable as it is absurd. The El/Elohim stories of the Hebrew bible reflects the evidence of their connection to the larger Canaanite culture, and in several cases their dependence on the broader mythological past of ancient Mesopotamia. The rough edges to these stories left by the Jewish editors are due largely to the fact that El was well known in the broader culture. Recasting El as Yahweh was less a problem than dealing with the fact that El was not alone.

There remains great speculation over the use of the masculine plural Elohim for El, but there can be no doubt that the notion of El being the father god of many persisted. In the end Yahweh creates by word ex nihilo, including the heavenly hosts of angelic beings, and has no consort. He does apparently make an exception with Mary in the New Testament, but we'll come back to that. El on the other hand has children, and ironically the Jewish redactors failed to completely edit them out of these older stories.

Those nagging plurals where they shouldn't be constitute some of the best evidence we are dealing, not with an inspired text, but a collection of writings based on source material from the larger Near Eastern culture. Equally problematic is the content of several stories, particularly the stories recorded in the first chapters of Genesis. There of course is El saying "Let us make humankind in our image" in the first creation story, and later in the Garden expulsion is this passage:
Then Yahweh-Elohim said, "See, the man has become like one of us, knowing good and evil; and now he might reach

out his hand and take also from the tree of life, and eat,
and live forever" --
For El to be talking with the other gods is not a problem
from a Canaanite point of view, but for the monotheistic
god Yahweh to be having this confab is more than
remarkable.

While there is little doubt that the El of the Hebrew
Scriptures is the same El venerated by the broader
Canaanite clans hundreds of years prior to the emergence
of Yahweh worship, the historical connections to the larger
Mesopotamian region are perhaps the most fascinating. If
we grant some measure of veracity to the stories in Genesis
then we can conclude that early Hebrew ancestors
originated in Babylonia during the Chaldean period (1200-
1000 B.C.E.) and made their way into Canaan. They are
described as nomadic shepherds who travelled the Fertile
Crescent trade routes between Babylon and Egypt.

These ancient Nomadic peoples may have originated
in Babylon bringing the mythology with them, but we also
know they returned to Babylon in the days of
Nebuchadnezzar's conquest. The Israelites of the northern
kingdom had already been conquered, enslaved, and
dispersed by the Assyrian invasion over a century earlier.
The Jews of the southern kingdom of Judah were taken
into exile and didn't return to rebuild Jerusalem until the
time of Ezra and Nehemiah as a vassal state to Persia.
Once again this remnant of Abraham's descendants had a
close relationship to the Babylonian world. The influence is
unmistakable.

Scholars have known for some time that the Hebrew
Scriptures bear the witness of multiple pens over a long
period of time. We have the stories where god is El, the

stories where god is Yahweh, some when god is both together, historical narratives and collections of traditions where the editor reveals himself as a third party, and material that appears particularly influenced by the temple priests in Jerusalem. There are other writings included as well like the wisdom material, Proverbs, etc. Writing was prolific after the exile period and continued into the period when the Greeks conquered Palestine.

Canonization or the formal setting of stories in a final form seems to have begun following the Ezra/Nehemiah period around 400 B.C.E. and continued in stages until near the end of the first century C.E. Books written in Hebrew and Aramaic were given status over books written exclusively in Greek, like what most know today as The Apocrypha. What is important to know is that some of the Babylonian stories and even El stories predate the Hebrew bible by more than a thousand years. Granted, the El stories in the Hebrew bible may also reach back into antiquity, but even then they bear a direct relationship to the myths of the older Babylonian cultures.

In ancient Babylon where formal writing seems to have originated came stories of creation, the beginning of gods, their roles, and their creation of human mortals. There are stories that depict the reason why humans can't be immortal, why innocence is lost, and why animals sense fear in our presence. There are also flood stories, not surprising in a land bounded and intersected by great rivers, and the most influential was perhaps told in the Epic of Gilgamesh. It certainly was the source for the biblical account of Noah and the Ark. I can't imagine anyone who reads the epic for him or herself viewing the biblical account as unique ever again.

Now Gilgamesh was a great warrior and king. He was part god and part mortal not unlike Hercules who would come about in Greek mythology many years later. In the beginning of the epic there is a man named Enkidu who is also remarkable in his heroism and agility. His innocence like Samson's hair has given him the ability to run with the gazelles, and all of the animals in nature befriend him. Alas he meets a beautiful woman, a harlot who seduces him. He is enthralled with love, and lust. Afterward his knees have weekend. He can no longer keep up with gazelles, and all the animals who had befriended him were now afraid.

In the bible the affection of animals isn't lost until after the flood when El gives up the animals to Noah and his descendants for food. As for innocence, it is lost in the Garden of Eden when Adam and Eve taste the forbidden fruit of "knowledge." As for Enkidu, he learns from the harlot about Gilgamesh, and as heroes are wont to do, sets out to make his acquaintance. The epic unfolds. As time goes by the aging Gilgamesh is fraught with the reality of his mortality. He learns though of a secret, a magic plant, that can bring him rejuvenation. The journey to it is well nigh impossible, a heroes journey to be sure, so he sets off to acquire the boatman that can take him across the mystical waters to the isle of paradise that resides on the edge between worlds where the sun rises on the horizon.

Once there he will meet Utnapishtim and his wife the only two mortals to ever receive immortality from the gods. Gilgamesh succeeds, but is exhausted. Utnapishtim tells him his story and is kind enough to reveal to Gilgamesh the location of this one plant. It is prickly and painful to the touch, but if ingested it will rejuvenate one

to the days of youth. Unfortunately it is at the bottom of the sea. Gilgamesh is not thwarted. He ties stones upon his feet and is drawn quickly down. He retrieves the plant, cuts himself loose, and swims back up to the boat.

He and the boatman return for home. Nibbles from the plant provide just enough stamina to recover from the ordeal, and once he reaches shore Gilgamesh refreshes himself in a nice pool of fresh water. The restoration of his youth and the extension of his great reign capture his imagination. Ah, but just then a serpent, damn sneaky snake, comes up from the pool and makes off with the magic plant. Snakes too are a prominent nemesis in the mythology of several cultures. Any creature that slithers about and can shed its old parched skin for a fresh new one has got to be a villain.

Naturally we find the snake in the Garden of Eden story, a story that is less about original sin than, like Gilgamesh, squandered immortality. It is worth noting to readers that in the biblical story the snake doesn't really lie. The fruit from the tree of knowledge of good and evil isn't going to cause death per se, but by eating it, as we have already seen, El and the others with him, presumably the other gods, will expel them from the garden paradise and deny their access to the magic plant, the tree of life.

To regress just a bit, during the epic story Utnapishtim revealed to Gilgamesh how he and his wife became immortal. It had come to pass that Enlil, one of the high Babylonian gods, god of storm among other things, decided to be rid of mortals. Ea the wise god wasn't a big fan of Enlil's plan so he made it possible for Utnapishtim to learn of it. Enlil was going to bring a deluge to destroy

the mortal humans and the creatures of the earth. Even the gods would shutter and flee from the calamitous event.

Ea bid Utnapishtim to abandon worldly goods and save his life. Utnapishtim commits to the endeavor of building a massive ship, an ark that was to be as wide as it was long. The building of the ark follows the pattern of a seven day cycle and it is complete on the seventh day. Utnapishtim has used all of his resources to bribe the townspeople to assist in the massive work, and just before the great storm he is able to gather the animals, his wife, children, and household all onto the boat and get it launched onto the water.

The Epic of Gilgamesh records this mythical story in great detail, and there can be no doubt this is the prototype for the biblical story of Noah and the Ark. "On the fifth day I laid her framework. One (whole) acre was her floor space. Ten dozen cubits the height of each of her walls, ten dozen cubits each edge of the square deck (Tablet XI)." Later Utnapishtim states "All my family and kin I made go aboard the ship. The beasts of the field, the wild creatures of the field, all the craftsmen I made go aboard. "The flood ensues raging for seven days until all is deluged. Then "the sea grew quiet, the tempest was still, the flood ceased. I looked at the weather: Stillness had set in, and all of mankind had returned to clay."

The ship comes to rest upon a Mount Nisir, and for seven days the waters subside. "When the seventh day arrived, I sent forth and set free a dove. The dove went forth but came back; since no resting place for it was visible, she turned round. Then I sent forth and set free a swallow. The swallow went forth, but came back …. Then I sent forth and set free a raven. The raven went forth and,

seeing that the waters had diminished, He eats, circles, caws, and turns not around. Then I let out (all) to the four winds and offered a sacrifice." The gods smell the fragrant offering and eventually Utnapishtim and his wife receive immortality though they must dwell far away at the "mouth of the rivers" – a mythical place no ordinary mortal will ever find.

This too can be compared to the Garden of Eden story where the Tree of Life at the heart of mythical Eden is blocked by Yahweh-Elohim such that mortals will never eat from it. The rainbow does not occur in the Gilgamesh flood story, but it does come about in the Enuma Elish creation story where the god Enlil presents his bow to the victorious god Marduk. The bow-star, as it were, was stretched forth in the sky as a sign honoring Marduk's greatness.

Anyone who has read the biblical story of Noah can see the way the Epic of Gilgamesh provided source material. There are some interesting differences that give us a clue about the use of myths from one culture to the next. When we break down the Noah story we can see an early version that involves the god El or Elohim. This version may reflect the way the ancient Canaanites who worshiped El appropriated the story from the even more ancient Babylonians and replaced one god for the other. By the time the story reaches its present form with Yahweh being involved, that is the Yahweh worshiped by the post exilic Jews, it is obvious they want to elevate their own emerging religion.

The story of Noah is such an awkward story. It is so problematic for a rational mind that most preachers don't even tell the whole story when they talk about it before

their congregations. There are after all usually small children present. For this reason clergy, especially conservative evangelicals like to skip Genesis 6:1-4 and go straight to Yahweh's displeasure with human beings who's every thought were evil all the time. The story actually begins with a throwback to the Canaanite god El who had seventy or so sons who were also gods.

"When people began to multiply on the face of the ground and daughters were born to them, the sons of Elohim saw that they were fair; and they took wives for themselves of all that they chose…. The Nephilim were on the earth in those days – and also afterward – when the sons of Elohim went into the daughters of humans, who bore children to them. These were the heroes that were of old, warriors of renown." Yes this is what happens when gods come down and have sex with mortal women. Their offspring, like Gilgamesh, Hercules, etc. are not immortal like the gods, but they are mighty heroes, a tour de force.

El's disdain for gods mixing with mortals leads him to destroy the humans of his making. He can always make more if he wants. Yahweh on the other hand doesn't do that kind of thing nor did the Yahweh of the post exilic Jews have sex with goddesses who bore little gods as their children. These heavenly hosts could no longer exist and soon find themselves being replaced by angels, created and not begotten. Nevertheless this messy rough edge remains in the text and probably as a slight to the Babylonian myths that by the 4th century B.C.E. had become loathsome to the Jews.

Still even for the casual reader of scripture the first reason "God" chose to deluge the earth was because heavenly beings were having sex with human women and

producing half god half mortal heroes. This is pretty untenable even for people who claim to be devout believers. An amazing statistical fact is worth mention here. While millions of people may still attend churches, the number of them who attend bible studies is miniscule in comparison. I contend a story like this is one of the reasons. One doesn't get very far into the bible before encountering things so absurd that the cognitive dissonance is unbearable. It is best left up to preachers to deal with it and let them be the ones to bargain us back into a comfortable denial where god really exists.

We clearly see the evidence where cultures have evolved one from the other. We see the rise and fall of gods based upon the success or failure of human conquests. It is also easy to understand why ancient peoples with no understanding of meteorological climate patterns would presume it was gods bringing about floods, famines, droughts, earthquakes, and the like. The post-exilic Jews who gave us the Old Testament were no different. Ironically they thought they had Yahweh set up pretty well as the high god and had put an end to the shenanigans of gods past.

This lasted only until Christianity begins to emerge, a religion that evolves from several sources one of which is Judaism. It is not difficult to understand why Jews of the late 1st century C.E. and afterward were both threatened and appalled by those who were asserting the divine origin of Jesus. Yahweh becomes quite the hypocrite when he decides to procreate with the mortal Mary and bring forth his "only begotten son."Indeed is there a better model for the adage "Do as I say not as I do?" If I were Jewish I would have been upset too. Even worse perhaps

is the adulterous context of the Joseph, Mary, Jesus, virgin birth story.

In a move that resembles the use of *Prima Nocta*, a practice implicated in the Epic of Gilgamesh and perhaps part of the crime of the Nephilim in Genesis 6, "God" impregnates Mary the young virgin who is already betrothed to Joseph. As such she was technically considered Joseph's wife. By the standards of the Torah given by Yahweh such an act would constitute adultery and be punishable by death. Of course if we put the whole debacle in the perspective of David and Bathsheba, then maybe that is why Jesus had to die.

As with cultures past and the stories they used to legitimize their authority the eventual rise of Roman Christianity assimilated the rough edges and negated the contradictions they revealed with the point of a sword. In this particular case Jesus replaced Zeus. One could accept it or rot in prison, die by sword, be burned at a stake, etc. What did a god have to do with any of it? From the cradle of civilization in ancient Mesopotamia where the stories of gods were first written, carved in stone actually – a process unsurprisingly emulated by the Jewish Moses, to the Canaanites, the Egyptians, the Greeks, the Romans, the Christians, the Muslims, and one might argue the emerging hybrid god of conservative fundamentalist minded Americans, the story is always the same.

Rarely do any of the gods die. They vanish as the people who once believed in them vanish. They are replaced as though they never existed by the might of humans who wield a new story. As long as there is a king, a parliament, a president, an ayatollah, a national interest

or political authority with the right weaponry a god needn't worry about fading away.

The fact is no such thing as a god has ever existed, and the day has finally come for us to put this undeniable reality into perspective. What does "God" have to do with any aspect of our lives? Absolutely nothing and whether the shock of this realization brings one hope or despair, the acceptance of its truth is good news for the future of the human species.

(Quotations, allusions, and paraphrases of ancient texts have been drawn from Ancient Near Eastern Texts: Relating to the Old Testament, Edited by James B. Pritchard, Princeton University Press, 1969. Bible passages are from the NRSV. As it is the author's intention to write for a predominantly lay audience standard academic notation is not being used though sufficient information is given to access any particular work in question. It is suggested that readers research and read these texts for themselves. Most can be acquired at libraries and in some cases through internet sites.)

The Subjective Journey

It was many years ago when a friend ask me if I wanted to join him on an excursion through local corn fields in pursuit of arrowheads. It was a completely legal endeavor, but one I thought to be a ridiculous waste of time. It had never occurred to me that throughout the Ohio River valley all one needed to do to be in contact with an ancient civilization was look down.

Later as a student of archaeology and cultural anthropology my appreciation for history was sharpened, and a world filled with evidence of distant pasts came alive. Today more than any other time in human history we have the capacity to examine the footsteps of ancestors. There will always be more to learn, but what we know at present is as enlightening as it is remarkable.

How far back should we go in order to appreciate the immense struggle our species has endured in order to survive to modern times? The days when we first began to walk upright couldn't have been easy. The thousands upon tens of thousands of years migrating in relatively small groups, gradually settling throughout the globe's broken continents, facing the tough odds of shifting climates, predatory species, and disease honed our human kind into the resourceful and resilient beings we are today.

We found a way to fit in, to survive, to endure; though the fact is modern humans are but a remnant of what once was. The majority of our species perished along the way, and some close relatives like Neanderthals survive only by the fraction of their DNA we have within

us. By the end of the last ice age the stage was set for the trek to modernity.

By way of comparison it is fair to suggest that our distant ancestors didn't "know" much about their world, but they were ever learning. With each successive generation the collective memory grew, and the experience of the past was incorporated and passed on culturally as well as genetically. Tools were refined, wheels were invented, and new patterns of social organization developed. While bit by bit knowledge was gleaned, what people believed shaped the world and gave it meaning.

In this respect we can think about our collective journey as a species as a subjective journey. It is as much a history of ideas, presuppositions, guesses, and even superstitions as anything else. If we think about the last 15,000 years as a scale with the subjective/faith context on one side and the objective/knowledge context on the other, then it is obvious that what we didn't know, or what we believed to be true was the weightier side.

Gradually we gained and accumulated knowledge. We learned what foods could be eaten and what foods were poisonous, which ones had medicinal uses, and which ones could be used for technological purposes. One can only imagine how horrible it must have been to be the guinea pig, the one chosen for trial and error experimentation. Were enemies chosen? Was it the elderly, weak members of the clan, or was it just gradual observation as when one in the group tried the red berries and became ill and died? "Hmm, guess we can't eat that."

Perhaps it would have been nice if there were compassionate divine beings to help lead along the way, to point out the things that were toxic or dangerous. But

there weren't. Human knowledge, ingenuity, and evolution have required incredible fetes of courage wrought with obstacle and sacrifice. To suggest anything less is a gross insult to the dignity of our species in its quest to survive. We have made very costly mistakes, and in fact still do, but to date we face them, learn from them, and do our best to rise above them. There has never been any help from outside.

Actually there is a humorous touch of irony entailed in the notion of gods helping humans. When things were going well for a culture it was generally assumed the gods were pleased. On the other hand when calamity struck, drought, famine, floods, quakes, pestilence, etc. the gods were not happy campers. In many of the ancient myths the personality attributed to gods often includes significant disdain for human beings. Even in the bible is there ever really a time when Yahweh is content to bless the people? Mostly he is depicted as being perpetually angry, jealous, dissatisfied, and condemning of his "stubborn, obstinate, and stiff-necked" people. For everyone else it seems his preference is genocide.

Calamity has not been the sole temptation to our subjective faculty over the many millennia where the positing of gods and spirits is concerned. Early on humans drew many conclusions about reality based upon a variety of experiences. Perhaps the earliest great mystery that led to beliefs regarding a spiritual world was the simple observation of life and death in nature. Living things breathe, and when they die the breath vanishes. Soon after, one withers and returns to the earth. Everything in this world is magical, divine, capable of influencing events, and worthy of reverence.

The veneration of elders and ancestors soon emerges along the path of our subjective journey. It is not difficult to understand why people would believe that those departed were still present as spirits, or that they were available to render assistance. All it takes is an uncanny moment of discovery, or a sick person recovering from an illness, a victory in a conflict, or a successful hunt to render honor to those whose spirits now dwell in the winds. If the physical resemblance the young had to the old wasn't enough to prove a continuity that lasted beyond death, then the human capacity for dreaming provided additional certainty.

The dream world was a spirit's world. The incorporation of shamans, seers, and "witch doctor" figures in ancient clan structures is well documented. The dreamers who had visions or who were perceived to manifest a knack for clairvoyance and the interpretation of omens rose in status. These seers along with their skills for extracting the "magic" from the plant and animal world were among the first humans we can trace who offered "spiritual" or divine explanations for natural phenomena. It is also worth noting that along the way humans discovered the psychoactive properties of many plants. This too enhanced and contributed to the formulation of religious experience in many cultures.

The veneration of ancestors and magical views of nature date back at least to the hunter-gatherer cultures that migrated around the globe after the last ice age. Archaeological evidence also reveals that veneration and worship around mother figures was also practiced quite early. Again it is not difficult to understand why ancients would posit the existence of a great mother or mother

goddess figure ruling over nature. The womb is the sacred source of life, and the mother is the one who nurtures and brings it forth. The birth-life-death-birth cycles in nature revealed a power beyond comprehension, one that was to be revered. During this time clear patterns of social division become evident. Males hunt, gather, support, and protect the clan. Females sustain, proliferate, and in some cases govern.

While it is clear that matriarchal cultures centered on a feminine divine existed in early clan societies, there remains a significant debate over the extent to which these groups existed, the duration of their influence, and the specific details of how they were organized. One likely reason this social structure found it difficult to thrive was conflict among tribal groups especially during times of limited resources.

With males, and likely the strongest males, out hunting, the women, children, and elderly would have been more vulnerable to raids by competing clans. We don't have a lot of data on warfare for the times that predate writing, but artifacts from many prehistoric sites reveal the existence of a variety of weapons that most certainly were used for more than hunting.

Just as superstitions about nature, the veneration of elders, ancestors, and mother figures influenced our subjective journey from prehistoric to modern times, so too did the veneration of great warriors and heroes. Again it is not difficult to understand why our distant ancestors would have placed value on such things as agility, strength, valor, and courage. Success and victory are easily attributed to the will of spirits and eventually gods. Further, those who rose as great warriors claimed power,

power that could only be thwarted by defeat. Gradually alliances are established and the politics of civilization begin to emerge.

By the onset of the Bronze Age about 3500 B.C.E. in ancient Mesopotamia human civilization has advanced immensely. The scale measuring subjective faith based assumptions verses what humans can claim to know objectively is shifting. Over the next two millennia we witness the emergence of writing, great architecture, art, and technological advances that reshape virtually every aspect of human life. Agriculture, the domestication of animals and the capability to sustain urban populations has been evolving for nearly 10,000 years and culminates in the great civilizations from Babylon to Egypt. Other parts of the world including India, China, parts of Europe, and later South America are also experiencing similar advancements.

In most every case regardless of where we venture on the ancient globe the spirits that once explained the unexplainable have become gods and goddesses. The human subjective journey is rooted in the questions "Why?" and "How?", and to this day we struggle to make sense of life, whether it has meaning or purpose. The ancients knew there was male and female, they understood it took both in order for life to continue, and they knew their own ability to survive was inexplicably connected to the natural world.

It is not surprising that the majority of ancient religions could be essentially construed as fertility religions. The earliest of the primordial gods are often likened to some monumental force in nature. In what may be the earliest creation myth ever written, the Enuma Elish,

Tiamat (salt water) and her husband Apsu (fresh water) are the progenitors of the first great gods. The gods procreate and give birth to gods, and each has its role to play or comes to represent some aspect of nature. In time it is assumed that divine activity is present in all aspects of the cosmos, behind the scenes as it were, though evident in the human sphere by such things as the success or failure of military conquest, whether a culture prospered or languished, and in the outcome of geological and meteorological events as it pertained to human activity.

Over time oral traditions and the stories that are passed on from one generation to the next are replaced by the written mythological poetry and narratives extant today. It is likely we will never know the songs sung or stories told by numerous human cultures as they passed on their versions of how we came to be or why the natural world behaves as it does. We can only assume that some of their imaginings are preserved in the written history before us. Effigies of pregnant mothers or phallic statuary can only tell us so much.

If the long steps along the road of human progress were marked by trial and error as knowledge was gained, then no less important was the pursuit to understand cause and effect relationships. The ability to accurately observe the unseen forces at work in nature would be a long time coming. Spirits and gods would direct the fate of human affairs and as religion became more formalized rituals for understanding and influencing the will of the divine developed into a plethora of traditions.

The aspects of life that were crucial for human survival were also crucial to the gods. Breath, blood, procreation, and vanity would become the core conduit

between the human and divine worlds. Gods too like humans want to be remembered, glorified, and recognized for their power. Everything from small effigies kept in personal dwellings to the rise of great temples with elaborate artwork are found in most every place human civilization evolves.

If the gods created human life then all aspects of human life played a role in the veneration of the divine. Incantations speaking the "correct" words the gods wanted to hear were written, songs celebrating the attributes of the gods and their mighty deeds were sung, and dance was no less important for pleasing and entertaining the heavenly realms. We see these patterns emerge in most cultures even though the gods have different names.

The gods also required offerings. Sometimes the offerings were as simple as food and drink. It certainly didn't take our distant ancestors long to figure out the gods really loved the smell of fat roasting and wafting from a nice barbeque. Other times though the gods required blood. Perhaps the most horrid imagination in human history has been the notion that sacrifice, one life for the sake of others' lives, animal and at times human, is required to appease the gods, quell their anger, and bring about the restoration of blessing, fertility, and peace.

It is more than disturbing that today, in the 21st century C.E. the largest and most powerful religions in the world still choose blood as the defining characteristic of their connection to the divine. Jews celebrate, if even symbolically, animal sacrifice on their holiest day of the year. Christianity regards the human sacrifice of Jesus as the "good news" and only path for human salvation.

Islamists regard the slaughter and annihilation of "infidels" as the ultimate will and pleasure of Allah. Blood though is more than simply a tribute to the gods for the life force they made to run through mortal veins. Its origin surely culminates in war and the reality that so many die in order for one people to prevail over another.

Sex too, like death, takes its place along the subjective journey, and early in the development of human civilization it was regarded as a primary way to emulate the gods and pay tribute to their ability to bless the earth with abundance and fertility. The relationship between the feminine and masculine has been one of the most mysterious and confounding in human history. Only as science has emerged in modern times have we come to discover what really takes place in human reproduction.

While the role of a feminine divine was influential in some early human cultures, and continued to be represented in the various goddesses of polytheistic religions, the preferential status of domineering males took center stage. One can see semen. The ovum, on the other hand, required a better pair of eyes. In the patriarchal world the woman was a receptacle, the lesser of the species whose primary role was to receive the male seed and bring forth his issue. It is easy, though the ignorance is quite embarrassing, to understand how women were relegated to the status of property and how polygamy emerged as a dominant structure in the rise of human civilization.

The Hebrew Bible offers an excellent glimpse into many of the common practices of ancient Near Eastern cultures. It is pretty much all there. One sees vividly the social conflicts between rural and nomadic peoples over and against the rise of powerful empires that sought to

centralize authority and bring religion in from the hillsides to the city temples. One sees the broad range of fertility religions, the people's devotion to various gods and goddesses, and the violent evolution toward a male dominated monotheism.

To read these ancient texts without understanding the role of sex in their world is a fool's errand. The overwhelming majority of readers haven't a clue about the rituals, beliefs, and customs associated with fertility based religions, and the relative immaturity of our present day society in regard to sex frequently prevents adequate examination and discussion of the topic. The prevalence of cultic prostitution alone in both Old and New Testaments should require an "R" rating before one ever turns the first page.

To be sure the act of sexual intercourse had meaning on numerous levels. To the ancient mind the male's semen carried the magical ambrosia that made life possible. Its use could certainly be pleasurable as well as procreative, but it could also influence the forces of nature and nature's gods. Intercourse was also an act of power, domination, and authority. What a man did with his "magic wand" didn't necessarily have to involve women. At times animals were used, at times other weaker males were forced to submit, and at times, particularly in the absence of cultic prostitutes, males could voluntarily have intercourse with males. The act itself held meaning and the release of seminal fluid was riddled with superstitions.

Properly understood there are no passages in the bible that adequately address the questions of modern sexuality especially homosexuality. The Levitical code defines incest, prohibits adultery, though its harsh

punishment has more to do with inheritance rights than sex, and prohibits male on male and male on animal intercourse in what appears to be a slight against cultic fertility rituals and possibly rape. One should note that women are not forbidden to have sex with women. In the ancient mind such behavior had no consequences since women were perceived to have no causal relationship to fertility.

Eventually the fertility aspects of polytheistic culture begin to give way to more complex speculations about what it means to be human, and about the destiny of humanity in this life and beyond. For the Jews of the post-Babylonian exile Yahweh emerges as the one true god, a male with no need of a consort, and a god who creates via "word." While Yahweh worship predates the exile period, there is no evidence that the god with his Moses who becomes the center of the canonized Torah by the second century B.C.E. (if even then) has the same characteristics understood by previous generations. By the time of the last editors of the Hebrew Scriptures new and influential ideas have emerged along the subjective journey, and as we have noted, when cultures change so do their gods.

To step back in time just a bit one has to consider the general cosmology of the ancient Near Eastern world. There are other cosmologies, some almost as ancient as with Hindu concepts, but none as influential for human history as that reflected in biblical writings. The world of Genesis is the world of ancient Sumer, Babylon, Canaan, and in most respects Egypt. There is the expansive heavenly realm, the earth, and the netherworld below – Sheol – the shadowy abode of the dead. In the Old Testament there is no "hell" per say, no notion of life after

death or a judgment that separates the righteous from the wicked. These ideas come later, and as with Greek mythology there does develop divisions in the underworld where heroes fare a bit better than the average mortal.

For the Israelites, like most throughout the Fertile Crescent who sought the blessing of gods through rites of fertility, sacrifice, and incantation, the emphasis was on the land of the living. All will eventually "go the way of the earth," but the "blessed" will carry on through their offspring. The favor of the gods meant continuity. The problem was there wasn't continuity. Wars, floods, famines brought calamity in due season to all peoples. The explanation was almost always the displeasure of the gods. Even the Hebrew prophets claimed their god was so displeased with the people that he chose their enemies to conquer and enslave them. What else could be the reason?

Gradually human beings began to realize the "magic" didn't work. The silent voice of the gods was only known through the words of prophets and priests who all too often spoke for the status quo. Some prophets were dissidents, but most held the company line cajoling the people to do more and give more or succumb to fate. The priests carried the weight of authority imbued upon them by kings, and for all the pomp and circumstance the will of god was only shown to them through the casting of lots. Gods do not speak, but when the dice are thrown they nod their heads.

These superstitions sadly persist to this day. There are preachers who in seeking god's inspiration for their sermons write several verses on separate slips of paper, toss them in the air, and whichever lands closest is god's will. Numerous people in their devotion to reading the

bible will open it randomly and subsequently believe that god led them to a particular passage. Worst of all is when preachers pick a current event or situation that bothers them then go searching the bible for a passage they can make fit the conclusion they have already drawn.

Emotions, political biases, theological presuppositions, and social opinions lead easily to the subjective assumption that "god has put this in my heart." This delusional pattern of supplanting reason for superstition is as troubling now as it was for our distant ancestors. The root problem is the same – gods do not speak, and beyond that, the maxims revealed to mortals that offer guarantees for a good and prosperous life do not work.

The traditional wisdom of the Hebrew Bible came to suggest that "the righteous will prosper, but the wicked will perish."This always sounds good in principle, but life doesn't work that way. The Book of Job provides the counterpoint. The same fate happens to all. Sometimes really wicked people succeed and prosper, while all too often good, righteous people are stricken with illness or calamity. The gods do not weigh in or keep their promises. Worse, for cultures who believed the promise of continuity, that their land and way of life was secure, to be passed on to their children and children's children, the will of the gods rang hollow and empty.

For millennia the religious ideas associated with primitive cosmologies were weighed and measured, but they were found wanting. It was time for something new. To the subjective mind there had to be more than this one mortal life. If for no other reason than justice there had to be something else something that brought judgment upon

the unrighteous and reward to the good and deserving. What happens next along this journey in speculation is essentially a philosophical revolution, and its long history is only now beginning to wane as human evolution is poised for a new step into the expanding universe.

The Jews who returned to Palestine after the Exile brought with them more than their own ethnic and cultural history. It is clear that the influence of Babylonian mythology compelled the editors of the Torah, Genesis in particular, to create a distinctly Jewish version of these ancient traditions. More so they sought to establish a distinct monotheism centered on the authority of the Jerusalem temple cult. Under Persian governance they were permitted to establish their religion, but there would be no monarchy. The books Ezra and Nehemiah reflect a stringent and ultra conservative attempt to demand radical faithfulness from those who returned. Obviously they believed such measures were required to please Yahweh and win his favor. The ambition for a restored empire would linger long though come to naught.

The question as to whether Yahweh would be pleased became rather moot because the people were not. From the 5th century B.C.E. to the end of the 1st century C.E. following the Roman destruction of Jerusalem and its temple the "biblical" world was riddled with conflict and division. More to the point, it was being challenged by new ideas. It had become painstakingly clear to many that the "old" days would not return, that times where one could live in peace and abundance passing this life on for future generations were not to be – at least not in this world.

As we have seen through the discovery of the Dead Sea Scrolls the period when the Hebrew bible was being collected, edited, and set into a permanent form was a prolific time of writing for the Jews. There was also the Apocrypha which protestant Christians do not include in their bible. The Dead Sea Scrolls revealed a much larger community with ideas that in many respects contradicted the Jerusalem authorities. And there was also the rabbinic tradition of the Pharisees, the teachers of the law, and the development of non-temple based synagogues where the traditions expanded and evolved. By the end of the 1st century C.E. the foundation for modern Judaism was formed.

Once again it suffices to point out that in spite of the fervor of modern religious fundamentalists who assert the bible or even Koran stands alone as the inspired "Word of God," there are many books, many writings, and many ideas that shaped the course of Judaism, Christianity, and Islam. Creationists may find it an easy trek to deny the antiquity of fossils, but it is impossible, save through the eyes of denial, to avoid the written history that exists layer upon layer over the last 5000 years.

One of the most important contributors to the evolution of modern religions is a person rarely mentioned. A harmonizer of sorts, the Persian Zoroaster brought ideas from early Hindu thought into the Babylonian world. The idea of the divine that emerged with his synthesis set forth a course that would shape the thought of philosophy and religion for centuries to come. It was Zoroaster that began to speak of a cosmic eternity where good is rewarded and evil negated. His dualistic universe where good brings good into the world and evil

brings chaos was simple and seemed to provide a more rational explanation for cause and effect relationships. Zoroaster placed emphasis on human choice, and in fact could be credited with originating the concept of "free will."

From his thought it was plausible to imagine an afterlife, the existence of heaven and hell, a final divine judgment, a harmonious union with an infinite divine, a division between good and evil, light and dark, noble and ignoble, and an ultimatum for human beings to be accountable for their choices. If there was appeal to the Persians where the Jewish religion of Yahweh was concerned, it was in the potential for their one god to represent the Zoroastrian divine.

The Greeks too incorporated the ideas of Zoroaster, and none perhaps more completely than Plato. As Hellenization transformed the Mediterranean and Near Eastern world philosophical schools emerged and though polytheism would continue for a few more centuries it was waning. The gods of stone were giving way to more transcendent and ethereal imaginings of divinity in the cosmos. By the time of the Pax Romana the influence of Plato's notion of pure forms was widely felt.

Gnostic communities began to develop and spread their newly calibrated ideas about what was "really" going on in the larger universe. Taking their cue from the Greek word for knowledge Gnostics generally came to believe that the true divine was spiritual perfection. Knowledge, truth, goodness, honor, peace, and all things virtuous were the ultimate realities. The world, all that is physical, all that is flesh and blood is corrupt, impure, and temporary. Human beings, or at least some, through the unfolding of

cosmic conflict carry within them the light of the great heavenly divine. The destiny of this light is to be freed from its fleshy bonds and return into an eternal union with its divine source. How this "soul" is to be liberated from its earthy prison becomes a matter of grand speculation and heated debate.

Perhaps the most successful illusion in history is the religion modern readers discover in the New Testament. Scholars have tried for well over a century to discover the historical Jesus, but mostly to no avail. This may strike some readers as a peculiar thing to suggest, but in truth the person called Jesus is more taken for granted than anything else. The evidence does not bode well for Christianity.

We do know a good bit about the first century C.E., and when we begin to fit the pieces of the puzzle together what most people have come to believe about Jesus and the existence of the New Testament church isn't the picture that forms before us. Zealous preachers love to enthrall their congregations with the notion that Christianity exploded like a wildfire after the resurrection of Jesus. But did it? It is rather disconcerting to that claim when one discovers that scant mention of such a movement was recorded by Jewish or Roman historians of that period. Josephus in a brief section of Antiquities of the Jews (III.3) mentions Jesus as a wise teacher and doer of wonderful works who had a following among some Jews and Gentiles. He states that the "tribe of Christians, so named from him, are not extinct at this day."

Josephus mentions John the Baptist, James the brother of Jesus, and acknowledges that Jesus was called Christ. One has to be careful here. Josephus hardly makes

a big deal of it. The tradition that rose around the person of Jesus was that he was a descendant of David, a wise teacher, and his followers may have believed he was "anointed" to be the heir to David's throne. The term "Christ" as with the word "messiah" in Hebrew is not a divine name, but a title meaning "anointed" that applied to the Davidic monarchy. The hope for a renewed monarchy and independence from Roman occupation was a major issue for some Jews in the first century.

We know from the Dead Sea Scrolls that a rival community of Jews, possibly the Essenes, had come to believe in the coming of two messiah figures. One would be priestly and the other the heir to David's throne. We also know from the War Scroll that there remained a belief that Yahweh would sustain his righteous remnant in a victorious holy war. Naturally he did not, and after numerous insurrections and persistent conflicts dealing with the Jews of Jerusalem and Palestine the Romans leveled Jerusalem and its temple in 70 C.E. The remaining dissidents were pursued to Masada where they either starved to death or committed suicide before the Roman siege could overtake them. This ended the authority of the Jewish priesthood, temple worship, most apocalyptic or messianic forms of Judaism, and left primarily the rabbinic Jews who formed the basis for modern Judaism.

What we know from Josephus is that the Jesus he mentions was executed by the Romans, presumably for treason over his "Christ" moniker, John the Baptist a bit earlier for offending King Herod, and James a bit later for his criticism of the high priest. These events all occurred prior to the time any writings emerged from groups that identified themselves as Christian. The most likely

scenario is that there was a movement rooted in messianic Judaism, in the apocalyptic thought similar to if not connected to the Dead Sea Scroll community and one which involved some pairing of Jesus and John the Baptist.

Using the gospels and New Testament writings as historical documents is problematic for several reasons; however they connect Jesus and John the Baptist and also suggest that both individuals had a following after their deaths particularly with Jews and some Gentiles in the larger Mediterranean world. What seems to be the case is that the idea of one god, a god that required compassion, generosity, and the values already established by Plato, Aristotle, and others was catching on.

The New Testament, like the Old, is confusing to the average reader largely because it is a collection of writings arranged in such a way as to imply a chronology that is inaccurate to the writings themselves. The letters of Paul, for example, predate the gospels. The gospels themselves are actually anonymous writings given their titles by the community that produced them. Mark is generally thought to be the oldest dated to around 65 C.E., Matthew and Luke-Acts c. 80 C.E., and John closer to the beginning of the second century. We also have the explicitly Gnostic Gospel of Thomas which is as early if not earlier than Mark.

What this confirms beyond any doubt is that one of the reasons the mythos of Jesus continued beyond his execution was its connection to the emerging popularity of Gnosticism. At this point trying to find the "real" Jesus is a bit like playing "Where's Waldo." We know Paul was writing and evangelizing less than two decades after Jesus' execution. To understand why, one must remove the

Christian glasses created at Nicea in 325 C.E. under the authority of the Roman emperor Constantine and read the texts with the broader understanding of what we know today.

The stories about Jesus suggest he grew up in Nazareth in the region of Galilee. We now know that the town of Sepphoris was located just next door. In the days of Jesus' childhood it was an eclectic community with theatre and opportunities for education. If there is truth that he was the son of a carpenter or possibly even stone mason, he would have been quite familiar with Sepphoris. He would have been fluent in Greek and would have learned much about the ideas permeating the larger world. If he was in fact a wise teacher and we can assume the gospels reflect some of the things he taught -- love, compassion, forgiveness, self-denial, mercy, generosity, giving up worldly possessions, etc. – he was the perfect Gnostic sage.

Scholars that have sought him out through the pages of the gospels have endured a near impossible task. The Jesus written about on these pages had already been chosen by several varieties of Gnostic communities before the first words were ever put to parchment. They wrote about their Gnostic redeemer, their magi, and the one who had solved Gnosticism's largest philosophical problem. Mortals, in spite of the potential for good, nevertheless are flesh and corrupt. How exactly then is one to liberate the divine light held within? Momentarily we'll thank Paul for the answer, but even Zoroaster had taught that a savior figure would come at the end of days to bring about harmony, judgment, and resurrection.

The gospel writers used a common biographical genre to write about their hero. Jesus was not the only "great" person or legendary figure to have his life chronicled in a heightened mythical form. The common pattern meant a virgin or divine birth, a life characterized by miraculous or heroic deeds, and a remarkable tale. It was the Greco-Roman way. The gospel writers also cast their stories about Jesus through the lens of both Jewish and contemporary cultures obscuring the chance for a genuine glimpse at an historical person. Jesus is depicted like Moses, Poseidon, enacts Old Testament scenarios, and even quotes Psalms from the cross.

In the end it is clear that the gospels are created from source material. There were common sayings and oral traditions that were worked into written accounts. Matthew and Luke used Mark and then expanded it in ways pertinent to their communities. The gospels do not agree with each other where the persona of Jesus is concerned and at times with major details like his resurrection. Further when we begin to look at the larger presence of Jesus in the Gnostic world we find a significant amount of conflict surrounding who he was, what he taught, and what was required of adherents in order to benefit from his salvific ministry to humankind.

Scholars will likely disagree to some extent over the suggestion that Gnosticism as a full blown movement existed in the Greco-Roman world. In some respects it did not. Numerous philosophers from Plato onward were positing a variety of ideas and developing followings. The period from the 4th century B.C.E. into the 4th Century C.E. was a prolific era for faith claims and subjective speculation about the cosmos. It was evident that the

traditional polytheistic mythology was no longer sufficient to explain nature or the nature of humanity. Gnostic thought, that is a world view that divided reality into physical versus spiritual, temporary versus eternal, good versus evil, mundane versus sublime, etc., was at the forefront of many minds. It is fair to describe this era as Gnostic because the value being placed on concepts like knowledge, reason, and transformation from the corporeal into the incorporeal marked an evolutionary step along the human subjective journey.

As anyone who has embraced Christianity or read the New Testament knows Paul more than any other created the foundation for the religion that eventually became Christianity. By his own admission Paul never met Jesus in person. He appears to be a member of the Pharisees, a zealous Jew but also a Roman citizen, and committed to the persecution of a rival group of messianic Jews who were proclaiming that Jesus as the Davidic messiah was raised from the dead and would soon return. Not only was such a movement troublesome for Sadducees and the official priesthood of the temple who wanted to avoid conflict with Rome, it was also problematic for the Pharisees who had achieved a relatively solid status of authority in the larger synagogue based community in Palestine and beyond.

In spite of the emerging traditions that suggested the followers of Jesus sought to help the poor, encourage peace, and devote themselves to esoteric pursuits, those proclaiming Jesus were considered heretics, blasphemers, and dangerously close to insurrectionists. Paul though has a change of heart, an epiphany, and in a transition that reveals his affinity for contemporary philosophy he creates

a remarkable hybrid that combines Judaism with Gnostic cosmology. The result is a movement that can speak to the broader culture and gradually transcend both the waxing conflicts within his native Judaism and the waning ideas that undergirded the polytheistic structures of the Roman world.

As a Pharisee Paul had already embraced the notion of resurrection and divine judgment, yet one key that he has been influenced by Gnostic thought is the fact that he has given up on this world as the venue for human transformation. For Paul Jesus is the conduit between worlds. At the same time, however, Paul is not the only one positing Jesus as the Gnostic redeemer. The textual evidence we have today suggests at the very least that the Thomas based community was as early as any and likely contemporary with Paul. One should also keep in mind that Thomas, or Didymus, meant "twin," and it was likely meant to imply that the followers of the Gnostic Thomas tradition mirrored the "authentic" Jesus.

Paul did not agree. For him there was a genuine flaw in the human condition and one so severe that no manner of devotion, sacrifice, abstinence, or study could remedy. It was exactly at that point that he found his cosmic Christ. Jesus could represent the fulfillment of all that Judaism brought to the table. He was the sacrificial lamb and scapegoat of Yom Kippur, but also the incarnation of the divine the Jews knew as Yahweh but others knew as logos, gnosis, and truth. Paul imagined that it was grace, unmerited favor, which was the heart of god's will. It was generosity, mercy, and kindness that represented the yearning will of his creator to act in such a way that would differentiate between all that was good and that which was

corrupt and false. What no ordinary human could achieve was achieved in Paul's "second Adam."

Persons reading Paul's letters through the historical take of Roman Catholicism, and even worse through the lens of the Protestant Reformation, are doomed to misunderstand Paul and his grounding in what ultimately became a centrist Gnostic point of view. "But now apart from the law, the righteousness of God has been disclosed…the righteousness of God through faith in Jesus Christ for all who believe….it was to prove that [God] himself is righteous and that he justifies the one who has faith in Jesus." (Rom. 3:21-26) The point here is in the nuance of the Greek text. Paul is not talking about whether you or I have faith, but is asserting that Christ's faith on humanity's behalf is sufficient.

Paul became convinced Jesus' resurrection was the proof that god had acted on behalf of humanity, and now the pathway to perfect union with the divine was open to all that would simply believe. This view was at odds with other Gnostics who believed much more was required. For Paul the burden was on god, a burden that would be enacted and active in the human sphere through the "Holy Spirit," god's gift to those who acquiesced to the proposition.

Paul, like other Gnostic thinkers, viewed the material world as corrupt. The human condition was characterized as idolatrous in so much as human beings were preoccupied with being human. By following Jesus one's earthen vessel would be filled with the divine and prepared to exchange the mortal for the immortal. Yet unlike most other Gnostic teachers that emerged Paul's

view of day to day life in the world was a balance between the sacred and mundane.

People could go about their lives, continue to participate in the broader culture, marry and have families if they wanted, or not, work, and fulfill their social obligations. The presence of Christ meant an inner transformation that would continue to grow until death and ultimately find fulfillment in resurrection and union with god. Male, female, Greek, Jew, slave, or free were all irrelevant since all would be one in Christ. The general view held by Gnostics was that only the spiritual was "real," and Paul was no different.

The failure to recognize Paul's theology as reflective of the emerging Gnostic paradigm has led many to think of him as liberal and egalitarian. Unfortunately he was not, and while, for example, it appears at times that he elevates the status of women, which in some cases he does, it is only in the context that gender is ultimately lost in the spiritual. Like Plato before him eternal bliss will not require the existence of a feminine component. Paul does not struggle against political corruption, fight to elevate the rights of women, or work to end slavery. On the contrary, the task at hand is to transcend the world not change it.

On the other hand Paul does struggle quite frequently. From his letters we know of conflicts in most every community he seeks to proselytize. He has rivals within the Jewish synagogue community, rivals in the secular world, and rivals within the Gnostic Jesus movement he represents. It is obvious that Paul met with some measure of success in developing a following, but it

is equally evident that he wasn't the only "evangelist" out there seeking the patronage of followers.

There is a core assumption that Christians as well as New Testament scholars fail to challenge. At first glance a quick read of the New Testament gives one the sense that there existed a rather homogenous movement of the divine that begins with Jesus' birth, sweeps through the 1st century as a tour de force leaving behind a well organized church, and culminates poised for Christ's triumphal return in the book of Revelation. Paul's epistles and the subsequent writings of his students that carried his school of thought beyond his death form the center of what becomes "this church." The problem in contemporary terms is that such a conclusion is based on a "photoshopped" portrait of church history.

While there is evidence that Paul wrote, travelled to different communities with his message, and developed a following, there is no evidence that the communities to which he wrote agreed with him or obeyed his teaching. In fact the best evidence is to the contrary. The transition from small groups embracing the notions of itinerant Gnostic philosophers into imperial Christianity is nearly a three hundred year journey fraught with conflict and competition. It is not until after Paul's death that the gospels depicting Jesus' earthly life and teachings are written. By that time there are numerous groups vying for recognition and authority. Paul's writings provided a common thread, but were by no means understood the same way by the various sects that used them.

By the 2nd century the title Christian had wide usage, but there were significant disagreements over what was considered authentic. The politics of Rome undulated back

and forth between tolerance of Christian groups and outright persecution. The Christians that lent themselves to a more ascetic Gnostic world view were perhaps more clandestine than those who advocated a vigorous public proclamation, but on both counts Rome could view Christians as either a positive community known for austerity and compassion or a dangerous and seditious threat. Christian groups were winning converts, and from Rome to Alexandria churches were becoming well established.

It is rather ironic that a movement which celebrated the inner transformation of adherents via the presence of god's spirit, a spirit that was to produce peace, love, kindness, gentleness, godliness, and self-control, could be so harshly human in its persistent conflicts and contentious debates. The early traditions that originated within the Jewish world had become predominantly Gentile, and the mythos of Jesus had stolen or transformed Yahweh into the Titan "Father" whose begotten son made even Zeus tremble with fear.

Many early Christians were content to focus on inner transformation, spiritual enlightenment, and a path that would transcend the physical world. But the emerging mainstream was increasingly concerned about transforming the political, religious, and socio-economic world at hand. The 2nd and 3rd centuries saw the rise of dedicated apologists like Clement, Polycarp, Justin Martyr, Ireneaus, etc. Their writings were intense and frequently critical not only of those within the broader movement with whom they disagreed but also against Rome and its polytheistic cultus." These church leaders represented an emerging orthodoxy, consensus was being honed, and

alliances were being built upon formalized confessions. Once again we see that where gods fail to act human beings are quite prepared to act in their stead.

An accurate picture of the rise of Christianity reveals the rough edges, the diversity of views, and most importantly its origin in Gnostic thought. Gradually over three centuries churches emerged with institutional form. Their polity emulated Roman guilds and temple cults, and the primary rituals were comfortably centered on Aristotle's four great elements. The "church" had its watery baptism, its earthy meal of flesh and blood, its airy breath of holy spirit, and of course its tongues of fire proclaiming the ethereal divine. This emerging religion was different though. The trek from the days of Zoroaster to Jesus came to represent a major shift in the way human beings would construe the universe and our place in it.

For all the guesses made along our subjective journey that proved unsatisfactory, all the totems, magic, spirits, goddesses and gods that in impotence fail, Christianity seemed a logical conclusion. God alone causes all things and cannot be affected by mortals. The will of god is supreme and eternal. All mortals are sinners, flawed, and in need of salvation. The atoning sacrifice of the one sinless being in history is the only remedy. The benefits to be bestowed upon human beings as well as punishment to be meted do not occur in this world. God cannot be tested, thwarted, or even known save through his Christ. One will either choose the good and be rewarded after death or choose wrong which means a more likely imminent death in this world and hell to follow. With the onset of the 4th century only one thing was lacking to see this world view rise to a lasting prominence in human history.

One must muse a bit about the evolution of civilization had Christianity not captured the interest of an emperor or matured into political expediency. Great minds from Aristotle on were making substantive strides in understanding mathematics and in applying an objective methodology toward knowing the natural world. Even the existence of atoms had been postulated well before Plato and possibly before Zoroaster. And one must celebrate with a bent toward melancholy the contributions to reason being made by persons like Hypatia of Alexandria who was murdered by Christians at the height of her genius.

The older religions were waning and many had disappeared altogether. One must wonder the extent to which Judaism would have survived had it not been for the periodic sympathy of Christians who somewhat reluctantly held them dear for Jesus' sake and their inclusion in New Testament prophecies. Frankly one must wonder if Christianity and Gnostic schools of thought would have withstood an age of reason. But as in all times past the gods change as politics change, as power secures its authority, and as peace is forged through war. To this end Christianity has proven the near perfect religion though Islam shares the stage.

The story of Constantine the Great is remarkable to say the least. His rise to power is a notable mix of military expertise and political cunning. His mother Helena was sympathetic to Christianity if not a Christian herself. Constantine came to share her sympathies. At the turn of the 4th century Diocletian had initiated what was perhaps the worst period of persecution endured by Christians. Their bishops were imprisoned, property confiscated, and writings burned. Constantine does not seem to have been

party to the persecutions, but at that time he appeared neutral at best.

As Constantine rose in status through his military victories he gradually gained his place among Rome's conflicted tetrarchs. With control over Rome's most formidable army Constantine in what was part defense and part ambition began the campaign to defeat the other Caesars and claim for himself the sole unified title of emperor. In October of 312 Constantine was approaching Rome and preparing to engage his rival Caesar Maxentius. The night before the battle at the Milvian Bridge Constantine claimed to have a vision where Christ bid him to use the chi-rho (sign of Christ) as he went forth to conquer his enemies. The next day Constantine's army advanced with the sign of Christ upon their standards and shields. It was a decisive victory for Constantine who now shared power with only Licinius his brother-in-law.

In 313 they signed the Edict of Milan which ended the persecution against Christians, restored their property, and returned their treasures. Christianity was now a legally recognized religion in the Roman Empire though it would be another decade before it took another step toward prominence. By 324 Constantine had defeated Licinius and been elevated as the sole ruler of Rome. In 325 he initiated the Council of Nicea. Constantine himself presided though technically he was still a pagan and didn't accept baptism as a Christian until the time of his death.

At this council the church "universal" was born. The ideas and practices of what would be recognized as Christian were weighed and measured. Those outside the accepted religion would be branded heretics, imprisoned

or executed, and their scriptures destroyed. This and subsequent councils of church officials under the scrutiny of government created the New Testament and the religion of Christianity. As for Constantine he had one great god whose authority on earth resided in one great priest and one great king.

It is doubtful that this is the religion envisioned by Paul when he took the ailing concepts of his native Judaism and translated them into an esoteric way of life that could have appeal beyond ethnic lines in the larger Roman world. His risen Christ had acted on behalf of all humanity and established the ultimate pathway to the divine. Paul's Christian paradigm successfully connected the dots between Zoroaster, Plato, and the Gnostic philosophical ideas that were gaining appeal in his day. Paul created a concrete connection to an abstract cosmos that seemed to make sense, but there were problems that he likely did not anticipate.

While Paul was alive it is clear that he struggled to press the particular nuances of his ideas. But there were obviously others with competing views that also impacted the development of this nascent movement. Jesus had to be defined and explanations for why him and not someone else were needed. The gospel writers attempted to address this problem. For Mark the story of Jesus' rise as the Christ figure begins with his baptism by John the Baptist. For Thomas the evidence of Jesus' divinity was in his secret teachings, the light of his knowledge which could only be the appearance of the true divine.

Matthew and Luke however went further in their attempt to connect Jesus to Yahweh and link the emerging divine father of the Gnostic world view to the god(s) of the

ancient past. Those who followed in Paul's footsteps seem to decry this step as foolish and unnecessary since the resurrection was all that was required to show god's approval. The genealogies of Matthew and Luke do not agree and apparently became a point of division and conflict. The idea of a divine birth may have appealed to gentile followers who would have expected such a thing for a great hero, but it was certainly anathema to those within Judaism.

While it was important to Jews to be able to verify that Jesus was a descendant of David, it was absurd that Yahweh would have sex with Mary and impregnate her with his seed. This was after all the very reason Elohim/Yahweh decided to deluge the world. Worse, that god would choose a young woman who was already pledged in betrothal was adultery. Modern Christians should consider this vain contradiction before taking the virgin birth literally. The one verse in Isaiah which was a metaphor promising Yahweh's love for a fledgling Israel was a tough sell for Matthew and Luke. The conflict it generated wasn't resolved until an emperor put his stamp of approval on the notion that Jesus was both fully human and fully divine.

The author of John fares a bit better as he describes the coming of Jesus into the world with the language of Greek philosophy and Gnostic thought. Jesus is the "Word," the "Logos," "the light of the world," and the "way, truth, and life." Christianity was emerging and leaving Judaism behind. From the early apologists to the church authorized by Constantine the Hebrew Scriptures were the fodder for picking and choosing whatever passages were necessary to give grounding to Christianity.

After Nicea it didn't matter because the authority of the church would control the story for the next 1200 years until the Protestant Reformation. By the vote of councils or decrees from the papacy Mary would become known as the "Mother of God," the will of the church would on pain of death be extended as the "will of god," and the sharp point of an upended cross would assist multitudes in accepting the "good news."

Any student of history must truly marvel at the ease of which gods fade and disappear. The great Marduk of Babylon whose bow star once marked the heavens with the sign of his power vanished like the colors of the rainbow as the sun retakes a stormy sky. Horus, Isis, with all the pharaohs of Egypt contently joined Anubis only to become quiet stones dug up by scholars and displayed for tourists. O Olympus, how uncanny is the silence of your departure, a fading mist without even the slightest clap of thunder from a disgruntled Zeus. And what of the many others, Odin, Loki, and Thor whose best destiny has been the big screen where the cult of followers sip soft drinks and munch buttery popcorn? The evidence provided by history is overwhelming. In all cultures, and in all places, regardless of the subjective imaginings that brought gods into the human sphere, they all vanish when we vanish, or perhaps better stated, when we are vanquished.

Christianity did in fact take much of the world by storm though it did experience significant division from within. This too was as much political as it was religious. By the 7th century Christianity was divided into the west with its allegiance to the Vatican in Rome and the Byzantine east centered in Constantinople. The Roman Catholics controlled most of Europe and portions of North

Africa, and the Eastern Church had begun to expand as far as Russia. Palestine, much of the Near East, the Arabian Peninsula, and much of Egypt felt the waning influence from conflicted Christianity, and as the case tends to be, nature abhors a vacuum.

Mohammed, a well travelled and knowledgeable Arab, sees the opportunity to unite the Arab peoples who until then have persisted in being divided into warring clan structures. Mohammed was a cunning politician and a capable warrior. He knew Judaism, Christianity, the story of Rome, as well as all the polytheistic traditions still alive in Mecca. Like pulling a name from a hat he plucked the name Allah from the Kaaba shrine, a name which was easily connected to Yahweh and to the broader culture of Abrahamic peoples. As most religious mystics are wont to do, he journeys to a solitary cave where no one can verify the grand revelation that gives him the Koran. Mohammed pulls a Paul. Unsurprisingly this new religion, Islam, takes the world by storm, and like Christianity, at the point of swords in war.

Islam for many is a case of "one upmanship" over Christianity. One, it eliminates the middle man, sort of. Two, it preserves the Zoroastrian and Gnostic notion of divine judgment after death leaving the work of Allah in human hands on earth. Three, it essentially has but five tenets that can be observed anywhere. One must confess there is no god but Allah and that Mohammed is his prophet, pray five times a day facing Mecca, give alms for the poor, fast and practice self-piety during the holy month of Ramadan, and if possible at least once in one's life make a pilgrimage to Mecca.

Mohammed appropriated both Jewish and Christian traditions as the unfinished work of Allah and recognized Moses and Jesus as lesser prophets. In Islam there would be two classes of people, believers and infidels. Tolerance for infidels continues to be a matter of debate, but putting them to death has been a recurrent remedy in the history of Islam. Islam, like Christianity, experienced serious conflict early on and it has been warring within itself ever since. Sunni Muslims have historically been the majority community and trace their status of authority to the decision following Mohammed's death where the religion and empire was to be ruled by caliphs or ones who were deemed "rightly guided." Abu Bakr was the first.

Shia Muslims disagreed with the way authority was to be passed on and favored a polity where the direct descendents of Mohammed would rule. Ali, Mohammed's cousin and son-in-law was their favored choice, and he did rise as the fourth caliph. However he was eventually assassinated which created the rift that is still violently present to this day.

This chapter has with admittedly broad strokes attempted to articulate nearly 15,000 years of the human journey to the present. The emphasis has been on the subjective presuppositions that in some sense we have been forced to assume or posit to explain why we are here and what it all means. Readers are challenged to recognize the common patterns that have emerged. There are some very important questions to ask. There is a tremendous amount of evidence to evaluate. No doubt to religious readers this has the potential of being a disheartening exercise.

It should be painfully evident that the reason any of us in our culture, whether it be a Christian culture, Muslim culture, Jewish, Hindu, whatever, believe what we do is largely because our ancestors wrought forth these ideas and traditions with a boot upon their necks. The great religions serve first and foremost to legitimize political ideology. In a true step forward in the evolution of human civilization and governance the framers of the US constitution realized that religion had to be separated from power. They had come to believe that reason, not religion, was the basis for human community. Rule of law, law negotiated openly by the governed and based upon the inalienable right to liberty, justice, and the pursuit of happiness in this mortal life was a better process for achieving a balanced and functional society than the whims of divine beings in the hands of tyrants.

How did they come to these conclusions? With the 16th century came the Protestant Reformation, the invention of the printing press, and the birth of modern science. Until then the scale we've been watching that measures human experience between what is subjective or faith based and what constitutes objective knowledge has been leaning toward the subjective. That was about to change.

The Protestant Reformation was just as violent and political as the Roman Church it challenged. For all that is lauded about Luther, Calvin, and others who parented modern theology their work was a travesty of ignorance. Their only source material was the bible which they were doomed to take a face value, and their motivation was a bitter distaste for both Roman Catholicism and the Holy Roman Empire that had dominated Europe for too long.

At a time when the baby should in fact have been thrown out with the bathwater these reformers did not have access to the Near Eastern mythology that gave rise to much of the Old Testament, the Dead Sea Scrolls, the Gnostic texts found at Nag Hammadi, or even the broader range of New Testament texts and fragments we have today. They created a new Christianity rooted in medieval thought and with Catholicism as their frame of reference. They threw out the bathwater but kept the baby.

The greatest contribution made by the reformers was they opened the door for an era of new questions. Soon the Enlightenment with philosophers like Immanuel Kant and Rene Descartes would bring fresh speculation to the table, and with the printing press more and more people would be exposed to emerging ideas. Even more important were the discoveries being made by scientists. Copernicus, with his discovery that the earth moved around the sun challenged one of the oldest assumptions in human history. We were not the center of the universe. We were not the focal point and something else was afoot. Indeed, today with what we know about the universe, and with Carl Sagan's "Pale Blue Dot" narrating our reflections, any viable subjective moment we might entertain transcends the paltry need for ancient gods.

By the 17th century there was a world of interest turning away from the Kings James and popes so and so due largely to discoveries being made by names like Galileo, Kepler, and Newton. Human beings were evolving better pairs of eyes, and we were discovering that physical laws with natural explanations, not gods, were the real rulers of the universe. These discoveries along with philosophical treatises rooted in rational process led

the Jeffersons, Washingtons, and Franklins of the 18th century to posit "a new secular order." To be sure they were deeply religious, or perhaps philosophical, but as their general commitment to Deism and in many cases Freemasonry suggests, these intellectual politicians were poised to embrace a world where explanations based upon evidence superseded superstition.

The weight of the scale between the subjective and objective was shifting and all the more rapidly throughout the 19th and into the 20th century. We were not the center of the universe, gods were not required to exude their sovereignty to make nature run its course, and with Darwin we discovered that creation itself was a myth. We, like all living species on the earth, have evolved over millions if not billions of years. The process itself is one of the most fascinating things ever comprehended through objective methodology, and while we still don't understand every detail, no aspect of any ancient religion is as exciting, inspiring, or enthralling to the human mind as evolution.

From a faith perspective religious readers must grapple with the question "Why?" Why continue to place trust in ideas and world views that quite frankly deserve extinction? Our subjective journey continues. It continues in our musing, in our poetry, in our imaginations, in our speculations about what might be or what comes next, for all of which we have learned to be patient, to wait until we have evidence. We are dripping with faith. Not because faith is knowledge, but because there is so much more to know and we won't know it if we keep drawing conclusions when we simply want to be comfortable with the fiction we are espousing.

Have you ever considered that there is not one piece of information in the bible, not one single revelation or tidbit of knowledge about the natural world or the larger universe that we have discovered through objective, testable, and verifiable evidence, that wasn't either known or assumed by the authors in their time period? For example, Pasteur discovered bacteria in 1862. Germs were the cause of disease not curses from gods. One can understand why an all knowing, all powerful god would not want humans of say the Iron Age to know about fossil fuels, combustion engines, machine guns, or nuclear technology. But what kind of god tells people how to clean and destroy mildew or what kinds of food they can and can't eat, but doesn't tell them about germs?

Really? God couldn't have said "Thou shalt wash thy hands after relieving thyself." It is unfathomable to calculate over all the long ages the number of infants and mothers who have died in the process of childbirth simply because of infections due to unsanitary conditions. Imagine the human suffering that could have been prevented with just a heads up about germs, bacteria, viruses, and the communicability of disease. The gods were pathetically silent.

Subjective aspects of being human will always be part of who we are. There will always be a balance between what we know and the horizons that frustrate our acumen with limitations. One thing we have learned, or at least should have learned, is that "god" is never a suitable filler for the gaps between what is known, yet to be known, or may never be known. "I don't know" is honest, a starting place, but continuing to stick a god in where explanations are lacking is lazy and futile. It is not that

science is the enemy of religion. Science is not a metaphor for a belief system. It is a method, and to date the best method we have for understanding the natural world and our part in it. It just so happens that all these places where gods have been used as answers have been proven false.

Letting go of god is admittedly a difficult and at times disheartening task. In some ways we are hardwired or programmed through thousands of years of experience to believe in supernatural forces. Superstition at times has served us well and has enabled us to be cautious or attentive where potential dangers are concerned. But mostly superstition has been a setback. Where angels fear to tread is usually the place we need to be. Still our emotions confuse us. We think we feel something, something out there that stirs us, which touches us, so it might be god, a divine, and so we are afraid to let go.

Even here science has once again inadvertently removed god from the shelf. We now understand quite clearly that how we feel, our emotions, and moods are caused by the complex chemistry of our brains. This helps us understand why people of most all religions can share similar experiences even though they worship different gods or gather around very different sets of beliefs. Further the person who feels moved to tears in the solemnity of a church service where the organist is softly playing Amazing Grace during communion may discover the same emotional experience as the national anthem is sung before a baseball game. Persons moved to ecstasy in a Holy Ghost revival service where the music is uplifting, the crowd is swaying with hands held in praise, and the preacher is rolling with spirited speech are having the

same chemical experience as someone enjoying their favorite symphony or rock and roll band.

In the end there is nothing unique about religious experience that isn't replicated in similar contexts of non-religious experience. The scale that once gave weight to subjective presuppositions about the mysterious workings of nature and gave gods the glory has given way to the preponderance of evidence and knowledge gleaned through objective research. For those who want to maintain the possibility of a divine out there somewhere it might be well to remember that to date 100% of the gods written into our history have identifiable human origins. Even the notion of a divine intelligence is a human concept.

In every case where people have imagined that gods were at work the evidence has proven otherwise. Gods do not form the galaxies or solar systems, control the orbits of planets, cause the rising of tides, or control the geological and meteorological activity of the earth. Gods neither inflict human beings with disease nor heal them when they are sick. God's did not create the earth, nor is there a shred of evidence that any living thing continues to live in some form beyond its death save through DNA that is passed on or through the brief memory that lingers with those who shared its experience.

God has suffered the fate of humpty dumpty. It is time to find acceptance and move on. Where our subjective journey goes from here is a mystery, as it should be, but it must move forward leaving the past with the dinosaurs to be studied, reflected upon, at times celebrated, but also lamented. Let us remember Ozymandias. Is this not El the ancient bull god of the Canaanites with his consort

Asherah, the original god of the Hebrews? His remains are broken stones, not flesh and bone, or a lasting breath. There was never an El apart from the cultures that carved him into existence. Therefore changing his name to Yahweh is simple math. Zero plus zero still equals zero.

Without El, there is no Yahweh. Without Yahweh there is no heavenly father for Jesus to be his only begotten son. Allah too succumbs to the dissipation of his sources. Zeus went quietly, is it too much to ask that the rest do the same? Do we really need more Joseph Smith's with golden tablets from angels named moron whose grand revelations mysteriously don't exist to be examined? Do we really need to demoralize ourselves with pejorative labels like "sinner" and concoct elaborate schemes that discriminate and pit one against the other for salvation? Can't we just learn to be accountable for what we do, face our mistakes, and even occasionally practice forgiveness for its own sake?

The subjective journey has led us to this point. A substantial characteristic of our species is the capacity as well as necessity to trust, to believe, to act in faith, good faith, and to look ahead with hope. It is a profound act of faith to leave the failures we own through religion behind us and move forward with what we've come to know as a starting point. It is a profound act of faith to accept what we don't know with courage until our questions can be answered with evidence. If there is a divine out there somewhere, then the time has come for it to act without our help. The path ahead we see a little more clearly now than in times past, and though it has taken us a very long time, perhaps now we can venture boldly on knowing it is our journey, a human journey.

Objective Consequences

Persons who actively embrace some form of religion clearly constitute a global majority. That there are so many types of religions and groups with an interest in "spirituality" is a testament to the subjective context of human experience. This fact alone should give one pause to question any group or individual that claims to possess the ultimate truth. Diversity is important in nature as a component of evolution and we shouldn't be surprised to discover that human belief systems follow a similar pattern. But that's just it – human belief systems.

In some cases as with Wicca or modern Pagan groups differing practices and beliefs tend to reflect individual preferences for exploring what adherents take to be spiritual connections to the natural world. Diversity in this context often reflects a creative, almost artistic, expression of subjective imagination which frequently incorporates cultural and ethnic traditions. For these and many other types of "faith" community there is a relatively comfortable ambiguity surrounding perceptions of a divine presence in the universe. And while there is no more evidence for a Gaia, "Force," or magical dimension in nature than the existence of a god, there is a certain appreciation for liberty and tolerance that even the most skeptical among us can respect. After all leprechauns and fairies helped point us to the microscopic, atomic, and quantum world we now find to be so much more intriguing.

The world's major religions, Hinduism, Judaism, Christianity, and Islam, are a bit different. In these

religions diversity is most often expressed as conflict. Hindus for millennia used the caste system to enforce religious, political, and social discrimination. The three monotheistic religions have bitter divisions within them, so much so, in fact, that each of these religions has tainted their history with a legacy of horrific violence and acts of unconscionable atrocity. This fact draws into sharp focus the urgent need to question their authenticity as viable expressions of human community.

These religions may have their point of origin rooted firmly in subjective faith claims, superstitions, and pre-scientific assumptions about nature; but that they exist historically and are manifest institutionally in human civilization means they have objectively measurable consequences. The initial observation involves the prevalence of internal conflict. Each of these religions claims to be ordained by the one true god, a god who is with them, working through them, and whose will guides them. How then is it that each of their internal institutions is perpetually marred by conflict, disagreement, and division? By comparison much can be said about the similarity between the types of conflicts that occur in each of these religions, but Christianity has perhaps the broadest range of divisions. In fact Christian beliefs, rituals, and traditions are so numerous and divergent to explain that counting grains of sand on a seashore might take less time.

There used to be a small church that sat overlooking the windy mountainous route from US 23 that led travelers up along the Tug Fork River to Williamson, West Virginia. The sign across the front read something like The Regular Apostolic Missionary Baptist Holiness Church of Jesus

Christ. The fact is each name represents conflict. Conflict and division have gone part and parcel with the evolution of most of the world's religions, and this disturbing reality gives us evidence that can be examined. The divisions in the above church could reflect differences in theological interpretations, arguments over polity and how decisions are made, or a bitter disagreement over which color to pick for the new carpet.

In the moment of religious experience there is often a heightened sense of euphoria, a feeling that one is transcending the earthly plain, and at its most sublime peak an assurance that such things as love, peace, and harmony are available to those who participate and believe. "God" is touching the human heart. Forget the brain chemistry because the voice of a visionary is interpreting the moment on a thoroughly emotive and subjective level. The language is inspiring, bonding, inspirational, and enticing. Human beings need community. We want to be loved, accepted, assured that our worst fears – including mortality – can be mitigated, and we want security.

The New Testament's Paul was surely this kind of preacher lulling his audiences with promises from above. The step too far is of course in the promises that the gods ultimately fail to fulfill. Nevertheless small groups form into communities and communities into institutions. The rules are negotiated; rites, customs, and rituals are formed. Boundaries are established. That which constitutes being in versus out is defined and methods of differentiation are set in place. Roles are defined and everything from who governs, protects, and articulates the community's ideals

to who performs various, even mundane, tasks is determined.

This human process for group organization and the promotion of social cohesion is replicated in countless ways and in countless contexts because, well because it is human. We have evolved to enact certain processes which assure the formation of groups centered upon some set of criteria that involves agreement and mutual benefit. Churches ultimately are no different.

Unfortunately the methods for protecting a group's boundaries have frequently proven volatile, even heinous and unconscionable. It doesn't matter whether we're talking politics or religion when a community wants to assert itself as "right," exclusive, authoritative with a claim of primacy, winning control at all costs has too often been the choice. Christianity is replete with examples of genocide and murder as is Judaism's scriptural claim to their history. Islamist groups still today in the 21st century are rife with the blood of those from outside they deem infidels and the blood of "heretics" within the purview of their own conflicted religion. Even as this paragraph is being written the news announces ISIL militants in Syria have just used crucifixion and beheading to express their interpretation of god's will.

In countries like the United States where rule of law implemented through a well established system of justice has made it a crime to murder people with whom you disagree, religious adversity has had to take another course. The religion of Paul with its one god, one faith, and one baptism has demonstrated quite effectively just how devoid of supernatural influence it is through persistent divisions and disagreements between adherents. Since

Christians can't simply kill one another they divide and start their own offshoot churches.

American Christianity is divided economically, politically, theologically, and racially. It has at times been said that Sunday mornings from eleven until noon is the most segregated hour in America. While occasionally there are exceptions, generally there are not. Churches form as likeminded enclaves each with their own interpretation of the bible, their own take on the mission of their church, and their own socio-political agenda. While at first glance one might think the divisiveness of Christianity is a benign matter of preference among those who to varying degrees choose to be religious, nothing could be further from the truth

Several trends have developed over the last few decades that demand the hypocrisy of religion be confronted. There is an overwhelming mountain of evidence that monotheist claims of being empowered by the divine are fraudulent and destructive. For all the long history where a god supposedly existed and participated in human affairs, there is but silence, not a fossil, nor a footprint, not a sliver of evidence that such was ever the case. There is, however, evidence to the contrary, human action, behavior, will, and the manifest intention to control, manipulate, and order the lives of others all on the authority of an imaginary tyrant.

If that sounds harsh then one needs to look more closely at the real world of religion. Fundamentalist, conservative, and evangelical Christians in the US have for years openly and intentionally been seeking political offices with the design of creating a Christian nation. Their alliance and influence with the Republican Party is a

matter of great concern. The hybrid religion they call "Christian" brings together a preferential status for wealth, a partnership with the NRA and a coupling of religion with gun ownership, a painfully discriminatory notion of family values which demeans the rights of women and demonizes LGBT persons, and advocacy for social policies in regard to both low income Americans and Latino immigrants that smacks cruelly as a reinstitution of slavery.

More and more frequently the spokespersons for the evangelical fundamentalists are politicians like Rick Perry or Michele Bachmann, and celebrity figures like Sarah Palin and the Duck Dynasty family. These persons have no qualification to speak as religious leaders, but use very narrow and typically misguided interpretations of the bible to inflame the common populace with their conservative agenda. Equally disturbing is the role fundamentalist Christianity has played on a national level.

During the administration of George W. Bush several fundamentalist preachers, including the likes of Tim LaHaye, author of the Left Behind series, and 700 Club's Pat Robertson had the ear of the president. Of particular interest to these fundamentalist Christians, who also includes a long list of well known evangelists not the least of which over the years have been people like Billy Graham, Jerry Falwell, Rick Warren, and Ted Haggard, is the US relationship to Israel. Their belief in the second coming of Jesus, the rapture, seven years of tribulation, Armageddon, and the role of Israel in what they naively take to be prophecies soon to be fulfilled has been a tragic and disconcerting influence in US foreign policy. While these motives may seem behind the scenes, Israel has

received preferential treatment almost since its inception, and as such resolving tensions in the Middle East has been virtually impossible.

The trend for conservative Christians to influence US politics is not the only coup d'état they seek. This fundamentalist movement within American Christianity which began as a reaction to Darwinian evolution around the beginning of the 20th century is experiencing a surge of influence that strains credulity to any rational mind. Children in the US have already fallen behind students in many countries particularly in the areas of math and science. Arguably the future of our species will depend greatly upon our ability to advance through science and technology. At a time when we need more chemists, biologists, physicists, and mathematicians it is quite disconcerting to witness the popularity of creationist and intelligent design ideologies.

Numerous states have implemented strategies to teach biblical creation theology as an alternative view to evolution, and the clear consequence is the perpetuation of ignorance. Further it is the promulgation of a narrow minded view that is not held by many Jews and Christians. The preferential status coveted by conservative Christians is being forced into public education through the manipulation of political process. In ultra conservative states like Texas and Tennessee legislators have found little resistance implementing their subjective faith perspectives as an alternative to scientific knowledge.

The US Supreme Court has largely been impotent when confronted with cases that involve the first amendment religion clause in so much that it has failed to recognize the deleterious effect of religion on community

well being in light of scientific advancement. While citizens are secure in their right to believe as they wish there are numerous examples where the court has limited actions stemming from religious ideology that violates the right of government to legislate laws that protect the liberty and dignity of citizens. One cannot practice human sacrifice or execute unruly children even if a person's ancient religious tradition demands one to do so.

In the case of education and for that matter many aspects of public activity, we have reached a crucial point on many levels where personal or even community religious opinion has waxed beyond the rights granted in the first amendment. Evolution is a fact understood to be so by every credible scientist on the planet. That denial plays a monumental role in the minds of some religious fundamentalists is unfortunate, but to deny children a viable education or to confuse them with myths that have been demonstrated to be blatantly impossible is an act that damages both the psychological well being and the future opportunities of the child.

States that insist on institutionalizing religious education are using the power of government to impose religion on the most vulnerable citizens and as such violate one of the most important guarantees of the constitution. This is indubitably selfish. It is the equivalent of saying "You might be free to believe or not believe what you want, but here your children will be taught to be Baptist or Catholic, or to believe what we believe." This trend is callous and reactionary. It is the willful and seditious action of a politically motivated segment of the larger population who because they cannot control or convince their own adherents to act voluntarily they feel compelled

to use political process to force their narrow ideology onto the larger community.

Christian conservatives and fundamentalists live in a paradigm where they are at odds with other Christians, where their children are as likely to reject abstinence, become pregnant out of wedlock, choose to have an abortion, use drugs and alcohol, or be same gender oriented as any other population in the country. While the god these Christian evangelicals and occasionally Orthodox Jews use with almost militant fervor remains silent and inactive on all counts, their behavior, thoroughly human behavior, is verifiable, quantifiable, and clearly a divisive force in contemporary society.

If the trend for those clinging to fundamentalist religious ideologies pressing their agendas into the realms of politics and public education weren't enough, the use of religion for monetary gain, the ease of perpetrating fraud against the unwary and unlearned, an unfettered greed seemingly protected by the first amendment, is perhaps the crème de la crème. There is, to be sure, a certain type of viability in the notion of belonging to a church community. While most churches fulfill a variety of societal needs, and express in various ways normative cultural traditions, not all churches are the same.

Historically church congregations in the US have been comprised of relatively small numbers of members who affiliate with a larger denomination. These congregations are usually spread across geographical regions with the larger churches in city and urban areas. Numerous sociological factors including shifting demographic and economic trends have contributed to significant change in the contemporary church landscape.

With the passing of the parent generation of the "baby boom," and the graying of the boomers themselves, most traditional mainline denominations have experienced significant decline. Yet over the last three decades there has been not only the rise of conservative politically motivated church organizations but also the rise of prosperity motivated religious movements.

A traditional church community certainly celebrates its theological bias, invites people to attend, join, assist in furthering the church's mission, and make donations to support the church's work. While congregants embrace in varying degrees the claims that the divine is with them and will bestow benefits upon them, still in a traditional church community there is the recognition that their support of the institution covers a broad range of mundane activity. The staff has to be paid, the church building maintained, and programs that benefit the congregation must be funded. Many of the benefits of belonging are realized as budgets are implemented. Congregants enjoy the singing of the choir, the ethereal light beaming through stained glass windows, the comfort of padded pews, the brief hiatus from parenting as children are safely sequestered into a nursery, and the occasions for gathering in a spacious hall to enjoy pot luck meals with good company.

The traditional church has not been without conflict, and all churches have discovered the difficulty of what is entailed in attempting to promulgate a healthy social institution. But with the rise of televangelism, the rise of charismatic "spirit" based denominations differentiated from traditional churches by offering high energy, technologically savvy environments, and the rise of mega-

churches tailored to the social and economic ideals of a younger generation, the landscape of religion changed. The health, wealth, and prosperity movement was born.

It is true that these "holy ghost" churches and organizations share the same institutional needs as any other group. Bills have to be paid and infrastructure maintained. Their congregants understand this. There is also an exchange that takes place. Benefits are derived from belonging to a 5000 member institution, from being on television, from the social networking that takes place, and even from applauding the ministers who prance about as symbols of opulence and success. The culture of the US from the late 20th into the 21st century has been characterized by materialistic individualism so it is not surprising that the most popular and successful forms of religion exacerbate those values. Religion has always been an easy scam. It has resided comfortably in the hedge betting illogic of Pascal's Wager dangling the possibility of a better life after death, a proposition safe from falsification or prosecution. The preachers always have the advantage as they are like Wimpy in the bistro proclaiming "I'll gladly pay you next Tuesday for a hamburger today."

However, there is a line that is being crossed. We all know the saying that "there is a sucker born every minute," and if one doesn't understand Caveat emptor, well sometimes we just have it coming. It is but a moderate fraud to state with genuine subjectivity belief in an afterlife and invite others to join the conviction. The constitution protects the mild neurosis of make believe and secures one's right to entertain a fiction. It does not protect the right to commit blatant acts of fraud.

The health and wealth evangelists cajole the arenas of their devotees with promises of blessings, worldly blessings, and financial returns for investing substantive dollars into their ministries. The more one invests, the more the return. These claims can be tested. Beyond the coincidental occasions where networking through the larger group lands one a better job or the stock market rises at just the right time, the evidence suggests that it is the evangelists themselves, their close inner circles, and the "ministries" they are building that receive the rewards. Followers with means can hang on for a long time, just in case, but not everyone has that luxury.

We don't have good data on the number of people who have fallen through the cracks of these ministries. We do see data that demonstrates more and more people are becoming unaffiliated with religion, that significant numbers of people are realizing the promises are hollow and deceptive, and the god they hoped would bless their lives didn't. These churches are equipped with as many excuses as they are promises. Persons who are failing in the rewards department are often told it is their own fault. They are not living right, don't have enough faith, or need to give more. Many leave these churches wounded and demoralized.

This isn't religion; it is criminal fraud rooted in unethical emotional abuse. If these churches are going to make claims that donations will result in material returns to donors, then they should be held accountable for the claims. If it were any other institution than religion it would be. Beyond the multitude of convictions that would come from crunching the numbers, there is neuroscience. We know for a fact that such things as emotion, trust, and

perception of meaning are influenced by the stimulation of chemicals in our brains. To create environments where mass numbers of people are being stimulated then prompted to give their money, especially when the chemistry is being intentionally mislabeled as "other worldly," is an act of deception on par with a Ponzi scheme, or more personally, a violation of trust between a counselor and client.

Religion for too long has hidden many deceptions either under the guise of authority backed by violent force or laws that guarantee free speech and the free exercise of subjective beliefs. There are limits. Polygamy is not a legal family system, nor is it legal to abuse animals in religious rituals, stone adulterers to death, or yell "fire" in a public setting when there isn't one. Of equal concern to the cause of justice must be the unsubstantiated claims of religions so divided within their own ranks that their fundamental claims are inherently contradicted.

As we will see religion has historically proven itself to be a volatile and divisive force. It might be different if the objective consequences that can be observed, quantified, and understood were different, but the evidence in regard to religion is unmistakably clear. The initial critique of religion based on its internal coherence, Christianity in particular, eliminates its right on any level to influence politics, education, or act as a viable strategy for upward economic mobility. For every church that says "yes," there is another that says "no." Is religion, a crap shoot with fewer odds than a lottery ticket, to have unbridled access to the institutions that govern, educate, and determine the moral and ethical standards of a world which has the evidence of better empirical choices? To the

extent that such has been the case it must be so no longer. For all that this season of religious fervor has yet to become the answer must be "absolutely not."

The objective examination of religion on an internal level, Judaism, Christianity, and Islam in particular, yields disturbing results. The conflicted views of interpretation, diverse range of disjointed claims, and complete lack of evidence for anything but human activity is more than compelling. What about when we examine the external relationship of these religions to the larger world? At least three criterion emerge with empirical weight as to be worthy of consideration. First is the assertion that human beings are a created species. Second is the assertion that religion is the source of morality and the basis for just community. And third is the historical behavior and activity of these religions and the question of accountability for those who would embrace their ideological paradigms.

One of the most ancient questions humans have pondered is "How did we originate?" Pretty much every culture we've been able to study has some myth or tradition that explains its origin and how the first human beings came to be. Some stories are really imaginative and creative. In almost all cases our distant ancestors drew from the celestial bodies, the waters of the earth, and the earth itself to depict the scenarios they believed led to the beginnings of life. We are sentient creatures after all, so what we see and touch and feel influences what we can understand about reality.

Motifs where humans, like plants, come from the earth -- a drop of divine blood mixed with soil and perhaps a wisp of breath -- are fairly common. Likewise

the notion that humans were made for a purpose factors into the equation. The ancient Mesopotamians were likely the first to translate their oral traditions into written form which depicted a world where the supreme deities were personified natural forces who gave birth to the great ruler gods who in turn begat lesser gods to govern over lesser forces. Humans were their earthly servants, fashioned from soil to make their beer and such. This hierarchy worked well for the rising city states and empires who saw fit to emulate this pattern of stratification on the earthly plane.

The Hindu religion developed equally early with a cosmology of similar result. In the broader Fertile Crescent the influence of changing empires from Babylon to Egypt meant undulating loyalties to the various mythical paradigms and the formation of hybridized traditions by those who settled in ancient Palestine. For the Canaanites El was the supreme creator god. His primary wife or consort was Asherah, and there was reputed to be at least 70 divine sons of El, including gods like Baal, who were venerated by various tribal groups. As the Hebrew Scriptures attest El was the original god of the Israelites.

By the time that Yahweh emerges synonymously with El as the creator god of the southern tribes of Israel, Judah in particular, rivalry between Canaanite tribes expressed through wars was well established. As demonstrated in the previous chapter the victors' god received the tribute and exaltation. Yah, which some scholars identify as one of the sons of El, gained prominence as the god of Jerusalem and was the supreme deity of the Jews who returned to the land in vassalage to Persia after the Babylonian exile period. Still as the first

creation story in Genesis attests the influence of El and the ethnic connection to Canaanite ancestors was widely felt by the Jews who wove these stories together into what became the Hebrew Scriptures.

These scriptures became the foundation, not only for Judaism, but Christianity and Islam as well. The estimates for world population in 2012 were just over 7 billion people with approximately 2.1 billion Christians, 1.6 billion Muslims, and only about 14 million Jews. Roughly half the world's population affiliates with the monotheistic traditions derived from the Hebrew Scriptures. Geographically the influence of these religions spans the globe and has been felt historically even in countries like India where around 1 billion people still adhere to Hinduism and in China where largely due to communism over 1 billion people consider themselves secular or non-religious.

The political, social, educational, and cultural evolution of the Americas, Europe, Russia, the Middle and Near East, Africa, and Australia has been dominated for centuries if not millennia by Judeo-Christian-Islamic ideology. Those tempted to suggest there must be viability in the beliefs of such a great majority with such massive influence should remember how frequently the masses have been proved wrong by the discoveries of even one individual. Such is indeed the case thanks to Charles Darwin.

The most widely held erroneous and arguably self-destructive belief in human history occurs in the first three words of the book of Genesis. This dependent clause is perhaps best translated "When Elohim began to create," but traditionally translators like to cheat a little and give us

the grand opening "In the beginning Elohim (god) created…." The real crux of the fallacy comes a little later in the first chapter when it states "Then Elohim said, Let us make Adam (man or human) in our image; according to our likeness; and let them have dominion … So Elohim created (Adam) in his image, in the image of Elohim he created him; male and female he created them. Elohim blessed them, and Elohim said to them, be fruitful and multiply, and fill the earth and subdue it…."

Genesis 1 has all the marks of an ancient Canaanite creation myth. It uses the seven day pattern, articulates the same cosmology that was commonly accepted in ancient Mesopotamia, and has El in conversation with his divine counterparts presumably his consort and children. The Jews clearly reworked this myth and placed it first in their scriptures to emphasize the Sabbath day. Within the myth are three notions that were taken for granted and unfortunately still are by a lot of people. Human beings are created by god, look like gods, and have authority over the earth like gods.

In the 2nd chapter of Genesis there is another creation story which technically contradicts the first but explains how Yahweh Elohim fashioned man and all the animals out of the dirt, but only as an afterthought made woman from the man's rib to be his "helpmate." This myth resembles the Babylonian creation story where humans were created out of the dirt to basically do work for the gods – build their temples, make their beer, etc. In Genesis one will notice that the man was put in the gods' nice garden to till and keep it. The Jews used the story as an etiology for marriage, but more broadly the myth has been used to subjugate women.

So we are created by gods, look like gods, pretty much have carte blanche to do as we please on the earth, and women are servants to men. Of course each of these tenets is blatantly false. Granted the ancient minds that recorded these myths weren't privy to science although in Genesis life does originate in earth's oceans, nevertheless these stories fail miserably to conform to the natural world and universe we observe. If you are a religious person you owe it to yourself and to humanity to scrutinize these beliefs and the impact they have and have had on the earth.

Even the most liberal views about the bible do not change the fact that these ancient texts were written from the bias of patriarchal cultures where women were either regarded as property or were treated as lesser beings than men. These ancient texts were also written without any knowledge of biology, genetics, or understanding about the crucial role female anatomy plays in the evolution of the species. That woman's existence is dependent upon the rib of a man is almost so farfetched a notion that paying it serious lip service seems beyond imagination.

Unfortunately the idea continues to be taken seriously and the uphill struggle for women to be treated equally and be able to define themselves without reference to males continues on a global scale. While most would argue that Hinduism and Islam have historically oppressed women the most severely, Christianity has been equally destructive to the rights of women. One need only remember the long trek through American history before women were able to vote and be recognized as equal citizens under the law. Even now women are less likely to receive the same wages as men, and are locked in a

persistent battle against religious bigotry where their reproductive rights are concerned.

Perhaps the most disturbing reality is the number of women in both Christianity and Islam who accept being subjugated to men as a divine plan. This fact presses the issue of denial on a psychological level into a serious consideration of what constitutes mental illness. Propaganda can be a form of abuse, and to essentially brainwash children, young girls in particular, with the notion they are to be subservient to men, that their place is in the home, and that god made them with specific gender roles is tantamount to a crime against humanity. The guise of religion has for too long been the cradle of abuses that deserve closer scrutiny under law.

The deleterious consequences to the emotional wellbeing of children, including males who are taught gender prejudice, and to the opportunity of women to be raised in the full stature of liberty are unmistakable. In the same way courts will often intervene when it comes to the health of a child in a religious tradition that rejects medical care, the same needs to be the case when conservative Christians, Jews, or Muslims attempt to indoctrinate their daughters and sons with ancient patriarchal myths that contradict the anatomical facts we know through genetics and biology, and foster gender discrimination otherwise prohibited by law. Children raised under these circumstances are disadvantaged emotionally and academically. In the same way it is illegal for adults to have sexual relations with children; it should be illegal to distort a child's understanding of human sexuality by nurturing gender discrimination as the will of a god.

The root of the problem is the notion of creation in the first place. Not only does the creative act of the biblical god diminish the dignity of women and give preferential statues to men, if one reads further this creator god discriminates based upon ethnicity. Of Noah's three sons only Shem is chosen for divine favor. Japheth goes his own way, and Ham who appears to head toward Africa is unfortunately doomed to servitude because he walked in and saw Noah, the "man of righteousness," sprawled out drunk and naked.

Of Abraham's two sons Isaac is chosen over Ishmael. Naturally the Muslims see it differently. Any way one cuts it the ethnocentrism is appalling and immature. Historically each culture has its god, the status of being the people of the god is bestowed, and the stage is set that will justify everything from racial discrimination, to slavery, to genocide, and war. It is fair to point out that with disturbing frequency one notices this glazed look in people's eyes, especially creationists and religious fundamentalists, when confronted with the plausibility of a god who creates two people roughly 6000 years ago, deluges to death about 1500 years later all but four pairs of men and women, three technically since Noah and his wife have no more children, then picks one lineage over the other two as the one that will receive divine favor. And of course we have now populated the earth from this massive genetic bottleneck less than 5000 years ago from three breeding pairs to over 7 billion human beings.

That is some impressive math. That is some impressive sex, and frankly one has to wonder how our ancestors had time for all those wars, the building of empires, all the geographic mobility, and all the genetic

and cultural traits that would develop diversely throughout the earth. Talk about be fruitful and multiply. The glaze in the eyes almost always translates into the same oblique words of denial "With god all things are possible. God can do anything; he's god."

Whether one is religious or not it is important to pause and think for a moment about what could be significant enough in our experience as humans to enable belief in a god as the explanation for the existence of all things, a god whose alleged revelation is at odds with everything we have come to know about physics, biology, genetics, the geographical origins of humans, the geological age of the planet, and the universe. Certainly until the 19th century we were socialized almost entirely in a creation culture. Those who doubted such was the case faced tremendous hostility, could at times articulate such blasphemy on pain of death, and at the very least faced rejection and censure.

The discoveries of Charles Darwin had a subtle impact at first, but gradually as more and more evidence has confirmed evolution is in fact the process that explains the origins of life on the earth the error of a creationist paradigm has become painfully obvious. For those who persist in denial and cling to religious ideology there is a comfortable package of assurances. Humans are created in the image of god, are special to god, loved by god, or at least potentially so if one's life measures up, can take for granted that god is in control of the universe, and can rest in the peace of life eternal. These are powerful beliefs, rooted deeply in culture, engraved in history, and difficult to exchange for the real universe.

There is, however, something, dare it be suggested more sinister lurking in the psyche here. While the influence of religion on a sociological level is compelling, as is the challenge for the institutions of religion to transition away from mythical paradigms into healthy reality based communities, the creation culture finds its greatest ally whenever we simply look in the mirror. We are a species that is capable of pattern recognition. We see in ourselves a pattern that seems to be different than anything else in nature, emphasis upon "seems," and we are infatuated with ourselves.

The idea that we are created does not come from outside our realm of experience, from a transcendent designer who once upon a time spoke a word then blew life into a dirtball; it comes from our own anthropocentric hubris. Historically we created religions to codify and legitimize the things that were important to us. We see ourselves as intelligent, powerful, imbued with a soul, different from other living things, and ultimately superior to them. The problem is we are wrong. Because we have inflated our own significance we have taken liberties with the earth and its species in ways that may prove destructive to our own survival. The creation paradigm that has dominated our history is leading us to a brink with consequences we must face.

Some might argue that greed and human ambition are the real culprits, but religion remains the underlying authority. It gives us permission. It condones our ignorance and deludes us with naïve notions that what we do is irrelevant. Especially for religious fundamentalists the earth is quickly abandoned for the better world they imagine inheriting one day. But there is no such place, and

this "pale blue dot" is all we have. Religion in this respect feigns goodness while masking a pernicious evil that would rob future generations of the chance to live this one remarkable life.

Human activity is altering the climate and landscape of the planet. Our arrogance has left islands of waste floating in the oceans, debris orbiting the planet, created dead zones in water and on land from pollution and waste, decimated forests, and threatened the survival of species that contribute to our own survival. The list could go on. Perhaps religion cannot be blamed for the many mistakes we have made, but the last thing we need as we seek solutions to serious problems is the irresponsible fanaticism of religions whose core beliefs exalt the significance of humans and diminish the significance of the natural world.

The first step is a psychological shift, a therapeutic salve for the ego which admittedly was bruised in the discovery of evolution. The knowledge that we are part of nature, that minute amounts of DNA separate one species from another, that we share elementary particles with all living things, and that we are intimately connected to an evolving, albeit indifferent universe is both unnerving yet inspiring. Creationists ironically find it difficult to embrace faith in truth, and prefer the almost childish rants where evolution is mischaracterized by pandering emotionally charged words of denial.

They love to inflame passions by equating the word "theory" which is a plausible explanation of facts with the word "myth," or as though it means to guess in the face of mysterious circumstances. The emotional barrier renders them blind to evidence and leads to ridiculous taunts like

"If evolution is true, why don't we see monkeys turning into humans?" Equally they love to ridicule the notion of gaps, missing links, and the ongoing research to discover that moment when chemistry turned into biology. It is true we may never be able to discover every detail concerning the earth's past, but just as Cambridge scientists recently discovered a metabolic process that could have led to the building of multi-celled organisms on the earth four billion years ago even before oxygen existed, the case that a god was involved has run its course.

A good analogy for describing the position held by those who cling to the notion we are created beings is found in the Monty Python film "The Holy Grail." It is the scene where Arthur fights The Black Knight. Even after the knight is completely dismembered and wallowing on the ground spewing blood like a gusher he continues to insist he's capable of fighting. The consequences of this prideful resolve in those who refuse to let go of the culture of creation and the fallacy it represents are less than humorous. It is immoral, an affront to reason, a source of violence against the earth and between human societies. It is a paradigm that leads to discrimination, indifference, and the degradation of life.

The creator who imbued his creatures with life also saw fit to give them authority, perhaps a dangerous and unbridled authority where the planet itself is concerned, but a bit less leeway where morality is concerned. With god there is always a "good book." Stone tablets, gospels, the lone prophet in a cave with an angel saying "recite," more angels, golden tablets, a bible, Koran, etc., and why exactly is it there are never any witnesses or in most cases original artifacts? Religion's most successful ruse

sometimes implemented through force and sometimes through gullibility has been its assertions through the texts it labels sacred.

Among the most spurious claims made by those who defend the importance of religion is the notion that religion is the source of morality, goodness, integrity, and ethical standards. For the Jews the first five books of the bible, or Torah is the source of the laws, commandments, and authoritative traditions handed down to govern their way of life. They attribute these writings to Moses though it is clear that multiple authors used a variety of sources over a long period of time to create these writings. Christianity and Islam utilize these scriptures as well in their traditions though Islam developed its own specific "Sharia" law tailored to the Arabic culture from which it emerged.

In all cases a variety of rules and laws are handed down and attributed to the will of a god. A variety of blessings and curses are prescribed. The righteous obey these laws and those who violate them are punished accordingly. The development of laws and standards by which a community is organized, however, is not unique to religion, and in fact has been an ongoing part of the evolution of human civilization. Many of the laws in the Old Testament, for example, mirror the laws of Hammurabi or other secular codes that predate the Israelites in ancient Mesopotamia. Some of the oldest forms of written language ever discovered are business contracts or legal adjudications which define rules for right dealing in commerce. It is obvious that human beings discovered that communicating norms and standards through language and writing was essential to

maintaining a social order. It is not surprising that when a king or empire made laws the weight behind them was attributed to a divine authority.

Obey or else, and "or else" quite frequently meant death. "Lex talionis" or the legal standard where punishment mirrored the offense became one of the earliest written codes. If one kills another, he should be put to death. If one steals, his hand should be cut off. The use of capital punishment could also extend to other types of violations especially if they were perceived to be a threat to the community standard or national interest. In the Torah as the rule of Yahweh emerges worshipping the traditional fertility gods of Canaan was punishable by death, adultery which violated inheritance laws was punishable by death and even children who struck or cursed their parents were to be executed. Not many modern day adolescents would survive to adulthood if these standards governed society.

Are these ancient cultural and religious laws moral and are the stories of the bible which tell of the comings and goings of the descendants of Noah, Abraham, and so forth genuinely appropriate as the standard for human dignity and community? There are many religious conservatives who seem to think so. In an ironic twist fundamentalist Christians whose religion has traditionally diminished the Old Testament in favor of New Testament ideology have over the last couple of decades drawn heavily from writings in the Hebrew Scriptures.

In what amounts to the pushing of a fundamentalist socio-religious political platform the tenets that appeal to the interests of these extreme conservatives are being picked and chosen according to their bias. They want

"god" in virtually all aspects of the public sphere, and they are clearly intent on defining the United States as a Christian nation. Their narrow view of marriage and family has led them to use theological presuppositions to infringe on the rights of women, and their inability to embrace equality for LGBT persons is reflected in their selective and hurtful use of a few bible passages.

The present conflict has reached a critical stage as creationists press for a place in public education, as conservative Christians insist on prayer in all things public, and as there is a renewed passion for setting forth the bible as the ultimate moral standard. This passion includes using the bible in contexts that involve children and public schools. Fortunately the hypocrisy of these Christians has yet to seek the ban of pork ribs and barbeque since it too is written as an abomination to Yahweh.

The religious right has become fond of the rhetoric which claims that secularists are waging a war against religion. In spite of the historical majority and preferential treatment of Christianity in the US they just can't let the sleeping giant of liberty rest. For generations the bible has sat prominently on tables in businesses and public settings, and has waited reverently in bedside drawers in motel rooms. Less than a majority of people actually read it, but it has always been popular to think one should raise children to live by its teachings. Even Blue laws continue to exist in many states and communities and have gone unchallenged in deference to Christians even though Sunday isn't the biblical Sabbath and Christians typically don't observe it anyway. To date all that has been asked of religious institutions is that they respect the constitution of

the United States, the rule of law that guarantees all citizens religion and government will be separate.

Now that this promise has failed to be kept inviolate it is time for people to see the bible for what it is. Is this a book to be displayed in public settings? Is this a book to be shelved in school libraries and made available to children? How many people actually read it? When put to the test the bible isn't the moral standard for all to live by, it is one of the most immoral, heinous, divisive, and unconscionable books ever written. At best it is an adult book to be read at a college level by those who are interested in studying Near Eastern history and mythology or the formative background for what became the Christian religion. Much the same could be said about the Koran.

The bible condones slavery, the genocide of whole cultures, the implementation of barbaric standards for criminal justice, and includes numerous sexual narratives that if given to children in any other packaging would be grounds for an indictment. Consider just a few of its teachings. Genesis 4: Cain murders his brother Abel. His punishment, El casts him out to be a nomadic wanderer instead of a farmer. Genesis 6ff: Elohim deluges the world killing all but his chosen few. 1 Samuel 15: In god's name Samuel commands King Saul to commit genocide killing everyone including every child and infant and animal. Psalm 137: The psalmist expressing his resentment toward the Babylonians after the exile which was purportedly Yahweh's judgment against his own people says "Happy shall they be who take your little ones and dash them against the rock!"

In these few passages one sees the violence and reasoning of a tyrant, the bitterness of war, and lust for blood and revenge. The god of the Old Testament is celebrated as loving, good, and kind to those who fear him and obey his commandments, but to every other living thing he is a jealous, malicious, and vindictive deity who is intent upon inflicting pain, disease, calamity, and death. While such a god doesn't actually exist, it is evident that these stories reflect the horrific circumstances of cultures at war and the brutality that has tainted human history.

Contrary to what many Christians like to believe about meek and mild Jesus, The New Testament version of this god ultimately promises more of the same. This Yahweh of old, now the heavenly father, sees fit to impregnate a young woman who is someone else's bride, bring forth his semi-divine issue for the purpose of a human sacrifice, and promise to love all humans that take his blood upon them. Those who do not believe are to weep and gnash their teeth, be cursed with plagues and destruction, and be cast off into hell.

Naturally Muslims share similar beliefs but from their own tradition which is pitted against the others. Here we are in the 21st century. Christians and Jews are content to slaughter the children of Muslims, Muslims are dedicated to the slaughter of Christians and Jews, and each claim they will persist until the other is annihilated. Each has its "good" book, the bastion of moral fortitude.

If the frequency of violence in the bible isn't enough to concern parents who want this book placed into the hands of their children with the guidance of a bobble-headed smile, then perhaps paying attention to the sex and lewdness will encourage a bit of a re-think. Genesis 6

portrays divine beings having sex with mortal women. Genesis 9 describes the righteous Noah passed out drunk and sprawled out naked. In Genesis 12 Abram passes his wife Sarai off to an Egyptian Pharaoh as his sister since she was beautiful and Abram was afraid he'd be killed to make her available. That was really courageous and moral.

In Genesis 19 Lot offers his two daughters to town revelers who are threatening to have sex with his male guests. In a bid to stave off this affront the traditional hospitality code, Lot is willing to let them gangbang his daughters. Later in Genesis 19 Lot's daughters take center stage. They take turns getting their father drunk and have sex with him. They become pregnant through incestuous sex. Genesis 34 has the story of Dinah's rape and the subsequent slaughter of the Shechemites. Genesis 38 has the story of Onan who masturbates his semen onto the ground instead of impregnating his late brother's wife. And it has the story of Judah being tricked into having sex with his daughter-in-law who pretends to be a prostitute. Genesis 35, by the way, let us know that Reuben slipped in and had sex with his father's concubine Bilhah, technically his step-mother.

Skimming on through the "good" book one can pause at 2 Samuel 11 and take in the rather bawdy, adulterous affair of David with Bathsheeba. This story has the sex, the conspiracy to cover it up, and murder, all of which go unpunished according to Torah law. Don't fret; Yahweh does take the life of the unwanted child. 2 Samuel 13 has the nail-biter story of the incestuous rape of Tamar by her half-brother Amnon. He feigns sickness and has his father David send her with food to make him feel better.

Once there he grabs her, rapes her, then tosses her away shamed and tainted.

These are some of the stories children will encounter if they read the bible. There is also Song of Songs which is laced with metaphors, euphemisms, and innuendo, but children aren't likely to figure out the allusions to intercourse, cunnilingus, etc. In all fairness Songs is one of the finest examples of erotic poetry in any ancient text. Some will nitpick with that assessment and say it is about the beautiful love between a husband and his wife. It is attributed to Solomon of course who if memory serves was rather prolific in the love department.

When considering objectively the evidence of what the bible is, what it contains, and how it has been used historically and in fact continues to be used, it is impossible to conclude that this is a moral book or that it has contributed to the moral development of human beings. Quite the contrary, the bible is a dangerous book, as is the Koran. By all rational standards it is immoral, and at best incapable of contributing to what any civilized society deems worthy as a foundation for justice or rule of law where equal rights for all citizens is valued.

While the bible may contain some moral precepts that are generally accepted as valid, like it is wrong to murder, steal, cheat, or lie, nevertheless it is not the source. Further these precepts which occur in ancient writings like the bible or Koran are immature in their formation. They fail to reflect the substantive developments that have been made in the way we understand social organization, the nuances of what is just, the biological forces at work in our evolution, or the progress we have made toward

understanding the social and psychological aspects of what it means to be human.

Our moral progress and development has largely been part of our subjective journey. One has to realize that there is nothing inherently moral or immoral, right or wrong, good or evil. We are animals. We are carnal. We are omnivores with an emphasis upon the carnivorous. We have survived as a species over and against tremendous odds, and at times our survival has been at the expense of other species even close primate relatives. We have forged our path through history without apology and without remorse.

The stronger of our species have been given to killing, raping, and taking what they want as far back in time as we can assess our cultural history. There is no inherently moral consequence, no lightning bolt to strike me from on high if I kill my neighbor, rape his wife, and enslave his children. There is of course the possibility that another neighbor will do the same to me, and all the more if his religion justifies it. The bible makes this clear, but we only have to go as far back as today's news to witness these very acts being perpetrated by Islamic extremists, brazenly so, in the name of Allah.

Most human beings and their societies upon the earth no longer behave this way or tolerate such behavior. The argument made by Christian conservatives and other religionists that without belief in a god or the authority of the bible people would succumb to barbarism and be ruled by their whims is absurd. In part this is so because we've already been there and done that. It is what we have learned, experienced, negotiated, and come to value through the evolution of civilization that demonstrates

that such is not the case. The only people to date who act with such disregard for human life are a low percentage of individuals who for a variety of reasons violate the law or religious fanatics. Of all possible worlds persons who believe a god sanctions or even commands violence against others are by far the most problematic and dangerous.

It is not difficult to see how laws and moral standards developed over time. While it may be possible for stronger individuals to dominate weaker individuals, the duration is not sustainable. Humans also discovered that banding together in groups, the adage "there is safety in numbers," was a way to better protect against attack and an equally efficient way to conquer other groups. Still as communities developed aggressive and ambitious tendencies proved unsustainable over time, and the complexities of social organization led to the development of rules, standards, and laws.

The undulating rise and fall of nation states, empires, and civilizations brought about many exercises in futility while at the same time honing the trial and error process of what is needed to make a society function with efficacy. The development of diplomacy and sophisticated strategies for trade and commerce gradually has proved to be more sustainable than war and conquest. Even ancient civilizations developed very early with non-religious codes that regulated fair dealing in the market and made it illegal to lie, cheat, steal, rape, and murder. These standards were enforced within communities and were incorporated into the religious ideology as a way to empower political authority.

It took a bit longer, even until modern times, for nations to develop far reaching ethical standards between nations, though treaties have been negotiated and signed for millennia. Political systems themselves have evolved significantly and most countries have found that rule of law with some form of representative government provides the most stability for their society. It is not a perfect world by any means, but the vigorous debates that have led to a broadening concern for human rights and normative international standards have been human endeavors. While there are competitive national interests and ethnic tensions that make moral progress difficult, religion remains the most volatile, divisive, and destructive aspect of the struggle.

Superstition has played its role in influencing human behavior and the beliefs that have led to governance. There are many examples in history where people believed that human activity influenced meteorological and geological events. The same is true whenever drought or disease brought decimation to a region. The bible is full of these erroneous assumptions. The story of Jonah portrays a tempest that is quelled once Jonah who has angered his god is cast from the ship.

Beyond myth and literary license the sad truth is that innocent people have indubitably been blamed and persecuted due to the ignorance of superstition. Some groups of Christians blamed Jews for the Medieval "Black Death" because fewer Jews were getting the plague. Christians of that era had begun associating cats with witchery, though Jewish enclaves believed no such thing. Jews were persecuted for bewitching Christians with the disease. The likely scenario is that religious ignorance and

superstition led to an overpopulation of rats which were infested with the fleas that carried the plague. Areas with higher cat populations had less rats and less exposure to the plague. Unfortunately innocent people were still exposed to ignorant people.

Much of the progress that has been made developing just laws and viable moral precepts over the last couple of centuries has been due to eliminating the influence of religious ideology and unfounded superstitions. Many of the conflicts and points of injustice that remain are due to the infusion of religious views into the political and judicial arena. The religions themselves are exclusive, discriminatory, and by their own definitions make it inherently impossible for those outside the boundary of the religious ideology to enjoy the full blessings of liberty. For all that is argued about the contribution religion has made to the moral framework of society there remains an inherent intolerance at the core of the main religions in question. It is all smiles for those who embrace the ideology, but whether church, synagogue, or mosque there is always a grimacing and malevolent reality waiting to pounce upon the skeptical and unaffiliated.

The irony is that religious institutions and the broader ideology upon which they are formed lack the one thing which humans have evolved to embrace as a primary tenet of morality. At the very center of our capacity for moral reasoning, the development of ethical standards and laws that promote justice and fairness is empathy. Our species has evolved with the intuitive ability to imagine ourselves in the situation of another. We understand that what happens to one can also happen to another or more particularly "me." The impetus for not

killing, raping, stealing, harming, abusing, cheating, etc. is found in the needs of a society to be able to function efficiently.

Our survival depends on our ability to eliminate war, revolution, and conflicts that destroy the delicate balance of networks that connect us as human beings and as a species to the earth itself. The bitter truth is that religion is part of the problem and not the solution. Christianity, Islam, and to some perhaps lesser extent Judaism are wolves in sheep's clothing. It is the strings they attach to their version of compassion and justice which essentially condemns the world beyond them to misery. They cannot embrace empathy because the exclusivist message they harbor forbids it. Those beyond their purview are sinners, infidels, gentiles, the unsaved, and the damned.

The evidence speaks quite clearly where religion is concerned. It is not a moral force. It is a divisive and tumultuous energy that threatens to unravel the very moral progress made by the human species for the sake of its humanity. As an atheist I value compassion and see altruism as an important component of a just, rational society. It makes good sense to eliminate poverty, suffering, and to guarantee education and opportunity to all. It is indeed mystifying to witness in the US conservative Christians, those who claim to be most rooted in "the love of Jesus," being the most adamant against health care for all citizens, the most blatantly indifferent toward those who immigrate here for work, to those who struggle in poverty, and the most harshly judgmental of those whose way of life differs from theirs. Their fears, anger, prejudice, and lack of empathy speaks for itself.

Historically religious morality has functioned in two ways. In contexts where government and religion were yoked religious precepts were used as law and as a way to protect the authority of the ruling class. One of the most significant points of rebellion in the Protestant Reformation had to do with the favoritism being shown by the Roman Catholic Church to the wealthy and powerful. Sins could be forgiven by purchasing indulgences from the church. The church as well as ruling authorities who collected these "sin taxes" had quite a racket. The greed led to appalling abuses, and most any sin, including murder, could be forgiven for money. Naturally the plight of peasants and commoners combined with the self interests of wealthy separatists eventually led to war.

The approach of religion where morality is concerned has not been social advancement through education, the development of mutual interests, or rational consideration of what constitutes common good, but to coerce or scare people with threats of other worldly punishment. The "shalls" and "shall nots" of religion defer one's actions to heaven or hell. In this respect there are no consequences in the temporal sphere, and it doesn't take people long to realize that if they do not get caught what guilt they may have otherwise incurred can dissipate in the notion of forgiveness. The effect diminishes responsibility. To not take responsibility for one's actions is considered immoral by most reasonable standards.

The telling of "little white lies," cheating a bit on one's taxes, spreading gossip or rumors about persons in the community, the occasional sexual affair, and perhaps many worse things are easily cloaked under the guise of religion. Churches are well known for their hypocrisy. On

Sunday morning even the vilest among us, the rudest, the most contentious, the most greedy, selfish, manipulative, and indifferent can sing Amazing Grace while donning formal attire, shake the preacher's hand, and leave acquitted.

Morality from a secular perspective does not necessarily make one a better person. Human beings are human beings and what is considered right or wrong can be arbitrary. The difference is one has to be honest and accountable first and foremost to one's self. In a healthy moral environment we scrutinize our choices and actions based upon the connections we value in the larger community. One's self image plays a substantial role. To be seen as honorable, respectful, dignified, intelligent, compassionate, generous, or kind rates pretty high on the list of values we have evolved to appreciate. To be sure we disappoint ourselves, and forgiveness has tremendous value in the wake of personal failure. However, properly understood forgiveness both as a personal and communal act enables one to move forward, begin again, and proceed to rebuild whatever trust was broken. It is acceptance and accountability that assuages guilt, not forgiveness. The paradigm created by religion which enables a false sense of well being by deferring responsibility to a god or savior figure is impotent and flawed.

Those of us that have significant experience with churches and particularly as clergy see the hollow and even emotionally harmful results that come from teaching people that a god will help them or forgive them or that all they have to do is trust Jesus. Ultimately these ideas encourage avoidance and some people who are never really led to face the things they've done carry the burden

throughout their lives. God never does anything, doesn't "wipe away their sin," thus the source of their angst revisits them. It can be the worst pathos and its persistence is debilitating.

The other side of this coin lends itself to arrogance, indifference, and callousness. The message of salvation, of being "God's Chosen," of being the forgiven, sanctified, even holy gives license to a heightened sense of self-importance that often leads to a blatant disregard for others. Some if not many are content with a blanket forgiveness that exempts them from accountability. Whatever they do is sanctioned by grace or at least will be. It is bad enough when those fallen from their high pedestal quickly return as though nothing happened, or to see the humiliated and disenfranchised faces looking for a new church because of the emotional wounds sustained from the last one, but when acts of sexual abuse or acts that rob people of their dignity are tolerated and glossed over as we have seen so frequently in recent decades, the immoral shifts to the unconscionable.

Within church life there is an even deeper moral conflict which again provides evidence that religion is flawed and incapable of honoring its promises to those it proselytizes. The old blues tune "Nobody Knows You When You Are Down and Out" provides a fitting analogy. In this case those often left by the wayside are the elderly. One must consider that churches are institutions and play an important role in society. The integrity of such organizations is based on their ability to function as advertized. In the case of religious communities there is an unmistakable void due to the idea that a god is with the

people, sustaining them, and providing them with assurance and comfort.

The absence of this divine countenance is not so noticeable to those who are actively participating in their church. In reality it is the human connections people find meaningful, and the value of belonging to a supportive group should not be underestimated. A church community offers a wide range of opportunities for persons to develop friendships, participate in important duties, and utilize various skills. One may join a choir, a men's or women's group, work with children and youth, serve on a church committee or board, perform important rituals such as offering prayers, lighting candles, serving communion, or collecting the offering. What takes place inside the church becomes an important marker for how people see themselves in relation to the larger world.

While all of these things may be important on a number of levels the delusion that becomes a haunting menace is the persistent proclamation that "god is with you." Like a lie that is rehearsed so frequently in one's mind that the liar comes to believe it as truth, the god language of religion that seems so empowering at the time is actually a slow growing cancer that will lead to bewilderment and estrangement. What many church people and church leaders as well fail to recognize is that the times they "feel" closest to god, "lifted up," or that something deeply spiritual has happened are human moments. If the human connections are not present, the sense of a divine dissipates. How one perceives a church is based upon how one fits in, how one is welcomed, included, or connected. If the relationship one has to a particular group becomes toxic the "god be with yous"

turn into "goddamns" and one is off in search of new connections.

The notion that a church group is anything more than a human community is perhaps naïve, but the sensationalist promises that are made come to affect the elderly the most severely. The trend for younger families to attend prosperity churches is understandable, even predictable in a materialistic culture. The recent comments made by the Osteen's, Victoria in particular, to their mega-church in Texas that people go to church to make themselves happy, and if they are happy, god is happy is the self-serving message a lot of people want to hear. But what happens to those who can't be there, who no longer wear the happy face, receive the blessings, feel the warmth of hugs and handshakes?

Small town churches and even less flamboyant urban churches have seen declining numbers for years. Church buildings like people age and are less appealing to those who want all things new. The gods seem to go with the "in crowds." It takes a lot of responsibility, time, and resources to maintain an institution. It takes even more to maintain connections with people who are the "down and out." For most churches "absence does not make the heart grow fonder," and clergy learn this very quickly. What many ministers do not realize is they will be expected to maintain the primary connection, "the god connection," with church members who can no longer join in the public gatherings.

Most churches do have some committee or group that occasionally visits the nursing homes or persons who are homebound, but typically the lot falls to clergy. As time passes average congregants become reluctant and

uncomfortable visiting with people, even those that were close friends, and all the more so if the person in question is seriously ill. It has also become more common for the children and extended families of seniors to live too far away for frequent contact. This makes visits from friends all the more important, and all the more hurtful when it doesn't happen. The loneliness experienced by some is nearly unbearable, and it is not uncommon for seniors to feel resentment or bitterness toward those they feel betrayed their trust.

There is a deep melancholy awaiting those with heightened expectations that god will not abandon them. It does not occur to people that their experience of god is tied to the human connections they enjoyed through most of their lives. Many people find they are left waiting, watching, hoping they aren't forgotten. The days can turn into weeks, the weeks into months, and the months into years with only sparse contact from church members, occasional visits from a pastor, and sadly it is often the neglected senior that maintains the connection with the church by mailing offering checks to the church office.

Aging is difficult for all of us, and all the more when facing a debilitating or terminal illness. We are hardwired to want to survive, so it is not surprising we struggle against letting go as death becomes imminent. It is equally understandable that we imagine life may go on in some form even though all of the evidence suggests otherwise. Death will always be a mysterious darkness, but how we approach it depends greatly on how we are socialized. Religion not only provides false hope for those who seek companionship during their waning days, but it also interferes with one's ability to make end of life choices.

Gods vanish as the human connections that carry
them vanish, but even the ability to believe in a god
vanishes as the brain becomes impaired. Persons with end
stage dementia, Alzheimer's, certain types of cancer, and
various brain injuries may languish and suffer seeking to
endure to the bitter end largely because they have been
socialized to do so by religious ideology that says it is
sinful to choose death. Loved ones share and endure the
agony of "fighting the good fight," and all the while
praying to a god that does not answer, does not heal, nor
lessen the suffering. This is immoral.

It is immoral to promise people that a god will be
with them when the human touch subconsciously equated
with the presence of a loving god will not. It is immoral to
teach people, especially beginning at childhood, that they
will go to an eternal hell if they end their lives by choice. It
is immoral to proclaim the sovereignty and omnipotence
of a god whose will determines all things and has control
over our destiny when there is no evidence to support
such a claim. Religion becomes an impediment to moral
reasoning that cajoles people out of their dignity and all
the more so as our graying years come upon us.

When we step back and view the consequences of
religious belief objectively, the dissension between
religions and within the religions themselves, the arbitrary
way religion is used to control others, influence politics,
dilute and distort the education of children, affect the way
human beings view and treat the planet, and use
antiquated stories whose moral grounding contradicts the
standards of justice and human rights we embrace as law,
a question of accountability emerges. A popular question
posed by religious persons to atheists is "What difference

does it make to you if we want to believe in god?" At first glance this seems to be a fair question especially in a free society. If what we are talking about is a right to utilize one's subjective capacity to imagine, wonder, ponder, or even have faith there is more to the universe than meets the eye, or that maybe there is life after death, then by all means, imagine away.

But if what one means, which is frequently the case, is the right to associate with a particular religion, like Christianity, Judaism, or Islam, religions that have institutional structures and historical baggage, then there is a problem. It is a problem of accountability. If one is going to affiliate with an organization or institution, call her or himself by that name, take upon oneself the message and content as a badge of identity, then is it not reasonable to expect such individuals to also be responsible, at least on some level, for the actions of the community in question? Too frequently the answer is no, or worse, to simply ignore the question, to not understand its relevance, or pretend it does not apply.

The average person who joins a church in the US and likely the same in most places does so for two primary reasons. Community influence, the need to fit in with peers and significant others and the benefit of belonging to a "respected" group are paramount. This satisfies a basic human need to belong to a community, to have standing among friends, and to enjoy the blessings of hospitality, friendship, and acceptance. The second reason is more personal. For many joining a religious community is a way of assuaging guilt or finding atonement for one's perceived mistakes or sins. Likewise dread in the face of

mortality meets the open church door with hope that "living right" will ensure forgiveness and eternal life.

Rarely does it occur to people to investigate beyond the surface. If their immediate needs are met whatever may have happened in the past is someone else's problem. It could be said that the first act of denial is to take upon one's self the benefits of the religion without also accepting responsibility for the consequences of its actions on an historical scale. This is a flippant standard that is not tolerated on any other level. If one says "I belong to the KKK," or "I've joined a Neo-Nazi group," immediately the flags go up and people expect accountability. If someone said "I just joined ISIL, but I don't believe in violence," the person would still be branded a terrorist.

Why should the standard be different for those who affiliate with Christianity or even Judaism or Islam? The majority of Muslims will claim they are not supportive of radical Islamists though at least one quarter of the world's Muslims are embroiled in war and acts of heinous violence. The Jewish community has perhaps done a more thorough job of facing the genocidal acts portrayed in their scriptures, yet their religion remains divided and claiming to be "Jewish" carries with it the connotation of being the people of the Old Testament god and the parent religion of Christianity and Islam. In Christianity it is a real game of hot potato as each division tries to distance itself from the others all the while claiming to carry the "true" version of the religion.

At the heart of it all is real history, and a legacy on all counts that has meant unbearable suffering for millions of human beings and the decimation of invaluable culture and world heritage. The apparent inability for religious

affiliates, or blatant unwillingness, to take responsibility for their religions is a matter of grave concern. It is even more troubling when one considers that the two most successful waves of evangelism within Christianity have been fundamentalist denominations like the Southern Baptists who press a message of being "Right," and the prosperity churches who preach wealth and "success." The self interest of the latter is appalling, and the potential for violence from the former is underestimated.

For years demographic research has shown a decline in membership in churches that expect a measure of accountability to accompany church membership. Many of these churches are part of the old mainline Protestant community and typically have clergy that are more formally educated and as such aware of the historical problems of the religion, the necessity of non-literal biblical interpretation, and the abusive tendencies that stem from traditional theism. These churches attempt to call congregants into a more costly discipleship that requires social justice, personal sacrifice, and a broader appreciation for diversity. The failure to attract people is evident not only in the declining numbers but also in the fact that when the media wants a "Christian" point of view they generally turn to the fundamentalists or harbingers of health and wealth.

Accountability is tough, and it sort of takes the wind out of one's sails. Imagine being in a service where one is being invited to become Christian and join the church community. Imagine the preacher has lulled the audience with promises of eternal heaven, gates of pearls and streets of gold. Perhaps you have gotten past the fact that your salvation is based on the merits of a human sacrifice or that

the birth of your savior was the act of a god who took someone's virgin daughter, a man's betrothed prior to their consummation in marriage and made her pregnant. Perhaps the part about only a few actually receiving the rewards of heaven while every other person that has ever lived and every other living thing will be condemned to hell and destruction goes over your head as you are convinced it is not your fate that is in question.

What if you were then asked to sign a disclaimer which states that henceforth you would be called Christian and therefore accept the legacy it entails and endorse the acts of its leaders as holy from the church's inception to the present? This along with the fact that they will also require a fair bit of your money may possibly give you pause to read the fine print.

You would learn that from the beginning of Christianity there were numerous groups of people who made claims about the man called Jesus of Nazareth even though there is scant evidence that he was a real person. There were many different writings that disagreed over who he was and what he taught. You would learn that there was significant conflict among these groups and that eventually violence and imprisonment was used to narrow the field into what became the church. You would discover that the collection of books called the New Testament was only part of the written witness to this movement, that other writings were censored, made illegal, and when possible, destroyed. You would discover that councils of preachers and bishops under the supervision of Roman emperors decided what the church would be and that its authority would be enforced by the use of persecution, torture, imprisonment, confiscation of property, and death.

To wear the Christian moniker would entail embracing centuries of conquest, genocide, and preferential treatment of the nobility and ruling classes. You would be party to inquisitions where disagreement with the church or its authority could mean being executed in vile ways like being burned alive. The long history of crusades and wars against rival Christians, pagans, and Muslims would be added to the atrocities committed by the church and its conquistador nations as whole cultures of indigenous peoples were decimated, enslaved, and slaughtered.

If you choose to be Protestant versus Roman Catholic the stain of blood remains. Denying responsibility for what "they" did doesn't change the war ravaged landscape or the fact that Protestants used puritanical violence to purge "sinners" and heathens from their midst. Every place and in every generation where Christianity has spread, its "good news" has been a bitter poison to indigenous peoples and to those forced into slavery. If you choose to be Roman Catholic then you can add to the centuries of genocidal violence the fact that your church contains the largest population of pedophiles ever recorded in any culture. Equally disturbing is the fact that the Roman Catholic Church with its papal façade has repetitively covered up this criminal perversion that has devastated the lives of innumerable children and families.

In fact the evidence against Roman Catholicism is so overwhelming that just deserts would entail dissolving the Vatican, trying its pope and leadership for crimes against humanity, giving over its library and collection of artifacts to the open review of the academic community, and the emptying of its vast treasury for reparations to all of the

indigenous peoples and cultures it has robbed and decimated. Ultimately the world has a responsibility to view religion for what it is, and while the gods themselves remain elusive and unobservable, the consequences of the actions of religious institutions speak for themselves.

Accountability itself is a measure of credibility. What we find when talking to persons who affiliate themselves with Christianity, Islam, and in some cases Judaism is they generally refuse to be responsible for the actions of their religion unless they are directly involved. People who are deriving a personal benefit from being involved in a religious community easily appropriate a posture of denial when it comes to the broader historical context. This institutionalized hypocrisy and the persistent passing of the buck it entails leaves these religions incapable of trust. The majority of Muslims may be unwilling to commit acts of violence in the practice of their religion, but estimates suggest around one fourth of the world's Muslims are committed to using violence and are dedicated to forcing Sharia law upon the world. Radical Islamists, at least as numerous as the population of the United States, are dedicated to war and genocide, yet somehow we are not supposed to be concerned about the merits of the religion in general.

Much the same is the case for Christianity. The majority of Christians may be part of moderate or liberal traditions that may be committed to non-violence, but how are we to trust the rise of Christian fundamentalism whose militant agenda has already pressed its way into government, education, and is very closely associated with the NRA and the increased interest in an armed citizenry? These religions lack any form of internal mechanism for

policing their own, manifest a rather clandestine fluidity whereby adherents can shift from one interpretation of the religion to another without scrutiny, and they defer responsibility for deleterious consequences resulting from the practice of the religion to someone else.

The fact is these religions fail miserably to provide effective models for human community. This doesn't mean that some aspects of what it means to belong to a church type organization aren't viable or important to the well being of society. It does mean that significant change needs to take place. The question "What's god got to do with it?" remains. The time has come for people to take a close look at what they really believe, face the evidence, and take responsibility for the consequences these many centuries of religious experimentation have left in its wake.

We still don't have a god. We do have dissension, hurt, discrimination, fear, ignorance, fraud, and war. When we measure the outcome of what it means to belong to these historical religions the result is an indictment against reason and a conviction against sanity. To the extent that we have believed in the existence of a supernatural deity we have consistently been proven wrong. To the extent that we have implemented institutions on behalf of a divine we have consistently done wrong. The gods have never been accountable to human beings and as such we emulate them in our failure to be accountable to one another. There is most certainly a better way.

If you consider yourself to be religious, especially if you are connected to one of the world's monotheistic religions, you owe it to yourself as a matter of self-respect to seek the truth. Likewise as a matter of moral obligation

to others and to the future of humanity it is necessary to press beyond naivety and examine the evidence, to learn the history, and to objectively evaluate the consequences of what your religion has been complicit in bringing about during the evolving course of human civilization. It is also an exercise in honesty to challenge yourself, and to think sincerely about what you want, about why a religion might appeal to you, and whether it is really worth sacrificing one's dignity and integrity by participating in charades that are primed to damn us all in the name of salvation.

Is it not possible to reassess? Is it not possible to face one another in sober judgment and winnow out the chaff of hypocrisy, fraud, ignorance, fear, and superstition? It is possible. In fact if there is to be a salvation, a lasting hope, or a faith that moves mountains, it is surely before us now. It is a courageous endeavor to bury our gods and stand humanly undimmed by our vulnerability to mortal days and press on with a brighter vision than the one bequeathed us when our time began.

Overcoming Denial

A few years ago there was a family that faced a devastating crisis. They were devout Christians, Southern Baptists, very kind people, and the epitome of what most folks would consider the perfect family. They were clean cut with a pleasant demeanor, never cursed or gossiped about others, and were exemplary hard working citizens. They were upper middle class with the father holding a really good job at a local chemical plant and the mother worked as a bookkeeper for a major construction firm. Both sons had done well in school, attended college, and neither had ever had so much as a traffic violation. One son was married, and the other engaged. They all went to church together and seemed genuinely happy.

Most in the community regarded this family as a model of decency and they could have been on a poster advertizing the goal for a Christian lifestyle. It certainly seemed the axioms where god blesses the faithful were working for them. The shock came the day the mother was arrested for embezzling funds from her workplace. It had been going on for years, and in fact it later came out that she had done the same at a previous job but they had been content to dismiss her quietly. Her husband and family were clueless, and even more devastated when they found out she had stolen nearly two hundred thousand dollars over nearly a decade.

The embarrassment and subsequent depression led the mother to attempt suicide, which was thwarted, but she required several years of therapy to recover a healthy state of mind and be able to put what she had done in

perspective. Her husband and sons struggled for some time to cope with all that had been revealed. The mother avoided jail time, but had to pay restitution to the company. Even worse was the shock that the IRS required them to claim the money she embezzled as income and pay back taxes on it with penalties and interest. Between the two fines the family had to exhaust their savings, sell their home, and work several years living in much more meager circumstances in order to pay the debts.

Everything in their lives changed, but to their credit they worked through it. In spite of the father's solid income over the years and what the mother could earn it wasn't enough to pay for their really nice home, the upscale furnishings, new cars, and still provide the best of the best for their children. That's what she wanted. She had the image in mind which was projected perfectly to all who knew them, but the only way she could achieve this for her family was to steal and lie.

One of the hardest things the family faced, for the sons and father in particular, was that their whole lives had been based on a lie. Months were spent in denial as each in his own way tried to look back for the clues they missed, and they languished in an agony of self blame and guilt. To be sure, much about this family's life changed. They lost many friends, were actually asked to leave their church, and genuinely began to question how their god could be so aloof. Eventually they paid the debts, made new friends, and started a new life. In some respects it was a cleansing experience, painful, but renewing. Much of what she had done was fueled by the notions of success and blessing taught by their religion and the desire to measure up. In the end they found that their love for each

other in the family and the resilience that comes from facing adversity and change were what meant the most.

This story is a good place to start. It functions as a suitable metaphor as we deal with the problem of denial in regard to religion, and it has a happy ending. This family dealt with loss, loss of a status, loss of resources, and a loss of invested time. They also faced what it feels like to live through a lie, something that they believed in but was false, and something that was too good to be true because it wasn't true. Yet they overcame and found a way to salvage the good and begin again.

Denial is an interesting artifact of human evolution. It would seem at first glance to be a flaw in our ability to make accurate assessments of situations and thereby a potential threat to our survival. It is balanced however with the human capability of acting too quickly, making a rash decision, or the potential to make an unwarranted change. In this sense denial actually serves the cognitive faculty and the ability to think critically and base choices on incontrovertible evidence. If it wasn't for our ability to defer decision making, temper emotional reaction, and reserve judgment we would be swayed by any and every opinion, will, or whim.

Denial also functions as a protection mechanism. It enables us to be duly suspicious and skeptical of potentially fraudulent claims. It is valued as an aspect of justice in so much as we demand one is considered innocent until proven guilty. And in times where significant change is implicated, rightly or wrongly, it is the force of resistance. This is especially the case when the exchange that is sought appears unbalanced. In the case of religion the crux of the problem is in fact this, at least on

the institutional level. For one to accept the evidence that god is a contrivance from pre-scientific cultures rooted in myth and superstition is untenable especially if it is perceived that the institution is in danger of collapse. Change is the logical and correct choice, but the consequences seem too disruptive to the survival of the community in question, so resistance appears to be the safer choice.

Denial is also kindred to procrastination. Many of us practice it daily. At times our ability to resist duties or responsibilities is humorous. The old story of the farmer asked about his leaky roof to which he replies "When it's raining it is too wet to fix, and when it is not raining the roof doesn't leak" makes the point. Urgency is a factor. If the need to do something or face something doesn't appear to be pressing, then putting it off is the easier and more comfortable choice. We see this frequently where the death of a loved one has occurred. It may take a person or family a really long time to alter the home environment, donate the decedents clothing, or move beyond the feeling that the lost loved one still cares about these things.

The same context applies to failing institutions like churches and small family businesses where demographic shift and competition has winnowed or eliminated essential support. Hundreds if not thousands of US churches have declined so severely that only a paltry number of members remain to care for the church building and conduct services. Most of these churches have constitutions or governing documents that specify the terms of dissolution, but many of them also have funds in savings and endowments that enable them to enjoy years of palliative survival. So much of their lives are invested in

the church, the names of their families are on plaques and stained glass windows, and their memories linger there. There is always hope in their faces that some new folks will wander in to carry on their legacy, repair their decaying facility, and bring back the "good ole days." In many cases the denial persists until the death of the last members and a trustee of sorts distributes the assets to charitable causes.

Denial also takes the form of repetition. It is not unfair to label human beings as creatures of habit. There may always be a better way to do something, but we place a high premium on the way we were socialized to do the things we do. Repetition frequently takes the form of ritual. Ritual can be daily habits like driving the same route to work or something more formal like saying a prayer before a public meeting. Repetitive behavior is habit forming, and like addictions habits are hard to change or break. Consider your kitchen where you have just decided to move a common item to a new location. For some time you will catch yourself reaching to the old location even though consciously you know it is no longer there. I like to call this a "Pavlovian Move."

When denial takes the form of repetition it is usually manifest as embracing a persistent familiarity even though the activity in question isn't working. This condition frequently happens to persons who try to lose weight by dieting without increasing their regimen of exercise. They may lose some weight, typically water volume or muscle mass, but not fat. They soon discover they have gained even more weight, but laboriously return to the same strategy. A rather deleterious cycle ensues. A few more examples are worthwhile.

A friend used to tell of a co-worker who frustrated her immensely because he used repair techniques on machinery that were ineffective and wasted her time. Bolts would break inside the equipment which required them to be drilled out and the hole rethreaded. He would always attempt to cajole them out with wrenches and screwdrivers and such because it had worked for him once when repairing the engine on his truck. It never worked on the factory machinery, but still he seemed convinced that his method was viable.

When I was a teen I was hit by an oncoming vehicle near my home as I returned from the grocery store. My automobile was damaged on the driver's side such that the front fender and quarter panel were scrunched into the tire. It was not drivable as it was. The accident wasn't my fault and once the police left the task of moving the car was at hand. My father and two other neighbors had ascended the scene and began debating what to do. Being the "ignorant" teenager who had now studied the situation for about an hour meant that somehow my suggestion to let some of the air out of the tire and drive it the remaining block fell upon deaf ears. As one of the neighbors emerged from his garage with a 2x4 they concluded they could bend the steel frame with wood. Three boards and six scuffed elbows later one of them said "Hey, why don't we just let some air out of the tire, and he can drive it home?" Needless to say as a moderately rebellious youth I did take pleasure in their denial.

On a more serious note denial as repetition, especially when solutions to problems are being sought from a subjective perspective, through assumption, or on the basis of perceptions stemming from unsubstantiated

fears, can be extremely problematic. The drug war in America, as a dismal failure, is case in point. Initially the criminalization of marijuana and other substances was deeply motivated by an overreaction to the hippie culture of the 1960's amidst concerns to keep these substances away from children.

Black markets were created which actually increased availability to minors. The response was to make stiffer penalties. The result over these many years with harsher and harsher laws is more serious problems with drug addiction, more drug related crime and violence, and what is likely the largest prison population in the world. The logical solution, largely supported by science, is obvious, but denial is legal. Taxpayers seem equally infected by the "D-bug" which is clearly reflected in the malaise of gullibility that applauds the religious pundits and politicians who keep saying the same things over and over, the same fears, the same plans, and achieving the same null results.

Denial as resistance, procrastination, and repetition is difficult to overcome though not impossible. These characteristics function in a variety of ways and contexts on a personal emotional and psychological level, but also, and perhaps more importantly, on an institutional and societal level. The institutions of religion are the frontline. If we were to think of the problem in medical terms these institutions, Christianity and Islam in particular, are ill, cancerous, contagious, not necessarily terminally so where the institutions themselves are concerned, at least not immediately, but potentially so for life on earth. A societal, if you will, sociological disease is possible, and just as dire

for the future of humanity as is late stage lung cancer for an individual.

The more advanced stages of the disease are evident in the groups that have bought into a fundamentalist mentality but the symptoms are not absent in more moderate groups. When asked to confront evidence the guard goes up, the resistance takes hold, the procrastination proclaiming comfort in the way we do things quickly dismisses the need for scrutiny, and the approved language repeating the by-lines and "politically correct" defense strategies are unleashed. As much as I hate to say or admit it, in this context science, reason, and rational argument based upon solid evidence is the equivalent of treating someone with an antibiotic to which the person has become immune. It alone will not be sufficient to cure the infection.

I have the deepest respect and admiration for fellow atheists Richard Dawkins, Lawrence Krauss, and others. They are pioneers to be sure, the avant- garde of those who champion reason and science in this day of waning superstition. And while it would seem logical that it be sufficient to simply present people with evidence, denial creates a social and psychological barrier that reason alone does not overcome.

One of the best examples I have seen, and one available for the analysis of readers via Youtube is an interview Richard Dawkins did a while back with Wendy Wright, a creationist, and the director of Concerned Women for America. Presumably this interview was planned in advance with both parties agreeing that it be filmed. It appears to take place in her office setting and there seems to be a defensive posture from the very

beginning. Office staff can be seen going about their work, and as Professor Dawkins arrives and asks where they are to go, Wright indicates they can just stand there outside the cubicles. No chair or beverage is offered which in terms of etiquette even among enemies is bad form and indicates both her level of intimidation and the degree to which resistance is embedded and formalized in her position.

Richard Dawkins appears willing to engage in conversation, and listens to her views with a reflective interest while formulating viable questions in what comes across as fair and unthreatening. One will notice that Wendy Wright maintains a resolve reflected in her demeanor and facial expressions that reveal she is unwilling to listen, engage the questions, and consistently throughout the interview relies upon rehearsed lines. When Professor Dawkins begins to ask if perhaps there is something else, an agenda, she becomes defensive and accuses him of an ad hominem attack. It was an honest question based on an accurate observation and her ill applied use of "ad hominem" was clearly planned.

It is interesting to note that her position when confronted with the scientific evidence for evolution was a theological agenda. She reiterates an unwillingness to recognize evidence as evidence and relies on two basic points: "We believe god created every individual person out of love as unique and loved," and that only through her loving creator god was there a moral basis for love, respect, and human dignity. Both of her tenets are biblically false. Forget science for a moment. There is no biblical creation story that specifically states god's motive in creating humans was love. In order to draw this

conclusion one has to twist the contexts of a few New Testament passages and essentially put thoughts into god's head – creating god in a human, rather utopian, image. Secondly, she is obviously willing to dismiss biblical violence, the preferential status of one ethnic people over all others, and the Christian problem that either states god predestined some people for damnation or foreknew the masses that would be damned. In either case we are not dealing with the loving creator she imagines.

Further she speaks in the vaguest of terms when arguing the notion that non-religious societies have committed atrocities, yet doesn't seem to be aware or the least bit willing to be accountable for the religious violence that has plagued human history. In short her view is a grand delusion. The fact which we see over and over is that Wendy Wright and the fundamentalist community she represents is entrenched in a world view of their own creation. As such there is a monumental investment at stake. For her to have listened to the scientific evidence presented by Richard Dawkins and drawn the logical conclusion would have meant the dissolution of her institution, her culture, and the comfort afforded by the world view she protects.

Denial in this interview was in full force. Resistance was maintained through defensive postures which made a genuine exchange impossible. Repetition was used through the reiteration of propaganda and codified "mantra" to stave off any chance that change would occur. And perhaps more subtle but symbolized by the office activity in the foreground is the element or procrastination. It says "we are busy doing business as usual, and unless

you have something of equal or better value to offer, we're just going to wait this thing out and hold on to what we've got." Unfortunately intellectual advancement, embracing truth, aligning one's self with facts, and coping with reality are a matter of insufficient funds where so much is at stake.

Ironically the transformation of denial involves evolution. The painful side of this is that extinction is part of natural selection. There will be some who cling to their denial unto the bitter end. The important thing to note is while change does in many respects equal loss it is not optional. It is necessary. In fact the debate between secular and religious perspectives at present isn't so much a matter of winning adherents to an ideological position, it is about survival and the future of our species and the planet itself. Those who continue to endorse the supernatural world view of the ancient monotheistic religions put not only themselves but everyone at risk.

The heart of denial involves very important social and psychological dimensions. Naturally there are deeply felt personal dimensions as well. At this point we can assess a few things about what denial entails at these various levels and make a few general observations about meaning itself which takes us to the true "teeth" of the problem.

Denial manifests itself in observable ways such as resistance, procrastination, and repetition, but hidden beneath is the fundamental question that probes how we determine meaning and significance in life. It goes to the very essence of identity, how we define ourselves, and how we perceive who and what we are.

Meaning is about connection. Everything meaningful in one's life involves one or more connections. Whether to a person, thing, or idea meaning is about connection. There are different kinds of connections, some positive, some negative, but whether something means anything to someone directly involves the level of connectedness. We are made of connections, billions of them, billions of connecting atoms, molecules, cells, and networks, interconnecting and interacting. Break a connection, like a clot that prevents blood going to the brain, and there is a real problem.

Our species has evolved to be able to recognize connections and it is important to us to believe they "mean" something. It is very popular for people to believe that "everything happens for a reason," that things are "meant to be." Long ago people imagined that supernatural forces must be at work in the universe, whether gods or forces like karma, to supplement the gaps in what we could understand. We needed a "meaningful" connection to explain who we are and "why" we are here. We believe life is meaningful because we are connected to it, to air and water and earth and sun, to lifelines, to sources.

When we love we are profoundly connected to others. Equally so when we hate; yet indifference is a profound lack of or avoidance to connection. Our human capacity for empathy is rooted in the fact that we can connect with each other and perceive equivalence. I muse a bit about the many times I have known a white person who held deep prejudicial opinions about persons of color, even referring to them with pejorative generalizations, until actually meeting a person of color, perhaps a co-

worker where a meaningful connection was established. Suddenly that person is a "friend," no longer thought of in terms of color, or at least less so, but still all other persons of color succumb to the generality of previous indifferences.

We negotiate meaning in our lives by qualifying our connections. One's mother is more meaningful than an aunt, usually. One's spouse is more meaningful than a secretary unless of course there is an affair that leads to a change in status. One's child is more meaningful than the kids next door though they can be important too. We speak of boon companions and best friends forever and a broad hierarchy of relationships fills our lives. Likewise we have our favorite sports teams, books, movies, music, art, foods, but could care less for things never seen or experienced.

We also have the capacity to disconnect. In this case we reduce or even eliminate meaning. I am particularly fond of this ability in regard to cooked peas, carrots and other vegetables I had the profound displeasure of meeting and can say quite glibly as a matter of self-determination and personal liberty that they mean absolutely nothing to me at all. Our capacity to eliminate connections that prove unsatisfactory or disconnect from situations in our lives that yield undesirable consequences is very important when facing the debilitating prison of denial. Change may equal loss, but sometimes loss is liberation.

Connections occur in many forms, and not all of them are beneficial. Duration is a factor. Sometimes we find meaning in a connection but it runs its course. Being able to let go, especially if the connection has taken on an

adverse meaning, is worth its weight in gold. Toxic connections abound, though sometimes as with certain addictions and bad habits we love them in spite of themselves. They still have valuable meaning in spite of our selves.

The most potentially damaging toxic connections are to illusions. This means one is connected to or vested in something that isn't real. Consider an act of fraud as in the Madoff scandal where investors where intentionally misled to believe in something that was false. Religion poses a similar problem. Islam promises an afterlife which naturally cannot be verified in the human sphere, but uses the notion of reward or punishment very effectively in what is otherwise a very human religion. There is not much promise that Allah will intervene in human affairs, and followers have a rather simple set of laws to obey in order to secure the guarantee of heaven.

Allah does not have to prove himself, and unlike Christianity there is no complex paradigm of supernatural activity, no holy spirit to interact with, and no expectation of miracles. The will of Allah is supreme and sufficiently expressed in the Koran. This simplicity is attractive to many and accounts for the significant rise of Muslim converts over the last several decades. It is also extremely dangerous. Only one illusion need be peddled as truth, and given the ambiguity of the Koran in regard to violence against those they expect to be damned by Allah, Islam becomes a profoundly volatile threat against all of humanity. The religion itself is designed to be an ethnic theocracy. One can only hope that in time that Allah, who was Yahweh, who originated from El the Canaanite fertility deity whose only real existence was stone carvings

of a god with bull horns, will be exposed for the illusion he is. The task before Muslims is to embrace their ethnicity while reforming their culture in favor of reason and human rights while distancing themselves from the barbaric, grossly patriarchal religion.

Christians face a similar challenge. In both cases and with some other religions as well there is change experienced as loss. But what is lost is the illusory aspect of the connection to the religion. The illusion is the existence of a god, and of course the supernatural and mythical paradigms. In the past when gods died it was through war. This isn't so difficult to comprehend since daily we are confronted by Islamist extremists who appear intent on continuing this age old tradition. It may come to all out war once again, but there are other evolutionary avenues available. Surely we are reaching a saturation point where the toxicity of being connected to illusory gods who leave global and universal affairs to the will of human beings is sufficient to thwart our persistent retreat into denial.

Already the majority of adherents to these religions appear to be moderates, and within Christianity, especially among clergy, there is a substantive base ready to take an evolutionary step. One great fear in the face of change, particularly when we recognize the substantial investment in the institution and social significance of religion, is that the "baby gets thrown out with the bathwater." The perception of destruction and upheaval is too great, and denial remains the "safe" choice. Not to sound overly macabre since the intention is to provide some measure of comfort, in the case of religion it is in fact the "baby" that must be thrown out, but the bathwater is worth keeping.

The extent to which atheists also experience denial, especially in the context that reason alone is sufficient to awaken the religious, is in missing the importance of this point.

Christians have two basic types of connections they consider meaningful. One is generally viable, but the other is illusory and thus toxic. The toxic connection of course is god and the fraudulent supernatural paradigm that goes with it. If one faces the biblical evidence then it is clear that the long history of the religion is a maze of human fumbling about trying to make sense of incompatible ideas. Human beings are not sinners, nor were they born into "original sin." The human sacrifice of a savior is unnecessary, barbaric, and immoral. There is no holy spirit that supplements human experience or the genetic predispositions of individuals with a special chemistry that makes life turn into a pool of joy, bliss, and spiritual perfection. Prayers go unanswered, angels do not descend from the sky to waft saints away from tribulation, and heaven is no more real than Olympus or Valhalla.

Even though church rituals like communion and baptism appear to carry spiritual meaning, when closely observed it is the bond between members of the community that is being formalized and upheld. The god language is unnecessary. In fact the god language is what threatens the community the most. At best it offers false hopes that simply fade into nullification when one dies. At worst hopes are dashed to pieces and people's lives are shattered when their ghostly expectations fail to materialize in the midst of need or crisis. And when the god language falls into the wrong hands it is easily used to

manipulate, coerce, defraud, and pit people against others without justification.

The uneasy part of church life is god. That moment when a human being is speaking for god is an awkward moment that most people hope passes quickly. The most successful preachers are always the ones whose countenance is human and connected to the people in "down to earth" ways – not the ones whose face glows like Moses with a lofty holier than thou gaze. This should be a sign to folks, and subconsciously it is. The exception to this is found in Pentecostal, charismatic, and holiness traditions. This is so only because the goal of preaching is to share the heightened emotional and ecstatic experience equally throughout the community. Everyone shares the "spirit," and it becomes a way to differentiate their human community from others.

I remember a story I was told of a minister in a mainline church, a church with relatively formalized liturgy and tradition, who encountered an unusual moment during the church's invitation. A new, non-member family with a sick child had wandered into their service. When the invitation to join the church was given the family brought their child forward for prayer. They asked the minister to lay his hands on the child and for the congregation to pray for its healing. This had never happened before, but the preacher obliged. When the family returned the next week elated that doctors had determined the child's condition had improved unexpectedly it caused quite a stir. The church board held a special meeting following the service and fired the preacher. They indicated they did not do that kind of thing

in their church and were concerned about the kind of people news of miracles and such would bring.

Change is hard. Change means losing something. In the face of change denial is a common pattern response. Fight the change; keep things the same, resist! Deep down most people know a change is coming where religion is concerned. For liberals and moderates denial is most comfortably expressed through procrastination. Conservatives and fundamentalists however sense it the most. Our religious culture has seen this coming for a long time. If not from the times of Copernicus and Newton, certainly the advance of science from Darwin to the present has been signifying a death knell. This coupled with our best science applied to biblical study seals the deal. Their fear and resistance is entrenched.

The stakes may not be as high as some fear. Without god the church as a form of human community remains a viable possibility. The primary things that draw people into altruistic, non-profit institutions are human things. The blessed ties that bind us to the ways of our parents and grandparents are as humanly constructed as the stained glass windows and bronze plaques that bear their names. Church, a word that simply means assembly or gathering, in many respects offers healthy connections.

We are a communal species. Most of us, at least during some parts of our lives, feel drawn to gather with others. We want to celebrate our rites of passage through life, the birth of children, their graduations, and weddings. We find meaning in being connected to friends and sometimes professionals who help us through life's ups and downs. We value a community in which we can say goodbye and find comfort in the face of death, the death of

loved ones and a measure of assurance and appreciation in the face of our own. To all of this the question stands – What's god got to do with it?

The church as an institution has lingered long like a spouse whose true love has passed on. It is time to move on and return to living life. We do not need an imaginary friend to help us along the journey, but we might need each other. It is not that god is dead, just that no such being has ever existed. The evidence is more than compelling and the consequences for not facing the truth are dire. A doctor observes symptoms, conducts tests, and renders a diagnosis. In the same way there are patterns we can observe that clue us in to one's emotional, psychological, and social status. If you find yourself in resistance, locked into repetitious perspectives you are unwilling to challenge, and are putting off the inevitable because it seems uncomfortable or not immediately necessary, then you have a pretty solid case of denial.

Nothing including a virus wants to die. Living things vie to survive. Denial has its antibodies, its defenses. Frequently its frontline is clergy. If you are a church person you likely have one of about five different types of pulpit masters. Many ministers are already atheists, but they are naturally reluctant to inform their congregations of where they stand and why. They do however provide subtle leadership gradually nudging their congregations toward a humanist world view. They have great potential for leadership and will likely be the first to translate denial into transformation on a community level.

Many other clergy are close and are perhaps better thought of as agnostic. They know the academics, but have bargained their way into a milder malaise of denial by

embracing non-theistic theologies. They too have great potential for leadership, but for now the baby stays in the bathwater. Similar to these clergy in terms of academic preparation is a more conservative class. These include Roman Catholic priests and some fundamentalist Protestants. They are apologists whose primary function is to protect the institution at all costs. As too many lay members of these churches have discovered individuals within these traditions are expendable. Persons whose life situations take a turn that crosses the narrow boundary that defines and protects these institutions discover a less than compassionate god and all the hurtful human behaviors that go with it.

Numerous persons who are considered ministers or pastors by their church tradition are simply ignorant and unqualified. They have no academic preparation beyond an unaccredited bible college degree, if that and some have purchased a certificate labeling them as a minister, or doctor of ministry for a paltry sum of money. These individuals almost always represent evangelical and fundamentalist groups who label themselves as independent and call their own clergy based upon emotional evidence. This class of minister is most likely to misinterpret the bible, use it as a bludgeon, and lead people to believe terribly erroneous and ridiculous things. On an emotional level persons who attend these churches stand to lose the most if their denial encounters truth.

Finally there is a class of clergy-like leaders who simply put are frauds. Most televangelists and prosperity preachers fall into this category. Their interest in religion is money and material gain. Their success is possible because it mirrors the values of masses of people who want the

same thing for themselves. Denial here takes a slightly different form though similar to certain aspects of procrastination. It resides in the notion that we can get something for nothing, or that there are gimmicks that allow us to succeed without going through established means that require diligence and hard work. These preachers sell positive thinking, self-help recipes, and common sense at prices way above market value. It's an old game. The fact that they can use god with impunity is unfortunate. The toxic connection they create is more delusion than illusion. In the end however we may find that it is easier for people to emerge resilient and transformed who have merely been cheated than in some of the former examples where followers are likely to experience a sense of profound betrayal.

Within Christianity those who affiliate with communities led by apologists, uneducated clergy, and prosperity preachers constitute almost entirely the population of those who endorse creationism, intelligent design, religion in politics, and the marginalization of those outside the boundaries of their world view. To them the non-existence of god comes as the greatest shock on both personal and institutional levels. Denial as a pattern of defense and resistance is in some sense the expected and natural response. Penetrating these barriers of denial is a difficult task that requires bringing a broad range of treatment strategies to bear against the problem. But like finding a cure for cancer, the problem of overcoming denial as it pertains to individuals with religious belief and the institutions which encapsulate and promulgate it, should be tailored more to a therapeutic approach and less to methods of confrontation and conflict.

The expression which is of course quite cliché that "Denial is not just a river in Egypt" is perhaps rather appropriate in this case. In some respects the problem we face in saying farewell to ancient gods and superstitions did begin at the Nile, the Red Sea, or on the ancient flood plains of the Tigris and Euphrates. In some sense we are all victims of epigenetic traits bequeathed us by ancestral cultures that have latched onto our DNA like excess baggage. Overcoming denial is the process of losing the luggage that is carrying the clothes we didn't need in the first place. This might not be the kind of baggage we can confidently entrust to United Airways, but it is in the hands of evolution.

Rage against the Dying Light

Emotional reaction is a guaranteed human response to just about anything we experience. If someone is having one, be somewhere else. I say this in jest, but also to underscore the point that emotional moments are generally irrational, unpredictable, and not the best time to attempt intelligent discourse. Our emotions move us into the subjective realm of feeling, and though there are times we are moved to emotion as a result of rational experience, frequently our emotional states incapacitate us at least momentarily from objectivity.

One factor that complicates our ability to interpret emotional responses is the human proclivity to not express emotion or feelings adequately especially in moments of conflict or contexts when we perceive it is inappropriate or self-deprecating to do so. We are socialized with numerous axioms that suggest many things are best left unsaid. As a result we hold in many emotions, feelings, and opinions which translate into forms of stress on a variety of levels. Unfortunately our subconscious mind keeps track. Expressions like "ticking time bomb," "pent up with frustration," and "about to go off on somebody" can represent very accurate descriptions of emotional status.

A person whose boss is condescending and disrespectful will likely not express her or his feelings directly for fear of reprisal but may quickly release the stress as hostility toward another motorist during the commute home. Someone who has tension and unresolved conflict at home may be the one who unleashes a tirade at a committee meeting over what seems to be an

insignificant matter. Communication skills are not generally our high suit, and too frequently we discover our undoing is in the unplanned expulsion of the stresses we mistakenly believed could be suppressed. With the force of projectile vomit the stress is released as hostility.

In these moments where our emotions have gotten the best of us we frequently find ourselves lamenting that we said things we didn't mean to say or did things we didn't mean to do. Guilt over the fact that we can't "take it back" further complicates our emotional status. Where forgiveness is an option there is the chance to move on with mild embarrassment and a lesson learned. But this is not always the case. Denial can play a role. It is sometimes easier to blame others as the cause of the outburst than to accept responsibility for one's own actions. Likewise a grudge factor may play a role and this on both sides of the coin.

Resentment becomes a subtle though obstinate barrier in relationships. The one who behaved with hostility may resent the other as the perceived source of the stress that led to the outburst, and the recipient may harbor resentment because a trust has been broken that resulted in injury. Consider a mother who is burdened with marital and economic pressures and subsequently overreacts to the child that spilled its juice by issuing a brutal spanking. The child may never forget the trauma. The husband seeing the whelps resents the mother, and she resents him for being the "ass" that caused her frustration. Emotion on this level becomes a cycle of instability that can have complicated and lasting consequences.

The things that matter the most to us in our lives are always dripping with emotive potential. Family, community, employment, national identity, and of course religion are prime movers. These things represent our most meaningful connections in life. It is in our self-interest to protect them. I can't easily curse my wife, friends, employer, or my god, but the people I don't know like the girl at the fast food window who hands me the wrong food or the cashier at the store who is taking too long when "I" am in a hurry are fair game. Typically we don't really get mad at people we don't know. There's little to no emotional investment in them. We do however cart a lot of baggage around with us just in case the opportunity presents itself to make an unsolicited donation to that unwary stranger who is perceived to be incapable of reciprocation.

Recently when I was leaving an area shopping center a woman cut abruptly through my lane to get into the lane for a right turn. Her bumper sticker said "Honk, If You Love Jesus." I did honk when I saw it though with facetious intentions which were rewarded. Immediately she gave me the middle finger with a sustained vibrato indicating her interest in amplifying the gesture, and I'm pretty sure the string of words she uttered weren't from The Lord's Prayer. Ironically it is really easy for people to lose their religion; unfortunately emotional moments are the least successful time to press the issue.

It is only natural for human beings as a communal species to be human in public. This means our emotions will always be at work and play a role in how we interact. Yet if it is so easy to express ourselves emotionally to strangers, perhaps due to empathy on the positive side –

smiles, friendly gestures, shared humor, handshakes, or kindly compliments, but the occasional unsympathetic finger and fuck you on the more negative side, then it is no wonder that emotion is exacerbated when it intersects with meaningful connections. In fact we might say that one thing that identifies a connection as meaningful is that we have vested it with emotional bonds.

When someone views an obituary of a person he doesn't know it is easily scanned over without reaction, but if the phone rings and the dreaded news is about a loved one or close friend then a flood of emotion ensues. On almost a daily basis we see stories about jihadists sacrificing themselves in suicide bombings in Middle Eastern communities and marketplaces and we perhaps lift a brow or shake our heads. But when Islamist sympathizers placed bombs at the Boston Marathon or used hijacked planes as tactical weapons we were moved to tears of rage. When life gets personal we feel it.

One of the most basic ways we succeed in building viable community is through connecting groups of people through emotional attachment. We have learned to utilize the universality of human emotional experience as a means to build cohesive structures and provide motivation for individuals to join together in sets and subsets of group activity. Emotion joins such things as ritual and consensus as a way to engage in shared experience. It is part of the glue that holds us together. Every year on New Year's Eve the whole US population and many other nations as well are engaged in jovial celebration, imbibing champagne, and preparing to kiss at the stroke of midnight.

On July 4th a nation is called together to celebrate independence, liberty, and freedom, and on September 11th

it is called into mourning and solemn remembrance. On all levels of society from national to state to community to family human beings connect through shared experience and arbitrarily value the experience according to the significance it holds for the individuals in question. We feel something or it means nothing. If someone wants to start a community, sell a product, persuade others to adopt a point of view, or attract the interest of others, then there better be an emotional appeal or the endeavor is likely to fail and fall short of the desired goal.

The same is pretty much true when trying to persuade others to have a change of mind, perspective, or a change in their patterns of behavior. There has to be an exchange on an emotional level or at the very least there has to be compensation. You may offer me a job. It might even have less pay than my current job, but if there are aspects about the offer I "feel" good about I might agree to take it. Conversely if the server at my favorite restaurant convinces me to try a new entre instead of my regular choice and I don't like it I may feel disappointed even slighted because the exchange I made was unsatisfactory. I will continue to eat there but will stick to what I have found to be most satisfying.

If one takes candy from a baby then a tantrum can be expected. If one exchanges the candy for a nice piece of fruit the odds are better that the child will adapt. This underscores a significant point when dealing with change or loss. In fact one of the reasons loss of a loved one is so devastating emotionally is because there is no exchange or compensation. Death is often experienced as an abrupt and sudden disconnection, indifferent to the emotional investment one has. Something is taken that cannot be

replaced. It takes time to stabilize, adjust, and reorient one's self to the new reality.

For all the emphasis that is placed upon the notion of finding comfort in the bible a thorough read reveals just how problematic that is for modern culture. In fact one of the most morally reprehensible testaments to the huge disconnect between the bible and modern views of family, life, love, and loss is found in the Old Testament book of Job.

Clearly rooted in a primitive patriarchal culture where family was viewed economically Job demonstrates a completely naïve understanding of the psychological power of emotional connections. After god has finished his game of testing Job which included financial calamity, inflicting Job with illness, and causing the death of his children, god makes it all better. Job's illness is healed, his fortunes restored, and he gets new kids. That the authors of these stories ever thought it was appropriate to suggest a god who was so emotionally inept as to think a family who had lost a child could be appeased by "Here, have a new kid" is beneath the commonest of sense as we would measure it.

And this is supposed to be a divinely inspired story. The loving god celebrated by conservative Christians whose platform is "family values" did after all offer up his own child as a human sacrifice. Why would this god care about how we feel? Yet the stories of the bible themselves are woven into interpretative frameworks that are guided by our emotional needs. In some respects it doesn't matter what is actually written in the bible, only the way we can bargain a collection of thematic material into an ideology that supports the structures of our emotional,

psychological, and social well being. The house is built well with great attention to detail, but it is a glass house.

Ideology, principle, and world view are no less potent in meaning to individuals than the loved ones of close interpersonal relationships. In fact to the extent that personal identity is often wrapped in a life perspective the two can be virtually inseparable. Say something like "It was god's will" at a child's funeral where the family holds a strict Calvinist view of god's sovereignty and they might take it as comforting. Say the same thing to a moderately religious or non-religious family and you have committed a callous offense that will evoke ire in the worst way and possibly an ass chewing.

Those of us that are interested in seeing religion evolve or even dissolve from its superstitious and supernatural underpinnings in place of secular, humanistic, and evidence based forms of community cannot afford to dismiss the importance of emotional attachment. Again confronting a creationist with scientific fact is an exercise in futility. While perhaps it should be, it is not merely the information that is relevant. There is an intricately woven emotional network that must be replaced. Currently the perception of religious fundamentalists is that secularists and atheists want to take their candy with not even a nice piece of fruit in exchange. And yes there is a tantrum.

Being right as a matter of principle has its own intrinsic value, but it can get you killed, or slightly less unpleasant, excommunicated. This is the unfortunate fate for many of us who have been so bold as to come out of the closet of ignorance in favor of reason. I have nothing but the sincerest sympathy for the many of you that have

revealed to your family and friends that you do not believe in god, gods, supernatural forces, or divine shenanigans for which there is no evidence. Your courage rivals that of Rocky Balboa and is analogous to the announcer's comments in film IV when he points out that Rocky is not only contending with a near invincible Drago, but a hostile crowd, and the Soviet politburo looking on.

Similarly there are many of you out there who know you are agnostic, possibly atheist, and struggle constantly deferring to silence in the face of the hurtful consequences that may follow if you are honest with significant others in your life. Many clergy are also in this boat of dilemma. Statistics show there is an increasing number of people who identify themselves as atheist, secular, or unaffiliated with religion, and no doubt a significant population is emerging seeking a fresh context of understanding in light of what we now know about the universe. There are hundreds if not thousands of clergy persons who are poised, if they can begin to act with honesty and integrity, to aid congregations with a transition away from archaic biblical motifs into viable forms of non-religious community. At present though the stakes are high and emotionally charged.

If we revisit the Job story there is an interesting caveat. While this story fails miserably to connect with our humanity that values life and the loved ones we embrace in its living, it does provide an analogy worth noting. The church and perhaps the synagogue and the mosque as well are like Job's finale. The institutions of religion themselves have a meaningful place in society and may well come to prosper without religious ideology. Religion after all is the disease. It is a leprous lesion that once eradicated leaves

the opportunity for a healthy life. And those new children, perhaps come to represent new perspectives, a new kind of faith where the subjective journey turns toward the future propelled by reason and science instead of ignorance and superstition. Whatever the case whenever something new or different challenges the old and normative with change, it must do so with passion, with conviction, and with emotionally viable opportunities.

We can kind of think of emotion as infrastructure. It is an underlying substance that gives meaning its meaning. In the same way that everything meaningful to us involves some type of connection, for something to be meaningful requires an emotional charge. I can look at the stars and galaxies and marvel in enlightenment as I absorb photons a billion years from their source, or get pissed as hell at the insensitive neighbor that bombards my celestial view with photons from his porch. Meaning entails emotion. Sometimes the emotion is built in and occurs naturally, but sometimes it develops over time as the connection itself becomes increasingly meaningful.

A death brings to light fears one may have held many years. To love is to risk. In some respects we all know it is coming but "just not yet." If the death is tragic and sudden the outburst of emotion is deafening and no words can bring comfort. A course must be run. Early on, however, when two people are first meeting and attraction takes a step toward commitment the infrastructure of emotional substance is being gradually woven throughout the connection. In time two people are in love. The wedding rings are an outward sign of the meaningful connection that has evolved within.

Those who have already revealed to their families that they no longer believe in god have likely experienced repercussions, and possibly very hurtful consequences. I have heard the stories of many especially from those in conservative Christian traditions where the reaction, more often it seems from fathers and male siblings than mothers and sisters though I don't have good science on that, has been to be disaffiliated from the family. "If you are not going to be with us in heaven, then you are not welcome with us now" is a common mantra expressing the emotional reaction.

A lot has changed in a brief period of time. A death event has occurred. The more literally persons believe in the bible the more likely their identity is woven into a community with highly protected and defended boundaries. Not only is there an "emergency" situation where my child is in danger of hellfire, but I have failed to safeguard a loved one. An internal struggle with guilt ensues and the search for someone to share the blame begins. The home is engulfed in a storm and it is not uncommon for family members to articulate their resentment. "Couldn't you have just kept this news to yourself?" Cognitive dissonance has few greater friends than the moment one who is raised to be honest and to have integrity faces condemnation for doing so.

There is also embarrassment where one must face the community with the news. In this case the community is more an angry mob than a support network. "We all know what must be done." There is also denial expressed by persistent disbelief that this could be happening to "me" on one end and a more hopeful resolve on the other held in the notion that the fledgling atheist is merely going

through a phase and will repent to good sense. Naturally this is offensive and hurtful to the one who has "come out," and perhaps worse is the ache of melancholy held in the realization that the peer pressures from less significant others is overriding the family relationship.

A religious family is most often a subset of a religious community. Emotional energy charges the connections with meaningful shared experience. It is not simply what "I" believe, but what "we" believe. It doesn't matter if what is believed is accurate or genuinely consistent with the biblical witness – and usually it isn't; it is what "we" believe.

There is a picture here, a comfortable world view, and in it we are all the same. We believe in god, go to church, believe in the bible, say grace before meals, drop what we are doing and gather at Thanksgiving, Christmas, Easter, and Mother's Day, believe the world has gone to hell in a hand basket because they took the bible and prayer out of schools, and preferably vote republican. There is some leeway for deviation, but not too much. "I am an atheist" is the bubble burster. It comes across as an act of desecration akin to taking a can of spray paint and smearing a giant "A" across Grant Wood's classic painting American Gothic.

Like death and in most cases change in general no one wants it to happen, but it does. Ultimately it is how we adapt to change that defines us. Religion has to change and in some sense die like everything else. Yet a new world view must emerge, a new portrait with renewed and freshly defined connections that are equally meaningful to the old must be painted. This takes time. Those in this situation already know the difficulty and struggle in a void

of brokenness. Patience is no longer a virtue; it is a challenge against emotional instability and heartache.

Longing has set in, but it is the same on both sides of the equation. The emotional infrastructure of the broken relationships has to be rebuilt. This is complicated and may not have the happy ending people want. It can be the case that the repairs on the family end are taking place by strengthening their bonds to the religious community while at the same time new connections of support and assurance are being developed by the ousted other with another sympathetic and like-minded community. Like the days when one left the homeland to venture to a new world, the goodbyes were said and never the twain shall they meet again. It doesn't have to end this way, but it might and it would be disingenuous to offer a trite hope that this is an easy fix. There is no snake oil to sell.

One thing is certain. Where emotional reaction is engaged, or a situation is highly emotional, there is no headway to be made in the relationship. Arguing ideology with someone who is in denial is only going to trigger emotional defenses and the stalemate will stand. In fact it may grow worse as an intractable perception of the situation is reinforced by repetitive arguments. All ones have to do is look at each other and they're right back in the thick of it. A positive emotional connection has to be established, but it can't be accomplished emotionally. The connection has to be established on a different level.

If it follows that eventually we face change through a phase of bargaining or negotiation, then there is some opportunity here for progress. A word of caution though, rational discussion may be possible but there are trip wires everywhere. Say the wrong thing, push too hard, trigger

an ideological position the other has yet to modify or reconcile and its do not pass go, do not collect your $200, straight back to denial. The goal in conversations at this level should focus on reestablishing the shared humanity, the good and special things that have meaning but are clouded by the conflict. You want cognitive dissonance to emerge and work in your favor. "I know what my religion teaches, what my community takes for granted as normative, but I love my son, daughter, spouse, etc." The hope here is to move into emotional reflection.

Persons that have yet to reveal their agnostic, secular, or atheist perspective to friends and loved ones are in a slightly more creative position. Chances are you have worked through what it means for gods and heavens and hells not to exist and have come to a point of resolution and contentment. Some families take the news in stride and in fact may see it as permission to articulate doubts they too have always experienced. Remember few people actually attempt to live their religion by the book which is an indicator that at least subconsciously they fear no repercussion from a deity. The majority of people create their own religious paradigm which essentially means "If I am a good person I will go to heaven when I die."

Our imaginations are capable of doing better than that. Becoming aware that the gods of the bible are not real and that the message is flawed serves as an impetus to think about what is and what might be based upon evidence and knowledge. As we recognize the importance of this life our humanity glows a bit brighter which means that conversations with family members about a non-religious life and a world without gods can actually deepen the meaning of our relationships and strengthen

the emotional bonds. Unless you are only interested in dropping the "atheist" bomb as an act of resentment because you are angry with your significant others take the time to lay some emotional groundwork.

We want a rational environment where trust is not threatened to allow time for our emotions to adjust. A reflective posture and language that poses new questions as opposed to shattering conclusions creates an atmosphere where acceptance and transformation are possible. Kübler-Ross was wrong that DABDA was a uniform process that took people through the stages of grief. We do however find a useful model for understanding how some cultures have been socialized to handle change. There is fluidity without guarantee that a process of going from start to finish happens every time. We can muddle around going back and forth, or like by-pass surgery we can reroute and skip the clogged arteries.

Families who have the opportunity to deal with the impending loss of a loved one over a period of time have shown that resilience not grief is the outcome. This is largely due to the fact that they have spent much time in emotional reflection and have prepared to embrace life through an inevitable change. The loss of gods and superstitious world views is no different. To be sure the task is markedly more difficult where conservative religious views are entrenched and where a family's social identity is firmly rooted in a fundamentalist culture. If you sense that it is impossible to make headway with finding acceptance from them then it probably is.

Human beings need to have meaning in their lives. We accomplish this by establishing connections to which we can attach emotional value. To be alone and

unconnected is to be in a limbo of meaninglessness. If you are an atheist and you know your family will reject you begin building ties and relationships with others who share your world view. Families who can't have children of their own find that adopting a child can be equally meaningful. The reciprocity of love becomes more important than fertility itself. Atheists too need love, community, meaningful ties to others, and affirmation. One's biological connections might not be the best place to sink these roots.

It is a mistake to think that you will be able to convince or even convert a conservative Christian parent or sibling to a secular or atheist perspective. Some have approached this dilemma from that point of view and have unfortunately reaped a whirlwind. The temptation to try is rooted in the hope of maintaining the meaningful connection one has enjoyed, sort of the desire to continue after the fact with business as usual. Think Rolling Stones – "You can't always get what you want." If Richard Dawkins, Lawrence Krauss, and Bill Nye can't convince the Wendy Wright's, William Lane Craig's, and Ken Ham's of the world with rock solid facts, then the chance of any one of us convincing our Southern Baptist, Pentecostal, or Catholic families that god doesn't exist is somewhere between a crap shoot and a death wish.

It comes as a rude awakening but we are not necessarily the most important game in town, not even to our parents. There are limits whether we like to admit it or not. If what we come to represent is threatening to their well being, threatens to undo all they have come to value, then we can easily be parlayed into a less meaningful status in their eyes. While biology seems to trump all else,

we are social creatures, and the biggest mistake is to underestimate the importance of social connections and institutional affiliation.

When someone asserts "I am a born again Christian" he or she is not just making a personal faith claim, it is an establishment clause that carries with it the huge emotional, psychological, and social investment one has made with time, energy, and personal resources. This confession carries with it a life spent in the perception of an honorable duty worth defending at all costs. This isn't blood is thicker than water; it is blood on blood with all the marrow, sinew, and flesh attached.

Conservative and fundamentalist minded persons rarely change their views through conflict. They must see it for themselves. Fortunately when they do their social make-up has prepared them to stand up for what they believe is right. We have reached a turning point in our time on planet earth and it is evident that religion must evolve into secular forms that dismiss divisive supernatural claims in favor of a human and earth species centered perspective. This shift has to occur on both personal and social levels. Until those convinced their investment in traditional religion as the model for a moral and just civilization is deficient and this by the emergence of secular institutions that demonstrate a greater efficacy, the battle will continue to exacerbate and rage.

Let's talk about rage. First, as an atheist I too am optimistic about the rising number of those who are unaffiliated with religion, or coming out as openly secular, atheist, or agnostic. It is a hopeful sign. However I am a tad suspicious and concerned that part of what we are seeing reflected in statistics involves many people who are

jaded and lashing out through a phase of emotional reaction. Saying you no longer believe in god because you are wounded by betrayal, which religion does to people on a rather frequent basis, is not the same thing as having come to a well adjusted acceptance of the real universe where archaic religions have nothing to contribute. Without transformation the process isn't complete.

Emotional reaction is indicative of instability. It may well be that many who are now angry, bitter, and disenfranchised by the hurt religion has caused them will move into a healthy non-religious perspective, but religious apologists abound. Many persons feel cut off and alone. To date there are very few forms of secular community for persons to identify with, and the religious always have their eye on the vulnerable. While it is a bit bawdy and satisfying seeing the many Facebook comments on atheist pages where the brazen and courageous say "Fuck Jesus" and "The god of the bible is a sadistic, malevolent, piece of shit motherfucker," it also gives pause for concern. Are these people really happy atheists expressing a moment of righteous indignation, or are they merely venting the hostility of their wounds?

Many of us know too well the proselytizing interests of Christians and Muslims and the tactics they will use. Persons in an emotional phase are vulnerable. There is always a sympathetic ear followed by a soothing voice to assure someone that "our church" or "our religion" isn't like the one who hurt you. If the expression "There's a sucker born every minute" was only a humorous cliché we could rest easy and let nature take its course. But then again we are part of nature and natural process involves competition. Without viable alternatives for social

affiliation that have winnowed out the fraudulent and manipulative wiles of religion, many "unaffiliated" are fair game to those who will prey upon them.

Jesus told a parable about a person's "house" being swept clean of demons, but because nothing positive came in to fill the void soon the demonic clutter was exponentially worse than in the beginning. Christian and Muslim evangelists are locked in a bitter competition. They want flesh. They want money. They are struggling to bolster their institutional presence. They want power and they will stop at nothing to get it. Their eyes are on the vulnerable and those who have felt the emptiness of religious experience. The gods never follow through leaving us empty and confused. Still many of us are reluctant, even in our anger, our rage, to accept a world without some supernatural activity. There remains a persistent "maybe," and this works to the advantage of those who would use us, salve our emotional distress by tricking us back into a prison of denial.

Christianity is experienced and quite proficient in this endeavor. It has softened some over the ages from using brute force and now prefers a more psychological approach. Exacerbating guilt has always been effective, and of course telling people they are going to get lots of money and blessings and eventually a heaven with more money and blessings is playing pretty well especially in the US. The single most lucrative population they proselytize is persons whose meaningful connections to the larger society have been disrupted and whose emotions are in flux. This along with the fact that fundamentalist Christians seem intent on arming themselves and pushing their agenda into the political

sphere should be a monumental concern to free thinking people, secularists, agnostics, and atheists who to date lack a competitive social structure.

Islam is another matter. We should not be confused about what is happening here, and it is entirely irrelevant that the majority of Muslims claim they are peaceful and offer their religion as a way of life with greater intrinsic value than other religions. Both Christianity and Islam are inseparably rooted in a mutually exclusive paradigm that states that only the faithful adherents within their religion will ultimately be loved, saved, and rewarded by their god. Everyone else is destined for destruction. Regardless of the toned down versions and the gentle smiles that accompany their moderate messages, the god of the Koran and Bible is intent on carrying out a moment of mass genocide and global destruction. As was the theme of the Highlander films "There can be only one."

There is a rage loosed in the world which some like to say isn't about religion or ethnicity but fanaticism. There is a tension between respecting freedom of choice in regard to the practice of religion and certain ways the religion is practiced. The actor Ben Affleck recently expressed this sentiment in conflict with Bill Maher and Sam Harris arguing that most Muslims were ordinary or moderate people who do not practice or endorse violence. From the rather egalitarian point of view popular in the West and enshrined in the US Constitution he is correct, but from the perspective of the religion itself he is terribly wrong.

Historically Judaism, Christianity, and Islam have demonstrated that it is completely irrelevant what majorities or moderates within the religions think or feel.

In fact as we reflect upon the power of emotion and the potential volatility it represents, it is worth noting that many persons in these religions, moderates and liberals in particular, exhibit less emotion than they should. Large numbers of people affiliate with Christianity but don't believe the bible should be taken literally, cull out the "good" themes that appeal to them, and rarely view their religion as exclusive. This bent toward universalism is naïve and breeds an apathy that makes it easy to dismiss accountability beyond a personal level.

The religions themselves are flawed paradigms with a maelstrom at the center and there is always a gravitational pull toward extreme literalism. This is so because the source material of these religions, the bible and Koran, demand an exclusive world view where violence is necessary to achieve faithfulness to the god's will. It doesn't make any difference how many people interpret verses to be symbolic or passé, there will always be some who are drawn to define themselves as the "true" believers and subsequently take to themselves the authority to act with indifference to the "opinions" of the larger community.

1st century Judaism spanned the Mediterranean. The majority of Jews were connected to a mainstream characterized by tensions between the conservative temple priesthood and the more moderate synagogue community of Pharisees and rabbis. Both struggled to be cooperative with Rome and had generally accepted their place in the larger Roman world. A smaller community of insurrectionists, not that dissimilar to modern jihadists, upset the apple cart. These more radicalized groups believed they could fight Rome, that god was on their side,

and that their "faith" expressed through violence would lead to the restoration of a Jewish kingdom. Their repetitive "bee stings" against Rome led to the destruction of Jerusalem and its temple.

The history of Christianity is so replete with acts of violence, persecution, and war that it would take volumes to tell of it. Yet consider the period of inquisitions where extreme conservatism sought to deepen the Vatican's authority by purging the church of anyone who held dissenting opinions. Puritan Colonists were equally brutal in persecuting what they deemed heretical. And even though contemporary fundamentalists have yet to resort to violence as they persistently try to influence government, there are the occasional extremists who bomb an abortion clinic or murder a physician in what they deem a greater act of love for god's will.

Islam is unquestionably the most violent and potentially lethal religion in the contemporary world. It is also the most complex. It certainly can be argued that the religion is being used to legitimize extreme political ambitions especially in the Middle East where war has ravaged societies and left them bereft of infrastructure, resources, and access to fair representation in newly formed governments. There is also the age old internal conflict between Sunni and Shia interpretations of Islam. In a perfect world, or rather in a different world, the views of someone like Ben Affleck should have merit. Unfortunately with Islam it is not possible to separate the politics and ethnicity from the religion. Islam is inherently Arab and theocratic.

Islam, a word generally taken to mean "peace," more accurately means "contentment in submission to the will

of Allah." Koran, a word that means "recite," is technically only carrying the force of Allah's inspiration when read or more particularly heard in Arabic. From its inception Islam was essentially an Arab nationalist movement. Mohammed lived at a time when a divided Christendom had waned in its influence over Palestine, the Arabian Peninsula, and much of Africa. Mecca, a cultural and economic center had for centuries drawn the diverse interests of Arab clans and with them came their various deities. Allah was one among many.

Mohammed was well travelled, well connected, and recognized the opportunity to unite his people in such a way that would enable them to rise as a great nation. For such a great task he knew he needed a god, a divine mandate, much like that claimed by Rome under Christ. At age forty alone in a cave he encountered, oddly enough, the very same angel who had once prepared Mary to lose her virginity. Under the auspices of divine revelation, and in fact what would be the final divine revelation, revelation that had begun with Adam, continued through Moses and Jesus, Mohammed would emerge with the last word and the religion to complete all religions.

Islam became the ultimate example of "one-upmanship," but it would have to be sold along with its requirements for a new social order and government. Some bought into it but many clans did not. War ensued. By the time of his death in 632 Mohammed had not only received the complete Koran, but had also succeeded in conquering the Arab world and imposing Islam as its religion, its rule of law, and as a culture to be spread throughout the world.

The following decades and centuries saw the expanse of Islam through military conquest. The acts of genocide and brutality quickly matched that of Christianity and the two religions have checked each other ever since. The rule of Islam has not always been brutal; in fact several periods in its history have produced great cultural and intellectual achievements. Unfortunately recurring periods of fundamentalist rule characterized by intolerance and violent upheaval have laid waste to hopes for a more moderate and cooperative Islam co-existing on the global stage.

The important thing to acknowledge is there is an inseparable root of militancy at the heart of Islam, and as long as the religion thrives there will always be an element of extremism beckoning to rise. At times the religion does assume moderate forms. The overtly patriarchal dominance of women softens, and education returns as a matter of prominence for all citizens. Culture and economy take on a more inviting global perspective, and the world is lulled into a sense of progress. Yet the harsh words of death to infidels and to Muslims who would defect remains in the text. As with Christianity and Judaism spiritualized and symbolic interpretations of the harshest verses come to the forefront, but a volatile literalism always looms.

Christianity is content in the moment where war is concerned largely because the US and western allies fight insurgency, radical aggression for global dominance, and the religious extremism prone to committing genocide and crimes against humanity on political and economic grounds. The rhetoric of terrorism suffices, and for Christians the label terrorist has finally given them a term

equivalent to infidel. Fundamentalist Christians however see their role in it lusting to continue where the Crusades left off, and will have an undying devotion to Israel until Jesus returns to the Mount of Olives.

Neither religion can be trusted, and with Islam actively engaged in militant jihad the argument that most Muslims are peaceful is somewhat of a façade. The swelling ranks of Islamist extremists enraged with a lust for blood and a desire to force Islamic law upon the world are not being bolstered by converts from the secular world. Granted there are great wounds of injustice suffered by many in the war torn regions of the Middle East, and the desire for revenge on personal levels transcends the institution of religion. The rage in some cases is understandable. Still it is inseparable from the religion itself and there is no corrective mechanism that can hold extremists accountable to the larger "peaceful" community.

If this were a new thing, whether on the part of Christians or Muslims, it might be different. But the violence is a recurrent pestilence. The gods have sat back and watched perhaps enjoying cold beers and tubs of buttered popcorn while wars and blood feuds have transitioned from swords to bullets, from bullets to bombs, missiles, and lethal gasses. We sense the appalling nightmare of what's next. Gideon's army of 300 will indeed level the playing field against the drone wielding superpowers when they acquire the magic button that wafts up mushroom clouds as a pleasing sacrifice unto their god. Damnation can finally be the fine point on human history.

Evolution is up against some serious odds. The gods of past cultures died out occasionally because people traded up and found a more suitable deity to venerate, but most often the gods crumbled to dust beneath the feet of war and conquest. The present conflict portends similar results. It is not Arab culture or ethnicity that is the problem. It is the toxic connection to an unreal supernatural specter that as with Christianity breeds instability, dysfunction, and volatility into what could otherwise be meaningful institutional structures.

As it stands the emotional charge makes reason impossible. It is bad enough when denial reacts with hurtful and hateful words, when families are torn apart by blind loyalty to failing ideologies, but when the emotional reaction reaches violent rage, hostility unleashed as blood lust and murder, all arguments for the legitimacy of a world view fail. There are no excuses. Humpty-Dumpty cannot be put together again. In this respect these religions have forever lost face. Those who affiliate with them must face this fact.

"The Bargain Marketplace"

There is nothing like an old fashioned market where the price of goods is open to barter and negotiation. A bustling crowd meanders through the plethora of choices politely squeezing in and out from one vendor to the next. The rich colors of fruits and vegetables and the aroma of freshly baked breads tantalize the senses, and discerning needs from wants becomes a game of frugality as the purse lightens. It is a magical place where endless possibilities seem to abound. There is something for everyone.

The mind is like such a marketplace. Ideas abound. We assign them values and negotiate their importance. In the mind we can imagine anything, explain everything, and rationalize even the most absurd contemplations. We can justify the unjustifiable. We can un-contradict any contradiction. We don't have to be right, accurate, or correct, just convincing, plausible, or placated from any angst the thinking may cause.

In the mind we create worlds, tomes of reality, and paradigms that make sense of our experience. Sometimes we change our minds because it suits us or because we must. It's a fickle game, thinking, talking ourselves in an out of just about anything. Sometimes our minds talk us out of changing our minds sending out thoughts to end where they began steadfast and resolute. It's a real mixed bag in there.

The mind has proven to be the greatest asset for human survival. Conversely it has also proven to be the greatest adversary. We appear to be the only species riddled by such ambiguity. At the heart of it surely lies the

fact that we like ourselves so much, that life means so much to us, that we just can't accept its inherent impermanence and temporality. We want infinite stability. We want the utopian dream, to live happily ever after. It is a centerpiece at the dinner table, a cornucopia of plastic fruit which unfortunately looks delicious but can't be eaten.

Reality is full of all the things we don't want. We don't want to die, age, be sick, in pain, poor, too hot or too cold, lonely, infringed upon, betrayed, wounded, disrespected, deceived, cheated, scorned, embarrassed, or made the butt of a joke. What we don't want is known as a matter of stark contrast because mostly we get what we want but can't hold on to it. And it is not for lack of trying.

It is amazing the lengths we will go to in order to convince ourselves that change is not afoot. We order our lives with habits, routines, and rituals the repetition of which creates the feel of sameness. It is both blessing and curse that our eyes lack the capacity to see the subtle changes constantly taking place as we live the course of our lives. That not one second that has passed is identical to the one that followed is a certainty we work diligently to ignore. And as the days come where hair thins and grays we evoke the skills of childhood where pretending was the norm and thus tease our mirrors with antics of tomfoolery. O to be the young lad I remember who upon exiting the shower could merely imagine the pretty girl and have a place to hang his towel indefinitely.

Until it is utterly impossible denial is a default state in the human mind. Everything is OK until it is absolutely not. The man who "knows" where he is in spite of his wife's chiding to look at the map is all good and quite sure

of himself until he crosses the Texas line when he was supposed to be aiming for Oklahoma. We laugh at our capacity for stubbornness and blind refusal to pay attention largely because it is a common faux pas, yet we seem quite content to let such things stand without corrective measures. It is as though we prefer stupid especially when smart means having to change something.

The reason we can identify denial as a default state of mind is when you poke it or unsettle it in the least way you get an emotional reaction followed by a defense strategy that restores its comfort zone. Denial is like my dog Annie who now owns the bed and couch. She'll move if you lay down, but will quickly return and snuggle up. If you move or disturb her in the slightest, she'll give a disgruntled growl and storm off like you violated her person. Fortunately she does not hold a grudge which is more than can be said about many humans. Intractably she returns.

In Kübler-Ross' stages of grief she believed people went through a cycle of stages from start to finish where denial moved to anger to bargaining to depression and eventually to acceptance. As previously acknowledged this model fails as a universal theory that explains the stages of grief, but it holds pretty well with some modification as a model for understanding the patterns of human behavior in the face of change. Denial functions to minimize the impact of change and at times to maintain the illusion that change is not occurring or is unwarranted. Because most things in life we trust as stable or foundational have meaning to us they are emotionally charged. But being upset in the face of something that challenges the comfort and security of something we deem immutable is merely

reactionary and insufficient at restoring the equilibrium denial affords.

A stage where we bargain or rather negotiate over the impact of the situation is inevitable. The first line of defense is to defend denial and seek to discredit the experience that a change has occurred. A second line of defense is to acknowledge the change but to reinterpret the event in question such that the "change" didn't change anything. The motivation on both counts is not to process the change into a new understanding of reality where the old is simply gone and something new must now emerge, but to protect the point of denial at all costs. It is a circular process that is rarely disrupted by debate or reasoned argument on behalf of the change event. The "What ifs" can have infinite recourse.

Acceptance has to happen simultaneously at the point where change occurs, where the shock hits the system. This may happen immediately or after the cycle between denial and bargaining finally plays out and the inevitable is realized. This is one of the reasons the Kübler-Ross theory fails as a series of stages one must move through in order to emerge from grief, and why research has shown that resilience in the face of loss is more common. Acceptance does move us to a post bargaining phase of emotional reflection where the new situation is processed and internalized. At that point acceptance as transformation is ready to begin, but if one is found bargaining then there is still a long way to go.

There was a recent story done on NPR that examined motives in medicine where terminal illness was concerned. It was a debate between a prompt trek into palliative care for patients whose illness had progressed too far for a cure

and the potentially unethical practice among some physicians to milk the system at the patient's expense through endless referrals to specialists for treatments that were unsupported by evidence to be effective. One family whose experience was chronicled revealed that the wife was diagnosed with an advanced stage cancer.

Initially she tried surgeries, radiation, and chemotherapy. Her condition failed to improve, but she was encouraged to continue trying new treatments. Her last round of radiation therapy had left her near death and in a state of great suffering, still she was told there was some improvement and a bit of hope. She and her husband finally revisited the initial diagnosis, accepted it and chose hospice care. They had a little more than a week to reflect upon their lives and say goodbye with dignity. The husband lamented the massive expense, the exacerbated suffering of his wife, and some remorse over the quality time they might have shared had they accepted the inevitable sooner.

The man's wife was a fighter, a courageous person, who like many of us had been socialized to hang in there, not give up, and defend what we hold dear. These are important values that apply in many cases, but not always. Religion, like those whose illness has progressed beyond cure, is case in point. Religion, and for example Christianity in particular, is two things. First it is an institution, a social structure woven into the fabric of society and is characterized by the performance of specific roles considered to be meaningful on many levels. Second it is personal, functioning in the lives of individuals as a network of support for subjective faith claims. The two are related and can support each other, but are not identical.

Not everyone believes in god the same way nor do the things people believe connect them to god fall neatly into a simple unified framework. There is a gambit to be run. Numerous factors have to be taken into account not the least of which include culture, economic status, degree of education, political affiliation, and the historical ties one has to a particular world view. The one thing held in common is the fact that in every case there will be those whose serve as apologists for the belief system in question. Typically this lot falls to clergy especially when viewing religion on an institutional level and in some case when dealing with issues of personal faith as well.

Somewhere around half of the world's Christians identify as Roman Catholic. In spite of the notion that the priests fundamentally serve the people their primary role is to serve as professional apologists for the institution of the church. The way Roman Catholics believe in god and connect to their faith in the religion on a personal level is different than that experienced by Protestants. In Catholicism the institution is everything and must be defended at all costs. It has still been well less than a century since the Latin mass was modified to vernacular languages where congregants could understand the liturgy being spoken on their behalf. It didn't really matter if they understood the words, scripture, or the details of the church's theology since their relationship to god was being mediated through the priests.

In Roman Catholicism the words attributed to Jesus in the gospel of Matthew where Jesus renames Simon Peter "the rock" upon which the church would be built and gives him the "keys to the kingdom" are taken literally. Legend states that Peter was the first bishop of Rome.

Subsequently each pope is his successor and receives the authority to act as the Vicar of Christ on earth. It is the church that mediates salvation to individuals through the sacraments.

For those born into Catholicism the first sacrament is baptism and one's place as a child of god is secure. Years of catechism follow where the pertinent dogmas of the church are taught. At the onset of adolescence one's baptism and learning are confirmed in a rite of passage that translates the youth into adulthood. Marriage too is considered a sacrament, and as the sacraments are the vehicles of god's grace it is not surprising the church is reluctant to modify its stance on divorce and same gender relationships. The church has typically held that procreation is the primary reason for sexual union in marriage and as such forbids the use of birth control. What better way to have a constant rate of growth tailored to support the institution?

The Eucharist is the magic sacrament and this for two reasons. According to the doctrine of transubstantiation when the priest blesses the bread and wine a miracle occurs. It is literally transformed into the body and blood of Jesus Christ. The ability to feast upon the divine and be refilled with god's grace on a regular basis throughout one's life is a prerequisite for heaven which the church controls. It is the sacrament of consistent grace and to be forbidden from it is to be put in jeopardy of divine punishment and hellfire. The church grants and revokes permission to ingest this salvation and in so doing has found a powerful way to manipulate adherents into obedience.

The sacrament of confession likewise plays a significant role. The priest alone has the authority to absolve one from sins which must be privately confessed to the priest preferably on a regular basis. This brings to light a special sacrament that most Catholics never receive, Holy Orders. Those individuals who are drawn to become priests upon completion of their studies and ecclesiastical requirements are set apart, sanctified by the church, and empowered to perform the sacramental rites. Celibacy has been required for many centuries as a testament that the priest is now wed to the church. While many people may see priests as a bit odd in so much as they are married to an institution and live on limited means, for Roman Catholics their priests have great power and authority.

We don't know why the Roman Catholic Church has been a magnet for pedophiles, but surely being in a frequent and private position to interact with young boys where power is virtually absolute factors into it. That a priest would console the youth with assurances that fellatio was an act that reciprocates Christ's love is an egregious perversion of trust. The church's response to this gross crime against children, a crime that we have discovered has been recurrent and pervasive within the institution perhaps for centuries, is equally perverse and unconscionable. What greater evidence exists that this monstrous expression of religion is concerned foremost with self-preservation than the fact that these priests were hidden, protected, transferred from one congregation to another in attempts to avoid embarrassment to the church, all the while knowing that repeat offenses would occur and that the church would do everything in its power to cover up the truth?

It is true that much outrage has been expressed by Catholics over this vast scandal. Many priests have been imprisoned and the church has paid hefty civil penalties. Still the institution, from the Vatican to the parish, maintains its credibility, its authority, and denies any real culpability for the atrocities past or present it has perpetrated against humanity. To the death one must suppose, the Last Rite, which is also a sacrament wielded by priests too bring to closure the church's tyranny over souls, will be this institution's stance. If you are Roman Catholic will you not see this façade for what it is?

If the stakes were not so high one could muse in whimsical humor at the creative dogmatism the Roman Catholic Church has brought to the world of religion. It is the master of fixing contradiction with fallacy. After Nicea where Jesus was proclaimed both fully human and fully divine as a definitive resolution to the competing forms of Christian Gnosticism, a new problem emerged. How does one get around original sin, and what about Mary? She now had become "the Mother of God." The church declared her a perpetual virgin in spite of gospel traditions that said otherwise, and decided that she too ascended up to heaven like Jesus. Of course this problem wasn't completely resolved until the 19th century when it was decided that Mary's soul had been cleansed of original sin in her mother's womb before she was born – the Immaculate Conception.

Sin has always been a real nemesis for this church, or perhaps actually it is the problem of grace as unmerited favor. If this loving god was actually willing to freely forgive human transgressions because he recognized it was his entire fault in the first place, then one wouldn't

need the church. What to do about post baptismal sin led to the doctrine of penance. What to do about un-confessed sin led to the wonderful place we know as purgatory. And of course when the church needed extra funds to build cathedrals and such it learned it could sell indulgences to the wealthy as a means to forgive really nasty sins like political corruption, greed, and murder.

One must also give a tip of the hat to the efficacy of this church for restoring at least a semblance of pagan polytheism to the heavenly realms. To think of all the trouble the post-exilic Jews went through to establish Yahweh as the lone god, sovereign, without consort or heavenly kin, concerned only with directing the affairs of mortals in the right direction is almost disheartening. Well, leave a religion up to a Roman Emperor or two and one is bound to be on the fast track to getting a goddess back in the mix and a saintly pantheon to receive prayers and bestow favors.

The priest who stands before the people is the grass roots marionette and he is loyal to the puppeteer. The best priests are the ones who make us feel like we are loved by them and the church for our own sake, for who we are. We are assured that they are here to serve us, have our best interest at heart, and that they are on a divine mission that translates into our eternal well being. The fact is much more profane. This institution exists to maintain its political, social, and economic power, and it uses the most basic human fears to manipulate people into its service.

The Roman Catholic Church has proven that with enough money, power, and desire to direct the affairs of the world gods are entirely unnecessary. Once they appropriated the words of Jesus "Whatever you bind on

earth will be bound in heaven, and whatever you loose on earth will be loosed in heaven (Mt 16:19)" god was remanded to the ceiling of the Sistine Chapel and Jesus to the crucifix. For all of the religions that claim their origin stems from visions of a lone mystic on a mountaintop or in cave none surpass the Vatican's prolific license to manufacture words for god. One may rest assured that as need arises, whether by circumstance, conflict, or contradiction, the will of god will be adjusted accordingly. The Roman Catholic Church has honed apologetics into a veritable art form, but they have been at it for a very long time.

Protestants too protect their institutions. Consider for a moment the great importance placed upon church membership. Anyone who has ever visited a church knows the pressure felt when the offering plate is passed and more so when the invitation is given. A preacher's success depends on being able to convince people to walk down the aisle affirm their acceptance of Jesus Christ and pledge themselves in dutiful support of the particular church. It is perfectly acceptable to convince people who belong to other churches to join your church, and in fact it is quite the game. With declining numbers of new converts it is essential to the survival of the institution to "rob Peter in order to pay Paul."

Small congregations particularly those with an aging population have for years felt the sting as their children and younger prospects have migrated to newer churches which offer popular programs for youth and more vibrant worship styles. Sometimes evangelism takes the form of competing convictions as when Baptists work to convert Methodists or when churches claim their interpretation of

the bible is more accurate than others, but frequently the key for drawing new members to a church is presenting an agenda or format that has social appeal. As the prosperity churches have discovered promising newcomers that god wants them to be happy, blessed, and rich works pretty well. Flamboyance works as well especially when congregants get to be on television or have their ego stroked by affiliating with what they perceive to be a really popular "in" community.

The initial point here is that many of the tactics being used to draw and keep people actively engaged in the religious institution are not religious. This should be a sign for folks. The preachers and clergy who "run the show" while perhaps devoted to their religious convictions are nevertheless professional apologists, negotiators, and bargainers. Whether the method is to tell people what they want to hear or argue for the churches political and theological correctness it is the institution they are being paid to serve and defend. God as an invisible ally is a significant asset. Claims can be made for which there is no falsification, and everything the church does to survive can be cloaked with divine countenance. Even grandma's fried chicken and a friendly game of horseshoes can take a step heavenward after the blessing at a church picnic.

We mustn't forget that the church as an integral institution has been around a long time. The pilgrims were landing at Plymouth before the Age of Enlightenment began in Europe. The work of Isaac Newton, John Locke, Hume, Kant and many others would be a while coming and even longer, if ever still, to the minds of most ordinary folk. Yes before Newton, before Darwin, before Pasteur, and before most every scientific discovery we know today,

including critical biblical scholarship, the Puritans, Anglicans, Baptists, Presbyterians, Methodists, Quakers, Lutherans, and Catholics had settled on these shores. Churches were built of one variety or another in most every community and the cemeteries that honor the memories of our ancestors frequently repose in the shadows of their steeples.

There was a lot of brick and mortar invested in a way of life that no one expected to change. Time though has left its mark. Gradually the buildings fall prey to wind and rain and even gravestones stand nameless leaving only the knowledge that "someone" was interred in history. Like erosion in nature ideas also decay. Knowledge condemns the imagination to the fetters of reality. God has not escaped these bonds, or at least that suspicion has nagged away at the social subconscious mind and persists like a recurring toothache. Deep down we know the tooth is dead, but it is a front tooth we dare not lose less an unsightly gap remain.

The image of landscapes devoid of their steeple incisors is too ugly a painting to paint. It doesn't immediately occur to us that there is recourse to a different kind of salvation so we exhaust ourselves fighting windmills for their indiscretion. "How dare they reveal the winds of change, and in broad daylight!" It is not god however we defend, at least not from the institutional vantage point, it is tradition. God, mom, and apple pie is a national self-image, and just after the national anthem we sing "Will the Circle be Unbroken."

To see things otherwise can easily be perceived as unpatriotic, and so we don't want preachers to be truth tellers. They can claim to be truth tellers as long as their lie

is the truth we expect, but if undeniable facts pertaining to the real universe are to be shared during the Sunday sermon, well then don't bother. One of the reasons for the decline in mainline churches is that many of their educated clergy have a conscience. Albeit most do a half-assed job sharing their knowledge with their congregations, partly out of fear for their livelihood no doubt, but still they can't sit back and not defend the rights of GLBT persons or a woman's right to make her own reproductive decisions.

These more liberal clergy also struggle to keep god in the mix, and perhaps for reasons on a personal level that go beyond institutional concern. It is after all a natural response to change, especially change experienced as loss, to bargain our way back into a comfortable position that either lessens the severity of the loss or negates it altogether. Their more conservative counterparts defend the religion with absolutes – The bible is the word of god, literally true, inspired, and without contradiction -- believe it; don't question it! – God created us, period! – God is all powerful, all knowing, unchanging, and infinite, and because I said so makes it so! The problem for more moderate and liberal clergy is they have seen the evidence and their integrity will not allow them to deny it.

The congregation needs an apologist, a negotiator who can maintain continuity in spite of changing times, and ultimately a leader who can inspire their faith. The preacher who knows the bible is not factual and in fact contains many horrific and immoral stories has a decision to make. This is not a new dilemma in the theological community and adequate bargains have been struck that keep church doors open. Over the last century theology has grappled with science, faced the discovery of ancient

textual material that sheds new light on the biblical witness, and has struggled to understand human subjectivity and spirituality against an ever increasing backdrop of new information about who and what we are.

The institutions of religion with or without gods are as much part of our evolution as opposable thumbs. To date liberal Christianity and progressive branches of Judaism have worked diligently to save face. There has been naïve optimism that the religions can be transformed by transfusing the institutions with palatable concepts of the divine that mesh with science and eliminate over reliance upon antiquated mythical paradigms. On the broad scale it has been a massive failure.

The two most popular theological strategies for reinterpreting the biblical god are Liberation and Process. The professional apologists bargaining with these paradigms have a new bag of tricks. Liberationists cull from the bible stories that celebrate deliverance, compassion, social justice, and inclusivity. The god of liberation sets people free, welcomes humanity, and loves all people. Naturally the problem here is entailed in the scissors that are required to cut snippets from the scriptures so they can be pasted into a more palatable story. God is remade in the image of liberalism.

Process thought frequently overlaps liberationist perspectives and in some respects the two are mutually inclusive. Those who embrace process theology, and the numbers among moderate and liberal clergy are very high, have dismissed the anthropomorphic god of the bible as a myth fashioned by ancient humans, and have given themselves to the assumption that the divine is a force in nature connected to all things. If you are thinking "Star

Wars" you are not too far off the mark. God becomes a metaphor for expressing themes of love, compassion, and justice that have gained value through the course of evolution. The god of process is persuasive, encouraging faith in the midst of choices, a god whose hope is present in all experience as the universe unfolds. This god is part of nature, intimately and subtly at work, but does not create, cause, determine, coerce, threaten, judge, or act contrary to natural process.

The god of process theology is "with us," shares human joy as well as suffering, and is divine only in the sense that entailed in the Big Bang is an energy that pervades all things for the good. Clergy who have appropriated this theological position tend to collapse all religions into the common themes that seem to emancipate human beings from fear, distrust, hatred, violence, ignorance, and injustice. Sacred texts as well as literature in general to the extent they all express the human struggle are welcome fodder for sermons and meditations, but science, especially quantum physics, becomes the sharpest lens for eying the divine. The more we know about how nature works, the more we know about god.

The problem with process thought is that it is pure speculation. Once again it represents human beings taking the things they value and hope is important and projecting them onto a universe that to date gives no evidence that such is the case. While some of the ideas are interesting and even on track for what subjective faith looks like as we ponder the meaning of the universe in a post-religion world, that a "god" concept is proposed is disingenuous. What process and liberationist thought do for the multitude of clergy who buy into their paradigms is

empower them to be dishonest with their congregations, but with a sense of integrity and intellectual hubris.

With a straight face they serve the institution and benefit from the status and respect afforded clergy in a religious society. They talk about god, Jesus, read from the same scriptures as fundamentalists, but they don't mean the same things when they use the words. Intellectuals in their congregations may appreciate the fine nuances and be on the same page of reasoning, but many sitting in the pews don't get it. There is always ambiguity, the subtle complications of context, and the twist where even the harshest bible stories represent humanity's struggle and frequent failure to connect with the true will of the divine.

Process is content to view transformation in small steps. Everything and everyone is in flux, evolving, and as such there are no absolutes. While the approach of the more liberal clergy appeals to those who deep down have already abandoned the biblical gods, it doesn't bode well in a culture of denial, rooted in fear, and seeking a definitive stance against change. On average the moderate and liberal churches decline through the perception that they are "wishy-washy," while the literalists, conservatives, and fundamentalists who speak with clear "rights and wrongs" seize the day. The mistake that liberal clergy make in not telling the truth, in not striving to transform their congregations through education, is the perpetuation of words, words like god, savior, sinner, spirit, angel, demon, miracle, heaven, hell, and judgment, words they interpret as metaphor when most others are not prepared to hear past the first entry in a Merriam-Webster's dictionary.

Denial requires a bargaining stage to maintain its health. If you are a clergy person or intellectual person of faith holding on to the institution of religion via reinterpretation of the divine into a palatable energy that works on behalf of an evolving humanity, you are bargaining. And while you may find some comfort on a personal level, there is nothing in the world view of process thought that can't be equally stimulating to the subjective mind without gods, divines, or notions of supernatural beings. The cost, however, of maintaining this façade is the perpetuation of ignorance, war, violence, discrimination, and indifference. It is one thing to teach children not to play with fire. It is quite another to give them matches and think they won't use them.

Playing with god words one thinks have been diffused is like casting a smoldering match near a pile of leaves on a windy day. Even if the forest doesn't catch fire, it was a grossly negligent and irresponsible act. This is peaceful Islam, liberal Christianity and Judaism. It is all well and good until someone strikes the words and ignites a jihad or a crusade, acts in fervor for religious extremism because the words beg to mean what they mean. "It's not our fault because we didn't mean it that way" is also denial seasoned with a good measure of bargaining.

The institutions of religion regardless of denominational flavor are socio-economic systems. In many cases they are also committed to influencing political structures and have spent decades establishing connections that enable them to extend the boundaries of their influence into the larger society. At this level god is irrelevant, and the task of leadership is to protect and extend the institution's viability. The rank and file is

always welcome to join, but as multitudes know all is well until a personal issue conflicts with the larger interests of the organization. Then it is time to change churches. This church-hopping phenomenon is a common form of negotiating one's place especially in American Christianity.

Clergy and church leaders' first priority is to serve the church. Members are needed and coveted, but are also expendable. This highlights a divide that exists between the communal and personal needs entailed in religious affiliation. The personal quest for spirituality and religious faith is rooted in our subjective desire to understand life and death in ways that are palatable and meaningful. The "divine" experience is not the same for everyone though there are some common patterns that have emerged that enable us to be drawn to likeminded enclaves.

The bargaining or negotiating phase is as much about how we make sense of our changing lives as it is a place for apologetics to argue a defense for denial. On a personal level we are listening for the explanation that speaks to us and offers us the opportunity to create a god that meets our needs. Science isn't the only thing that shakes the foundational claims of religion and makes us feel the uncanny pit in our stomachs that god doesn't really exist. Life experience is full of let downs and changes that shake us. We don't need a Rhodes Scholar to remind us of unanswered prayers, miracles that didn't materialize, or the fact that we are moving quickly to the end of our days.

The meaning of something being subjective is that it is personal perhaps analogous or similar to what others experience, but it is what "I" think, feel, contemplate,

perceive, need, or imagine that matters. Human beings exist uniquely between individual and communal contexts of living. "I" seeks out "we" and the "we" seeks out the "I's" that will reinforce the connections that hold meaning.

God as a concept is quite generic. As previously noted the evidence of how people live their lives in relation to the demands of sacred texts is thoroughly ambiguous. Simply put if we really thought a god was going to get us we wouldn't be so at ease with making god fit into our lives. Christians, for example, would in dire earnest sell all their possessions, give to the poor, and practice the radical discipleship Jesus commanded. People don't do this, but they do other things instead which resonate with what they need or want. The default position that is most widely embraced is that if one is a decent person, does good to others, then heaven awaits. Specific embellishments follow depending on one's subjective context.

The following sketches will be helpful to fellow atheists and secularists toward developing a more clear understanding of the problems associated with various expressions of Christianity in the US and by analogy similar types of nuances that can also exist in other religions. There really is a bargain deal out there for everyone. Many factors influence a person's religious beliefs and affiliations. Geographical location, socialization, level of education, and socio-economic status are always key indicators to be considered. It is never as simple as merely showing people scientific or even biblical evidence to awaken them from their ideological slumber.

There is a substantive population of Christians in the US, generally in working class or lower socio-economic

communities where ignorance is valued. This isn't a pejorative statement. Ministers in these churches are never educated in order to be qualified to preach, they are "called." "Book learning" is shunned, except the bible which is to be understood literally. Many persons in these churches have a very low level of public education and have virtually no interest whatsoever in understanding biology, physics, or neuroscience. To them "city preachers" are just as full of the devil as atheists and people of other religions. These churches include many types of "hardshell" Baptists and some Pentecostals.

I remember a story from a book recounting the life of a mountain preacher in North Carolina where a lively revival meeting was being held out at a brush arbor on the mountain. He prayed "Lord, I thank you that I'm ignorant, and pray you make me ignoranter." This about sums it up, and the thick wall protecting the boundary of these types of religious communities is virtually impenetrable. A similar motif is frequently found in holiness churches like Nazarenes and Churches of God. Congregants see themselves as being set apart, sanctified, suspicious of any biblical education outside of their own denomination, and equally suspicious of people who call themselves Christian but wear suits and ties and fancy dresses while attending church.

The economic and educational divide is clear in these expressions of religion. The people are usually good, down to earth, hard working folks who like to think common sense is their forte. The bible is their only book and shaking it at someone who is in conflict with a political, social, or moral opinion that is being espoused is also considered "the word of god." It doesn't make any

difference what it is, the bible open or closed keeps denial in good stead.

It is like the story of the young seminary student who comes out to the country to visit his old grandfather who is sitting on his front porch reading the bible. When asked, the grandfather says he's reading about Moses parting the waters and leading the Israelites through the Red Sea on dry ground. The educated grandson provides an intellectual corrective and tells his grandfather that it was probably a geological event that made that spot on the sea only four inches deep at the time the Israelites crossed. The grandfather starts praising god, and bewildered, the grandson who thought he'd effectively rationalized away the miraculous inquired about his grandfather's optimism. The grandfather replied "God destroyed all of Pharaoh's army in only four inches of water."

By way of extreme contrast there is a substantive number of Christians who value intellectualism and sublimity. The question of transcendence in contemplative repose is particularly meaningful. For many of these Christians the institution of the church has great intrinsic value both as symbol for goodness on earth and as a connection to the mysteries in the larger universe. These Christians are more likely to value process thought, have higher levels of education and income, and attend moderate to liberal mainline churches. The bible is food for thought but rarely taken literally.

Ritual and formality are also very important factors for many Christians. Roman Catholicism speaks for itself, and for Protestants, especially those above, churches that are firmly rooted in sacral tradition are very appealing. Clergy are robed, worship is well ordered, and a

perception of "high church" is the norm. These churches offer rich symbolism marking the rites of passage through life, invite parishioners to value contemplation, and are likely to incorporate solemn hymnody and periods of silence during worship. The theology of these churches will typically be diverse entertaining ideas expressed in mostly progressive views of the divine with a nod toward Deism and the rather Gnostic portrayal of the divine through metaphors like love, peace, and justice.

Among the most successful and appealing expressions of Christianity are what we might call the experiential churches. These include most Pentecostal and charismatic type churches and many of the non-denominational "fellowship" congregations that have emerged over the last two or three decades. Many of the mega churches sporting televangelist ministers fall in this category. The emphasis is upon being "moved" by god, receiving and experiencing god's spirit, and knowing god through emotional connections.

These churches will frequently be informal, offer vibrant music, and have preaching that emphasizes faith, blessing, and prosperity. Clergy rarely have academic degrees, possibly denominational training, but like the first group rise to the pulpit via "divine calling." Christians in these congregations generally claim the bible is literally true and inspired, but typically pick and choose their texts based upon the emotive capability verses have for affirming their core values. These churches have been very appealing to young families, especially middle class conservatives, and form a major component in the overall landscape of the American fundamentalist movement. There is overlap to be sure and elements in each of the

sketches can be manifest on personal levels that defy generalization, but many Christians "feel" their religion very deeply. "Faith" is an emotional reality, and turning to god in prayer for everything from finding a good parking place to healing for a sick friend or loved one is a daily experience.

An interesting caveat emerges here. Numerous persons dispersed rather broadly throughout the church world but certainly represented in the more experience based churches are those who are drawn to themes invoking spirituality as an avenue to the supernatural. It would come as a shock to many preachers to discover just how many of their congregants believe in ghosts, follow their horoscopes, purchase the occasional crystal for positive energy, do yoga, or believe in various tenets of magic and superstition. Once again "god" can be quite arbitrary and easily defined as the one who rewards general good with earthly rewards and heavenly bliss.

At the heart of the religion felt by innumerable people especially the masses of ordinary folk who affiliate with churches but order their lives through contemporary culture is a common set of core propositions. These propositions that many take for granted as true have been exacerbated by preachers who have been overly eager to succeed by telling people what they want to hear especially at funerals. These propositions look something like this. Openly saying one believes in god, Jesus, or is a Christian is equivalent to making it so. Being a good person is the primary thing god expects. All one has to do is ask for forgiveness and it is done without condition of further responsibility or reciprocity. Heaven is a real future

place where friends and loved ones will be reunited to live forever in perfection and joy.

Hymnody perhaps more than preaching reinforces these presuppositions. Amazing Grace, Just as I Am, and When the Roll is Called up Yonder have made their mark. The fact is though that most of these popularly held assumptions are not biblically accurate any more than they are rational in light of the evidence we have concerning the real universe. Nevertheless persons who hold these general views about their religion can be highly invested emotionally in them. Against the impending reality that gods do not exist any and every defense bargaining can muster will do to restore order to the denial that defines their world.

The most pronounced and markedly visible characteristic valued by serious adherents of religion is correctness or "right" belief. This is certainly true for Islam, and is the defining characteristic for evangelical, fundamentalist, and conservative Christianity. One must believe the right things or believe correctly in order to enjoy a "personal" relationship with god. There is always a list, a set of "fundamentals" that if endorsed and appropriated qualifies one for salvation and more than that affirmative social status.

For many it becomes a mantra reinforced by preaching to the sound of "amens" chiming from agreeable parishioners. We believe in god, in the virgin birth, in the bible, in god's word, in the death, burial, and resurrection of Jesus Christ, in the rapture, and so on. These things are easy to remember and difficult to challenge. A person struggling with issues in her or his life succumbs to invitations from others to attend church and

start living "right." A simple set of propositions is hammered into god's will, a sinner's prayer for salvation is provided, and a moment of goose bumps translates into a trip down the aisle to accept Jesus into one's life. The accolades from others affirm that one has done the right thing.

This is easy religion. This is dangerous religion. A person has just been convinced that all life's troubles have been covered over by the blood of Jesus with no real emphasis on personal responsibility and no moral obligation to examine the claims made by the church in regard to the "fundamentals." One has made an "A" on the test and so it never crosses one's mind that the test itself was flawed. Reason has little chance of mounting a defense here because persons who fall for fundamentalist ideology have embraced a cycle of endless tautology. Everything they have been taught was absolute truth must be true because they were taught it was true. In the case of most average persons who opt in for this conservative trek when questioned about their beliefs or challenged in regard to accountability they will defer to the view of their favorite bargainer (preacher).

Bargainers for fundamentalist ideology are genuine experts at their craft. They have honed circular arguments into a juke box with one record that plays automatically every time a coin hits the slot. Their institutions, like the Southern Baptist Convention, are powerful and well established so there is a lot of spit and polish to their persona. One of the most notable apologists for Theism and fundamentalist Christianity is Dr. William Lane Craig. For years he has deceived audience after audience with tautological thinking and his popularity is profound

evidence that all denial requires to be sustained is a broken record.

For Dr. Craig god exists. It doesn't matter that a preponderance of evidence suggests otherwise. He is resolute in his conclusion, and therefore he cheats. In a debate with Lawrence Krauss he argued: Every existing thing has an explanation for its existence…The universe is an existing thing. Therefore the explanation for the existence of the universe is god. For this to be a valid argument obviously the existence of god would have to be proven objectively without assuming god exists. This has never been done. Hence Dr. Craig has to insert an unsubstantiated faith claim and attempt to make it look reasonable.

Dr. Craig maintains it is more rational to believe god exists than not, and he uses this assumption to justify everything from an intelligent designer for the universe to the existence of morality in human civilization. The overwhelming evidence from human history demonstrates that we are usually wrong when using presuppositions from superstition to explain natural phenomena. Religion was wrong about the relationship between the earth and the sun. Religion was wrong about the causes for natural events like earthquakes and storms. Religion was wrong about the cause of disease. Religion was wrong about the origin of life on earth.

Religion has rarely been right about anything. A multitude of religions along with their gods and goddesses have come and gone over time. They were proven empty, hollow, and devoid of supernatural power. People either stopped believing in them or were forced to believe something else through war and conquest. For Dr. Craig

only one of these gods exists, the god of the bible. Yet here too we have the problem of stories that show human activity, the merging of gods and ideas of the divine into one generic being, and thoroughly clear human manipulation in the process of combining multiple sources into one contrived narrative. Based on the laws of probability alone it is not only irrational to suggest a god for the cause of anything, it is downright absurd.

More reasonable by far is the assertion that if Muslims, Christians, and Jews ceased to exist in history, naturally, through the course of time and preferably not through violence, the gods Allah, Jesus, and Yahweh would cease to exist. Still the Dr. Craig's of the world persist is supplying weary and troubled minds with the impetus they need to avoid the inevitable. This frequently happens by creating false depictions of biblical themes that strike a contemporary chord in listeners. It is easy to present biblical themes out of their original context, create the appearance of absolutes that resonate with contemporary values, and misdirect the audience into a false dualism between positions that must be interpreted as either right or wrong.

Dr. Craig likes to argue that without god we could not have a moral society. Take adultery for example. He would argue that it is morally wrong to commit adultery because god told us it was wrong and reprehensible. Dr. Craig views adultery as sin, a law of god given to uphold the integrity of sexual relations in a monogamous marriage, and ultimately something that places one in a position of divine punishment. In his view not science nor the secular advancement of rule of law in society, but the bible sets the moral standard. This sounds "right" to

conservative congregants especially when they are told they can merely repent and ask forgiveness to put any indiscretion behind them. Ultimately this kind of moralistic sensationalism makes a great talking point, exacerbates the flow of self-righteous adrenalin, but means absolutely nothing beyond the hypocrisy it engenders.

Most everyone realizes that adultery was a big sin in the bible and that the penalty was death. We all understand the potential for volatile consequences when a spouse is caught having sexual relations with someone else. Jealousy, betrayal, and the rage that can be unleashed when one feels something personal and sacred has been violated by another is why the ensuing violence is deemed a crime of passion. But is the capital offense of adultery in the bible really about sex as fundamentalists suggest?

There's a lot of sex in the bible. Incest is of course taboo as is sex in the context of idolatry in regard to fertility religions. Lesbian sex is never prohibited nor mentioned. This is likely due to the ignorance of pre-scientific societies in regard to reproduction. A woman merely offered a womb for the male to implant his semen which was generally thought to be the whole ball of wax. Prostitution happens and may have been considered fornication, but not a big deal unless it was temple prostitution. The bottom line is that men could have all kinds of sex. They could also divorce their wives, quite liberally in fact, though with some financial obligations under certain circumstances.

In the patriarchal culture of the bible monogamy was unheard of. A man could have many wives, a lot of sex, and even slaves for sex. Each wife had her concubines who also did double duty for the man of the house. Wives and

concubines alike were essentially the property of the man and his exclusive right to have sex with them was enshrined in law. There is more to this than sex though.

Upon close reading one will also discover many laws that governed inheritance rights. The key blessing of Yahweh to the people was the land and the right to possess the land from one generation to the next. It was a religion without a heaven in those days so being able to pass your estate as an inheritance to your children; firstborn son in particular, was a big deal. Adultery posed a viable threat to that endeavor. A wife that would risk bearing another man's child who might in turn receive her husband's inheritance was to be executed, not so much for the sex, but for the potentially polluted bloodline.

Today, largely thanks to science and the evolution of law as a secular standard for just community, women have rights too. Most often people are married because they love each other and rarely for economic or political alliances, Islam excepted. No one enters a marriage thinking it won't last. We recognize that sometimes things change, relationships drift apart, and both men and women are free to choose other sexual partners. We place great value in consensual relationships even while there may be adverse consequences.

We do not permit murder. We allow divorce and in fact most states have gone to "no fault" divorces where households are divided between the two parties fairly. If there is a pregnancy involved, instead of taking the woman out and stoning her to death we use DNA from a paternity test to determine who gets to pay the child support. And along similar lines we equally disapprove of the biblical ignorance which commanded the death of

children who cursed or dishonored their parents. Hormones can do some crazy things to adolescents and psychology has helped us understand such things as autism, Turret's Syndrome, hyperactive disorders, and other forms of mental disability that can sometimes affect our children.

Fundamentalist apologists like Dr. Craig use oversimplification and misdirection to appeal to people's desire for order and simplicity. In a world where change is constant and where denial is persistently begging for an impermeable stasis, the promise of absolutes regardless of how false and impossible they might be is reassuring. For conservatives change is the enemy. Thus welcoming GLBT persons as full members of society, supporting women's rights to make their own reproductive choices, facing the fact of evolution, and acknowledging the gods of old as the fodder of superstition are laden with fear and resistance. For all they say about truth, in the end it is their nemesis.

What people believe about god is arbitrary, but for many that belief is what gives them the comfort and security to face life. We are poorly socialized to deal with change, especially change experienced as death. If it is hard for parents to talk to their children about sex, the difficulty is greatly exacerbated when it comes to presenting life as a temporally limited process that is finite with a beginning and an end. It is easier to forestall fact with fairy tale. As adults we are no better and perhaps worse as we get older. We want someone to be out there, someone who is for us, someone who is helping us and guiding our destiny. Bargaining helps maintain the lull between the beginning and the end with optimism. It can also give us "fighting words." By rationalizing denial we

have ground to stand on, albeit a slippery slope, but if we feel that we are fighting back, hanging tough, staying the course, it is almost like being god.

Bargaining, negotiating, or engaging in apologetics is a normal but futile exercise in the pursuit to cope with change. It may be hardwired into our genes through evolution or something that is culturally determined through socialization, but we do it. Whether we are protecting institutions and meaningful social structures or our own personal world view it is a step that will likely be repeated until we finally get a grip and face the facts. This is especially true when it comes to religion and the gods we rely upon for security.

We use the expression "different strokes for different folks." This holds for the way people connect with the idea of the divine, but the diversity entailed should stand out as yet another piece of evidence that the bargains we strike are thoroughly conditioned by human need and preoccupation.

While it may seem to be a simple question concerning the existence of a divine in the universe, either there is or there isn't, the fact there are so many different ways people approach the question makes it very complicated. We could say that one's culture and social status shapes what persons believe to be evidence for the existence of god, and one's psychological predispositions shape how one experiences what is perceived to be god. Churches become an interesting testament to human migratory behavior. "Birds of a feather flock together" rings true when it comes to the way people gather to the themes they need in order to maintain belief in god or conversely the way people gather to a god that functions

as a metaphor for the type of community they need to find meaning and validation.

What speaks to some people is a god in conflict with the larger culture, a god that calls them apart and gives them a special identity. What speaks to some people is a god that moves them emotionally, either in solemn contemplation or through vibrancy and charisma, but they gather to "feel" the presence of god. What speaks to some people is mystery, the sublime, and the possibility of a great transcendent intellect that is present in shared rituals, symbols, and philosophical imagination. What speaks to some people is a god of compassion and hospitality who calls people together to do the work of peace and justice. What speaks to some people is a god of order who provides absolute rights and wrongs, a literal word, and unchanging will. And then what speaks to some isn't so much a god as it is fellow human beings who offer friendship and community where it can be taken for granted that god is present in acts of kindness and fellowship.

In every case there is an angle, a hook, a bargain that works to ward off the nagging pathos of a universe without supernatural explanation. In every case bargaining serves denial, and the task at hand which is to face one another as human beings without help or hope from a divine magician who can fix anything and everything is forestalled. Gods do not exist. All the bargaining in the world cannot change this simple fact, and yet the funny thing, by way of paradox, is that they do exist when we create them. Our bargaining negotiates the terms of their existence, and it must be "their," plural, because never has one word worn so many faces.

Hence "god" is always dependent upon us, limited in power to our power, limited in mind to our thoughts, limited in compassion to our willingness to show compassion, and limited in judgment to our choices for what we consider to be right or wrong. When you see this for yourself your denial will have finally failed you; it will have lost its hold. God will no longer need defending which believe it or not is a hell of a burden to be lifted from a mere human's back.

And be not dismayed, we atheists are a gracious breed that will not seek an undue penance for the years spent imprisoned in fairy tale slumber. On the contrary, it is a new day with much catching up to do. It is a human hand of genuine partnership now extended, mortal, but sincere in its embrace, warm with real blood flowing with the courage to face fate with dignity and humanity.

It is ironic though, that god's death is so much easier than ours. No pyre, no digging, no expense, nor tears from grieving friends and family, no, it is like erasing a misspelled word from a page or trading in an old car for something new. The path ahead may be new and untested, uncharted, but as research has shown we are more defined by our resilience than our grief, and adaptation has been our forte. The only thing that the gods of history have ever done is divide us. Perhaps without them at least one obstacle over which we stumble into peril will be removed and a better course of evolution may proceed.

Emotional Reflection

At a recent trip to the dentist the assistants were preparing to do the fillings on a couple of teeth. One is a captive audience in such a situation, awkwardly numb, and best content to be a listener in spite of moments where verbal interaction seems desirable. A lot of discussion had taken place between them about their families, bills, the coming of winter, and regressions into childhood experiences. The "story-esque" atmosphere and a momentary lull in activity seemed an appropriate invitation to suggest they might enjoy my book A Kentucky Tale.

One of the assistants replied "I am a Christian, and right now I only have time for the good book." She apparently had just started going to church and for the first time in her nearly forty years she was going to try reading the bible. Her pastor told her to start with the Gospel of John because it was the "easiest" to understand and insisted she read the "authorized" King James Version. I opted to hold my tongue in the assumption it wasn't to my benefit to rile the person who was about to work on my teeth.

I felt sorry for her for several reasons. The Gospel of John might be the easiest book to misinterpret, but it is not the easiest to understand. That she was told to read King James meant she was attending a fundamentalist church and it was unlikely her pastor understood it either. I felt like telling her to read Mark next so she could see how incredulous it is that these texts are referencing the same individual, but I didn't. She was struggling with her life

situation, with raising her children, and had just turned off her cable television and internet services in order to save up for the high cost of winter utility bills. This church offered her respite, a larger community with which to share common struggles, and though delusion comes into it, she likely won't notice as long as the sense of welcome and friendship holds.

Her church no doubt is a creationist church. As a lay person she will not detect the obvious flaw that stands out to the trained eye. They make history so simple. They just count backwards from Jesus adding up the numbers, the times, dates, and genealogies, and voila, the beginning of the universe. Never mind the image of a great flood used by almost every ancient culture to wipe away the primordial days before writing emerged to record our history, the days before memory when gods roamed the heavens and earth at leisure.

She like most won't catch the fact that even at best the memory of the ancient Hebrews passed first orally then later in writing from the 2nd millennium B.C.E., but knew nothing of the 3rd or 4th when the cultures of the Sumerians and Akkadians and others were already recording their stories. It is hard to recount what one never knew in the first place. Yes when we follow the Hebrew story back it just stops while the stories of Mesopotamia, Egypt, India, China, and the larger world keep going further and further until even Neanderthals have something to contribute to the long narrative of human history. And the god El wasn't the first god, except to Hebrew memory, a god shared throughout Palestine and the Levant by many clans. El and his progeny like Baal were real in so much as they were the subjects of human

temples, stone carvings, and mythical stories tapped into clay tablets with cuneiform symbols before alphabets stole the show.

Yahweh, god of the southern tribes might have had a shot at authenticity if he hadn't latched on to El. But alas none have a life of their own beyond human intervention, contrivance, innovation, and conquest. It is a lamentable saga to be sure. A poorly laid foundation always spells disaster for the house built upon it, and that is where we find ourselves today. These religions have run their course, and though there is a major effort on the part of billions to keep them alive, all the guns, bullets, and bombs, all the beheadings and crucifixions, all the sermonic tirades, bible thumping, and pleas for denial that can be mustered will not breathe life into something that does not exist.

Gods do not exist. God does not exist. There is no supernatural friend or foe waiting quietly in the wings of dark energy to suddenly pop out and make everything alright or right every wrong. Life is an exclusive experience of living things which in this universe is a remarkable attribute. If gods could rise from the pages they are inscribed upon they would demand humanity and sacrifice their literary immortality for even one real breath.

It is reality that stirs our emotions and draws us into reflection. Kübler-Ross believed depression was one of the stages in the grief process that most encountered before finding acceptance and the ability to move on. It is more complicated than that, but we do generally find ourselves needing a time to reorient our perspectives when the throws of change have shaken us. Depression per se is not required though serious reflection which emerges from

being a cognitive and emotive species is a key factor in healthy transitions.

So what does it mean that god does not exist? Interestingly enough unlike a real death or loss where there is an adjustment to a physical absence such is not required here. That doesn't necessarily make it an easy or unemotional task, but it does bring into sharp focus that the change at hand is a change of mind or a change in perspective. When a child learns there is no Santa Claus there might be a few tears though most children figure it out for themselves and sort of play along with their parents' reluctance to fess up. They develop a new perspective based on an exchange which involves both a maturation of thought about the meaning of the holiday and the continuation of tangible connections that make the event meaningful. In other words they still receive presents and enjoy family traditions but learn to view the larger season as a time of cheer and good will to all.

Much the same process is at work when we accept the absence or non-existence of supernatural beings or forces. Tangible changes may or may not be necessary, but the initial brunt of change comes to our perception of intangibles. This has both disheartening and liberating potential, or aspects that can be viewed as positive and negative at the same time. Naturally the most immediate concern involves death in a universe where divine intervention is off the table.

Death itself is pretty tangible. No one disputes it. Everything and everyone dies. The religions, though occasionally making some bold statement, don't really posit a god that steps in and prevents us from dying. Whether by accident, illness, violence, or attrition death

comes to us all and gods are content for life and death to runs its course without miraculous interventions. Belief in god can make it worse by drawing out the inevitable where the notion one must suffer unto the bitter end or face punishment is the sadistic grace offered like a carrot on a stick. But essentially our mortality is not a matter for debate.

It is the question of an afterlife that both haunts and inspires us. It is also the question of every afterlife scenario ever imagined by religion that vanishes with god into thin air. There are no mythical places in the real universe. Likewise there are no mythical souls or spirits within us that transcend the mortal neural network. And if someday we discover some near mass-less particles that leave us upon death like neutrinos from a star it won't be magic or anything we have previously conceived or imagined.

Some people like to derive hope from accounts of near death experiences, from stories of astral travels and visions of light, but "near death" isn't death. While research is showing that the brain can experience an intense surge of activity as it is about to die, death remains the equivalent of turning off a switch. Once a permanent disconnection has occurred there is no evidence of any activity beyond natural process.

We don't dispute the fact of death. We just don't want to die. The late Christopher Hitchens nailed it fairly well when he pointed out that our angst in death is not only knowing we must die, but that we leave while others remain as if life is a party that continues without us. But that dilemma is on this side of death and we all face it in our own way and without the aid of a god. It may be consoling in the hour of death to dream of "distant shores,

green fields, and a swift sunrise," as subjective creatures we all have points of faith and imagination, but that too is a characteristic of our humanity. Even irrationality has its moments of applicability, why diminish ourselves further by attributing it to something outside of us?

Heaven isn't just about having a nice place to go when we die. Its origin goes much deeper than that, and it addresses an irreconcilable problem we have with life. To this Jews and Muslims probably have a less convoluted view of an afterlife than Christians. It is not just heaven that waits, but hell. Life can be full of missed opportunities, botched chances, unrequited loves, and unfulfilled dreams that an eternal heaven renders less problematic. But life is also full of unfairness, injustice, and all sorts of bad form that we experience as untenable. The problem of evil has long perplexed the moral mind, a problem given over to religion because justice is a paltry remedy that too frequently goes unserved.

Two things make what we think of as evil impossible to resolve within the sphere of human experience. One is time. Time is a linear proposition, a constant, that moves ever forward. So many times we wish we could take something back, to not have said what was said, to not have done what was done, or to speak or do when we didn't. Rule of law is the best we've come up with to address injustice and unfairness. Yet frequently laws are not preventative. We know from law that there is a consequence if certain behaviors are enacted, or perhaps better stated given that law is a community standard, if one is caught enacting certain behaviors. People weigh the odds and negotiate within themselves whether or not compliance is meaningful

People cheat on their taxes, exceed speed limits, drive under the influence, and use illegal drugs. These are minor offenses compared to theft, rape, and murder, but could have damning consequences under certain circumstances. The person who speeds or drives drunk may have gotten away with it a thousand times, but in the moment when an innocent pedestrian or motorist is killed something has happened for which no measure of justice will be sufficient. The loved one lost cannot be restored and even the death of the defendant is insufficient funds. It just sucks and we can't fix it.

God in this respect does become the Marxian "opiate of the masses." While it might seem at first glance appropriate to defer injustice to a future recompense that too is adding insult to injury. The existence of a heaven for the righteous and a hell for the wicked is a twisted game of subjective relevance that means nothing to the dead and tortures the living with false expectations. We have been working ourselves into heaven and casting others into hell for millennia. It is a distraction that either leads to apathy, "let go and let god," or a lax of procrastination where we fail to advance our own evolution because we assume there is something else.

For the living time is a present reality. We will never be able to take back hurtful things or change past experiences. We can forget them, learn from them, and make modifications to the way we approach being a civilization, but to defer our problems to an infinite future is to bear them infinitely without resolution. The god of Judaism, Christianity, and Islam is a god who keeps a tally, who intends to dredge up the past and in the case of Judaism and Islam will separate the righteous from the

wicked. It is a little different with Christianity because there are a few more nuances, but regardless, this isn't justice.

It is revenge, and what we have learned about revenge is that it is an archaic concept bereft of what we need to accomplish civility, morality, and justice. The biblical view beyond its fairy tale landscapes and its dreamy superlatives is impotent and immature. A god who was inactive in the past and ignores the present is hardly worth trusting for the future. Revisit the conclusion of Job. Is a god who will allow your demise and the demise of all that you love off the hook because a thousand or million years from now he will make it better, give you a new life, new family, a new world? The blessing of this heaven is the promise of amnesia. If there is to be progress in our world it will be done amidst the solemn sadness for all of the things we can't change and take back. It will be done in the dignity of the human spirit that values the uniqueness of life and strives through empathy and reciprocity to evolve.

Heaven may have come about in human thought as a way to reward bravery, honor, and nobility in life. Our heroes get to go on in eternity and that is a pretty good sales pitch especially for children at a formative age. Hell too seemed a logical deterrent. Torment, weeping, gnashing teeth, boils, sores, the curse of worms eating one alive, and fire burning without relief forever and ever certainly turns the stomach. I don't really understand why freezing didn't get in there because goddamn it hurts. Oh, well the ancient Near East being close to an equatorial climate had somewhat less experience with ice than fire.

Nevertheless humans seem to have struggled with the ideas of good and evil for a long time.

The hard word in the matter is there is no such thing in nature. As sentient creatures with a capacity for empathy we have a real problem with this. This is the second problem we have with the notion of evil. We are likely not the only species on the planet that has evolved with a sense of differentiation between what is considered good and productive versus bad and counterproductive, but we are certainly fixated on making these distinctions. We like things that stimulate and gratify our senses. We don't like pain or things that deprive us of pleasure and well being. There is a big difference between a fart and the aroma of freshly baked bread.

The fact is neither good nor evil exist as absolutes. These are species relevant concoctions that only apply to us and the notion of gods we have created to establish a context where what we value has meaning in the larger universe. The universe takes issue with us on this. Our planet and biosphere take issue with us on this. In nature violence assumes a rather organic disposition. It is impartial and indifferent to experience and unsympathetic to the wake left behind any particular event.

The hurricane, avalanche, tornado, earthquake, tsunami, or volcanic eruption that obliterates a community didn't mean it personally any more than an asteroid that hits the planet causing the death of millions of life forms. Insurance companies call these "acts of god" so they do not have to pay the flood of claims that would force them into bankruptcy. Even here in this example as a matter of business there is an impersonal element. One pays a premium for insurance, if an accident happens, the

company pays the claim. It is a gamble against averages and mathematical probability. Not everyone perhaps, but someone will experience a random act of violence. We don't know who, when, or how often, but we bank on the rate working in the company's favor.

It is interesting that we don't seem to blame nature even when it devastates and destroys us. If we can we pick up the pieces and move on, but we don't generally damn nature as evil. Millions and millions of supernovae have blasted their elements into space making possible our own existence, but how many of them may have obliterated solar systems like our own killing billions in a blink of an eye? Still it is not evil. It is simply what happened and can't be undone or reversed. In order for something to be evil in our eyes there generally has to be intent, malice aforethought, and a motive that disregards the dignity of fellow human beings.

The concepts of good and evil are only applicable in the sentient world. To the extent we have come to recognize and respect the sentience of other species we have begun to extend our rule of law to them as well. The mistreatment of animals has become a matter of grave importance to many people, and we frequently work to protect species that are in danger of extinction. Still the lines between what is considered natural and outside the designations of good and evil are drawn. We don't regard the pollens that inflame our allergies as evil; we treat the symptoms to make ourselves feel better. We do not regard viruses that attack us and make us ill as evil. We kill them if we can without giving it a second thought. A can of bug spray comes in handy for annihilating hundreds or even

thousands of living things with no moral challenge or guilt to the average conscience.

God's role in good and evil has only been relevant to what human beings do to each other. Our cats aren't perceived as damned for eating mice, nor hawks that swoop down to nab a cute little squirrel. It is only the carnality of the human species that is called into question. In this god's universe a trillion acts of indiscriminate violence can be happening every second, but the only one that matters is a human act. This god is never to blame nor accountable except to us, and even then only as a metaphor that calls us to be accountable to one another.

Our struggle has been against ourselves. The problem is that we too are animals, like cats or hawks, but we have evolved into a higher form of awareness and intelligence that challenges us to be more. We have created the categories of good and evil partly to differentiate ourselves from other species, but also as an attempt to set a standard for our ongoing evolution. The fact is god is no longer useful for this endeavor and as a concept has become counterproductive to the process. The gods we once imagined would determine right from wrong, adjudicate between us, and apply the appropriate rewards and punishments have on the one hand succumbed to our carnality and on the other failed to adequately represent the best of our humanity.

While facing the question of a universe without a heaven or hell seems at first quite morbid to those of us who were hoping not to die or at least stay dead, the heart of religious faith beats in the hope that there is an invisible friend to help us now in the present. Perhaps the problem is we can't evolve fast enough, get all the hungry fed, the

homeless sheltered, or the sick made well. To be sure there remains a lack of trust which pervades humanity especially disadvantaged regions of the world where even the most basic ethical standards, rule of law, and opportunities for economic and educational advancement languish in human conflict. Turning to god for hope remains a popular alternative.

Ironically the goal of such faith is human awakening and response. The cries sent up to god are always meant for human ears. One sign this is true is the way god continues to be reinterpreted from one generation to the next in increasingly diverse ways. The god we imagine loves us today is so much larger and expansive, inclusive and welcoming than the god written on the pages of the bible. We use the same words and stories that have been handed down, people will still talk about being "Christian," but the god being referenced has been reinvented many times.

The god of Judaism and Islam is ethnically challenged in a world where we have learned diversity is a key and necessary component of evolution. Judaism is largely content to see their story as an ethnic story with little interest in proselytizing the world. If it wasn't for the politically inflamed Middle East and the fact that Islam and Christianity appropriated their god, the world would likely view Judaism with humor and tolerance much as we do other indigenous cultures that maintain their heritage over and against the modern world.

Most stories that depict divine favor for one ethnicity or culture over all others are morally reprehensible to everyone else, but they are just stories to everyone else and unless used to discriminate against and marginalize others

they are dismissed as benign. In fact if people actually sat down and thought about just how ridiculous the process has been trying to make sense out of ancient religious ideology and the course of its transmission from one generation to the next and from one culture to another over time trading the idea of "god," even in the face of death, for an honest "I don't know" seems quite genuine and refreshing.

The dental assistant will soon read John 3:16. "For god so loved the world." Really? Ok, this would be the god who deluged the world killing every living thing except a boat load of animals and eight people. Four of these people, half of humanity, were women who the story doesn't give names. Noah has three sons from whom all people on earth would descend. God cursed one them, ignored one of them, and picked Shem. From the line of Shem god picks Abraham, and from his two initial progeny god picks Isaac. Muslims argue he kind of picked Ishmael too. God's will is for Isaac to pick Jacob over Esau and so on and so on. Was it that tough just to go ahead and pick everybody?

It would have been a better human story if the eight would have all been chosen to go into the world, be fruitful and multiply, and bear the will of a loving god. "We are the World" would probably have been written three thousand years ago, but Judaism would not have had an ethnocentric creation myth for its culture. It is precisely here that a much greater concern arises in regard to Islam. What could be construed as a relatively benign presence the Jewish god represents in the global configuration of cultures is metastasized into malignancy with Islam.

Islam does proselytize. It does utilize violence in order to promulgate its notion of world order, largely through the advancement of an ethnically prejudicial system of belief where once in one cannot leave without condemnation, and is rooted in exactly the same ethnocentricity as Judaism. In their view Allah/Yahweh chose Ishmael and ultimately his descendent Muhammad over all others. Death in Judaism is a bit vague depending on the type of rabbi one consults. It can be a transitional state where one rests under the purview of a creator who can restore life and will ultimately order the universe with less ambiguity or a temporal hiatus until a messiah figure comes to sort things out and order life anew upon the earth. Death in Islam isn't vague at all.

Death in Islam is two things. It is closure to an earthly life whereby Allah will decide one's reward or punishment. And more pertinent to present world considerations it is a means to an end – no pun intended. Death is a tool, a weapon in an arsenal sanctified to enable mortals to act as the agents of divine prejudice and retribution. Of course it is a human act to cause death and use extermination to limit competition, a human act and an old story. Most all religions share a like reputation at some point in their history for happily sending people off to meet their maker, but few seem to revel in the carnality of it as much as those given to a jihad. Perhaps that is because Islam's heaven is the most carnal of them all. It is a man's heaven to be sure. It is the only one where sex is explicitly guaranteed which is certainly one up from Judaism or Christianity. One has to wonder though about the virgins promised to faithful jihadists for their murderous devotion. Will Allah make them from scratch or just rise

up the innocent daughters slaughtered by ignorant and ambitious humans from time immemorial?

Semitic ethnicity drew first blood in the game of religion, was the first to write of it, and as a result has bequeathed the world an oversimplified version of life and death that cannot be squared with reality. It put pen to the page at a time when heavens and hells made more sense to warriors and potentates who needed leverage to build their empires than to common folk. As such we face a quagmire of inconsistencies that leaves us wondering if these heavens were ever worth the cost.

Islam as an expression of violent ethnocentrism that borrowed its god, heaven, and hell from archaic Semites and Roman Christians must stop, it must be checked, for it has neither the wisdom nor the vision to resolve the existential dilemma human evolution begs to be addressed. Who and what we are and how are questions these antiquated religions are impotent to answer. A god that demands from us obeisance and devotion on the promise of a future resurrection and recompense is an excuse for tyranny and meaningless to the task of what real living and dying entails. What this type of religion does is heighten our concern for objective status in the present and in spite of all the meandering about spiritualized themes it destroys faith as a part of our subjective faculty.

There is more faith in accepting death as death, non-existence as non-existence, and facing the unknown as the unknown than in any of the paradigms offered by formalized religions. This is their hypocrisy. They promise something that cannot be delivered in any material sense, and call for belief in intangibles outside of us that actually

reside within us. And to this ruse against sanity, Christianity, while it may not currently be the most violent, is certainly the most damaging to everything it means to be human.

All three monotheistic religions postulate a very confusing heaven. On the one hand afterlife is perceived to be out there somewhere. It is a journey only souls can make, and perhaps at the end will rematerialize in a world of infinite perfection. Yet on the other hand is the earth world we cannot get beyond. The core ambition for these religions is a transformed earth where a perfect king messiah figure rules with absolute clarity and goodness. Getting there is the problem and for Islam and Christianity in particular it is a divine mission to prepare the world for god's final coming.

Technically it is not what happens after death that matters but what happens in life that counts in both perspectives. At times it is not clear what we fear most, dying or living. The various writers of the New Testament were equally perplexed and in case you haven't noticed do not provide a consistent vision or reliable description of what an afterlife might entail. The kingdom of heaven is coming, is elsewhere, is already here, is within us, is to be strived for, and is in the process of being prepared.

Sometimes Jesus is the Jewish messiah who is returning to rule upon an earth transformed by Yahweh's final purge, and sometimes he is the pure light of divine truth ready to translate us into an infinite spiritual harmony with our creator and heavenly father. Sometimes flesh and blood does not inherit the kingdom of god and sometimes it does. Sometimes the faithful are promised tangible rewards a hundredfold what was given up on

earth, and sometimes we just morph into angelic spirit beings without physical relationships, have our minds wiped free of memory, receive new names, and spend eternity prostrate before god's throne worshipping. Sometimes we are told to forsake the world and tangible things in pursuit of lofty spirit ideals, but then also promised an eternity in a city made of gold, giant pearls, and precious gems.

It is a theological cluster fuck if there ever was one. The rules for getting into one of these heavens are equally ambiguous. Matthew's Jesus was a tough nut that demanded radical measures of discipleship and says quite frankly that not many will measure up. Paul's Jesus was a bit more interested in belief; trust that god had sort of taken care of everything on our behalf. Most of what we are taught about Christianity is a synthesis of views constructed out of the mish mash. Of course this is what one gets when a 4th century council under the oversight of a Roman emperor creates a religion from competing ideas. It is no wonder the Roman Catholic Church preferred that average people not read the results and simply take their word for it.

The massive division between Protestant Christians is but further evidence of the confusing blend of ideas that have come to weigh upon the minds of mortals. Yet a few things stand out which condemn Christianity to absurdity. Like Islam, it is a religion that seeks global domination. While it shares the same ethnic origin as Judaism, its Jesus has since been globalized. The Jesus who once was quoted as saying he did not come to bring peace on earth but a sword has proven that he meant it. Christianity wounds us with its dualisms and false pretenses. One is either saved

or damned, loved and welcomed or condemned and rejected, in or out. We are deprived of our humanity, and relegated to a status without dignity, labeled sinners, and cajoled to feel blame for our mortality.

Only with this god in the picture are we incomplete, unworthy, shameful, and loathsome. And death, while it may come too soon for some and not soon enough for others is life's natural counterpart. We might not want to leave the party, but it is not unfair. It is hard that we cannot control the circumstances when death presents itself, but death is not the wage of sin. It is completion, and the result of having lived. Surely there is peace and contentment in having lived. But religion would take this from us, and Christianity essentially tells us that living isn't meant for living and dying isn't real.

In fact Christianity basically tells us the world isn't real. The Gnostic roots of Christianity leap quite boldly from New Testament pages with passages like "Do not love the world or the things in the world (1 Jn 2:15)," and "Adulterers! Do you not know that friendship with the world is enmity with God (Jas. 4:4)?" Early forms of Christianity placed great value in the notion that we are essentially spirit beings trapped in fleshy bodies which count for nothing. Salvation was not only a purifying act which prepared unworthy sinners to join the realm of god it was also perceived to be an act of liberation that made it possible for the divine spirit within us to be reunited with the heavenly father. The debt owed to Plato is unmistakable. By the 4th century when Christianity was formed under Roman authority a balance was struck. Those who leaned toward the radically Gnostic were purged, the "body of Christ" on earth would amass great

wealth and power, and the average human could await her or his "pie in the sky."

While there were indeed sincere mystics who believed life was a spiritual struggle best lived through acts of self-denial, prayer, and the contemplation of higher philosophical ideals, there was also a pervasive and terribly misinformed world view that placed the earth at the center of a universe where divine and human interaction was the reason anything existed. The universe was about us. It was our training ground, our testing ground, and it was temporary with "real life" out there awaiting god's will to unfold.

It is easy to see how those with affluence and power came to view their status as blessed with divine foretaste, but how the masses of ordinary people, many of whom lived under oppressive circumstances, longed for a better life. It wasn't a life that was going to be realized here. Their religion was their hope. Unfortunately some of the hardest realities we face as human beings are inequity, poverty, disease, and hardship on massive scales. Still today millions of children die from malnutrition, illness, and the repercussions of regional violence. It is too often a world of "haves" and "have-nots."

Of course this is a human problem the divine has never seen fit to address. The fact is life is not about us, and not everyone who lives has a "good" life. Life isn't fair in this context, and our similarity to all other creatures on the planet is never more evident than when storms with massive floods indiscriminately flush away the dead, humans bobbing along with rotting livestock, refuse, and debris. Our vulnerability to nature is evident and death is a more certain proposition for things that live than any

presumption that life will always be worth living. Life does not come with qualitative guarantees.

It is always condescending and particularly odious when a Christian apologist like Dr. William Lane Craig defends biblical acts of genocide or brushes off massive deaths and global calamity as being alright because god saves the children and will make everything OK in the end. Such religious ideology is a charade of lies that diminishes the true struggle we endure to survive and distracts us from working to alleviate the conditions that make life untenable for so many. Our evolution has led us to appreciate life on increasingly significant levels and has taught us to respect the delicate balance between life and death. Empathy, reciprocity, and altruism have made it possible to view life through a distinctly human lens. As such there is concern to make life better, to diminish suffering, cure disease, and develop sustainable strategies that will enable life to continue on the earth.

We have a much different understanding of the universe and our small place in it than did philosophers and mystics of old whose guesses weren't even close. The Christian view of life was and is naïve if not blatantly ignorant. One had better stop and smell the roses, savor sentient experience, and seize the day. This small little planet upon which we have evolved is pretty unique, and to date far enough away from any other habitable world that going elsewhere is impossible. If heaven and hell are metaphors for the kind of life circumstances one can expect to encounter along the way, then they are earthy circumstances of the ongoing present and nothing else.

To suggest we should not love the world is suicide and the annihilation of all that is potentially good and

meaningful in life. The world is what we have, and until there is some piece of evidence of another, real evidence, not mythical tales, as Lawrence Krauss likes to point out, written by iron age peasants who didn't even know the earth revolves around the sun, then loving the world and everything in it is our pleasure and duty. To live this life as though there is another is arrogant, flippant, and irresponsible. To live and not want others to live fully because you imagine death as some kind of portal to another more exclusive life is egregious and selfish.

Likewise that "I" must die and leave life behind is not a sufficient excuse to deny others their day in the sun. In morbid moments there can be flirtations with psychopathic ambivalence where envy gets the best of the imagination, where one's imminent departure seems just cause for the departure of everyone else, but it is a fleeting moment, at least for normal people who ultimately find joy in seeing the faces of newborns taking their first breaths. Alas a last breath is also a beautiful thing, untimely as it may often be, but it signified something meaningful, something unique. It returned unto nature that which had been lent, not given to possess, but to use for a little while, and then returned to be recycled and used again.

Life is a wonderful process of give and take, full of symbiotic relationships, which ironically is missing when god enters the picture. The very idea of god is primitive, a flirtatious preoccupation with an alter ego whose primary role is to sit there and be quiet. God was invented too long ago. Humanity in spite of its mortal trappings has outlived god and evolved beyond the need to rehear the opinions of "divine intelligence" that peaked with a human sacrifice. Even the idea of an afterlife or heaven requires a better

imagination than what 1st century Gnostics or a 7th century Arab prophet could design while brooding in a cave. From what we see of today's youth and young adults a heaven without gaming, reality television, and social media will be rather disappointing.

Whoever said heaven is what we want. According to scripture it is what god has in store for us whether we like it or not. Again I think of Christopher Hitchens who conversely to the last reference suggested heaven as a party one is forced to attend and not allowed to leave. Suddenly death as an end, a silent repose like a sleep from which one never wakes, a quiet finale without reflection or hindsight, without remorse or anticipation seems quite appealing.

In fact as we get down to it heaven is an untenable concept. There is either a forced servitude to a god no one has actually met save through sketchy Judeo-Christian-Islamic writings that address humanity through the lens of archaic cultures or the promise of a non-sentient eternity where a spiritualized existence somehow incorporates the things we value most in our human experience like love, peace, loyalty, intelligence, and compassion but without the capability to experience these high ideals in tangible ways. There is of course the popular view many hold where the rewards of eternal life give us the things, including material things, we want the most. This hope isn't biblical or even religious, but it too suffers from the fact that we are a communal species and many of the things we would want personally require the cooperation of others.

What if your heaven isn't my heaven? Given the diversity in the world such a place where all is one and

one is all would be impossible, or horribly unbearable. One person's heaven becomes another person's hell with no way to reconcile the differences but to kick someone out. Not to get too bawdy but consider gender. Surely a heaven for everyone fumbles about with the nuances of sexuality, him wanting her to fellate and swallow and her wanting him to stimulate her with conversation. If she complies she remains ungratified. If he complies he loses interest. Heaven and hell become two sides of the same coin.

Humor aside, the biblical and Islamic heaven is a man's heaven. Patriarchy prevails, or as Plato seemed to believe gender is morphed into an eternal masculine. If women are allowed into heaven as women then the whole thing unravels and we are right back to being human. The visionaries who created heaven were ignorant but powerful men who either saw no need for the feminine in a world where procreation wasn't necessary or viewed femininity as perpetually inferior and subservient to the masculine.

Sex does come into it. Gnostics were content to eliminate sex as a base and carnal activity unbefitting the divine. The vagina was rendered unnecessary and represented temptations best left behind with this world. In other paradigms for the afterlife sex is still on the table but more as a reward for men. Frankly, that anyone would postulate virgins as a reward for devotion to god is blatantly demeaning and insulting as well as immoral. Does anyone really need more evidence that god was created by man in a man's image, and a stupid insensitive man at that? Would not a real intelligent designer have at

least hinted at the notion of gender equality or shown some sense of maturity in regard to human sexuality?

What heaven fails to give us on all counts is what we can only have here in this life. There is no heavenly vision that promises intimacy, touch, warm embrace, companionship, and certainly not the passion of mutually shared orgasms. The god of heaven is inept and incapable of feeling, connecting, or participating in the risk of relationship to another. Only humans endure this risk, and in spite of the frequent difficulties of being alive it is our defining characteristic. To be perfect, without vulnerability, complete in one's self without need for others, invincible to failure, and not at risk of losing anything is to be dead.

Life is none of these things. It is frail, imperfect, and fleeting, and yet deep down we don't really want another life. We don't want to give up this life; we just want it to be better. We want for it all of the things we imagine god could do but doesn't. From our absentee god we have learned that the chance to live longer healthier happier lives depends on human ingenuity and progress. In fact never have we been more aware that the assumption that god exists is an impediment to our evolution, a conclusion supported by mountains of evidence accumulated over thousands of years.

What we lose with god's exit from our world are things that never existed in the first place but have teased and haunted us none the less. Dismissing the notion of god might be the one time we actually get something for nothing. With god go heaven, hell, ill fated promises of punishment and reward, delusions of grandeur, sins, saviors, and the authority of religious frauds who use

these various fallacies to manipulate us and cheat us out of the little time we do have to live life. It may seem that we lose hope as well, but our subjective journey does not end with god. Faith ironically transcends religion because it is innately human. One may find losing god to be more blessing than curse, and an opportunity for a more viable and realistic kind of faith to emerge. What we lose with god is that which was at best unnecessary and at worst a crime against our humanity.

For many people the task of facing the loss of god is emotional, painful, disruptive, and fraught with sadness. As with any death or catastrophic change one may feel anger, betrayal, despair, or a sense of hopelessness. No, we won't get to see departed loved ones again. No, the person who committed a crime against someone you love will not be punished in an eternal hell. No, resurrection into a grand redo is not forthcoming. What we have in this life, for good or ill is all the evidence demonstrates is real. If there is something else, or someone else, the gods of the holy books aren't it. And no, myths, fairy tales, lies even little white ones, and masterful fabrications no matter how elaborate do not become true or real just because people want them to be.

We have the earth. We have each other. We have opportunity but not guarantee. While we have time we have time. We have within us the capacity for making meaningful connections in a multitude of ways that enrich and inspire us and make life worthwhile. We have dreams not all of which will come true but to dream nevertheless. We have hearts that can be broken but also filled with great joy. We have accountability, not to an invisible deity, but to ourselves, others, and to a living world, a

responsibility renewed with each day to look into living eyes imbued with dignity and respect.

We also have the capacity for reflection, the ability to engage ourselves with critical thought. We have the ability to challenge ourselves and press ourselves beyond the superficial or the oversimplified. We climbed mountains then we aimed for the stars. We are resilient, a species with a long history of adaptation. We have even been known to overcome our worst fears and evolve. We are better than gods and don't need them. And so what if we die? So do they. We are the ones who really lived.

Toward Acceptance and Transformation

Billions of people throughout the world adhere to a religion. Christianity, Islam, and Hinduism are the largest with Judaism chiming in as perhaps the most influential. Each has specific beliefs that are celebrated across a continuum of interpretations and a variety of social and cultural expressions. There is significant disagreement between the religions often expressed through exclusive claims and equally significant disagreement within the religions over who holds the correct interpretation. While the point of these religions would seem to be about connecting to a divine being it is the humanness that stands out with unmistakable clarity.

Thus far we have explored biblical evidence which makes belief in gods like El, Yahweh, and subsequently Allah antiquated and irrational. When we add the knowledge gained through scientific study of our world and universe the idea that there is a supernatural cause or a god out there somewhere dissipates into the stark reality that such a thing has never been the case. One primary claim of this book is that we, at least subconsciously, already realize gods do not exist. Many do not want this to be the case for both personal and societal reasons and the response is a common psychological pattern where denial is reinforced through emotional and cognitive strategies.

Religion has played an incredibly important role in the evolution of human civilization, important but not always positive. Still we don't know how to let go of it, how to change or replace it, and as such it is nearly inconceivable to imagine a world without the gods who

authenticate our churches, synagogues, and mosques. Many fear a world without religion, without god, would be a world of anarchy and chaos. But fear is the key word since it is reason and mutual respect not religion that has been the impetus for social advancement. In fact it is the religions with mutually exclusive claims that resort to violence that create chaos and instability. We all see this.

At the heart of religious culture we find certain common themes being enacted regardless of the particular religion. At the heart of religious faith we find common concerns being addressed regardless of the particular religion. On both counts we see common human ground. The former occurs as a communal expression of humanity and the latter, personal. Both are deeply meaningful on subjective levels and strike an intimate chord at the heart of what it is to be human. The pertinent question of course is "What's god got to do with it?"

In reality the simple answer is nothing, or at least nothing viable or essential. What people believe about god varies, is arbitrary, and constitutes a focal point of conflict within and between similar institutions. In the US, churches as well as synagogues and mosques, are considered 501 c. 3 non-profit organizations. Religions celebrate a status quo and are formally protected by the 1st amendment. But what draws people to churches isn't necessarily religious, and in fact when we examine the function of churches and like organizations we find tremendous similarity in the types of activities people expect to find. It is generally the god language that is divisive, and sometimes "god" is intentionally used to separate the wheat from the chaff, sell one's brand over and against that of others.

This is particularly true in conservative churches that lure congregants with assertions of correctness or right belief. The need to be "right" is like a fetish to some of us, and if that is one's forte then shifting to a secular view should be a short step. Based upon evidence, history, and experience belief that a god exists is incorrect, and therefore the right thing to do is not believe in god. Yet belief in god for many people is more than a personal faith claim, it is about being part of a community, a church. This is a crucial point for atheists and secularists to consider.

If losing god means losing community, losing one's church which functions as a support network on many levels, then the exchange isn't sufficient. This is a key reason science alone frequently fails to convince people to alter their views about religion. The Wendy Wright's of the world have their whole lives intertwined with a broader community that operates on religious, but also social, economic, and political levels. The religious aspect is only a small part of the bigger picture. While it may be true that some types of churches cannot survive without their god claims, Roman Catholics and Christian Fundamentalists would indeed struggle most, it is not necessarily the case for moderate and more open minded religious communities.

What we discover as a matter of human interest is that community is necessary. Community doesn't always happen the same way, and not everyone participates in community with the same frequency. Being connected to others is intrinsically human. Some people are finding a sense of friendship and community through social media and what we think of as constituting viable community is always being revised. Not all Christians attend church on a

regular basis, and some may almost never attend. But it is amazing how passionately some people can feel about being a "member" even though direct participation with the group or financial support is markedly absent.

This being said there remains a multitude of people who do attend churches, and even those who do not participate regularly derive comfort and meaning knowing their church is there if they need them. The fact is, from an institutional point of view, church type organizations are where we have located some of the most basic forms of human interaction. "Church" is that institution human beings have woven into the fabric of society to meet some of our most basic needs. Secular minds must grapple with this.

There is never going to be a time when people give up a venue for celebrating life's rites of passage. Again, "church" is not an inherently religious word; it simply means a gathering of people. People are always going to want to gather with others to celebrate the births of their children, their kid's graduations, and moments of coming of age like entering adolescence or young adulthood. True, some couples elope, but most want the church wedding, especially the families and friends. And in that moment when the benediction bids "God bless you," what we really mean is we bless you and wish for you the best life has to offer.

Community stirs us with powerful moments. Equally meaningful are the opportunities to share the mundane, to relate to friends and share the experience of living day in and day out. For many a church community offers a norm of affirming routines, connection to a variety of interest groups, and a consistency that diminishes the angst of

aging and life passing on. The church becomes a place to go through life together, share joys and sorrows, and find counsel and support in the face of difficult choices and circumstances. The church is also that place where we say goodbye, where life is honored and memorialized, and where hands are held and hugs exchanged when the human touch of reassurance is needed the most.

The evolution of the church institution is a matter of coming of age, of realization. It is not a god or a religious ideal that makes a church concept meaningful or worthwhile; it is the broad expression of humanity encountered in such a community that matters. An interesting affirmation of this point is experienced by most clergy who discover their popularity with a congregation usually resides in how human or down to earth they are perceived to be. It makes church folk really uncomfortable to have a "saint" in their midst who talks religion all the time. Preaching and praying have their place, when the folks are prepared for it and the right stage is set, otherwise it is best to keep one's feet on earthy ground.

If taking away gods, even false gods, mean obliterating the community structure where life is lived and celebrated, then there will always be resistance and denial will continue to prevail. This kind of shift has been done before. One sees evidence of it in the bible where various festivals of the people continued but were reinterpreted to honor a different deity or hold new meaning. When Rome appropriated Christianity it didn't rob the people of their holidays, it renamed them. The solstice Saturnalia festival became Christmas, and the spring equinox veneration of Ishtar and the rising of new life was remade in the language of Jesus' resurrection.

They even kept the name Ishtar (Easter). In fact most every holiday celebrated by modern Christians was once a pagan festival where customs were kept but the names and meaning were remade to suit the religion.

The concept of secular church institutions is not only worthy of consideration, but the transition will likely be necessary. We need community where the rites of passage can be celebrated, and also a format for altruistic expressions. Evolution has taught us that it is important to our survival to balance competition with cooperation. It is not healthy for society to be mired with disparate populations, to have masses of people without access to basic goods and services. The higher we rise on Maslow's pyramid the more we find ourselves willing to assist others both for the betterment of a common good and as a matter of personal fulfillment and self-actualization.

The church as an institution has for many been the place where good deeds could be done, where compassion and good will could be offered to others, and where charitable endeavors could find patronage. It is perhaps here that the church as a religious institution has failed the most and outlived its right to status. Because of competitive religious ideology, political ambition, and self-preservation churches have lost their efficacy to provide society with effective benevolent opportunities. The vast resources they consume to promote themselves leaves little in the coffers for anything else.

The majority of funds given to churches support only the particular church, and what "good deeds" are done are usually tied to some form of evangelism. It doesn't occur to churches that supporting education, scientific research, or promoting sustainable solutions to social problems are

viable avenues for altruistic behavior because their god isn't in it. A paradigm shift to secular type church communities opens the door for a much more effective way to interact with the larger world and maintain the foundation of voluntarism that supplements our social framework.

Religion has disproven and disgraced itself. We are not unworthy sinners in need of salvation. We do not need gods to make us be good. We do not need ancient myths that have lost credibility to shape what we believe to be meaningful in life or contradict what we know to be true about the universe. We certainly don't need to be lied to or manipulated with the threat of hell or promise of heaven by those who would have our money and sway our votes. And we most certainly do not need gods with guns. We do need each other and the platform where our humanity can be celebrated and developed. As suggested earlier, in the case of religion it is the baby that needs to go, but the bathwater, perhaps redrawn, must stay.

There is a significant opportunity looming for atheists, secularists, and humanists to reinvent what it means to be human community. There are many in churches that already put little stock in the god stuff, and many more on the fringe with nowhere to go. They want to be part of something good, fulfilling, meaningful, and affirming. They want a place to raise their children, a safe environment for developing relationships, and viable opportunities for personal enrichment.

Before this type of community can materialize a measure of clarity will have to be reached among secularists and a willingness to engage people with substantive alternatives to religion on an institutional level

must become a priority. Perhaps soon even the clergy who know full well god does not exist will instead of resigning begin to lead their congregations into fuller and more mature expressions of what it means to live as human beings. They do have the skills and academic credentials to do this. They only need the courage to be honest, and a sharp pair of scissors to begin cutting away the denial.

To date a good many secular minded people are content to not be involved in organized communities and prefer free association based upon personal interest or need. Some join the American Humanist Association, follow The Richard Dawkins Foundation, or perhaps occasionally attend a Unitarian Universalist service. There are not many opportunities for secular group affiliation though we are seeing the rise of non-religious organizations that seek to offer a venue for likeminded individuals to meet and greet, hear guest speakers, and express concern over issues that deal with church/state separation.

Still there are many occasions when non-religious persons face life situations without the support that group affiliation provides, and many who are on the fence between religion and non-religion are reluctant to publicly alienate themselves from friends and family when scant alternatives exist for being connected to a larger community. Weddings and funerals can be particularly awkward, and the church world for the most part owns the rituals, language, and customs that define normative subjective behavior on a social level. When good things happen people are supposed to give thanks. When bad things happen people are supposed to repent. There are invocations, intercessions, and benedictions for most every

occasion. What we are talking about here are forms of accepted social behavior that are relegated almost exclusively to religion. The god language functions to authenticate forms of human behavior that society has historically endorsed as meaningful.

There are patterns and forms for the way we are "supposed" to do things. There are normative and acceptable ways to raise children, get married, get buried, start meetings, initiate public events, and face changing life situations. "God" is the normative word for authenticating the various rites and rituals we use to nudge people to fall into line. Freethinkers, atheists, non-conformists are cast as rogues who threaten an otherwise stable system. Thus it is easily perceived that the removal of "god" from the mix means the disruption of social order. The lack of secular models that demonstrate such is not the case gives an edge to the religious status quo, gives them control, and allows them to remain the keepers of social stability.

The patterns for behavior that are used in a religious context to promote various aspects of social order, interesting enough, do not require religion to be meaningful. Prayer for example, exemplified by a child or group of people with hands folded and heads bowed says less about a supernatural presence than it does a human moment of deference, respect, solemnity, and focus. "Let us pray" draws hearers into a collective agenda and constitutes a moment of shared experience intended to be meaningful to everyone. Frankly the god language is disingenuous, even abusive, as it asserts an authority held by the speaker, either as an individual or as a representative for a larger institution, that suggests everything that follows is to be accepted without question.

"God" is on the side of the particular church, the winning football team, the government. "God" is a power word; a ploy used to gain an advantage that otherwise would be given to debate. Christians demonstrate this every time they blatantly ignore Jesus' own rebuke against hypocrites who pray in public as they persistently use public prayer as a means to press their socio-political ideology. They don't care what god thinks, only about creating the narrow parameter for the social order they endorse.

Prayer itself as a collective form of behavior has intrinsic value as a human endeavor. There is nothing wrong with calling a group into a moment of silent reflection before an event or even having a guided meditation that names the context for the group gathering. To pause before sessions of congress with words that remind legislators to honor their solemn duty, to proceed with respect, honor liberty, and remember their decisions affect many people is a worthy use of time. Much the same can be said about prayer in other contexts. Properly understood these are human moments where hopes are shared for the well being of others. When we are ill, facing adversity, dealing with unexpected change or stressful circumstances it makes us feel better knowing that others care for us, wish us well, and keep us in their thoughts.

In fact throughout life's journey we discover it is the points of human contact that have meant the most. Many pastors will affirm this, that when they have shared in the last moments of a person's life, often the words the person needs to hear aren't words about god or Jesus or heaven, but words that confirm her or his life meant something, words that say thank you for your contribution, words that

give permission for one to leave in peace. The things that move and inspire us are human things, earthy things, things to which we can connect with in meaningful ways. God is no substitution for a genuine smile or warm embrace.

The possibility for secular based communities to do "church" more effectively than religion is dripping with potential. Such an institution is not religious in the traditional sense. There are no supernatural assumptions or imaginary friends. It is human community for the sake of humanity and for the betterment of the one earth we have to share with all life. Secular community does not have to completely emulate religious community in order to be viable. In fact it offers opportunities for enrichment and personal growth that religion is impotent to provide.

As a form of voluntary community a diverse range of activities are possible that can unfold without the constraints or pretense found in religious institutions. Such a place would certainly be a venue to celebrate rites of passage, a focal point for benevolent and altruistic endeavors, but also a venue for continuing education, for incorporating the arts, and for bringing reason and science to the hearts and lives of ordinary folk. The traditional church where people go to sit in uncomfortable pews, sing morbid hymns about a human sacrifice, and listen to a preacher ramble thirty minutes on some bible passage has been waning for some time.

Granted many still go, and even more to the churches that wave their hands, use rock bands, and preach about achieving prosperity. It doesn't hurt to toss in nationalistic fervor, patriotism, and a message that gives people a heightened sense of control over their world. But

what does god have to do with any of it? The answer is obvious, and the fact is more and more people are realizing that religion is a fraud that has reached a limit. It has peaked, and the scramble among fundamentalists to force ideology into politics and public education seems powerful, but only because last ditch efforts to hold onto a fleeting moment are flooded with passion and energy, like a dying brain that produces visions of light in a heightened awareness just before it shuts down forever.

Many, including me, have reached a point where we wouldn't give a plugged nickel to sit and have Yahweh/Jesus/Allah smoke blown up our arses, but the thought of gathering in community with others to celebrate humanity is still on the table. I can see gathering with others to sponsor events, perhaps a wine tasting for a charitable cause with a nice local jazz band playing then topped off by a speaker like Lawrence Krauss or Richard Dawkins or Sam Harris to enthrall the audience with the latest in theoretical physics, evolutionary biology, or neuroscience. In fact there are a plethora of creative possibilities that emerge when the idea of community is expanded to incorporate who we are today and the mythical ignorance of ancient cultures is cut loose.

Willingness must emerge among those who see the failure of religion, the fraud, the hurt, the danger it represents to gather with a vision for community that transcends and surpasses the crippling supernaturalism that demeans human culture. Without a viable exchange people are content with the false security of denial, and as long as "god" is held close to the human bosom in the form of family, friends, and the social institutions to which one is attached acceptance and transformation will be slow

in coming. While I respect the autonomy of atheists, and the rather non-evangelical posture of simply expecting people to examine evidence and draw correct conclusions, because we are fleshy sentient beings with subjective underpinnings there is more to it.

The "build it and he will come" motif from the film Field of Dreams resonated with many as a motivational mantra. Perhaps a bit cliché, still it speaks to a foundational truth at the heart of most any successful endeavor. First one has to believe something is worthwhile. Second, particularly from an institutional perspective, what is presented has to be worthwhile. But third, people want to be invited and welcomed into something worthwhile, and if they are not invited, if nothing meaningful exists, they certainly will not come. The challenge for atheists and secular minds who envision a society where evidence based thinking is normative and where our subjective journey is informed by objective reality is to build it.

The message of a universe without an antiquated Jewish or Arab god or a Christian savior with a heavenly realm is not a negative message. It is not a message that must thwart our dreams or kill our optimistic moods. The fact that we die like everything else doesn't put the kibosh on what it means to be alive or discredit our yearnings to understand life more completely. The human imagination remains quite intact without gods. The amazing thing is what we know to be real and factual about ourselves, our planet, and our universe are much more interesting and worthy of interest than the limited view of the universe espoused in ancient myths.

Christian fundamentalists like William Lane Craig get stuck like a broken record on the idea that life could happen without a creator, a divine intelligence that ordered everything to be just exactly what it is. That is a faithless viewpoint that wallows in fear of faith. True faith, the subjective muse of agnostic uncertainty, marvels in evolution and that we ever came to be at all. In a universe full of events leading to consequences, courses set and forces following, elementary particles and gravitational fields, accelerating, expanding, we are here. 13.8 billion years or so into this evolving conundrum we look back and forward and want to know all we can.

Guessing hasn't really panned out. We fortunately have come to know a few things. We know the moon is not made of cheese. We went there and it wasn't. We know there are no little green alien men on Mars. We are there now and as of today they have made like gods and haven't revealed themselves. The next time a comet passes we can be assured it is not an angel gracing the heavens since we just hopped on one for a ride. We know life does utilize and depend upon death for its evolution which kind of adds a new twist on the expression "thank your lucky stars."

Scientists now know that some of the water on earth is older than our solar system. Chemists in Cambridge recently witnessed the spontaneous emergence of the type of metabolic process necessary for life to begin, and in conditions similar to what the earth's oceans experienced billions of years ago before oxygen existed in our atmosphere. We know life originated in the earth's oceans.

Almost daily we discover new information that deepens our understanding of how life came to be. Equally

important we continue to discover the complexity of the human brain, the vast amount of information collected and passed on through our genetic material, and that our sentience, perceptions, and ability to comprehend are part of our evolution. Each step forward teaches more about how we as individuals experience consciousness and are able to live meaningful lives.

What we are able to know about life objectively is both the basis for substantive community and personal growth. If spirituality means those moments we are connected to emotions of deep appreciation, awe, and enlightenment, then knowledge is the key. Faith is what we need to work together as human beings. It is the trust required to translate our knowledge into meaningful applications and structures while leaving an open end for our ability to continue learning about ourselves and the larger universe. Religion can no longer help us. It is the fly in the ointment.

Whatever is ahead, even the course of what we come to believe about the universe, about life, and the degree to which meaning is involved cannot be informed by ancient myths and stories. In fact with religion behind us there is a genuine liberation to see the world for what it is and discern the vast interconnectedness of life. The deceptive flaw of the monotheistic religions is the assertion that we are different, special, or above nature. We might be special in our own right, but we are very intimately part of nature. Everything about us is a shared commodity, and the first time one sees this reality it is truly an awakening experience.

It is a bit ironic that we place so much stock in the notion of individualism given the fact that each one of us is

a veritable community if not universe. A glance in the mirror is a trick of the eye when one considers we are made of the same elements as everything else and are teeming with billions of interactive molecular parts. So is everything else in nature. Every plant, animal, bird, and insect are doing the same things in their various and diverse ways, utilizing the same fundamental building blocks, and together we are a wonderful testament to a great common ancestor we call life.

Why is this not an obvious joy to behold? Are we that selfish as to want it all for ourselves? And how arrogant is monotheism, the ancient testament to our species' hubris, that only we are important, only we have souls? Every parent's answer to the child who asks about squirrels and butterflies, the pet dog or cat, is "Of course they go to heaven." Only humans face condemnation of the soul – a concept by the way that is not good enough for conservative Christians who also want the body to reappear with it. If such a thing as a soul existed would it not be a component of everything that lives? There's no evidence for the existence of a soul, or that consciousness exists as an ethereal energy held in magical memorial particles, but we muse "what if?"

Ah but once again a reality check demonstrates just how small we are in our ability to imagine, guess, or perceive what is. It is the physical components that connect us. It is the elements, the hydrogen, nitrogen, carbon, iron, and oxygen that connect us, which transcend us, and continue beyond us to be shared and reused by others. The breaths we breathe have been breathed before. The oxygen once utilized by those we've lost to time still sustains us and if their essence remains surely it is in

nature. Perhaps our capacity to look beyond ourselves and feel connected to the vastness of space and time is inspired by the billions of neutrinos passing through us every second or the photons we absorb when gazing into starlight that has travelled eons and continues long after its star has died.

The holy books of old cannot help with these things. There is much we do not know about life, about the universe, about ourselves, but whatever there is in here or out there -- even immortal souls -- will be proven or disproven through the work of reason and science. To this task god is at best useless or worse a harmful delusion that robs us of time and dulls our wits. God is a crutch still used long after the broken leg has healed. Acceptance is throwing away the crutch and walking again on one's own. Transformation comes to us as we reclaim our humanity, our dignity, and live freely with clarity and appreciation.

Still there will be many who want to keep god in the mix. It's a comfortable word, a metaphor personalized by the individual to represent the possibilities we hope exist. For many god is a higher power, a loving being that is there for us, knows us, cares about what we face in life, and welcomes us to share an infinite future. These projections of our selves onto the universe are natural. While we are living it is hard to believe we are less than infinite or to perceive a time when we cease to exist. When one buys a lottery ticket the ensuing fantasy isn't about losing, going back to work the next day, or a dream that one will become impoverished and forgotten. No, it is a brief flirtation with wealth, being invited to dine with Bill Gates, hobnob with celebrities, and sail into sunsets on

one's new yacht. An important trait of our evolution is to forecast survival, success, and to deny vulnerability. Who wants to get up every day expecting to fail? I cannot remember my second grade teacher's name and only vaguely remember her appearance, but she taught these indelible words "Can't never did."

Even in our senior years we still have days where we feel young and think maybe there will be some new thing that comes along to make rejuvenation possible. We keep at it. The future seems so distant and the idea of not existing doesn't seem plausible. We are hardwired to survive so it is only natural that our capacity for empathy is projected out and reflected back. This is the "god" we see when we look out into space, when we reach for the one who is there for us, and imagine life eternal. It is the alter ego our finitude begs us to believe beats our hearts, breathes our breaths, and thinks our thoughts.

Some will persist that god cannot be disproven, but this is an error. It is the unknown that cannot be disproven. We have proven that "god" does not exist. We have proven that the idea of god was created by humans to explain natural phenomena. We have proven that the gods of the bible were generated by human cultures and human sources. Every claim where the word "god" was used to explain an objective reality has been falsified, and as such the word itself becomes inherently fallacious.

Gods did not create the universe. Gods did not cause life to begin. Gods do not cause storms, earthquakes, pestilence, or disease. Gods did not give rise to empires or sanction the genocide of millions. Gods did not create morality or teach human beings to discern right from wrong. Gods do not intervene in human affairs, heal the

sick, raise the dead, or perform miraculous feats that contradict the laws of nature. Gods do not cause our feelings or influence our emotional experience. In all of these things claims for a divine cause have been falsified either through self-contradiction or by objective evidence verified through scientific analysis.

The "god" word is an unworthy word. It is beneath us to use it. To cling to it is to evoke millennia of ignorance, conflict, violence, and fraud. To say "I believe in god" is a demeaning confession that either belies one's intelligence or asserts one's callous disregard for humanity. As a generic word that expresses faith or hope in the existence of things like a soul or an afterlife it is inappropriate, misapplied, and unnecessary. It is like calling an apple a peanut. The word carries with it enough historical baggage to confine its parameters of meaning to a simple set of definitions that are no longer open for debate. The word rape cannot mean consensual sex, and the word "god" must mean what it means.

> God: 1. an imaginary being used to explain natural events before scientific method was developed; 2. a symbol of power and authority used to justify the rise of empires and their conquests; 3. a concept frequently used to grant authority to discriminatory social and political ideologies; 4. a placebo used to pacify the distress of humans facing adverse circumstances; 5. a common misconception of a general populace used to assign meaning to natural experiences and to emotions generated by biochemical processes.

Ironically "god" has become an antonym for faith. As previously stated it is the unknown which remains unproven. The words "I don't know" are the appropriate words of confession which clearly identify the subjective condition for faith to be active. Too often people assume that an atheist is a person who doesn't believe anything as though no subjective faculty exists. And sometimes atheists are quite defensive in regard to "faith" as though it is exclusively a concept synonymous to myth or religion. Both views belittle what it is to be human.

If asked I would likely respond to someone by saying "I am a believer." I don't mean this in any way that contradicts the wonderful film by fellow atheists "The Unbelievers." The following question indubitably would be "In what?" This is precisely why most people are unnerved by faith as a subjective context where knowledge is not available. There is this nagging need for an object when the clear requirement of faith is to remain open ended. "I don't know." This can just bug the shit out of some people.

We seem to be very confused about the difference between operating on subjective versus objective levels. People often ask "Do you believe in evolution?" It is not a viable question. It is a subtle confusion, an attempt to mix and match opposing concepts. One can ask "Do you understand evolution." It is a fact and "believing" in it is irrelevant. A math teacher doesn't ask which do you believe is true 1+1 = 5, 1+1 = 3, or 1+1 =2? The question is "Which is the correct answer?"

When one seeks to objectify or concretize a subjective faith question the same subtle confusion, a fallacy applies. "Do you believe in god?" If by this one is wrestling with

"god" as an undefined concept, a question in and of itself that is unanswered, a possibility still cloaked in an unknown conclusion, a word without semantic clarity that could mean any number of things was it verified objectively, then it is a legitimate subjective query. But that's not what people mean. The "god" of the question has objective characteristics that can and in fact have been tested. So the accurate question is "Do gods exist outside of human imagination, activity, and experience?" The answer based upon evidence is "no," and as such writing in "yes" to the belief question is a good way to get an "F" on the final exam.

The thing is when we put god in the box it deserves and face life accordingly our subjective journey continues. Nature demands we be believers, but what it is our faith will discover is unknown. We press forward with sobriety and humility because rarely does a thing we assume or guess exists prove to be true. God is a major case in point. Could there be life in other dimensions of the universe, or is dark energy the realm of infinite consciousness? Is there such a thing as karma or reincarnation? Are our loved ones out there and will we join them? Does the universe have intrinsic meaning, consciousness, purpose, or an evolutionary goal? We don't know.

There is nothing wrong with thinking about these things. Who knows, a pertinent discovery that can be tested, verified, and open for falsification may just be on the horizon. We may evolve and conquer death or may vanish in an instant without a trace in a quantum bubble that negates the whole universe. We simply don't know. Not knowing is the posture of good faith, and the freedom to exercise our subjective faculties is indeed a human right.

When we pause to listen to one another sometimes we learn, sometimes we pick up ideas that further our own thoughts on a matter, and sometimes, well, we just hear stupid. If it becomes an occasion for a mutually shared laugh then even stupid is worth the faith that claimed it.

If it comes to people claiming to know things they don't know, can't verify, selling snake oil, peddling salvation or ultimate truth, making promises they cannot keep, or worse, attempting to force others to acquiesce to their view, then we have a serious problem. The use of god in human history has proven this beyond any reasonable doubt. The fear of many imprisoned in denial is that a godless path is an immoral and fated trek into doom and destruction. Sadly it is their fear that gives us the doom and destruction. It is the acceptance and subsequent transformation beyond that fear that gives us emancipation, faith, and a ground for hope in the evolution of a better humanity.

Historians have referred to the time following the rise of Christianity through the downfall of Rome into the centuries where the Holy Roman Empire was forged with blood and conquest as The Dark Ages. In spite of many optimistic twists and turns, periods of renaissance and enlightenment, the last chapter of that book has yet to conclude. Its weighty clouds loom above us still though the light signifying closure to its days of tyranny shines ever more brightly. We have all been wounded by the naiveté of religion, the ignorance, the barbaric carnage of jihadists, and the insolent bigotry of fundamentalists. The scars will take time to heal though it is uncertain how much time we have.

There is an urgency implied with the rising of each new day's sun. For some of us that urgency is equally poignant in the graying of hairs and the longing to see it before we leave, that step, that next step forward in the evolution of our species, our civilization, our humanity. For each of us as individuals the earth itself offers incredible opportunity for experiencing and connecting to life. There is meaning in most every process and a genuine delight, even reverence, in witnessing the life cycle shared by so many living things. The clues of our own existence are hidden in the very stones upon which we tread. Our senses bid us to pay closer attention, and to not take for granted the brief chance we have to participate in a universe laden with flowers and butterflies, stars and galaxies, radiant light, and mysterious darkness.

Our own endeavors, the human contributions, are no less compelling. The art, literature, music, and dance, the knack we have for figuring things out, innovating, discerning, and understanding how it all works, this human interim between species where in spite of flaws, errors, and gross injustices we melt in tenderness at the promise of a kiss or smile or simple embrace. Are not our tears worth shedding and laughs worth laughing? What other world could there possibly be where love can be made in so many ways or where flavors and fragrances could mingle with dreams of succulence and satisfaction then dissipate only to rise again?

And that's not the half of it. Who is content to go it alone? If it tasted good, looked good, sounded good, felt good, and smelled out of this world it has to be shared. There is hardly one star in the sky or a single gene encoded with all the bits that make it real. It takes pairs and

partners to make the spiral swirl, dance, and come alive with zest and flamboyance. "We" is the relevant word, and the opportunity to take "that" step is a global construct, like the mass pregnancy that occurs during a blackout when everyone is making the most of the moment and the power that was is no more. In this case it is not a power that can be restored, or even should be. It was faulty and outdated, and when the lights return a new infrastructure will have been implemented that utilizes a better source of energy, one that is renewable and less prone to failure.

To date a "god delusion" has gripped the world, but it is waning. It wanes with every jihadist use of beheading and murder, with every Christian fundamentalist's immature rant against beautiful people, and with every Catholic priest who suckles a child to his penis. It wanes with every unanswered prayer prayed to the sky in the name of an ancient deity made of stone. It wanes with every act of ignorance that confuses a child's mind with a mythical world where people and dinosaurs lived together and drowned together for the whims of a being that couldn't pass a high school biology course. It wanes because our level of gullibility has been surpassed and because our devotion to life outweighs our fear of death.

Yes these are words intended to inspire community, the rise of community, and the outing once and for all of the many of us who have held our tongues, waited and watched, but can do so no longer. Yes some Muslims have guns, bombs, and big knives. Yes Christians have mega churches, tons of money, opulence, popularity, rock bands, political clout, and as rumor has it, even a Starbucks on occasion to service their congregations. But what's god got to do with it? This is good news because finally we can see

the evidence that what people yearn isn't god, but people, meaningful connections, and a sense of viable community.

Even the most individualistic among us eventually get bored enjoying Keats with sips of fine scotch beside a warm fire. It takes a while, but we do. In most every community there are five or ten, fifteen or twenty, thirty or forty, perhaps even a hundred or two freethinking secular minded atheist folk. It is not that difficult to get the ball rolling. What we fail to realize is there is a whole world of wonderful human beings waiting to evolve, but needing welcome, an invitation, an opportunity.

Denial, for all the comfort it seems to afford, is burdensome. It is not real and at the heart of it is an emptiness that requires fuel to keep it going. Fuel is costly, demanding, and it exacts a toll that can even decimate the love that bonds parent to child, friend to friend, and neighbor to neighbor. This is god's legacy to humankind. The indifference is unbearable, unsustainable. This is not our world, and the time has come to bring reason to the forefront and end the madness. This too is a time for faith, but faith in our selves because we have no other in whom to place hope or trust.

Over the long years we have laid a foundation. It isn't perfect, and its architecture is constantly in revision. It changes as we come to know more about life, about the universe, about the consequences of our choices. It has integrity precisely because we refuse to be bamboozled by conjurers and shamans whose guesses have not measured up. There is too much at stake. Our world, our "Pale Blue Dot" is at stake. "We" are on the line. If there is to be trust, a basis for community trust, then it will be built from what

we know and not from what we assume, or believe, or conclude from unsubstantiated fears.

"Amazing grace…that saved a wretch like me" may be some world, but it is not this world, our world. What we become as individuals and as communities will beat to a different drum, and sing a different song. Perhaps it will be John Lennon's Imagine or maybe Bob Thiele and George David Weiss' tune sung by Louis Armstrong:

I see trees of green, red roses too
I see them blue before me and you
And I think to myself
What a wonderful world….

Our world is a wonderful and amazing world and no less the universe beyond. Sometimes this swirling mass of energy and matter is hard, even indifferent, to the beauty we experience, to the dreams we dream, to the hopes we have for a meaningful existence. But always it is a world filled with life, with living connections and interconnections that tease us to know them more fully. Herein we find a reality so sublime that ancient seers would have paid good money to see what we see, and would have laughed hearty laughs that they ever thought it could be gods. They would have been the first to ask the question, not as a matter of contempt or insult but with joy and awe in the presence of quantum particles and genes. They with us would salve the pains of ignorance past in rhetorical jest "What's god got to do with it? They would boldly share with us a toast and venture on "to where no one has gone before."

Printed in the United States
220758BV00004B/11/P